Newport

A LIVELY EXPERIMENT · 1639-1969

Newport

A LIVELY EXPERIMENT · 1639-1969

Rockwell Stensrud

The Redwood Library and Athenæum gratefully acknowledges the generosity and support of
Gilbert S. Kahn and John J. Noffo Kahn which made possible the publishing of this book.

Published by Redwood Library and Athenæum, Newport, Rhode Island 02840

Edited by Jason Weiss
Image research by Jane Carey, Cheryl Helms, and Erin Zielinski
Research by Brian Stinson
Index by Thomas Kozachek

Publication design by Poulin + Morris Inc., New York, New York
Typeset in Galliard and News Gothic
Printed on 135 gsm StoraEnso Lumisilk
Printed and bound by C S Graphics Pte Ltd., Singapore

Jacket illustrations:
James Nicholson, *Newport Harbor*, 1888, oil on panel, Newport Historical Society, Newport,
Rhode Island, 2000.40; Joseph Frederick Wallet Des Barres, cartographer and publisher, London,
A Plan of the Town of Newport in the Province of Rhode Island, 1776, engraving,
Newport Historical Society, Newport, Rhode Island, 2000.43.6

Library of Congress Control Number: 2006930502

ISBN 978-0-9754879-3-8

Newport: A Lively Experiment is dedicated to
Gilbert S. Kahn and John J. Noffo Kahn,
whose generous gift has made its publication
possible . . . and to Ralph E. Carpenter,
whose half-century commitment to the city
has inspired it.

Contents

PROLOGUE ix

FOREWORD xiii

1 THE BIRTH OF NEWPORT · 1639–1655 2

2 THE CHARTER OF 1663 · 1655–1698 44

3 TOLERANCE AND PROSPERITY · 1698–1740 80

4 THE ROAD TO REVOLUTION · 1740–1776 124

5 INDEPENDENCE AND DECLINE · 1776–1790 194

6 UNION AND SURVIVAL · 1790–1843 246

7 SOCIETY ASCENDANT · 1843–1880 294

8 THE QUEEN OF RESORTS · 1880–1914 342

9 THE GRAND REVIVAL · 1914–1969 414

EPILOGUE 461

ACKNOWLEDGMENTS 463

SOURCE NOTES 467

BIBLIOGRAPHY 483

INDEX 497

Prologue

From the earliest years of North America's colonization by Europeans, a few towns played dominant roles in defining the diverse character of the territory that would become the United States of America. As the country matured from its initial imperial roots, chose democracy, and struck out on its own, these towns (soon to become significant cities) continued to exert their influence in moral, artistic, and political spheres, and set the tone for the nation. There were many differences among these centers, but the tension produced a dialogue that has led to a clearer understanding of the values that have shaped America's destiny.

Newport, Rhode Island, was one of those defining towns, and it continued to play a pivotal role in the country's consciousness while America emerged as a world leader. Lessons learned in Newport over the centuries—religious tolerance, political freedom, artistic experimentation, architectural grandeur—helped transform the nation at every phase of its development. As times and tastes changed, Newport remained a bellwether, an independent voice, a place where opposition to the ordinary was the norm.

Founded in 1639, the City of Newport measures approximately eight square miles on the southern tip of Aquidneck Island in the State of Rhode Island and Providence Plantations. It is a small city by twenty-first century standards (population 26,500 according to the 2000 census), easily traversed, almost intimate compared with its rival colonial cousins of Boston, New York, or Philadelphia. But its very human scale helps define and highlight Newport's abundant charms.

Surrounded by water on three sides, with an easily accessible, splendid natural harbor, and blessed with a temperate climate, Newport was established by nine Englishmen who had fled or been banished from the Massachusetts Bay Colony. The town rose to prominence in colonial America as a leading trading port and center of mercantile and artistic creativity; it suffered and declined under British occupation during the Revolution, but slowly revived by rediscovering its commercial acumen, its intellectual and aesthetic foundations, and finally by becoming one of the most prominent and prestigious resort towns in all of America.

When people who have not ventured to the town are asked what they have heard about Newport, they often focus on its splendors and excesses during the Gilded Age, its America's Cup sailing heritage, and its jazz and folk festivals. But on coming to the city, these people discover a canvas far broader and more complex than the mythic Newport. They see the beautifully well-preserved colonial architecture; the grandeur of the Redwood Library, Trinity Church, and the Touro Synagogue; and examples of the furniture that made the city famous in the eighteenth century. They observe firsthand the extraordinary "cottages" of the nineteenth century along Bellevue Avenue and marvel at their craftsmanship and elegance. They experience a wealth of cultural attractions, from its art museums and galleries to its classical music programs and the renowned Newport Symposium. Here is a city that enlivens and entertains year round, one that offers a narrative in myriad tongues.

There is another Newport as well, one more deeply ingrained in America's psyche than the quest for entertainment. The case can be made, and easily defended, that if a few brave men and women in Newport in the middle of the seventeenth century had not held out stubbornly and courageously for freedom of conscience, America might not have had the chance to flourish as it has over time; that if Dr. John Clarke had not fought for and obtained the signed and sealed Charter of 1663 from King Charles II ensuring the "lively experiment" in religious concernments, England's colonies in the New World could have tilted precariously toward the despotism and religious intolerance of the Massachusetts Bay Colony, Connecticut, and elsewhere. Instead, the king took a gamble on the future. As the historian Carl Bridenbaugh observed, "It is well known that the Merry Monarch acceded graciously to this shrewd plea with the unprecedented religious clause of the Charter of 1663, which, in an age of faith, legitimated the first secular state of modern times."

What Newport and Rhode Island brought about was nothing short of revolutionary in the ideas of how individuals and their government should interact. Roger Williams, the founder of Providence, led the way in the quest for religious freedom in the colonies, and he was joined by others who would not tolerate the Bay Colony's bigotry. What stands out is how absolutely radical, how *new*, this idea was. Throughout history, governments had dictated how people were to think and believe. Now, a group of English subjects in America's smallest colony were insisting on a fresh notion—that people could and should have the freedom to make up their own minds regarding their beliefs. This was untested territory, frightening to those who wished to dictate a community's mores. But by insisting that the individual had integrity beyond state control, Newport and Rhode Island changed the direction of the American ethos and created an indelible legacy.

In an age when multiformity is taken for granted in the United States, it is well to remember that the situation could have turned out quite differently. Newporters demanded religious freedom as the basis of the community's existence. For nearly a century they had to fight off their more powerful neighbors to the north and west, who labeled Rhode Island "Rogue Island," "the Island of Error," or "the cesspool of heresy," and sought, in innumerable and devious ways, to bring the colony into their harsh Puritan fold.

Those efforts to subjugate them proved futile. As if Newport's founders did not have enough to contend with—clearing fields, protecting livestock, building rough houses, making a living in the raw wilderness—they also chose to fight a long-simmering battle for freedom of conscience, freedom for men and women to profess their faith in God in a personal manner. Newporters did not imprison or execute people for their beliefs, as Bostonians did; they did not ban ideas that might endanger the clergy's autocratic hold on society, as the leaders in Salem did. The first settlers of Rhode Island, particularly those in Newport, broke with history and pointed America in the direction it would ultimately travel—becoming a country that values diversity, that mandates private freedoms, that protects what individuals believe in. Newporters set in motion a new way to live and coexist in society; and they did so in an astounding manner.

So there are two Newports to celebrate. One is the tangible community, founded in the seventeenth century, with a rich history of victory and defeat, valor and ignominy, heroism and scandal. It is a city where American heritage comes alive on every street, where every era of the American experience is represented, from the colonial to the postmodern. The physical city is convivial, often light-hearted, even frivolous, known since the 1840s as *the* place for summer entertainment and recreation. Newport offers the resident and visitor alike a fresh perspective on the delights of seaside city life.

The other Newport is a more metaphysical, even spiritual place. This Newport is a state of mind, and it engages us because the ideas and tenets espoused there are so deeply engrained in the American experience—ideas once considered dangerous or seditious that ultimately prevailed and became mainstays in the quest for a free and democratic existence. This is the Newport where the soul of America first found its mooring.

Foreword

Newport: A Lively Experiment 1639–1969 highlights the evolution of this magnificent city and underscores a defining moment in the history of the New World—when democracy was introduced to Newport in the form of the Charter of 1663. The Charter is probably one of the most insightful documents written on liberty and the role of government. It is a work of persuasive diplomacy; each sentence conveys clarity of purpose. Altogether the Charter provided the Colony of Rhode Island and Providence Plantations more freedoms and privileges than any other English colony.

The Rhode Island colonists were permitted to hold forth "a lively experiment" that "a most flourishing civil state may stand and best be maintained" and "that all and every person and persons may from time to time, and at all times hereafter, freely and fully have and enjoy his and their own judgments and consciences in matters of religious concernments." The language of the Charter defined more liberties than those specified in the Constitution, written nearly 125 years later. Its radical ideas predated Locke's "life, liberty, and property" by twenty-seven years and Jefferson's "life, liberty, and the pursuit of happiness" by over one hundred years.

My first thoughts of Newport's past and future came to me during my frequent trips to Newport in the 1930s. I would drive up one street and down another, passing by public and private buildings dating from the sixteenth, seventeenth, eighteenth, and nineteenth centuries—most were shabby and rundown. Collectively they constituted a massive remnant of colonial and federal Newport. On Bellevue Avenue I would pass by a tired nineteenth-century business block that included the Newport Casino and its tennis courts, both the worse for the wear.

At the end of each visit, I would have mixed emotions. I hoped that there would still be time to restore and preserve these iconic relics of some fifteen generations. Newport's historic significance had been neglected for years, as had its buildings, which constitute the most comprehensive concentration of architectural styles in America. For years the question of when and how to rejuvenate the city went unanswered by those who failed to recognize the rich cultural heritage that surrounded them in their daily lives.

After World War II, I found myself having lunch in Newport with Katherine Warren. She told me her vision for rescuing Newport. She had drive, courage, and a contagious enthusiasm. I found myself totally immersed in her newly formed Preservation Society of Newport County. We soon began our first major project, the restoration of the Nichols-Wanton-Hunter House.

At the same time, Mrs. Michael van Beuren and Mr. Archbold van Beuren commissioned the publication in 1952 of Antoinette F. Downing and Vincent J. Scully, Jr.'s seminal *The Architectural Heritage of Newport, Rhode Island*. Here was a powerful catalyst that encouraged the formation of organizations, like Operation Clapboard and Doris Duke's Newport Restoration Foundation, that aimed to restore and conserve more than seventy colonial houses. Their accomplishment has no counterpart in America in scope, diversity, and historic significance. This long period of restoration created worldwide interest in this fascinating and diverse city.

Written with style and grace by Rockwell Stensrud, the author weaves a tapestry of Newport's historic past—exploring and commenting on people and events in the dynamic culture that has always characterized the city. It is a story of radical ideas, religious reforms, military occupation, and ingenious initiatives in science, literature, politics, art, architecture, medicine, the decorative arts, and sports. Newport's many achievements in these diverse areas owe their success largely to the city's culture of freedom and liberty. Newport has long encouraged those with adventurous ideas to pursue their dreams.

Newport has had a complex history. It has often been described as the home of "the otherwise minded," with a culture of its own. The reader's image of Newport and Rhode Island will undoubtedly be reshaped by the following pages.

Ralph E. Carpenter

" . . . And whereas, in their humble address, they have freely declared, that it is much on their hearts (if they may be permitted) to hold forth a lively experiment, that a most flourishing civil state may stand and best be maintained, and that among our English subjects, with a full liberty in religious concernments; and that true piety rightly grounded upon gospel principles, will give the best and greatest security to sovereignty, and will lay in the hearts of men the strongest obligations to true loyalty . . . "

—from *The Charter*, Granted By King Charles II, London, July 8, 1663

Newport

A LIVELY EXPERIMENT · 1639-1969

TRAMONTANA   TERRA

TE INCOGNITA

NVOVA FRANCIA·

TERRA   DENVR   VMBEGA

Flora

Le paradis Port Real.   Port du Refuge

C. de breton

Brifo.

C. Breton

Jsola   de Bretoni

Jsola della rena.

OSTRO

The Birth of Newport

I

The Founders

Newport was settled by eight men of distinction—and one would-be tyrant.

Giacomo Gastaldi
La Nuova Francia
(detail) from
Giovanni Battista
Ramusio, *Terzo volume
delle Navigationi et
viaggi* (Venice, 1556).
Courtesy of
The John Carter Brown Library
at Brown University
Providence, Rhode Island

The names of the founding fathers are etched into the bedrock of Newport's geography. Travel the streets of the present-day city and you weave through a tangible narrative that pays homage to these venerable men. At the southern tip of Aquidneck Island you will come upon Brenton Point, Hazard's Beach, and Coggeshall Ledge; to the northeast is Easton's Beach. In the heart of the city are streets commemorating Dyer, Bull, and Clarke. Each of these pioneers contributed to Newport's success; each risked his life to create a colony where free men and women ruled themselves and religious tolerance was the law. They were balanced, able men who sought to design a civil government that offered social equality in the midst of Puritan oppression. And then, as you meander into northwestern Newport, you will arrive at Coddington Cove where you will encounter the specter of perhaps the most perplexing of the first inhabitants—a man who prized freedom of conscience yet attempted to establish his own mini-monarchy on the shores of North America.

From the beginning, Newport has never been lacking in color, controversy, or contentious characters.

William Coddington's bid for lifelong control of Aquidneck Island came just twelve years after Newport was founded in 1639. The small settlement was besieged by powerful forces, any of which could have ended its brief existence. The government of the nascent colony of Rhode Island and Providence Plantations was in chaos, split into four uncooperative spheres: Providence, Warwick, Portsmouth, and Newport. Massachusetts Bay Colony and Plymouth to the north and east, and Connecticut to the west, coveted their neighbor's rich lands and natural harbors in Narragansett Bay and disdained the personal liberties Rhode Island espoused. Various Native American tribes were potentially hostile. Meanwhile, at home in England, King Charles I had been beheaded for his stubborn support of the Anglican Church and his defiance of Parliament, and Puritan forces under Oliver Cromwell were engaged in civil war against the royalists. Amid this turmoil, Newport—conceived as a theocracy but only a year later evolving into a civil government dedicated to self-sufficiency—had to defend itself from the power-grab by its most influential and richest founder, William Coddington, who in 1651 had arrived from London with a commission from the Commonwealth's Rump

Parliament naming him governor of Aquidneck Island for life.

Other settlements might have accepted their fate and acceded to Coddington's authority. Not Newport. Unlike the Puritan religious communities surrounding Narragansett Bay, where most inhabitants acknowledged autocracy as the only way of life, Rhode Islanders were unconstrained and fervent about their autonomy in politics and faith. Their insistence on "soul liberty," a belief embraced by Roger Williams, was the reason they had escaped—either on their own or by banishment—the ignominy witnessed in the Bay Colony.

The freewheeling, rambunctious spirit later associated with America's Wild West had found its origins in Yankee Newport. Its inhabitants were not about to accept Coddington's commission without a fight. No one, regardless of his presumed importance, was going to take away their liberties. And the man they chose to direct the battle was another leader, although of very different temperament, Dr. John Clarke.

The struggle between these two protagonists illuminates the story of Newport's first thirty-five years. Coddington was a risk-taker, but mostly when the long odds were in his favor. He was a big man in many ways—physically, financially, and paternally, having had three wives in succession and thirteen children. (Clarke also had three wives but no progeny.) These same qualities fed his ambitions for domination. He liked to win, to control the course of events. William Coddington was a merchant-prince. John Clarke was a preacher-everyman. Strong of conscience and conviction, Clarke was at heart a conciliator, a pastor and healer, not a power-hungry ruler. One was overbearing, the other humble. One wanted to dominate, the other strove to share. Both of them held their community in high esteem but differed greatly in how to achieve the best lives for its inhabitants. Coddington and Clarke had taken the measure of each other since meeting in Boston in 1637. They knew each other well, and, from the scant reports we have, they loathed each other.

Putting aside for a moment the arrogance of his bid for permanent despotic leadership, William Coddington undoubtedly believed he was doing the right thing for his fellow colonists, in procuring his power and "protecting" Aquidneck Island from the more radical forms of Puritanism and the chaotic governments on the mainland. His fellow colonists, aghast, immediately rose up against him, deputizing John Clarke to have Coddington's commission annulled. And here is the irony: if Coddington had not been granted his hegemony, Clarke would never have had cause to travel to England and remain there another twelve years as Rhode Island's agent to Parliament and the Crown, a sojourn in which he secured from King Charles II Rhode Island's prized possession, the Royal Charter of 1663—the most liberal secular and religious contract ever granted by a European monarch.

William Coddington and Dr. John Clarke were lightning rods, the two central characters in the early drama that largely fashioned Newport's future. But they could not build a community by themselves. The other seven men responsible for settling the town in May 1639 were a diverse band who had survived the rough passage from England to America, honed their skills in the Bay Colony, and then either by force or free will had abandoned Boston and helped establish the Pocasset (Portsmouth) settlement at the northern tip of Aquidneck Island in 1638. One year later, they had left Pocasset and were beginning again.

WILLIAM CODDINGTON (1601–1678) brought wealth first and foremost, but he also exhibited legal and administrative skills, and political leadership, to say nothing of his business acumen.

DR. JOHN CLARKE (1609–1676) was a physician, preacher, scholar (fluent in Hebrew, Latin, and Greek), surveyor, farmer, part-time merchant, and, as time would witness, a first-rate diplomat.

JOHN COGGESHALL (C. 1591–1647) was a wealthy merchant, a solid administrator and a successful farmer; he was a descendant of one of England's most consequential families that dated back to the Norman Conquest.

WILLIAM BRENTON (C. 1600–1674), one of the richest Bostonians, was a highly successful merchant and farmer; he was an able statesman, who held a surveyor's commission from Charles I.

JEREMY CLARKE (C. 1598–1661) (no relation to John) was a surveyor and merchant who helped train and lead Newport's military force.

HENRY BULL (C. 1608–1693) was the town's sheriff and keeper of the peace and at the end of his long life, Governor of Rhode Island.

NICHOLAS EASTON (C. 1600–1675) was a tanner, house builder, farmer, miller, and diarist.

WILLIAM DYER (C. 1605–1677) was a merchant, soldier, and later served as Attorney General.

THOMAS HAZARD (1610–C. 1665) was a farmer and surveyor.

Historian Antoinette Downing asserts, "Many of these settlers were men of broad culture and outlook, outstanding both politically and socially. William Coddington had not only been accounted the richest man in Boston, but, like William Brenton, John Clarke, and others, he had been eminent in England before his departure for the new world." While the mainland and Pocasset drew a humbler, less educated, and poorer population dedicated mostly to farming, Newport was the locus for a more vibrant intellectual, mercantile, and artistic expression. In the coming years most of the nine men would hold the highest offices in both Newport and Rhode Island government, adding luster to their reputations and, more importantly, guiding the colony in ways advantageous to their business ventures.

The founders had some factors for success in their favor—it was springtime when they arrived in Newport after abandoning the Pocasset settlement, so they had six months of good weather to survey their holdings, begin clearing and sowing fields, erect their initial crude structures for shelter and safety, and, according to tradition, clear the harbor. The perhaps-apocryphal story, told by a descendant of Henry Bull in 1832, says that the land "fronting on the harbor where Thames Street now is, was then an impenetrable swamp, which circumstances so discouraged the settlers that they concluded to locate the town near Easton's Beach; but on further survey, they found the roadstead there unsafe for shipping, which obliged them to resort again to the spot where Newport now stands." Having purchased the island from the Narragansett Indians the previous year, the founders now hired them to burn and clear the swamp and then fill it in "for the gift of a coat with brass buttons."

By May 16, 1639, just over two weeks after Nicholas Easton and his sons landed at Newport, the other founders had made their way south along crude Indian paths to their new settlement. On that day they held their first official meeting and declared that "the Plantation now begun at the South west [*sic*] end of the Island shall be called Newport." Tradition holds that the town was named after Newport, capital of the Isle of Wight, where the original Puritan fleet had assembled in 1630. But it is possible that Newport, an agricultural town in East Shropshire, England, was the inspiration. They also set boundaries and directed that "the Towne shall be built upon both sides of the spring & by the sea-side Southward."

Newport's excellent saltwater harbor was the primary allure for these merchants, but they had to have a steady source of fresh water to survive. They began to build their town houses around the abundant stream that ran from where today's Spring Street intersects with Touro Street and then meandered on to the cove. The spring at that time was large enough to accommodate small boats. Local historians have offered various scenarios for the placement of the first houses, but all agree that Newport differed distinctly from Bay Colony towns, which centered on the village green, meetinghouse, and church. The new settlers were *not* congregationalists—it was precisely this melding of church and state that Newporters were fleeing, and their new town reflected their rejection of conservative Puritan order and containment. From the beginning, the hamlet had a haphazard look. Newport had no early church building as a focal point and the first Colony House was not erected until 1687, so the founders spread their four-acre town lots along the fresh spring and toward the harbor in order to monitor their primitive commercial adventures. Thames Street ("by the sea-side Southward") was built up for domestic and mercantile purposes with huts and small wharves, while plots along West Broadway, Farewell, and Marlborough streets were desirable for their easy access to the spring, which watered orchards and gardens as well as supplied family needs. Many, including Coddington, Easton, and Bull, had houses in this vicinity; others scattered farther afield.

According to Newport historian Lloyd Robson, "With the early summer weather facing the settlers, they lived first in tents and temporary shelters. When they began to build, they probably constructed frame houses sided with half logs and consisting of one room with a chimney and fire place at one end." The chimney would be made of wood, plastered with coarse mortar, or built with cemented stone. The Rhode Island "stone-ender" became a classic form of seventeenth-century New England architecture. Within a decade, however, more sophistication was introduced. Downing adds: "The character of the boxlike houses they built lay in the typical framed and braced medieval construction. After they had hewn, squared, and dressed the heavy oaken timbers to a smooth face, usually with an axe alone, they chamfered them along the edge for a decorative finish. Then they framed them together with interlocking joints of mortise and tenon, dovetail and half dovetail, as expert and self-sufficient as the stone vaulting system of a Gothic church."

These houses in town were only an aspect of a larger scheme. One of the most important points of business at the first meeting of townsmen was the allotment of land. In 1639 there were only about five

thousand colonists inhabiting the small settlements throughout New England. Of these, the majority were farmers eking out a sparse existence on small plots of land. Most had come to escape religious persecution in England; some were merely adventurers seeking economic opportunities that were closed to them at home. Most had few belongings and fewer illusions about the difficulties they faced. But from the outset Newport was different—and the city has exhibited a slight air of superiority ever since.

While Pilgrim and Puritan settlers in the Massachusetts Bay Colony, Plymouth, and Connecticut subsistence farmed on rough four- to six-acre parcels, most of the founders of Newport rewarded themselves with large estates "in the country," in addition to tracts of land by the harbor. As Englishmen still adhering to feudal concepts, they made sure that land was doled out according to a person's standing in society. Of the nine founders:

WILLIAM CODDINGTON was allotted 750 acres as well as additional pasture land near Coddington Cove and a town lot of 6 acres;

WILLIAM BRENTON got 399 acres for his Hammersmith estate;

JOHN COGGESHALL received 389 acres along what is today, appropriately, Coggeshall Avenue;

NICHOLAS EASTON was given 389 acres along Sachuest Beach;

WILLIAM DYER was awarded 200 acres;

JEREMY CLARKE had 186 acres;

DR. JOHN CLARKE got only 148 acres.

It is not known how the land division was devised nor why there is no record of Bull's or Hazard's holdings, but as the community leader and largest investor in the purchase of the island Coddington made most of the rules. Given Dr. Clarke's superior education (which should have bestowed more social prestige than the lower-class Easton would have been accorded), could his small land grant reflect that rivalry between the two men was already under way?

At that time the tracts of property in the hands of the founders were extensive, taking up most of today's Newport and beyond. Had the founders stayed in the Bay Colony or even in the original Pocasset settlement, it is doubtful they could have amassed so much pasturage. But by abandoning the island's northern settlement, where political infighting had become severe, the Newport founders could do as they pleased—and that was to replicate the large-scale agricultural holdings so profitable back in England. Coddington, Brenton, and Coggeshall would, during their tenure in Newport, become wealthy merchants, selling animals and crops raised on their estates to an ever-expanding market; they were savvy businessmen and administrators, as had already been proven in England and Boston. So, while it is accurate to point to religious differences with the authorities in the Bay Colony as the conflict that caused these men to abandon their first homes in America, it would be naïve not to consider that they probably plotted their exit from Massachusetts as much for worldly riches as for matters of spiritual conscience.

The Road to Newport

The developments that led, in a mere two decades, from the landing of the Pilgrims at Plymouth in 1620 (creating the second extant colony in the New World based on a social contract; Jamestown, Virginia, had been the first in 1607) to the founding of Newport were dramatic and remarkably swift, given the pace of life at the time. And like most incidents throughout the seventeenth century, appropriately remembered as the Age of Faith, everything revolved around religion. Most of Europe's wars were fought over religion (usually Catholic versus Protestant); the civil war in England was an intense combat between traditional Church of England royalists and radical Puritan republicans. Puritans, Calvinists, and Anglicans might spend days at a time arguing matters of theology or interpretation, forever debating the exact location of their gateways to God. The celebrated conundrum "How many angels can dance on the head of a pin?" may be held up to mockery in the twenty-first century, but in the seventeenth its implications were momentous, even deadly.

The Scrooby Pilgrims (most were from the village of that name in Nottinghamshire, England) were Puritans, but they took a more severe stance than the majority of their brethren: they had entirely separated from the Church of England, because they believed it had become too lax in discipline and observant of excessive rites—in short, too Catholic. Anything that smacked of Rome was anathema to these radical Protestants whose predecessors had suffered under (Bloody) Mary Tudor some seventy years before. "The sulphurous path leading to the Roman Church was, in the opinion of Puritans, thoroughly adorned with such trappings as surplices, altar rails, crucifixes and statues. These were to the Puritans horrifying and idolatrous symbols; even the celebration of Christmas was denounced as being a piece of Popish flummery." While the Pilgrims were not physically persecuted by the authorities, they fled to the more liberal Holland for nearly a decade to escape their Anglican neighbors' mockery and disdain at home. Feeling more and more marginalized in their adopted country, they decided to re-form their community and churches in America. Intending to land at the mouth of the Hudson River, they mistakenly made landfall on Cape Cod in November and made their way to Plymouth the following month. They had few skills to cope with their new existence and for ten years eked out a bare subsistence, often aided by the native Indians.

Then in 1630, the Great Migration of about a thousand hard-line Puritans began, led by John Winthrop, to the shores north of Plymouth to form the Massachusetts Bay Colony. These believers had known legal and bodily persecution at the hands of Charles I and William Laud, Archbishop of Canterbury, and most of those who made the journey did so to seek religious autonomy—and to run for their lives. Unlike the Pilgrims, this group of Puritans had not detached itself from the established church, but strove to change its nature from within. While Laud was pushing for elegance and ceremony, Puritans stressed the sermon. As the name connotes, they sought to purify the church along the lines of John Calvin's austere teachings. "They wanted to reduce Christianity to its most primitive form of four bare walls and the literal words of the Bible." But in England, the more radical the Puritans became, the more repressive was the Crown. They had little choice but to seek a less hostile environment, and the besieged king bid them good riddance.

One historian, writing at the end of the nineteenth century, contrasted the settlers of Virginia with their brethren in Massachusetts: "Instead of men 'in gentlemanly conformity to the Church of England,' pleasure loving and easy and indolent in manners, we must deal with stiff, solemn individuals, devoted to schools, colleges, and learning, to whom amusement was a crime, whose lives were completely absorbed in religion, and who were among the most unrelenting fanatics the world has ever seen."

The civil leaders in Massachusetts believed themselves to be smarter and better than everyone else. As Arthur Schlesinger relates, "Not only were the founders themselves drawn from Britain's rural and urban gentry but also, as good Puritans, they considered their superior station divinely ordained. In the words of their first governor, John Winthrop, 'God Almightie in his most holy and wise providence hath so disposed of the Condicion of mankind, as in all times some must be rich some poor, some high and emminent in power and dignitie; some mean and in subjeceion.' Accordingly, they immediately assumed the key positions in government and society, sharing the honors with the foremost clergymen."

Unlike the angels on the pinpoint, theological differences among the Puritans in Massachusetts were of utmost consequence, and the internecine battles of the 1630s ultimately led to the creation of new colonies, such as Rhode Island, by those who could not abide the oppressiveness of the Bay Colony. Using Puritan logic and exhibiting his reputed arrogance, Governor Winthrop reasoned that a few good men could rule better than the common people and observed that "meere Democratie" was the "meanest and worst of all formes of Government." Winthrop was not alone in this belief. Democracy in the form we know today was virtually untried outside of ancient Athens, Venice, Iceland, and a few Swiss cantons. And it was highly controversial. In the seventeenth century, aristocrats and men of wealth reigned over the masses throughout Europe, and the idea that common subjects might embark upon self-rule was not only suspect, but seditious as well.

Nonetheless, the road to Newport began in Boston and Salem. The very harshness of their uncompromising elites forced those of a more liberal spiritual—and mercantile—persuasion to seek destinies free of the theocratic handcuffs of the Bay Colony.

The problem centered on control. Governor Winthrop and his cohorts in the clergy wanted domination over every aspect of a colonist's life. The Massachusetts churches

did not restrict themselves to the control of ecclesiastical matters. As early as 1631 it was enacted that none should be admitted to the exercise of political privileges except members of churches. This measure, adopted with the idea that the enfranchised should consist only of Christian men, formed what was practically a theocracy, being the Calvinistic idea of a commonwealth designed to protect and uphold the framework of the church. This made each local church the center of political authority and threw all the power into the hands of the clergy. A man could not become a freeman unless he was a church member, and he could not attain to that standing unless he was approved by the minister in charge. By this means the clergy administered the temporal power, using the state as an instrument to carry out their will. They soon showed that they would, if the occasion required, avail themselves of the civil executive power to severely punish those who had committed no crime against the civil authority, but merely differed concerning ecclesiastical affairs.

The church and the state were essentially the same, but the church set the tone for society's behavior.

Although the royal charter granted to the Bay Colony in 1629 was merely a license for a trading company, Puritan leaders were quick to establish their strict religious community of nonseparating congregationalism. England was three thousand miles away and already in the throes of a downward spiral to open revolt against the king and civil war. What would London care about a few thousand dissidents in barbarous North America? For thirty years the Puritan fathers bet correctly, ruling by the Bible as much as by civil law, increasing the penalty for "heresy" (most of what they didn't like was condemned as heresy) from a day in the stocks to disarmament, to banishment, and ultimately to death by hanging for disagreeing with their tenets. The tighter Winthrop and his faction turned the screws, the more people looked for an escape. Historian Stephen Foster maintains that "Puritans, it seems, were a nervous lot, even if they did not always know what they were nervous about."

The leaders were determined to repress what the populace thought, not just what they did. "There is no question that the Puritans were opposed to liberty of conscience. Their denial of it was the foundation of their system. It was preached against in Massachusetts as the cause of all immorality, and nearly every eminent man has left his written protest against it." Given the atmosphere the leaders created, it is not difficult to understand why the Newport Quaker Mary Dyer was hanged in Boston in 1660 or why the Salem witch trials of the 1690s took such a drastic toll. Massachusetts had a functioning civil government and a general court, but these lay bodies, tied as they were to the Puritan churches, were subordinate. When a government is dominated by theological interpretation instead of secular laws, the miscarriage of justice becomes a daily occurrence.

Among the first to fall prey to the Bay Colony's draconian measures was Roger Williams, a brilliant young

preacher from England. As most American schoolchildren once knew, Williams was the founder of Rhode Island. But not by his own choice. He came to America to find freedom to practice his faith, not to become the originator of a New England colony. That burden was thrust on him by the unrelenting magistrates in Boston.

Born near London in 1600 or 1601, Williams studied law and theology at Pembroke College, Cambridge, and arrived in Boston in 1631. He immediately alienated the authorities by accusing them of not being true Puritans, since they had not completely divorced themselves from the Church of England. Williams was young, energetic, and popular with his parishioners—and, as an ardent Separatist, far more radical in his beliefs than most inhabitants. He befriended the local Indians, particularly the Narragansett sachems Canonicus and Miantonomi, and learned their language in hopes of converting their tribes to Christianity. He later abandoned his efforts to sway them to his faith, but remained on good terms with them until the outbreak of King Philip's War in 1675.

While preaching in Salem, then Plymouth, and back again in Salem, Williams further offended the Boston magistrates by challenging their right to Indian land without purchasing it, and embroiled himself in several ecclesiastical controversies by demanding a clear separation of church and state. He was an unrepentant renegade in search of a spirit appropriate for the times. "Williams, having lost faith in every form of religion of his age, and believing the ordinances of every church to be invalid, had necessarily no confidence in the doctrine of exclusive salvation [taught by the Puritans], and hence his belief in religious liberty." The conservative rulers viewed these "sins" as a direct threat to their power base. Williams was espousing a brand of Puritanism at odds with Governor Winthrop's evolving New England Way, which created a biblical commonwealth based on Judeo-Christian tenets that stressed *conformity*. In October 1635 the Boston magistrates had had enough of his dangerous ideas and brought Williams to trial. With undue haste they found him guilty and banished him from the Bay Colony. When Williams fell ill, the authorities put off his exile until spring, as long as he behaved. That was impossible for a man of his character; he continued to preach his seditious doctrines.

Fearing that his messages were being heard too well by his supporters in Salem, and ready to do anything to be rid of him, the officials conspired to seize Williams and force him onto a ship bound for England. It is at this juncture that we get a glimpse of the complex relationships forged by the original settlers. Although John Winthrop despised Williams's revolutionary ideas and voted for his banishment, it was he who secretly warned Williams that Sheriff John Underhill was on his way to deport him, and urged Williams to leave his wife and infant immediately and flee south to the safety of his friends, the Narragansetts. (A few years later, Williams and Winthrop would jointly buy Prudence and Patience islands for grazing sheep and cattle.) At the human level, the stern, conservative Winthrop obviously cared for his wayward younger friend; but when it came to the authority of the clergy being challenged by theologies counter to his own, he didn't hesitate to act against Williams.

Roger Williams was furious at his treatment by Boston's clergy and remained so for the rest of his long, productive life. He spent his first winter of exile with the Indians at Seekonk. When spring arrived, he was joined by his wife, child, and twenty-seven other followers anxious to be free of Massachusetts Bay tyranny. They then moved farther south. Practicing what he preached, Williams bought land from the sachems at the head of Narragansett Bay and named the settlement Providence. There he forged America's first real attempt at secular government. The separation of church and state, and tolerance for conflicting religious beliefs, were the hallmarks of the community from the beginning, in 1636. Thanks to Williams's constant vigilance, even when severely threatened, he never allowed those basic doctrines to be relaxed. The initial seed that would grow to become Rhode Island had been planted.

The Great Antinomian Crisis

The next threat perceived by the Bay Colony leaders was far more serious, and it led directly to the acquisition of Aquidneck Island and the founding of Newport. Known as the great Antinomian Crisis (the word means "against law"), it pitted a vigorous, strong-willed woman who believed in freethinking Puritanism against the increasingly suspicious and rigid Boston officials and clergy. Just as Providence would not have taken shape the way it did without Roger Williams's leadership, Newport would not have evolved as it has without the actions and influence of Anne Hutchinson, who believed that inner faith and the actions of grace were all that were necessary for salvation, not blind obedience to biblical moral law.

When Hutchinson and her wealthy merchant husband and nine children arrived in Boston from Lincolnshire, England, in September 1634, they were among the most respected people in town. That was soon to change. Anne Hutchinson, labeled by Winthrop the "American Jezebel," spearheaded the most serious assault ever on the Massachusetts orthodoxy and split the Bay Colony into two rival camps, legalists vs. spiritists. By attacking the majority of the colony's preachers on doctrinal grounds, and accusing them of having no true knowledge of the significance of the Holy Spirit, she caused a storm cloud to gather over Massachusetts Bay. The spiritists (Anne Hutchinson and her followers) "were united by a belief in the radical transformation wrought when an individual received saving grace, a transformation so overwhelming that such individuals believed themselves thereafter set apart from other human beings by the fact that in some form or other the Holy Spirit dwelled in them. This notion of 'free justification by grace alone,' of an ecstatic and overpowering intimacy with the divine, formed the basis for a startling number of religious, social, and political ideas that thoroughly alarmed those among the Puritan population who perceived such notions as a threat to their world-view."

Anne Hutchinson began holding weekly discussion meetings in her home (directly across Cornhill Road from John Winthrop's house), so women of the town could review the Reverend John Cotton's latest sermons. Cotton, more liberal than most clergymen in the Bay Colony, was gaining popularity, to the dismay of his ecclesiastical peers. In time, Hutchinson began to sermonize on her own. While already popular with women, who had no legal or ecclesiastical voice in the colony, Anne Hutchinson's meetings began to attract men as well, and that is when her problems began. Sometimes as many as forty to fifty people gathered at her house to hear her opinions. It all seemed innocent at first; but Hutchinson's spirited preaching of the indwelling of the Holy Spirit and a covenant of grace rather than laws sent a deep chill down the spines of the rigid Bay Colony clergy, because it threatened their influence with parishioners by showing another way to salvation. One can almost hear them pleading, "Why should they heed our sermons about the need for constant vigilance against evil if they believe they might be saved without it, simply through the grace of God?" A rift opened in the colony's towns between those who agreed with Anne Hutchinson's mystical discourses and those who were terrified of their implications.

According to the historian Emery Battis, "Many members of the local congregation became enthusiastic followers of Mrs. Hutchinson, including a majority of Boston's prominent and influential citizens, most notably the governor, young Henry Vane. Indeed, Anne's relatively permissive doctrine seems to have been most attractive to the affluent merchants and craftsmen of Boston, men who had been constrained in the performance of their entrepreneurial roles by the doctrine of responsible social organicism preached by the clergy and legislated by the gentry and yeomanry." Sir Henry Vane, one of the most important men in England and later a close aide to Oliver Cromwell, had come to America to witness the Puritan settlement in Massachusetts. Because of his social prominence and despite his youth (he was twenty-four at the time), he was elected governor for one term, briefly replacing John Winthrop. Vane was headstrong and rebellious, and was firmly in Anne Hutchinson's camp; his position further opened the void between the warring parties. Others who backed Hutchinson were William Coddington, John Coggeshall, and William Brenton.

Throughout 1635 and 1636 the controversy raged. More and more people were taking Anne Hutchinson seriously, and the leaders were scrambling for a solution—anything to get her out of their sight. They feared that the strict structure they had so carefully built was about to be destroyed, so "these ecclesiastical dictators" resorted to their usual means when confronted with anyone who disagreed with them: they dragged her into custody and brought her to trial for proselytizing her iconoclastic views.

The Antinomian Crisis came to a head in May 1637 when Sir Henry Vane was replaced by John Winthrop as governor of the colony. With Vane's removal from office Anne Hutchinson had lost a loyal protector. Winthrop had seethed on the sidelines biding his time while the Antinomians dominated. Now, with a vengeance, it was his turn. Probably at his behest, the colony ministers held a synod in August to denounce Hutchinson and put the errant John Cotton in his place. Attacked for his more accepting views of the Bible and of human nature, Cotton capitulated to their discipline. Once Hutchinson's most devoted defender had deserted her, the clergy and magistrates in tandem could remove her—and her ardent followers—permanently from their midst.

In November 1637, Dr. John Clarke arrived in Boston from England and immediately became embroiled in the Antinomian debate. It was the same month that the General Court had met to deal with Anne Hutchinson, and the colony was in crisis. Clarke, as a newcomer, could have stayed out of the fray but he took Hutchinson's side at once, appalled that people in the Massachusetts Bay Colony could not voice their own opinions without suffering persecution.

The historian William McLoughlin puts the controversy in perspective:

> By labeling her an Antinomian, the Puritan leaders branded her as a lawless fanatic who would govern by direct revelation. Her mystical reliance upon the spirit of God within would undermine all law and order; it would prevent the enforcement of the word of God by civil authorities. . . . Considering themselves practical, realistic, level-headed reformers, they branded Hutchinson as visionary and dangerous. That division between the pragmatist and the perfectionist has been at the basis of American cultural conflict ever since. It poses the binary tension within which the people of this country have oscillated for more than three centuries—a tension between noble idealism and hard-headed expediency.

The trial of Anne Hutchinson was a serious matter in those deeply religious times. She had opened a veritable Pandora's box with her preaching, and Winthrop was determined to snap the lid shut before more people questioned his rigid vision of the New Jerusalem, the City on the Hill, the American utopia he so clearly believed in. Although she was weak and ill, Winthrop made her stand as the accusations spewed forth from the legalists. When her ordeal was nearly over, Anne Hutchinson, having defended herself skillfully against the magistrates who were in utter confusion about how to handle her, was baited into the confession that doomed her future in the Massachusetts Bay Colony. "She had very nearly cleared herself of the charge [of traducing the ministers and their ministry] when she impulsively announced to the court that God had revealed to her that he would destroy her persecutors. This startling declaration, which seemed to impugn and threaten the whole state, created so conclusive a presumption of guilt that her horrified inquisitors, without further ado, sentenced her to banishment from the colony." Many of her followers were disenfranchised, disarmed (such was the fear of an uprising), and also banished from the Massachusetts Bay Colony.

But there was more. From the back of the room in Newtowne (later Cambridge), across the river from Boston, a venue chosen by the magistrates to attempt to limit the attendance of her followers, William Coddington rose and declared his support for Anne Hutchinson. "I do not for my own part see any equity in the court in all your proceedings. Here is no law of God that she hath broken, nor any law of the country that she hath broke, and therefore deserves no censure."

William Coddington was one of Boston's most prominent citizens. He was born to the English mercantile rank in 1601, and armed with wealth and a knowledge of the law; from the time he landed in the Massachusetts Bay Colony in 1630, he had taken on the air of a gentleman and felt himself superior to almost all other colonists in New England. His legal and administrative skills were obvious, even as a young man. He had been chosen an assistant in the Massachusetts Bay Company and Governor Winthrop depended on his counsel; from 1633 to 1636, he served as treasurer, so he had experience in complex financing; from 1636 to 1637, he served as an elected deputy of the corporation. All were high offices in the colony. He had a thriving mercantile business, property in Boston (reputedly he built the first brick house in town), and a farm in Braintree. In short, he had a great deal to lose by defying his peers.

Most historians treat Coddington's defense of Anne Hutchinson as the brave and futile act of a man of principle. Swayed, perhaps enthralled, by the teachings of his own preacher, the brilliant John Cotton, Coddington was clearly a man who valued spirituality. And as conservative as he was later to show himself to be, he was surely more open-minded than other Boston leaders when it came to Williams's concept of "soul liberty." In a 1640 letter to John Winthrop, written at Newport, Coddington affirms his adherence to principle when he asserts that "concerning Mr. Weelewrights Banishment. What I did

VANITY, VANITY
In a 1643 letter to John Winthrop, Coddington produced this mea culpa: "the Lord hath let me see the vanetye of my own spirit, and need of attending him in all his ordenances."

Edwin Austin Abbey
Trial of Ann Hutchinson
from William Cullen
Bryant et al., *Scribner's Popular History of the United States* (New York: Charles Scribner's Sons, 1897), 1:555.
Courtesy of the
U. S. Naval War College Library
Newport, Rhode Island

[handwritten marginalia:] march but beeing put by our journey by the Disention in the Contry where ye vane was turd out from beeing governor they went vnto Roud Jland in Jvne

Nahum 1. 3:4:5.6.

and builded at porch muth at the cove and planted After this yeare 1638 m 15.4

and such like things which stood upon Shelves, to clatter and fall down ; yea, people were afraid of their Houses : and it was so, as that some being without doors could not stand, but were fain to catch hold of Posts and Pales to prevent them from falling. About half an hour after, or less, came another Noise and shaking, but not so loud nor strong as the former. It was not onely on the Land, but at Sea also ; for some Ships that were on the Sea-coast were shaken by it : so powerful is the mighty hand of the Lord, as to cause both *the Earth and Sea to shake, and the Mountains to tremble before him : His way is in the Whirlwind, and the storm and the Clouds are the dust of his feet ; the Rocks are thrown down before him : Who can stand before his indignation ? and who can abide in the fierceness of his anger ?*

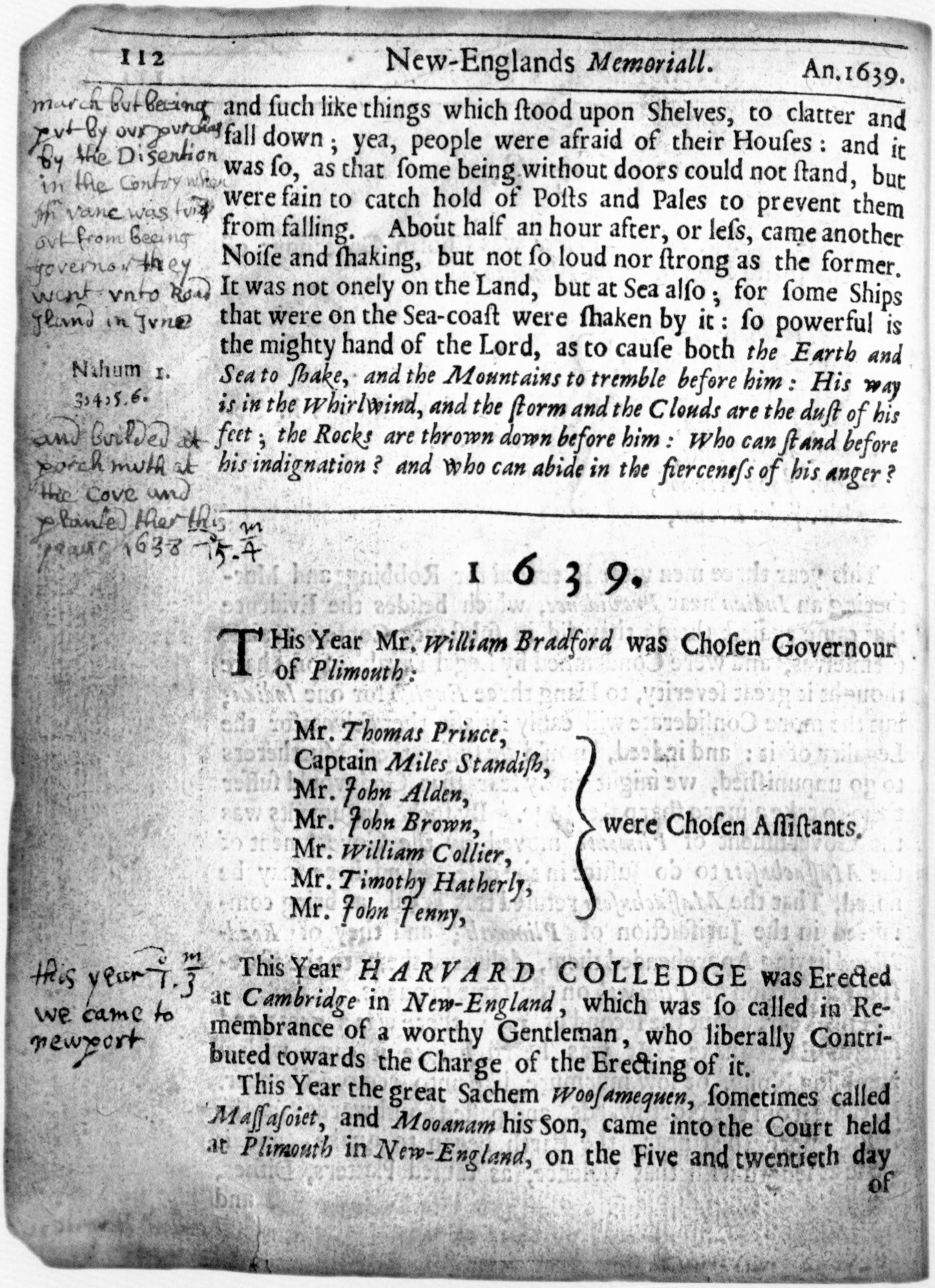

1639.

THis Year Mr. *William Bradford* was Chosen Governour of *Plimouth* :

> Mr. *Thomas Prince*,
> Captain *Miles Standish*,
> Mr. *John Alden*,
> Mr. *John Brown*,
> Mr. *William Collier*,
> Mr. *Timothy Hatherly*,
> Mr. *John Fenny*,

} were Chosen Assistants.

[handwritten marginalia:] this year m 1.3 we came to newport

This Year *HARVARD COLLEDGE* was Erected at *Cambridge* in *New-England*, which was so called in Remembrance of a worthy Gentleman, who liberally Contributed towards the Charge of the Erecting of it.

This Year the great Sachem *Woosamequen*, sometimes called *Massasoiet*, and *Mooanam* his Son, came into the Court held at *Plimouth* in *New-England*, on the Five and twentieth day of

therein was in discharge of my conscence [*sic*] in my place. And truly Sir to my discerning whether you did well or I, depends of the truth of the cause." So it is fair to give the man his due in the Antinomian affair.

However, the nagging question of Coddington's real intent looms large. Bostonians had been traversing the Atlantic coast from the time they arrived in the Americas; cartographic knowledge was shared at the wharves. Coddington was a merchant at heart, eager to increase his business interests. In his journal, John Winthrop refers to the excellent harbor on Aquidneck Island as early as 1634, and if Winthrop knew of it, it is fair to assume that his close friend and confederate William Coddington also was aware of the promises that lay to the south. At the time of Anne Hutchinson's trial in November, Coddington's good friends John Coggeshall and William Brenton, along with more than seventy like-minded and generally prosperous citizens, had already been disenfranchised because of their support for Hutchinson and for her brother-in-law, the liberal preacher John Wheelwright, who had been found guilty of sedition earlier in the year.

It was obvious they had to find new lives for themselves. But where? It is possible that Coddington and his wealthy friends had Narragansett Bay in mind from the start. Was his defense of Anne Hutchinson in any way bound up with his determination to quit his home for fields more fertile than the small, sandy tracts of the Bay Colony? Given the hostile climate of the times, he knew that by standing up for this "evil woman" he would be sealing his own fate. Conscience or commercial cunning, or a little of both? Historian Carl Bridenbaugh is unequivocal about the real motives of the group. "The migration of Anne Hutchinson and her followers to Rhode Island was much more than a flight from religious persecution. It was an agricultural-commercial experiment that had been thoroughly and minutely planned in advance in Boston and adequately financed by men who were thoroughly familiar with the management of estates."

Shortly after the trial, a number of Hutchinson's followers chose the recently arrived Dr. John Clarke and a few others to seek out new territory for settlement. The party ventured north and experienced a harsh winter, returning to Boston to regroup. They had little time to spare. The Massachusetts courts had banished Coggeshall, Bull, and many others (Coddington was urged to depart, but was not officially banished); if they were not out of the colony by early May, they would face imprisonment. Now joined by Coddington and his faction, in early spring a small party headed for Narragansett Bay and in Providence encountered Roger Williams, "by whom we were courteously and lovingly received." Williams advised them that Aquidneck Island might be purchased from the Narragansett Indians, and accompanied Coddington and Clarke to Plymouth to ascertain if the territory was free of that colony's claim. The magistrates there declared "that if the provident hand of God should pitch us thereon they should look upon us as free, and as loving neighbors and friends."

Meanwhile, the outcasts had been busy making plans in Boston over the winter. There must have been a number of clandestine meetings, because the authorities were still nervous about being toppled by a popular revolt. On March 7, 1638, the Aquidneck Compact was signed, either in Boston or Providence, by nineteen men (some sources put the number at twenty-three) whose lives in the Bay Colony had been compromised. "We whose names are underwritten do here solemnly in the presence of Jehovah incorporate ourselves into a Bodie Politick and as he shall help will submit our persons, lives and estates unto our Lord Jesus Christ." The Compact then goes on, "We that are Freemen Incorporate of this Bodie Politick do Elect and Constitute William Coddington, Esquire, a Judge amongst us, and so covenant to yield all due honour unto him according to the laws of God." The founders of Aquidneck had established not a democracy, but another quasi-religious community based on Mosaic, or biblical law, not the laws of England. The main difference between their modus operandi and that of the Bay Colony was that church membership was not a requirement for citizenship and no taxes were to be assessed for the support of any denomination.

The exiles, a majority of whom had been part of John Cotton's church, had formed a government and decided on a destination. Now they had to purchase the land; to do so, they turned again to Roger Williams for assistance. On March 24, 1638, less than three weeks after signing the Compact, Williams negotiated a deed for Aquidneck Island (already being called Rhode Island by some) with the Narragansett sachems Canonicus and Miantonomi, for the payment of forty fathoms of wampum in the form of white beads. (At the time, those forty fathoms equaled about $70 to $80.) The deed reads, in part, that the sachems "have sold unto Mr. Coddington and his friends united unto him, the great Island of Acquednecke," as well as the grasslands on nearby islands. It is evident from later events, when Coddington tried to become governor for life, that he felt he owned the island. He was not only the elected judge, but undoubtedly had also put up most of the capital for the purchase.

The relationship between Williams and Coddington appears to have been cordial at the time, although it is difficult to believe Williams completely trusted Coddington; after all, the latter had been part of the government that had banished Williams from the Bay Colony several years earlier. In later times, after their friendship had withered to mutual hatred, Williams maintained that the sale had little to do with Coddington's riches: "It was no price or money that could have purchased Rhode Island, but 'twas obtained by that love and favour which that honored gentleman, Sir Harry Vane and myself, had with the great Sachem Miantonomo [sic]." Earlier, in one of his plaintive letters to John Winthrop, Williams asserted, "a thousand fathom would not have bought either [island] by strangers. The truth is, not a penny was demanded for either, and what was paid was only a gratuity, though I choose, for better assurance and form to call it a sale."

Why did the Narragansett sachems agree to sell Aquidneck Island to the English? The relationship among native tribes was complex, with hostilities dating back hundreds of years, centered on control of land and military might. When Roger Williams trekked south from the Massachusetts Bay Colony in 1636, he had already formed close ties with Miantonomi and Canonicus of the Narragansetts, had learned their language, and had been generous with gifts to the tribal leaders. Williams had also become friends with Ousamequin, sachem of the Wampanoags, the traditional enemy of the Narragansetts. Ousamequin was the first to deed Williams land, on a parcel controlled by the Wampanoags, but claimed by the Narragansetts. Months later, Miantonomi and Canonicus welcomed their friend when he left Seekonk and founded Providence.

But the Narragansetts were in a quandary. Although large, the tribe was constantly aggravated by the Wampanoags, who had already made a pact with the English in Massachusetts. In the west, militant Pequots (another enemy) were preparing for war against the settlers. When Williams appeared, the policy of the Narragansett sachems crystallized. By giving away (or selling for a token amount) lands in Narragansett Bay, they strove to create trade with the English settlers while at the same time keep their distance from the Wampanoags. Later, when Williams asked Miantonomi and Canonicus to cede Aquidneck Island, they were more than willing to oblige. Historian Sydney V. James contends that the Narragansetts were solidifying their "buffer zone by selling territories (claimed by the Wampanoags) to other newcomers who created settlements south of Providence. Thus it is quite realistic to think of the colony of Rhode Island as in part a product of Narragansett Indian policy."

Pocasset

For William Coddington, John Clarke, and their allies, the sojourn at Pocasset lasted just one tumultuous year. There is scant documentation about why the encampment failed to thrive, but probably the clash of too many oversize egos in too small a space, quarreling over scripture and social science, was the prime culprit.

In one corner we have the presumptuous Coddington, a fountain of contradictions. Vain, self-righteous, and elitist, he was also a man of integrity who stood up for his opinions, sometimes at great cost to himself. He could be both petty and principled. "Coddington, as we shall see in his later life, strongly believed in centralization of power, especially when that power was centralized in him." At several key junctures in his life, Coddington behaved like a spoiled child, who, not getting his way in a neighborhood game, angrily picks up his ball and stalks off, leaving his friends stranded and his enemies perplexed. Pocasset was one of Coddington's abandoned ballfields.

In the other corner stands Anne Hutchinson, newly arrived from her ordeal in Boston in 1638 and still full of fire. We have already seen a glimpse of her stubbornness and belief in her own views. She was the first true American heroine and the most influential woman in the colonies in the seventeenth century, a tireless crusader for her covenant of grace no matter what the opposition. In the larger context of the Massachusetts Bay Colony, Coddington took her side in the Antinomian affair because he felt she was being treated unjustly and perhaps used the crisis in order to extricate himself from an atmosphere unfriendly to entrepreneurs. Now, at Pocasset, the two began to quarrel from the outset over policy and religious interpretation. One conservative, with his eye on the purse and posterity; the other radical, with her eye on revelation and redemption.

Then six months later, we add to this spicy stew a third ingredient, Samuel Gorton, a rabble-rousing English extremist who questioned Coddington's power at every turn and proclaimed that he had as much right to lead the community as anyone. Already banished from both Boston and Plymouth because of his outspoken rebellion against authority, Gorton came to Pocasset and made himself immediately unpopular with the majority of citizens. "He had freed himself, like Roger Williams, from every kind of dogma, formalism, and church organization. Sermons, he said, were lies and tales, churches divided platforms, and baptism a vanity." The Puritan leaders in the Bay Colony cringed at his teachings, which denied the existence of heaven and hell and the Holy Trinity. Gorton provoked an uproar wherever he was—which was never one place for very long.

On May 13, 1638, those freemen who had signed the Aquidneck Compact held their first town meeting of record. Over the previous three weeks Bay Colony exiles had been trickling onto the island. By the time of the meeting there were approximately a hundred people at Pocasset. Who chose the plantation's location is unknown, although Anne Hutchinson and her disciples seem to have arrived on the island in March,

WAMPUM

Exportation of silver coin from England was forbidden, so the early colonists had to create a monetary system all could agree on. The new legal tender became Indian money called peage or wampum. The black wampum was fashioned from the dark eye of the quahog shell and was twice as valuable as the white peage, which came from the thick neck of the more abundant "perry-winkle" shell. Edges were rounded and a hole bored through the center to string the shells together; 360 wampum disks were called a fathom. This currency had value because it could be exchanged for furs, which in turn could be sold for real English silver.

a full month before Coddington's group. On April 26, John Winthrop wrote in his journal, "Mr. Coddington (who had been an assistant from the first coming over of the government, being, with his wife, taken with the familistical opinion) removed to Aquiday Island in the Narragansett Bay." From the outset Pocasset's position at the northern tip of Aquidneck proved to be a poor one for large-scale commercial enterprise. Perhaps its proximity to the small gathering at Providence and the mainland was thought to be advantageous; or perhaps, in the haste to quit Massachusetts, no one had seriously explored the island. Pocasset offered an inviting cove large enough for pinnaces or small shallops. But a serious harbor for ocean-going vessels was needed in order to support enough commerce to sustain the community. Apart from bitter religious and political infighting, the issue of geography may have doomed the settlement for the aspiring merchants.

The new freemen, numbering fourteen, led by their judge, proceeded to set their lives in order during the summer and fall of 1638. The records show that the leaders proclaimed "that the Town shall be builded by the Spring . . . that a General Fence be made from Bay to Bay," and "that every Inhabitant of this Island shall be always provided of one muskett, one pound of powder, twenty Bulletts & two fademe of match." A week later the government met again and allotted plots for building houses, nearly all of which were five or six acres. Even Coddington, the chosen judge and leader, had to be content with this meager acreage. Stocks and whipping post were voted on later, as were plans for a prison. A good indication that more religious dissidents were expected to flow in from the Bay Colony or England was the order "that Will. Balston shall Erect & set up a house of Entertainment for Strangers, and also to Brew beer & to sell wines & Strong waters."

In the meantime, the colonizers were busy erecting huts or tents and evidence exists that Nicholas Easton built the first house in Pocasset, just as he would a year later in Newport. There is conjecture that some lived in caves during the first year as well. The daunting work of clearing fields, planting, hunting, and fishing went on daily. Summer turned to autumn and the settlement was growing, but not always with the most desirable newcomers. Winthrop asserts that at Aquidneck "there came over this summer twenty ships and at least three thousand persons." This number is pure fantasy on Winthrop's part—either he meant that three thousand people came to all parts of New England or he was seriously misinformed. Aquidneck would not harbor that many people for a decade or more. Among those who did migrate to Aquidneck, most were probably Antinomian adherents who were not allowed to land in Boston, but there was fear that some criminal-minded might think the new settlement to be free and easy. The stocks were put to use as the authorities scrambled to pass more laws to maintain order.

With the basics covered, Pocasset leaders got down to what they did so well—argue over divinity and plot for power. The problem was that while Coddington ruled because of his economic and social status, the Hutchinson faction, albeit poorer and less educated, could garner more votes when the freemen met. Coddington was thwarted regularly as Hutchinson supporters were voted into government positions, particularly monetary and military, that Coddington wanted to control. It galled the judge to have his authority questioned at every turn, and at some point he must have felt the same way about the talented Mrs. Hutchinson as John Winthrop had the year before: she's *trouble*! Relations between Coddington and Hutchinson deteriorated quickly. Ruling by Old Testament law was proving to be as difficult on Aquidneck as it had been in Boston, even though religious tolerance was observed. These radical Puritans, obsessed with minute doctrinal issues and persuaded that the strict orthodoxy of the Bay Colony's governance was overly severe, were now learning that creating a working government without the benefit of a strong consensus among the leaders was tricky indeed.

The strain must have intensified when Samuel Gorton, fresh from his expulsion from Plymouth, arrived in December 1638. Given their widely differing attitudes toward governance, Coddington and Gorton undoubtedly distrusted each other from the time they met, and that enmity lasted their lifetimes. One reason Coddington would not later dignify Roger Williams's 1644 Patent for Rhode Island was because it included the town of Warwick, founded by Gorton after he had been banished (yet again!) from Aquidneck Island. If Coddington felt besieged in trying to rule his growing community before Gorton's entrance, he really had problems now. An ardent believer that only the laws of England were to be followed, Gorton immediately sided with the Hutchinson faction and went to work on the autocratic judge, challenging his biblical domain and asserting that he had no right to rule because the regime was not sanctioned by English authority. "Gorton's extremely liberal civil ideas, and his religious proselytizing would inevitably have thrown him into any party opposed to Coddington's strong theocratic government. It is not surprising that Gorton and Mrs. Hutchinson, although teaching antagonistic creeds, should have temporarily united to oust from civil power one of a different mind."

Yielding to Gorton's demands and boxed in on all sides, Coddington conjured up his political acumen and arranged enough votes for a proposed alteration of the government structure. On the surface, adding three elders "to assist the judge" looked like a move to a more egalitarian solution, thus mollifying Gorton. In reality, the change only strengthened Coddington's hand because the three elders elected on January 2, 1639, were solid Coddington men—Coggeshall, Brenton, and Easton. Coddington's tactics alienated the Hutchinson party even more, partly because he had outmaneuvered them and partly because Coddington and his crew now had the power to impose their biblical rulings as they saw fit. Everything religious had become a political issue, and the reverse was true as well. Soon afterward, Anne Hutchinson and her clique declared that they would follow their own consciences concerning religious practices, regardless of what Judge Coddington said. The standoff was complete—and increasingly bitter. Metaphorically, swords had been drawn, and perhaps literally too. The early town Record Book (the official ledger of legislation) alludes obliquely to civil strife that needed to be contained. Pocasset was growing steadily. The burgeoning settlement was rife with rumor and tension as spring approached.

The climax came on April 28 when the government held its mandated quarterly meeting. What form of demonstration Hutchinson and Gorton had devised is unknown, but the historian H. M. Chapin describes it as "the *coup d'état* of 1639." Others conjecture that Coddington was shouted down at all points and in outrage and frustration gathered up the Record Book, with its vital data, and stormed out of the meeting followed by his allies. Coddington, the judge, was not going to be treated this way. Two weeks later, Governor Winthrop wrote in his journal, "At Aquiday the people grew very tumultuous, and put out Mr. Coddington and the other three magistrates, and chose Mr. William Hutchinson only, a man of very mild temper and weak parts, and wholly guided by his wife, who had been the beginner of all the former troubles in the country, and still continued to breed disturbance." For the moment, Hutchinson and Gorton had won the battle. They were not to win the war.

William Coddington was too keen a politician not to have seen the uproar coming in advance, and his decision to retain the Record Book—*his* Record Book, by God!—only strengthens the hypothesis among early historians that once again he and his friends had plotted their exit long before it came. They had had a year to explore the island by land and sea; any of their group would have immediately recognized the advantages of the exceptional southern harbor. These were men who envisioned large-scale trade in surpluses produced by large-scale farms. They knew what they wanted, and now it was within their grasp.

Later that same decisive day, the nine Newport founders met privately and proceeded to draw up yet another new compact. Were they disheartened by the events that had unfolded or relieved to be free of the shortsighted, quibbling rabble that had stood in their way to prosperity? For most of these men, probably the latter, even though it meant they had to undertake another exodus. Still, the unknowns were enormous, and their decision to move on could not have been easy.

Symbolically, William Dyer, the clerk for the previous year, turned to a fresh page in the Record Book and wrote, "It is Agreed By us: whose Hands are under written to Propagate A Plantation in the midst of the Island or Elsewhere And do engage ourselves to bear Equal charges answerable to our Strengths and Estates In Common and that our determinations shall be by Major voice of judge & Elders the Judge to have a Double voice." They had turned over a new leaf, literally, and were on their way south.

Pocasset was history.

On the horizon lay Newport.

Life in Early Newport

Early on the morning of April 30, 1639, just two days after signing the Newport Compact, Nicholas Easton and his two sons, Peter, aged seventeen, and John, fifteen, untied their shallop from its mooring in the harbor in Pocasset. Their voyage south along the western coast of Aquidneck Island, in the midst of other islands large and small, must have been idyllic, coasting past patches of a forested landscape that in many places ran clear down to the shoreline. As they sailed the nearly fifteen miles toward their new destiny, the Eastons experienced essentially the same scene described by Giovanni da Verrazzano in 1524 on his voyage to discover the fabled and elusive Northwest Passage to Cathay. In his report to his sponsor, King François I of France, Verrazzano laments his failure in the ultimate quest but offers the first description of Narragansett Bay written by a European.

> We frequently went five to six leagues into the interior, and found it as pleasant as I can possibly describe, and suitable for every kind of cultivation—grain, wine, or oil. For there the fields extend for 25 to 30 leagues; they are open and free of any obstacles or trees. And so fertile that any kind of seed would produce excellent crops. Then we entered the forests, which could be penetrated even by a large army; the trees there are oaks, cypresses, and others unknown in our Europe. We found Lucullian apples, plums, and filberts [hazelnuts], and many kinds of fruit different from ours. There is an enormous number of animals—stags, deer, lynx, and other species.

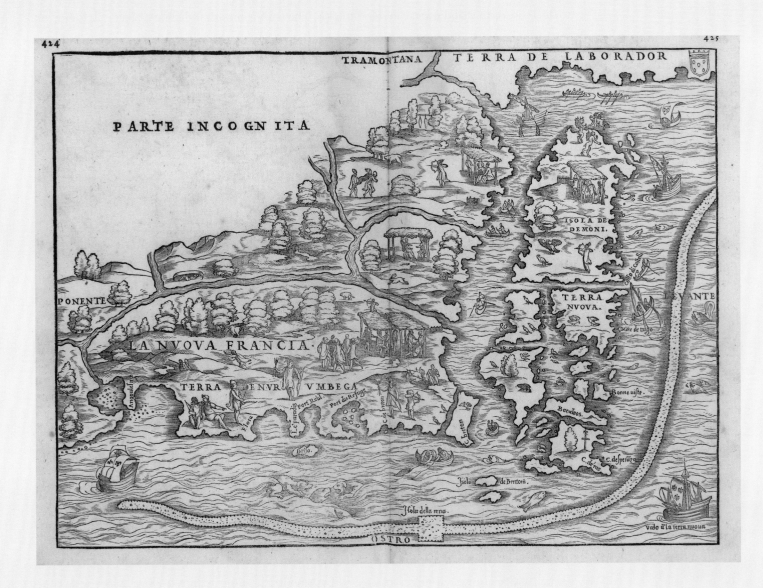

TRAMONTANA   TERRA DE LABORADOR

PARTE INCOGNITA

ISOLA DE
DEMONI.

PONENTE   TERRA   LEVANTE
                                                           NVOVA.

LA NVOVA FRANCIA.

TERRA   DE NVR   VMBEGA   Bonne uiste.

                    Port du Refuge   Bacalaos.

                                                           C. de las   c. desperança

                    Briso.

                                              Isola   de Bretoni.

                              Isola della rena.
                                                           Vedo a la terra nuova
OSTRO

FAR RIGHT

Howard M. Chapin
*Documentary History
of Rhode Island*
(Providence: Preston
and Rounds Co., 1916)
2:73.

Redwood Library
and Athenæum
Newport, Rhode Island

In 1669, Peter Easton recorded the founding of their new home: "1639 . . . In the beginning of May this year the Eastons came to Newport in Road Iland and builded ther the first English building and ther planted this year and coming by boat they lodged at the Iland . . . the last of Aprill 1639 and the first of May in the morning gave the Iland the Name of Coasters harbour and from thence came to Newport on the same Day."

Verrazzano described the vista at Newport this way:

> The coast of this land runs from west to east. The harbor mouth [which we called "Refugio" on account of its beauty] faces south, and is half a league wide; from its entrance it extends for 12 leagues in a northeasterly direction, and then widens out to form a large bay of about 20 leagues in circumference. In this bay there are five small islands, very fertile and beautiful, full of tall spreading trees, and any large fleet could ride safely among them without fear of tempests or other dangers. Then, going southward to the entrance of the harbor, there are very pleasant hills on either side, with many streams of clear water flowing from the high land into the sea. In the middle of this estuary there is a rock of 'viva pietra' formed by nature, which is suitable for building any kind of machine or bulwark for the defense of the harbor.

A league was generally considered to be about three miles in Verrazzano's time, so his measurements appear to be far too generous.

In the next weeks eight other colonists and their families, taking the overland route from Pocasset with their farm animals and simple belongings, joined the Eastons. After all the previous turmoil, with the hardships of constant dislocation, and the rugged trek along the narrow Indian paths from the north, these people might well have trembled as they came upon the last rise and looked out over the sheltered harbor below to contemplate the uncertainty ahead. Yet we can also imagine a corollary (there being no contemporaneous records): a collective sense of awe and expectation, a determination buoyed by the gentle May breeze to make *this* experiment work, a newfound conviction that the future lay before them as splendid as the view they were taking in for the first time. Newport, in fact and in spirit, had been born.

The treasure that is Newport took a long time to evolve. Three and a half centuries after its founding, the city has grown from its rich colonial roots and flowered into a display of perennially innovative architecture: Peter Harrison's classic Palladian designs, Federal and Greek Revival houses, solid Victorian and stick-style edifices, ornate European-inspired mansions created by America's leading architects along Bellevue Avenue and Ocean Drive, and distinctive Modernist houses of the twentieth century. No other city in America can claim a collection of buildings as diverse, magnificent, and well maintained.

But in 1639 what promise did Newport hold? It was backcountry that had to be quickly tamed and cultivated—a collection of muddy trails for streets, crude dwellings built only to keep the elements at bay, and despite its fine deep-water harbor and roadstead, there were no wharves or warehouses essential for commerce. Existence was bare bones. Only a collective indomitable spirit and dedication would transform the settlement's raw reality into the grandeur that lay in the distant future.

The founding families were getting accustomed to their new surroundings and faced the task of making some progress, somehow, every day. They had moved their possessions, started again the process of allotting and surveying land, started again the arduous task of creating arable fields, building houses and barns, finding food, clearing the harbor. The men of these families were mostly farmers and they understood what it meant to work. Many of them had come from counties in southern England known for advanced agricultural methods. During their tenure in Massachusetts, the farmers had discovered the vast differences between the climate at home and that of the New World, so they had an advantage. Then, in Pocasset, they gained a year's crucial experience with the soil of Aquidneck Island, which differed markedly from the sandier, rockier soil of the Bay Colony. They could exercise their freedoms without the distractions of the bitter feuding that had gone on the previous year at Pocasset, and they could concentrate on building a community of their own.

The fair summer climate, the benign soft breezes, so frequently noted in descriptions of Newport from Verrazzano to the present day, helped make their labors more bearable. Access to Indian maize, the fruit available in woods and meadows, and the endless opportunities for fresh fish and bivalves and crustaceans gathered along the bay and ocean shores, as well as the good hunting, alleviated any immediate culinary concerns. And they had help. There is ample evidence that many of the Indians still inhabiting the island were hired to aid with the backbreaking toil, at least during the first year.

After the Indians had helped construct the new town and had taught the settlers their methods of cultivating crops, such as maize, beans, and tobacco, they were looked on with suspicion, as if they had fulfilled their allotted tasks and could now be dismissed. The bloody Pequot War of 1637 in Connecticut, where dozens of colonists were attacked and killed by Indians, was fresh in everyone's mind, even though the Pequot had been subsequently slaughtered in return by the settlers. Unlike Roger Williams, who kept in close contact with the Indian tribes for decades (trading furs and helping them negotiate with the Bay Colony authorities) the leaders of Newport were wary of the Narragansett and Wampanoag and paid many of them to leave the island. Their fear of being attacked by angry tribes superseded their gratitude for the sale of Aquidneck and the assistance the Indians had given. Although relations between the two groups were generally quite good for the times, the English were steadfast in wanting to have the plantation to themselves. Coddington summed it up in a December letter to Governor Winthrop: "Our Indians are peaceable, though we trust them not."

There were a few skirmishes over the years. In April 1641 Indians were responsible for burning down one of Nicholas Easton's houses. This provoked a spate of laws by the government aimed at containing the Indians—no one could "sell, give, deliver, or any other ways convey any Powder, Shott, Gunn, Pistoll, Sword, or any other Engine of Warr, to the Indians." Furthermore, it was illegal for Indians to trap animals, take canoes or boats, loiter around town, or break a promise once given. The English were nervous.

More families were trickling in. Coddington, Brenton, and Coggeshall, with the largest estates and the wherewithal to hire tenant labor, began delegating the responsibility of sowing crops, planting orchards, and erecting fences to protect crops and livestock from predators and possible theft by Indians. Although the

CLAIMS

June 20th 1639

Received from Mr. William Coddington and of his Friends unitted to him in full satisfaction of grownd broken up or any other title or claime whatsoever formerly had of the Island of Aquednecke, the sum of five Fathom of wampum peage.

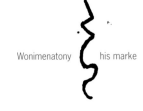

Wonimenatony   his marke

island location meant that wolves, foxes, and other dangerous animals could be hunted to a point where they were no longer a threat, since their numbers could not be easily replenished by migration, for at least a decade these animals were a serious nuisance. The Record Book contains numerous entries stipulating bounties for the heads or hides of slain wolves.

We will never know for certain how much of the land needed to be cleared in Newport proper for crops and grazing animals. Evidence points to the probability that over the course of centuries, resident Indians, primarily Narragansett and Wampanoag, had exposed much of the land nearest the water and had been harvesting maize for their own uses. One hundred and fifteen years before Newport's founding, Verrazzano had attested to the acres of open land: "they are . . . free of any obstacles or trees. And so fertile that any kind of seed would produce excellent crops." Given the speed with which the Newport farmers were in full operation, producing acceptable yields within two or three years and major surpluses within a decade, it appears that a good proportion of the settlement was available for planting during its first summer. By contrast, many settlers in the Massachusetts Bay Colony began their agricultural pursuits by feeding their livestock in grassy salt marshes because it took up to twenty years to clear their homesteads.

In terms of government structure, nothing essential changed with the move to the south end of Aquidneck Island. Coddington was in control, still ruling under ecclesiastic, not common law, and the Record Book reveals a series of haphazard efforts to govern the burgeoning town. Jeremy Clarke was chosen to be constable for protection against the Indians; a "Train Band," or military force, was established to drill the men; Henry Bull continued in his role as sergeant, and the building of stocks, a whipping post, and a prison were mandated. Further, it was decreed "that no man shall go two miles from the Towne unarmed eyther with Gunn or Sword." Civil order was paramount.

As the judge and elders ruled on numerous civil concerns, both weighty and mundane, a true slice-of-life account of the issues facing the government emerges from the documents found in the Record Book. The laws involved the erecting of fencing, who could build a sawmill, how the corn supply would be surveyed, hunting and fishing rights, trade with the Indians, and which newcomers would be admitted to the rolls of freemen. By autumn the leaders were discussing the need to reunite with their "Brethren of Pocasset" to present a united front against incursions by Indians, foreign powers, or other colonies.

But now the Newport government faced a fundamental predicament. Any détente with the more radical leadership in Portsmouth (as Pocasset was renamed later in 1639), under Gorton and Hutchinson, would necessitate a restructuring of Newport's religious compact: two days after Coddington's group was driven out, the newly formed Pocasset/Portsmouth government voted to adopt the laws of England as its standard and jettison the religious composition. It embraced civil authority over theocracy, probably at Gorton's insistence, and in doing so, was a step ahead of Newport. Pocasset/Portsmouth would never consider a reconciliation if Newport did not change its biblical mandate.

The Newport leaders were also deeply concerned about the precarious ground they stood on with King Charles I and Parliament. They might have purchased the island from the Indians, but unless they were recognized by the English government their town had no standing, which meant that both Connecticut and the Massachusetts Bay Colony could lay claim to their territory. The threat was serious, particularly because the Boston Puritans were so vengeful regarding the Newporters' desire for freedom of conscience. They were not just another group of settlers; they were despised traitors of the orthodox cause, the "cesspool of heresy," and would continue to be the target of opposition.

With that sword of Damocles hanging over them, "the Courte," as Newport initially styled its assembly, voted in November 1639 to change its governing structure from one ruled by the Bible to one dictated by English law. "In the fourteenth yeare of ye Raign of our Soveraign Lord King Charles. It is agreed, That as Natural Subjects to our Prince, and subject to his Laws, all matters that concern the Peace, shall be by those that are officers of the Peace, Transacted." This was a critical turning point for Newport because its leaders, even though conservative compared to many of Portsmouth's firebrands, were still precariously out of step with the majority of politicians and clergy in England who believed that for a society to flourish church and state had to be joined. By embracing English law, even while asserting their intention to follow their own heterodox spiritual paths, Newporters would be viewed more favorably by their fellow subjects back home who were also openly examining the traditional relationship between church and Crown.

This shift in policy could not have been popular with Coddington because it diluted his control, but it was necessary if any headway were to be made either in gaining official recognition in London or with the leaders of Portsmouth for joining the two towns under one government. The Court further ordered Nicholas Easton and Dr. John Clarke to write to Sir Henry Vane, now

Sir Anthony van Dyck
King Charles I of England out Hunting,
c. 1635
Oil on canvas
Louvre
Paris, France
The Bridgeman Art Library/
Time & Life Pictures/
Getty Images

a powerful Member of Parliament, and inform him "of the state of things here and desire him to Treat about the obtaining of a patent of the Island."

Negotiations between Newport and Portsmouth went on through the winter. Each town was forced to compromise to achieve reunion. Portsmouth ended up yielding political power to Newport in order to gain legal access to the land titles in the Record Book that Coddington had spirited away the previous year. Newport ended up abandoning the self-appointed, no-limits-on-term judge and elder system and accepting yearly elections of officers by the island's freemen. Coddington could salve his wounds knowing that he was able to garner more votes. He would still be leader, regardless of title. Gorton and Hutchinson might have hated the idea of once again being under Coddington's thumb, but they were outvoted by their fellow freemen. The island's safety, both physical and legal, necessitated federation.

Thus, on March 14, 1640, representatives of the two towns met in Newport. Gorton stayed away. The wording of the new compact, naming all the Portsmouth men—"presenting themselves, and desiring to be reunited to this body, and . . . readily embraced by us"—clearly indicates that they had come supplicant and were accepted. The reconciled leaders proceeded to establish courts in each town, accept a number of new freemen, and change the title of judge to governor; the elders were now to be called assistants. A vote was taken and, as expected, Coddington was elected governor of Aquidneck Island.

The intention was clear: the Island of Aquidneck was henceforth to be treated by its neighbors and the Crown as a unified, formalized government adhering to the laws of England. It did not constitute the style of democracy we recognize today, but it was on the right path. While London would eventually agree with its claims, Newport's avaricious neighbors continued to go to great pains to gain control over this valuable and productive piece of real estate dominated by so-called heretics.

The melding of Newport and Portsmouth went quite smoothly considering the animosity that had existed between the towns. There were troubles, to be sure, with so many diverse religious views being advocated: some, like Gorton's, were outrageous and incendiary. Nicholas Easton entered the fray by insisting that God was the creator of all sin. But, by and large, peace prevailed as people moved on with their lives. In Newport a sawpit was established to provide beams, planking, and clapboard at a fixed price for housing. A few wharves were erected at the harbor for lading the boats used in the nascent trade in hides and crops with nearby towns. Weather was a problem in the first years, delivering harsh, snowy winters and cold, wet summers that diminished crop yields and made for miserable conditions.

In March 1641 "the Courte" convened again and solidified its determinations on several crucial issues. The enacted statutes reveal how radically different, how modern, Aquidneck was when compared to its neighbors. "It is ordered and unanimously agreed upon, that the Government which this Body Politic doth attend unto In this island, and the Jurisdiction thereof, in favour of our Prince is a DEMOCRACIE, or Popular Government; that is to say, It is in the Power of the Body of Freemen orderly assembled, or the major part of them, to make or constitute Just Laws, by which they will be regulated." Furthermore, the freemen declared "that none be accounted a Delinquent for Doctrine; Provided, It be not directly repugnant to ye Government or Laws established."

Freedom of religion had become law.

Later, in Newport, the General Court (as the government was now called) again made its intentions manifest: "that the law of the last court made concerning liberty of conscience in point of doctrine is perpetuated."

Now, in Rhode Island, a subject's rights were spelled out clearly. Aquidneck led the way in granting autonomy for all. The historian Edward Field maintains: "These laws, so contrary to the prevailing spirit of the age, permitted enthusiasts, visionaries, and fanatics to live and work and talk side by side with orthodox thinkers . . . it was precisely the absence of such laws that induced these settlers to leave England and later Massachusetts. They had no intention of allowing posterity to belittle them for denying the free discussion of religious problems—the very principle for which they themselves had contended." At Newport and Portsmouth a majority of freemen (property owners primarily), not the clergy, made and upheld laws.

They also made history.

This radical idea—the formalized separation of church and state—was extraordinary, and it sent a deep chill down the spines of those in the Bay Colony and beyond who believed that order in society could only be maintained by strict religious symmetry. But the men of Providence and Aquidneck, particularly Roger Williams and John Clarke, who dared to be innovative in their thoughts and actions, were pointing away from the past and toward the future of society. This transformation led to turmoil and uncertainty at times; these men were throwing the gauntlet in the face of overwhelming odds in their "attempt to invert the enduring axiom of nearly fifteen hundred years: that civil and political cohesion alike depended upon a general and coerced uniformity of religious belief."

There is no doubt that life in Rhode Island was disordered because of this social experiment, but too many historians have overemphasized the negatives and not focused on the advantages that diversity brought to the community. Newport welcomed even nonbelievers and nonchurchgoers (of whom there were many).

The genius of Newport has been its enduring commitment to the principle that freedom begets creativity and productivity. When people are delivered from assault against their beliefs or morals, they function at a higher level than those who are shackled by daily uncertainty. "The prime fact about religion in Rhode Island and Providence Plantations was the absence of a priesthood, or hierarchy, which permitted the growth of a secular state, the expansion of settlement, and the development of a laissez-faire economy."

To increase commerce and communication between the two island towns the General Court mandated that a road wide enough to allow cattle to pass be cleared. What is today Broadway was the Newport terminus of that road. Other streets were being cut within the town, mostly dusty or muddy paths filled with horses, carts, wandering animals, and scampering children. There were, of course, no stores; most things people needed for daily life, like candles, pots, and some furniture, were made at home by both men and women. The historian Pieter Roos points out that most pottery had to be imported because Aquidneck has few clay deposits. Likewise, early clothing would not have been made at home because of the lack of wheels and looms. Sheep were prized for their wool, much of which was shipped to England and France

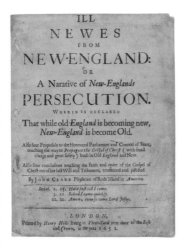

DIFFERENT UNDERSTANDINGS
In his seminal defense of Aquidneck's policies, *Ill Newes from New-England* (1652), John Clarke wrote, "Notwithstanding the different understandings and consciences among us, without interruption we agree to maintain civil justice and judgment, neither are there such outrages committed amongst us as in other parts of the country are frequently seen."

The religious freedom that was mandated by the March 1641 decree of the Aquidneck Island General Court was rare in North America at this early period. While some historians contend that Dutch New Amsterdam was first in allowing religious multiplicity, Russell Shorto gives this interpretation: "Cultural diversity management was about the last item on Peter Stuyvesant's list of job skills, and it's safe to say he was less than thrilled to see Manhattan's streets becoming an ethnic kaleidoscope. Religion was at the root of it: Stuyvesant despised Jews, loathed Catholics, recoiled at Quakers, and reserved a special hatred for Lutherans. Which is to say, he was the very model of a well-bred mid-seventeenth-century European. Religious bigotry was a mainstay of society. The four New England colonies to the north were founded on it [with the exception of Rhode Island]. Across Europe it was universally held that diversity weakened a nation. . . . It's strange that the one nod that history has given to the Manhattan-based colony—as a cradle of religious liberty in the early America—is off base."

for manufacture, while the meat was considered a staple of the colonialist's diet. With no church at which to congregate, people would meet in the streets, at the harbor, or at the Parade (now Washington Square) to trade information and gossip. Slowly a sense of "townness" was beginning to develop among the two hundred or so people.

With all the attention paid to religious practices during these years, one might imagine the settlers would immediately establish their new churches and continue their pious ways, finally free of the fanatics in the Massachusetts Bay Colony. But no. Evidence of any real church building is scant. In a letter back to Winthrop in the Bay Colony in December 1639, Coddington claims to have "gathered a Church, & do intend to chuse officers shortly." Howard M. Chapin quotes a report by Thomas Lechford, an Englishman who had visited sometime in 1640: "At the Island called *Aquedney*, are about two hundred families. There was a Church, where one master Clark was Elder: The place where the church was, is called *Newport*, but that Church, I hear, is now dissolved; as also diverse Churches in the Country have been broken up and dissolved through dissention."

The "dissention" that Lechford notes may well refer to the long, slow dissolution of friendship and trust between William Coddington and John Clarke. Speculation abounds over this matter and documenting it is impossible, but disparate pieces point to a probable scenario. The increasingly inflexible Coddington was content to rule the government, but his predilections were closer to John Winthrop's in the desire to control everything. John Clarke, given his exposure to Gorton, Anne Hutchinson, and other freethinkers, probably became more radicalized. When the men arrived in Newport, Coddington concentrated on civil matters and Clarke began his church, a Baptist congregation, and probably the only "church" in town, albeit without an actual building.

Unlike the strict parishes of the Massachusetts and Connecticut Puritans where one preacher would sermonize for endless hours, Clarke encouraged others to take over the pulpit and espouse their views, called for sweeping discussion, and welcomed all who entered. He was opposed to a priesthood and believed that church bureaucracy led to moral rot. As Clarke's ideas about governance and theology matured, he became more open than most of his contemporaries and rejected rigid structure. He was a fervent advocate of the separation of church and state—and this is where he and Coddington presumably began to fall into their irreparable discord. Coddington, a member of Clarke's church at first, probably seethed at the direction the pastor was going; it was *too* open, too disorderly, and Coddington craved order above most things. When Clarke called for the rebaptism of all adults because people could only find true grace of their own free wills, Coddington must have blanched: Anabaptism was a step too far for him.

When the split came, in the summer of 1641, it was undoubtedly something Clarke endorsed that drove Coddington out the door forever. It could well have been a disagreement over a point of religious doctrine. One astute historian believes that the defining issue was probably separation of powers. As the next few years would demonstrate, Coddington was never a firm advocate of separation. After all, he would soon secretly entreat John Winthrop to take Aquidneck into the Bay Colony fold, an indication that he approved of the joining of church and state at some fundamental level. At any rate, the schism was complete. Coddington and his well-off, estate-owning friends Brenton, Easton, and Coggeshall, left Clarke's church, never to return. Sidney V. James believes there was a class issue as well. Those who remained with Clarke were farmers or laborers, many landless, thus not allowed to vote as freemen, and perhaps not the kind of people with whom Coddington wanted to associate. Clarke went on leading his flock for years, officially founding the second Baptist church in Newport, in 1644, while Coddington and his friends embraced Quakerism in the 1650s—an odd choice for them since it is a faith that espouses no hierarchy and no creed.

A decade later, in 1651, when Coddington returned from England with his Commission and Clarke immediately joined the opposition to it, the chasm between what these men valued and believed had become enormous. William Coddington wanted to procure his personal fiefdom. John Clarke wanted to realize freedom for all.

The Search for Security: The Patent of 1644

Newport had more to worry about than religious matters. Even though the General Court on Aquidneck was enacting statutes to govern the island, the administration was proceeding without authority from England. The governor and the assistants were renegades—there was no patent, no commission, not even a letter mandating their existence. Legally, Providence had no right to exist, nor did Portsmouth and Newport, and the leaders of Connecticut and Massachusetts never hesitated to remind their wayward neighbors of this lack of legitimacy. Newport's efforts to obtain some kind of recognition from Sir Henry Vane had come to naught, and as the early years passed the magistrates became increasingly alarmed at their vulnerability. Royal or parliamentary recognition was crucial.

When Indian militancy began to rise throughout New England, as a result of intertribal competition and growing resentment against the English, the settlers in all colonies became even more concerned about safety. But Coddington and his government were isolated, especially after being haughtily rebuffed in 1640 in their request to Massachusetts authorities for a united front against Indian uprisings. Then in May 1643 Newporters found even more cause for alarm when Massachusetts Bay, Plymouth, Connecticut, and New Haven banded together to form the United Colonies of New England. Providence and Aquidneck were blatantly omitted. It was now markedly evident that their neighbors would continue to spurn solicitations for any kind of friendly union, even for common security. It was time to act. Letters were insufficient. Someone had to travel to England to plead their case.

Roger Williams of Providence, not the men of Aquidneck, was responsible for the first patent securing Rhode Island's legal status. Although there are no records indicating that Williams was acting on behalf of Aquidneck, "Historians agree that 'the movement was made by the colony of Aquidneck, Providence united in it, and Roger Williams was selected as agent.' He was, because of his friendship with Sir Henry Vane, perhaps the best representative that could be chosen." Unable to collect public funds to finance his journey, Williams sold his half-share in Prudence and Patience islands, which he had purchased with John Winthrop in 1637. Still barred from setting foot in Boston, Williams was forced to sail from Dutch New Amsterdam in the summer of 1643.

On the two-month voyage to England, Williams wrote his famous *A Key into the Language of America*, a study of the Indians' speech and way of life. Since little was known in England of the natives, the book (printed in London in late 1643) was widely applauded, "winning commendation from the Board of Trade, and forming a substantial basis—in the details which it gave concerning the Narragansetts and their country—for the application for a patent." Upon arriving in London, Williams found the country of his birth in a state of crisis. Charles I had been forced to flee the capital to Oxford because of the bitter opposition of the Puritan forces in the Long Parliament, now in control of much of the country. The Civil War had begun.

But Williams was lucky in his friends. Three of the most powerful men in England—Sir Henry Vane, Oliver Cromwell, and the poet John Milton—sympathized with Williams's views on the need for independence from the Massachusetts Bay Colony and Connecticut and aided him in his applications to Parliament. Vane had firsthand knowledge of the ecclesiastical ruthlessness in his old home and had no love for John Winthrop. As a staunch supporter of Anne Hutchinson, he shared many of Williams's views on religious tolerance. Sir Henry had become even more radical in his social and religious outlook since returning to London from America and undoubtedly talked about his ideas with the visitor from Providence. Williams spent much of his free time with Sir Henry and was often a guest at his house.

Roger Williams argued his cause well. On March 14, 1644, the Parliamentary Commission (Vane and Cromwell were among its seventeen members) awarded Williams his Patent for "the Colony of Rhode Island and Providence Plantations." It reads, in part, that the Commission shall grant

> to such Persons as they shall judge to be fit for the better governing and preserving of the said Plantations and Islands, from open Violences and private Disturbances and Distractions. And whereas there is a Tract of Land in the Continent of America aforesaid, called by the Name of the Narraganset-Bay; bordering Northward and Northeast on the Patent of the Massachusetts, East and Southeast on the Plymouth Patent, South on the Ocean, and on the West and Northwest by the Indians called Nahigganneucks, alias Narragansets; the whole Tract extending about Twenty-five English Miles unto the Pequot River and Country.

The boundaries established in the Patent would prove to be a serious source of contention between Rhode Island and its neighbors for well over a century. Connecticut and Massachusetts would go to great lengths to have this pact, and all subsequent ones, voided, often using questionable tactics or downright fraud to prove their case.

The Patent continues:

> And whereas divers well affected and industrious English Inhabitants, of the Towns of Providence, Portsmouth, and Newport in the tract aforesaid, have adventured to make a nearer neighbourhood and Society with the great Body of the Narragansets, which may in time by the blessing of God upon their Endeavours, lay a sure Foundation of Happiness to all America. And have also purchased, and are purchasing of and amongst the said Natives, some other Places, which may be convenient both for Plantations, and also for Building of Ships, Supply of Pipe Staves and other Merchandize. . . . Robert Earl of Warwick . . . and the greater Number of the said Commissioners . . . out of a Desire to encourage the good Beginnings of the said Plantations . . . give, grant, and confirm, to the

aforesaid Inhabitants of the Towns of Providence, Portsmouth, and Newport, a free and absolute Charter of Incorporation, to be known by the Name of the Incorporation of Providence Plantations, in the Narraganset-Bay, in New England.

The Patent spells out what were, at the time, very liberal conditions for how the colonists could manage their lives.

> Together with full Power and Authority to rule themselves, and such others as shall hereafter inhabit within any Part of the said Tract of land, by such a Form of Civil Government, as by voluntary consent of all, or the greater Part of them, they shall find most suitable to their Estate and Condition; and, for that End, to make and ordain such Civil Laws and Constitutions, and to inflict such punishments upon Transgressors, and the Execution thereof, so to place, and displace Officers of Justice, as they, or the greatest Part of them, shall by free Consent agree unto.

The document adds that any laws passed by Rhode Island and Providence Plantations must "be comfortable to the Laws of England, so far as the Nature and Constitution of the place will admit." This glaring loophole would allow almost any law to pass. Nothing is said about religion; whether Williams thought broaching that sensitive subject might jeopardize the civil compact, or whether Vane warned him off is unknown. England (indeed, all of Europe) at that time was in such unrest because of religious differences that any mention of it could have been fatal to the cause of securing a legally sanctioned patent—even though in 1644 Puritans had gained control of Parliament. The discussion of religion was probably unnecessary. "While the words 'civil government' warrant the construction sometimes placed upon them that their use precluded the establishment of theocracy and effectually guaranteed the liberty of conscience that was dear to all good Rhode Islanders, the 'full power and authority to rule themselves' left no doubt that the inhabitants retained soul liberty in complete functioning."

Roger Williams had secured the first patent for a political civil state in the New World, as opposed to a trading company like the Massachusetts Bay Colony or a proprietary colony like Maryland. It was a landmark political achievement.

The entire colony should have let out a sigh of relief and raised a glass in appreciation of his efforts when Williams returned to Boston with the Patent on September 17, 1644. He was able to land there because he also carried a letter from authorities in England urging the Bay Colony leaders to ease off their treatment of him and his followers. Boston was not about to go that far, but the magistrates did allow him safe passage through their realm without arresting or harming him. At Providence he was hailed as a hero. But not everyone was pleased with what Williams had accomplished in London.

Most Newporters, like John Clarke and his allies, were delighted with the scope and fairness

WAYWARD PURITANS

Secular though it was, Rhode Island was constantly in the throes of religious agitation throughout the seventeenth century. The founders of Newport were all, at heart, radical Puritans broadly held together by their mutual abhorrence of the spiritual corruption within the Church of England. But *everything* was a matter of nuance and interpretation. As people kept dissenting and debating and dividing into more and more branches of Puritanism, schisms arose causing ongoing suspicion and recrimination. It was a period of unprecedented religious turmoil and confusion, when conservative Presbyterians and Congregationalists were contemptuous of the beliefs of the more liberal Baptists, Seekers, or Quakers. As the historian Stephen Foster writes, "Puritanism was above all else a *movement*: a loose and incomplete alliance of progressive Protestants, lay and clerical, aristocratic and humble, who were never quite sure whether they were the vanguard or the remnant."

In the spring of 1640, a preacher named Robert Lenthal made his way from Weymouth, Massachusetts, to Newport and was later admitted as a freeman. He probably held forth in Dr. John Clarke's Baptist gatherings and he must have been admired because he was chosen to be the town's first teacher. "And *August 20*, Mr. *Lenthal*, was by Vote called to keep *publick School* for the learning of Youth, and for his Encouragement there was granted to him and his heirs one hundred Acres of Land." The venture was short-lived. Less than two years later, Lenthal had returned to England and the Record Book is silent about any further orgvanized schooling for the town's growing population.

of the Patent. Here, finally, was a powerful weapon against Massachusetts and Connecticut, a badly needed protector from the designs so clearly antagonistic to Newport's own. And here, with Parliament's recognition of the settlements as a separate colony, was the legal authority to proceed with cooperation among the towns. Clarke's sympathies were for union. He had chaired a meeting of freemen in January 1644 (which Coddington did not attend) and later sent a letter over his signature addressed to "The Inhabitants of the Town of Newport unto the Inhabitants of Providence." The letter clearly puts forth an offer of cooperation. But rivalries were such that a small faction—the Coddington faction—spurned the Patent completely and continued to do so for the next three years.

The crux of the problem lay with the perpetuation of power. The Patent meant that Coddington would be forced to relinquish a fair part of his domination and to share power equally with Portsmouth and Providence. But Coddington looked down his nose at the rabble in Providence, who were poorer, disorganized, and far more radical than he liked. He had no intention of dividing his domain, and he made his displeasure known.

In fact, Coddington had begun his slippery slide down the slope toward despotism months earlier. In order to secure his unmolested grip on leadership of Aquidneck Island, he was ready to offer allegiance to the hated Bay Colony rather than submit to the vote of the majority in Rhode Island. It is almost beyond comprehension that Coddington thought he could persuade *any* Newport inhabitant to be again associated with the Boston bigots. Yet on August 5, 1644, more than five weeks before Williams arrived home with the Patent, Coddington sent a secret letter to John Winthrop in Boston:

For Gorton as he came to the Island before I knew of it, and is here against my mind, so shall he not be by me protected. I could have heartily desired for the good I profess of both plantations that we had not been rejected in alliance with you about the Indians, which now the generality here will be averse from. The truth is here is a party which does adhere unto Gorton and his Company, in both plantations, and Judge them so much strength to the place which be neither friends to you nor us.

Now the truth is I desire to have either such alliance with yourselves or Plymouth one or both as might be safe for us all. I have my chief interest the Island it being bought by me and my friends, and how inconvenient it might be if it were possessed by an Enemy lying in the heart of the plantations and convenient for shipping I cannot but see but I want both Counsel and Strength To effecte what I desire.

I desire to hear from you and that you would bury what I write in deep silence, for what I write I never imparted to any, nor would to you had I the least doubt of your faithfulness, that it should be uttered to my prejudice.

Coddington, so fearful of a union with Providence, so determined to keep Aquidneck under his thumb, was even more motivated by the reappearance of the loathed and irrepressible Samuel Gorton. Coddington would have rather sat at the table with the Devil than with Gorton, such was the bitterness between them.

Coddington continued to pursue his separate strategy in secret. It was not the first time he had acted with imperious majesty—nor would it be the last.

For three years Williams and his supporters attempted to form the colony of Rhode Island and Providence Plantations under the 1644 Patent, and for three years they were stymied by numerous attempts to have the treaty nullified by Connecticut and Massachusetts. The angry and cunning magistrates in Boston even went so far as to create and backdate a bogus "commission" claiming Narragansett Bay as their own. The intercession of Sir Henry Vane put a halt to the trick, but it is a good indication of the means these punctilious Puritans were ready to pursue.

Closer to Newport, things were no better. Coddington continued to chafe under the Patent's democratic implications. Clarke and his coterie wanted union, but Coddington constantly intervened. He had no intention of joining a colony that "did not even recognize the Island in its title of incorporation. The feeling of distrust must have changed to one of fear, when [Coddington's] faction realized that the Gortonists had been admitted to equal parliamentary privileges in the new ship of state. On November 11, 1646, we find Coddington writing to Winthrop: 'The Commissioners have joined [Gorton and his company], in the same [Patent], tho we maintain the Government as before.' " Now, in addition to Providence, Portsmouth, and Newport, Rhode Island added Warwick as an official town. Coddington simmered.

When representatives of the four towns finally met in Portsmouth for three days in May 1647 to accept the Patent and form an authentic government, they produced a document that was a credit to their belief in finding a common ground. Some writers contend that there must have been weeks or months of prior negotiations before the General Court of Elections officially convened. The laws were well executed, there was a minimum of wrangling, and the usual contentiousness of the past was absent. It was a large gathering, including a majority of the colony's freemen, such was the importance of the occasion. Lloyd Robson writes:

> They came on foot and on horseback over the rudely cut trails; by canoe, by rowboat, and by shallop; down from Providence and Warwick and up from Newport. Men in knee breeches, home spun coats, and broad-brimmed hats—the minister, the merchant, the surgeon, the soldier, the smith from his forge, the farmer from his plow, the carpenter from his saw, the tavern-keeper from his pots of ale, the hunter from his traps, the sailor from his vessel—all came hurrying to Portsmouth, ready to cast their votes for the new officers and to "set their hands to the engagement of the Charter."

These pioneers, much like the men who would assemble in Philadelphia a century and a quarter later to create the United States of America, began by acknowledging that the laws already adopted by Aquidneck Island's government were the model for their labors. Titles and duties changed again. They elected John Coggeshall president of the colony, William Coddington assistant for Newport, William Dyer secretary, and Jeremy

ANNE HUTCHINSON

When her husband, William, died in 1642, Anne Hutchinson, weary of the continual harassment of the Boston officials and arguments with Samuel Gorton, took her brood of children, and with some devoted followers moved south to Pelham, on Long Island Sound, north of New Amsterdam. (The Hutchinson River Parkway in today's Westchester County, New York, is named for her.) In his journal, Winthrop relates: "The Indians . . . began to set upon the English who dwelt under the Dutch. They came to Mrs. Hutchinson's in way of friendly neighborhood . . . and taking their opportunity, killed her . . . and all her family . . . and put their cattle into their houses and there burnt them." Actually, one of her daughters survived, but the sad end of the fiery Anne Hutchinson in such a slaughter is testament to the dangers of the times. Was her fate simply bad luck, or was there a design in her being targeted? "Until recently, most scholars were convinced that the attack was an act of reprisal against whites for taking Indian territory. However, some scholarship speculates that Puritan authorities incited the Indians to attack. The wealth of detail reported about the massacre suggests that English observers had been present."

Clarke treasurer. Of the seven officers, four were Newport men, a nod to the fact that the most potent political power lay there—and would continue to do so for the next one hundred years.

Then they got down to the substantive work. The representatives adopted a bill of rights and code of laws far more forward-thinking than might be imaginable for the time: "The form of government established in Providence Plantations is Democratical, that is to say, a government held by the free and voluntary consent of all, or the greater part of the free inhabitants." They adopted a trial and jury system; proposed plans for an army and a colonial police force; they secured the rights of the minority, guaranteed liberty and property, and defined crimes and legislative powers. They dealt with the anxieties of their Puritan neighbors with the clause that their government would not become "(as some conjecture it will) an anarchy, and so a common tyranny, but willing and exceedingly desirous to preserve every man safe in his person, name and estate."

Rhode Island created a fledgling democracy that would become a template for other colonies in the decades ahead. Almost every civil concern was dealt with fairly, soberly, thoughtfully—even though what looked good on paper was not necessarily always followed in practice. But the fifty-plus page document the freemen produced went further than secular edict. It protected liberty of conscience, the bedrock principle of Rhode Island's existence. "These are the laws that concern all men, and these are the penalties thereof, which, by the common consent, are ratified and established throughout the whole colony; and, otherwise than thus which is herein forbidden, all men may walk as their consciences persuade them, everyone in the name of his God. And let the Saints of the Most High walk in this colony without molestation in the name of Jehovah, their God."

It was a brave beginning, more farsighted and bold than any other colonial attempt at self-government—but this experiment in representative democracy would nearly be wrecked by a new wave of internal dissension, apathy, and finally by the scheming machinations of William Coddington.

Coddington's Folly

The first difficulties arose when William Coddington's attempt to maintain his domination over Aquidneck Island was thwarted by the new charter agreement, which allowed Portsmouth to elect its own officers and act autonomously. Portsmouth set about doing just that. The freemen voted as one to act alone, not jointly with Newport. They were determined to be part of the *colony* of Rhode Island and Providence Plantations, not a satellite of Newport. Elections were spoiling Coddington's long-sought plan to rule by fiat, but he viewed the vote by his Portsmouth neighbors as merely a temporary setback.

The drama heated up in May 1648 when the General Court of Elections met again. A new leader had to be chosen because John Coggeshall, the first colonial president, had died the previous November. Amazingly, given his increasing conservatism and intransigence, William Coddington was elected by the freemen—and this is where the farce begins. Because of the scarcity of records, there are conflicting views about exactly what happened. What we know is that immediately upon his election, Coddington was suspended from office because certain legal complaints had been brought against him that he had not answered. Some believe it had to do with an assault-and-battery charge brought by fellow Newporter William Dyer. Others say the issue was a long-standing legal dispute with William Brenton. Still others believe that his traitorous letter of August 5, 1644, to John Winthrop, about joining Aquidneck with Massachusetts, had become known. (The first instance of political "leaking" in America?) In any event, Coddington was charged with contempt, and Jeremy Clarke was elected to replace him until the matters could be cleared up.

They only got murkier.

In a May 1648 letter to Governor Winthrop, Coddington continued to curry favor with the leader of the Bay Colony: "Sir, this bearer and Mr. Balsone [William Baulstone], and some others of this island, are in disgrace with the people in Providence, Warwick and Gorton's adherents on the island, for that we will not interpose or meddle at all in their quarrels with Massachusetts and the rest of the colonies; and do much fear that Gorton will be a thorn in their and our sides, if the Lord prevent not."

The political battle lines that had been emerging for years became fully drawn. John Clarke, Jeremy Clarke, Nicholas Easton, William Dyer, and others were firmly in the anti-Coddington camp. They had become utterly frustrated with their leader's continual attempts to thwart the 1644 Patent and keep himself lording over Aquidneck. Roger Williams, who was trapping for beaver in Wickford temporarily to replenish his finances (the government had reneged on its promise to repay him for his travels to England to obtain the Patent), reviewed the troubles in a letter to John Winthrop, Jr., of Connecticut: "Our poor colony is in civil dissension. Their last meetings at which I have not been, have fallen into factions; Mr. Coddington and Captain Partridge, &c, the heads of one and Captain Clarke, Mr. Easton, &c, the heads of the other faction."

Coddington had some support in Portsmouth, but almost none in Newport where the men favored the full Providence Plantations government over Coddington's Aquidneck Island compact. Coddington's refusal to acknowledge the duly elected administration stemmed not only from his quest for domination, but also from his aversion to Samuel Gorton. Williams was at wit's end watching all he had worked for come unraveled because of unchecked egos unwilling to work for the good of all Rhode Islanders. He pleaded for a conference where all parties could meet and heal the wounds, and even asked John Winthrop, Jr., to come act as arbiter, but Coddington would have nothing to do with the idea. The former governor was pursuing yet another treacherous design.

In September, probably in secret, Coddington and his henchman Captain Alexander Partridge (a former Roundhead soldier now living in Newport) left Aquidneck and bowed before the magistrates in Plymouth. They requested "that we, the islanders of Rhode Island, may be received into combination with all the United Colonies of New England in a prime and perpetual league of friendship and amity; of offense and defense, mutual advice and succor upon all just occasions for our mutual safety and welfare, and for preserving peace amongst ourselves . . . and to this motion we have the consent of the major part of the island."

Coddington had no such consent, except perhaps from his few followers—and in his own fervid

RHODE ISLAND
On March 13, 1644, at the meeting of the Aquidneck General Court the following law was passed: "It is ordered by this Court that the island commonly called Aquethneck shall be from henceforth called the Ile of Rhods, or Rhod-Island." In 1524, when Verrazzano first encountered what is now Block Island, he likened it to the Greek Isle of Rhodes in size and shape. During the next century, due to the imprecision of cartographic knowledge, the name became associated with Aquidneck, not Block Island, and the tradition held. In a 1637 letter Roger Williams alludes to "Aquedneck, called by us Rhode Island, at the Narragansett's mouth." However, in this book, "Aquidneck" is used throughout to describe the island in order to lessen the confusion when referring to the whole colony or state of Rhode Island and Providence Plantations.

imagination. Newport, along with the rest of Aquidneck, was being surreptitiously bartered to the devil. In the end it did not matter; the Plymouth leaders asserted that they would only accept the petition if Aquidneck came under the total control of their colony—a Puritan oligarchy where church and state were one. No more democracy. No more soul liberty. One has to step back a moment and ask a basic question: what in the world was Coddington *thinking*? For a decade he had upheld religious tolerance, not least in Anne Hutchinson's courtroom in the Massachusetts Bay Colony itself, and now he was proposing to give up all the hard-fought gains simply so he could remain in control. He clearly appears to have become addicted to power. One must also wonder how much his thriving mercantile pursuits might have influenced his reasoning. For the second time Coddington had attempted to sell out Newport, and for the second time he had been rebuffed.

Like a cat with nine lives grasping on to the end of a string, Coddington would not let go. More determined than ever to separate Aquidneck from the rambunctious Providence Plantations government, he decided to seek out the ultimate authority, London. Roger Williams wrote to John Winthrop, Jr., "Mr. Coddington went to the Bay with his daughter for England and left Capt. Partridge in trust withall the last week at Newport." That was January 1649. William Coddington was a man possessed.

After years of civil war between royalists and parliamentary forces, Charles I was captured and tried by his enemies. The Regicide judges tried him and the House of Commons found him guilty of treason. On January 30, 1649, Puritan forces executed their sovereign Stuart monarch by chopping off his head before a large gathering at the Palace of Whitehall in London. The day was bitterly cold and the king, brave to the end and not wanting to be seen shaking lest the large gathering took his actions for fear, wore three sets of garments.

The Interregnum was on. The Commonwealth was installed. The House of Commons ruled alone because the House of Lords had been abolished as well. England was in the grips of republican mayhem under Oliver Cromwell's Protectorate.

Into this scene stepped William Coddington—a royalist at heart, no matter his protestations, hell-bent on a mission to become a monarch himself. Because of the governmental chaos with the switch from majestic rule to that of Parliament, Coddington was kept waiting for more than a year before he could submit his petition to the Council of State in his quest to become "king" of Narragansett Bay. In the interim, he made as many new friends as he could who might help him through the loopholes of Commonwealth justice. He dined with his old friend Sir Henry Vane, but it is unlikely that he admitted the real purpose of his mission. Vane, of course, was allied with Roger Williams and was instrumental in his achieving the 1644 Patent—the instrument Coddington was seeking to circumvent. Edward Winslow of Plymouth was in London, also vying for the rights to Narragansett Bay, claiming it came under Plymouth's original charter, an appeal he probably never would have made had Coddington not stirred up trouble by seeking jurisdiction under Plymouth the year before. Several official meetings were held by a subcommittee of the Council of State to determine who should get the spoils.

Coddington swore that he had discovered and bought the island himself, and desired to rule Aquidneck (as well as Conanicut Island) under Commonwealth law (this from the man who had set himself up as a biblical judge and had been forced to yield to representative government against his will). He must have been convincing, because on April 3, 1651, he won the title of governor of Aquidneck Island—for life. He was given the authority to choose and confirm six assistants who would lend an aura of respectability to his sham rule. He could make laws, raise a standing army, and do as he pleased with Newport and Portsmouth.

Edward Field insists that

> there is not the slightest doubt that Coddington obtained this commission under false pretences. His representation as to personal ownership of the island was certainly untrue, and was expressly denied by him a year later [under great duress]. That his neighbors so regarded it, is shown in Dexter's [a member of the Providence Council] letter to Vane of August, 1654, in which he says, "We were in complete order, until Mr. Coddington, wanting that public, self-denying spirit which you commend to us in your letter, procured by most untrue information, a monopoly of part of the colony, viz., Rhode Island to himself, and so occasioned our general disturbance and distractions."

Coddington believed he had finally won his battle for control. But, such was the extent of his egotism and arrogance, he probably did not have a clue about the troubles he was sailing into—most of which were of his own making.

The town that William Coddington returned to in August 1651 was markedly different from the unbroken expanse he had encountered just twelve years earlier when he helped found Newport. He brought with him his new English wife, Anne Brinley, his third, the previous two having died. Anne had just given birth to William Coddington, Jr., who would be a future governor of Rhode Island.

If the Coddington party had taken the overland route from Boston, they would have traveled by horse and cart along the dusty paths used by Indians and colonists alike, taken a ferry from Tiverton to Portsmouth, then made the fifteen-mile trek down what is today East Main Road into Newport. It would have been a slow journey, laden with baggage and goods collected in London. The party would have passed numerous small and large farms, by now mostly fenced in and orderly. In 1648 Edward Winslow described Aquidneck as being "very fruitfull and plentifully abounding with all manner of food the Country affordeth, and hath two Townes besides many great Farmes well stocked in the same." Being the height of summer, crops would have been abundant, and Coddington could smile over his new domain. *Mine, all mine*, he might have reflected, like some deluded Shakespearean prince.

In his 1908 history of Rhode Island, Irving B. Richman offers one of the most romantic descriptions of early Newport, which is worth quoting at length for the abundance he chronicles. A few later historians are skeptical of his account because it may be idealized; nonetheless, the scene he depicts is valuable in painting a particular picture of life at the time.

> Two of these farms, indeed—the one owned by Coddington and the one owned by William Brenton—were, even in 1650, magnificent estates. The former (comprising some seven hundred

and fifty acres) was in two tracts. The first extended northwestward from Newport as far as Coddington Cove, and northeastward as far as Miantonomy Hill. It was diversified by upland and vale, meadow and wood; possessed on the west of a wide bay frontage; and stocked generously with horses, cattle, and sheep—the latter the finest of English ewes and rams (black and white), and in a special sense the pride of their owner. Upon taking the estate into possession, Coddington built a house on this tract at the cove. The second tract lay to the south of town, and was more diversified and picturesque even than the first. Here were hills crowned by spruce, cedar, and hemlock trees, interspersed with oak and maple; here were luxuriant valleys enshrining bright-eyed pools and ponds; and here, too, were masses of rock, fantastic in outline and hoary-headed, that ere long by sheer force of their presence dictated the bestowal of the appellation "Rocky Farm."

The Brenton estate comprised some four hundred acres to the east of the first Coddington tract. Later on, Brenton purchased land near the present Fort Adams, where he built, with materials brought from Boston, a large brick house capped by four chimneys, and laid out the grounds in orchards and gardens. He named the place Hammersmith, in honor of Hammersmith, Middlesex, England, the home of his youth.

Richman goes on:

> Upon both the Coddington and Brenton farms, as upon other less opulent Aquidneck estates, good English wheat, oats, rye, barley, and peas were harvested, to say nothing of good hemp and flax, and good English apples; while, as for cheese, butter, honey, venison, fowl and fish, wild strawberries and blackberries, hickory nuts and chestnuts—all were to be obtained in ample measure.

In describing what the town itself was like, Richman is equally expressive.

> As residents of Newport in 1650 (when all told the population may have been about three hundred) we find the Eastons, the Bulls, the Dyers, the Hazards, the Clarkes, the Goulds, the Shearmans, the Cranstons, the Jefferays, and the Coggeshalls. . . . The company, it is needless to say, was distinguished. It was so in the threefold aspect of extraction, education, and wealth.

Contemporary accounts claim that although their houses were small, they were well built and many had glass windows. While possessions were more crude than those found in England, housewares like earthen dishes, beds, and tables were serviceable and far less expensive than transporting items from across the ocean.

If the Coddington entourage had come from Boston by sea, their boat would have sailed up Narragansett Bay, past Castle Hill, into what many observers declare was the finest natural harbor in all the colonies. They would have seen dozens of people at the wharves, in their small warehouses and hurrying along Thames Street—shipbuilders, coopers, joiners, masons, rope makers, carpenters, smiths—all engaged in some kind of maritime activity. Commerce was beginning to thrive, because without it Newport could not survive. Trading for articles unavailable in town was the only way to acquire certain necessities. Farmers were beginning to produce surpluses of most crops and animals, sufficient to send along the coastal routes from Newfoundland to Dutch New Amsterdam and beyond, to the English colonies in the West Indies. Trade at this time with Boston was minuscule, the Puritan oligarchs still wary of any association with the dangerous Newport freethinkers.

The Record Book, compilations of contemporary letters, and Winthrop's journal abound in references to livestock and grains shipped, merchandise received, and who owed what to whom. These documents alone are testament to the rapid growth and accumulation of wealth that the Newport stockmen-merchants were able to achieve in such a short period. Until the British and Hessians arrived to occupy Newport during the Revolutionary War, it would only get better.

We do not know Coddington's mode of transport or whether he arrived home by land or sea. Nor do we know what he was thinking, although he must have been pleased with himself. But we do know that the new "Governor of this Colony for His Life" was returning to Newport a marked man.

Newport Revolts

How utterly humiliating it must have been for him that his ungrateful townsmen treated him the way they did. How thanklessly they behaved, this rabble of republicans that did not want to submit to his wisdom and higher authority. When Coddington unveiled his Commission to his fellow citizens and the implications of it began to sink in, the citizens simply revolted—immediately and unequivocally.

The fact that Coddington not only controlled who could live on the island and who could vote was bad enough, but, because the entire freehold was in his name, the Governor-for-Life also had full power over who could own land. If he wanted, he could withhold or withdraw tracts of land from anyone he might disagree with, and the leaseholder would have no recourse. Richman asserts: "No sooner did it become known that he had been made Governor of the islands for life, than a protest of indignation and consternation was raised throughout the colony."

Once more, it was the conservatives versus the liberals, and the latter held the numbers. In Newport sixty-five freemen met, a majority by far, and selected John Clarke to go to London at once to get the Commission repealed so the colony could be ruled by the Patent of 1644 again, rejoining the mainland towns and Portsmouth in democratic government. The freemen signed a resolution that urged Clarke to "address unto the parliament of England, in point of our lands and liberties." In Providence forty-one citizens met and raised a £100 subscription to send Roger Williams to London for reconfirmation of his parliamentary Patent. Warwick joined Providence and pledged another £100. Since Williams and Clarke were both *personae non gratae* in the Bay Colony, they were forced to petition the authorities for permission to pass through their territory without being arrested. Williams and Clarke sailed from Boston in late autumn 1651 accompanied by William Dyer whom Coddington had sued years earlier, accusing him of stealing ten head of cattle.

While the three men were in England over the next year, Newport inhabitants mounted several

SAMUEL GORTON

The last time we encountered Samuel Gorton he was giving Coddington headaches in 1639. His career as a nuisance did not diminish in the least in subsequent years. While still at Portsmouth, Gorton got into several battles with townsmen, the most famous of which came in 1641 when he was defending one of his servant maids. In court, he shouted down the magistrates, calling them "Just-asses," and demanded that Coddington, who presided over the trial, be sent to prison for his corruption of justice. He was promptly brought up for contempt of court and arrested. When he and a few of his friends resisted, they were tried and sentenced to the whipping post. Later, he and his cronies were disenfranchised and banished from the island. Gorton found his way to Providence next and fell into violent arguments with Roger Williams, but while there he bought a large parcel of land at Shawomet from the Narragansett Indians. When a troop of Massachusetts militia tried to oust his band, because they claimed the land was within their jurisdiction, the two forces clashed for hours before Gorton was finally defeated. While he was imprisoned in Massachusetts, the leaders got so tired of his constant badgering that they banished him (again), and he returned to Aquidneck in 1644 (referred to by Coddington in his letter to Winthrop). Gorton then traveled to London to obtain a commission for his land south of Providence and upon returning named his settlement Warwick in honor of the man who signed his patent.

uprisings against the Coddington government. One incident brought an armed gang to the governor's door when he was meeting with a delegation of Dutch from New Amsterdam (an unwise encounter since England and Holland were about to declare war on each other). A more serious outbreak against Coddington's ally Captain Alexander Partridge, the governor's chief (and hated) lawman, resulted in a pitched battle between factions in which one man was killed and another wounded. The report of this riot is ambiguous in parts, but in March 1652, Captain Partridge was dragged from his jail cell by a mob of Newporters, hastily tried and found guilty for his crimes, and shot to death. Not even Coddington could contain this outrage. His government was coming undone, and his handpicked council was against his rule. More open rebellion was in the offing, and Coddington, instead of defending his realm, fled to the safety of Boston from which (unlike most of his colleagues on Aquidneck) he had never been officially banished. The "king" had been driven out.

The Lord Protector of England, Oliver Cromwell, having been informed of the strife by Roger Williams, had had enough of the infighting in Rhode Island and wrote Coddington a letter ordering him to give up his Commission and submit to the Patent of 1644. What transpired during William Coddington's exile in Boston is unknown, but on April 14, 1652, he issued a signed, witnessed statement admitting that he was not the sole owner of Aquidneck Island: "there was an agreement of eighteene persons to make purchase of some place to the southward for a plantation." He then went on, "I, the said William Coddington, Esq., do by this writing promise to deliver the said deeds of the purchases" to the other freemen as evidence and finally, "I . . . have no more in the purchase of right, than any other of the purchasers or freemen received, or shall be received in by them, but only for my own proportion."

With this confession, the first obstacle in voiding the Commission had been overcome. Williams and Clarke removed the second one on October 2, 1652, when they successfully persuaded the Council of State to rescind the Coddington Commission and reinstate Williams's Patent of 1644. Sir Henry Vane again helped his old friend Roger Williams through the legislative thicket, probably with gusto after he realized how Coddington had duped him the year before. Vane and Williams had far more in common than Vane and Coddington ever could.

Coddington's coup d'état had been squelched, but his actions over the previous years had put a severe strain on discipline and the respect for law throughout Rhode Island. There was increasing turbulence in the absence of a legitimate government. Providence was near anarchy and the acting General Assembly implored Williams to return home and help put things right: "The honour of this Collonie lyeth at stake, to keep ourselves in order and union till the return of our agent from England, that provisions be made that wee be not then found in a rout."

Williams came home but was unable to find a remedy for the mayhem. Newport, too, was rent with division, and Samuel Gorton in Warwick was always liable to explode. From London, an exasperated Sir Henry Vane wrote: "How is it that there are such divisions amongst you? Such headiness, tumults, disorders and injustice. The noise echoes into the ears of all, as well friends and enemies, by every return of ships from those parts. Is not the fear of God amongst you to restrain? Are there no wise men amongst you?" The fault for much of the agitation can be laid at the feet of William Coddington.

Part of Clarke and Williams's petition for cancellation accused Coddington of conspiring with the Dutch to send soldiers to Aquidneck—a clear act of treachery and a capital offense now that England was officially at war with the Netherlands. The English were contemplating trying Coddington for his alleged crimes. Had they done so, he could have been hanged for treason. But nearly three years after his commission had been granted, a humbled ex-Governor Coddington stood before the Newport Court of Trials and stated: "I, William Coddington, do freely submit to the authority of his Highness in this Colonie, as it is now unified, and that with all my heart." Quite unlike what might have transpired in the Massachusetts Bay Colony, remarkably Rhode Island opted not for revenge but chose to forgive Coddington's misadventures and sent a letter to Clarke, still in London as their agent, asking him to request that Parliament drop the charges. The Protectorate was too distracted with its own crises to pursue indictment.

William Coddington got away with his life, but his brief stint as "king" of Aquidneck Island had finally come to an end.

The Charter of 1663

The Road to Freedom

Dr. John Clarke was a singular man.

      Unlike William Coddington, he was modest, thrifty, and utterly moral. He championed few causes but pursued them relentlessly: liberty of conscience for all and separation of church and state. Clarke didn't leave behind much signed evidence of his thoughts and beliefs, as John Winthrop and Roger Williams did. Yet the consequences of his meager output have been immense in their impact on the political and social development of both Rhode Island and America. Aside from writing some of Newport's legislation, John Clarke authored only two major works: *Ill Newes from New-England* in 1652, which is a devastating record of the Massachusetts Bay Colony's persecution of fellow Puritan dissenters, and, more famously, the Royal Charter of 1663, granted by King Charles II.

      Clarke never sought the limelight, even when he was preaching. Clarke was briefer than John Cotton and his brethren, and more apt to share his pulpit with others, even common parishioners. He did his work diligently and retreated into his Baptist faith for strength and courage. He was serious and scholarly. Although he held civil office numerous times—he served on the General Court in 1648, was treasurer of the colony in 1649, and deputy governor in 1672 and 1673—he appears to have done so out of a sense of responsibility to his town and colony, rather than to garner personal political power.

      Unlike Roger Williams, who is practically a household name, John Clarke is virtually unknown beyond students of Rhode Island history. Yet Clarke's impact, in the long run, eclipses what Williams achieved. Williams founded and guided a small colony expertly and fairly; he fought for what he believed in, obtained the Patent of 1644 from Parliament, and Rhode Island benefited from his labors. Clarke's social engineering was at a higher level. He envisioned, and was able to implement, a revolutionary shift in the way a dominion interacts with its subjects in the realms of secular discourse and religious sovereignty. In the 1663 Charter he achieved the establishment, by royal decree, of the first enduring republican government in the New World, based on an individual's right to choose his or her own faith freely without temporal control or punishment. John Clarke wrote the formula for the future—untried, dangerous, prescient in ways unimaginable at the time. He laid down the destiny for Newport, Rhode Island, and consequentially the United States of America.

Guilliam de Ville
Portrait of a Clergyman, possibly John Clarke
(detail), 1659
Oil on canvas
Redwood Library
and Athenæum
Newport, Rhode Island
RLC.PA.125

These advances would have come in time; they were written on the wind. But the concepts were Clarke's to believe in and battle for at a time when few others could even conceive of such liberties. And he had the luck of timing: Charles II, a receptive monarch, was troubled by the way the tyrants in Massachusetts behaved toward its inhabitants and visitors; he had lost his father to the Puritan chopping block in 1649, and the hanging of Mary Dyer in Boston in 1660 for her Quaker beliefs, just as the Restoration was beginning, left a lasting impression on his memory.

Dr. John Clarke set a new tone in the English colonies. He had the imagination and intelligence to envision a society in which inhabitants would be free to choose their own leaders and equally free to follow their spiritual instincts without fear of persecution. More than a century after Clarke wrote the Rhode Island Charter, Thomas Jefferson penned the Declaration of Independence—a document that, in a variety of ways, echoes Clarke's plea for human liberty.

John Clarke was born on October 3, 1609, Westhorpe, Suffolk, England, the sixth of eight children in a moderately prosperous family. It is evident that he had a university education because he could read Hebrew, Greek, and Latin, but where he went is unknown. If it was in England, he would have attended either Oxford or Cambridge. The same mystery surrounds his medical and legal training; these could have been obtained in England or, like other dissidents of his era, he might have gone to Holland for instruction. A John Clarke of England was enrolled at the Students of the Academy at Leiden, Batavia, in 1635, and it is likely this is our Clarke, although there were many John Clarkes in that period. Whether he was officially ordained in any church is also not clear; he may have joined the ministry in Holland, because Baptists were active there at that time. Although he preached and ministered for years, he never officially took the title of elder. In 1634 he married Elizabeth Harges, which appears to have been a step up for him but down for her, according to Sydney V. James, an expert on Clarke. In 1637, when the couple immigrated to Boston, they were accompanied by two of his brothers and one sister.

It is clear that Clarke was a freethinker, open to new ideas, accepting of other people's reasoning. Although raised as a Calvinist Puritan, he sought his own conscience, and once he had embraced the Baptist creed, he did not waver. Both in Pocasset and Newport, Clarke preached, practiced medicine, drafted laws, tended his own fields, helped survey and clear farmland, and assisted in laying out roads and building bridges. He was at once a simple man, part of his community, and a complex thinker, steeped in the Bible and the classics, and ready to entertain new concepts of theological and societal expansion. Clarke was one of the best-educated men in early America. As he matured, he became more open-minded. The religious agitation and the profusion of beliefs churning around him in the colonies broadened his thinking and, at the same time, intensified his own Baptist outlook. He witnessed outrages, and every affront to soul liberty offended him. He had his own problems as well. In *Ill Newes from New-England*, he details his personal confrontation with the tyranny of the Massachusetts Bay Colony. This ordeal affected him deeply, and it led directly to his choice of language in the Charter of 1663, the language of emancipation.

In 1651, a few months before he traveled to England to seek annulment of William Coddington's Commission, Clarke, accompanied by fellow Newport Baptists Obadiah Holmes and John Crandall, was

Guilliam de Ville
Portrait of a Clergyman,
possibly John Clarke, 1659
Oil on canvas
Redwood Library
and Athenæum
Newport, Rhode Island
RLC.PA.125

invited to Lynn, Massachusetts, to aid and comfort another Baptist, a blind man named William Witter, and conduct total immersion baptisms of new believers. Clarke knew that his presence would lead to trouble, given the strict laws against proselytizing within the Bay Colony. He didn't care; in fact, he was looking for a way to provoke the rigid Massachusetts authorities. On Sunday, July 20, while he was conducting a service in the privacy of Witter's house, two local constables forced their way in and arrested the three men. Their warrant allowed them to search for and detain "certain erronious persons, being Strangers; and them to apprehend and in safe custody to keep and tomorrow morning be eight of the Clock to bring before me—Robert Bridges." Later the same day, as Clarke wrote, "so to their Meeting we were brought, while they were at their prayers, and uncovered [worshipping without wearing hats]; and at my first stepping over the threshold I unveiled myself [took his hat off], civilly saluted them, turned into the seat I was appointed to, put my hat on again, and so sat down, opened my Book, and fell to reading: hereupon Mr. Bridges being troubled, commanded the Constable to pluck off our hats, which he did, and where he laid mine, there I let it lye." Clarke tried to convince them of their error in treating strangers in such a manner, but for naught; they were guilty of showing disrespect by not keeping their hats off in church. When Clarke accused the Puritans of not being true Christians, he and the others were arrested again, carried off to "the Ordinary" for the night, and watched over "as Theeves and Robbers."

The next day they were taken to Boston and imprisoned for three weeks before their trial by Governor John Endicott. All three were found guilty of rebaptizing Witter's associates and of several other offenses and heresies. The court ordered fines of £30 to Holmes, £20 to Clarke, and £5 to Crandall, and added that if the fines were not paid they would be whipped (the immediacy of the sentence recalls the ordeal of Anne Hutchinson). Friends came forward and paid Clarke's fine (against his will), Crandall was let off, but Holmes refused on principle to pay. He was taken out and flogged thirty times, enough lashes to kill or cripple a man. He wore his punishment as a badge of honor, a small inconvenience for his Baptist faith. Endicott, the ultimate Puritan bureaucrat, his face drawn tight, eyes simmering with righteousness, almost as an aside told Clarke that his transgressions should have brought him the death sentence. We do not know Clarke's rejoinder. Eventually, all three men escaped the Bay Colony and returned to Newport.

Sydney V. James maintains that "when Williams had gone to England in 1643 to petition for a charter giving the four [sic] towns a colonial jurisdiction of their own, he had written *A Key into the Language of America* to advertise his value in converting Indians—and by implication, to point out Massachusetts's failure in this regard. This was a marvelously indirect method but it worked." Perhaps Williams shared this tactic with Clarke on their voyage to England in 1651 to overturn Coddington's Commission, because, early on in London, Clarke penned *Ill Newes from New-England* as a way of informing the English authorities of what was really going on in the Bay Colony. The work served as an object lesson in a colony out of control with its attempt to rule all aspects of secular and religious life—the same conditions that would prevail if Coddington were allowed to maintain his near magisterial reign. Under the 1644 Patent, Rhode Island wasn't denying people's rights, he asserted; Rhode Island let people live by their principles. It was Massachusetts, with its punishments and brain-deadening dogma, that was the real culprit. *Ill Newes* was well received in an England hungry to learn about life in America and went through at least two printings. It was particularly well regarded in Newport.

Writing *Ill Newes* helped topple the Coddington Commission and was the beginning of a long creative process of refinement and enlargement for Clarke that would culminate in the language he chose in the 1663 Charter. And it is magnificent language, as lofty and compelling as we will ever see in a diplomatic document. *Ill Newes* was a first draft of Clarke's persuasive argument that separation of the civil sector from the religious actually enhances the workings of government; that by letting people freely choose their own faith and staying out of their way, the secular body is empowered and can operate in a more orderly and rational fashion. In the eleven years between *Ill Newes* and the Charter of 1663, Clarke would continue to hone his statement and clarify his argument and was able to convince not only the English king but also his myriad advisers (who had deeply divided agendas) of the worthiness of this revolutionary approach.

John Clarke and his wife stayed in England for twelve years. Roger Williams tarried in London for over a year after the repeal of Coddington's Commission, then returned to Providence in 1654 to try to get all four towns back into a single government. It took him three more years to do so, such was the depth of division among the Narragansett communities. On paper, the towns had agreed to reconstitute themselves into a colonial government; in reality, they acted as separate fiefdoms with withering disdain for the needs or wishes of the others. In Rhode Island, chaos ruled and in that regard it was very much like battle-fatigued England.

Clarke acted as the official agent for Newport in London, but he was really the de facto representative for the entire colony. In February 1654, Clarke submitted a petition to Parliament requesting an expanded charter for Rhode Island, but he received no answer. He became an itinerant Baptist preacher, practiced medicine and law at Gray's Inn, and was involved in radical politics to the extent that he (or another John Clarke; the record is hopelessly muddled) was arrested and jailed for six months in 1658 for his opposition to Oliver Cromwell's rule. Whether he was still incarcerated at the time of Cromwell's death in September 1658 we don't know—but the demise of the Lord Protector completely changed the political balance in England. Cromwell's son Richard took over, but was not strong enough to keep control. The center was collapsing. The twenty-year Puritan rule, so full of fury and revenge with their hatred of the Anglican hierarchy and jealousy of the monarchy, was burned out, and the English people called for old-fashioned royal stability. When Charles II, having waited for over a decade, crossed the English Channel and made his way from Dover to London to ascend the throne on May 25, 1660, the citizens cheered and celebrated for days.

The experiment in radical republicanism, the Interregnum, was over. The Restoration had begun.

Newport acclaimed the return of royalty and quickly sent the king a congratulatory letter in support of his reign. But now two interrelated problems confronted the Newport leaders. The first was that Williams's Patent of 1644 had been granted, and reconfirmed in 1652, by Cromwell's Parliament, the body that had voted to execute Charles II's father in 1649. How kindly would the new king look upon that document? Would he void all contracts entered into by his avowed enemies? When he assumed the throne, Charles II was the great unknown. He had spent the previous nine years wandering around Europe, impoverished and ignored, trying to gain support for his restitution. Would he act vindictively toward colonies supported by the Protectorate or let those sins pass? If there was not some panic on the part of Rhode Island's magistrates, there should have been.

PAYING FOR FREEDOM
In a 1665 letter, Roger Williams pleaded with the town of Warwick's leaders to raise money to reimburse Clarke for his efforts:

Now let me say these 2 things which mine Eyes have seen: First when I left Mr Clarke in England to negociate the Affairs of the whole Colony I saw with what a low sail he stood along, with what Content, patience and self denial, which Course I know he hath continued having received but little supply from us, nor of his own Estate which he Continually wrote for.

Williams's appeal for justice went for naught. Warwick refused to pay.

The second dilemma concerned Dr. John Clarke. For the eight years he lived in London before the Restoration, Clarke was a conspicuous antiroyalist, signing petitions and becoming deeply involved with a movement known as the Fifth Monarchists, which ardently believed that Christ was about to return and rule the world. Sir Henry Vane's association with the Fifth Monarchists and other activities would earn him his place on the chopping block in 1662, becoming a martyr for those who still yearned for militant Puritan standards. Granted, Clarke had opposed Cromwell late in his rule and was imprisoned for his actions—but how would the royalists deal with the Newport agent when he was so clearly associated with religious radicals? The royalists wanted a return to Church of England hierarchy, not innovation. The problem was compounded by a second arrest of Clarke in 1661 after a brief and futile Puritan uprising against the king; he was released without charge due to insufficient evidence, but his intimacy with rebels would have made him highly suspect to the Crown. For Newport, this association of its agent did not bode well. Shock waves from the shift in government in England and from Clarke's shaky reputation with royalists were washing across the Atlantic to Newport.

The leaders at home had been in regular correspondence with Clarke during his absence. One letter pleaded with Newport's agent to supply powder and shot, which Clarke did, in 1656—using his own money. In fact, his financial plight was severe because Newport had furnished him with few or no funds. Clarke was forced to mortgage his home and farmland in Newport to Richard Deane of England, in the early 1660s, just to meet living expenses. Legally, he never got his property back, although he lived on it upon his return from England. The failure of Newport's leaders to adequately repay their agent is a lasting enigma. The issue remained unresolved after Clarke returned home, and even after his death. Lawsuits were entered, promises made, legislation passed—and still Clarke was never adequately compensated.

Massachusetts and Connecticut increased their assaults on Rhode Island's sovereignty during the years Clarke was away, sending agents of their own to petition Charles's court to nullify Rhode Island's government. Whether in letters to leaders in Providence and Newport or in official documents delivered to London, the Puritan colonies were going to great ends to rid themselves of the heretics among them. And there was more. As the Narragansett Indian tribes lost population and influence, they began a wholesale sell-off of their lands (to pay fines levied on them by the Puritans in other colonies), much of it not to Rhode Islanders, but to citizens of Massachusetts and Connecticut trying to usurp their hated neighbor. In a giant pincer movement, Rhode Island was being strangled from all sides. It had no legitimacy.

Jarred into action by the multiplicity of threats against them, the politicians finally got ready to relay Clarke his orders on October 18, 1660. And then for some unknown reason, they dithered and debated about deputizing other agents and did not get around to sending the letter until August of 1661. A precious year had been lost, and that added to Clarke's dilemma. Addressed to "our trusty and well beloved friend, Mr. John Clarke, physician, one of the members of the Colony, late inhabitant of Rhode-Island . . . and now residing in Westminster, our undoubted agent and attorney," the letter asked that Clarke obtain royal approval of the 1644 boundaries and demand the halt of "unlawfull userpations, intrusions, and claimes" of any outsider. That was a tall order for a man known as a Baptist with Fifth Monarchist sympathies, who knew almost none of the new bureaucrats of the Crown, and had almost no money with which to pay advisers and lawyers (or make bribes), and was associated with the Puritan rebellion. With all the work the royalists had in front of them to restore their government, why should they be concerned with a tiny colony in far-off America? Clarke's predicament was dire.

Battling for the Charter

The man to whom Clarke was appealing was a complex character. Charles II had lost his father to the Puritan cause; his mother was Roman Catholic. He himself had been born into the Church of England—and was to die a confirmed Catholic. While on the run from Cromwell's troops after the royalists were defeated at the Battle of Worcester in August 1651, Charles had been hidden by loyal English Catholics for days on end, at great peril. Having witnessed their bravery, and benefiting handsomely from their support, Charles reportedly stated to Father John Huddleston, "If it please God, I come to my crown, both you and all your persuasion shall have as much liberty as any of my subjects." It was the despised papists who were responsible for the 21-year-old Charles's later compassion for the spiritual conscience of others. "The King was by temperament, conviction, and (by the implications of his word at Breda) personally inclined to toleration." Too many lives had been lost for the lack of it.

Still, the challenges facing John Clarke were many. Once he received his commission, he started to work writing his first letter of petition (he wrote ten versions) to the king and his council on behalf of Rhode Island. In it, Clarke concentrated on religious, not territorial, themes. This was his strong suit, and given that Charles II had endorsed religious toleration in his April 1660 Declaration of Breda, Clarke must have felt he was on a solid footing. The Breda document begins, "We do declare a Liberty to tender consciences: and that no Man shall be disquieted, or called in question, for differences of opinion in matters of religion which do not disturb the peace of the kingdom." Charles's motives for issuing the Declaration of Breda, just a month

Sir Peter Lely
King Charles II, c. 1675
Oil on canvas
Collection of the
Duke of Grafton
Photograph by Ian Smith/
Time & Life Pictures/
Getty Images

before his restoration to the throne, were highly complex, having more to do with healing wounds in internal English politics than anything else. Yet the monarch did sign the declaration, and Clarke was familiar with its tenets. In the course of rewriting his petitions, Clarke incorporated some of those ideas into his documents.

Clarke asserted in his letter that the original founders of Rhode Island had escaped religious persecution in England and Massachusetts and that they had a right to their newfound liberty. The petitioners "were necessitated long since for cause of conscience, with respect to the worship and service of God, to take up a resolution to quit their dear and native country. . . . He prayed that 'under the wing of royal protection' they might 'not only be sheltered, but caused to flourish in civil and religious concernments in these remote parts of the world.'" Sydney V. James maintains that Clarke "bolstered this plea with strong professions of loyalty to the crown, a topic on which he probably decided to say what he knew was necessary and trust the Rhode Island people to accept his judgment. Vigorously stretching the truth, he claimed they had always been the most loyal of subjects." Here we see Clarke's diplomatic skills at work. It was essential to appeal to the king's vanity, regardless of the fact that Newport had favored republicanism over royalty during the previous decade.

Clarke delivered the first letter in January 1662, but he must have had second thoughts. Perhaps the language was not strong enough, *precise* enough. Constantly revising, he drew up another letter, delivered a week later, and for this he went back to some of the rhetoric in *Ill Newes*. Now he added the famous phrases that would become the heart of the Charter: that the residents of Rhode Island

> have it much in their hearts (if they may be permitted) to hold forth a lively experiment, that a flourishing civil State may stand, yea, and best be maintained, and that among English spirits, with a full liberty in religious concernments and that true piety rightly grounded upon gospel principles will give the best and greatest security to true sovereignty, and will lay in the hearts of men the strongest obligations to truer loyalty: Now, know ye, that we, being willing to encourage the hopeful undertaking of our said loyal and loving subjects, and to secure them in the free exercise and enjoyment of all their civil and religious rights.

"A lively experiment." The phrase is exquisite, charming, seemingly innocent. But its implications are enormous. Clarke was asking the king to try something new in his American colonies—something brave and revolutionary. Clarke's appeal hit a responsive chord. Charles II had an adventurous mind. He helped establish the Royal Society for scientists the same year he granted Newport its Charter; he loved experimentation in all things.

But there were other reasons for Charles to grant Clarke's petition. Parliament had denied the king the religious toleration he had declared at Breda and in fact had gone in the opposite direction, reverting to harsh, punishing strictures against Puritans and all others outside the Church of England by passing the Clarendon Code. The code saddened Charles, but there was nothing he could do; he had to accede to Parliament's demands. He could gain revenge against both Parliament and the Puritans by granting the tiny New England colony what was being denied him in his own realm. And finally, Charles was repelled by the excesses of Massachusetts and Connecticut in repressing religious dissent. The reports out of the Bay Colony of whippings, banishments, and public hangings did not jibe with his sense of justice. By making an example of Rhode Island, the monarch was sending a not-too-subtle message to its neighbors to relent.

The Charter continues (again, the language is Clarke's):

> [We] do hereby publish, grant, ordain and declare, That our royal will and pleasure is, that no person within the said colony, at any time hereafter shall be any wise molested, punished, disquieted, or called in question, for any differences in opinion in matters of religion, and do not actually disturb the civil peace of our said colony; but that all and every person and persons may, from time to time, and at all times hereafter, freely and fully have and enjoy his and their own judgments and consciences, in matters of religious concernments.

These statements that Clarke was asking the king to sign were extraordinary. He had nothing to lose in making these appeals for religious toleration, and everything to gain, if they were granted.

Again, note the phraseology Clarke employed. He wrote of people having the right to "enjoy"—enjoyment was not a concept usually associated with seventeenth-century religious matters. Yet Clarke was looking to the future by writing those words. His concept of "enjoyment" was elaborate and subtle; he was not championing frivolity but arguing that it was everyone's essential right to revel in—"enjoy" at the deepest level—their relationship with God, without secular control. John Clarke predated thinkers like John Locke, David Hume, and Immanuel Kant, and in a sense presaged the Age of Enlightenment in the eighteenth century. In 1776, Thomas Jefferson wrote: "We hold these truths to be self-evident, that all men are created equal, that they are endowed by their Creator with certain inalienable Rights, that among these are Life, Liberty and the pursuit of Happiness." Enjoyment, happiness; the gift of life.

Historians have long debated whether America's Founding Fathers were influenced by Clarke's 1663 Charter when framing the new nation's Constitution in the 1780s. While some writers assert that Roger Williams's insistence on a clear separation of church and state and absolute freedom of conscience and Clarke's appeal for a "lively experiment" had little impact more than a century later, others strongly disagree. The legal scholar Patrick T. Conley has reviewed the writings of numerous experts and concludes, "The Founding Fathers were well aware of the Rhode Island system of disestablishment and soul liberty, which was still intact under the same frame of government when the Bill of Rights was drafted and ratified; the guarantees in Rhode Island's famed charter of 1663 influenced similar grants of religious liberty in the proprietary charters of East Jersey, West Jersey, and Carolina issued shortly thereafter; and Williams's views on religion and the state were distilled and reiterated by Algernon Sydney [*sic*] and other English writers of the Whig libertarian tradition with whom our Founding Fathers were quite familiar."

The Charter of 1663 is a complex document, outlining rights and obligations in the civil sphere. Clarke had help from London lawyers in preparing it, and many of the concepts are based on English law. Sydney V. James enumerates some of the special qualities Clarke added to the Charter.

> He spoke for a unique society with no parish taxes, no specifications of parish boundaries, no grants of land to endow churches, no exemptions from taxation for church property, no laws

to require attendance at public worship, no laws to call on the citizens to teach religion to their children or conduct family devotions, no legal authorization for clergymen to create marriages, no public support for education. Nor did the operations of government have the slightest flavor of religion. There were no invocations before the deliberations of courts or the legislature, no chaplains for the militia, no election sermons, no allusions to God in oaths of office or oaths to give testimony—in fact, no oaths whatsoever, but instead a solemn promise made in the awareness of the laws against perjury. With this background in mind, Clarke appealed boldly for a guarantee of religious freedom, adding the argument that this liberty would support rather than undermine both social prosperity and loyalty to the king. And the king took notice of it.

After sending another application to the king in the winter of 1662, Clarke waited for a response. And waited. But now there was a new development to make his life miserable for the foreseeable future. John Winthrop, Jr., from Connecticut, the son of the same John Winthrop who had banished Anne Hutchinson and her followers two decades previously, had arrived in London seeking a charter for his colony. Unlike Clarke, he had a number of important contacts in high places; he used them to his advantage, and to Clarke's distress, he came with his pockets full of money, while Clarke was penniless and borrowing heavily. The details of what ensued between these two men over the course of the next year are complex. The dispute centered on border variances, not religion. Winthrop was claiming most of Narragansett Bay for Connecticut, as he had been doing for years—only now he had a friendlier audience. If his claim were to stand, the territory of Rhode Island would be cut by over two-thirds, much of it fertile grazing grounds needed by its farmers in order to create viable commerce. The Rhode Island for which John Clarke was attempting to get a charter would cease to exist. Clarke scrambled, wrote plaintive letters to Newport authorities, and could not have been happy as Winthrop outwitted him, time after time, with the parliamentary committees. Clarke was a diplomat of the first rank, but this kind of bureaucratic infighting did not play to his strengths: he was too honest.

As a frustrated Clarke waited for word from the Privy Council and some advice from Newport, Winthrop got his charter speedily passed in April 1662. It was a disaster for Rhode Island. Clarke's application to the Crown had carefully laid out the dimensions and proportions of the colony's borders. But now Winthrop had apparently won title to all that land, with the exception of the four existing Rhode Island towns. When Clarke "discovered that all this had been done, he bestirred himself in earnest. He sought out Winthrop and found him on the point of embarking for America. He prevailed upon him (either directly or by an appeal for fair play, or indirectly through the Lords of Council) to postpone his journey. The question of the conflicting territorial claims of the two colonies was then carefully taken up."

A panel of arbitrators was convened to solve the border dispute. Each man presented his claim, Winthrop stretching the truth so much that Clarke accused him of "base treacherous & under hand dealing." At the same time, Winthrop was writing letters to his business associates in America traducing Clarke. No solution was found; the matter became even muddier. More alternatives were proposed, but by now Clarke and Winthrop were so wary of one another that the suggestions were all dismissed. Clarke, out of funds, was nearly out of options. In a letter to the authorities at Newport, he spewed forth at "the cruel deceitful Barbarous

Treacherous dealing of a professing People against their Neighbors who have fled together with Themselves to the extreme peril & hazard of their lives to enjoy their spiritual liberties in those remote parts."

Finally, Clarke petitioned the king directly and informed him of the dispute with Connecticut. Months went by. More meetings were planned, then canceled. The new year of 1663 arrived and Clarke must have been frantic. Connecticut had had its charter, with the disastrous boundary implications for Rhode Island, for eight months. If he couldn't persuade the Council on Foreign Plantations of his rightful cause, all would be lost. More negotiations between Clarke and Winthrop ensued, but to no avail. The question was where to establish Rhode Island's western border—at the Pawcatuck River or the Pequot River. And the problem for Clarke was that Winthrop not only had more leverage, he also held a stake in a private enterprise, the Atherton Company, that laid claim to most of Rhode Island's mainland—Point Judith to Wickford and beyond to the west, many thousands of fertile acres that were rightfully part of Providence Plantations. Winthrop had reasons beyond political ones not to back down.

After more rounds of meetings and negotiations, more panels of arbitrators, Clarke and Winthrop, weary of the battle and each other, came to an uneasy agreement. Under the guidance of the earl of Clarendon (ironically, the same Clarendon associated with the punitive religious code prevailing in England—one has to wonder how in the world he accepted Clarke's tolerance clauses), it was ruled that the Pawcatuck River would form the boundary between the colonies. This seemed like a logical and just conclusion, but it was not to be. Connecticut and Rhode Island would fight over their borders for nearly eighty more years, partly because of the imprecise language incorporated in the 1663 Charter. Clarke's defense of religious liberty was magnificent; his understanding of the geographical and economic consequences of the land question was flawed.

But the task at hand was completed. Clarke labored in London, steering the Charter through its many revisions and final signature. He got a modicum of revenge against Winthrop by removing a clause that would permit members of the Atherton Company the right to vote for jurisdiction under Connecticut or Rhode Island. Having learned what Parliament might or might not allow, Clarke copied many civil clauses from the Connecticut charter, and the two documents are quite similar, except in regard to religious tolerance. The Charter of 1663 granted another important freedom, one that removed a constraint that had been challenged by Rhode Islanders from the beginning. The colony now had the right "to transport goods to and from it in commerce, so long as the king's customs duties were paid. For Rhode Island, the right to travel within the king's dominions had special significance: it meant that the actions by Massachusetts in the past to banish Rhode Islanders on the pain of death were rendered null."

In the eyes of English law, the Charter "created a corporation under the name 'The Governor and Company of the English Collonies of Rhode-Island and Providence Plantations, in New England, in America.' Its members, the freemen and their successors, would be 'a bodie corporate and politique, in fact and name.' The political entity was often called the Governor and Company, by which was meant either the chief officers or the whole body of freemen."

Against great odds, John Clarke had succeeded in writing and obtaining the most liberal Charter ever granted by a monarch. It allowed for a religious independence found nowhere else in North America, a self-governing body of freemen not beholden to the English Crown for supervision; in fact, a literal free republic within the royal domain. One of the most curious and unexpected clauses is the complete release

of Rhode Island from any obligation to the Church of England (again, how did Lord Clarendon let *that* one slip by?). It allowed for fishing rights, commercial rights, an independent judiciary, freedom of political assemblies, the sustaining of a military force, and many other privileges not granted in the past to any colonial government. The Charter was so thorough and democratic that it remained the law of Rhode Island until 1843, when a new constitution was ratified.

Roger Williams was pleased and a little perplexed at the array of liberties Clarke had managed to procure. In a letter to an old friend, Williams remarks: "This his Majesty's grant was startled at by his Majesty's high officers of state, who were to view it in course before the sealing, but fearing the lion's roaring, they crouched, against their wills, in obedience to his Majesty's pleasure."

Clarke's Charter represents a milestone in Western history because his requests created, according to Professor Sydney Ahlstrom, "the first commonwealth in modern history to make religious liberty (not simply a degree of toleration) a cardinal principle of its corporate existence and to maintain the separation of church and state on these grounds." It is an irony of history that few people even know John Clarke's name, let alone anything of his great accomplishment. Scores of twentieth-century historians spent their careers dissecting and exalting Puritan Massachusetts's intolerant New England Way without even mentioning the revolution brought about in tiny Rhode Island by Clarke's successful petition for human dignity and self-control.

John and Elizabeth Clarke stayed in England for another four months, but he arranged for the Charter (in a box under lock and key) to be brought to Newport by Captain George Baxter. Word seems to have already reached home that Clarke had achieved something significant, so when Baxter landed in late November 1663, the town was filled with anticipation. The event is recorded in the Colonial Record:

> At a very great meeting and assembly of the freemen of the collony of Providence Plantations, at Newport, in Rhode Island, in New England, November the 24, 1663. . . .
>
> Voted, 1. That Mr. John Clarke, the Collony Agent's letter to the President, Assistants and Freemen of the Collony, be opened and read, which accordingly was done with good delivery and attention.
>
> Voted, 2. That the box in which the King's gratious letters were enclosed be opened, and the letters with the broad seal thereto affixed, be taken forth and read by Captain George Baxter in the audience and view of all the people; which was accordingly done, and the said letters with his Majestyes Royal Stamp, and the broad seal, with much becoming gravity held up on high, and presented to the perfect view of the people, and then returned into the box and locked up by the Governor, in order to the safe keeping of it.

The "lively experiment" had officially begun.

The four settlements on Narragansett Bay have, far too often, been portrayed by most twentieth-century historians as unstable, chaotic, and irreverent. The colony's reputed factionalism has been viewed negatively instead of being seen as the predictable birth pangs that accompany the arrival of a new idea. This nearsighted depiction of the small colony is prejudiced and unfair. "In fact," maintains historian Ray Irwin,

Rhode Island's early strategies for survival underscore enduring themes in the history of the United States. The leaders of the colony found ways to govern effectively a socially and religiously diverse populace, while mastering and applying the art of pragmatic politics within the Anglo-American empire. They devised a way to live peacefully which emphasized both the separation of religious and civil spheres and dependence upon English law and tradition. So, whereas orthodoxy stressed morality, vocation, and social and political order, the Rhode Island experience amplified the notions of benign diversity and flexibility. Thus, Rhode Island and Providence Plantations not only more closely resembled early modern England than its neighbors, but it also prefigured more truly American religion, politics, and society.

Newport Comes of Age

The Clarkes returned to a town on the march, in the midst of a great transformation. It must have looked very different to them, having been gone so long. By the mid-1660s, Newport was home to over seven hundred people. Many were fresh from England, although most newcomers were migrants from other New England colonies who desired either more openness for their religious practices or more opportunity for financial advancement. Newport was alive and thriving. Houses were being built along Thames and Marlborough streets and all along the hillside rising from the harbor. The rudimentary lean-tos with thatched roofs and crude chimneys were being superseded by more substantial houses, while the Gothic building techniques brought from England were creatively adapted for the more stringent New England climate. With experienced carpenters and builders now part of the community, homes were often two stories with four rooms per floor, either plank-framed or stud-framed, and with a central, enclosed chimney. Some of the houses were built in what became known as Rhode Island stone-ender style, sturdy dwellings that kept out the cold. William Coddington built a stone-ender on Marlborough Street around 1641 that was the pride of the community because of its size and (for the time) grandeur. William Brenton lived in a distinguished four-chimney brick mansion at his Hammersmith Farm plantation. By 1680, the population had reached about twenty-five hundred and there were more than four hundred houses, well over half of them in the town proper. New streets were being carved out of the landscape, and physically Newport was truly resembling a town, not a village outpost.

Newport was growing in prosperity as well. The great farming estates of the Brentons, Coddingtons, and Coggeshalls were doing exactly what the founders anticipated: yielding substantial surpluses that could be traded along the coastal routes and, more frequently, in the West Indies. Carl Bridenbaugh contends:

> This was no accident, no simple, hit-or-miss accomplishment but rather a very complex combination of able leadership, vision, daring, ample capital, hard work, and (not to be underestimated) a generous measure of chance. . . . From the aborigines they borrowed methods and plants freely; they exploited safe pastures on the islands; they made the several wooden by-products of forest clearing yield them profitable cargoes. But the real secret of their success was grazing, breeding, and fattening of livestock to vend to distant markets and the growing of only such selected grains as they required for their own provisions and the feeding of their beasts.

The "beasts" in and around Newport—horses, goats, sheep, pigs, and cattle—were engines of economic growth. William Coddington was shipping horses to Barbados as early as 1649, and the steady stream of exports only continued to grow over the coming decades. Husbandry was lucrative and relatively easy: just turn the animals loose in protected fields and let them eat and fatten—and reproduce. Herds doubled in size within a few years. Many of the estates had planted imported, and expensive, English grasses, the most fertile and healthy diet for livestock in the New World. Corn was plentiful. Nearly everything planted on the island thrived. As the farmers prospered, the standard of living kept rising and new opportunities for growth presented themselves.

The same men who had begun toiling on the land were looking to the sea as the source of expanding wealth. New, larger wharves were built in the harbor. Ships were being constructed in increasing numbers; not large craft at first, but mostly coasting vessels to accommodate animals and agricultural products. King Charles II sent a Royal Commission to America in 1664 to survey his holdings. After a tour of Rhode Island, the commission reported: "The Narragansett Bay is the largest and safest port in New England, nearest to the sea, and fittest for trade. Its citizens have increased and prospered and are seized and possessed,by purchase and consent of the natives, to their full content, of such lands, islands, rivers, harbours and roads as are very convenient, both for plantations and also for building of ships, supply of staves, and other merchandise."

During the 1650s, as Clarke lingered in London, two other developments occurred that would markedly alter the social and religious balance of Newport and fuel economic growth for nearly a century— the appearance of a new generation of well-to-do merchants and the arrival of Quakers and Jews.

The first Quakers to arrive in New England were two English women, Mary Fisher and Ann Austin, who had shipped in from Barbados, in 1656. They were greeted with the usual good-hearted and salubrious welcome that Boston was famous for meting out to those who did not acquiesce to their orthodox Puritanism: five weeks of imprisonment, the public burning of their religious books, a rigorous inquisition to determine if they were witches, and banishment. A few days after Fisher and Austin arrived, eight Quakers landed from England and were held in confinement for eleven weeks before being sent home. Then the Massachusetts leaders passed a law forbidding shipmasters from bringing Quakers to their colony and imposed a £100 penalty for such a crime. Any Friend who eluded their net by "coming into this jurisdiction shall be forthwith committed to the House of Correction, and at their entrance severely whipped and kept constantly at work." Two years later, they invoked the death penalty for any Quaker trying to re-enter the Bay Colony after an initial banishment. Connecticut was no better.

English Quakers knew that Rhode Island would not treat them harshly. They began arriving at the port the next summer, first arriving in Newport in 1657 where they quickly made converts among the town's most prominent citizens. Coddington, Bull, Easton, Coggeshall, and other worthies quickly became Quakers. For these men, who had disagreed with John Clarke fifteen years earlier over fine points of Baptist dogma and had probably been in the spiritual wilderness ever since, finding a body of faith that appealed to them must have been reassuring. Some religious historians assert that Coddington and his group had been quasi-Quakers for years—without knowing it. The affinity between their beliefs and those championed by George Fox and his followers was very strong. "The Society of Friends espoused the new democratic ideal: all human beings were equal. Quakers should not doff their hats to anybody. Unlearned men and women need not defer to clerics with university degrees, but must make their own views known."

With many prominent men and women embracing Quakerism, acceptance in town was swift. Whether for purely religious reasons or economic ones, many of the new merchants began to worship with Friends. Newport hosted the first General Meeting of Friends in William Coddington's living room, a four-day affair that organized business matters and leadership. Known today as New England Yearly Meeting, the General Meeting in 1660 predates the better-known establishment of Quakers in Pennsylvania by twenty years.

QUAKERS

The Puritan movement, which began in 1560, was burning out; the Quakers were the last flash before extinction. Started in England largely by George Fox in the middle of the seventeenth century, the Society of Friends, known as Quakers, believed that Christ had come to teach his people himself without the need of a priesthood, ecclesiastical rites, hymns, and sacraments The teaching of divine truth was accomplished by waiting silently to be searched by an "inward light," illuminated by the Holy Spirit. Communication with God was a personal matter, and Quakers refused to join any established churches because they were all the creations of men and nations, not of God. Quakers were persecuted heavily, in both England and America. Three of the hallmarks of the Quaker faith to this day are the refusal to be bound by oaths, the refusal to participate in state lotteries and gambling, and pacifism. Most Quakers will not bear arms. Their official name, Friends, is said to come from John 15:15 (KJV), in which Jesus declares, "Henceforth I call you not servants; for the servant knoweth not what his lord doeth; but I have called you friends."

Within a decade, the Quakers were the commercial and political leaders of Newport. For the rest of the seventeenth century, Newport remained the capital of Friends throughout New England, regularly hosting the Yearly Meetings that were the foundation of Quaker cohesion—and a source of Quaker commercial success.

But the rapid integration of the Quakers into Newport society was a traumatic event for its fearful neighbors in surrounding colonies. Quakers were avid proselytizers and, just as had occurred with Anne Hutchinson and the Antinomians, Massachusetts authorities moved quickly against any incursions that might divert the focus of their subjects away from strict congregationalism. In a September 1657 letter to Benedict Arnold, then president of Rhode Island and Providence Plantations (the great-grandfather of the Revolutionary War traitor) the Commissioners of the United Colonies wrote that they were informed that: "divers Quakers are arrived this summer at Rhode Island, and entertained there, which may prove dangerous to the Collonies." The letter continued, "We suppose you have understood that last year a companie of Quakers arrived in Boston upon no other account than to disperse theire pernicious opinions . . . and all Quakers, Ranters, and such notorious heretiques might be prohibited coming among us." Yet, the commissioners complained, Newport had the audacity to embrace them, "from whence they may have opportunitie to creep in amongst us. . . . We therefore make it our request that you . . . take such order herein that your neighbors may be freed from that danger; that you remove those Quakers that have been received, and, for the future prohibit their coming amongst you; . . . and further declare that we apprehend that it will be our duty seriously to consider what further provision God may call us to make to prevent the aforesaid mischief."

President Arnold waited a month and then replied, "as concerning those quakers (so called), which are now among us, we have no law among us, whereby to punish any for only declaring by words, &c, their minds and understandings concerning the things and ways of God, as to salvation and an eternal condition. . . . And as to the dammage that may in likelyhood accrue to the neighbor collonys by their being here entertained, we conceive it will not prove so dangerous as the course taken by you to send them away out of the country as they come among you."

The Quakers were in Newport to stay, even though in 1658 Massachusetts made threats to cut commercial ties with Rhode Island if Friends were allowed to remain. That would have been devastating for the economy of the small colony. Newport authorities were so nervous about the possibility of a trade embargo that they wrote to John Clarke in London asking him to intercede with Parliament on the colony's behalf "that we may not be compelled to exercise any civil power over men's consciences, so long as human orders in point of civilization are not corrupted and violated." Massachusetts never followed through with its intimidation—instead, that colony's learned leaders started executing people for heresy.

Mary Dyer

One of the great insults to the people of Rhode Island occurred in June 1660 when the Massachusetts oligarchs executed Mary Dyer, wife of William Dyer, a founder of Newport. It is a troubling story, cleaved on both sides with entrenched suspicions and fears. It epitomizes the ugliness of seventeenth-century religious controversy, and over three centuries later, it still sickens.

The incident is well documented. When William Dyer went to London with John Clarke and Roger Williams in 1652 to gain the cancellation of Coddington's commission, his wife, Mary, accompanied him. William Dyer returned to Newport with the news of the restoration of the 1644 Patent, but Mary remained in London and came strongly under the sway of Quakerism. In 1657 Mary sailed to Boston and was incarcerated for her beliefs, which she boldly broadcast. Like her old friend Anne Hutchinson, Mary was not intimidated by the Massachusetts authorities or clergy and seriously provoked their ire with her speeches about their waywardness. Like them, she was convinced of her righteousness, ready to debate with anyone who tried to dissuade her from her mission.

Informed of his wife's predicament, William Dyer immediately posted bail for her release—it was granted, on the condition that she never set foot in the Bay Colony again. But Mary Dyer was a missionary. For a year or more she sought converts to Quakerism in Rhode Island and Long Island in New Netherlands, but she returned to Boston in the summer of 1659 and was arrested. Her husband again had to appeal for her release, and wrote a letter of petition in which he said: "It is a sad Condition that New England professors are come unto, in exercising such Cruelties towards their fellow creatures & sufferers in old England upon the same acount." Perhaps because of William Dyer's standing in Newport government and society, Mary was released, but clearly warned that if she tried to return, Boston would enforce the newly enacted death penalty against Quakers.

Howard Pyle
*Mary Dyer on her way
to Execution,
June 1, 1660, in Boston
Common*, c. 1905
Oil on canvas
Newport Historical Society
Newport, Rhode Island
NHS 90.1

A sensible person would have complied. But Quakers of this period believed in suffering for their faith. Mary Dyer chose to obey her God rather than the Bay Colony Puritans. Within a month she marched back into Boston, accompanied by two other previously banished English Quakers, Marmaduke Stephenson and William Robinson. Duly arrested and hauled before the Massachusetts General Court, they were indicted for "rebellion, sedition, & presumptous obtruding themselves upon us . . . and should be put to death." The court further ordered that "one hundred soldiers . . . completely armed with pike, musketteers, wth powder & bullett, to lead them to the place of execution, & there see them hang till they be dead." Without her knowledge, her son William had pleaded with the court to spare his mother, and the court again relented. But they wanted to teach Mary Dyer a vivid lesson. The three convicts were escorted to the scaffold on the common, in front of a large crowd. The hangman placed the nooses around all three of their necks, Dyer in the middle. First Stephenson was dropped, then Robinson swung. Both men strangled to death, only a few feet from Dyer. Her arms were bound and a kerchief placed across her face. She awaited her end. And then the reprieve was read, probably to Dyer's horror since she was set to die. The rope was removed, she descended the gallows, and was returned to prison to contemplate the murder of her friends.

From jail she wrote a letter to the authorities excoriating them: "With wicked Hands have you put two of them to Death. . . . I rather chuse to Dye than to live." She meant it. For the third time, she was sent out of the colony to Newport, with the hope that her husband and sons could restrain her. She spent part of the winter at home, then disappeared. She went to Shelter Island on her mission, then up to Providence, and ventured back to Boston in the spring, knowing full well what fate awaited her. Was she haunted by the execution of her associates, consumed with guilt that she alone had been spared? With modern eyes, it is easy to see that she must have been somewhat obsessed in spirit to leave her family and walk willfully into a certain death sentence, for that is exactly what she did. Her faith demanded action.

At her trial on May 30, Mary Dyer testified that she had come again to Massachusetts to bear witness against their laws and further denied that their sanctions held validity. Nonplussed, the judges then announced her death sentence. In the meantime, her husband had written another plea for her life, which the authorities chose to ignore: "I only say this yourselves have been & are or may be husbands to wife or wives so am I: yea to one most dearly beloved oh do not you deprive me of her, but I pray give her me once again . . . pity me, I beg it with tears."

At nine o'clock on the morning of June 1, 1660, Mary Dyer was paraded through the streets of Boston to the common and hanged by the neck until dead.

Back in Newport, the news of Mary Dyer's hanging galvanized the resolve of the small Quaker community to persevere. Reports traveled widely throughout the colonies and back to England. With the restoration of Charles II to the throne and Parliament's institution of the Clarendon Code, which Charles was powerless to suspend, opening the way to greater persecution of Quakers, more Friends fled England for the safety of Newport.

About the same time, 1658, another religious group, one that had known severe persecution for over fifteen centuries, arrived in Newport harbor. The first Jews to settle in New England, these outcasts were accorded the same welcome given to various Christian sects. Because of the loss of the Newport Town Records from 1644 to 1679, it is impossible to trace their point of origin. That they were Sephardic Jews driven from Spain by King Ferdinand and Queen Isabella in 1492 is almost certain; beyond that, almost nothing is. Such is the confusion that one historian asserts that they came to Newport by way of Brazil after the Portuguese defeated the Dutch there and the Jews lost what little freedom they had. Another claims they came from Holland; a third is sure they emigrated from the West Indies island of Curaçao; and a fourth believes they could have come from New Amsterdam, which had thriving trade relations with the Narragansett Bay settlers, so that the Jews there would have known about Newport's record of tolerance. The Dutch West Indian Company, which ruled New Amsterdam until the English won it back in 1664 and named it New York, was glad to take Jewish investments but did not allow Jews religious freedom; they could set up shop and trade but could not form a synagogue or gather for religious reasons.

Wherever they came from, it seems their stay may have been short—or maybe not. Rev. Edward Peterson (some historians question his reliability) wrote in 1853: "In the spring of 1658, Mordecai Campannall, Moses Packeckoe, Levi, and others, in all fifteen families, arrived from Holland. They brought with them the three first degrees of masonry, and worked them in the house of Campannall, and continued to do so, they and their successors, to the year 1742." There are few existing records to support the author's statement; he seems to have had documents, which have now disappeared, or was relying on oral tradition. In fact, Peterson is right about the 1658 date but wrong about the Newport visitors' origins: they came from Jamaica. We know they bought land for the Jewish cemetery on February 28, 1677, because the deed is entered in an extant town ledger. It is assumed that they formed a synagogue, but where it was located is unknown. The famous Touro Synagogue was not built until the next century.

And we know that some Jews were formally granted the same rights as Newport Christians because seven years after the cemetery had been purchased, the General Assembly of Rhode Island voted: "In answer to the petition of Simon Medus, David Brown, and associates, being Jews, presented to this Assembly, bearing date June 24th, 1684, we declare, that they may expect as good protection here, as any stranger, being not of our nation residing amongst us in this his Majesty's Collony, ought to have, being obedient to his Majesty's laws."

Throughout the 1700s, Newport's Jewish community would grow and prosper, and, along with the Quakers, form a solid commercial base that spurred the town's international trade expansion.

The New Guard

The founding fathers of Newport were getting on in age. Many were still active in commerce and government, and the majority of them had attained real wealth through their efforts. Most of these men had sons who

AND IN ENGLAND . . .

While the people of Newport were creating their future in the untamed outpost of America, every ship arriving from England would remind them of what they had left behind, both good and bad:

With the restoration of the monarchy, the Puritan ban on theaters was lifted; dramas and comedies flourished, and the Drury Lane Theatre was opened.

The Royal Society was founded in 1663, ushering in the new age of science and ending the Elizabethan cosmological worldview.

The Great Plague in London in the summer and fall of 1665 devastated the city, leaving fear, confusion—and sixty-nine thousand people dead in the course of six months. "The surviving fashion for blessing one who sneezes . . . has its origin in the days of the plague, since to sneeze was considered to be the first sign of an attack."

Sir Isaac Newton developed the theory of gravitation.

The Great Fire of London in 1666 was a disaster almost unimaginable: during the five-day wind-blown horror, 12,500 wooden buildings were destroyed, and that did not include 109 churches that burned. Because of the Great Fire's destruction, Charles II was forced to rebuild the capital. He was fortunate to have the genius Sir Christopher Wren as architect; many of Wren's masterpieces, including St. Paul's Cathedral, built with stone, survive today.

John Milton published *Paradise Lost* in 1667.

England fought a frustrating war with Holland between 1665 and 1667 that featured costly naval losses and a lessening in Charles's prestige.

having Sued me for account of 3200 of Sugar which the Court hath Ordered me to give him an account of: and is Fallen indebted unto me. I having made him debter for the list of debts here inclosed.

Peleg Sanford was brought to trial in Boston for his debts and spent some months in jail; it appears he was not at fault, but either because of a ship being lost or another misadventure, he was held accountable, and paid the price. After getting out of that scrape, he was in correspondence with a London merchant, William Pate:

> JANUARY 10 : 1667. Sir I have given order unto mr Wm Sanford to Remit with what Speed he Can Sugar unto your self for my account the which if you Receive and you be paid the Balance due: then if you please to Send in Bone lace to the Value of Five pounds & in taffetty & other Silk as also Some good Silk Buttons for Breast and Coat with Some Stitching & Sowing Silke: ferrett Ribon and Silk fallune to the Value in these Sorts to Five pounds and if any thing more should Come into your hands please to Send it in Nails Carseys green say yard wide Cottens duffles and Stript blankets with one dozen or two of good Ivory hafted knives in pairs.

Sanford eventually received this order from Pate, but, again, not everything went smoothly in the world of trade. Some things never change.

> Mr William Pate the goods you Laded on Board the John Pearse Commander I have Received, with Invoice of what was in the Lady but find my Self Extremely abused in the prices & also by the Badness of the goods . . . you are also pleased to Charge 26s for a saddle & furniture but there was not any furniture to it more than a mean Snafle Bitt & I can purchase a far better in the Country with all furniture far Cheaper.

Peleg Sanford's letters span three decades and offer the most comprehensive view we have of the tribulations facing early Newport traders in the seventeenth century. Their ships were often lost at sea or seized by pirates, agents cheated them, tradesmen pushed the limits on pricing, and the land-locked merchants had little recourse. They faced imprisonment for debts unpaid and financial ruin if their bets didn't pay off. Yet without the security of the large and inclusive Quaker network, based on a common belief and trust, little could have been accomplished at all. And when everything went right, they stood to earn tremendous profits. Like it or not, they were all gamblers.

Empire

During the first two decades of Newport's existence, the period of the interregnum, the town had been virtually ignored by the republican Parliament in London. With the return of the king, however, the focus of England changed from primarily internal issues centering on religion and the power of Parliament vis-à-vis the monarchy, to the operation of the external empire; this forced aggressive foreign policy to the forefront of the agenda, priorities began to change dramatically, and an entirely new mandate was created that stressed the royal and imperial prerogatives of the nation. Charles II faced constant problems with the Dutch (England waged three wars in twenty years), with the French (England's traditional enemy), and with Catholic Spain and Portugal.

The consequences for the American colonies were swift in surfacing. When the Dutch, possessing a superior navy, closed off the Baltic Sea to British shipping in the 1660s, England became dependent for the next century on the American colonies for masts and spars to supply its growing fleet. Parliament passed the Navigation Acts of 1660, 1662, and 1663, all of which reduced the freelance fervor of colonial sea trade and made it mandatory that all goods flowing into America must be laded in English- or American-made ships. The 1660 act demanded that many colonial products, such as tobacco, sugar, and cotton, were to be sent only to England. Good-bye to the Dutch and French markets, hello to decades of illicit trade by colonists. Further tightening the noose, the 1663 act required that all foreign goods had to pass through English ports (so tariffs could be collected) before being shipped to America. These acts distinctly subordinated the needs of the colonies to the dynastic needs of England. The colonies were increasingly to be operated under the strictures of royal governance, and under the thumb of a Parliament eager for the revenue.

It was a new age. At the time of the Restoration, the century-old struggle between Protestant sects was waning and Anglicanism was on the ascendance, becoming the unquestioned authority at home. In America, except for Massachusetts and Connecticut, toleration was gaining approval, with Rhode Island leading the way. This did not mean that religion had lost its appeal, simply that fanaticism had lessened and that people had begun to focus more on physical, not spiritual, concerns. Within a generation, instead of counting the number of angels on the head of a pin and discoursing endlessly on theological fine points, Newporters were casting their eyes on the busy harbor and counting the number of ships entering and leaving, while reckoning the number of shillings in their pockets.

As England tightened the screws on the colonies, the whole mercantile system—the great machine for growth so vital to survival and prosperity—came under cumbersome scrutiny. Charles II needed an immense amount of money to fight his imperial European wars, and he looked greedily to America to add to his coffers. England, after twenty years of civil war, was financially distressed. Parliament passed more and more acts trying to squeeze every asset out of its colonial cousins, mostly in the form of raw materials like wood for shipbuilding and a large array of agricultural products. These official actions cut, like a double-edged sword, in two ways: for many tradesmen, the parliamentary imperatives put a crimp on their activities and forced hardships; for others, they opened the door of opportunity.

The Newport elite of the 1670s, the Quakers, vowed to play by the new rules and began to consolidate their power. By voting as a bloc in the 1672 elections, they took over the colonial government and held it for six years. Nicholas Easton of Newport was elected governor; even William Coddington returned to the political scene as governor in 1674, totally contrite, a confirmed Quaker, and obviously forgiven for his previous political sins. The Quaker Walter Clarke was next elected with John Cranston his deputy. But after a disastrous and bloody contest with the Indians in 1675 and 1676, called King Philip's War, the colony's freemen voted to return Benedict Arnold, not a Quaker, to the office of governor.

This period witnessed the ascendance of Peleg Sanford, Arnold, Walter Newbury, William Coddington, Jr., Caleb Carr, John Cranston (most of them Quakers), and others of the second generation.

In the summer of 1672, Roger Williams challenged the Quaker leader George Fox to a debate while the latter was visiting Newport (and staying in William Coddington's guesthouse). Williams was not a supporter of the Friends; in fact, he violently disagreed with most of their tenets—but being Roger Williams, he never contested their right to settle in Rhode Island. This was to be a strictly theological dispute and Williams relished the prospect of telling George Fox how utterly wrong his beliefs were.

But it was not to be. Before Roger Williams, then seventy years old, rowed himself all the way down the bay from Providence, Fox had departed Newport. Williams was furious and accused Fox of wiggling out of confronting him in his broadside *George Fox Digg'd out of his Burrowes, or an Offer of Disputation*. Fox then refuted Williams in his rebuttal *A New-England Fire-Brand Quenched, Being an Answer unto a Slanderous Book*, by asserting that he never received the challenge invitation and would have enjoyed the confrontation.

In front of a packed house, Williams conducted the almost-great debate with three of Fox's followers for three days in Newport and one in Providence. There was a good deal of name-calling and dissension, acrimony and bitterness; in the end, nothing much was settled. The Quakers did not quake or waver, and Williams, the Seeker, was even more convinced of the error of their ways. Perhaps the angels *were* still dancing on the head of the pin.

In Newport the merchants *were* the government, and since none of Rhode Island's other towns approached the influence of Newport, the whole colony followed its example. Quakers expanded their reach over most of the islands in Narragansett Bay to gain grazing land for their growing herds and to add to the tonnage of exportable commodities. When the islands didn't prove big enough for their plans, they joined the already rampant land rush going on in Narragansett County—the same huge tract of land John Clarke had succeeded in rescuing from Connecticut's grasp in 1663. But there bedlam reigned. Too often, in an attempt to settle scores with the English settlers, the Narragansett Indians had sold the same plot of land to more than one buyer. Massachusetts and Connecticut businessmen, forming partnerships like the Atherton Company, seized the opportunity to buy land as a way of weakening the sovereignty of Rhode Island and cheat the Indians while doing so. Although the legal wrangling over this part of the colony went on for decades, it did not stop the Newport merchants from placing their immense herds of sheep and horses across the bay, taking the risks and reaping the benefits.

According to Sydney V. James: "Land lust, just as it replaced religion as the root of acrimony within Rhode Island towns, also superseded religion as the chronic source of conflict between the heretic colony and its orthodox neighbors. . . . It was always political at heart, not legal. The contest did not end until trade took the lead over land as the foremost source of wealth and made agriculture the handmaiden of commerce."

At the same time, Quakers enacted laws that favored their commercial aspirations and invested their growing wealth not only in land, but also in shares of ships, many of which were now being built in and around Newport. They passed laws mandating new and better roads throughout the colony so produce and animals could get to Newport, and hence to distant markets, faster. Nearly every action they took was in accordance with their commercial agenda. In so doing, they fattened their wallets while they did the king's bidding.

The Quakers pushed for as much control as they could leverage and still hew to parliamentary demands. Power and capital were the best controls available. The effect of their success rippled through the succeeding decades because the Quaker Grandees, as Edmund Andros called them, managed to make Newport into the second-most active seaport in New England, thus attracting and patronizing artisans who worked in new industries and trades that supported myriad Quaker ventures. Carpenters, coopers, ropemakers, tanners, dressers, ironmongers, weavers, and others flocked to Newport in search of religious freedom and a living wage. A portion of the Long Wharf was built by Benedict Arnold, Jeremiah Bowen, Walter Newbury, and others in the 1680s to accommodate the burgeoning number of vessels coming to port. More and bigger warehouses sprouted up to hold the goods that would be carried by Newport seamen and captains to all parts of the world. Things were getting *busy*. In 1679, the General Assembly "ordered that masters of all vessels more than 20 tons must give notice upon entering Narragansett Bay and intention of departure three days before leaving port." Three years later, a naval office was established in Newport to register lading and supervise other maritime activities. By 1680, Newport's population would be in excess of twenty-five hundred people, and nearly half of them were Quakers in trade.

King Philip's War

King Philip's War, between colonists and Native Americans, engulfing most of southern New England from June 1675 until September 1676, was the deadliest conflict on North American soil in the seventeenth century. It led to the final demise of the power and influence of Indian tribes in the region. The reasons for the war are complex, having to do with fifty years of Native Americans being cheated, lied to, subverted, and driven off their ancestral lands by English colonists. That issue is beyond the scope of this book, because Newport itself was not directly affected except by the large influx of colonists fleeing the conflagration on the mainland. As a result of the war, Newport added around five hundred refugees, many of whom had lost their homes and possessions to the fires of the enemy Indians.

But while Newport escaped physical damage, the same cannot be said for dozens of Massachusetts, Connecticut, and mainland Rhode Island communities. Both Warwick and Providence were torched to the ground by King Philip's tribesmen. Thousands lost everything they had, and probably between two thousand and three thousand colonists and as many as seven thousand Indians lost their lives. For the Native Americans, that added up to about forty percent of their entire population. In the end, the very Indian tribes that had welcomed the English settlers over the previous half-century, had taught them their farming and hunting techniques, which helped keep them alive in the early years, and had sold the land the white man now

S. G. Goodrich
Philip
from *Lives of
Celebrated American
Indians* (Boston: J. E.
Hickman, 1843) p. 190.
Redwood Library
and Athenæum
Newport, Rhode Island

inhabited, were utterly defeated. After King Philip's War, the Europeans were ascendant, never again to lose dominion over the land.

Very briefly, after years of perceived abuse, broken promises, and failed arbitration by the governments of Massachusetts, Connecticut, and Plymouth—but not Rhode Island—the chief sachem of the Wampanoag tribe, Metacomet (or Metacom), known to the pioneers as King Philip, attacked the encampment at Swansea in Plymouth Colony on June 24, 1675, killing about ten inhabitants. He was resolved to retrieve the land stolen from his people by the colonists and drive the English out of his territory. Colonial authorities had been expecting hostilities from the Wampanoag for years and had prepared accordingly.

While Philip and the Wampanoag were the primary belligerents, the Narragansett Indians' sachem, Canonchet, received overtures from the Newport Quakers, who were opposed to joining the war effort. For a time, the Narragansett professed their peaceful intentions and allied with the Rhode Islanders; but the treaty they had made didn't last; there was too much pent-up suspicion and hostility for it to work. Even Roger Williams, a devoted friend of the Indians for forty years, wrote to John Winthrop, Jr., that "all the fine words from the Sachems to us were but words of policy, falsehood, and treachery."

That autumn Philip and his allies went on a several-month rampage throughout southern New England, making forays into dozens of Massachusetts towns, burning houses and killing settlers. They waged a violent war of hand-to-hand combat, and the results were devastating to the colonists. In December, a force of about twelve hundred United Colony soldiers attacked the Narragansetts at their stronghold in what has become known as the Great Swamp Fight, at a site where South Kingstown, Rhode Island, now stands. The Indians were routed and many of the wounded settlers were transferred to Newport for convalescence. "Major Peleg Sanford alone furnished quarters at Newport for a large body of wounded, supplying (besides many other things) 244 pounds of mutton, 66 pounds of butter, 74 pounds of sugar and 28 5/8 gallons of rum."

The quandary for the pacifist Quakers of Aquidneck: what to do? Their neighbors were beseeching them to enter the fray, but their religious principles forbade combat. Political and military leaders wrote increasingly frustrated and angry letters to Newport. Yet Walter Clarke, then governor, resisted involvement. The Assembly advised its neighbors on the mainland to "repair to this Island which is the most secureist" and when they arrived, they would be given land to farm. Almost all the inhabitants of Warwick heeded the invitation and headed for Aquidneck.

Devastation hit the Rhode Island mainland in March 1676. Warwick and Providence were destroyed by Philip's men. There seemed to be nothing the colonists could do to stop his assaults. Newport leaders started to get nervous. With the specter of losing all they had achieved to the bows and arrows and muskets of the Indians, the Quakers belatedly began preparations for war. Governor William Coddington had finally seen another light and in a letter commissioning John Cranston as Major for Rhode Island, Coddington implored him to "use his utmost endeavor to *kill*, expulse, expell, take and destroy all and every the enemies of this his Majesty's Collony." So much for Quaker nonaggression.

But already the fortunes of the Narragansett and the Wampanoag were beginning to subside. First Canonchet was captured near Pawtucket in April and executed. In August, an Indian deserter tipped off Colonel Benjamin Church that Philip was hiding at Mount Hope, in Bristol, Rhode Island. A force of soldiers surrounded his lair and the sachem was ambushed and shot in the heart by a member of the tribe loyal to Church, then his body was drawn and quartered. Brutality on both sides was rampant. The war was all but over, the Indian nations vanquished, the threat to the white colonists nearly eliminated.

Mainland Rhode Island lay in ruins; it took decades for it to recover. But Newport, now the home of hundreds of new settlers displaced by the conflict, was unscathed. With Warwick and Providence having to start over, Newport became the undisputed leader in the colony—prosperous, optimistic, and full of the kind of energy freedom and creativity engender. Evidence of that can be found in the buildings they erected in which to work and live.

Solid Architecture

Roger Williams, in a poignant letter to the inhabitants of Warwick in 1665, wrote of the two "Jewells" John Clarke had managed to guarantee with the Royal Charter of 1663. The "first is peace," and "The 2 Jewell is Libertie." True on both counts in the metaphysical realm. Peace and liberty allow inhabitants to be free in their creations, to experiment and have the confidence to build solidly for the long decades or centuries ahead—and nowhere is that optimism more evident than in Newport.

A third jewel is the tangible, lasting legacy of significant colonial architecture that is still, in part, with us today. Much of the grandeur exists in the eighteenth-century examples. Yet the remaining buildings of the seventeenth century give an excellent glimpse of what was to come; although altered over the years, those still standing from this period were restored in the twentieth century with the benefit of recent knowledge of proper methods. They are a showcase for the way life was once and serve as historical evidence of a pride of workmanship. But the larger point is that these edifices were well built from the beginning because Newporters had faith in the future.

The best-known and best-preserved structures of seventeenth-century Newport are:

THE WHITE HORSE TAVERN, corner of Farewell and Marlborough streets. According to Antoinette Downing, it was built before 1673 on a portion of William Coddington's original six-acre town plot. Around 1687, it is believed, William Mayes obtained the house and a license to open a tavern. When it passed into the hands of the Nichols family by marriage, they maintained it as a public house until the Revolutionary War. Before the Colony House was built in 1739, the Newport Town Council, the General Assembly, and the Criminal Court all regularly held meetings at the White Horse Tavern, and one can only wonder about the quality of legislation or justice passed at these sessions. The White Horse fell into disrepair in the early twentieth century; it was slated for demolition to make way for a gasoline station, but was purchased by Archbold van Beuren for and restored by the Preservation Society of Newport County in the 1950s. Since then, it has become once again a tavern and restaurant.

THE WANTON-LYMAN-HAZARD HOUSE, at 17 Broadway, is often said to be the oldest house in Newport, but debate has been raging since the 1950s over the precise date of its construction. A commonly accepted estimate is sometime between 1690 and 1695; however, some historians believe a more accurate date would be the first decade of the eighteenth century. It is beautiful in its proportions, a two-story, plank-framed

The facts are these: a stone structure sits in Touro Park on Bellevue Avenue; someone built it. Beyond that point, there is only tireless debate accompanied by a dozen ideas, most of which lack any pretense to serious scholarship. The five most popular conjectures are:

THE NORSE THEORY. Vikings in North America in the tenth century coasted down from Newfoundland and built the tower as a Catholic Scandinavian church.

THE ARNOLD/COLONIAL THEORY. In his will, Benedict Arnold refers to his stone-built "windmill" for grinding grain; the tower sits on land Arnold once owned and recent carbon-dating seems to indicate a seventeenth-century origin.

THE PORTUGUESE THEORY. Some say sixteenth-century explorer Miguel Corte-Real built it as a church and watchtower while waiting to be rescued by his brother around 1502.

THE IRISH THEORY. Not well known, but it asserts that Irish monks sailing to America in the seventh or eighth century built it. *Why*, is the question.

THE CHINESE THEORY. An amateur historian asserts that the tower was built by marooned Chinese sailors around 1422 when part of a fleet of ships that had circumnavigated the globe washed up in Narragansett Bay.

All of these speculations are muddied by a poem that Henry Wadsworth Longfellow wrote in 1841 called "The Skeleton in Armor," which mythologizes the Norse theory. He was simply creating folklore, although countless people have come to believe in the Viking origins.

Much of the evidence to date favors the colonial hypothesis. Near Arnold's birthplace in England stands a windmill very similar to the one in Newport. Carbon dating of mortar from deep within the structure performed in the 1990s points to its seventeenth-century origins. According to Newport historian Pieter Roos, a 1712 map drawn by Stephen Mumford, later meticulously copied by Ezra Stiles, clearly depicts the mill on Arnold's land with its wind vanes still in place, indicating that it was a working mill and not some sort of lookout. That cartographic evidence drives another nail into the other four presumptions. Moreover, a reputable Scottish reporter visiting Newport in 1744 wrote: "I called upon Dr. Moffat [sic] in the morning and went with him to a windmill near the town to look out for vessels but could spy none. The mill was a going and the miller in it grinding corn, which is an instance of their not being so observant of Sunday here as in other parts of New England." Most historians contend this was Governor Arnold's mill because the writer, who was a keen observer of the unusual, never even mentioned that it was built of stone, indicating that such structures were not at all uncommon in that day. Another clue comes from the fact that during his fifteen-day sojourn on Aquidneck Island in 1524, Verrazzano never mentions the tower, which would have been quite prominent at that time. Verrazzano had a sharp eye. Something as noticeable as the tower would have stirred his curiosity, yet there is no mention at all.

But speculation continues to abound because other carbon studies point in a different direction. In 1993, Danish scientists collected some samples of the mill's mortar, analyzed it, and came to the conclusion that the construction was around 1500, thus, if correct, making Corte-Real the probable builder. The mystery continues.

The End of the Century

Peleg Sanford was a very good prevaricator when he needed to be. In 1680, the Board of Trade in London, overseer of colonial affairs, gave him need when it sent Rhode Island a long list of inquiries to be addressed so that tariffs and taxes could be set. As we all know, it is not prudent in

END OF AN ERA
King Philip's War marked the end of an epoch. The feared tribes were now subservient. All of Newport's efforts could be devoted to gainful pursuits. In May 1676, the Quakers were swept from government by Benedict Arnold; after the catastrophe just averted, Aquidneck freemen rethought their commitment to nonviolence and decided it was better to be prepared than perish for religious principle. Arnold died in office and was replaced by William Coddington, Quaker though he was; the island's respect for him had rebounded greatly since the fiasco of the 1651 Commission. And now the old guard was vanishing:

William Brenton passed on in 1674, "undoubtedly the leading grazier of New England." Brenton left six farms to his children; on Hammersmith Farm alone, there were 1,613 sheep at the time he died. He was rich indeed.

Dr. John Clarke had died, almost unnoticed, during the height of King Philip's War in 1676. The longtime Baptist author and procurer of the Charter of 1663 was survived by his third wife—who was a Quaker. His will stipulated the creation of a charitable trust to provide scholarships for poor boys: Clarke's is believed to be the oldest testamentary trust in America; it still makes grants to students and possesses assets of over $5 million.

William Coddington also died in office in 1678; in his later years he had mellowed considerably. Whatever else might be said of him, Coddington took his civil duties seriously.

The governor's office must have had a jinx on it during those years because Coddington was succeeded by John Cranston, who died after serving the colony for less than two years.

Samuel Gorton, firebrand to the last, passed away in 1677.

And the man who started it all, Roger Williams, strong and opinionated until the end, died in 1683, age about eighty.

such circumstances to brag of your successes. So when Governor Sanford and his Council responded, point by point, some latitude (to say the least) was taken:

> TO THE SEVENTH WE ANSWER, that our coast is little frequented and not at all at this time with privateers or pirates.

> TO THE 14TH, That the principal matters that are exported amongst us, is Horses and provisions, and the goods chiefly imported is a small quantity of Barbadoes goods for supply of our families.

> TO THE 21ST, That as for Merchants we have none, but the most of our Colloney live comfortably by improvinge the wilderness.

> TO THE 22ND, That we have no shipping belonging to our Colloney but only a few sloops.

> TO THE 23RD, that the great obstruction concerning trade is the want of Merchants and Men of considerable Estates amongst us.

> TO THE 26TH, we answer that those people that go under the denomination of Baptist and Quakers are the most that publiquely congregate together, but there are others of divers persuasions and principles all which together with them enjoy their liberties according to his Majesties gratious Charter to them granted, wherein all people in our Colloney are to enjoy their liberty of conscience provided their liberty extend not to licentiousnesse, but for Papists, we know of none amongst us.

Sanford's creativity is evident in nearly all of the twenty-seven statements. Except for the answer concerning religious tolerance, Newport's response is an astounding understatement of the reality. In fact, Newport was on the cusp of entering its Golden Age—which would last until 1776—and the town was bustling with economic activity. To assert that the colony had no merchants was to bend the truth as far as it could go. Presumably the governor could claim he meant that the town had no merchants on the level of those in Boston or London, but his answer is still audacious. His assertion about pirates is equally stunning. Since the 1650s, Narragansett Bay had harbored a long roll call of privateers, and many had turned to outright piracy with a vengeance. But the governor had good reason to play down all this. The less known in England about Newport's accumulation of wealth, the better. Misleading the tax man has a noble heritage.

Rhode Island's friend, Charles II, died in February 1685 and was succeeded by his brother, the Duke of York, who became James II. Like his older sibling, James was a confirmed Roman Catholic married to a staunch Catholic wife, but unlike Charles II he was also an autocrat with a short temper. When he suspended the Clarendon Code limiting freedoms for Catholics and attempted to pack high royal positions with them, defiance to his rule escalated. Parliament was awash with plots and intrigues already, but when the queen gave birth to a son who would succeed his father, Whigs and Tories alike went into action.

James's daughter, Mary, by his first marriage to the daughter of the Earl of Clarendon, had been wed to the Protestant William of Orange; they were living in Holland. In order to stop the Catholic line of succession, Parliament invited William and Mary to England to replace James. With a large armed force, the Protestant royal couple landed in England in 1688. The Glorious Revolution was at hand. King James II had few friends or defenders; he was forced to flee London for France while his daughter and son-in-law usurped the throne. England was delirious. After an unsuccessful attempt to regain the throne, James died in exile in 1701, a broken man. But during his three-year reign, King James II took actions that threatened Rhode Island's autonomy and caused the biggest political storm New England had experienced.

In an attempt to consolidate his far-flung colonial holdings into a coherent, remunerative body, James and Parliament created the Dominion of New England (1685–1688) from all the northeast colonies and installed Sir Edmund Andros as its governor. The new body, detested throughout the region, was disastrous for each colony for different reasons. First, all the original charters and patents were rendered void and were to be surrendered to the governor for destruction. Andros would make and enforce the laws; all colonial assemblies and courts of law were suspended. With the most far-reaching and liberal Charter, Rhode Island stood to lose heavily. Second, as he had in England, James II demanded tolerance for all religious beliefs, so, along with Catholics, the hated Quakers, Baptists, and other sects deemed heretical in Boston were now to enjoy the same rights as Puritans. For Newport this was a moral victory and a comfortable continuation of its own status quo—but the Massachusetts orthodox theocracy was diminished by the directive, never to emerge in force again. Third, Massachusetts, as the foremost mercantile center, was hit hardest by the levying of import/export duties and taxes, monies that would henceforth be sent to London instead of remaining in the colony.

Edmund Andros was hated in America. He was not only the figurehead for fundamental, constricting changes that none of the colonies wanted to see implemented, but also personally overbearing and imperious. Yet Newport found a way to live within his regulations (mainly by ignoring them)—and to best him at his own game.

In November 1687, Governor Andros and his entourage paid a visit to Newport to survey the situation and collect the Royal Charter of 1663—so they could burn it. Walter Clarke, son of the founder Jeremy Clarke, had been governor of Rhode Island and Providence Plantations at the time of the suspension of his office, so he was still the leading politician. Luckily, Clarke had been forewarned of Andros's appearance and, for safe measure, had given the Charter to his brother to hide.

Andros came to Clarke's Newport house and demanded the Charter. Clarke replied that he had no idea where it might be, so Andros's posse searched Clarke's house, and came away empty-handed. Apparently, the Dominion's governor wasn't overly upset, but in an effort to demonstrate his authority, he called for the Rhode Island and Providence Plantations seal and promptly broke it in two when Clarke produced it.

Edmund Andros didn't know it, but his time as chief executive of New England was about to expire. In April 1689, word reached Boston that the Glorious Revolution had been accomplished—William and Mary were on the throne and the hated Catholics were deposed. Boston rejoiced and immediately rioted

In the 1930s, the legal scholar and historian Charles Carroll wrote a fitting epilogue for seventeenth-century Rhode Island and Newport:

In the weakness of authority lay the salvation of this venture in democracy; the merit of the "lively experiment" lay principally in the fact that there was no authority that could suppress this exuberant venture in a freedom never before known in man's history. In an age when mankind suffered because of strength of government, when the individual was helpless, when in neighboring colonies, called free, tyranny was practiced, there was one place where the citizen was exalted, and that was Rhode Island. If for no other reason than recognition of an ancient and honorable period in its history, Rhode Island is justified in keeping the heroic figure of the Independent Man on the pinnacle of the State House, and in preserving the inscription that circles the marble dome: "for the times an unusual happiness, that one may say what he thinks and think what he pleases."

against Andros's authority. The crowd captured the governor but he escaped to Newport, where Peleg Sanford seized him and packed him back to Boston; from there he was sent to England as a prisoner. In a letter of complaint against Andros sent to London, the new Boston authorities asserted: "That he & a few with him, imposed what Laws or orders they pleased, without any concent of the People, either by themselves or Representatives," and further that Andros "invaded the property of many, denying that the people there had any property, but sayd that all was the K's."

In Newport, the government that had been interrupted by the Dominion of New England reconstituted itself and went on ruling as if Andros's reign had been but an impolite hiccup. The following year, Henry Bull, the last of the founders, was elected governor, to be replaced a few months later by John Easton—the same John Easton who had coasted down Narragansett Bay from Pocasset with his father and brother in April 1639 to settle Newport. He remained governor for five years and helped bring stability back to the colony by halting Connecticut's assault on Narragansett County's borders and promoting a new wave of shipbuilding along the Bay.

It is evident from seeing the same names appearing over and over again that Newport, for all its democratic values, operated in fact as a semi-oligarchy. That was the norm at the time. Dynastic families rose to the top and stayed there. And that, apparently, was what the town's freemen wanted: the division between the haves and have-nots was not a matter of rebellion, but one of acceptance, even pride. Most of these family members had good educations, and they possessed wealth, an essential element at a time when officeholders were paid nothing for their toil. They were suited to rule, and they took their responsibilities seriously. The other working freemen were obviously content to let these men make and enforce the laws and guide the future of the town and colony.

It was time-consuming labor. Before Andros's appearance, William Coddington, Jr., had been governor for two years; William Brenton served three terms; John Easton's brother, Peter, was governor for two years. And Samuel Cranston, son of John Cranston (former governor; the first licensed physician in Rhode Island and possibly all of America), was to leave his mark on Newport like almost no other politician in the eighteenth century: he held the highest office in Rhode Island from 1698 to 1727.

The names we see so frequently in our excursions around Newport—on street signs, wharves, coves, and parks—are there for good reason. They honor the men who helped make Newport the city it has grown to be—and remind us forever of their deeds.

Newport had existed for a mere sixty-one years as the seventeenth century gave way to the eighteenth. With its well-planned origins and its stubborn dedication to freedom of conscience, the town had fought and then prospered against long odds. By 1700, Newport had earned the same standing among the colonies as Boston; in some venues, Newport was beginning to surpass its old competitor. Because of the town's openness to new ideas and conflicting points of view, Newport was a diverse mix of citizenry: wealthy businessmen and poor beggars, speculators and scoundrels, artists and artisans, sailors and shipbuilders, pirates and preachers. Newport was slowly shedding its English roots and was on the threshold of becoming one of the five great American cities of the eighteenth century. It was forming its identity and liking what it found. The lively experiment was a success.

Tolerance and Prosperity

3

Stability Out of Chaos

The tumultuous roller-coaster ride of Newport's first sixty years finally began to level off at the turn of the eighteenth century with the election of Samuel Cranston as governor, in 1698. Cranston, a Newport man, was the catalyst for unifying the fiercely independent colony, delivering direction and cohesion at a time when London was again threatening to rescind the Charter of 1663. Not only did he save Rhode Island's unstable government from ruin, he also served as leader of the colony for the next thirty years, being elected to the governorship twenty-nine times without interruption, a record no other major officeholder in American history has ever achieved.

Samuel Cranston was respected for his political acumen and revered for his integrity and tact. Occasionally he used strong-arm tactics or sleight-of-hand maneuvers to achieve his ends, but mostly it was through compromise and clear-headed logic that he effected the changes Rhode Island needed in order to prosper. He was Newport's first professional politician, and in the long history of the town, one of its finest.

The times called for, and summoned, a man of his character and skills. Ever so slowly, like the stubborn mule being lashed by its frustrated owner, Rhode Island was being forced to abandon its willful independence and cleave more closely to the dictates of England. Since the granting of the Royal Charter of 1663, Rhode Islanders, led by Newport, had been nearly autonomous, their dealings with London haphazard and infrequent at best—which was just the way the colonists wanted it. Newport was too insignificant for Whitehall to care about, given the turbulence in seventeenth-century England. But when Cranston ascended to the governor's chair, such unchecked independence carried perils as well as advantages.

Unlike other American colonies, ruled (except for Connecticut) by a royal governor or representative directly responsible to Parliament, Rhode Island had few high-level English Crown officials within its borders. Consequently, Newport merchants had a far easier time evading customs taxes and importing goods from enemy ports during wartime, measures that ensured higher profits. It was a burgeoning quasi-democratic territory, controlled by the now sizeable number of voting freemen, responsible for its own day-to-day functioning as long as the government appeared to uphold the laws of the 1663 Charter.

Rhode Island had more freedom than other colonies. But now circumstances were in flux and

Artist unknown
View of Newport (detail),
c. 1740
Oil on panel
Collection of
Alletta Morris Cooper
on extended loan to the
Newport Art Museum
and Art Association
Newport, Rhode Island

without a voice in London, without a steady dialogue between Rhode Island and English authorities, the colony was beginning to suffer commercially. The territory was tiny compared to its neighbors and its murky borders still unfixed. Rhode Island had no influence within the increasingly bureaucratic imperial system. It had no voice there. Boston continued to exert its dominance and pressure, both on New England and on the Board of Trade in London that controlled colonial affairs. It was becoming manifestly apparent to the most powerful Newport residents—the merchants hankering for wider and more profitable trade—that a closer, albeit less freewheeling, connection with London must be developed lest they be locked out of the imperial mercantile system. Here was the choice: growth or eclipse, prosperity or stagnation.

By 1700, Governor Cranston saw that the towns could no longer go it alone and shrink into isolationism. Massachusetts and Connecticut were still trying, largely through chicanery, to absorb Rhode Island into their holdings. Just a few years before, the Massachusetts Bay Colony had taken over and subsumed the proud colony of Plymouth, so there was ample precedent for Rhode Island to be carved up and tucked within the borders of one of its more powerful neighbors. And London cared not a whit if Rhode Island lived or died. In fact, the majority sentiment in Parliament was tilting toward ridding the empire of this problematic, renegade colony filled with feisty freethinkers. Cranston understood, far better than many of his cantankerous peers, that all of Rhode Island had to come together as never before and govern itself by the dictates of the 1663 Charter. Or it was likely to disappear altogether.

Rhode Island venerated the many freedoms granted under the Charter. Yet in the fast-changing imperial political world, the Charter itself was a dilemma. London was ambivalent about officially recognizing the validity of the royal decree. Under King Charles II, the Charter was safe because he had granted it; but under James II, Newport had nearly lost its rights during Governor Edmund Andros's failed three-year attempt to bring the New England colonies under one umbrella. With King William III, after years of muddled messages and uncertainty concerning the legality of the document, in the mid-1690s London reluctantly reaffirmed the Charter's legitimacy—on the condition that Rhode Island maintain a militia to fight in the Crown's wars. The commercial-minded English Whigs were beginning to hold sway, and their philosophy of a mercantilist economy that included all of the colonies for the moment saved Rhode Island from extinction.

After more than a half century of unruliness, it was time to put the colony's house in order. In May 1696, Governor Walter Clarke called the General Assembly together. The colony's freemen faced the future: they debated and finally voted to institute a bicameral government loosely modeled on the English Parliament's House of Commons and House of Lords. Officials were to be elected annually, and various executive, legislative, and judicial duties were more fully defined and brought closer to England's wishes.

Now Rhode Island had a working legislature and it could present a cohesive (to some extent), cooperative (to some extent), and loyal face that Whitehall could recognize. The evolution from the chaos when the four original towns went their own way to the stability of a valid, representative, colony-wide, government where the collective freemen (now numbering about 70 percent of the male population) possessed power was finally achieved, at least on paper, sixty years after Roger Williams had come to Providence. This stability might have fallen apart—such was the history of Rhode Island's rambunctiousness—but because of the skills of Samuel Cranston and the cooperation (to some extent) of the legislators, Rhode Island, with Newport in the leadership role, entered the eighteenth century on stronger, if still precarious, footing.

There is another dimension, more profound and defining, to be entertained. This evolution from the attempt at Aristotelian republicanism to a struggling representative government emulating the structures of England had enormous long-term implications for Newport and Rhode Island. Experimental democracy, along with the genuine religious tolerance that among the northern colonies only Rhode Island enjoyed, was encoded in Newport's DNA. For the first half of the eighteenth century, all the other American colonies bowed (to a large extent) deeper and longer to the monarch's dictates, all the other colonies believed what London wanted them to—that they were mere outposts of the dynastic English system, subservient and essentially powerless. Not Newport. While the Crown stressed compliance and loyalty, Newport strove to maintain its self-determination under the Charter, and its officials used all the subterfuges at hand to accomplish that end.

The spirit of the Revolution of 1776 can be witnessed in Newport from the beginning. The manifest desire to control one's own destiny without interference from Whitehall is the nucleus of the rebellion that led to the foundation of the United States of America. It took other colonies decades to come to the conclusion that many Newporters had reached over a century before Lexington and Concord: freedom is essential to growth, to prosperity, to control of one's life—to happiness. The liberties Americans now enjoy did not exist in 1700, but the debate in Newport and the experience of the freemen there contributed to the crystallization of the American idea of democracy, which achieved its now-classic formulation in the writings of Thomas Jefferson. He understood the link between freedom and happiness and made it a mainstay of the Declaration of Independence. But John Clarke had made the same link a full century earlier when appealing to King Charles II that the people of Rhode Island be entitled to "enjoy" their religious and civil freedoms in their lively experiment (Clarke specifically used the word "happiness" in his 1663 document when he wrote that he desired "by the blessing of God" to bring "happiness to all America"). The heart of the Revolution was not as simple as the issue of "no taxation without representation," as some writers have posited. The real heart of the revolt was the yearning for a spiritual split from a parent no longer beneficent or supportive, a hunger for psychological as well as temporal control. And in control lay that enjoyment.

In an 1818 letter to Hezekiah Niles, John Adams framed the question, "But what do we mean by the American Revolution? Do we mean the American war?" He then answered himself: "The Revolution was effected before the war commenced. The Revolution was in the minds and hearts of the people; a change in their religious sentiments of their duties and obligations."

The Revolution was one of America's defining moments. After a century and a half as stepchild to London's niggling dominance and arrogance, Americans reluctantly concluded in the mid-1770s that their freedom was the only course for a future that might lead to happiness. It was a radical departure, unprecedented in the Western world's history of rebellions. And there was a genuine sadness for many that the gulf between England and America had become so wide and so deep. The colonies had witnessed no mass tortures, no major massacres of innocents, no upheavals from oppressed lower classes to cause the final split. The American Revolution was more ephemeral, more sedate, less outwardly emotional, perhaps more intellectual than others before or since. Nonetheless, freedom and individuality were at the core of the Revolution.

That lesson had been learned in Newport.

In his seminal work, *Colonial Rhode Island: A History*, Sydney V. James states: "Governor Samuel Cranston presided over a transformation of Rhode Island from a beleaguered cluster of villages to a flourishing agricultural province organized to aid the growth of Newport's trade." This accomplishment alone would make Cranston one of the most memorable of the colony's chief executives, but the story of his life and political endeavors is far richer. Cranston's saga is fundamental to an appreciation of the vagaries and varieties of life in Newport in the early eighteenth century, just as William Coddington and John Clarke's were in the previous century.

Samuel Cranston was born in Newport in August 1659, the first son of John Cranston and Mary Clarke. The senior Cranston, a descendant of a powerful Scottish laird, had a distinguished career in the town: he was one of the first licensed doctors of medicine and surgery in the American colonies and served in numerous official positions, including governor from 1678 to 1680, the year he died. He was fair-minded, liberal, and an inspiration for his family. Samuel's mother was a daughter of Jeremy Clarke, one of Newport's founders and also a former governor. When young Samuel married, he took the hand of Mary Hart, a granddaughter of Roger Williams, with whom he had seven children. During his long tenure as governor, Samuel's ties to the powerbrokers of Providence through the Williams family proved crucial. Like so many successful Newport men, Samuel Cranston had useful connections.

Cranston's early years are shrouded in uncertainty and myth since many records have not survived. He was reportedly a small man with sharp, darting dark eyes, generous and kind to everyone around him. He was genuinely well liked. Some historians contend that he was a goldsmith and active in the militia; others say that he went to sea, because he was often referred to as "Captain." But the most dramatic, and probably apocryphal, legend that surrounds Samuel Cranston is that as a young sailor he was captured by pirates (a regular occurrence in those days) and, as nothing was heard of him for many years, he was given up for dead. According to another writer in 1881,

> It is related by Bull, in his *Memoirs of Rhode Island*, that "his wife having an offer of marriage from Mr. Russell of Boston, accepted it, and was on the eve of solemnizing the marriage ceremony. But Cranston, having arrived in Boston, hastened homeward, and at Howland's Ferry, just before night, was informed that his wife was to be married that evening. With increased speed he flew to Newport, but not until the wedding guests had begun to assemble. She was called by a servant into the kitchen, a person being there who wished to speak with her. A man in sailor's habit advanced and informed her that her husband had arrived in Boston, and requested him to inform her that he was on his way to Newport. This information induced her to question the man very closely. He then told her that what he said was the truth, for he had seen her husband at Howland's Ferry that very afternoon, and that he was on his way to Newport. Then, stepping toward her, he raised his cap and pointed to a scar on his head, and said, 'Do you recollect that scar?' from which she at once recognized her husband as in her presence. He then entertained the wedding guests with the story of his adventures and sufferings."

Mr. Russell of Boston apparently took his change of fortune gracefully.

The story is probably romantic fiction, but what Cranston went on to accomplish in his long political career was genuine. He became chief executive in the spring of 1698, at the age of thirty-nine, when his Quaker uncle, Governor Walter Clarke, refused to take an oath to enforce the newly issued Trade and Navigation Act drawn up by the Board of Trade, and resigned. Right away, Samuel Cranston was confronted with a major crisis. Although born a Quaker himself (he was never affiliated with any denomination, yet he was assigned Pew 1 at the Anglican Trinity Church and some of his children were baptized there), the new governor realized that the security of the Charter was at risk by defying the powerful board and quickly signed the edict in order to assuage the authorities.

But that was just the beginning of his travails. Richard Coote, the Earl of Bellomont, was the Royal Governor of Massachusetts, New Hampshire, and New York at the time, with the commission of captain-general over Rhode Island; he was not amused by the colony's independent behavior on a number of counts, the most serious being harboring pirates. The Board of Trade had instructed Bellomont to investigate Rhode Island because "their favoring of pirates and carrying on illegal trade has been so often complained of, and the instances hereof are so manifest, that we cannot doubt the truth of it." Bellomont was abetted by a group of prominent royalist Newport merchants—Peleg Sanford, Francis Brinley, and Nathaniel Coddington among them—who sided with the Crown and desired closer ties with London for commercial reasons; they, too, wanted to see the end of the Charter government, because they believed it obstructed their business dealings and was too lax on outlaw pirates who sometimes plundered their ships.

With his conservative allies, Bellomont was relentless in his assaults on Rhode Island's Charter and, in November 1699, petitioned the Board of Trade and the Privy Council to nullify the republican government, bringing twenty-five distinct charges against it. The accusations were devastating and offensive in the extreme. Along with the serious piracy issue, Bellomont asserted that the government had neglected numerous royal decrees, that "the generality of the people are shamefully ignorant, and all manner of licentiousness and profaneness does greatly abound, and is indulged within that government," that no records were being kept by officials, that they were taxing citizens illegally, and that the colony's military was not supportive during a time of war. His most damaging salvo was aimed at Cranston himself, attacking one of the governor's speeches to the General Assembly regarding the laws of England and his majesty's government's relations with Rhode Island as "basely insinuating it to be little better than *bondage* and *slavery*."

If Samuel Cranston actually used those words, he already understood the implications of imperial repression, and in this he had the jump on Thomas Paine and Patrick Henry by three quarters of a century.

Clearly, the noble Bellomont did not appreciate nor understand Rhode Islanders. Cranston himself concluded a letter to the earl by remarking, with ironic understatement, that his "Lordship had taken some displeasure against us." Bellomont's aristocratic English worldview could not encompass the desires of a people who wished to live free of London's strictures. The very caricature of a proper English gentleman and snob, Bellomont could hardly conceive of underlings having any capacities or entitlement to think for themselves. The historian Gordon S. Wood offers this view: " 'The title of gentleman,' wrote one early-eighteenth-century observer, 'is commonly given in England to all that distinguish themselves from the common sort of people, by a good garb, genteel air, or good education, wealth or learning.' " As a colonial American, Cranston had little concern for such distinctions. He was a commoner of Scottish, not English, blood, and proud of it. He was of course also a member of America's "aristocracy," given his lineage in Rhode Island history, but Cranston would never have thought of himself as anything but an ordinary, hardworking man.

Aristocrat or commoner, Cranston was in an extremely precarious position, as was the Charter. In April 1700, the Board of Trade sent a document to the king "and recommended that it be referred to the law officers of the crown 'to consider what method may be most proper for bringing the colony under a better form of government,'" stating flatly that Newporters were "thirsting for independence." No other colony had been accused of seeking a break with the monarchy at this early a date. Rhode Island was in the forefront of the agitation that would grow steadily throughout the century, culminating in the American Revolution.

But at this time, Governor Cranston's first line of attack was to write a strong petition to King William III saying that Bellomont's charges were full of falsehoods and that the people of Rhode Island were eternally devoted to the sovereign and his laws. Hoping to avoid confrontation, he then turned his sights on the Board of Trade; in a carefully crafted, diplomatic response, insisting that his government had been overhauled and was now in full compliance with English regulations, including the prosecution of outlaws, Cranston urged his superiors to disregard Bellomont's attack. He also swore that there were no pirates operating from Narragansett Bay, and he would not countenance such activity. Like everyone else in Newport, Cranston knew very well that both pirates and privateers used the many safe and secluded anchorages in

Narragansett Bay to hide from English navy ships and customs collectors, but, with the survival of the Charter at stake, he vigorously stretched the truth.

Rhode Island was in grave danger. Even as small as the colony was, London was clearly not in the mood for unconstrained thinking in America. As Cranston and the General Assembly waited for the other shoe to drop, the Fates intervened when Lord Bellomont died suddenly in March 1701 while in New York. Cranston must have sighed in relief. It looked as if no one else was about to take up the cause of persecuting the colony, and with the death of William III in March 1702 and the ascension of Queen Anne, the whole issue of Rhode Island's outlaw ways lay dormant.

But not for long.

Imperial Wars

In the twenty-first century, citizens of the United States are so accustomed to thinking of themselves as a free people that it is often difficult to remember that for the first seventy-six years of the eighteenth century, the American colonies were a mere appendage of the British Empire—an increasingly important holding, no doubt, but an outpost nonetheless, far removed from the prime focus of concern in Europe. The colonies became important mainly when Parliament needed revenues to extend the Crown's influence. And the dynamics of empire continued to shift as the ramifications of each foreign-policy decision taken in Whitehall rippled across the Atlantic.

England's wars with France and Spain inevitably spilled over to North America. The so-called French and Indian Wars actually stretched, with brief respites, from 1689 to 1763, and in America, each installment carried the name of the English monarch on the throne. As the European powers battled to increase their empires, block their rivals, and dominate the political front at home, their colonies were drawn into the fray. At stake were the English settlements along the Atlantic coast; French Canada; Spanish Florida; the Dutch, French, and English West Indies; and the vast unknown territory of the American West.

King William's War (1689–1697) did not involve Rhode Island directly on land, and its citizens did not take action in the futile attempt by the English to capture Quebec from the French. But it was Newport's very inaction that angered Lord Bellomont and his superiors in Parliament. The Privy Council thundered, Where were those colonists when we needed them? Although Newport commissioned numerous privateers to harass French and Spanish shipping—sometimes with admirable results—the Crown was unhappy with the colony's pacifists and blamed the governing Quakers for discouraging military action. Rhode Island was forever doing something *wrong*. King William's War was concluded with the Treaty of Ryswick in 1697, but peace was not to last. The contest between European powers, and the impotence of their diplomatic endeavors, ensured that a grinding war would dominate most of the eighteenth century.

When she took the throne, Queen Anne was soon drawn into the conflict known in Europe as the War of Spanish Succession (1702–1714) and Queen Anne's War in the colonies—yet another melee featuring England against France and Spain. With the hostilities spreading to North America, Newport was finally drawn into the imperial combat; it was at this juncture that Samuel Cranston was again challenged by his English overlords. He'd had just enough time to catch his breath before this assault on the colony's sovereignty began. Surviving Lord Bellomont's crusade had been taxing on the young governor, but in 1702 when Parliament

FAR LEFT
Michael Dahl
Queen Anne, 1705
Oil on canvas
National Portrait Gallery
London, England
NPG 6187

appointed Joseph Dudley—a London bureaucrat with ambitions to succeed where Edmund Andros and Lord Bellomont had failed—to the post of Royal Governor of Massachusetts and New Hampshire, Cranston's burdens grew heavier.

The Dudley affair was almost a carbon copy of Bellomont's attempt to bring Rhode Island under the royal heel. Dudley accused the colony of promoting piracy, of not obeying English laws, of running a corrupt and inept government, and a host of other charges. But he went farther when he arrived in Newport one day in September 1702, in his capacity as captain-general of Rhode Island and demanded (which he had the power to do) to be given command of the militia. The governor and his assistants greeted Dudley and his royal followers cordially, but Cranston hemmed and hawed and finally objected to the request: he showed Dudley the 1663 Charter, which explicitly gave the General Assembly control of its military force, and essentially told Dudley he would not yield on the subject. When Dudley attempted to exercise his other royal prerogative as vice admiral, Cranston again rebuffed him by pointing out the fact that Newport had had its own admiralty court since 1695. Dudley was dumbfounded at Cranston's refusals to bow to his will and angrily departed Newport for Narragansett County, where its officials, without argument, turned over control of their armed forces to the Massachusetts royal governor. Newport continued to provoke trouble.

Back in Boston, Dudley wrote to his superiors in London: "My Lords, I am humbly of opinion that I do my duty to acquaint your Lordships that the government of Rhode Island in the present hands is a scandal to her Majesty's government." He further asked the Board of Trade if it would be possible to repeal the Charter, and for the next two years the authorities mulled over that option, leaving Cranston and the General Assembly hanging in limbo. England giveth, and England could taketh away. During that tense time, Governor Cranston did all he could to curry favor in London and build his case for the colony as a good vassal of the Crown. He sent soldiers to fight under Dudley against the French and Indians. His issue was not about aid to his fellow countrymen: it was about control and stopping London's encroachments on the Charter. Cranston understood that if he gave way on one point, any point, the Charter could be attacked legally by the Lords of Trade. So, privateers were issued letters of marque, armed and fitted out to capture French and Spanish ships, the colony was placed on war footing, and whenever Governor Dudley requested assistance, Cranston made certain it was forthcoming. Yet no matter what Cranston did, nothing mollified the demanding Dudley. He was obsessed with bringing Rhode Island under his thumb and teaching Newport a lesson in humility.

To that end, in November 1705, Dudley delivered to the Board of Trade a scathing thirteen-point attack on the colony's behavior, much of it a rehash of previous charges, and all of it prejudiced. This is not to say there was no truth in his accusations. Still, the document pained Cranston because he had tried to abide by the new rules, and he realized that, again, Rhode Island was in danger of having the Charter annulled because of one man's grudge. The governor replied to the charges, reminding London of Rhode Island's services during the war, the number of men it sent to the front being far more than requested, of the financial sacrifices that the citizens had made, and, boldly, that Dudley's indictment was full of fault and unfair to Newport and the rest of the colony.

Some solution to this antagonism had to be found. Both sides awaited the outcome in London. First, the Board of Trade sided with Dudley and suggested that it was time to bring an end to the two chartered colonies (Connecticut being the other), because they were causing too much trouble, evading taxes, and, in Rhode Island's case, displaying an independent spirit contrary to royal decree. Then the lawyers for the Crown weighed in against Newport on the premise that if the governor were charged with "neglect," that might be enough to scuttle the colony's independence. Months passed, and eventually a bill reached the House of Commons calling for "the better regulation of the charter governments." Given Dudley's prestige and the number of agents he had to lobby in his favor, the bill passed with no trouble. Finally, in February 1706, the measure reached the House of Lords. Newport's future was at risk. Arguing on behalf of the Colony of Rhode Island and Providence Plantations was the skillful and respected William Penn, founder of Pennsylvania, and, Quaker though he was, a favorite of Queen Anne and many of the aristocratic lords. Penn, a brilliant litigator, was serving as resident agent for Rhode Island in England, and his rational and persuasive rebuttals to Dudley's clearly self-serving allegations carried the day. The Lords debated and voted to reject Dudley's petition.

Rhode Island's 1663 Charter was saved, never to be seriously challenged again. It remained the foundation of the colony and state until 1843, when a new Rhode Island constitution replaced it. The language of Dr. John Clarke enjoyed a longer life than any other colonial document.

Pirates and Privateers

When Andros, Bellomont, and Dudley leveled their accusations against Rhode Island, at their core was the charge of ongoing piracy permitted within the colony. No matter how much the leaders dissembled, the reality remained that it was a friendly port of call for many outlaws of the sea for nearly a century. And despite its official denunciations, the town was proud of the fact. Newport supplied a number of America's finest seamen; that some of them resorted to illegal activities should come as no surprise. Respect for English laws, particularly those governing seaborne adventures, was noticeably lax in Newport.

In truth, piracy was rife throughout all the colonies for close to forty years. Some historians call the period from 1690 to 1730 the Golden Age of Piracy, because it represented the most overt campaign of terror on the seas. One reason for the high volume of piratical attacks on foreigners was simply avarice: seamen were not well paid, and one successful pirate raid could put thousands of pieces of eight in a sailor's pocket. But there was a deeper, political element as well. Parliament continued to pass "unpopular trade laws that encouraged smuggling in cheaper goods on which no duties had been paid and no questions asked. By the end of the seventeenth century a pirate ship route was operating out of New England. It was manned by a company of seamen, paid, outfitted and armed by wealthy merchants to go to the Far East, plunder the ships of native traders and scurry back with luxury goods to sell in the colonies." Piracy provided a convenient way to rebel against the Crown, and it only began to decrease when colonial ships became targets after the 1720s, interfering with the profits of American merchants, who then acted to curtail it.

But until that time, as A. B. Hawes states, "For most American colonies, there were many economic advantages in acting as a home base for piracy. Pirate operations gave lucrative employment to

DEFENDING THE CHARTER
Why did Cranston and the majority of Rhode Island inhabitants go to such lengths to protect the 1663 Charter—and particularly in Newport? Why not simply submit to the imperial bureaucracy and get on with their lives? In many ways, such a move would have lessened their burdens. The answer is complex because the relationship between the people and their unique rights under the document was emotional as well as practical. At the metaphysical level, the Charter provided citizens with a sense of independence—they were different from their neighbors, better protected against incursions from the Crown. Any child who is different (a little smaller, a little smarter) knows the relentless pressures to conform, to be like everyone else. And, deep down, that child also knows he or she has to struggle for his or her ideals, his or her sense of individuality, his or her pride. The Charter was worth fighting for because Rhode Islanders were stubborn, proud, and fiercely self-reliant. In the economic sphere, the Charter kept royal tax collectors away, allowing Newport merchants to bend the rules to their advantage. On another level, "the charter became an object of veneration in a way that foreshadowed respect for constitutions after the American Revolution, because Rhode Island saw in the charter what Americans later would see in their constitutions—that is, a form of higher law above the expediency of the day."

mariners, shipbuilders, craftsmen, and suppliers. They also sometimes furnished an opportunity for profitable investment. If booty were brought in, many desirable commodities could be bought at bargain prices. Any gold, silver, plate, bullion, and coins imported by pirates would supply means for payment against the generally unfavorable balance of trade with the mother country."

Part of the problem that Cranston and others faced when answering Parliament's charges was a matter of semantics, because there was a fine line between who could be labeled a pirate and who was a privateer. When authorities accused Newport of harboring pirates, town officials would retort, No, no, no, those people were really legitimate privateers—here are the papers. Pirates considered any ship on the high seas a potential target; they respected nothing and were usually quite ruthless when they seized a ship. Privateers sailed in legally sanctioned vessels commissioned by colonial governments, at the behest of London, to plunder ships of an enemy nation during a time of war. But with the wars of the eighteenth century stopping and starting abruptly, and with communications being spotty at best, a privateer could easily cross the line into outright piracy without knowing it—or, in other cases, caring. Many a privateer captain, having obtained his papers from the colony, was likely to hoist the skull and crossbones flag once over the horizon. In Newport, most citizens did not care if a ship in the harbor groaning with valuable plunder was a pirate or privateer: if the captain could enrich the town, what did it matter? Nearly everyone turned a blind eye.

The sea is the soul of Newport. This island-bound town sought its release and outlet through the vast Atlantic Ocean at its doorstep. Possessing a superb natural harbor, but with little hinterland to exploit, Newport always looked to the sea as its life-support system. Men went to sea because it was one of the most rewarding, though dangerous, ways of spending one's life. Men went to sea as privateers because it was a patriotic duty and appealed to their sense of adventure. And men went to sea as pirates because it was romantic, exciting, and often highly lucrative. A number of former pirates made Newport their home after giving up the lure of the chase and lived as well as the wealthiest merchants, with no stigma attached to how they had come by their money. The fact that many of these outlaws were no better than ruffians was conveniently overlooked by the majority of the populace.

Newport sent out a number of privateers to harass Dutch shipping during the wars of the 1650s and 1660s, and London authorities were pleased with the results. The English navy was not powerful enough at that time to dominate the seas; the aid of colonial privateers took some of the burden off its shoulders. When the enemy became France and Spain, the number of targets, and the spoils, increased. Colonial officials eagerly sold or offered privateering commissions to all comers, without looking too closely at their credentials. Some, they knew, were good, honest patriots, wanting to impress English authorities and pick up considerable rewards as well; some, they suspected, were not so pure. Thus it came to pass that Deputy-Governor John Greene commissioned thirty privateers during the year 1694 alone; among those John Bankes and William Mayes, who, along with Thomas Tew (who was denied papers by Governor John Easton because Tew tried to bribe him with £500), were the most notorious Newport pirates of the seventeenth century.

The adventures of Bankes, Mayes, and Tew are part of Newport folklore. Both Tew and Mayes came from prominent Rhode Island families. Some local historians contend that Tew's cousin was Henry Tew, deputy governor of the colony in 1714; Mayes's mother was a daughter of the notorious Samuel Gorton, founder of Warwick, while his father, William, Sr., started the White Horse Tavern on Marlborough Street and was the first pub owner to receive a liquor license in Newport (around 1687). Upon retirement from his career as a pirate, William Mayes, Jr., also ran the White Horse Tavern and reportedly died there, peacefully in his bed.

Thomas Tew's first sortie into piracy went spectacularly well. He had purchased a share in the 70-ton sloop *Amity* while in Bermuda, and in 1693 obtained a privateer's commission from that island's governor to hunt down French ships as his loyal duty during King William's War. He and another ship captain were given orders to raid French forts on the west coast of Africa. When his companion vessel became incapacitated in a storm, Tew, now on his own, apparently rethought his mission. Calling his crew of eighty together, he suggested that they "shape a course which would lead them to ease and plenty." The crew replied enthusiastically, "A gold chain or a wooden leg, we'll stand with you!" Knowing where the most likely targets were, Tew steered the *Amity* around the Cape of Good Hope to the Red Sea.

> Just as they were entering the Strait of Babelmandeb, a large and richly laden Arabian vessel hove into sight carrying about three hundred soldiers and much gold. Tew told his men that this was their opportunity to strike for fortune and although it was apparent that the ship was full of men and mounted a great number of guns, the Arabs would be lacking in skill and courage; which proved true for she was taken without loss. Each man's share in the gold and jewels amounted to over three thousand pounds sterling and the store of powder was so great that much of it was thrown overboard.

After spending some time on Madagascar in the company of a band of other swashbucklers and buccaneers, Tew and most of his crew (some elected to stay on the island) set sail and arrived in Newport in April 1694. When the spoils were divvied up, Tew's share was £12,000, a fortune. He was instantly famous as well. Thomas Tew "was suddenly the cynosure of all eyes, lionized by the gentry in their handsome frame houses on the hill overlooking the harbor. The shopkeepers, merchants and tavern owners down near the docks frantically elbowed one another in their haste to provide his free-spending crewmen with all the liquor, women and other necessaries demanded by mariners who had spent more than 15 months at sea."

Most men would have retired, but Tew was relatively young, and restless. Within months, word got out that he was preparing for another voyage to the Red Sea, and he was mobbed by men who wanted to sail with him. At this point Tew was joined by Bankes, Mayes, and a Boston pirate named Captain Thomas Wake, all of whom were also fitting out vessels for a trip to Madagascar and beyond. The Newport harbor was busier than it had ever been, given the preparations necessary for four pirate ships. Merchants counted their money as they supplied guns, powder, sails, and provisions. The conservative royalist Nathaniel Coddington, no fan of these men, relates that "great was the Comotion whilst they lay here, Servants from most places in the Country running from their Masters, sons from their Parents." It was at this juncture that Tew attempted to bribe Governor Easton, and upon his denial, went to New York and bought a commission from the royal governor, Benjamin Fletcher, for £300, the gift of a gold watch, and presumably the promise of a kickback. Back in Newport, he teamed up with Bankes in his bark *Portsmouth Adventure* and Mayes in his

It is evident that Newport privateering was widespread by glancing through notices and advertisements in the *Boston News Letter*, established in 1704, the first regular newspaper to be published in America. For example, on May 22, 1705, we read: "Captain Peter Lawrence is going a Privateering from Rhode Island, in a good Sloop, about 60 Tuns, six Guns, and 90 Men for Canada, and any Gentlemen or Sailors that are disposed to go shall be kindly entertained." The Newport ship had good luck, because on November 10 we are told: "Yesterday the Court of Admiralty was held here for the Condemnation of Capt. Lawrence's Prize, and she was Condemned; and on Wednesday, the 22nd Current will be exposed to Sale, together with all her Guns, Rigging, Ammunitions, and Furniture." Public recognition of privateering acknowledged its extralegal existence.

brigantine *Pearl*, and in his sloop *Amity*, the little armada departed for the East in November. Most Newporters waited eagerly for their return.

Hard evidence becomes scant at this point, and taking the word of pirates concerning their exploits is akin to believing in the Tooth Fairy. Apparently, the Newport ships met up with the famous English pirate Captain Henry Every at Madagascar; since his ship was much larger and because his reputation preceded him, Every was made admiral of the marauding fleet. The five ships, with Every in his *Fancy*, cruised northeast and strategically lay in wait at a narrow strait for a flotilla of Indian ships full of loot. But the pirates partied long and hard one Saturday night and the fleet of twenty-five Indian ships floated noiselessly past the brigands as they reveled. Our fleet of pirates didn't realize their loss for a whole day, and when they gave chase, the results were less ambitious than anticipated. They managed to capture only one prize, although that ship alone was carrying £60,000 in gold and silver.

Chastened and chagrined for letting such a huge prize elude them, the band of bandits headed east again and just off Bombay, sighted a huge Indian vessel, the *Gunsway*, belonging to the Great Mogul, Emperor of Hindustan, with forty guns and eight hundred men. Surrounding her, the ships began their attack. After a lucky shot that disabled the Indian mainmast, the pirates boarded the ship, found the soldiers less than eager for combat, harassed the women, and made off with a treasure in precious metals and jewels reportedly valued at over £300,000. The Englishmen and Americans sailed off, divided their take, and eventually went their separate ways.

Pirating had its disadvantages as well as rewards. Some years passed, and in a subsequent raid on another of the Great Mogul's ships, Thomas Tew took a shot in the stomach and died. Bankes disappeared from the books altogether, and many rumors surround Mayes's exploits following the attack on the *Gunsway*. His name was associated with numerous raids, none substantiated, and even though he was pursued by the English navy, he was never captured. Eight years after his adventures in the Red Sea, William Mayes turned up in Newport and took possession of his father's White Horse Tavern. The stories around the saloon fireplace, a glass of grog in hand, must have been highly entertaining.

When Mary Dyer of Newport was hanged on Boston Common on June 1, 1660, among the throng of people witnessing her execution was a young man named Edward Wanton, recently arrived from London, at the event as an officer of the Guard. Repelled by the sight of her body dangling limply from the rope, he had, by all accounts, an epiphany so deep and clear that it changed his life. He returned home and said, "Alas, Mother! we have been murdering the Lord's people." Wanton then took off his sword, vowing never to wear it again, a promise he kept. In a fine example of "the primacy of secondary consequences," the death of Mary Dyer at the hands of the Massachusetts Puritan fanatics changed Newport history because Edward Wanton that day decided to leave barbarous Boston and become a Quaker himself. In doing so, he gave birth to a family dynasty that would produce war heroes, hugely successful Newport merchants, and over the course of the eighteenth century, four colonial governors of Rhode Island proud to bear the Wanton name.

Two of Edward's eldest sons, William and John, were among the most colorful adventurers

Artist unknown
Governor John Wanton,
date unknown
Oil on canvas
Photograph by Daniel McManus
The State Archives,
the State of Rhode Island and
Providence Plantations
Providence, Rhode Island

Newport had ever seen. Privateering made them famous in America and England and launched the young men into long, illustrious careers in business and politics. It wasn't only pirates who cashed in on the high seas; successfully coming to the defense of one's town and colony could also lead to riches in another form.

Edward Wanton was a serious Quaker and a fine orator. He married in 1663, sired ten children, and brought them up in his faith. William Wanton, born in 1670, also kept the faith until he fell in love, at age twenty, with Ruth Bryant, the daughter of a strict Presbyterian deacon who was adamantly opposed to their union, as were his parents. Displaying a streak of creativity that would mark his life, William suggested, "Ruth, let us break away from this unreasonable bondage. I will give up my religion, and thou shalt give up thine, and we will both go to the Church of England and to the devil together." The proposal worked, and they were married, happily, for life. John, two years William's junior, gave up his Quaker beliefs as a teenager, but returned to the Society of Friends when he was forty.

In 1694, the brothers, then in their early twenties, got their first taste of adventure when a large pirate ship, carrying twenty cannon, appeared at Newport harbor, threatening every vessel that passed. William and John gathered about thirty friends in a small sloop, armed only with muskets and cutlasses, and gave chase. With most of the men hidden below deck, the sloop approached the outlaws and was fired upon. Unfazed, the Wantons steered their ship directly under the pirates' stern. According to John Bartlett, "Her men at once sprang upon deck, and with irons prepared for the purpose, grappled their sloop to the ship, and wedged her rudder to the stern-post so as to render it unmanageable . . . each man seized his musket, and taking deliberate aim, shot every pirate as he appeared on deck. After making great efforts to disengage

In a 1708 letter to the Board of Trade, Governor Cranston announced that the colony's annual exports to England now exceeded £20,000 and that the principle trade arena was the West Indies, where there had been a substantial increase in activity owing "to the inclination the youth on Rhode Island have for the seas." He also lauded Newport sailors' superior abilities, asserting that few native ships had been victimized because "they being light and sharp for runners, so that few of the enemy's privateers, in a gale of wind, will run or outsail one of our loaded vessels." Then Cranston boasted that since 1695, eighty-four vessels of all sizes had been built on Narragansett Bay and that twenty-seven of them were moored in Newport. The tremendous growth in shipbuilding and trade would begin after the 1713 Treaty of Utrecht brought a halt to Queen Anne's War and peace to North America.

themselves, and finding it impossible to do so, the rest surrendered and were taken into the harbor of Newport by their brave and gallant captors, and turned over to the authorities, when, after a trial, they suffered the penalty of their crimes by being hanged."

The brothers enjoyed their celebrity in Newport, and went into maritime business and other ventures that would make them wealthy and catapult them into colonial politics. Three years later, they were again lured to the chase when, just before the end of King William's War, another heavily armed French ship was taking prizes in Narragansett Bay, disrupting commerce and threatening Newport directly. When the brothers reported to their pacifist father what they intended to do, Edward Wanton failed to dissuade them and replied, "It would be a grief to my spirit to hear ye had fallen in a military enterprise, but if ye will go, remember it would be a greater grief to hear that ye were cowards." The young men fitted out two ships with eager Newport volunteers, engaged the French intruder, jammed her rudder, boarded, and "swept the enemy from her decks. This prize was very valuable, as she had the choicest spoils from the prizes she had taken, and the Wantons were greatly enriched, besides rendering a valuable service to the Colony."

The Wantons were called into service for Newport a third time in July 1702, at the outset of Queen Anne's War with France and Spain, when Governor Cranston issued a privateering commission to William for a five-month cruise in the hundred-ton brigantine *Greyhound*. With a crew of one hundred, the ship sailed north to the Gulf of St. Lawrence where, within just two months, Captain Wanton captured three French ships, all much larger and more heavily armed than the sturdy *Greyhound*. Wanton ushered all three vessels, filled with a huge cargo of dried fish, back to Newport, to much acclaim. But the town's archenemy, Massachusetts Governor Joseph Dudley, tried to claim the ships for his Boston jurisdiction and threatened to treat William Wanton and his crew as pirates. Governor Cranston claimed the prizes for Newport and carried the day when authorities in London sided with Rhode Island and told Dudley he had badly overshot his mark by interfering with Newport's Admiralty Court, the body responsible for the colony's maritime activities. This episode with Wanton's *Greyhound* spurred Parliament's change in attitude toward the colony; Dudley's accusations were so clearly wrong and overstated that the Privy Council began to wonder about the validity of all his other charges against Rhode Island.

Newport sent out many other successful privateers during the hostilities with England's French and Spanish enemies, but none achieved the notoriety of the Fighting Wantons, as they were affectionately known. Later in 1702, William and John were summoned to London to be feted by Parliament for their services to the Crown and presented to Queen Anne. An account written in 1878 states that "Their portraits were painted by the court artist. Queen Anne granted them an addition to their family coat of arms, which was considered a great honor, and, with her royal hands, presented each with two pieces of plate, a silver punch bowl and salver." These distinctions propelled the brothers' entry into Rhode Island politics: aside from running a busy shipbuilding operation, by 1705, William had been elected Speaker of the House of Deputies and his career was launched. He also made several more privateering runs during Queen Anne's War, each adding to his fame and bank account. In 1706, Captain John Wanton was privateering again, and brought a French ship into Newport as a prize. He entered the political arena later than his brother, but was equally successful. The family dynasty was well rooted and soon began to bear fruit.

Throughout his lengthy tenure as the colony's chief executive, Samuel Cranston was under constant pressure to prove his allegiance to the Crown. He had to balance his commitment to his constituents and those to suspicious English officials; like a seasoned circus performer, he was a master at both duties. As the maliciousness of Joseph Dudley's campaign against Newport subsided, Rhode Island was looked upon more favorably because it faithfully sent its quota of men and materiel, both on land and on sea, to help fight England's battles, not least through its privateers. But, as in a bad dream, some demons could not be exorcised and kept floating back to haunt Rhode Island—and the one that lingered longest was the piracy problem. Rumors flew around American and English ports of brigands who were stashing booty in Narragansett Bay, of port collectors who looked the other way, of merchants who provided provisions, no questions asked. No matter what the governor and General Assembly did to mollify the authorities in England, the colony's reputation as a friendly haven for outlaws of the ocean persisted. Those demons were finally put to rest in the summer of 1723 when Newport demonstrated without doubt its firm stand against crime on the high seas.

Two notorious pirate sloops, *Ranger* and *Fortune*, captained by Englishmen Charles Harris and Edward Low respectively, had been terrorizing the East Coast of the Atlantic and the West Indies for several years. Acting in concert, they plied the waters for fresh prey, stealing anything not nailed to the deck when they ran down an innocent merchant ship. They gained reputations for mistreating officers and men of the victim vessels, slashing them with cutlasses at will. How many sailors they actually killed is unknown.

In early June, the two pirates captured a Virginia sloop, took everything of value, and after harassing her crew with weapons, let her go. They had made their first mistake because the next day the Virginian came upon His Majesty's Ship *Greyhound* (not William Wanton's), which was patrolling the seas in search of pirates. When its captain, Peter Solgard, heard the tale, he took off after the brigands. Three days later Solgard came upon the pirate ships off Long Island, where Harris and Low made their second, fatal, error. Believing the *Greyhound* to be a merchant ship, *Ranger* and *Fortune* began to fire, under black flags, on the British vessel. Only as they drew closer did they realize they were attacking a well-armed ship of the Royal British Navy. Hoisting sail and changing flags, both pirate ships fled, but Solgard ran down Harris in *Ranger* after a bloody skirmish that left several men dead and brought him and his crew to Newport to be tried.

The town was abuzz. Rarely had so many pirates been captured at once, and no one had any illusions about their fate. William Dummer, the lieutenant governor of Massachusetts, members of His Majesty's council, and others joined Governor Samuel Cranston to open the judicial proceedings on July 10, 1723. Captain Solgard and various victims testified, and each of the defendants had his turn in the dock. Most of the pirate ship's crew claimed to have been forcefully impressed from captured prizes and claimed innocence. When the court rendered its verdict, twenty-six of the thirty-six prisoners were found guilty and sentenced to death. The fact that ten men proved their innocence indicates that Cranston conducted a fair trial.

A large gallows was erected on Gravelly Point, a spit of land projecting into Newport harbor. On July 19, with most of the town's citizens watching, all twenty-six men were hanged by the neck and subsequently buried on the north shore of Goat Island between the high and low water mark. Newport had finally proven its allegiance to the Crown, and the talk of the town's being favorable to pirates was forever silenced.

The Cranston Legacy

With the Charter finally secure from Joseph Dudley's overreaching grasp, Samuel Cranston and the General Assembly focused on moving Rhode Island closer to London for survival's sake. From 1707 until his death in 1727, Cranston managed to accomplish a sea change in the way Rhode Island conducted its business. He argued and cajoled, flattered and threatened, shifting alliances when necessary. Nearly every action he and his legislature took had one goal: to make Newport a thriving mercantile hub that could stand on its own, a port that would do away with Boston's dominance of New England.

In order for external trade to flourish in Newport, Cranston knew that internal communications had to be markedly improved, and quickly. The infrastructure was a shambles, partly because of the lingering border disputes; no one wanted to take responsibility for physical assets that might be deeded to Connecticut or Massachusetts. Old roads and Indian paths had to be widened and repaired, and new highways cut from the wilderness, so farmers could get their produce and animals to Newport for transshipment along the Atlantic coast and to the West Indies. Ferry services to Jamestown and the mainland had to be increased and made safer. Bridges had to be built and maintained. Docks and piers had to be constructed. In Newport itself standards for weights and measures as well as collection of maritime fees had to be strictly enforced. "Indeed, without the internal reconstruction, keeping the charter privileges would have been neither possible nor worthwhile. Though much was said about saving the charter as if it was an end in itself, the ultimate purpose of self-government was to foster the commerce of Newport and, by extension, the prosperity and cultural autonomy of the whole colony." In short, Rhode Island had to settle its domestic dilemmas before it could build and sustain orderly, profitable trade with the world at large.

In Newport, close to two hundred new structures had been built between 1690 and 1710, all of them wood frame, and mostly small and snug. The Point neighborhood was developing an orderly grid of streets either numbered or named after trees, not people, and for the first time, home addresses were introduced. A new highway and bridge made this mostly Quaker area accessible to town. By 1715, Queen and Thames streets were paved in stone, as was the Parade (paid for by a lottery or a special tax on African slaves entering the colony), and other roads were widened and resurfaced. Newport was growing so rapidly that the leaders divided the town into four wards, each equipped with a fire pump. In 1710, the town's population reached twenty-five hundred; by 1730, the number had nearly doubled. Newport was catapulting itself into a thriving mercantile center, ready to handle the expanding commerce brought about by the governor's legislation and the initiatives of the burgeoning merchant class.

But on a broader canvas, Cranston had to juggle numerous other burdens that were still inhibiting the growth of Newport. The border skirmish with Connecticut, simmering since the 1640s, was causing renewed anxiety in Rhode Island as Connecticut's sheriffs continued to arrest Westerly citizens and jail them in Stonington. Decades of uncertainty left Rhode Island farmers in a quandary over which colony's laws to obey: the legal deadlock was thwarting growth. Plus, the dispute was handing the Board of Trade in London ammunition for abrogating both colonies' charters.

Cranston appealed to his counterpart, Governor Fitz-John Winthrop, to put a halt to the divisiveness but for years made no headway. Then, suddenly in 1703, Connecticut yielded; a committee met and the border was negotiated at a point very near where it stands today. Narragansett County, with its vast agricultural holdings, was finally within Rhode Island's domain. Cranston, for the moment, felt secure. Again, because of internecine politics and simple greed, the agreement fell apart in subsequent years and the problem was not finally solved until 1727; but getting the interim treaty took pressure off the governor.

There was more, much more. To support stability and development, a solid colony-wide tax base had to be created giving the General Assembly powers that had previously been the prerogative of the towns. Laws had to be updated, revised, and fairly enforced. Bitter and expensive internal land disputes between Rhode Island's towns had to be curtailed in order to encourage settlement. The military had to be controlled by the colonial government, not the towns. In short, a complete overhaul of the system was mandated. Sydney V. James asserts: "To accomplish this business, the General Assembly had to subdue independent power exerted by the towns and landowners' organizations and secure control over many parts of public affairs that had been only nominally subject to its rulings." As towns lost their autonomy to the colony-wide government and courts, Newport became the de facto controller of everything. It was not only the colonial capital, but also such was the power of the town that every governor until 1760 was required to live and work in Newport. The Rhode Island General Assembly attempted to spread democratic practices throughout the colony by deciding in 1691 to meet five times a year, on each occasion in a different town. Thus was born the practice that the Assembly held its largest and most important meeting in May in Newport, then in later months the sessions moved on to Providence, Warwick, Portsmouth, and South Kingstown. Even with this equitable system, everyone acknowledged Newport as the leading town.

Although it took decades of numbing labor and dispute to achieve the ends that would launch Newport into the limelight of colonial commerce, Governor Cranston achieved most of his goals. After all, Rhode Islanders were a headstrong, contentious, and contrarian lot. Even his compromise with London to allow a royal vice-admiralty judge and a customs inspector in Newport, contrary to the Charter's intent, was seen as a smart political tactic; in the scheme of things, it was a small concession while sending the message to Parliament that Newport was a good team player. Within Rhode Island, the towns and villages did manage to coalesce and submit to a centralized colonial authority, albeit somewhat reluctantly. The hinterlands were developed and agricultural output increased apace. Even though New England was in an economic depression after the final years of Queen Anne's War, Newport not only held on, it also began to lay the groundwork for the phenomenal expansion that would follow the Treaty of Utrecht in 1713.

The significance of this treaty was immense for North America as well as Europe, because it allowed all parties to focus on internal needs instead of military ones. Commerce now trumped war; bellicosity found

GEORGE I

Queen Anne died in 1714 and was succeeded by George I, the first British sovereign from the House of Hanover in Germany. He was a great-grandson of James I and was chosen to inherit the Crown in the Acts of Settlement worked out by Anne because he was a firm Protestant, and Parliament intended to rebuff the claims of James II's Catholic son James Francis Edward Stuart and his followers, known as Jacobites (Jacob is Latin for James), who had the backing of the Catholic monarchs of France and Spain. George I was not popular in England because of his stiff manners and lack of conversational English, but his tenure was tolerated because he supplied stability to the Protestant cause. During his reign, there was a rise in national self-assertiveness and pride as Great Britain markedly increased its navy to surpass that of France. Its commercial fleets expanded. Britannia ruled the waves. National wealth ballooned, manufacturing of all kinds grew, and the slave contract, the *asiento*, negotiated from Spain at the Treaty of Utrecht, led to rapid development of ports like Bristol, England. George I favored religious tolerance, but widespread freedoms were never granted because of the fear of an uprising by Catholic Jacobites. He died in 1727 and was followed by his son, George II.

a new arena. Writing in the 1850s, the historian Samuel Arnold eloquently summed up the significance of the end of Queen Anne's War:

> The last war of religious and political principle was ended. A new era had commenced. Commercial privilege henceforth usurped the throne of priestly and kingly prerogative. Trade was to be the battle cry in future contests. Mercantile adventure and territorial aggrandizement were soon to become the occasional and the object of further strife, and colonial affairs, the conflict for the possession of the Western world, were ere long to assume an importance hitherto unknown. By the peace of Utrecht the crowns of France and Spain were forever disunited. Protestant ascendancy and the peaceful accession of the House of Hanover were secured in England.

With the Treaty of Utrecht, North America (but not Europe) now embarked on an unprecedented period of thirty-one years of peace. And Newport blossomed as never before. In the new mercantile world that was emerging, it should come as no surprise that the next battle to be entered into was over trade and how to finance it, manipulate it, and dominate it. In Newport, the matter centered around the controversial printing of paper money.

The first paper money circulated in North America was issued in 1690 by Massachusetts to cover the costs of the expensive military campaign against the French in Canada. The bills were later redeemed, as planned, by coin accumulated through taxes and trade. These government-backed notes were meant to be a temporary fix until "real" money, shillings and dollars, flowed into the coffers, but the paper bills were convenient for day-to-day transactions and the practice of printing more paper was initiated.

In 1710, the Rhode Island General Assembly issued the first round of paper money to cover its own extraordinary costs for Queen Anne's War and followed with four more placements in as many years. These bills of credit were to be covered by imposing a tax levy and creating new duties on goods sold within the colony by non-Rhode Islanders. The bills were to be redeemed in gold or silver after five years. No one balked at the need to support the military campaigns. But by 1714, two distinct points of view over the issuance of a new round had materialized, and a political upheaval on a scale not witnessed before had erupted.

On one hand were the "hard money" advocates, those who did not trust the validity or legality of paper money and wanted to use only specie (gold or silver coins) for transactions. These were mostly conservative farmers and ordinary citizens not directly involved with Newport trade. On the other hand were the strong supporters of "soft money," or paper issuances, who needed the influx of new currency to jump-start commerce, which had markedly fallen off because Spanish silver milled dollars and British coins had been siphoned out of the colony during Queen Anne's War. These were (at first) mostly the expansionist Newport merchants and others involved with commerce, who could not engage in trade with other colonies or the West Indies without some sort of working capital. The barter system used so effectively in the seventeenth century had too many limitations and London merchants only dealt in sterling, gold, or Spanish silver. Other colonies had their paper-based legal tender, they reasoned, why shouldn't Rhode Island create its own?

In the mid-1600s, the freemen of Newport rallied around either the conservative William

Coddington and his faction or the more liberal Dr. John Clarke and his followers; the ongoing debate between the two ideologies had much to do with religious matters, although how the town was governed politically had been clearly at stake as well. But now, with theological squabbles finally less compelling and commercial aspirations on the rise, we see the true beginning of a two-party system in Rhode Island, somewhat emulating the divisive Whig and Tory factions in England. The lines were drawn. Partly the problem was a purely philosophical argument over the present and future finances of the colony, but a more pervasive concern also lay behind the debate. There were two distinct societies emerging in and around Newport—the rural farmers, with their eyes on the earth, and the urban merchants and artisans, with their eyes on the sea. The two sides had been growing farther apart by the year, but the paper-money conundrum represented the first major battle cry. In 1743, when the majority of small-plot farmers north of town drew apart from Newport and formed the new municipality of Middletown, the seeds of their secession can be traced to the 1714–1715 currency debacle.

In the election of 1714, the hard-money party devastated the opposition so decisively that almost no one from the lower chamber of the General Assembly, the House of Deputies, was re-elected (the upper body, the House of Magistrates, was less affected). It was a stunning about-face, and a coup for the more careful, and as it turned out, more prudent freemen. Governor Cranston had remained mostly neutral and, because of his prestige, was re-elected. But the Newport merchants, reeling from their defeat and more convinced than ever that paper was the wave of the future and the answer to their problems, fought back and spent the next year gaining advocates from other towns, who agreed with them that the port—and indeed

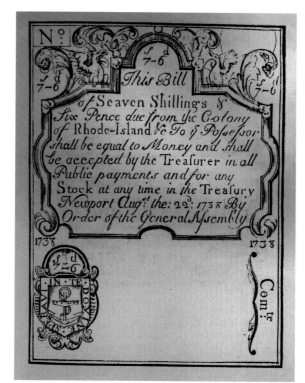

Seven Shilling and Six Pence Bill, 1738
Engraved by
William Claggett
Newport Historical Society
Newport, Rhode Island

the entire colony—would suffer greatly unless commerce were revived. And the only way to get it going was with newfound money. At the May elections of 1715, there was a complete reversal. The paper-money party, led by William and John Wanton upon their return to center stage, and aided by grandchildren of William Coddington, overwhelmed the specie party and swept back into control of the General Assembly—and held on for years. Even amid this turmoil, Governor Cranston was again spared, but he lost some of his power and influence from that election on. The Wantons were in ascendancy.

Now in the hands of the more liberal wing, the Assembly voted through a £30,000 land "bank" measure that would loan Rhode Islanders money at 5 percent interest for ten years, secured by mortgages on land. That action brought capital back into the system and did in fact spur business transactions, but numerous further issuances (too many and too ambitious) over the ensuing years, along with the serious mismanagement of collections and just plain sloppy bookkeeping, put a heavy strain on the colony for decades. Many economists contend that it wasn't the paper money per se that raised havoc in the marketplace but that the General Assembly printed far too much, flooding a fragile economy with costs it could not bear.

One of the primary problems with the issues after 1715 was that the new bills of credit, called "tenor," were not redeemed through direct taxes, which would have spread the risk, but were instead based on land ownership. Many large landowners grew rich, temporarily in some cases, and used the money to buy more land or invest in trade. Another problem was that colonial bills of credit were not recognized in England; they only had regional appeal. But the tenor enthusiasts had an answer. "The disadvantage to the merchant of paper being worthless in England would be more than offset by the stimulation of local production by plentiful money and perhaps also by bounties or direct public investment, which would assure the trader an increased supply of needed goods to ship to the mother country." Paper money was popular with a majority at home, but London frowned heavily on it and vigorously tried to bring its use to a halt, without success. Parliament was too busy fighting other battles, so that many of the same Newport merchants who had actively supported paper in 1710, but who now saw only the pitfalls of more issuances, were frustrated by the British government's inability to step in and take control.

As it turned out, both parties were right—and wrong. The hard-money men pointed to the rapid depreciation of the notes and the bankruptcies of neighbors when they couldn't repay their loans, and said, in effect, "I told you so! This is evil and will ruin the colony." The paper-money champions could point to the huge increase in commerce over the years and retort, in effect: "It isn't a perfect solution, but without the influx of cash, we'd all be starving."

There were other serious repercussions caused by the ongoing tenor debate. In 1729–1730, another issuance of £60,000 in paper money led to one of the most serious political and constitutional crises in Rhode Island history. It pitted Governor Joseph Jenckes against Deputy Governor John Wanton, and only King George II could resolve the dispute. In short, the General Assembly, under the control of Wanton, passed a new round of bills of credit to sustain commerce, but when it came to signing, Jenckes vetoed the measure because he was a hard-money man who loathed the prospect of more deflation. Furious, Wanton called an extraordinary session of the Assembly and pushed the measure through again, to the glee of some Newport merchants and Narragansett County estate-holders. A growing number of conservative and influential businessmen, Abraham Redwood and William Ellery among them, had by this time decided paper money was bad for their trade because it had become so unreliable and had lost so much value; they backed the governor. Jenckes, believing that as chief executive he had the power to nullify legislation, wrote George II to ask "whether an act passed by the General Assembly of this colony may be judged valid, the Governor having entered his dissent from it." In other words, who had the upper hand, the governor or the legislature?

Here was a problem never before encountered and, like most colonial legal issues, it was complicated. To the delight of the paper-money party (spiritually joined at the hip with the liberal, commercial-oriented Whigs in the House of Commons), the king's attorney general and solicitor general both demolished Jenckes's veto by reporting, "In this Charter no negative vote is given to the Governor, nor any power reserved to the crown of approving or disapproving the laws to be made by the colony . . . acts passed by the majority of such Assembly are valid in law." It was a decisive victory for champions of the 1663 Charter—and astounding that a British monarch would waive his own rights to meddle in Rhode Island affairs, especially since Parliament had already told Rhode Island to stop printing land banknotes. The ruling was a landmark in legal history.

The paper-money debate went on for decades, while the reputation of Rhode Island plummeted with merchants in other colonies, particularly in Boston, as the notes fluctuated wildly in value. "By 1740, about £340,000 in bills of public credit were in circulation, and they suffered from a high rate of depreciation. Merchants still generally supported the paper money policy, however. Not until 1750 did they come to view the steady depreciation of Rhode Island currency as a problem outweighing the advantages of plentiful currency." In 1750, after another issue of £50,000, the colony's debt to England stood at around £525,000 and by then crafty forgers were also adding to the problem; the General Assembly was so concerned with the rash of bogus bills that they passed a law making counterfeiting punishable by hanging.

Many speculators were hit with losses that wiped them out. In today's terms, according to its opponents, the printing of paper money without sufficient security was akin to going on a spending spree with a dozen credit cards when there isn't any money in the bank to cover the bills. Yet what, really, were the alternatives? "Those who were committed to the policy testified heartily in its favor. Gov. Richard Ward in a general survey of the subject, in 1740, referred to the absolute necessity of some kind of currency, if only paper, and then remarked, 'We never should have enjoyed this advantage had not the government emitted bills of credit to supply the merchants with a medium of exchange. In short, if this colony be in any respect happy and flourishing, it is paper money and a right application of it that hath rendered us so.' " Newport could never have launched itself into the mercantile world—and its Golden Age—without taking the gamble on paper.

The Golden Age Begins

What was the "happy and flourishing" Newport like in the 1720s and 1730s? The Golden Age of the town—for so many years a possibility—was finally dawning, and Newport was entering the ranks of being one of the five major colonial towns of the eighteenth century, along with Boston, New York, Philadelphia, and Charleston

PIECES OF EIGHT
Metal mattered. The most valued currency in the seventeenth and eighteenth centuries was the Spanish milled dollar, produced mostly in Mexico from the rich silver lodes in Central and South America. (No wonder so many pirates made the Caribbean Sea their base.) It became the international coin of choice; and just as today's slogan for the American Express card—"Don't leave home without it"—denotes instant acceptability, the Spanish dollar was all-powerful. But England starved the colonies of coin for decades because of its own shortage and also to keep the Americans subservient, so there was little hard money in New England to be used for external trade. The British gold guinea and silver shilling were highly valued but scarce. French, Portuguese, and other European coins circulated and were pegged to the British pound. But no coins in the world were more sought after than the silver Spanish pieces of eight.

(still known as Charles Town). The influx of new paper money was having its desired effect: spurring trade, drawing hundreds of new citizens eager for employment, stimulating an interest in the arts and learning among the merchant grandees, and enhancing Newport's architectural character as more lavish buildings were designed and erected.

Newport dominated every aspect of Rhode Island life until about 1750, when it was challenged by Providence in the commercial and political sphere. Add to that challenge three years of destructive British occupation during the Revolutionary War, followed by a friendly, yet still intrusive, foray by the French, and Newport would be nearly exhausted physically and rendered impotent as a major trading center. By 1800 Providence was thriving as a port because of its new manufacturing economy—a development Newport was never able to achieve because of its isolated island geography and the siphoning off of steady income—and it was becoming the dominant town in Rhode Island. This lack of industrial capacity hampered Newport economically for many decades to come, but the consequence of its absence allowed the town to remain in a virtual time warp and maintain its vast wealth of colonial architecture intact: derelict, unpainted, deteriorating by the year, but a treasure to be restored at a later time.

While other towns forged themselves into cities and modernized during the Industrial Revolution (only to decline into Rust Belt eyesores in the twentieth century), Newport remained backwater quaint and quiet for the most part. While railroads pushed America's frontier farther west and spread wealth along with industrialization, Newport scrambled to survive. The town was stilled in stasis. The great irony is that this very *lack* of factories belching fumes, laying waste to the countryside, and poisoning the water helped the town conserve its rich heritage: in the nineteenth century, it became the premier summer colony for the many rich industrialists who sought Newport as the perfect place to build their great mansions and frolic in their sailboats, precisely because it had *not* been devastated by their polluting businesses.

But in the first half of the eighteenth century, so much revolved around the flourishing town of Newport. The money, the talent, the ideas were all there, working together to create an entrepreneurial environment that welcomed change and rewarded ambition. It was the West Indies that supplied the first major expansion in Newport's trade, and served as the axis in the so-called triangular trade routes so prevalent throughout the eighteenth century. From the English islands of Barbados, Jamaica, Antigua, Nevis, and others, as well as French, Spanish, and Dutch ports, came the commodities used to expand trade and pay for English manufactures—iron, firearms, clothes, china, silver, fashions, and more—that were in great demand in Newport.

Men like William and John Wanton, Godfrey Malbone, Daniel and Stephen Ayrault, Benjamin Ellery, Abraham Redwood, and many others were moving beyond continental coasting voyages; they were shipping smoked fish from the Grand Banks, local produce, and animals to the Caribbean, and returning with mahogany, molasses, indigo, cloth, and a host of other goods.

By 1720, trade had continued to increase to the point that more than 600 ships passed through Rhode Island's ports yearly. . . . Increased demand for exports for the West Indian trade forced merchants to develop trade with other continental colonies, since Rhode Island could not produce a sufficient quantity of agricultural products for export. Rhode Islanders also began distilling rum, the first of several experiments in manufacturing products for export. During the 1720s, Newporters discovered that rum was an extremely profitable commodity on the African coast, thereby launching themselves into the slave trade. Ultimately this trade provided the largest source of capital for further commercial expansion.

Trade soared, more ships were built in and around Newport to take part in the procession down to the Caribbean, more men took to the sea. Although the merchants were gambling, gaining capital, and growing rich, Newport still had an inferiority complex when it compared its wealth to Boston's. The businessmen wanted more ways to raise hard cash. They had a major problem to solve: how to obtain English and Continental imports when Londoners wouldn't accept Rhode Island paper money. Over the years, Newport merchants developed a strategy that partially overcame this crippling deficit. They shipped homegrown produce (grain, fish, flour, horses) from Newport to the West Indies, trading it there for local products (timber, molasses, sugar). Then, by selling these West Indian products mostly in Boston and New York, which had much higher volumes of direct trade with Great Britain than Rhode Island did, the Newport businessmen got the hard currency necessary to buy English manufactured goods that could—finally—be sold for a profit in Newport.

That was the benign form of triangularity: Newport to the Indies to Boston or occasionally to England. But another pattern took a form all too prevalent in the 1700s, the one that still haunts America, and that was Newport's deep involvement—and success—in the African slave trade. That route went from Newport (with ships filled with hogsheads of rum distilled in Newport from West Indian molasses) to the

Triangular trade map

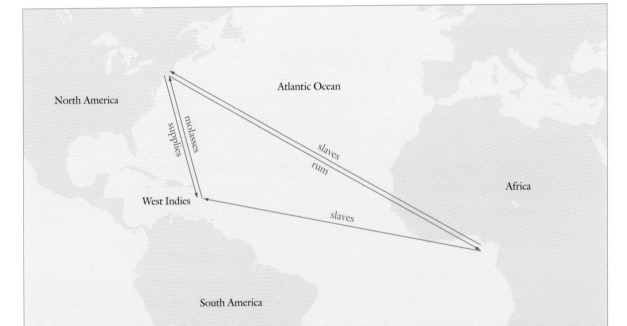

west coast of Africa, where the rum was used to purchase slaves; from Africa the vessels sailed to the West Indies—the dismal Middle Passage—where part or all of the human cargo would be sold to English, Dutch, or French plantation owners for hard currency, a portion of which would be used to buy more molasses to distill into yet more rum. Then the captain would set sail for Newport, often carrying slaves to be sold in Rhode Island and other colonies, and the whole course would be repeated.

England heartily encouraged the traffic in Africans. In 1708, Governor Cranston wrote to the Board of Trade that there were about thirty slaves coming into Rhode Island annually, all from Barbados. The number was small, he asserted, because of "the general dislike our planters have for them, by reason of their turbulent and unruly tempers . . . the inclination of our people in general, is to employ white servants before negroes." Unlike the Southern and Caribbean plantation owners, Rhode Island did not greatly change its attitude about owning black slaves for fieldwork. Those blacks in Newport before the Revolution, about 11 percent of the overall population, were employed mostly in domestic service.

During the eighteenth century, Rhode Island became one of the foremost colonies engaged in the slave trade, both in the triangular route or the bilateral one, which ran directly from Newport to the African coast and back to various ports (mostly in the South) on the Atlantic seaboard. Putting aside the moral issues concerning this practice and focusing on the economics, it is perhaps understandable why so many Newport merchants favored the African route: with a limited arena in which to expand because of their lack of capital or clout, as well as their shortage of high-volume, homegrown products to offer, the businessmen looked for profits wherever they could find them. When Great Britain won the rights to the *asiento* from France and Spain at the Treaty of Utrecht, which gave it the authority to enter the slave markets of Guinea previously denied it, Parliament opened the trade to colonials as well as home-port ships. Rhode Island merchants, already bringing large quantities of molasses back to Newport from the Caribbean islands and turning it into rum, learned quickly that rum was the preferred medium of exchange along Africa's west coast where slaves were held for shipment to the New World. Newport-produced "Guinea Rum," an especially strong concoction, "drove out most of the West Indian rum, as well as European gin, brandy, and liquor." Rum was prized more than Dutch cloth or English iron and guns. With this liquid currency, the merchants could fill a slave ship, unload it in the West Indies in exchange for much-needed hard cash, and, more often than not, turn a profit.

In the larger scheme of the European slave trade, Rhode Island's participation was relatively small. "From 1701 to 1810, Great Britain, one of the 'big three' slave-exporting nations, purchased an estimated 2.5 million African slaves." Rhode Island's contribution during the same period was a little over one hundred thousand. In 1731, Samuel Cranston's successor in the governor's chair, Joseph Jenckes, wrote the Board of Trade that the colony possessed "ten or twelve sail a year" going from Newport to the West Indies, and we must presume, to Africa as well.

Just nine years later, Governor Richard Ward was to tell the same body: "The colony's growing merchant fleet of 120 vessels was 'constantly employed in trade, some on the Coast of Africa, others in the neighboring colonies, many in the West Indies and a few in Europe.'" The historian Jay Coughtry estimates that of all Rhode Island shipping, about 6 percent was involved in the Africa trade, and that the real reason the commerce flourished was because the profits on homemade liquor were highest along the African coast, where Newport rum had replaced French brandy as the firewater of choice. In 1726, Rhode Island sent two ships to Africa and returned to North America with 232 slaves; in 1739, thirteen ships carried cargoes of rum and came back to the Indies with 1,499 Africans. Contrast these figures with England: in 1720, 146 ships were involved in the British slave trade. Massachusetts also had a thriving business in slaves, and it started decades earlier than Rhode Island's. "Although the trade was a unique branch of commerce and was viewed as such by those who participated in it, it was only one component in a complex colonial economy whose mainspring was maritime commerce."

The General Assembly understood that molasses was "an Engine in the hands of the merchant to effect the great purpose of paying for British goods." With an annual debt of £120,000 for the import of manufactures from England, the General Assembly focused on the payment of this obligation by saying it was "the great object of every branch of commerce" to use Newport-distilled rum as a medium for raising hard currency. It is estimated that the rum/slave trade alone contributed about £40,000 toward the reduction of Rhode Island's debt to Great Britain in the 1730s and more later on.

A number of prominent Newport men were involved in the slave trade in the eighteenth century, and part of the reason for their celebrity was the wealth they accumulated dealing with Africa. Every religious denomination in Newport was involved in the slave trade and many well-known families owned slaves. William Ellery, Sr., father of the same William Ellery who signed the Declaration of Independence and became a vocal opponent of the slave trade on moral grounds, sent several ships to the Guinea coast. Godfrey Malbone, a deacon at Trinity Church, grew rich on the trade. William and Samuel Vernon, sons of the famous silversmith, made their fortunes in numerous ways, and slaving was at the top of the list. Even the Quaker John Wanton, along with his brother William, engaged in the trade for years. Aaron Lopez, a Jew from Portugal, also grew rich in his vast mercantile pursuits, which included sending vessels to Africa. Christopher Champlin, a Baptist, was also involved in the slave trade. And the respected Brown brothers of Providence engaged in slaving briefly, but finding it unprofitable, changed their tactics; Moses Brown, youngest of the four brothers, ended up in the 1770s repudiating the trade and becoming a pacifist Quaker.

Unlike slaves in the South and the Caribbean, Africans in Newport generally lived in the same house as their owners and took their surnames and religions as well. Those slaves were put to work doing domestic service in the home or working in warehouses, rum distilleries, shipbuilding, and other maritime trades. The black population of Newport was fully integrated into the workings of the town, a case unusual for the era. Black Africans also had their own graveyard, now known as God's Little Acre, as part of the Common Burying Ground on Farewell Street. Nearly three hundred gravestones, or markers, still exist.

White America has always had problems coming to grips with the slavery matter. Whether out of denial, lack of care, or shame, non-blacks conveniently skirt the issue whenever possible. Today it is not unusual to look backward and pass moral judgment on a commerce that brought millions of humans under subjection for life, that treated people as chattel, and that must be reckoned with as one of the most deplorable episodes in American history.

Hindsight is easy, and illusory. Like their counterparts in the rest of the world, Newporters in the eighteenth century had few scruples about buying black Africans from other black Africans who had acquired the slaves through warfare or outright kidnapping. Product was product. British authorities and colonial

merchants knew that America was in dire need of men with sturdy backs and strong arms and didn't care where the bodies came from.

Some preachers, notably the Congregational minister Samuel Hopkins, railed against the trade and others joined the chorus as the century progressed. Very few people listened. Many Quakers were repelled by the practice, but theirs was a voice lost in the wilderness. It wasn't until the decade before the Revolution, when white Americans started to use the "slavery" analogy to describe their relationship with Great Britain, that the colonists began to face the gross inequities. How, many white writers asked, can we talk about "enslavement" by London when our colonies are awash with real slaves, of another color, purchased at auctions and not here of their own free will? By and large, Southerners didn't buy the argument; their moral compass was stuck on the status quo. Their plantations demanded large numbers of hands, and the black slave was the most economical alternative.

But the abolitionist movement began to gather steam in the North, and finally the long debate was joined. It took the Civil War for all to see how fractured the nation really was: clearly the root cause of the conflict was slavery itself. After a long hiatus, the civil rights movement of the mid-twentieth century reminded all Americans again of how much had not been accomplished, of how recalcitrant segments of society were in granting genuine equality.

Newport played a part in the slave trade and, according to the legal historian Patrick T. Conley, "The nefarious traffic in human chattel is the most serious blot on Rhode Island's libertarian reputation." Many of its citizens grew wealthy because of it and in a classic example of the trickle-down effect, the town itself prospered. Can the contradiction be rationalized today? Not really. Slavery has always been America's moral Achilles heel.

The Rise of the Wanton Brothers

William and John Wanton had elbowed Samuel Cranston aside during the hurly-burly of the paper-money episode; through their authority in the General Assembly, they had effectively taken control of political events by engineering numerous issuances of tenor currency, thus keeping some of the Newport merchants happy. But Cranston was by no means powerless, nor unpopular among his peers; he still functioned in many crucial roles as chief executive. "He was everywhere, serving as president of the Council of War, chief judge of the Court of Trials, moderator of the Newport town meeting, presiding officer of the town council, promoter of civic betterment, committeeman for assorted tasks, spokesman for the colony in some delicate negotiations, and prime mover in four or five landowners' organizations. It may be fair to picture him as the doge of a nascent New England Venice." In short, he was still needed, and in a godfatherly fashion, kept the colony in check emotionally as he catered to the needs of its inhabitants.

All that came to an end in April 1727 when Governor Cranston died while still in office. Samuel Arnold, writing in the 1850s, best sums up Cranston's legacy:

> The death of Samuel Cranston was no ordinary event in the history of the colony. In the strength of his intellect, the courage and firmness of his administration, and the skill with which he conducted public affairs in every crisis, he resembles the early race of Rhode Islanders. Thirty times successively chosen to the highest office, he preserved his popularity amidst political convulsions that had swept away every other official in the colony. He was the connecting link between two centuries of its history, and seemed, as it were, the bridge over which it passed in safety, from the long struggle for existence with the royal governors of Massachusetts, to the peaceful possession of its chartered rights under the House of Hanover.

Samuel Cranston was followed in office by Joseph Jenckes, a Providence man, who, during his five-year tenure as governor, was ordered by the General Assembly to move to Newport to be closer to the seat of power. Jenckes was an oddity, reportedly standing seven feet tall in his stockings. He had been deputy governor for eleven years, and was Rhode Island's representative in London in 1720 to solve the long-standing boundary dispute with Massachusetts (he didn't succeed). Newport lore bubbles with humorous anecdotes (veracity unknown) about powerful men and women who fall prey to the embarrassing gaffe, compromising situation, or perfidy of fate. Concerning the new chief executive we read that "when he was elected, feeling a desire to maintain the dignity of the station, and to wear a garb like that of other colonial governors he sent an order to England for a cloak. From some blunder, however, on the part of the correspondent, the order was made to read for a clock instead of a cloak, and a clock was sent." Whether or not he ever got his cloak we do not know, but the clock remained in the Jenckes family for more than a century.

Other than paralyzing the government with his veto of the paper-money bill, Jenckes's governorship was uneventful. The real nexus of power and prestige lay with the Wanton brothers. William Wanton was first to be elected governor, perhaps because John, as a Quaker, did not want to have control of the military. Given his privateering fame and his success as a businessman, William was trusted throughout Newport, and he proved to be a savvy politician. He was elected again in May 1733, but died in office the following year, at sixty-three years of age.

Now it was John Wanton's turn to govern. He was a swashbuckler—handsome, rich, elegant, famous in town for the lavish parties that he hosted with his wife. Ironically, he was also a recognized Quaker elder until the Newport Meeting censured him because he was forced to sign military commissions upon taking over the governorship. Like a true Renaissance man, John Wanton had one of the largest libraries in the colonies and was known for his interest in philosophical discourse and debate. He became friendly with the philosopher George Berkeley during his three-year sojourn in Newport and was a member of a group of men who met regularly to discuss issues of the day—the same core group that laid the foundation for The Company of the Redwood Library in the next decade.

John Wanton had spent seven years in the House of Magistrates, and in his capacity as deputy governor and leader of the paper-currency faction wielded considerable influence. His naval victories made him a celebrity, but what especially endeared him to Newport was his leadership role in a wild melee concerning the English customs collector Nathaniel Kay in 1719. Most Newporters had zero tolerance for the royal agents appointed by Parliament to the admiralty court and customs house. They resented their presence in the port and showed their disdain openly, regularly, vociferously. Being a representative of the Crown in Newport in the 1700s was akin to being on the front line during war, without the benefit of hazardous-duty pay.

The incident at hand was not an unusual one, given most Newporters' animosity toward any outside controls. In a September 1719 letter to the Board of Trade, the Englishman Caleb Heathcote reported, "the officers of his majesty's customs have been most grievously insulted and abused." Heathcote's dander was up, and he had a rousing story to tell his superiors:

> And 'tis very wonderful to me, who am thoroughly acquainted with the temper of the people, that none of his majesty's officers of the customs have been mobbed and torn in pieces by the rabble, and of which some of them have very narrowly escaped; an instance whereof happened in this town, to the present collector, who having made seizure of several hogsheads of claret, illegally imported, and notwithstanding he had the Governor's warrant, and the high sheriff, besides his own officers to assist, and took the claret in the daytime, yet the town's people had the insolence to rise upon them, and insult both them and the civil officers; and having, by violence, after a riotous and tumultuous manner, rescued and possessed themselves of the seizures, set the hogsheads ahead, and stove them open, and with pails drank out and carried away most of the wine, and then threw the remainder into the street.
>
> This tumult was no sooner over but one Mr. John Wanton, who uses the sea, and is a master of a sloop, a magistrate, of the people's choice (as may be reasonably supposed), for the keeping up the rage and humor of the mob, did immediately issue out his warrant for apprehending

Within months of Cranston's death in 1727, George I also passed away unexpectedly while visiting Germany. His son, the Prince of Wales, became George II. The latter was more comfortable in England than his father had been, spoke the language well, and had a better understanding of the English temperament. But George II was not terribly smart and was easily manipulated by his wife, Queen Caroline, and the brilliant Whig leader Sir Robert Walpole, who was able to keep England out of war for decades in order to bolster trade and build up the navy. When Walpole was driven from office in 1742 by William Pitt, England changed its tune and the Seven Years' War ensued. Pitt's leadership brought victory and vast new territories to Great Britain. During George II's reign (1727 –1760) the Jacobites were finally defeated, ending the panic over Catholic takeover by "Bonnie Prince Charlie"; John Gay wrote *The Beggar's Opera*; William Hogarth began producing *The Harlot's Progress*, his series of narrative, satirical engravings; Samuel Richardson wrote *Pamela*, often said to be the first novel in English; Henry Fielding penned the brilliant *Tom Jones*; and Samuel Johnson published *A Dictionary of the English Language*.

of Mr. Kay, the collector, under pretence of his taking other, and greater, fees for clearing of vessels than the laws of this colony allowed of (and which amounted to only two shillings sterling); but the matter being fully examined before the Governor, and it appearing that he had taken no greater fees than above mentioned, and which had always been accustomary, and that the prosecution was maliciously intended to expose the collector he was dismissed. But Mr. Wanton, not satisfied with what the Governor had done, and being willing to ingratiate himself amongst his neighbors, who had so lately advanced him, issued out a second warrant for the very same fact; and to magnify his zeal on that occasion, had him arrested and taken into custody in the custom house, while in his duty, and thence hurried him away amidst a crowd of spectators, refusing to admit him to bail.

This type of disturbance was not atypical in Newport—it was the norm. Governor Cranston had some explaining to do to the Lords of Trade, and the skirmish did not enamor him any further to his colleague. Wanton was a rebel; Cranston wanted to preserve order—and what in the world can you do with a man who wants to steal center stage? Neither was Nathaniel Kay too happy about the humiliation he endured. But after the Kay affair, John Wanton could do no wrong in Newport.

John Wanton served as governor for six prosperous years (1734–1740). During his term, all manner of mercantile activity increased in Newport because, paper-money man that he was, Wanton kept urging the General Assembly to issue more, and more extensive, land banknotes to keep the economy humming and to continue the pressure on Boston's merchants. But he also had to deal with new and highly restrictive trade laws forced on the colonies by London. The most damaging was the Molasses Act of 1733, which raised tariffs on the import of the key commodity from the West Indies. That meant more expensive rum for Newport, its most reliable export. When it came to satisfying its Caribbean colonies or those on the American continent, Parliament chose the islands, because they delivered more revenues back to the mother country. Newporters grouched and petitioned to no avail. Their markets for selling home-produced goods were being suffocated. Leading businessmen were in an uproar, furious at the greed of London on one hand and the lingering hangover of unstable currency on the other. The primary upshot of the Molasses Act was to spur full-scale evasion of the tax man by any means possible—while at the same time Newport merchants continued to deal with French, Dutch, and Spanish islands clandestinely. Midnight smuggling in the numerous coves sprinkled throughout Narragansett Bay increased.

In 1739, sugar was added to the list of items protected in the English Caribbean islands and, again, it showed London's favoritism to the West Indies. Governor Wanton wrote to the Board of Trade pleading with them to rescind this newest outrage because so many Newport merchants were being deeply hurt by the restrictions; the board was unmoved. These, and numerous other acts imposed on the colonies by Parliament, which were injurious primarily to northern trade, made it clear that London would play its colonial holdings off one another and cast its favor wherever tax revenues were highest. In the emerging cutthroat world of eighteenth-century mercantilism, which championed the need for a nation to build up and maintain its hard currency and in which profit was all, commercial competition was growing bitter and intense. Income from tiny Rhode Island was but an afterthought when compared with the amount of revenue that could be siphoned off in the West Indies.

But Newport, in another instance of self-protection and prescience (and perhaps collective paranoia), was keenly aware when any of its liberties were being threatened. In 1734, forty-two years ahead of events to come in Philadelphia: "Richard Partridge, agent for Rhode Island in England, argued that Parliament actually had embarked upon a policy that involved taxing the colonists as Englishmen without representation, in violation of a principle recognized in England, though sometimes violated, since the Magna Carta. Thus he anticipated one of the rallying slogans in use before and in the earlier period of the Revolution, that 'taxation without representation was tyranny.'"

Fighting John Wanton died in office in July 1740, bringing to an end the remarkable rise and success of the sons of a man who had left Boston eighty years earlier because of his horror at the hanging of the Quaker Mary Dyer. But John's passing did not put a halt to the fortunes of this remarkable family. Two more Wantons were destined to sit in the Rhode Island governor's chair in the decades to come.

Signs of Intelligent Life

The arrival of George Berkeley in Newport in 1729 altered the town's chemistry favorably and forever. By that time, Newport had spawned a number of men who, with their newly minted fortunes, desired to become more like "gentlemen" in the English sense of the word—refined, well dressed, debonair, but mostly, erudite and well-read. William and John Wanton weren't the only men in town with growing libraries of classics and current English science and philosophy. They were joined by Godfrey Malbone, Henry Collins, William Ellery, Nathan Townsend, and a select coterie of others, who also hungered for a position in the intellectual firmament and had the money to spend on intellectual pursuits. These men enjoyed talking among themselves; they traded books and ideas and yearned for the stimulus of London (Boston was still trapped in a religious quagmire that discouraged most secular scholarly adventures). But it wasn't until the illustrious and already famous Anglo-Irish philosopher and Church of England prelate George Berkeley alighted on the docks in January (after a bumbling four-month voyage) that the aspiring patricians of Newport found their beacon.

George Berkeley was born in Kilkenny, Ireland, in March 1685, a grandson of a follower of King Charles I who was rewarded for his loyalty with a royal position in Belfast by Charles II. The brilliant Berkeley studied at Trinity College, Dublin, showing promise from the beginning; he read the classics and turned to writing philosophical tracts that brought him early recognition in the British Isles and on the Continent. Like most educated men of his day, Berkeley spoke Hebrew and Greek and often penned his works in flawless, persuasive Latin.

While lecturing at Trinity College, he was ordained a deacon in the Church of England in 1710. As his philosophical works, particularly *Treatise Concerning the Principles of Human Knowledge*, gained readership, his fame spread. Here was a man who could defend the belief in God, and do it eloquently. He spent several years in London and became friends with the leading thinkers of the time, particularly Jonathan Swift, Alexander Pope, and the essayists Sir Richard Steele and Joseph Addison, for whom Berkeley

TAKE FIVE

As organized religion began to lose its influence on the hearts and minds of Newport's people and more leisure time was being spent in secular pursuits, the tavern became more popular. Regardless of what it was called—dram shop, inn, coffeehouse, or boardinghouse—the tavern was a place of entertainment and lively conversation for all segments of society. Unlike the later hotel or stand-alone bar, an eighteenth-century Newport tavern was normally housed in a room or two attached to the owner's house, a public house that served liquor, cider, beer, food of some sort, and offered a few beds for rent for the night. Being a busy harbor town, Newport had to put up its visitors someplace, and by the 1730s it hosted about twenty-five such establishments. None were lavish, but the King's Arms and White Horse Tavern were considered the best, attracting a wealthier clientele than taverns crowded along Thames Street, many of which catered to transient seamen in pursuit of strong grog and loose women. Taverns offered a place to play cards or billiards, gamble, have a shot of rum from one of Newport's twenty-odd distilleries, trade news and gossip, and take a break from life's rigors.

John Smibert
Bishop George Berkeley,
c. 1727
Oil on canvas
National Portrait Gallery,
Smithsonian Institution
Washington, D. C.
Gift of the Morris and
Gwendolyn Cafritz Foundation
NPG 89.25

Geo.Berkeley S.T.P.
Dec. Derenſis.

wrote articles for *The Guardian*. He then spent nearly five years traveling Europe as a tutor—France, Naples, Venice, Rome—rounding out his already extensive education and developing a keen eye for great art.

Pursuing his teaching career, his philosophical writing, and his duties as a clergyman came naturally for George Berkeley. In response to the skeptical John Locke and Isaac Newton, he advocated that the substance of an object does not exist beyond the mind's recognition of it and that all phenomena are merely ideas and visions. His school of philosophy became known as immaterialism, and at the basis of his thinking was the need to disprove the "new" (read scientific) ideas in currency that attacked the primacy of God. His doctrine held that a table, say, had no more reality or existence than a collection of perceived sense data. Berkeley was an idealist, a traditionalist, a religious conservative in the Anglican mode, and he was distressed by the growing assault on spirituality. He believed that if he could prove that physical objects did not "exist" beyond the imagination, then the connection between God and humans would be shown to be immediate and direct. In his spirited and nuanced writings, atheism is attacked as being unnatural, therefore impossible to sustain.

In 1724, the Episcopal bishop of London elevated Berkeley to the lucrative position of dean of Derry. He now had a sinecure of £1,100 per year and a seat of power within the establishment, and he went to work on his ambitious idea of converting whites, blacks, and Indians in the New World to the Anglican creed and training them to become clergymen. After consulting with colleagues, he decided that Bermuda, roughly equidistant between North America, Europe, and the West Indies, would be the best place for his new school, to be called St. Paul's College. King George championed his cause and gave him money. After years of intensive lobbying and private fund-raising, Berkeley convinced a reluctant Parliament to put up £20,000 toward the project. Berkeley was ecstatic about the possibilities of his endeavor, and he determined that Newport would serve as his base of operations where he could hire staff and obtain materials for his school. In 1728, he married the daughter of the Chief Justice of Ireland and they sailed to America in September of the same year.

The choice of Newport was no accident. Berkeley was the highest-ranking Anglican ever to disembark in North America; the religious fervor of the previous century, while ebbing, was still a decisive factor in the dean's wanting to reside in a community that promoted religious freedom. Although small in the colonies and still stigmatized by the majority of Puritans in America, the Church of England had been active for three decades in Newport, and the new Trinity Church had recently been completed on Spring Street, a building so grand that it was then the centerpiece for Anglicanism in New England. Would Dean Berkeley have been as welcome in Boston, New Haven, or Hartford? The answer is unequivocally no. The resurrection of the powers of the Church of England bishops made the dissenters uneasy, to say the least.

As sophisticated and gentlemanly as the Newport grandees might have thought themselves to be, the appearance of George Berkeley was a real event—here was an international celebrity, a man who knew Europe well, a man of the latest ideas. The colonies had never entertained the likes of him. People flocked to see him, listen to his sermons at Trinity Church on most Sundays (even Quakers and Baptists filled the pews), and engage him in worldly conversation. Along with his new wife, Anne, Berkeley also brought to Newport the Scottish painter John Smibert, who became the most influential artist in the colonies in the early eighteenth century. Suddenly, Newport was feeling itself to be a little bit like London.

The Berkeleys and their young son Henry soon set up headquarters in a gracious two-story house that the dean had scrupulously renovated and enlarged, named Whitehall, on a 96-acre farm a little over three miles north of the harbor in today's Middletown. They went about collecting materials for the college in Bermuda, enjoying the fine climate, and taking part in the town's activities. While the winter was "sharp," Berkeley noted that summer was "exceedingly delightful," and autumn "is said to be the finest in the world." He went on to describe his new surroundings:

> This island is pleasantly laid out in hills and vales and rising grounds; hath plenty of excellent springs and fine rivulets, and many delightful landscapes of rocks and promontories and adjacent islands. The provisions are very good; so are the fruits, which are quite neglected, tho' vines sprout up of themselves to an extraordinary size, and seem as natural to this soil as to any I ever saw. The town of Newport contains about six thousand souls, and is the most thriving flourishing place in all America for its bigness. It is very pretty and pleasantly situated.

Dean George Berkeley thoroughly enjoyed his thirty-three months in Newport. And in a sense, he had already anticipated what the colonies had to offer. In 1726, at the height of his enthusiasm for his experimental college in the New World, Berkeley penned the poem (not published until 1752) "On the Prospect of Planting Arts and Learning in America." which ended with the famous lines:

> Westward the Course of Empire takes its Way;
> The four first Acts already past,
> A fifth shall close the Drama with the Day;
> Time's noblest Offspring is the last.

Westward, following the sun. The dean was a prophet. Berkeley was convinced that Britain was crumbling, veering into a nether land of freethinking atheism and rank materialism that would overturn the authority of the spiritual realm and lead to chaos. Like his Puritan adversaries, he too yearned for a solid melding of church and state. Berkeley was intent on rescuing the Anglican creed from destruction and saw America as the golden hope. In England, he alleged: "We have long been preparing for some great catastrophe. Vice and villainy have by degrees grown reputable among us; our infidels have passed for fine gentlemen, and our venal traitors for men of sense, who know the world. We have made a jest of public spirit, and cancelled all respect for whatever our laws and religion repute sacred."

The dean even believed that without the introduction of Church of England bishops in North America, "that noblest, grandest part of the British Empire of the WHOLE world will be lost; they [the colonies] will shake off the Mother Country in a few years." Berkeley was right about the shaking off, but wrong about the timing and the cause of rebellion. Reason, not religion, dictated the War of Independence nearly a half century away.

Before departing Britain, Berkeley had sent more than a thousand books to Newport, ultimately destined to form the core of the library at his college on Bermuda. While Trinity Church had started a small lending library in 1702, open to parishioners and non-Anglicans alike (made up primarily of religious tracts), the collection of valuable books that Berkeley had amassed was unprecedented in New England. Even Harvard College at the time couldn't match the dean's collection.

Not surprisingly, Berkeley's library became the magnet for Newport's eager intellectuals who wanted to absorb the dean's tomes and discuss ideas. The Trinity Church rector, James Honyman, who had housed Berkeley and his family until Whitehall was ready for occupancy and was probably the dean's closest friend in town, had already identified the men who were most interested in learning. In 1730, with Berkeley's encouragement, a Society for the Promotion of Knowledge and Virtue, commonly known as the Literary and Philosophic Society, was formed by the minister, his son, James Honyman Jr. (an attorney general of the colony), Daniel Updike (also a Rhode Island attorney general), Henry Collins (a rich merchant and patron of the arts), Peter Bours (a slave trader and merchant), Stephen Hopkins (a future governor), Samuel Johnson (later president of King's College in New York, which became Columbia University), and other leading lights. The Society was inclusive to the extreme, open to Sabbatarians, Quakers, Anglicans, Congregationalists, and Baptists. In Newport's open culture, one's personal theological beliefs were not a hindrance; the primary concern of these men was gaining knowledge and sharing ideas.

The men, numbering between twenty and twenty-five, met every Monday night to "converse about and debate some useful question in Divinity, Morality, Philosophy, History, &c." The Society drew up bylaws, elected a treasurer, and took itself quite seriously. The members also honored the confidentiality of their sessions by agreeing that "no member shall divulge the opinion or arguments of any particular member as to any subject debated in the Society, on penalty of perpetual exclusion." Berkeley may well have been the impetus for the Society, which continued to flourish during the 1730s and 1740s, eventually leading to the founding of The Company of the Redwood Library in 1747.

George Berkeley was convivial and outgoing with his fellow residents, treating them not only to sermons, but also to stories of his European travels and life in London; Newporters eagerly soaked up the great man's wisdom. He was respected widely, even by his philosophical opponents, because he was regarded as pious, moral, and fair. Newport itself was a balm for Berkeley, although he sometimes despaired over the religious wrangling going on around him. Yet his whole experience in the town turned out to be bittersweet. He truly liked America and Newport; he was able to think and write and dream about his future. But he had no direct control over that future.

As he waited—and waited—for word from Parliament about the promised funds for his college, he began to have doubts about the Bermuda location and contemplated constructing his dream in Newport. When he wrote to London with these thoughts, his adversaries (of whom there were few, but powerful) heartily latched on to his equivocations and mocked his sincerity. He was accused of being a utopian dreamer, of abandoning his position at Derry, of being out of touch with the "new" thinking percolating in London. With each month that passed, he realized he was being dangled by the lawmakers, and, from three thousand miles away, could not lobby for the success of his mission.

It was probably at this late and unsettling stage that Berkeley began writing what would become his most famous, and longest, treatise, *Alciphron: or, the Minute Philosopher*. He used the dialogue form, modeled on Plato, to argue his point that England was awash with infidels, knaves, and freethinkers out to abolish religion, and the New World was to become God's only savior. The author set seven extended

When George Berkeley ventured to Newport in 1729, he was accompanied by the Scottish artist John Smibert, an old acquaintance, who was intending to become professor of painting and architecture at Berkeley's proposed college on Bermuda. Born in Edinburgh in 1688, Smibert had studied portraiture under Sir Godfrey Kneller in London, spent three years in Italy copying Old Masters, and returned to London to set up a studio in Covent Garden, where he sought patronage and produced a number of well-received canvases. While he gained a considerable degree of recognition, competition in London was rough; when Berkeley sought his talents, Smibert accepted. In Newport, Smibert was almost as celebrated as his patron; America was devoid of classically trained painters and he was eagerly sought out by the art lover Henry Collins. During the year he tarried in town before moving to Boston, Smibert painted probably his most famous work, *The Bermuda Group*, a portrait of seven people gathered before Dean Berkeley, including the artist himself, perched behind on the left side of the picture. *The Bermuda Group* (now at Yale) remains one of the finest group portraits in American art, influencing numerous future painters, including Robert Feke. While in Newport, Smibert also painted portraits of Berkeley (alone), Henry Collins, and Mr. and Mrs. Joseph Wanton, among others. John Smibert's eyesight began to fail him in 1749; he died in Boston two years later. According to the critic Martin Kalfatovic, after his death, his studio remained intact and "became a pilgrimage site for generations of American artists including John Singleton Copley and Charles Willson Peale."

dialogues in a bucolic landscape he knew well: the beaches, woods, and meadows around Whitehall—Hanging Rock and what today is Second, or Sachuest, Beach, and the Norman Bird Sanctuary. Tradition has it that Berkeley would have one of his three black slaves carry his chair and portable writing table to a rugged, high, yet covered opening at Hanging Rock (known to locals in later centuries as Berkeley's Seat), which afforded him a majestic view of the ocean to the south; there he would spend part of the day thinking and writing, calmed by the sight of Aquidneck Island's beauty and the gently rolling sea and agitated by his vision of what was befalling his native land.

By arguing that all the beauties of the natural world are God's gift and God's gift only, Berkeley railed against those who tried to diminish "Nature" and turn it into a concept instead of a religious reality. "This remarkable, artful philosophical dialogue, defending ancient revelation against modern reason, hoary truths against recent sophistications, stable tradition against flighty fashion, and God against mammon, made only a modest splash in England." In America, however, it was very popular, and put his name, literally, on the map: ironically, liberal and progressive Berkeley, California, was named after the esteemed conservative thinker.

The end of his dream came in early 1731 when he was informed by the bishop of London, Edmund Gibson, that Sir Robert Walpole, then in charge of the treasury for Parliament, was balking. Walpole told the bishop, and he reported to Berkeley, "If you put this question to me as a minister, I must and can assure you that the money shall most undoubtedly be paid as soon as suits with public convenience: but if you ask me as a friend, whether Dean Berkeley should continue in America expecting the payment . . . I advise him by all means to return home to Europe, and to give up his present expectations." Defeated and depressed, the dean prepared to return to England.

The nearly three-year American sojourn was over. Anxious to get on with life, even if his most ambitious project had been snatched from him by Walpole's cunning, the dean gave Yale College the bulk of his valuable library: almost nine hundred volumes (one-third of the school's total books); Harvard received the remainder. He also deeded to Yale his property at Whitehall, the proceeds of which were to fund scholarships for students in Latin and Greek; they were the first graduate fellowships ever offered by an American college and helped hundreds of students for more than a century. Even back in Great Britain, Berkeley continued to be munificent: he sent more classics to both Yale and Harvard. But his most lavish gift was that of an organ for Trinity Church in Newport, in 1733, a rarity in the English colonies. Rev. James Honyman, ever-appreciative of the dean's gift, was nonetheless perplexed: he had to summon Charles Pachelbel from Boston to assist in assembling the complex instrument in 1734, yet he had no suitable organist to perform. Pachebel and later a member of the congregation filled in, but it was not until 1736 that a full-time organist arrived from England to play on Sundays.

A disappointed and bitter George Berkeley, with his family, sailed to London from Boston in September 1731. Although fashionable freethinkers mocked his idealism and assault on materialism, he was still beloved, still famous, and was received back in the fold enthusiastically by most Anglicans. One of his superiors, Bishop Atterbury, said of Berkeley: "So much understanding, so much knowledge, so much innocence, and such humility I did not think had been the portion of any but angels, until I saw this gentleman." In 1734, he was elevated to the position of bishop of Cloyne, in Ireland, a seat he held until he died in 1753, in Oxford.

George Berkeley and his fellow writers could scribble to their hearts' content, yet unless there was a way for other people to read their words, all was for naught. But printing presses were cumbersome, expensive, and rare in early eighteenth-century America. Rhode Island had no outlet for written expression until early 1727, when James Franklin settled in Newport, after constant woes in Boston. He brought with him his press and type, and talent, making Newport only the fourth town in New England to host a professional printer.

James Franklin, elder brother of the illustrious Benjamin, was born in Boston in 1697, but as a young man had to go to London to secure an apprenticeship with a printer to learn his craft. He purchased a used printing press and returned to his native town in 1717 to work at the *Boston Gazette*, then opened his own shop, where he produced mostly pamphlets and broadsheets, and a few books. Business was steady, and he had Benjamin as his apprentice to help out. With money coming in, James Franklin decided to try his hand in the newspaper trade and came out with the *New-England Courant* in 1721. Like his younger brother, James possessed a healthy, satirical sense of humor; aside from publishing advertisements and shipping news, the paper featured essays that veered dramatically from the proper, conservative so prevalent in Boston. In a short time, he made enemies of the establishment, particularly the esteemed and overbearing preachers Cotton and Increase Mather, who believed they and they alone could read the pulse of their town. When Franklin assaulted the government and accused it of being lax in its pursuit of pirates, the authorities went into action and jailed the printer for a month. During his incarceration, brother Benjamin took over and continued publishing the *Courant*.

Things didn't get any better after he gained his freedom. James Franklin continued to take on the authorities and the supposedly high-minded and pious Puritans, who were neither high-minded nor pious, he wrote, but a bunch of lying hypocrites. Such endearments were unwelcome, obviously, and Boston being Boston, he was headed for a showdown. Cotton Mather, for one, raged that Franklin's paper was "a wickedness never parallel'd anywhere upon the Face of the Earth!" The legislature quickly concluded that Franklin was insulting both the clergy and themselves by printing a contrary point of view, and banned the *Courant*. But the printer found an easy way around the official edict by listing Benjamin Franklin as the publisher. Frustrated, the government again pounced, and James was about to revisit his jail cell; he was saved by a grand jury that refused to indict him.

By 1727, James Franklin had had enough of the machinations in Massachusetts and moved his press, his wife, Ann, and their six children to Newport, where he could publish what he wanted without fear of being arrested. As in Boston, Franklin, now aided by his wife (Benjamin had escaped his older brother's strict discipline by running away to Philadelphia), published commercial pamphlets and an array of religious documents—not surprising in a town with so many different sects, each vying for attention and new converts. Earlier in the century, when Joseph Dudley and Parliament were pestering the General Assembly about the lack of written laws in the colony, Governor Cranston promised to have them printed and distributed. Since there was no press in Rhode Island, this did not come about for nearly two decades, and then

The Road to Revolution

4

On the Town

The very *bustle* of the place. Newport's Golden Age was in full flower, now a full century after its shaky beginnings. The wilderness that William Coddington, John Clarke, and their fellow founders confronted in 1639 had been tamed; their commercial aspirations were being realized; their insistence on religious freedom had been achieved and preserved under great duress; their pursuit of a civil government ruled by the votes of the colony's freemen had prevailed. Against long odds, the little enclave of Rhode Island and Providence Plantations had survived—and now it was prospering.

The town had successfully challenged Boston in coastal and international trade and was gaining an international reputation as the most sophisticated town in New England. Toward the end of the colonial era, Newport would boast of a more robust trade, both domestic and overseas, than New York. Shipbuilding in and around the town supported a variety of tradesmen, from ropemakers and carpenters to riggers and instrument-makers. Arts and crafts were flourishing under the influence of clockmakers, silversmiths, and fine furniture-makers; a solid and a growing array of artisans was creating treasures for the town's wealthy merchants, treasures that would be valued by generations for their craftsmanship and beauty and would command millions of dollars at auction in subsequent centuries.

The metamorphosis from wilderness outpost to hamlet to village to thriving town and now to the status of small city was nearly complete. As a result of Newport's extensive communications with other ports, word spread down the coast and into the West Indies celebrating its welcoming weather and culture. Dean George Berkeley likened Aquidneck Island's climate to that of Italy. Later writers, with better oceanographic knowledge, correctly attributed the nearby swing of the Gulf Stream as the source of Newport's delicate southern summer breezes and moderate winters. And the nurturing conditions beckoned visitors. While the most visible symbols of Newport's fame as "America's First Resort" are the vast nineteenth-century houses along Bellevue Avenue and Ocean Drive, as early as 1729, summer guests began flocking to Newport in significant numbers when a cluster of Southern and West Indies plantation owners arrived, fleeing the seasonal malaria that threatened their lives. Newport's reputation continued to spread as more people learned of the island's charms and of the respite it offered from the suffocating heat of the Carolinas, Pennsylvania, and the

John Banister account book, Journal B (detail), 1746-1749
Photograph by Daniel McManus
Newport Historical Society
Newport, Rhode Island

Caribbean. Unlike any other New England town, Newport opened its doors to a diverse mix of generally wealthy and sophisticated summer travelers and as a result became even more cosmopolitan, more open and accepting, more vibrant. Newness and change did not threaten the growing city; it thrived on the influx of the exotic. In taverns and inns along the harbor and on the hill above, visitors traded stories and experiences with local inhabitants, widening and gentrifying the horizons of all involved.

In 1742, Newport was home to 6,200 inhabitants, a 63 percent increase in just twenty-two years. Who were these people streaming into town from other colonies and foreign ports? Most were English, but Scots, Scotch-Irish, French Huguenots (still escaping decades after Louis XIV revoked the Edict of Nantes, which had protected Protestants' rights), German Palatines, and eventually Portuguese Jews; African slaves were also represented. But no Catholics—they were still considered dangerous and would have been deported had they ventured into Newport's harbor. Despite the town's reputation for toleration, welcoming Catholics at that time was beyond the ken of nearly all its inhabitants. With the exception of the year-long presence of the French army during the War of Independence, adherents to the Church of Rome would not have an impact on Newport and Rhode Island until well into the nineteenth century.

Given its independent spirit, it is a bit of a paradox that of the five great cities of colonial America, Newport retained its essentially English heritage longer and guarded it more jealously than Boston, New York, Philadelphia, or Charles Town (Charleston), by legislating that ship captains had to post bonds of £50 for any newcomer not from the British Isles. Busy, successful port cities like Newport were magnets for industrious, entrepreneurial men and women looking for opportunity. For the most part, it was this class of immigrants who were attracted to Newport, although some less-savory pirates were still liable to lay anchor in Narragansett Bay on any given day.

By the 1740s, Newport had amassed all the basic ingredients necessary for a relatively stable and predictable economy. Everything needed for it to expand was in place. Hard currency in the form of English coins and Spanish milled dollars flowed steadily into town from the triangular mercantile routes with Africa and the West Indies. Direct trade with select European ports, as well as London and Bristol, was meager at first but lucrative for those merchants who undertook it. Privateering brought large amounts of bounty into town. Real capital, as distinct from the endlessly confusing issues of old and new tenor paper money, was becoming plentiful and served as a magnet for the growing number of middle-class artisans and skilled workers, who would, in turn, nudge the economy to an even more robust level. As trade expanded, more goods were required for export. Tastes of the elite became more sophisticated, fueling the desire for better furniture, finer instruments, more elaborate mansions, the latest London fashions and books, plus other European luxuries. Expectations rose and items (window curtains, pewter plates, brass andirons) once beyond the reach of most Newporters became commonplace as growth continued on a steady upward spiral.

These crucial ingredients—a ready supply of hard currency; a splendid natural harbor so close to the Atlantic; a talented, ambitious, and disciplined workforce; a merchant aristocracy with a risk-taking, bet-the-farm mentality; and a dash of luck—were all in place in Newport in the middle of the eighteenth century. Remove those key components (to say nothing of the decline of Boston's commerce and Newport's constant evasion of the Crown's customs collectors) and the town would not have thrived as it did. But that combination was, for the foreseeable future, just right.

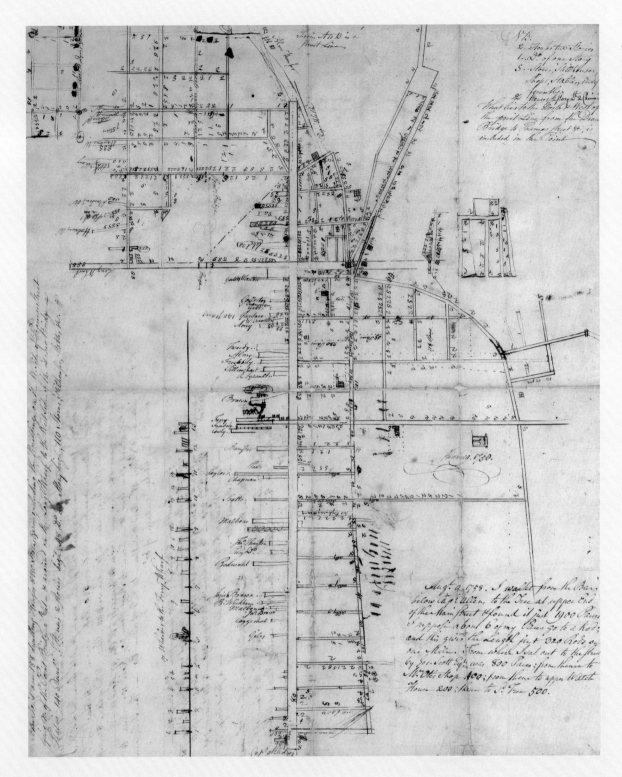

Ezra Stiles
*Manuscript map
of the city and harbor of
Newport,* August 9, 1758
Ink on paper
A unique record of
the thriving mercantile
city in the mid-18th
century, with town lots
indicated and labeled
with the names of their
owners (e. g. Brown,
Redwood). Stiles
recorded on the plan the
height of the buildings
on each lot, with a "1"
indicating a one-story
structure, "2" a two-story
building, and a slashed
"2" represented
a two-story house with
2 chimneys.
Photograph by
The Archival Image
Redwood Library
and Athenæum
Newport, Rhode Island

A continuum was in place. Prosperity begat creativity. Creativity begat production (works of art, books, artifacts, furniture), which, in turn, led to another level of prosperity (monetary, emotional, intellectual). Any soothsayer wandering into Newport at that period would have concluded that the stars were certainly in the correct alignment.

Newport's population by 1740 was composed of three distinct strata: the upper-class gentry of wealthy merchant-farmers and old-money aristocrats (the Coddingtons, Brentons, Coggeshalls, Eastons), who lived off the inheritances of riches gained by their ancestors and increased them by engaging in trade; the emerging middle class of artisans and skilled laborers, many of whom aspired to join the ranks of their social superiors; and the lower class of manual laborers, servants (indentured or free), and black and Indian slaves. As an essentially English town, Newport naturally emulated the social norms of the mother country right down to rigid class distinctions, which dictated that the upper-class gentlemen held most of the power, most of the capital, and merited a high degree of envy. But this being rough-stocking, hurly-burly frontier America and not hidebound Europe, the artificially inflated status of the *ancien régime* was soon to burst.

Newport's Elite

Centuries of English tradition were at play when the grandees of Newport strutted along the streets, or were hoisted into their carriages by their footmen (often African slaves) to be driven from their fine houses, to their stores and warehouses on their own private wharves jutting into the harbor for a few hours of looking over the books and giving orders to their clerks and accountants. After that, it was time for leisure in the taverns or coffeehouses, learning, and long repasts with their peers. They were the nobility of America, the privileged few who commanded respect wherever they went. The successful merchant princes of town, those who dared to risk their fledgling fortunes in order to create larger ones, were *entitled*—entitled to make the rules (and break them when they desired), entitled to wear fine London clothing and wigs and import the latest fashions in home furnishings and dress for their wives. They fell in lockstep with whatever was the rage in England, and having the wherewithal to carry through on their whims, did so. They reveled in conspicuous consumption, trying to one-up other members of their cohort by purchasing more ornate equipages, fine furniture from the

Advertisement dated Newport, June 6, 1763 by Thomas Teckle Taylor and Samuel and William Vernon
The Newport Mercury
Announcing the arrival of healthy Gold Coast Slaves available for purchase.
Newport Historical Society
Newport, Rhode Island

Newport. June 6, 1763.
ON Thursday inst arriv'd from the Coast of AFRICA, the Brig ROYAL CHARLOTTE, with a Parcel of extreme fine, healthy, well limb'd,
Gold Coast SLAVES,
Men, Women, Boys, and Girls, Gentlemen in Town and Country men now an Opportunity to furnish themselves with such as will suit them. Those that want are desired to apply very speedily, or they will have the Advantage of supplying themselves. They are to be seen on board the Vessel at Taylor's Wharf.
Apply to *Thomas Teckle Taylor*, *Samuel* and *William Vernon*.
N. B. Those that remain on Hand will be shipped off very soon.

Artist unknown
Potter Over Mantle,
c. 1740
Oil on panel
This painting of
wealthy plantation owner
John Potter and family
depicts a house slave
serving tea.
Photograph by Daniel McManus
Newport Historical Society
Newport, Rhode Island

Townsend and Goddard families, erecting larger and more lavish townhouses, laying out manicured grounds and gardens at their country mansions, and amassing the very latest books from their London dealers. The competition among a certain set, to be (or *appear* to be) au courant, has long been intense in this town.

Newport had developed a multiple personality as it grew. It was, and still is, a social mecca, a playground for the rich and wellborn, a place where American "society" has defined and developed its ornate pecking order. After all, three of the original nine founders were, if measured in today's currency, millionaires. And it has always been a town in which people of all strata could use their talents to prosper. Then there is the more cerebral Newport that gave America its first quasi-independent city-state, its first attempt at a real division between church and state, its first New England town (along with Roger Williams's Providence) founded on dissent from the existing Puritan orthodoxy, dedicated to liberty of conscience. This multiplicity has often led to a restrained friction. Over the first century, Newport's inhabitants pandered to the socially superior, aristocratic merchant and landlord class, just as if none of them had ever left England. Now the times were changing.

These outward displays of ostentation among the rich may have been perceived as a mark of arrogance by their neighbors of a lesser order who were beginning to chafe under the weight of the medieval European class structure. Living in America was beginning to tip the balance: something subtle, yet at the core quite radical, was emerging in colonial towns in the 1740s and 1750s—a nascent republicanism was brewing and the ascent of the commoner, ready to challenge (or, perhaps worse yet, *ignore*) the authority of the elite, was bubbling to the surface. The fervor of the era, which ushered in a new and broad debate about the very nature of "freedom," was dawning. Carl Bridenbaugh wrote: "Underneath the apparent calm routine of daily life, which went on with only an occasional interruption, society itself was passing through a fundamental change. In numbers the tradesmen and artisans held an increasing advantage over those above or below them, and they were aware of their strength."

In Newport, because the town had evolved in a more democratic fashion than others, this spirit was more keenly developed than in the adjacent territories controlled by Crown authorities and organized to be more obedient to London. Newport was *psychologically* farther along the road to independence because it had been practicing and working out the knots of representative government, for the most part unfettered by English officials, longer than its peers. The concepts of democracy, so taken for granted today, look relatively easy on paper; the *practice* of democracy was a far harder task to accomplish in the eighteenth century, because it was still highly controversial, suspect, and untried in an arena as large as America. Newport had a distinct advantage when the aroma of revolution began to fill the air: its inhabitants were already familiar with the rough-and-tumble nature of a (mostly) democratic system. When the final break with the monarchy came, the elite of Newport were not overthrown or imprisoned or murdered (think only of the French Revolution for comparison)—no, the gentry were outmaneuvered and *outvoted* by the rising multitudes.

Ever since the founding of Newport, the members of the rich upper crust had guarded their power and privilege through strategic intermarriages and almost perpetual control of the political process, through which they could pass legislation to increase their share of wealth. However, the strict social order was beginning to crack as the middle class asserted its mandate more forcefully. Before, one's place in the pecking order had been determined by birthright, not merit. For the common person to kowtow to his or her "betters" was expected throughout society, and firmly enforced. Whether the grandees, ensconced in their privileged world, actually understood the implications of the changes swirling around them is questionable. Nonetheless, within a few short decades, fueled by the liberating ideals of the Enlightenment, a looser, freer society was to materialize out of the Old World stranglehold, a more expansive culture that for the first time rewarded hard work, talent, and good deeds as well as the lineage of one's distant ancestors.

Regardless of the tectonic plates shifting beneath their slippers, the elite of Newport didn't neglect their civic responsibilities. It is a hallowed, time-tested obligation of the ruling class to foster goodwill throughout the larger community with munificent gifts and notable works. One of the most eminent was Henry Collins, a prosperous ropewalk owner and maritime merchant, who was an unflagging patron of the arts, contributing the land for the Redwood Library, commissioning paintings by John Smibert, Robert Feke, and others. Because of his unstinting contributions to the intellectual growth of his native town, Dr. Benjamin Waterhouse later dubbed Collins "the Lorenzo de Medici of Newport."

Born in 1699, Henry Collins was the youngest son of the renowned silversmith Arnold Collins, who designed and engraved the seal of the Colony of Rhode Island and Providence Plantations (still in use), which features an anchor along with the motto "Hope." Unusual for the times, young Henry was sent to London for his schooling, where he developed a deep appreciation for literature and the arts as well as a solid grounding in commerce. Returning to Newport, he went into the ropemaking business (a smart move, given all the ships being built around the port) and soon thereafter became a trading merchant, at which he excelled. His newfound riches allowed him to pursue his real love of the arts. He became active in the Literary and Philosophical Society where he befriended George Berkeley and the young Abraham Redwood; began his extensive art collection of personally commissioned portraits (of Berkeley, John Callender, and other Newport ministers, including the grim-looking Rev. Nathaniel Clap); and oversaw the construction of the Seventh Day Baptist Meeting House (most likely designed by Richard Munday, because it greatly resembles

Trinity Church), as well as the Redwood Library on Bellevue Avenue. Collins gave his time lavishly to the town as well. He served on the committees that oversaw the extension of the Long Wharf beginning in 1739 and the construction of the Brick Market, along with other projects.

Henry Collins was an aesthete par excellence. He lived sumptuously, both in town and at a large estate in the country, enjoyed the company of his well-read and inquisitive companions, and commanded respect. He also built up a fleet of merchant ships so extensive that there was one for every letter of the alphabet. Along with his partner Ebenezer Flagg, he ordered his flotilla into privateering during King George's War and later in the French and Indian War. For a long time the profits kept coming, but when the tide turned, the results were disastrous for Collins. It is unknown exactly how many ships of his were lost to storms or seized and sunk by marauding French and Spanish warships, but those losses, coming in rapid succession, plus the effects of a harsh enforcement of the Navigation Acts, forced his firm into bankruptcy in the early 1760s. After such a good, long run, Collins was ruined. All of his extensive properties were confiscated by London creditors and he had to live out the few remaining years of his life, destitute, with the family of his deceased partner. Having never married, Henry Collins died alone in 1764.

In 1744, Dr. Alexander Hamilton (no relation to the Revolution's patriot), a thirty-two-year-old Scottish bachelor, who had received a classical education and his medical degree at the University of Edinburgh before emigrating to Annapolis, Maryland, was recovering from a debilitating illness, probably tuberculosis. In an attempt to reinvigorate his life, Dr. Hamilton set out to explore the northern colonies, all the way to York, Maine. He kept daily entries in a journal that is nearly two hundred pages long. He made the expedition on horseback, accompanied only by his black slave and many letters of introduction from Maryland gentlemen to others of their class in major towns along his route. *The Itinerarium of Dr. Alexander Hamilton* is one

F. Scott Fitzgerald notoriously penned in his story *Rich Boy*, "Let me tell you about the very rich. They are different from you and me." To which Ernest Hemingway later waspishly retorted in *The Snows of Kilimanjaro*, "Yes, they have more money." That snippet of sarcasm set the stage for one of the more hilarious literary catfights of the last century. But in the main, Fitzgerald probably had it right, and an incident concerning the enormously wealthy Godfrey Malbone (slave trade, privateering) more than bears him out. According to the observant Dr. Alexander Hamilton, on Malbone's 600-acre estate just out of town at the foot of Miantonomy Hill was "the largest and most magnificent dwelling houses I have ever seen in America. It is built entirely of hewn stone of a reddish colour; the sides of the windows and cornerstones of the house being painted like white marble. It is three stories high, and the rooms are spacious and magnificent. . . . The whole stair case, which is very large, is done with mahogany wood. . . . Round it are pretty gardens and terraces with canals, from whence you have a delightful view of the town and harbour of Newport with the shipping lying there." So far, Hemingway's riposte is valid. But the next episode carries the day for Fitzgerald. In 1766, Malbone threw a large party for all the swells from town. But as the servants were preparing a meal, fire broke out in the kitchen and soon began to engulf the house and, stone though it was, clearly the end was at hand. "Romance now takes up the fact, and proceeding in a strain accordant with the style of the man and his life, relates that Colonel Malbone, seeing the inevitable destruction, declared that if he must lose his house, he would not lose his dinner; and, as it was early summer, ordered the feast to be spread upon the lawn, where he and his guests ate their dinner by the light of the burning house." Different indeed.

of the most detailed, consistent, and fascinating contemporary accounts of colonial life produced in the eighteenth century.

After visits to Philadelphia, Manhattan, Albany, and Boston, Dr. Hamilton arrived in Newport in mid-August. His first night was spent at the White Horse Tavern where, he reports, he "was almost eat up alive with buggs." He was entertained by Dr. Thomas Moffatt, an old friend and one of Newport's esteemed physicians, with whom he discussed medicine, and was shown around town. Newport's sometimes racy reputation is given credence in the following account:

> Dr. Moffat [*sic*] took me out this evening to walk near the town where are a great many pleasant walks amidst avenues of trees. We viewed Mr. Malbone's house and gardens, and as we returned home met Malbone himself with whom we had some talk about news. We were met by a handsome bona rosa in a flaunting dress, who laughed us full in the face. Malbone and I supposed she was a paramour of Moffat's, for none of us knew her. We bantered him upon it and discovered the truth of our conjecture by raising a blush in his face.

Dr. Hamilton was invited to a meeting of the Literary and Philosophical Society and was "surprised to find that no matters of philosophy were brought upon the carpet." The gentlemen were more interested in talking about privateering and shipbuilding, and Hamilton was not terribly impressed with the intellectual fervor of the group that evening. It seems he, being unmarried, had his mind more on the women of Newport. After dining with a Captain Williams and a Dr. Keith one evening, the trio had a mission:

> At eight o'clock we waited on the ladies and with them walked a little way out of town to a place called Little Rock. Our promenade continued two hours, and they entertained us with several songs. We enjoyed all the pleasures of gallantry without transgressing the rules of modesty or good manners. There were six in company at this promenade; vizt. 3 dames and 3 gallants. The belle who fell to my lot pleased me exceedingly both in looks and conversation. Her name was Miss Clerk, daughter to a merchant in town. After a parting salute according to the mode of the place, I, with reluctance, bid the ladies farewell, expressing some regret that, being a stranger in their town and obliged soon to leave it, I should perhaps never have the happy opportunity of their agreeable company again. They returned their good wishes for my compliment; so I went to my lodging and after some learned chat with my landlady concerning the apothecary's craft, I went to bed.

In all, Dr. Hamilton was most impressed with Newport, and not only because of the fair ladies. In fact, he was downright smitten.

They are not so strait laced in religion here as in other parts of New England. They have among them a great number of Quakers. The island is the most delightful spot of ground I have seen in America. I can compare it to nothing but one entire garden. For rural scenes and pritty, frank girls, I found it the most agreeable place I had been in thro' all my peregrinations. . . . Their government is somewhat democratick, the people choosing their governour from among their own number every year by pole votes . . . They have but little regard to the laws of England, their mother country, tho they pretend to take that constitution for precedent. Collectors and naval officers here are a kind of cyphers. They dare not exercize their office for fear of the fury and unruliness of the people.

Dr. Alexander Hamilton's firsthand account of Newport life in 1744 has the authenticity that carries down the centuries. He found the people in Newport "very civil and courteous in their way." Clearly, he was sad to leave, but his itinerary was set, so Dr. Hamilton bid farewell within a few days, happy to have made the town's acquaintance.

Among the mid century aristocrats of Newport—John Channing, Henry Collins, Godfrey and John Malbone, Henry Marchant, John and Peleg Brown, Sueton Grant, William Ellery, Samuel and William Vernon, Gideon Wanton, Daniel and Stephen Ayrault, and Samuel Freebody—none is esteemed more highly than Abraham Redwood. Granted, his legacy is more familiar because the Redwood Library and Athenæum, the oldest continuously operating lending library in America still in its original building, bears his name. But Abraham Redwood would have been remembered nonetheless.

Like Henry Collins, Abraham Redwood was a complex character. Having inherited his wealth early in life, he was self-assured, decisive, and independent-minded. Raised in his family's Quaker faith, he arrogantly defied the Friends' prohibitions against owning slaves and ostentatious living: he went his own way and later in life chose to leave the Quaker Meeting rather than free his slaves, such were his needs on his Caribbean plantation. Nevertheless, Redwood was firm and far-sighted, philanthropic and public-spirited, a lover of beauty and, to Newport's lasting benefit, of books and ideas. As a leading member of the Literary and Philosophical Society in the 1740s, Redwood understood the need to establish a permanent base for learning, and with his friends created a legacy that is still an integral part of the community over 250 years later.

Abraham Redwood was born on the West Indies isle of Antigua in 1709. His father, Abraham, Sr., an English seaman from a prominent Bristol family, had married one Mehitable Langford, the daughter of the largest estate owner on the island, and with that match his, and his children's, fortune was assured. But finding the climate on Antigua less than optimum, the Redwoods moved to Newport a few years after Abraham was born. The island estate, Cassada Garden, a large producer of sugar and molasses, was left in charge of business managers while Abraham, Sr., pursued his trading interests from Rhode Island.

The love of learning, and the focus on education as essential to a happy and rich life, must have run deep in the Redwood family. In the seventeenth century, Abraham's great-great uncle had given Bristol, England, a building for the town's first public lending library. Once settled in America, Abraham was sent

Attributed to
Samuel King
Abraham Redwood,
date unknown
Oil on canvas
In this portrait, Abraham
Redwood is holding
Alexander Pope's
Essay on Man, published
1732-1734.
Redwood Library
and Athenæum
Newport, Rhode Island
Bequest of
Mrs. Edward A. Grossman
RLC.PA.086

to school in Philadelphia, because of the limited educational opportunities for a young Quaker in Newport. When he returned home in his eighteenth year, he married Martha Coggeshall, also a Quaker of high birth, with whom he had six children.

Europe and Great Britain, and thus the colonies as well, still ordered their societies around the feudal concept of primogeniture, which dictated that all the wealth of an estate (land, money, possessions) passed directly to the firstborn son in the family; the other offspring had to make their way in the world through their own resourcefulness. The first Redwood son died young, when Abraham was about sixteen: his older brother Jonas was killed when thrown from his horse in Newport. All of the substantial family holdings, including the Antigua estate, passed into Abraham Redwood's hands. With his future now quite secure, he embarked in maritime trade, mostly sending produce and timber to the islands and returning with the usual staple of molasses and sugar from his own plantation. After spending three years on Antigua in the late 1730s (while his wife and children remained in Newport, and none too happy about it), to sort out management difficulties and carouse with friends and relatives, Abraham returned home for good and took up his responsibilities as one of the leaders of the town's elite.

The nabob of Newport could do as he pleased. One can imagine Redwood, dressed to the nines (to the constant consternation of his plainer fellow Quakers), being driven from his mansion, secluded behind a high brick wall and sturdy wrought-iron gates, down Thames Street in *his* English chaise, walking along *his* private wharf to *his* extensive warehouse overflowing with Newport cheeses and hogsheads of rum, inspecting goods and *his* ledgers, and then retiring to the White Horse Tavern for an afternoon of gossip and business talk. After taking an early dinner at home with his wife and children, he would probably seek the company of his male companions at meetings of the Literary and Philosophical Society or at the numerous taverns frequented by his social set.

The Redwoods lived in a finely appointed house on Thames Street (near the present intersection with Memorial Boulevard), one of the most splendid in town and directly across the street from Godfrey Malbone's lavish townhouse; but Redwood's real joy was the nearly 150-acre farm up the island in Portsmouth where he could indulge in his passion for gardens and flowers. He was among the first in the northern colonies to import an English gardener as full-time help, and his letters to London in search of certain seeds and rootstocks attest to how seriously he took his botanical endeavors. Numerous visitors remarked on the beauty and wide variety of what Redwood had suceeded in growing—lemons, oranges, limes, pineapples, and more. He had his gardener, Charles Dunham, who earned a salary far outpacing most common workers, build hothouses and greenhouses, and kept him busy year-round. The plantation in the Caribbean allowed him to import hundreds of specimens so he could experiment in cross-fertilization and cultivating hybrids, particularly with tropical fruits and flowers. Even to this day, Newport is noted for its extraordinary collection of exotic flora, much of it imported during the Gilded Age to grace the grounds of Bellevue mansions. The impetus and inspiration for the correct and glorious garden in Newport began with Abraham Redwood.

For all his other successes and good deeds, Redwood will always be remembered best for his gift that laid the foundation for the Redwood Library. The proposal for a temple of learning in Newport had probably been discussed among the members of the Literary and Philosophical Society for years, ever since George Berkeley deeded the major part of his extensive library to Yale College. If Newport was to remain an intellectual center in New England, an impressive collection of books and documents needed to be amassed for the community's benefit. In 1747, the Society took action. Leading the way was Abraham Redwood, who donated £500 sterling for the books that would form the nucleus of the library's collection. Then Henry Collins offered his land. The Company of the Redwood Library was created and a £5,000 subscription of "old Tenor" colonial money was started to raise funds for construction. A committee was formed to oversee the project, and the members sought out the services of Peter Harrison to design the edifice. The building, a neoclassical gem based on designs Harrison had assimilated from Edward Hoppus's *Andrea Palladio's Architecture* as well as the work of Inigo Jones, is a masterpiece of Doric order, sophistication, and refinement as yet unseen in America. Abraham Redwood, honored by having the new library named after himself, must have been very proud.

Redwood didn't limit his philanthropic largesse to the library. He also gave £500 toward the founding of a Quaker school and stipulated that another similar gift would be forthcoming if a university were to be built in Newport. The latter bequest was tied up in a long-simmering struggle between Newport and Providence over the site of the school; in the end Providence won, and what we know today as Brown University was founded. Redwood also served as an Assistant in the General Assembly in 1744 and 1747, but retired from public life afterward. At the time of the Revolution, he and his daughter (his wife having died) moved to a farm in Mendon, Massachusetts, to escape the torment of the British occupation; they returned to Newport after the evacuation and reclaimed the townhouse and country estate. Abraham Redwood died in March 1788, at the age of seventy-nine.

Decades later, in a letter to a friend, Dr. Benjamin Waterhouse offered this assessment of the man: "You do not remember Abraham Redwood. I do. He was an extraordinary man. He made the best use of his talents, and of his property of any man I ever knew. He was judiciously liberal; while a dignified economy run through all his affairs. He was the greatest public and private benefactor of any man I ever knew on Rhode Island; and his style of living, & appearance was the best."

Craftsmen at Work

On June 3, 1989, at Christie's Park Avenue auction house in New York City, in the middle of a large sale, a rare piece of furniture belonging to Nicholas Brown went on the block. The *New York Times* had speculated on how much this desk and bookcase might bring. The highest price ever paid for a piece of French or English furniture at auction had been $2.9 million; how in the world could a provincial piece, regardless of provenance, bring more? Optimistic experts were positing that perhaps as much as $5 million or $6 million might be spent, an unheard-of price tag for an *American* artifact.

But the bidding produced an unprecedented surprise when the auctioneer hammered down the Brown piece at $11 million (the commission brought the final price to $12.1 million), the highest price ever paid for *any* piece of furniture in the world. Only masterpieces that hang on walls had ever brought more. Even the most optimistic of oddsmakers shook their heads at the astounding outlay.

The piece is a nine-and-a-half-foot-tall bonnet-topped mahogany block-and-shell desk and bookcase made for Nicholas Brown of Providence between 1760 and 1770, and attributed to the master craftsman John Goddard of Newport. It had been a fixture in the Brown family ever since. Along with John and Job Townsend, John Goddard and about twenty other relatives by birth or marriage made up the Townsend-Goddard dynasty that was so influential in eighteenth- and nineteenth-century American furniture making in Rhode Island; some critics assert they were the most important in America. Carl Bridenbaugh says that the Townsend-Goddard evolution of the shell-carved block-front is "the most distinctively American product in woodwork." The men of these interrelated families produced a variety of pieces—desks, chairs, high chests, chest-on-chests, superb block-front secretaries, and more—that have been described as "the pinnacle of taste and design."

The Townsends and Goddards were master craftsmen, but they were certainly not alone in town. When Boston's economy faltered around 1740, Newport took up the slack and forged ahead of its old adversary, particularly in the furniture-export business. As C. J. Moore describes:

Attributed to
John Goddard
*The Nicholas Brown
Chippendale
Block-and-Shell Carved
Desk and Bookcase*,
1760-1770
Sold by Christie's
New York in June 1989
for $12.5 million, a
world auction record for
American furniture.
Christie's Images, 1989
Private collection

From 1740 to the Revolution, Newport had almost as many furniture makers as Boston, many of whom were making tables and desks for sale to the other colonies, especially the cities of New York and Charleston, and the West Indies. During the eighteenth century in Newport, there were at least 99 cabinetmakers, 17 chair-makers, 2 upholsterers, and 4 carvers, 1 turner, and 16 joiners who may have worked on furniture. . . . Furniture export was a vital component in the cycle of prosperity which colonial Newport enjoyed. Between 1764–1767, though records during that period are sketchy, at least 492 chairs, 71 case pieces, and 30 tables were sent to Annapolis, and 113 chairs, 71 case pieces, and 309 tables to Charleston.

It is no wonder that Newport furniture became famous throughout the colonies. But it took the genius of the Townsends and Goddards to elevate the craft to an art.

The Townsends and Goddards were all Quakers; they lived and worked near each other on Easton's Point beginning around 1725 until the middle of the nineteenth century; a number of their houses are still lived in. Fathers handed down to their sons and nephews not only traditions, but the tools of the trade as well. Job Townsend, Sr., and his brother Christopher were the first of their families to make the move from housebuilder (Christopher worked on the Colony House) to the more specialized craft of making fine furniture, at first in the Queen Anne style. Many, but not all, sons and cousins apprenticed with their elders in both families, intermarried, and the skills learned by each generation stayed within the ever-increasing clan. As the merchant class became wealthier during midcentury, their demand for finer, more elaborate, furnishings grew as well—not only among members of the Brown family, but also governors Stephen Hopkins and Samuel Ward, as well as Stephen Ayrault, John Wanton, Jr., and Aaron Lopez, among others. These men had built their stylish mansions and now wished to fill them with artifacts of comparable quality. As the orders increased, John Townsend and John Goddard grew in their craft, evolved an individual style refined with their hallmark shell carvings, and reached their artistic maturity. The lucky combination of riches and great talent in one small community produced the masterpieces that have had a lasting influence on America's decorative arts and are represented in the country's finest museums.

In his groundbreaking study, *The Arts and Crafts of Newport Rhode Island, 1640–1820*, Ralph Carpenter undermined the myth that "many, probably the great majority of Americans, think of our colonial furniture as crude and primitive." Carpenter's scholarship led the way in explaining how profound the influence of the Newport furniture makers had been and detailed the contributions of the numerous Townsends and Goddards in the eighteenth century, as well as a number of other cabinetmakers who toiled in town during that era.

Although the concept for the magnificent block-front desks and bookcases probably didn't originate in Newport (Massachusetts is a better bet), the genre was brought to unparalleled perfection by the Townsends and Goddards—and the crucial detail that distinguishes their work from all other colonial furniture makers is the convex and concave shell carvings that adorn their important pieces. This "unique interpretation of the form developed by Townsend and Goddard" as well as the detailed craftsmanship and use of mahogany rather than walnut brought the Newport artisans their deserved fame. The clan had "an obsession for understatement that allow[ed] no ornamentation to interrupt the smooth flow of the outline."

Another hallmark of their work was the precise dovetailing, the mass and line of the cabriole leg, the boldness of the ogee-bracket foot, and the undercut talon on the claw-and-ball foot.

The majority of the pieces now attributed to their workshops had gone unidentified for many decades, hence the obscurity of the Townsend-Goddard families. In some cases, the Townsends and Goddards did put their names on certain pieces, but in other cases their labels were not attached or possibly came unglued and were lost over the centuries. Carpenter brought them their overdue recognition. Since his book was first published in 1954, many more pieces have come to light, adding further luster to the Newport school of the eighteenth century. In the 1980s, Michael Moses supplemented Carpenter's study in *Master Craftsmen of Newport: The Townsends and Goddards*, and we have a far better understanding of why the Newport block-and-shell furniture is the most original and important contribution to American furniture design during that period. The term "Colonial Newport furniture" is synonymous with grace, beauty, and understated elegance.

What was it about the Townsends and Goddards that made them so unique in American furniture-making design? To begin with, as Quakers they were by nature and spiritual training independent minded; they savored their religious freedom in Newport, and that attitude perhaps contributed to the creation of innovative designs in their furniture. When the elder craftsmen turned from building houses to making furniture, they tended to copy the prevailing Queen Anne style until they had the confidence to expand and explore a more original style—the block-and-shell design for which they are so rightfully renowned. Certainly they were influenced by other craftsmen; the Townsends and Goddards borrowed features from French, English, and Chinese furniture, but they did not *copy*. Instead, they created their own American vernacular and hence their masterpieces. As Quakers, they believed in the self-sufficient character, and, as Quakers, they had an almost inbred dislike of ostentation. Paradoxically, Philadelphia, another Quaker stronghold and also a major furniture-making center, produced lavish, exuberant Chippendale cabinets and chairs, a style not in keeping with their religious tenets. Newport furniture, particularly by Townsend and Goddard, displays strength, stability, confidence, and a robust depiction of the emerging American spirit with a minimum of embellishment.

For decades, the majority of Townsend-Goddard pieces had been referred to by experts as "Chippendale." Carpenter asserts that recent scholarship places the signature block-and-shell case pieces, marble-top tables, and other similar forms in a category by themselves. He finds certain elements of design taken from or related to other directories, but what the Townsends and Goddards produced was unique. In his *New York Times Magazine* review of a major exhibition of John Townsend's furniture presented at New York's Metropolitan Museum of Art in 2005 (curated by Morrison Heckscher), the art critic Robert Hughes wrote of the block-and-shell cases, "This was a Newport invention. There is nothing at all like it in English or European furniture. It marks the moment when American furniture declares its independence from the pattern books and prototypes of Chippendale and other London makers."

These craftsmen learned their skills in the family workrooms. Techniques were passed down from generation to generation. While the clan connections are too intricate to list, a good example of the melding of the two families can be seen early on. Job Townsend, Sr. (married to a descendant of the original Easton family), and Christopher Townsend were joiners in Newport in the 1730s. Job, Jr., born 1733, apprenticed with his father or uncle and went into trade. When John Goddard arrived in town, after a career as a sloopmaster, he apprenticed with Job, Sr., and ended up marrying Townsend's daughter Hannah in 1746, after which he opened his own shop next to the Robinson house on Washington Street. John Goddard's brother James married another of Job Townsend's daughters, Suzanna. John Townsend married Philadelphia Feke, daughter of the famed artist, and had five children with her, most of whom carried on the family traditions. And so on. Most of these men became wealthy through their work. They held various offices in Newport politics and several of them held important posts, such as town treasurer and Surveyor of Timber.

Being appointed Surveyors of Timber may have given the Townsend-Goddard craftsmen a slight advantage in securing the very best wood for themselves; they, in essence, had an inside track, and could have used it for their own benefit. When mahogany arrived from Jamaica, Cuba, Santo Domingo, or Honduras, the surveyor would be on the wharf to inspect it. Depending on where the mahogany matured, it could vary in density anywhere from 25 to 55 pounds per cubic foot. Swamp mahogany grows faster and is lighter in density. Highland mahogany, growing more slowly, is solid and heavy. Cabinetmakers preferred the heaviest, sturdiest wood for their expensive, large-scale furniture. As inspectors the Townsends and Goddards may have had first dibs on the choicest wood (although some historians assert that might have been difficult, given the competitive conditions in Newport at the time). The mahogany remaining after the other Newport craftsmen had selected the top-of-the-line pieces was often sent on to England. At one point, the Surveyor of Timber received a letter from a London agent complaining about the poor quality of a recently arrived batch. We can speculate that being patriots and Newporters of an independent streak, the Townsends and Goddards may have taken pleasure in one-upping their English competitors.

How much and in what way all the brothers, cousins, and nephews collaborated is not well known, but some records from the time indicate that the extended clan not only competed with each other but sometimes worked together on a piece when meeting a tight deadline for an overanxious buyer. Also unknown is the artist who produced the exquisite shell carvings on the desks and secretaries that were produced by both families. Some authorities assert that the carving is so uniform it must have come from one hand; others believe that several of the men turned themselves into master carvers. Did men outside the extended families work in any of the Townsend or Goddard workshops? This is also unknown, but Carpenter has read documentary evidence which states that the best carver in Newport before the Revolution was a black African whose name is lost to history. Could he have plied his trade with one of the Townsends or Goddards? Whatever the answer, it is clear that long-term familial cooperation contributed to their collective success. And the $12.1 million purchase price in 1989 for a desk and bookcase is perfect testament to the Townsend-Goddard mastery of the fine art of furniture making.

The furniture of the Townsends and Goddards was notable in the extreme, but by no means the only example of superior Newport craftsmanship. The town continued to be a haven for a budding class of entrepreneurs and artisans who valued freedom of expression in all aspects of their lives. Religious openness was more or less taken for granted, of course, and that essential freedom led people to expect, even demand, other liberties—artistic, intellectual, social, political—all of which were implicit in the Charter of 1663. Thus the cabinetmakers, clockmakers, silversmiths, stonecutters, and other members of the growing middle class lived and worked in an environment that encouraged originality and creativity. Conversely, artisans of Philadelphia, while certainly resourceful and diligent craftsmen, tended to produce artifacts along more traditional English lines and were considered to be less innovative than their Newport peers.

One of Newport's most engaging craftsmen was the polymath William Claggett, best known today for his skills as a clockmaker, but in fact a man of many other talents. Born in Wales about 1696, Claggett came to Boston as a boy, apprenticed with a master clockmaker for five years, married at eighteen and moved with his wife and son, William, Jr., to Newport around 1716 to establish himself as a clock- and watchmaker who also specialized in repairs. The Claggetts lived on Bridge Street, in the Point section, not far from many other enterprising artisans, and quite close to the Townsends and Goddards. In those early days of chronometry, the artisan had to fashion the majority of the working parts himself, mostly out of scrap brass. He had to be part craftsman, part engineer, part mechanic. It was a time-consuming occupation, one that called for utmost patience, to say nothing of steady hands and keen eyesight.

William Claggett excelled at his occupation, but he must have been a restless, ever-curious fellow, a cross between mad professor and Renaissance man. He got into a raging theological debate with the elders at the Second Baptist Church over scriptural authority, and was so incensed that he wrote a 230-page rebuttal to their ways and means that James Franklin published for him in Boston in 1721. That screed got him thrown out of the congregation, and he didn't seem to care. Soon the clockmaker was busy in another discipline, branching out by making and repairing compasses—not a bad job for a busy seaport like Newport, and a natural evolution for a man talented in working with minute metal pieces. Whether driven by a need for money to support his growing family or because of his overeager personality, Claggett also took over his deceased father's bakery, selling bread and biscuits to ships in the harbor.

While he was turning out beautifully engraved clock faces and sturdy mechanisms with wooden cases made by the Townsend-Goddard dynasty and other local cabinetmakers, William Claggett was moving in yet another direction. In 1736, he offered to sell an organ to the Old North Church in Boston; whether he built the instrument himself or imported it from Europe is unknown, but representatives of the church ventured to Newport to assess its value and liked what they saw. They paid Claggett £300 (his original asking price had been £400), and the clockmaker-cum-music-maker traveled to Boston to install the organ. Richard L. Champlin, once the assistant librarian at the Redwood Library and an authority on Claggett, believed that Claggett's knowledge of these complex mechanisms was gained from his familiarity with the organ at Trinity Church in Newport (where he had supplied the tower clock), the gift of Bishop George Berkeley. Documentation is scarce, but when one is dealing with someone as far-ranging in intellect and talents as William Claggett, it is perhaps best to err on the side of believing he could accomplish just about anything when it came to building instruments.

His next venture outside the clock-making craft was electrifying—literally. Claggett somehow fashioned a large electrical machine to explore how these then-little understood forces actually worked; the apparatus encompassed most of one room in his small colonial house on the Point (we have no record of how his wife and children felt about these arrangements). Now we add the vision of the mad scientist at work, a forerunner to the Frankenstein creation of the next century. Trying to discern the magic of electricity was

popular sport in the mid-eighteenth century, so Claggett was not alone in his attempts to unlock the mysteries of nature's charges. Typical of his style, he became fully obsessed when something interested him. He gave demonstrations of his machine in Newport, and the gathered crowd was fascinated with his pyrotechnics. His reputation spread. "It is written that he was intimately acquainted with Benjamin Franklin who inspected his apparatus at Newport in 1746. Indeed it has been suggested that Franklin derived his interest in electricity from Claggett and his apparatus."

We have evidence of his antics from dispatches that appeared in the *Boston Evening Post*: "March 3, 1746. Boston. The wonderful account of the surprizing effects of Electricity, as lately discovered in several Parts of Europe, having raised the Curiosity of several Gentlemen here, Mr. William Claggett, Watchmaker, has fixed a machine, by which a great Variety of those Experiments have been repeated, to the Astonishment of the Spectators."

That was just an appetizer, because the next report went into more detail. "December 29, 1746. Boston. We hear from Newport, on Rhode Island, that Mr. William Claggett of that Town, has at last succeeded so far in the Electrical Experiments, as to set fire to Spirits of Wine, the most satisfactory and difficult of all."

But the best was yet to come. Claggett had been persuaded to move his electrical contraption from Newport to Boston so the multitudes there could revel in his discoveries. The next entry from the *Evening Post* chronicles his victory:

August 24, 1747. Boston. For the Entertainment of the Curious, There will be seen at the House of

Capt. John Williams . . . a Great Variety of curious Experiments of the most surprising Effects of Electricity, wherein will be shewn the wonderful Phenomena of Electrical Attraction, Repulsion, and flamistic Force; particularly the new Method of Electrifying several Persons at the same Time, so that Fire shall dart from all Parts of their Bodies, as the same has lately been exhibited to the Astonishment of the Curious in all Parts of Europe. Performed by William Claggett, Clock-maker, whose Business will not suffer him to make any long stay here, and therefore should be glad those Gentlemen and Ladies whose Curiosities may excite them to behold those Wonders, would attend as soon as possible.

Claggett's circus-like displays of electrical forces were a hit in Boston, and he raised £1,500 for charity from his efforts.

The last known artistic achievement of the prodigious William Claggett was engraving the currency for the colony of Rhode Island and Providence Plantations. Contemplating yet another distribution of the increasingly controversial paper money in 1738, the General Assembly was correctly concerned about the proliferation of counterfeit "bank" issues, so it decided to manufacture bills that would be harder to copy and turned to Claggett for help. The move made eminent sense: Claggett's talent for designing intricate and precise clock faces was well known. It was not a far stretch for him to engrave the plates for various denominations of currency. Along with creating the elegant bills, which stayed in circulation for decades, Claggett was employed to do the printing as well.

William Claggett died in October 1749 after producing approximately seventy clocks of various description, most of them signed. His business and tools were taken over by his sons William, Jr., and Thomas and his son-in-law James Wady, each of whom went on to create superb clock mechanisms and designs, many housed in Benjamin Baker or Townsend-Goddard cases.

Claggett was one of the most talented and original of Newport's early eighteenth-century craftsmen. He had verve and vision, irrepressible curiosity and nimble hands. His electrical experiments influenced other scientists, and his currency engravings deterred colonial counterfeiting. Some of his clocks would undoubtedly fetch prices in the high six figures if they went on the block today. His legacy endures.

Regardless of the era or economic circumstances, the people of Newport needed dishes and utensils for eating and drinking. In the early decades of the town, many of the settlers would have used wooden platters, leather buckets, and horns; only the wealthiest would have brought silver or pewter utensils and pottery from England or Boston. But as wampum gave way to hard currency gained through trade, Spanish silver coins and English shillings flowed into the port and the pockets of the merchants. Along with fine houses and furniture, the best way to let the world know you had arrived was by displaying objects fashioned from silver.

Much of the silver that survives today was made for customers who wanted to safeguard and display their wealth, as well as enjoy the use of the objects. In colonial days, someone with a surfeit of silver coins—easily stolen and untraceable—might go to the local silversmith and order a set of spoons and knives or plates, marked for easy identification. The smith would melt down the coins in a crucible, pour the molten liquid into a skillet to form an ingot that was then hammered into sheets of silver of various gauges, and proceed to create whatever was ordered. This manner of protecting one's own was not quite as safe as putting the money into a bank—which didn't exist then anyway—but the product was much more beautiful than a checkbook. Thus the customer was able to preserve his wealth (which could be melted down later if he were strapped for assets), while at the same time showing off his works of art.

Unlike carpentry and furniture making, silversmithing drew a large number of upper-class men. It was a highly respected craft that members of the colonial aristocracy felt comfortable in pursuing, and there was a very practical reason as well: these men possessed much more of the silver needed to make their cups, beakers, and porringers than the average artisans, who often dealt in barter for the goods they produced. So, it is no surprise to see the familiar names of Coddington, Brenton, and Clarke among the best-known silversmiths of Newport.

Boston set the tone for colonial styles in silver; the great smiths Edward Winslow and Paul Revere will forever be associated with that city. But the work done in Newport during the eighteenth century equals the execution and design of the best silversmiths in New York, Philadelphia, or Boston. Less florid than objects made in Europe, most colonial silversmithing displays a simplicity of shape and proportion and purity of line more fitting to the environment; Newport men rarely attempted to copy the overly ornate pieces being produced for the British gentry, nobility, and Church of England parishes. They certainly possessed the talent to do so (although they may have lacked the knowledge of some techniques), but the frontier American sensibility veered more toward unadorned austerity. Newport silversmiths followed the American custom

Samuel Vernon
American silver tankard,
1720-1737
Newport Historical Society
Newport, Rhode Island
Gift of the
Estate of Edward W. Gould
79.1.1

of impressing only their maker's mark on the pieces they produced (English pieces would have four hallmarks), thus identifying Newport silver does not present the problems that identifying Townsend-Goddard furniture does. We have clear evidence today and can identify who made which saltcellar or teapot.

The best known of the Newport silversmiths of the era was Samuel Vernon. Born in 1683 of good family (his mother was the granddaughter of Anne Hutchinson), Vernon was the father of William Vernon who, as president of the Eastern Navy Board for the patriots during the Revolution, was responsible for building up the American navy. Samuel Vernon was a careful, innovative craftsman who produced a wide variety of tankards, cups, spoons, porringers, and pitchers during his productive career. His designs are simple and elegant, reflecting an innate aesthetic and a pair of very skillful hands. His works reside in major museums in America. In 1715, Vernon was hired by the General Assembly to design and engrave the plates for the first issue of paper money in Rhode Island history; they were used until the 1730s. The bills were clean and easily readable, but proved to be too easy for amateur engravers to counterfeit.

Creating chalices, flagons, plates, and other ceremonial silver for the town's churches was another important activity of the smith. Trinity Church possesses some of the most distinctive pieces of colonial silver, particularly two flagons for the communion table made by Benjamin Brenton, grandson of Newport founder Governor William Brenton, and two baptismal bowls created by Daniel Russell, who also advertised himself as a goldsmith. Most of Newport's other established churches have silver plates and chalices produced by local artisans.

Other Newport silversmiths of note, and whose work can also be found in the best collections of colonial silver, were Arnold Collins (father of the art-loving Henry Collins), Jonathan Otis (married to a Coggeshall descendant), Thomas Arnold, and Jonathan Clarke (perhaps a relative of the founder Jeremy Clarke). All of these craftsmen left legacies for future generations to admire and use on a daily basis.

Down to the Sea in Ships

Newport was sustained by the sea. It was the town's lifeblood, its oxygen. With no virgin tracts of arable land stretching back into the hinterlands on which farmers could produce large quantities of crops and animals, no huge plantations on the southern scale (despite the colony's formal name), Newport's prosperity and growth depended entirely on its ability to trade with its sister colonies and the world beyond. Newport has long been known as the Venice of America, and the comparison is apt. Thus the ship, regardless of its size, configuration, or comfort, was the most prized instrument for expansion and livelihood, the one essential tool that Newport could not live without.

Shipbuilding around Narragansett Bay began when the first settlers arrived—by boat, of course. Being islanders now, not mainlanders who might become distracted with other enterprises, Newport men began constructing small pinnaces, shallops, and ketches of about 10- to 35-ton burden to get about locally and use as fishing boats. These smaller vessels were single-

TRADES AND ARTISANS
The other men and women who helped make the wheels of commerce go round during Newport's Golden Age were a varied and extensive lot, an amalgam of artisans (comprising between a third to a half of the steadily employed), craftsmen, mechanics, and laborers (many of them apprentices or indentured servants), who did the bidding of the ruling merchant princes and, by and large, were content to make an honest wage and go back to their small homes and families every night. A good portion were, like the Townsends, Goddards, and Claggetts, proprietors or freelancers, carrying out their assignments for a variety of clients. The majority of Newporters held steady jobs in fields in which they apprenticed young and never left. Booming Newport offered sustenance, opportunity for the gifted and energetic, a safe haven for private beliefs, and a pleasant urban environment.

If you were to picture life in Newport about 1750 or 1760, you would see carpenters and joiners to build your private homes and public buildings; spermaceti candlemakers to light the spaces in your snug rooms; clockmakers to keep you on time; thermometer makers to let you know what to wear outside. Cordwainers (an antique Spanish term meaning shoemaker) would keep your feet dry; hatmakers, your head; and the numerous tailors would keep you in high fashion, or merely warm. Millers would produce flour with which bakers would make your daily bread. Tanners would produce leather for a variety of your needs, including some kitchen gadgets as well as gloves, shoes, and upholstery; coopers would produce the vessels for storing bothyour liquid and dry

CONTINUED ON PAGE 146

goods; over twenty local distillers would concoct the rum to pour into the pewter or silver mugs made in various shops; and the forerunner to the apothecary might be able to sell you a cure for your hangover. Glasscutters would fashion panes for your windows and mirrors for your daily grooming. Blacksmiths would shoe your horse. Masons would build your fireplaces and repair roads; metalworkers would supply your home and Mr. Malbone's fleet with a vast array of goods; and the numerous mechanics would fix everything in sight. Gunsmiths would fit you with rifles to hunt game; and if you were unlucky enough to go shooting with a novice who made an errant shot at you instead of a buck, the stonecutters and engravers from the John Stevens shop on Thames Street would carve your tombstone.

masted, simply rigged, and relatively easy to build and maintain. They were the essential harbor craft, manned by three or four sailors, and used daily to ferry goods and people to surrounding points and back.

As Aquidneck farms and the adjacent Narragansett plantations began yielding enough produce for export, larger vessels were required for coastal, and eventually oceanic trade to the West Indies and across the Atlantic. Larger facilities (it would be a stretch to call these rough construction sites dotted along the bay shipyards yet) started constructing 40-ton sloops with two masts (fore and aft mainsail and jib) for the more arduous seaborne voyages. These sloops, and also the schooners, were the principal "big boats" of the early years and they were turned out in six to nine months on average.

New England was the shipbuilding capital of America, with Boston leading all other centers, until about 1740 when its economy stagnated. Boston's shipwrights formed guilds early on and were better organized and financed. Those in Rhode Island, true to the colony's more helter-skelter, go-it-alone worldview, were more like odd-job workers, hopping from site to site as work presented itself. New England, with its abundance of eager workmen, could produce ships at far lower cost—sometimes 60 percent less—than Old England, which was rapidly being depleted of its lumber, a commodity readily found in the vast forests along the western Atlantic seaboard. American ships were renowned for their speed, but because of the green wood used in their construction also disparaged for their poor longevity. By 1700, the American colonies were supplying England with over a quarter of its merchant fleet, and in the mid-1720s London shipwright guilds were complaining to Parliament that their best carpenters were fleeing to the New World. By 1770, American shipyards "had outfitted a third of Great Britain's merchant marine, which was then the largest, and the thirteen colonies ranked as a leading center of international ship production."

Around Newport and all along Narragansett Bay, shipbuilding was a major industry, probably responsible for employing more men than any other endeavor, including the manning at sea of the ships themselves. In 1721, Rhode Island reported to London that it had but 60 vessels, but in 1740, Governor Richard Ward told the Board of Trade that the number had ballooned to 120 ships, most of them owned and operated by Newport merchants. Thirty years later, more than 500 ships would crowd Newport harbor. And, because of less red tape and government involvement, Newport continued to produce ships at a cost about 20 percent cheaper than any of its colonial counterparts, so the business expanded until the eve of the Revolution. Merchants' needs were expanding as well, and larger craft were necessary for their increased loads. At the beginning of the eighteenth century, brigs, at around 60 tons, and snows, at 90-ton burden, began to slide down the ways into Narragansett Bay after about a year under construction. These were both two-masted designs, more complex to build and sail, but necessary for the Caribbean traffic. The next step up was to the barks of 90 tons and three masts, and eventually to the full-rigged ship itself, a three-masted, double-decked vessel of 140 tons and up, with a crew of fifteen. All of these, especially the very largest of ships coming in at 400 tons or more, were being built and maintained at Newport, to the delight of the city fathers who watched the town coffers surge with revenues from the boom cycle and an expanding tax base.

These ships, large and small, were constructed from the most rudimentary "plans." It is astonishing today to realize that all the shipwright had to go on was a few lines drawn on a piece of wood—yet the complexity of the task was enormous. The initial carving of a half-hull model also helped guide the builders in their design. The art of the shipwright was passed down, orally, through generations of men, and not until the very end of the seventeenth century do we find anything that could be called a real builder's plan. It wasn't until late in the eighteenth century that we see detailed plans concerning the variety of aspects needing attention in the building of a vessel.

Who used these ships? Nearly everyone in town at one time or another. As an island enclave, everything about Newport was maritime-focused. The largest proportion of the ships went to the merchants, but Newport built and fitted out close to fifty privateering vessels during the colonial war years as well. Fishermen turned to bigger vessels when they sailed farther afield into the expansive fishing grounds of the North Atlantic and Grand Banks, harvesting cod to be sold in the Indies. Slavers had to be fitted out in a particular way to transport human cargo. Ships carrying the famous Narragansett Pacers were provisioned with large girdles to suspend the horses during the voyage so they would not lose their footing in rough weather. Construction went on constantly, because many ships were lost to storms and enemy privateers, or to pirates. They had to be replaced, and made larger and more seaworthy than the ones lying at the bottom of the ocean. Finally, a few wealthy Newporters ventured early into a sport that the city has always been associated with—the pleasure sailboat, used for no other reason than to enjoy a peaceful sojourn at sea on a warm summer's day.

All of these vessels had to have a place to moor, and Newport harbor was among the best and busiest in all the colonies. John Banister, Abraham Redwood, Aaron Lopez, and many other successful merchants owned their own piers, and some sixty to seventy smaller ones lined the harbor along nearly two miles of shore, from Long Wharf and beyond, both north and south. Ships large and small could find docking space, plus the services of stevedores and draymen to move their goods to nearby warehouses and shops. Whatever the vessel, Newport could handle it, just as Verrazzano had predicted in 1524—but, ironically, this very achievement in efficiency spelled the port city's future doom. When the British Royal Navy considered strategic alternatives as it planned its occupation of the colonies prior to the Revolution's hostilities, Newport, not New York or Boston, was the clear favorite.

Shipbuilding, particularly the fashioning of larger vessels, was a complicated business involving numerous skills and keen management of the schedule to keep the approximately fifty carpenters and joiners working in tandem. Carl Bridenbaugh, in *The Colonial Craftsman*, enumerates some of the challenges: "A three- or four-hundred-ton sailing vessel was the most elaborate undertaking of our colonial forefathers. The almost baffling complexity of building, launching, fitting, rigging, and finishing a great ship of the eighteenth century called forth the services of workers from nearly every craft in a colonial city. . . . Thus, the construction of a large sailing ship represents, as does nothing else, the supreme achievement of early American craftsmanship." Once the vessel was almost complete, the complex job of stepping masts and running the astounding array of labyrinthine lines that controlled the sails could take a month.

SHIPBUILDING

Putting up a colonial house was child's play compared with constructing a vessel that had to withstand the rigors of the open sea. Bridenbaugh offers an extensive picture of what went into the making of a ship at that time, worth quoting in full:

Details about shipbuilding are hard to find, but among the papers of a leading Newport merchant, John Banister, is a set of accounts for the construction of the three-hundred-ton ship *Leathley* in 1740 that shows convincingly how such an enterprise distributed profits widely and gave work to nearly everyone in Newport. Artificers represented twenty-three separate crafts, including shipwrights, joiners, carvers, cabinetmakers, blockmakers, and small-boat builders; ropemakers, riggers, sailmakers, smiths, founders, braziers, glaziers, painters, coopers, tanners, and bricklayers. Ten ship chandlers supplied the nails, bolts, hinges, anchors, naval stores, cordage, and other equipment for the *Leathley*; while bakers, brewers, butchers, and tallow chandlers, in addition to day laborers, white and black, and draymen also contributed to the enterprise. Captain Peter Harrison, who superintended construction of the ship he was to command, carried eighty-three different accounts for supplies and services on his books, one of the last of which was a charge of £10 for the compass, quadrant, and navigating gear made by Newport's famous Benjamin King. In a very real sense, the building of a large ship was a community enterprise.

A great many of the crafts and nascent industries prevalent in the eighteenth century are with us today, but one key sector of the shipbuilding process has been lost to us: the ropewalk. How *did* they get such outstretched lines of rope for a ship's extensive rigging? Imagine a very long shed-building, taking up as much as a quarter mile, add men hauling lengths of fiber to and fro, and you will begin to get the picture.

The cordage needed to fit out one of Newport's larger ships was prodigious; and it had to be long, strong, impervious to saltwater, and pliable. The raw materials used to fashion ships' lines were hemp and tar, and the best hemp available was *Cannabis sativa*, the very same plant used in the harvesting of marijuana. Perhaps unaware of the occupational hazards of ingesting hemp in the workplace (or perhaps considering it a perk of being a ropemaker), the General Assembly actually encouraged *Cannabis sativa*'s growth in Rhode Island after 1722 and later offered a bounty for every pound grown within the colony's borders. In 1729, Newport employed two Hemp Viewers (can anyone imagine that public post being created today?) to judge the quality of the weed, but we have no direct verification of the uses or tests to which these officials may have put this now-outlawed specimen of flora.

Cannabis aside, the ropewalk was akin to today's nuclear power plant. It was a vital, and extremely dangerous, part of the maritime industry: vital because no ship could leave port without the miles of lines, cords, cables, and ropes made within its confines; dangerous because the constant peril of full-scale fire caused by spilled molten tar made the ropewalk a tinderbox waiting to explode. For this reason, almost every colonial town mandated that ropewalks be sited on the outskirts; in Newport, two walks lined what is now Kay Street, the others were on Farewell Street, leading out of town (one was owned by the art-loving Henry Collins). They were a necessary utility, but who could predict when the next Chernobyl might go into meltdown? No thriving shipping center could do without a ropewalk, and no God-fearing town of the period was ever at ease with the serious threat to life and property the walks represented.

The job of creating the lines for a ship's rigging was arduous, monotonous, and intricate; much of it was performed by African slaves. The ropemaker would begin the process by tying a heavy bundle of hemp around his waist and then back-peddle along the length of the shed as his assistant cranked a large wheel paying out more hemp. As the ropemaker receded, fashioning a distinct strand, he would lay the unwound line on sturdy floor brackets called "bearers" to lighten his load; when he reached the far end of the walk, he had created a stretch of strong, unbroken yarn. The process was repeated over and over. "Once he had three such strands of equal tension and equal size, he next 'laid' the rope. That is, he bound together the three lesser lines, using the same wheel to twist them in the same direction." Depending on the type of line he was creating, he would twist the strands in different directions or add a fourth strand to make a heavier cable.

Once the long "line" was shaped, the ropemaker and his apprentice would drag each strand through a large bucket of hot tar, and then force it through a small eyehole to remove the excess; at that point, the strands were twisted together to form the final rope. The danger inherent in the process is obvious: with such cumbersome lengths of rope being dragged through the tar, it was just a matter of time before someone knocked the bucket over and started a fire. Most colonial shipbuilding centers lost one or more ropewalks to the accidental conflagration: Newport suffered at least two, although one of the longest ropewalks in town, thought to be along Catherine Street, survived only to be dismantled by British soldiers during the Revolution and used as firewood.

Aside from Henry Collins, other notable Newporters were involved in the ropewalk industry; with so many ships being built, ropemaking was a lucrative business. A descendant of the famed pirate Thomas Tew made his living churning out lines, as did a relative of Godfrey Malbone along with the royalist Francis Brinley. Ropewalks were also an excellent training ground for young men who would move on to more prestigious employment within the maritime trades. To get an idea of the extent of the activity going on in Newport, consider Richard Champlin's report that "in 1770 William Vernon, owner of no small fleet of vessels, ran up a bill owed to Deacon William Tilley for cordage, spunyarn, lines and worming. It totaled £3,358." That figure represents many miles of rope.

Fat City

Between 1740 and 1775, Newport's Golden Age reached its peak and, at the time of such prosperity (discounting the recession of 1763–1766), it seemed to many of the inhabitants that the good times would be unending. Ships large and small were splashing off their ways all along Narragansett Bay, and reliable trade routes to the numerous islands in the West Indies and to Africa's west coast were constantly refined to meet new conditions (war, scarcity of product, oversaturation of a particular market). Well-established merchants continued, by and large, to flourish within a familiar pattern, while younger men set their eyes on what they believed would be an even more lucrative target—direct and sustained trade with Great Britain and the European Continent.

Until this period, Rhode Island merchants had never had the sway or sufficient specie capital to establish continuing links with their counterparts in London, Bristol, or Liverpool, and thus had to obtain the highly sought-after English goods from Boston, New York, or Philadelphia. But a new generation of businessmen, led by the wealthy John Banister (privateering and smuggling were specialties, as well as legitimate business), succeeded in establishing ongoing relationships with London merchants who were willing to extend credit for the hardware, home furnishings, and textiles Banister purchased to sell at the shops on his wharf, Banister's Row, in Newport. Seeing his initial success, a number of merchants, among them William and Samuel Vernon, quickly followed suit and found others in England who would deal with them directly. They were later joined by Aaron Lopez and Christopher Champlin, who were even more aggressive in pursuing European connections.

Like so many Newport men before and after, John Banister (himself the son of a rich merchant and a distant relative of the Duke of Newcastle, a distinction that gave him great social cachet) married an heiress who made his life even easier. Hermione Pelham, a descendant of Governor Benedict Arnold, had a dowry most men in Newport would have lusted over: large parcels of property along Pelham Street and what is now Touro Park. The Banisters joined Trinity Church and built a mansion on the corner of Pelham and Spring streets; their son, John, Jr., was among the first of Newport's gentry to attend Harvard College. Banister died in 1767, so he did not have to witness the insult his house endured a few years later: during the Revolution, his former residence was commandeered by the head of the British occupying forces, the hated

The next great phase in Newport colonial architecture followed shortly with the emergence of Peter Harrison, often referred to as America's first *real* architect. That distinction is bestowed on him because he initiated the tradition of sketching plans for others to execute, but he was not a builder himself. Since he didn't charge a fee for his services but only accepted gifts of silver plate, some authorities hesitate to label him a "professional" architect in the modern sense. Nonetheless, Peter Harrison was the real thing, and the distinct echoes of his work can be seen later in Thomas Jefferson's Monticello and his buildings at the University of Virginia.

More is known about Harrison's life than Richard Munday's. Born in 1716, in York, England, where he and his brother Joseph were raised as Quakers, Peter Harrison spent his youth onboard ships, eventually becoming a captain after arriving in America. He seems to have had an active mind and wide-ranging interests: cartography, shipbuilding, surveying, and obviously architecture. He liked to work with his hands. Around 1739, Peter followed his brother to Newport, where they joined in a growing and successful trading enterprise. (Peter Harrison was on his way up in the world, an opportunity that would have been denied him had he remained in rank-conscious England.) By then, it was clear that the Quaker Meeting House was not the route to upward mobility (so greatly had society changed in a mere few decades), thus he joined Trinity Church, like many other recently arrived merchants desiring for the good life.

The Harrison brothers had extensive business dealings with John Banister, and the wealthy magnate sent the young men to England on trading missions several times over the next seven years. It was undoubtedly at this time that Peter Harrison began to take interest in the designs of Andrea Palladio, the Italian Renaissance architect of pure line and form. Palladianism had reached England and was the latest fancy of the upper class. Harrison not only saw examples of how the Palladian concept worked well on British soil, but with his frequent forays to London also began to form a library of architectural books that was considered, at his death, the finest and most extensive collection in America. He was curious and motivated, and he had a consuming fascination with how things, particularly buildings, were made.

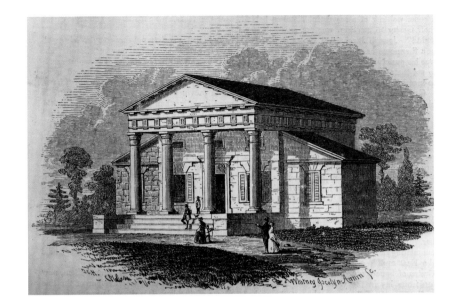

Peter Harrison, however, might have gone down in history as a footnote had he not won the heart of the most eligible young woman in Newport, Elizabeth (Betty) Pelham, another descendant of Benedict Arnold, first governor of Rhode Island. Miss Pelham was from impeccable lineage, but she was also an heiress and had recently come into a substantial inheritance from her father. Armed with a cloak of respectability through his Trinity connections, the dashing and talented Peter Harrison pursued Miss Pelham with vigor— perhaps too much vigor, because on the eve of their wedding in 1746, Betty Pelham was already pregnant, and her relatives were not particularly happy.

Be that as it may, Harrison was catapulted into high society and a life of leisure, given his wife's £20,000 dowry. John Banister was now an in-law, not an employer. Harrison made the best of his new situation: her money enabled him to spend more time at his drafting board, sketching plans for buildings derived from his growing library devoted to English and Italian architecture. He became a member of the Literary and Philosophical Society and through that association met the leading thinkers in town just when they were seriously contemplating the construction of a library for themselves and the community at large. How and why Peter Harrison was chosen to draft the sketches for this endeavor is not recorded. Many of the members must have known of his fascination with buildings and had probably seen the maps and house plans he had drawn. By the summer of 1748, nine months after The Company of the Redwood Library had been incorporated following Abraham Redwood's £500 gift for books, Harrison had submitted his plans and drawings for the building; with Henry Collins's donation of the plot on what is now Bellevue Avenue, building was ready to commence.

According to Carl Bridenbaugh, who wrote Harrison's biography, the fledgling architect relied mainly on three books from his collection to gain inspiration for the Redwood Library. From Edward Hoppus's edition of *Palladio*, Harrison copied the classic temple portico; from William Kent's *Designs of Inigo Jones*, he got the inspiration for the doorway treatment and the window placement; and from Batty Langley's

In their epic chronicle, *The Architectural Heritage of Newport, Rhode Island: 1640–1915,* published in 1952 and still the most authoritative study of early buildings in town, Antoinette Downing and Vincent Scully, Jr., state: "It is fitting that Trinity, as Newport's first important eighteenth-century building, was the first to be erected by a man whose name is known. The increased importance of the designer was concomitant with the changing approach to architecture. The housewrights and carpenters of the seventeenth century had been anonymous workmen who did not design buildings, but put them up according to traditional usage.... Only in the eighteenth century, when the design of the building came to be considered apart from the building itself, did one man occasionally gain eminence over others as a drawer of plans or an architect."

Treasury of Design, he replicated the elaborate panels on the bookcases. Those were just elements: what Harrison achieved in his Roman temple fronted with four curved Doric columns and flanked by classical wings was a result of his own inspiration; derivative, yes, but the Redwood Library is unique in Europe and America. Harrison created his own vernacular based not on the prevailing baroque fashion, but on a fusion of accepted Italian and English styles adapted to colonial realities. Palladio, Wren, and Jones worked mostly in stone, but the cost of replicating a similar design in that material would have been prohibitive in Newport at the time. Instead, Harrison used wood, but as the original contract reads, the exterior would "be plank'd in Imitation of Rustick," which meant that a bellows-like device blew sand onto the fresh paint to make the surface appear as if it were stone.

Harrison modified, changed what he needed to fit the environment, and delivered one of the most stunning and influential buildings in America. By introducing Palladian design to the New World, so soon after its acceptance in England, Peter Harrison was ahead of his time stylistically, yet in harmony with the emerging sentiments of its inhabitants. Bridenbaugh reported: "By returning to seventeenth-century models he became an innovator. This retrospective quality in design provides a significant parallel with current American political thinking, for colonial statesmen were beginning to seek inspiration in the republicanism of Harrington, Sidney, and Locke which was contemporary with the Palladianism of Inigo Jones—and republicanism in political theory together with classicism in architecture eventually became the mode of the new nation."

The Redwood Library (Athenæum was added to the name in 1833) opened in 1750 to popular acclaim from almost everyone, Newporters, colonials, and foreign visitors alike. People seemed to be frankly amazed that something so glorious stood on American ground. Because Harrison was the first to introduce such a bold classical design, the Library was a showpiece for decades (it still is). Until Jefferson began introducing his classical buildings in Virginia decades later, the Redwood Library was the primary working model for a Palladian public building in the colonies. The historian Jon Sterngass asserts that the Redwood Library "was perhaps the most important cultural institution of colonial America."

Share-owning Proprietors were welcome to browse through the newly arrived trove and borrow one book per month (others could borrow if they left a deposit equal to the cost of the book). The original collection, bought in London by Redwood's agent with the £500 gift, consisted of 751 titles in some 1,339 bound and unbound editions, or, as Bridenbaugh reports, "206 folio, 128 quarto, 712 octavo, and 251 duodecimo volumes." In 1905, the historian Irving B. Richman, perhaps feeling defensive that Boston received cultural kudos when they should have been directed toward Newport, wrote, "At a time when at Newport and in Narragansett private libraries contained books such as the *Faerie Queen*, *Hudibras*, *Samson Agonistes*, the plays of Ben Jonson, Pope's Homer, and the plays of Moliere, none of these was to be found in the library of Harvard College, the largest library in the Bay colony. Nor did Harvard possess a line of Addison, Steele, or Swift, writers with whom (through Berkeley) Rhode Islanders were intimately acquainted, and whose works were among those earliest secured for the Redwood collection." Redwood's original collection also contained philosophical, religious, and scientific texts that opened up a wider world to Newport.

The Redwood Library was expanded and renovated several times over the next two and a half centuries reflecting its growing collection and importance as a Newport institution. In each case, Harrison's lines, proportions, and details were retained with little modification. The little summer house now on the Library's grounds was originally on Abraham Redwood's country estate; it too is clearly a Harrison design, and one of the few from the eighteenth century to survive.

Word of the sophisticated new library in Newport spread quickly. Harrison was next commissioned to submit designs for King's Chapel in Boston because, as the Anglican minister Henry Caner wrote to Harrison in 1749, the building committee had heard of him "with Advantage for a particular Judgment and Taste in Things of this Kind, and for the Knowledge you have acquired by travelling and Observation." His plans were accepted and the new church, one of the first in America to be built of stone, was finished in 1754. In Cambridge, Harrison designed Christ Church, the oldest building in the city and the only one for which Harrison was rewarded with more than a piece of silver plate.

Back in Newport and now quite noted throughout New England for his elegant designs, Harrison was approached in 1759 by Rabbi Isaac Touro, Aaron Lopez, and other members of the Sephardic Jewish

Interior view of Touro Synagogue, 1763
Designed by
Peter Harrison

Photographer unknown
Newport Historical Society
Newport, Rhode Island

community, to draw plans for a synagogue. This commission presented unique challenges for the architect because there were no other such structures in America to draw on for inspiration, and he knew nothing of the Jewish ritualistic iconography that had to be incorporated in the interior. Again for no payment, Harrison held extensive discussions with Rabbi Touro to learn about Jewish sacred traditions, then returned to his library and scoured his many books. In Kent's *Designs of Inigo Jones*, Harrison found plates that helped him solve interior problems. He created a classical space, two stories high with a galleried hall, perfectly proportioned, that incorporated twelve prominent columns, in both Corinthian and Ionic styles, that represented the twelve tribes of Israel. The exterior of imported English brick, deliberately made plain so the synagogue would not appear ostentatious and possibly offend Christian sensibilities, is quiet and inviting in form. The hip-roofed building, which was not dedicated until 1763, was sited at a radical angle from the road, then called Griffin Street, so that the Holy Ark, as mandated by Jewish tradition, would face east toward Jerusalem. Many architectural historians have declared the Touro Synagogue, as it has been known since the 1800s, to be the high point of Harrison's career, his masterpiece in classical, understated design.

Based on certain style elements, it has long been assumed that Peter Harrison was probably involved in drawing the plans for one of Newport's most enduring domestic dwellings, the Vernon House, home to comte de Rochambeau during the Revolution. His last addition to the town's increasingly sophisticated skyline was a commercial venture known as the Brick Market at the opposite end of the Parade from the Colony House, at Thames Street. Land was purchased and designs were drawn up as early as 1760, and those plans were from the quill of Peter Harrison. The building was not completed until 1772, well after Harrison had left town, but the builders served him well. Again, he put his library to good use. Downing relates, "The scheme he selected, a single order embracing two stories set over a high arcaded basement, was . . . a favorite one in England at this time. This particular version was derived from Inigo Jones' design for Old Somerset House illustrated in Colin Campbell's *Vitruvius Britannicus* of 1726." Harrison's version was more American, and less grandiose, since this was intended to be a working market for butchers and grain merchants, as well as other dry-goods traders. Palladian-inspired throughout, the 33-foot by 66-foot Brick Market is an elegant public building designed to radiate stability and strength.

Brick Market, c. 1812
Oil on canvas
A unique painting by
a Hessian soldier
during his tenure in
Newport. Designed by
Peter Harrison, 1772
Newport Historical Society
Newport, Rhode Island
94.4.1

Peter Harrison quit Newport for New Haven to take up the prestigious job of Collector of Customs for the Crown. He did not end his architectural career, although he had far less time for it. After a very successful and fulfilling life, Harrison's end was chilling. As events leading up to the Revolution turned more violent in colonial towns, leading loyalists were singled out for harsh treatment by marauding rebels. Harrison, a high Tory if there ever was one, especially despised for holding the position of the customs man, attracted a mob one day in 1775. They broke into his house, destroyed his books and architectural plans, and trashed everything else. Peter Harrison died of an apoplectic fit on April 30, 1775, at the age of fifty-nine.

Gilbert Stuart

Considered by most art historians to be one of the finest portrait painters America has ever produced, Gilbert Stuart lived a life of peaks and valleys akin to a character out of a Charles Dickens novel. Brush in hand reaching for his palette, Stuart was a genius; pen in hand before an open ledger book, he was a disaster. He was a brilliant artist who was at pains to take care of himself and his family while at the same time producing works that enriched the course of Western art. One portrait alone, the bust of George Washington pensively staring in space that adorns the United States one-dollar bill, has secured Stuart's reputation forever. But it is well to remember that the Washington image was only one of some 750 known paintings that he created in his long and productive lifetime.

Gilbert Stuart was an American prodigy. Born to a Gilbert Stuart from Perth, Scotland, and Elizabeth Anthony of Middletown on December 3, 1755, in North Kingstown, Rhode Island, the younger Stuart seemed

to be fascinated with copying from life at an early age. The artist's father made snuff for Dr. Thomas Moffatt, but the business failed, so in 1761, the family moved across the bay to Newport. They took quarters, according to Stuart himself, "next to Abraham Redwood," but despite its being a good neighborhood, the artist went on to describe his surroundings as "a hovel on Bannister's [*sic*] Wharf." Bannister's Wharf is a long way from Redwood's house, so it is possible the family lived in two locations. He attended school at Trinity Church and befriended Benjamin Waterhouse, who later distinguished himself as a doctor of medicine. Throughout their youth, the two men were inseparable.

Stuart couldn't stop dabbling with images, but with little family money, paints and brushes were a luxury. Then the Fates intervened. Local lore has it that at age twelve Stuart was afflicted with a severe eye problem; there was fear he might go blind. Dr. William Hunter, who attended to the Newport Scottish community, was called in to see the young man. In his darkened room, Dr. Hunter was struck by a number of drawings on the walls made with stones or clay. He was fascinated and "he resolved to help the boy become an artist—that is, if his eyesight could be restored. Stuart recovered and, as soon as he did, Hunter gave him brushes and colors, and commissioned him to paint two spaniels lying under a table." That painting now hangs in the restored Hunter House on Washington Street. Gilbert Stuart's career was launched.

In 1769, Dr. Hunter fulfilled his promise to help the young man and arranged for Stuart to receive instruction from visiting Scottish artist Cosmo Alexander, who spent a year in Newport. Stuart and his teacher traveled through the South, then sailed to Edinburgh where, in 1772, Cosmo Alexander died unexpectedly, stranding the sixteen-year-old with no money. Eventually, Stuart hired on as a collier on a ship headed for Nova Scotia and made his way back to Newport in 1774. On his return, he painted two portraits, one of the prominent merchant John Banister, the other of Banister's wife and child. While lacking the nuances of his mature work, the portraits are remarkable nonetheless in his command of the human face. Both paintings are in the Redwood Library.

Before the advent of photography, the painted portrait was the primary means of visually fixing a person in history. Especially among the upper classes, having a record of what grandfather looked like was a source not only of pride but also a measure of family continuity. Talented portrait artists like Stuart or John Singleton Copley were kept constantly busy, such was the demand for prestige and posterity. When Stuart returned home, he quickly received commissions to paint a number of prominent Newporters, including Jacob Rodriguez Rivera (now in the Redwood), the Malbone brothers Francis and Saunders, and probably Aaron Lopez. But Stuart angered some people by refusing to paint a full-length portrait of Abraham Redwood, even after his parents and many friends urged him to do so. He gave no reason for his actions, which ruffled people even more (some scholars believe he was manic-depressive). Eventually he did do a half-length portrait of the founder of the library, but his patronage in town all but disappeared.

Sometime in 1775 Stuart decided London would offer a broader market for his skills and set sail. He had difficulty finding willing subjects who would pay him enough to live on, so, practically penniless, he became a church organist in order to survive. Benjamin Waterhouse, having completed medical studies in Edinburgh, joined his friend in London in 1776, and together they roamed around town and took in the sights. Waterhouse also helped Stuart obtain a few commissions, but it must have been a discouraging time for the artist. Almost reduced to begging on the streets, Stuart finally wrote his compatriot, the Pennsylvania-born artist Benjamin West, one of the leading painters in Britain, for aid. West hired Stuart as a copyist, took him on as a student for four years, and invited him to live in his home. Here Stuart became productive, submitting paintings to the Royal Academy annually. Stuart was learning his craft from one of the finest

teachers of the age. In 1778, he painted a self-portrait that now hangs in the Redwood Library (decades later he completed the only other known sketch of himself, for his wife; it is owned by New York's Metropolitan Museum of Art).

Stuart's breakthrough came in 1782 when he exhibited his *Portrait of a Gentleman Skating* at the Academy. The canvas won instant acclaim from critics and almost immediately commissions started coming his way from high-born Londoners eager to have their likenesses captured by this young phenomenon. For the next five years Stuart painted regularly, lived extravagantly, and was the talk of the artistic world, producing portraits that were compared favorably to those of Sir Joshua Reynolds and Thomas Gainsborough. In May 1786, Stuart married Charlotte Coates from Reading, Berkshire; together they would have twelve children. For the time, life was very good to Gilbert Stuart. But just over a year later, the darker side of the artist's personality caught up with him: his lack of business skills, his inability to even bill his clients for their paintings, and his high living necessitated a stealthy flight from London before his debts landed him in prison. He had thrown away his fame, sullied his reputation, and it would not be the last time he was to do so. The family moved to Dublin and during their five years there, the same cycle occurred. Stuart was popular from the outset, made good money, and squandered it spectacularly. What Stuart needed more than anything was a business manager.

Escaping creditors again, Stuart moved to New York in 1793 (paying for the family's passage by doing a portrait of the ship's captain) and, again, had no trouble finding willing, rich subjects to paint. But by this time, he had a vision of how to avoid penury: he would paint President George Washington, the most famous man in America, make multiple copies, and in so doing make a fortune. In theory, Stuart was correct. Washington's image was in great demand, both among the people and by institutions. After two successful years in New York, Stuart obtained a letter of introduction to the president from John Jay, then chief justice of the United States (Stuart had done a highly successful portrait of Jay in London and the two men had become friends), and moved to Philadelphia, which was the seat of the federal government before Washington, D.C., was built. The artist's first sitting with the president in 1795 produced the portrait (a bust) known as the Vaughan type, and Stuart made many replicas of it, even though he was not fully satisfied with the canvas. He also worked on portraits of George and Martha Washington, but never completed them. In April 1796, Stuart had his second sitting with Washington, and this time he drew a life-size standing portrait, with the president's arm outstretched to an unseen audience. This painting is known as the Lansdowne type, named for the man who ordered it. In the autumn of that year, a third sitting took place and that produced the famous image which is known as the Athenæum Head—the one that adorns the United States one-dollar bill.

Stuart made an unknown, but large, number of replicas of all of his portraits of Washington (one resides in Colony House in Newport). He had been right: demand was high. Every state house wanted an image of the man who saved America from Britain, and Stuart did a brisk business. Moving to Washington, D. C., in 1803, with a national reputation because of the presidential portraits, Stuart proceeded to paint nearly every important government figure, from Thomas Jefferson (who waited twenty years for Stuart to finally finish the canvas) to James and Dolley Madison. He was immensely popular, in great demand, and because he was an excellent conversationalist, someone to have around. But Washington, D. C., proved too

On the eve of the Revolution, Newport's elite still clung tightly to their wealth and the reins of power. The fifty richest men (twenty-seven of whom belonged to the Anglican Trinity Church) had protected and enlarged their fortunes and enjoyed a disproportionate affluence. And they did so with the tacit consent and cooperation of the rest of the town: nearly everyone prospered as a result of the mercantile risks taken by the more adventurous businessmen. But the Revolution would tear this coterie asunder: many rich merchants, whose profit margins would be compromised by the rigid enforcement of customs, fled Newport in 1776, never to return. Egalitarianism would arise. Many of the aristocrats were staunch loyalists and were forced to flee town when the British forces evacuated in October 1779. Money drained out of the port, not into it; commerce declined precipitously. The backbone of the proud merchant class had been broken by the British.

raw for Stuart, so he moved his family to Boston in 1805 and stayed for the rest of his life. There he continued to churn out copies of his Washington portraits and bring lawsuits against other artists and engravers who were selling Stuart's likeness as their own. He also produced portraits of the Boston elite, President James Monroe, and John Quincy Adams and his elderly father, John Adams.

In his later years, Stuart's health began to fail and he developed partial paralysis in his left arm; it was around this time that his daughter Jane Stuart began to help him with his overload of work, reportedly filling out the bodies of his subjects after he had concentrated on the face. He also made a nostalgic trip to Newport and reported, "I then visited the stone mill, and mentally renewed my questionings respecting that strange and meaningless structure; cast a glance at the Redwood Library building, admired its unique architecture, so classical, so refined; examined a few folios, and reverently gazed at their pictorial embellishments." Yet after all the success and fame, all the commissions and high-paying clients, when Gilbert Stuart died in his seventy-third year in Boston in July 1828, he was insolvent. All the money was gone and he left debts close to $20,000. The genius with a paintbrush simply never learned how to account for his talents.

In appreciation, one critic wrote of Stuart, "Often underrated because he painted only portraits (and so many of those were of Washington), Gilbert Stuart ranks not only among the very best artists of his time but also among those produced by the United States. He influenced a generation of American portraitists, both those who had been his pupils and those who never met him but knew his work and emulated his style. His oeuvre is a rich visual record of most of the leading personages of his day in Britain, Ireland, and America."

Hunter House and Its Inhabitants

One of the most majestic reminders of what it would have been like to live in Newport at the height of the Golden Age is the carefully restored Hunter House on Washington Street on the Point. Once known as the "Mansion of Hospitality," in its prime the house embodied dignified luxury, filled with detailed paneling, paintings, fine furniture from Newport's leading artisans, and artifacts from foreign voyages. Although its name derives from its last significant owner, William Hunter, who resided there in the nineteenth century, the refurbished house stands as a microcosm of colonial Newport, an archaeological record of the good life during one of the town's most memorable periods.

Local historians more properly refer to it as the Nichols-Wanton-Hunter House, acknowledging the three owners who created, enlarged, and endowed it with the lasting elegance so evident in the twenty-first century. Jonathan Nichols, Jr. (cousin of the owner of the White Horse Tavern), is credited with the first stage of development, when the house was certainly smaller than the one we see now. Nichols was a significant figure in Newport: a prosperous merchant, a longtime leader in the General Assembly, and for four years the deputy governor of the colony. He was an imposing man in all ways, physically, financially, socially. It is said that his wharf at the rear of the house (in those days considered the "front") was the longest private docking facility in the harbor, crammed with storerooms filled with merchandise from his many trading voyages.

Nichols died in 1756 and his "mansion" was purchased by another Newport notable, Colonel Joseph

Wanton, Jr. (born 1730); it is widely held that it was he who expanded the house to its current proportions. As a member of the powerful Wanton dynasty (his uncles and father were governors of Rhode Island), Joseph, Jr., prospered in trade, married Abigail Honyman, a granddaughter of the revered minister of Trinity Church, and set about to showcase his wealth and status in town. As long as sentiment toward England was positive, Wanton was in good favor because he was a staunch Tory who believed any disrespect toward the Crown was an insult. During the Stamp Act rebellion, Wanton and the rest of the loyalist Newport junto were clearly out of step with the majority of townsmen, yet their devotion to the king never wavered. Throughout the pivotal decade leading to the Declaration of Independence, Wanton and his clique lost prestige and power (he was voted out of the General Assembly for his views) but continued to hold their ground. If he and his wife were entertaining anyone at their mansion of hospitality during those dire times, the guests were likely to be fellow Tories, such was the depth of division in Newport between loyalists and patriots.

In June 1775, Joseph Wanton, Sr., was deposed as governor of Rhode Island by the rebellious General Assembly for his support of Great Britain; six months later, patriot troops arrested his son for his role in commanding three companies of loyalist soldiers. During the British occupation of Newport, Joseph, Jr., lived well, hosting a number of parties at his home for British officers and visiting dignitaries. But when the invaders departed in 1779, Wanton, a marked man, evacuated with British troops to New York City, where he died in 1780, age fifty. His second wife, Sarah Brenton, was forced to depend on the largess of the General Assembly to survive because all the Wanton assets had been seized by the state government.

The boom and bust cycles of the Hunter House mirrored the fate of Newport itself. French officers lived in the house in 1780 and 1781, before trekking to Yorktown. Thereafter, the house was neglected and fell into disrepair until William Hunter, Esq., and his new wife purchased it at auction in 1805 for $5,000, a fraction of what Joseph Wanton, Jr., had paid for it during the glory years of Newport's Golden Age. Members of the Hunter family lived in the house until 1854, when it passed from private hands and became,

The Hunter House,
1748-1754
Photograph by Jim Patrick
Courtesy of the
Preservation Society of
Newport County
Newport, Rhode Island

among other things, a boardinghouse, the headquarters of the Town and Country Club, and later a home for Catholic nuns. Then it settled into a long period of decline.

A great deal has been written about Hunter House because it is widely considered to be one of the ten most important colonial homes extant in America. By 1945, it was slated for destruction, its rich paneled rooms to be removed and reassembled in New York's Metropolitan Museum of Art. Realizing that a treasure-in-the-rough was about to be lost, a group of Newport citizens stepped forward, led by Katherine Warren, purchased the building, and formed the Preservation Society of Newport County with the aim of bringing it back to what it looked like at the height of Wanton-era elegance. Throughout 1952 and 1953, a team of experts led by Ralph Carpenter completely restored the two-and-a-half story Hunter House. The famous original main doorway, with its classic pilasters crowned by a polychrome carved pineapple (a symbol of hospitality in colonial days), was rescued from a nearby dwelling and installed in the front of the house, not the back, which is where it first resided when the gateway to the wharf made the bayside entrance more important. Inside, rooms were painted the original colors, including some rose cedar graining and marbling. With the restoration completed, the committee then set about filling the house with appropriate colonial period pieces: furniture by the Townsends, the Goddards, and other well-known eighteenth-century makers; clocks from William Claggett's shop; a painting by Gilbert Stuart (his first oil painting, of Dr. William Hunter's two dogs); fine silver, stoneware, Newport pewter, and dozens of other treasures. A visitor to Hunter House can experience the full range of what fine living during Newport's rich pre-Revolution era would have been like.

King George's Wars
When the Treaty of Utrecht was signed between England and France in 1713, few people imagined it would keep the great powers of Europe from lunging at each other's throats for very long, given the depth of their rivalry. Oddly, peace prevailed except for brief a skirmishs between England and Spain in 1718 and France

and Spain in 1719. On the whole, for over a quarter century Great Britain, France, and Spain focused on diplomacy rather than arms to settle their disputes. All three nations were exhausted economically and had to recoup their equilibrium before returning to the battlefield. Tension was always just beneath the surface, the enmity simmering, but for this period sanity was restored and the lure of wealth acquisition trumped the more belligerent voices crying for all-out combat with their traditional enemies.

In London, Sir Robert Walpole, often referred to as England's first prime minister (in spirit, perhaps, but technically incorrect), steered the dominant Whig party and King George II's government toward economic prosperity and control of the seas. He succeeded brilliantly for over two decades, and then, after dismissing a large number of his ministers who had defied him, he lost his majority because those very men who had once been loyal sided with the opposition Tories. Walpole had overreached; he was then forced into abandoning his pacific policy and had to advise the king that war with Spain was in the country's best interest. The sea war that ensued cast Britain into a succession of bloody international battles that raged on until the Treaty of Paris in February 1763 once more brought temporary calm in Europe and America.

The three imperial wars of 1739 to 1763 were more than just a settling of scores among three bitter foes; they also served as a harbinger for the struggle in the 1770s between England and its thirteen continental colonies over the issue of control. Britain needed its American colonies by its side during the mid-century conflicts: it needed their raw materials, their growing wealth, their men on land and on sea. The colonists obliged, sometimes willingly, sometimes not. They fought well, harassed French and Spanish shipping with deep resolve and excellent results, and helped Britain eventually win the contest. When France was forced to give up all of Canada and Louisiana and Spain abandoned Florida at the peace conference in Paris, the Americans, for the first time, did not have enemies (except for hostile Indians) on their borders. A threat that had been with them for 150 years was now removed, and they were finally able to examine, in a new light, the swiftly deteriorating relationship with the mother country. Britain was victorious, now astride the power structure of Europe, and more arrogant than ever in its demands. But Americans had learned a great lesson fighting England's battles: they had gained confidence in their ability to wage war, anticipate the enemy, and endure military hardships. They had seen the inside workings of the British army and learned of its general staff's pigheadedness and addiction to tradition, regardless of the military conditions. These wars were America's boot camp and training grounds, and the lessons were not forgotten when all other paths to peace were abandoned and rebellion was seen as the only answer.

Hostilities between England and Spain broke out in the autumn of 1739 in a bizarre, stage-managed fashion. Back in 1731, a British sloop master named Robert Jenkins had been loading merchandise in the Caribbean when he was accosted by a troop of Spanish guards. An argument broke out over his right to be trading, and one of the Spaniards cut off Jenkins's ear with his cutlass. Nothing more came of the incident until 1738 when the war party opposed to Walpole sought out Jenkins and invited him to Parliament to tell his tale. In one of history's strangest public-relations stunts, Jenkins did more than just relate his woes: on the floor of the House of Commons, he took out a kerchief and unwrapped the severed ear he had been carrying around for seven years. Parliament was aghast! How could an Englishman be treated in such a barbarous way? cried the

ministers. Sentiment was high because so many English businessmen were losing valuable cargoes and routes to Spain's aggressive merchants. When reports got out about Jenkins's ill-treatment at the hands of the hated Catholics, London went into an uproar. Public opinion was so stridently anti-Spanish that Walpole had no alternative but to relent and declare war. Thus the War of Jenkins's Ear was joined, Walpole's long domination of the Whigs was finished, and ten years of peace came to an end (dating from the 1729 Treaty of Seville).

The War of Jenkins's Ear was fought mostly on the sea, primarily in the Caribbean, and lasted just two years—until it kindled an even larger conflict. When news of the outbreak reached Newport two months after the declaration, seamen and merchants were joyous: it was time to arm ships, raise crews, and go privateering again. Everyone knew that the Spanish had the lion's share of silver, so the enthusiasm for capturing Spain's ships was high indeed. Spain had thrown its commercial weight around long enough; it was time to defend England and knock the new enemy off its perch. Most of Newport's leading merchants fitted out privateering vessels to head south and capture prizes. John Banister, the Wantons, and Godfrey Malbone all got involved, but their high expectations were rarely met. A few did capture well-laden Spanish ships and gained valuable cargoes. A Newporter, one Captain Hull, as reported in *The Boston News Letter* in 1740, captured a bounty so valuable that each of the crew's share was over one thousand pieces of eight. But Hull's success was unusual. The competition was heavy, the Caribbean was afloat with privateers and pirates from many nations, and in the end, the whole venture was not especially lucrative for the majority of Newport seamen.

At home, fear of a Spanish attack on the harbor, given the town's status as one of America's premier ports, caused Rhode Island officials to garrison Fort George on Goat Island and construct a network of watchtowers and beacons to signal the advance of the enemy. Spain never attacked Newport, but the preparations stood the town in good stead when the war with England broke out in 1776: the towers and lights became part of an intricate coastal warning system that was very effective for the patriots. Two hundred Rhode

Island men took part in the disastrous attack in 1741 on the Spanish stronghold at Carthagena, in today's Colombia; the force of a thousand colonial men was decimated by disease and Spanish superior might, and only about one hundred returned home alive. It was an incident that was never forgotten by the bitter colonists, because the campaign was so poorly planned by British officers and the New Englanders were no better than cannon fodder.

After Governor John Wanton died in 1740, Richard Ward was elected in his place. Ward, a Newport merchant who had had a long political career, served for three terms, during which the colony was on constant war footing. When King George II upped the ante by going to war with France in March 1744, Rhode Island greatly increased its commissions for privateers; in fact, more warships sailed from Newport than from Boston or New York, such was the enthusiasm to go after the French. The arena also enlarged: now the privateers could go north to the Gulf of St. Lawrence to lay in wait for French vessels on their way to Montreal or Quebec. One Newport ship had a particularly remunerative career. Under Captain John Dennis, *Defiance*, along with another Newport sloop, the *Queen of Hungary*, took seventeen prizes in one six-month period. Dennis then refitted her to carry sixteen carriage guns, twenty-six swivels, and a crew of 110 men. Roaming the high seas alone, *Defiance* went on to capture about fifteen Dutch, French, and Spanish enemy ships in a three-year period, making a healthy profit for the captain, crew, owner, and the English treasury.

But life on the sea was fraught with dangers that had nothing to do with national hostilities. The wife of any sailor knows the anxiety she feels when her husband leaves port. In wartime, given how many ships were being taken by enemies, how seamen were held for ransom or simply killed, wives' forebodings increased. Any major shipping center like Newport knew that disaster could come in many forms. By the autumn of 1745, the wealthy but unlucky Godfrey Malbone had finished building and fitting out two privateering ships, the 180-ton *Duke of Cumberland* and the 200-ton *Prince of Wales*, at considerable expense. "Then this reputedly wise businesslike owner became a victim of superstition. Horoscopes advised sailing on the eve of Christmas. Despite the violent northeasterly snowstorm then commencing the ships sailed out, never to be seen or heard from again. Presumably they both sank, making widows of 200 Newport women. Such heavy losses . . . eventually killed enthusiasm for privateering." Malbone quit the business and went back to being a merchant, as did many other owners who feared the dangers or simply couldn't make enough profit out of aiding the British Crown.

Colonial soldiers, along with English troops and officers, captured the French fortress at Louisburg on Cape Breton Island after a hard-fought series of battles aided by the best-known Newport warship of the era, the *Tartar*. This 115-ton sloop was built at the colony's expense of £8,679 to be employed for the defense of Narragansett Bay and for privateering excursions. She had admirable success under a number of different captains and burnished the reputation of Newport seamen, but her career ended ignominiously when *Tartar*'s last captain was convicted of smuggling contraband. Discouraged by the cost of maintenance and the uses she was being put to, the General Assembly auctioned the *Tartar* off in 1749 for £6,910.

BORDERS AND CHARTERS

All the colonies had disputes in the eighteenth century over the fixing of borders, partly because of local jealousies, poor surveying, and murky directives from London. Confounding the issue over territory was the fact that the thirteen original colonies had been established under a variety of legal frameworks; untangling the hodgepodge of laws and regulations was daunting. Who had jurisdiction? What statutes applied to a corporate rather than a proprietary or charter colony? This legislative jumble caused problems when it came time to write the United States Constitution because each colony had operated under a slightly different tradition, based on how London had granted the deed.

A corporate colony had a charter granted by the English monarch to its stockholders.

A proprietary colony was owned by an individual or small group under a charter from the Crown.

A royal colony was under the direct control of the monarch.

To wit: Virginia (1607), a corporate colony, converted to a royal colony in 1624. Massachusetts (1620), originally corporate, became a royal colony in 1691. New York (1664), a proprietary colony, converted to a royal colony in 1685. Maryland (1633), remained a proprietary colony throughout. Rhode Island (1636), was a corporate colony as defined by the 1663 Charter. Connecticut (1636), remained a corporate colony. Delaware (1638), was initially a proprietary colony under William Penn, and remained so thereafter. New Hampshire (1638), a proprietary colony, converted to a royal colony in 1679. North Carolina (1653), a proprietary colony at first, became a royal colony after 1729. South Carolina (1663), followed the same course as North Carolina. New Jersey (1664), initially a proprietary colony, was granted a royal charter in 1702. Pennsylvania (1682), was a proprietary colony under William Penn, and remained so thereafter. Georgia (1732), originally a proprietary colony, became a royal colony in 1752.

King George's War (in Europe, the War of Austrian Succession) came to an end with the treaty at Aix-la-Chapelle in 1748 and most Newporters were bitter over the results. Nothing, it seems, had been resolved at all, because the diplomats gave back to each country every possession lost in the hostilities. Thus, all the efforts put into the Louisburg campaign had gone for naught—the lives lost, the huge tax burden borne by Rhode Island, the pride of victory, and the security gained by not having an enemy on the northern border, were all snatched away by the negotiators. Worse still, the reasons for the war were in no way resolved between England on one side and France and Spain on the other. It was a peace forged from exhaustion, not because one side had gained a clear-cut victory; which meant, of course that war would be joined again in the near future.

In May 1745, the third member of the most dynamic political dynasty the colony ever produced took over the governorship of Rhode Island. Gideon Wanton, born in 1693, son of Joseph and nephew of William and John, excelled in the family trading business; he also became the treasurer of the colony for ten years. He served two terms, initially replacing William Greene of Warwick, the first governor in Rhode Island history influential enough not to be required to reside in Newport. As a prelude to the bitter Ward-Hopkins rivalry in the following decades, Wanton and Greene traded the governorship: Greene was awarded the job again in 1746–1747, but Gideon Wanton won it back for the 1747–1748 session. And then Greene defeated Wanton again the following year, whereupon Wanton retired from politics; he died in 1767.

Both men had to deal with the emergencies emanating from King George's War, and both were hounded by their counterpart in Massachusetts, Royal Governor William Shirley, who implored Rhode Island to send more men, more materiel, more money, for the siege at Louisburg. Pressure from London and other colonies was drawing Newport further into the vortex of the empire's strategies, and as much as they may have wanted to resist the pull for economic reasons, both Wanton and Greene could do nothing but comply. Wanton sent two hundred men to Boston during the war and was loyal to the cause. Still, Rhode Island was criticized by Parliament and Massachusetts officials for not doing more, a continuation of a pattern that had been prevalent for decades: even though Rhode Island had limited resources and manpower, the colony was expected to supply an unfair percentage of goods and personnel.

Unlike his illustrious uncles, Gideon Wanton was more conservative and less the showman; he never attained the popularity of his relatives, but was steadfast in his duties. Bartlett tells us that "though he was a Quaker, he was a belligerent one . . . distinguished for his talents and for the influence he exerted in the affairs of the colony." One of the major accomplishments during these years was the final resolution of the border dispute with Massachusetts, which had been simmering for over a century. Ever since Roger Williams founded the colony in 1636, its northern and western neighbors had been finagling to draw as much of Rhode Island as possible into its territory. As with Connecticut, Massachusetts was relentless in its refusal to officially recognize the borders granted to Rhode Island in the 1663 Charter. But Parliament had had enough of the bickering and mandated that an independent commission, made up of men from New York, New Jersey, and Nova Scotia, come to a conclusion regarding fixed, and *permanent*, borders. The commissioners heard evidence from Massachusetts and Rhode Island and came down firmly on the side of the latter. Once again, the Charter carried the day. Still, Massachusetts dragged its heels for five more years until May 1746 when the Privy Council in London ordered that the panel's findings be honored. Defeated, petulant Massachusetts officials refused to aid in the surveying of the line, so Rhode Island had to complete the job alone.

The territory gained by the colony comprised the five towns of Bristol, Tiverton, Little Compton, Warren, and Cumberland, about 120 square miles that added close to 4,700 people to Rhode Island's tax base. Finally, the colony was realized in the shape Dr. John Clarke had envisioned, measuring 48 miles north to south and 37 miles east to west, split nearly in half by Narragansett Bay. Still the smallest of the thirteen original colonies, Rhode Island was, at last, complete.

The culminating campaign for control of North America, the French and Indian War, stretched from 1754 to 1763, and it started out badly for Britain and its colonial cousins. Because the peace treaty of Aix-la-Chapelle had not settled land boundaries in the New World, both England and France eyed western expansion greedily. Skirmishes involving the two antagonists and their various Indian allies were a regular occurrence in the Ohio Valley. Tradition holds that a young surveyor named George Washington, in his capacity as colonel in the Virginia militia, began the conflagration when he let off the first musket shot at French forces garrisoned at Fort Duquesne in April 1754. "The firing of a gun in the woods of North America brought on a conflict which drenched Europe in blood." Word got back to London and Paris quickly, and although diplomacy was attempted, both sides were ready for a showdown. A formal declaration of hostilities was made in 1756 (hence the appellation Seven Years' War in Europe).

The French and Indian War was different from the three previous engagements, which had been driven far more by European power politics than by any real concern about the North American continent. Wars begun in Europe simply migrated to the New World colonies, yet they were Old World contests nonetheless. But this new campaign, although clearly an outcome of the failure at Aix-la-Chapelle, had distinct overtones of being an *American* war; the colonists, now accustomed to cooperating and fighting together in their militias, were determined to rid themselves of the feared and hated French and Spanish along their borders, in order to live with increased security—and plunge westward unmolested. There was an American purpose for wanting victory on their own soil, not merely an obligation to aid the king in his European adventures and travails.

With each decade, colonists were becoming less English, less concerned about Europe's preoccupations, and more focused on their own, very different needs and aspirations. They were becoming self-dependent, at first not fully understanding the consequences that must ensue from their newfound emotional freedom. The Englishman, particularly the haughty, disdainful, all-knowing army officer, was the butt of jokes among colonial armed forces throughout the French and Indian War. American soldiers soaked up what might be useful from their military masters, and jettisoned the medieval mindsets. By the end of the war, Americans had a far clearer sense of themselves as masters of their own destiny and territory. In short, a gap had opened between the mother country and "her" possessions, largely because colonists were beginning to refuse to consider themselves as possessions any longer. This last colonial war shifted the psychological balance forever: instead of thinking they were doing the king's bidding, Americans came to believe that they were a distinct people who were getting help from their English forebears in solving an American problem.

In the summer of 1754, delegates from nine colonies met in Albany, New York, to plan war strategies. Rhode Island sent Stephen Hopkins and Martin Howard, Jr., two of the ablest minds in the colony. The conference planned military operations and options for further colonization of the interior to thwart the French. The war was under way, but the British failed in their first attempts at capturing French forts in the west and north. In the Ohio River Valley, British General Edward Braddock was soundly defeated at Duquesne and a naval blockade against Montreal was a fiasco. The next year proved to be as frustrating, with 1757 even worse. No matter what the British and their colonial soldiers attempted, the French got the upper hand. From the outset, Rhode Island sent men to various theaters of operation, and they went with enthusiasm, only to return disgruntled and suspicious of British field leadership.

In England, King George II encouraged a parliamentary changing of the guard and the elder William Pitt regained his powers. He exhorted the colonists to commit more men and money and dispatched fresh forces from England. Pitt understood better than anyone the long-term consequences if the French were to gain a victory in North America. Then, the fortunes of war began to change. In 1758, Rhode Island sent a thousand men, the largest number ever committed, to take back Fort Louisburg; after a bloody seven-week siege, the French surrendered the strategic fort and the floodgate opened. Even though the British suffered defeat at Ticonderoga, they rallied and kept up the pressure, taking control of the Ohio Valley with the leadership of Rogers's Rangers and securing open passage to the great American frontier to the west.

The conquest of Canada was the ultimate goal and, for once, it was in sight. With the British navy, aided by Rhode Island privateers, blocking the St. Lawrence, the last great battles—for Quebec and Montreal—were almost foregone conclusions. But the British underestimated the skills of the French General Louis Joseph de Montcalm, who kept them at bay for months. In 1759, in the decisive encounter at the Plains of Abraham, British General James Wolfe took Quebec; both he and Montcalm were killed during the fighting. Montreal fell the next year. The invasion of Canada was a triumph: the French were driven from the land, and from power. At the Treaty of Paris in 1763, a humiliated France formally ceded Canada, and the rest of the North American mainland, to Great Britain.

In Newport, there was a profound sense of relief when the French and Indian War came to an end. Rhode Island had committed thousands of men to the many land battles, and even more through seaborne privateering. A great many of those men never came home. It was reported that "from 90 to 100 vessels were lost, three times as great as New York and four times as great as Massachusetts." Although some merchants got wealthier through their privateering efforts, many, like Henry Collins, lost everything. The war strained the economy to its very limit with large issuances of paper money to cover expenses, which later led to higher taxes and a disgruntled populace. One contemporary writer complained, "The merchants of the town of Newport have lost in the course of their trade, upwards of two millions of money since the commencement of the present war. The price of provisions and all other necessaries of life, being greatly increased by reason of the war, is an additional burden to, and greatly distresses the inhabitants of said town, who depend on trade and labor for their support." The deep economic depression cast its pall over most activities for years to come. To top off all those woes, Great Britain, at the insistence of King George III, decided in that trying period to get tough on the colonies and began strictly enforcing the many navigation laws that Newport sailors had been evading so successfully for decades. King George III needed money, badly. The attempt to tax America to the limit accelerated the already festering resentment against the Crown. Another nail was driven into the coffin named Concord.

The Great Ward-Hopkins Controversy

If religion was the force that dominated the seventeenth century, politics took its place in the eighteenth century. Nowhere was this reality more visible than in the raging battle that engulfed Rhode Island from 1755 until 1770 between Samuel Ward of Newport (and Westerly) and Stephen Hopkins of Providence. Their internecine brawl had all the elements of an ongoing soap opera, but at heart was a deadly serious competition between up-and-coming Providence and dominant Newport for power, prestige, and control of the colony's purse and patronage. The contest was almost Oedipal in its dimensions, son against father vying for the affection (i. e. votes) of the colony's freemen. Their rivalry cemented the two-party system of allegiances that foreshadowed the future feud between Federalists and Republicans during and after the heated debate over the United States Constitution.

Historians have long been divided in their depiction of the struggle between these two men and their factions. Depending on their political sympathies, geographical affinities, and the age in which they wrote, they have described the Ward-Hopkins controversy as a clash between the northern portion of Rhode Island versus the southern tier, merchant versus farmer, upper class versus middle and lower classes, loyalist versus patriot, conservative versus radical, Anglican versus Congregationalist, and hard-currency versus paper-money advocates. To a certain degree, all of those characterizations contain a modicum of truth. But the reality is more complex, and it is fair to say that the real roots of the argument were the purely political desires to gain power and keep it, in order to control the colony's economic and social agenda. The governor's chair was not the seat of power; that authority lay with the General Assembly. Thus, the yearly voting had more to do with the election of a slate of delegates loyal to one man or the other than it did with the man himself. Ward and Hopkins came to personify the struggle, but in truth it was a legislative scuffle more than the issue of who was governor.

Samuel Ward was born in Newport in May 1725, the son of former governor Richard Ward; the family was not only politically prominent but wealthy and socially well connected. Samuel married and took up farming in Westerly, but never lost touch with his Newport colleagues, and in 1756 was elected as a deputy to the General Assembly. The partisan line-ups often shifted, yet one source of the controversy originated in a bitter feud between Richard Ward and William and John Wanton over the issuance of paper money. Thus the Wanton faction, though Newporters, swung its allegiance to the Providence party financed by the Brown brothers and eventually led by Stephen Hopkins. There was bad blood from the beginning of Samuel Ward's political career. In 1757, when William Greene, another devout enemy of the Wantons, ran for reelection as governor, Samuel

GEORGE III

When George II died of a stroke in his water closet in 1760, he was succeeded by his grandson, the emotionally fragile son of the Prince of Wales Fredrick Louis. George III was only twenty-two when he ascended the throne, an insecure young man who could not read fluently until he was eleven and was plagued by mental-health problems his whole, long life. George III reigned for sixty tumultuous years, from 1760 to 1820 (although he was declared insane for the last decade of power), during which he witnessed two Treaties of Paris. The first, in 1763, awarded all French and Spanish lands in North America to Great Britain. The second, in 1783, officially acknowledged the independence of the United States of America after Benjamin Franklin, John Jay, and John Adams negotiated the pact that had been hailed as the greatest triumph in the history of American diplomacy. In just twenty years, King George III and his ministers managed to alienate and lose their prize possession. During his reign he attempted to reduce the powers of the aristocratic Whigs, but the political machinations were impossible to temper.

George III oversaw a vast change in his empire while on the throne: the economy greatly expanded; manufacture of iron, steel, ships, and other commodities grew as the Industrial Revolution took root; the British colonies, despite the loss of America, were added to in India and through the voyages of Captain James Cook in the Pacific. Intellectuals like Adam Smith, Edmund Burke, and Thomas Malthus ushered in advances in economic and social theory. In the arts, Laurence Sterne published *The Life and Opinions of Tristram Shandy*, the great equestrian painter George Stubbs published *The Anatomy of the Horse*, and Richard Sheridan presented *The School for Scandal* on the London stage.

Ward backed him and fueled the long-lasting rancor by writing a pamphlet not only critical of Hopkins, who was Greene's opponent, but also accusing him of corruption.

Hopkins sued Ward for slander, but lost the case in court. The rivalry now became personal and nasty, and it stayed that way for over a decade as Ward and Hopkins traded the governorship three times. Hopkins served from 1758 to 1762, when Ward won one term, only to turn the office back to Hopkins in 1763; Ward won again in 1765 and 1766, but Hopkins regained the office the next year for one last term. By that time, the political duel had become so intense and crippling for the colony that both men, seeing that the critical national agenda was more pressing, agreed not to continue the contest and Ward bowed out of elective politics. But most of the damage had been done by then.

Stephen Hopkins was born in Providence in 1707, and was eighteen years older than Ward. He spent his younger years as a farmer, surveyor, and merchant, who grew rich because of his association with Godfrey Malbone of Newport. Eventually, Hopkins made his way into local politics, working his way up through the ranks and collecting useful allies. He was elected to the General Assembly and was the colony's chief justice in 1751. By 1750, Providence was beginning to compete successfully with Newport for local and foreign markets, and the mercantile savvy of the four Brown brothers—Nicholas, John, Joseph, and Moses—was propelling the northern town, still only about half the size of Newport, into manufacturing as well. The Browns clearly understood that for Providence to continue to grow, they needed to shift the General Assembly's priorities away from Newport and spread patronage around to the northern towns. The only way for that to happen was to wage a full-scale attack on the status quo, take control of the Assembly by winning the governor's position, and installing a party slate loyal to their interests. The Providence elite needed a powerful advocate in government, and they found him in Stephen Hopkins. When he gained the governorship in 1755, the balance of power began to shift away from Newport forever. The hegemony that had been in place practically from the beginning of the colony had been successfully challenged; Rhode Island politics would never be the same again.

Although lacking in formal education, Hopkins had a brilliant mind, was well-read, and ever curious. For a long period, he was one of a handful of non-Newport members of the Literary and Philosophical Society. Hopkins founded a newspaper, *The Providence Gazette*, and wrote many articles for it. He was one of the leading statesmen before the Revolution who believed that the colonies needed to unite to prevent incursions by the British government into their rights. As a delegate to the Albany Conference in 1754, he met and became friends with Benjamin Franklin, who also advocated union. Even when he was deeply embroiled in his battles with Ward, Hopkins was looking beyond Rhode Island to the future of the colonies. Several times he represented Rhode Island at provincial congresses that were beginning the process of drawing away from Britain, and in 1764 he published the lucid and convincing pamphlet *The Rights of Colonies Examined*, which laid out the reasons for resistance to the mother country if Parliament did not reduce the onerous taxation being imposed on America. The colonial assemblies, he asserted, not Parliament, should be the only bodies to levy taxes. Always a patriot, early on he was convinced that the day would come when America would have to rebel.

During the period of their rancorous contest, Hopkins and Ward were not very far apart politically. Both supported military action during the French and Indian War, both did their best to protect Rhode

Island's interests vis-à-vis Parliament, and both were opposed to the various taxes London was proposing for the colonies. One of the primary differences between them was the attitude toward paper money versus taxation: Ward and his faction, controlled by conservative Newport merchants, wanted to be done with the practically worthless paper, while the more radical and rural Hopkins and his followers favored further production of colonial paper. Yet no matter how many differences are examined, the issue always comes back to power and the Newport versus Providence struggle. The fact that the men drew close to each other after they had abandoned their quests for governor indicates that the feud was not as personal as some historians have depicted.

And what did a Rhode Island election look like during those years of strife? Even later-day Texas politics couldn't compete with the wild ride Rhode Islanders were subjected to every year at the spring elections. Sydney V. James reports:

> The opposing parties waged their campaigns with vigor and cash to pile up the vital majorities in elections. Candidates and their backers made speeches, printed broadside appeals, and inspired useful items in the newspapers. . . . The political managers treated voters with food and drink. They hired men either to earn their gratitude when the ballots (known as "proxes") were cast or to keep them busy when the voting was in progress. They rigged spurious land transactions to get poor men admitted to the suffrage. They paid the undecided to vote for their own slate and paid the dedicated opponents not to vote at all. To make sure that those who had been bought stayed bought and to discover when partisan clerks falsified their reports, the managers watched in every town as the proxes were presented and kept lists that they checked with the totals later revealed in the count.

The two contingents brought the act of electioneering to a high art, producing broadsheets utterly filled with misstatements of fact and outright lies. Rhode Island elections had turned into wild drunken affairs filled with high drama and a healthy dose of comedy as well. A writer in *The Newport Mercury*, after the controversy had died down, lamented, "Party virulence had been increasing, until one general hostility pervaded the whole colony, which raged between the friends and supporters of the two candidates. It appears to have been a question of men, more than about measures. Between the mercantile and the farming interests, between the aristocracy of wealth and magnificence and the democracy of numbers, the colony was torn by domestic discord; town against town, and neighborhood against neighborhood; almost every freeman was enlisted in one or the other ranks, and felt towards each other that hostility which abated even the charities and hospitalities of life."

The irony of this acrimonious saga is that there was no one person at fault. Both Samuel Ward and Stephen Hopkins were good, upstanding men who cared deeply about the direction of Rhode Island and the other twelve colonies. Both of them were highly intelligent and informed; both good writers espousing freedom from an increasingly dominating King George III. Powerful as they had become, in a sense the two men were pawns of an ever more potent and mercenary party system run amok that had, in the collective lust for control, obliterated common decency and sown the seeds of longtime discord. Once the invective mud

In 1764, the Royal Navy enlisted Robert Melville, soon to become governor of the island of Grenada, to undertake a detailed study of Newport harbor, with the aim of establishing an extensive naval station there. After extensive surveys, Melville reported back.

The whole bay is an excellent man-of-war harbour—affording good anchorage, sheltered in every direction, and capacious enough for the whole of his majesty's fleet, were it increased four fold. There are no dangerous ledges or shouls within the Bay, or near its entrance, which is easy with all winds. Another advantage it possesses over any other harbor on the northern coast in the winter season, is, that it is very seldom obstructed by ice. . . . It has other advantages which cannot be found elsewhere in America. A whole fleet may go out under way, and sail from three to five leagues on a tack; get the trim of the ships, and exercize the men within the bay, secure from attack by an enemy. The vicinity of the ocean is such that in one hour a fleet may be from their anchorage to sea, or from the sea to safe anchorage in one of the best natural harbours the world affords. . . . The centre passage which is the direct one into the harbor of Newport as well as the bay, has a depth of water (from 12 to 26 fathoms) and bold rocky shores . . . with every point, height, and island being placed in the very best position for effectual defence.

It is no wonder that the British authorities chose to occupy Newport when war commenced.

slinging had begun, there was no turning back; the party hacks kept the contest going right up until the musket shots rang out in Massachusetts.

After Ward and Hopkins removed themselves from the destructive gubernatorial races that had sapped so much goodwill of the populace, the two men ascended to the national stage as a team and performed brilliantly. In 1774, as a member of the General Assembly, Hopkins urged the body to pass legislation calling for "the firmest union" among all colonies and to call a convention that would establish guidelines for their rights and liberties. The Assembly complied, and Rhode Island became the first colony to advocate the creation of the Continental Congress that met later that year, with Stephen Hopkins and Samuel Ward as its representatives. The longtime foes rode together from Providence to Philadelphia. Also in 1774, Hopkins drafted the Negro Emancipation Act for the General Assembly; it passed, in Newport, becoming the first piece of legislation in America outlawing the importation of African slaves.

The first Continental Congress brought all the colonies except Georgia together to debate options and voice grievances against British policies, particularly the so-called Intolerable Acts, which Parliament had voted on earlier that year. Delegates met for six weeks and tentatively voiced aloud the possibility that if the king did not back down, a break might be the outcome. Most of the members were still looking for ways to reconcile differences, but Stephen Hopkins rose from his seat and stated to the full assembly that, "powder and ball will decide this question. The gun and bayonet alone will finish the contest in which we are engaged, and any of you who cannot bring your minds to this mode of adjusting the question had better retire in time as it will not perhaps be in your power, after the first blood is shed." The stunned representatives were, for the moment, speechless.

Both Hopkins and Ward were elected to attend the Second Continental Congress on May 10, 1775. Only three weeks previously, the events at Lexington and Concord had taken place, and with British troops now firing on colonists, the mood of the Congress was decidedly more radical than the year before. Stephen Hopkins chaired a committee that established the Continental navy and also sat on a panel that drafted the Articles of Confederation. Samuel Ward was busy in various working groups, particularly one forming the Continental army. Along with John Adams of Massachusetts, he recommended that George Washington be selected commander in chief of the new force.

There was much work to be accomplished and little time to do it. Hostilities were in the open and the colonial leaders had to come to decisions about how to proceed. Congress stayed in session throughout the next year in Philadelphia, edging ever closer to making the final, inexorable split with Great Britain. While the debate unfolded, Samuel Ward, a firm defender of liberty, contracted smallpox and died on March 26, 1776, less than four months before Congress published the Declaration of Independence penned by Thomas Jefferson. Stephen Hopkins signed the document, and in place of Ward, Rhode Island dispatched William Ellery, a staunch Ward supporter during the rivalry with Hopkins, a graduate of Harvard College, and a lawyer of note in Newport. He too became a "Signer" and remained in Philadelphia as part of Congress throughout the war. Back home, the British burned his house and its contents in revenge for his activities. Tradition has it that William Ellery sat next to the secretary the day most of the delegates stepped forward to endorse the Declaration. As his colleagues approached the table, Ellery looked into their eyes as they signed their names to what he said "might be their death warrant" but witnessed only "undaunted resolution." When Stephen Hopkins, old and infirm with palsy, signed his name he reportedly announced, "My hand trembles but my heart does not."

With the weighty business of managing the rebellion to attend to, Hopkins remained with Congress until illness forced him to retire to Providence in 1779. He continued his duties as chancellor at the new Brown University and followed news of the war—and the Peace of Paris in 1783. Before his death in 1785, Stephen Hopkins was able to witness the fruits of his long labors. By challenging Newport's political and economic dominance, Hopkins and the Brown brothers had succeeded in turning Providence into a comparably robust hub of growth in northern Rhode Island. Population was expanding, manufacturing was increasing rapidly, and, having been spared the ignominy and ravages of British occupation, the city was poised to take a leadership role in New England when the chaos of the Revolution subsided. Hopkins had helped engineer an almost total reversal in the relationship between Newport and Providence; the latter's subordination of 150 years was finally brought to a close while Newport lay in virtual paralysis after British and French forces moved on.

Everything seemed to be changing at the time—allegiance to the king had ended, a new republican nation was being created, and patterns of commerce were sailing in new directions. Being a major seaport ceased to tip the scales toward prosperity and Newport probably would have suffered even without the British occupation: the engine of growth now lay in the manufacturing of iron, potash, textiles, and a long list of other products that were absent in Newport. Producing rum was not enough any longer. The Brown brothers got a head start on the new economy and drove Providence into the next century, turning it into a vital center for the region. Newport—with its population in steep decline, its mercantile system decimated, its vibrant cultural life depleted, and its physical infrastructure half destroyed—like Rip Van Winkle, fell into a long and languorous sleep.

Come the Revolution

But those somnambulant days lay in the future. Back in 1763, following Great Britain's assumption of European leadership after the defeat of France and Spain, a tumultuous two decades were about to unfold, catapulting Newport into a leadership role in America's struggle against Parliament and the Crown.

The road to revolution was long and winding, filled with many detours, as more and more Americans began to lose faith in its erstwhile parent. John Adams was right when he said that the Revolution had been achieved in the minds of the colonists before the first military engagement. Rules emanating in London kept appearing, one after another, until there was a palpable sense of a loss of control: for years, the acts of Parliament came like an avalanche, cascading into the lives of virtually every American. And one morning, a majority of people woke up and realized that the relationship had irredeemably soured.

The tribulations began directly after the 1763 Treaty of Paris when the ministry of George Grenville tallied up the costs of the recent war, looked into its empty coffers, and decided it was high time that the American colonies take on more of the burden. King George III agreed wholeheartedly, and thus began the imperious policies that led to the open rebellion of the following decade. Grenville initiated three broad inroads into the freedoms Americans enjoyed. The first was a stringent tightening of the already existing Acts of Trade and Navigation that had been so successfully evaded by Newport merchants; from 1763 onward, hundreds of new tax collectors would fan out in all the colonies to make sure the king was getting his due. The bitterly and almost universally opposed second measure, the one that led most directly to the break, was a series of taxes on the colonies for support of British troops in America and Canada. It was the tax issue that really raised the ire of Rhode Islanders, because it was a clear abrogation of their powers under the 1663 Charter, which left taxation to the discretion of the General Assembly, *not* Parliament. The third insult was the permanent garrison of nearly ten thousand soldiers throughout the provinces that the colonists did not welcome, whether they had to support them financially or not. Americans had already demonstrated their skills as militiamen; they did not want the incursion of British soldiers because they didn't believe they were needed, and they voiced clear sentiments about not wanting to host a standing army during peacetime.

The first two measures affected Newport directly and immediately. The subterfuge of the previous thirty years, when customs collectors winked at the illegal molasses pouring into port from foreign islands, was about to be drastically curtailed. When Grenville insisted on the renewal of the Molasses Act of 1733, which would ruin Newport's lucrative and dominant rum trade by collecting duties on sugar, and when British naval ships started harassing legal commercial traffic in the harbor, Newport fought back with violence sooner than any town in all the colonies. And it began by fighting back with words as well. Governor Hopkins pleaded with London to reconsider: "Upward of thirty distill houses, for want of molasses, must be shut up to the ruin of many families and of our trade in general. Two-thirds of our vessels will become useless, and perish upon our hands; our mechanics, and those who depend upon the merchant for employment, must seek for subsistence elsewhere . . . and as an end will be put to our commerce, the merchants cannot import any more British manufactures, nor will the people be able to pay for those they have already received." The entreaty fell on deaf ears. The Sugar Act of 1764 passed easily through the House of Commons and House of Lords in April. Five colonies, including Rhode Island, vigorously protested the bill, but they were unsuccessful in swaying a greedy king.

Newporters had to devise new ways to avoid the customs men; there was more off-loading of hogsheads at night in the coves surrounding the city, with a heightened us-against-them mentality among the natives. Now Crown officials were hated even more earnestly because they were actually doing their jobs. But there were ways to respond, and Newporters had proven their skills at evasion on many occasions in the past. While the new ordinances were odious to the merchants, for the time being, they only grumbled. That was to change quickly when the British Navy began patrolling Narragansett Bay, almost putting an end to commerce as Newporters had known it for a century.

The next year, 1765, Grenville pushed the Stamp Act through Parliament, the first direct tax to be leveled on America, and the colonies exploded. It was the first challenge affecting all the provinces equally—and a harbinger of the struggle to come. "The colonists could see that they would have to pay stamp fees at every stage of a lawsuit, that diplomas and deeds, almanacs and advertisements, bills and bonds, customs papers and newspapers, even dice and cards, would all be charged. But there was not much interest in details: every duty, however large or small, was felt to be an attack on the security of property because it was levied without consent. If Parliament succeeded in collecting the stamp tax, there was no telling how much would be demanded in the future." The colonists objected strenuously, asserting that the Crown could govern them, but not tax them directly, particularly since the colonists had no representation in the British government.

Official London did not care about American grousing, although William Pitt, now earl of Chatham, and Edmund Burke were wary early on of pushing the colonies in such a manner. These two famous defenders of American rights were not alone. In one stormy parliamentary debate over the passage of the Stamp Act, Charles Townshild, a Tory MP, took the floor and asked his colleagues, "These Americans, our own children, planted by our care, nourished by our indulgences, &c., will they now turn their backs upon us, and grudge to contribute their mite to relieve us from the heavy load which overwhelms us?" Another MP, Colonel Barre, with a vehemency becoming a soldier, rose and said: "*Planted by your care!* No! Your oppression planted them in America! They met all the hardships with pleasure, compared with those they suffered in their own country, from the hands of those that should have been their friends!"

The night after the Stamp Act passed Parliament, Benjamin Franklin, then in London, wrote to a colleague in Philadelphia, "The sun of liberty is set; the Americans must light the lamps of industry and economy." To which his friend replied, "Be assured, *we shall light torches, quite of another sort.*"

Newport took action. The 1663 Charter, defended so relentlessly for so long, was the reason. Rhode Islanders believed that the Charter was a firm compact with the British Crown and even Parliament could not abrogate the intent of Charles II; the colony had the *written* right of self-government, including the right to

tax itself, without outside controls. While some other colonies, not imbued with the self-protective instincts of rebellion when their freedoms were threatened, put forth milquetoast objections, Newport, in a lather, took to the streets. At first, the Town Council issued proclamations to set the tone: "It is for liberty, that liberty for which our fathers fought, that liberty which is dearer to a generous mind than life itself, that we now contend." Then the overt resistance began.

In July 1764, when the British schooner *St. John* was making life miserable for Newport shipping, she detained and seized a cargo of sugar from the New York brig, *Basto*, and steered her into Newport harbor. The populace was not pleased. The *St. John* was not only harrying legal commerce, her commanding officer, Lieutenant Thomas Hill, was on a mission to impress as many colonials as he could kidnap for duty in the Royal Navy—put bluntly, a job worse than death, as every Newport seaman knew. Hill's "obnoxious arrogance" incensed the townsfolk and that led to a skirmish not witnessed on American shores before then. With official approval, some men went to Fort George on Goat Island and began firing on the *St. John*, which prudently sought shelter at the stern of an even larger British ship, *Squirrel*, after her mainmast had been hit by the cannon. Officials went ashore and tried to patch up the quarrel, and eventually succeeded—but the fact is, the British flag was fired on by colonists willing to make a statement for their rights. Newport was not an easy place to be for the perceived oppressors.

Soon thereafter (and this is before the Stamp Act went into effect), HMS *Maidstone* made its appearance at Newport, charged with the same orders as the *Squirrel*: confiscation of trading vessels and impressment of Americans to slave as crewmen aboard their ships. After another seizure of men for service in the navy, a mob of Newporters stole one of the ship's boats, dragged it up the Parade and set it on fire, to the glee of most of the town's not-so-loyal subjects. A pattern was emerging: Rhode Island did not enjoy being subjected to the will of the British navy, and it was going to demonstrate its distaste to the hilt. But the most egregious display of rebellion was still to come.

The Stamp Act Congress of October 1765 met in New York City to air complaints concerning the new conditions. Such was the trepidation over Parliament's course of action that the delegates, who gathered from nearly all the colonies, debated and prepared a document called a Declaration of Rights and Grievances and sent it on to London. At the same time, Parliament was besieged by angry English merchants who were losing American trade because of the non-importation measures the colonists had enacted in protest to the new law; their voices, plus the Americans' stiff refusal to acknowledge the measure, encouraged the lawmakers to reconsider. After a forceful address by William Pitt, who declared that Parliament had no right to tax the colonies directly, the House of Commons came to its senses and voted to repeal the Stamp Act. Yet the stubborn ministers never learned the lesson that America was not going to accept external taxation, and kept concocting more laws to anger the provincials.

Before this repeal was even discussed in London, colonists had let their displeasure be known in the streets of America. Boston rioted against the act in the summer of 1765. In Newport, a pamphlet and newspaper debate was being waged between Stephen Hopkins, taking the patriot's position, and his old colleague at the Albany Conference of 1754, Martin Howard, Jr., who argued that the colony should obey Parliament in all measures. Howard, a lawyer and formerly respected citizen, went so far as to call those who did not agree with him "licentious, sordid, and incompetent." He was a mainstay of the so-called Newport Junto, a group of prominent loyalists who even went so far as to advocate a repeal of the 1663 Charter in favor of a royal decree. One can only imagine how popular *that* demand made them in a town devoted to near-autonomy and broad powers of self-government because of the Charter's forward-looking language.

The Junto members, many of whose names are familiar, were mostly High Tories, mostly rich, mostly members of Trinity Church, and mostly out of step with the times. They were trying to demonstrate their loyalty to the king at a moment when most Newporters had already thrown up their hands in despair over the dwindling economic opportunities and the assault on their freedoms by Britain. These grandees with divided loyalties because of their financial allegiance to Britain—Howard; Dr. Thomas Moffatt from Scotland; George Rome, who had confiscated the popular Henry Collins's property; John Robinson, the tax collector; and the architect Peter Harrison (recently removed to New Haven)—were now perceived as a repository of past discriminations by the majority of townsfolk.

Resentment over the Junto's devotion to the king came to a boil in Newport in late August 1765. Two popular Sons of Liberty patriots, Samuel Vernon and William Ellery (who was to sign the Declaration of Independence), saw an opportunity to get back at the Junto and make a bold statement in favor of freedom. They gathered a large number of men, created three effigies—one for Howard; one representing Augustus Johnston, the Distributor of Stamps; and the last for Dr. Moffatt—and dragged them through the streets to the courthouse, where they were hung from a gallows. At this point the crowd was in the thousands, and their blood was up. That evening, the effigies were cut down and burned, to the delight of the assembled, and not too sober, mob. Moffatt, Howard, and Johnston all took refuge outside of town.

But the symbolic act of annihilating the cloth-and-straw figures wasn't enough. The next day, hundreds of men carrying axes and clubs descended on the houses of the three Tories, destroying everything they could find. Furniture, china, books, and personal records were smashed and burned. Having taken refuge on the British man-of-war *Cygnet* conveniently anchored in the harbor, the shaken men of the Junto realized they could never live in Newport in peace. Soon after the two-day demonstration came to an end, Moffatt and Howard sailed for England, never to return to Rhode Island. The mob's revenge was complete.

But events were to become even more remarkable in the near future.

The *Liberty* and the *Gaspee*

Even in the face of increasing harassment by the British navy in Narragansett Bay, Rhode Island refused to relent. The most overt examples of this deep-seated spirit came three years apart when two marauding naval vessels were burned to the waterline by colonists furious over the incessant disruption of their trade, legal or illegal. Rhode Island was becoming unruly about any form of imperial domination, be it through the various taxes and duties proposed or by seaborne policing of the coastline. London's attitude toward the colonies was becoming clear: we don't trust you. Americans got the not-so-subtle message, further alienating their rapidly diminishing affections.

Author unknown
Burning of the Liberty Sloop letter, dated Newport, July 21, 1769, and addressed to Mrs. Edes and Gill of the *Boston Gazette*. Manuscript

The letter is a circumstantial narrative of the destruction of the *Liberty* by the townspeople, the first overt act of violence against the British authorities in America. The writer describes how incensed the citizens became with Captain Reid's behavior so that they "scuttled, dismasted, stripped and dismantled" the *Liberty*, trusting that they had taught Captain Reid better manners so that he would not further incur "the universal resentment of an abused, oppressed people. . . ".

Redwood Library and Athenæum
Newport, Rhode Island

Newport July 21st 1769

Messrs Edes & Gill

Please to insert the following in your next Gazette and youll oblige

Yrs

A few Days ago an armed Sloop in the Service of the Revenue, insolently named Liberty, appointed by the Commr of ye Customs, and commanded by the famous or rather infamous William Reid, arrived in this Port from a Cruize, and brought in with her a Brigantine from the W. Indias bound to New York, and commanded by Packwood, and a Sloop (Voyage & Capt. Name are both unknown to the Writer of this Advertisement) both belonging to and taken off New London.

Last Wednesday in the Afternoon Capt. Packwood went on Board his Brig. in Order to take a Shore his Wearing Apparell and finding his things turned out of the Cabbin he manifested his Surprize at it to the Officer of the Cutter, who had the Charge of the Brig. and asked him what it meant The Officer damned him, told him that he had a Right to do what he pleased on Board that Vessell, that he (Packwood) should not carry any thing out off her, and treated him with such abusive, scandalous, threatning Language, that Capt. Packwood unable any longer to bear such intolerable abuse, drew his Sword, which he had just taken out off the Cabbin, and told him that if he persisted in his insolent Behaviour he would infallibly run him through — The puissant Boatswain now thought it best to haul in his Horns, and permit Capt. Packwood to take his Cloaths into his Boat, but he had no sooner left the Brigantine's Side before the said Boatswain resuming his Courage, hailed the Cutter, & ordered her to fire upon that damned Rascal in the Boat — Matches were immediately applied to two Swivel Guns both of which flashed — The Armed

Newport had witnessed brawls and riots aimed at their overseers; the level of insolence and insults increased, and the disregard for government property grew as well. But never had the Crown been attacked in such a direct and destructive manner in all the colonies until July 1769 when a group of irate men scuttled one of his majesty's ships. London, while more than angry over the incident, still didn't get the point.

The affair with the *Liberty*, an armed sloop under Captain William Reid, began when she chased down two boats arriving from Connecticut suspected of smuggling and escorted them into Newport harbor. The skippers of the two brigs were brought on board *Liberty* and interrogated. It was not a pleasant interview, and as the men were rowing back to the wharf, sailors on the *Liberty* fired at them. Later that day, ashore on business, Captain Reid was surrounded by a large number of Newporters; armed with bludgeons and knives, they demanded that he call his crew on land to be questioned about their motives for shooting at unarmed colonists. Reid had little choice, and he and his men were taken temporary prisoners of the mob. Tempers were high, and with *Liberty* now unmanned, some provincials made their way to the British ship, cut her cable, and grounded her on the Point. She was stripped of her mast and valuables, then set ablaze, to the delight of most Newporters. Articles in *The Newport Mercury* indicate that she smoldered for three days.

London protested the actions loudly, but, oddly, did not press a legal case, as would have been expected. Whether authorities didn't want to fan the flames further, or knew they would never find sufficient evidence to convict, is unclear. But the fact that a royal ship could be destroyed right in Newport harbor, and the perpetrators suffer no retaliations from the mother country, sent another kind of message to the people of Rhode Island—one that would be remembered in the years ahead.

The firing of *Liberty* upped the ante for both sides. This act of aggression in Newport was the first violent outbreak in New England, a shot across the bow, warning, as nearly everyone sensed, that there was much more to come.

The next incident, the burning of HMS *Gaspee*, was far more serious, and the subsequent legal wrangle had broad implications in Rhode Island and in Great Britain. For the first time in the ongoing struggle, British blood was spilled at the hands of an American; that is why the *Gaspee* incident has been called the "Lexington of the sea," because "it was a demonstration in arms by irregularly organized colonial forces against the organized naval force of his majesty." Thus the real opening of hostilities in the War of Independence took place in Narragansett Bay three years before the land war commenced, an event little known outside of Rhode Island. Historians setting the agenda for studying America's past have been more rigorous in their scrutiny of Massachusetts and too often dismissive of Rhode Island, and so the tiny colony's contributions have been mostly overlooked. For example, the Boston Tea Party, while dramatic, was an action against a commercial trading vessel owned by the East India Company, which the Crown was trying to save from insolvency; the ship was unharmed. The total destruction of HMS *Gaspee*, on the other hand, was a direct assault on the Royal Navy and thus an offensive action against the king and Great Britain itself.

Like the patrol boats before her, the *Gaspee* had made herself unpopular with the sailors in Newport. The deputy governor wrote to Governor Joseph Wanton, Jr., of "a schooner, which for some time past hath cruised in Narragansett Bay, and much disturbed our navigation. She suffers no vessel to pass, not even packet boats, or other of an inferior kind, without a strict examination; and where any sort of unwillingness is discovered, they are compelled to submit by an armed force." Governor Wanton investigated; he demanded explanations and official papers from the *Gaspee*'s captain, Lieutenant William Dudingston, who arrogantly refused to submit to Rhode Island law. Harsh words were then exchanged between Wanton and Dudingston's superior officer in Boston, Admiral Montagu, who essentially told the governor to mind his own business and that his ships could do whatever they pleased. Wanton, who would later show himself to be a staunch loyalist, nonetheless shot back, "Please be informed that I do not receive instructions for the administration of my government from the King's admiral stationed in America."

Dudingston continued to assault Rhode Island shipping for months, never coming ashore because he knew he would be arrested, or worse, by furious Newport or Providence officials, who continued to fume over their inability to stop the *Gaspee*'s patrols. All along the harbor there was talk of measures to be taken against her, but the frustration increased for months before an opportunity arose. Then on June 9, 1772, Dudingston signaled the packet boat *Hannah* of Providence to submit. The little vessel's skipper, Captain Benjamin Lindsey, wasn't about to let Dudingston search his boat as long as there was the possibility of escape, and he sailed up the bay toward Providence, toying with the slower, more cumbersome, British ship. Dudingston, in a rage over the audacity of these upstart Americans, let his sailing skills lapse, because he followed the *Hannah* across a shoal at Namquit Point in Warwick and succeeded in grounding the *Gaspee* on a sandbar, just as Lindsey had intended. Lindsey proceeded on to Providence and toward sunset reported the incident to the merchant John Brown, who happened to own the *Hannah*.

Seeing their opportunity to strike back, the Providence men moved into action at once, knowing they had only eight hours before the tide would rise and float the *Gaspee* free. John Brown gathered about sixty volunteers, mostly prominent and upstanding Providence men, under the command of Captain Abraham Whipple (later famous during the war) in eight longboats, and in complete silence, rowed to where the *Gaspee* was stranded. Unlike the men at Boston during the Tea Party raid, the Providence patriots wore no disguises and in no way tried to hide their identities. When the flotilla got within hailing range, Whipple demanded to come on board, claiming to be the sheriff of Kent. Dudingston, prominent in the darkness in his white shirt, shouted back that his request was denied, at which point someone shot Dudingston in the groin and arm, and the melee was on. The Providence men took the crew by force and landed them on the Warwick shore while others took Dudingston to a private home in Pawtuxet and dressed his wounds. Then they set the *Gaspee* on fire and retreated to Providence. The ship was totally destroyed. The first armed battle of the Revolution was a victory for the Americans.

London was enraged over the wanton act of violence toward its navy. Legal proceedings were initiated, commissions formed, evidence taken, rumors tracked down, large rewards offered, threats made . . . and no one came forward to give testimony except a runaway mulatto slave whose word was easily dismissed. All attempts to find the culprits were in vain. Thus, after more than a year of investigation, the commission came up empty-handed, even though it was common knowledge in Providence and Newport that John Brown had been the ringleader the night HMS *Gaspee* went down. The whole colony came together to protect its men and thwart the British. When the Crown threatened to arrest any culprit and take him to England for trial, the public was outraged at the violation of Charter privileges. Even Thomas Jefferson, in the

Declaration of Independence, referred directly to the *Gaspee* affair when he accused King George of tyranny, "for transporting us beyond the Seas to be tried for pretended offences."

Endgame

From the summer of 1772, when the *Gaspee* was destroyed, until 1776, America was in a state of upheaval. These were no ordinary times. Resistance to London's attempts to raise revenues escalated after colonists tasted a small and temporary victory with the overthrowing of the Stamp Act. When the House of Commons (changing its leadership almost annually) had passed the Townshend Acts in 1767, levying duties on paint, paper, lead, glass, and tea, Americans again raised a howl of protest; three years later, those acts, with the exception of the duty on tea, were repealed.

Clearly Parliament was divided, unable to come to a conclusion about the right way to handle its wayward American colonies. Burke said to let them go; we've lost them already. Lord North, in power in 1770, demurred, swearing the British would teach America the error of its ways. So much had gone wrong, cooperation was nil, and the battle of nerves was wearing both sides down. British soldiers were stationed throughout the colonies, ostensibly to "protect" them, but everyone knew this was a standing army of occupation. Writers agitated, pamphlets and newspaper articles championing rebellion grew more numerous: something momentous was about to occur.

In May 1773, Parliament passed the Tea Act and, in December, Boston hosted its Tea Party. London retaliated by producing the Coercive Acts mandating the closing of Boston harbor, abrogating the Massachusetts charter, and ordering General Thomas Gage, commander of the British army, to occupy the city and assume the governorship. Now Parliament was not just imposing taxes, it was deliberately shaping the future of an American colony that had long enjoyed a healthy measure of autonomy. The stakes in the game had been raised. This was an out-and-out takeover. In sympathy, Newport sent provisions and food for the besieged inhabitants who had completely lost their commerce. It was just a matter of time—a short time—before the bonfire exploded in New England. It was these and other alarming events that caused the Rhode Island General Assembly to propose the meeting of the Continental Congress. Unity among the colonies was crucial.

In Newport, given the constant patrols by various naval ships, commerce was in chaos, which left more men idle. Small demonstrations of defiance took place with regularity. Any British sailor walking the streets was in imminent danger. An eerie sort of peace prevailed, but just barely, given the anger and resentment on both sides. The Newport Light Infantry was formed; men and women alike readied themselves for an invasion.

In November 1774, Captain James Wallace entered Newport harbor for the winter in the *Rose*, a frigate with twenty-four large guns, enough to level the town if he so desired. Like the *Gaspee*, the *Rose* was meant to put a halt to Newport shipping and to make life as miserable as possible for townspeople. To a large extent, Wallace and the *Rose* succeeded, because by the hundreds Newporters began to flee fearing a bombardment, but more so because there were virtually no monetary opportunities to be had. The economy was at a standstill—no shipping in Newport meant the loss of thousands of jobs. By the following spring, Wallace was rumored to be ready to raze the town if smuggling didn't stop. Taking him seriously, more people

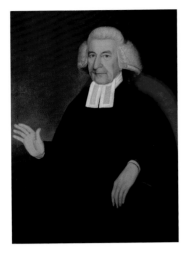

decided to exit for safer climes. The General Assembly voted to form a navy in order to challenge the *Rose*, but realized it had neither the finances nor the manpower to achieve positive results. Thus the job of creating a colony-wide navy was passed along to the Continental Congress and Stephen Hopkins.

By late summer of 1775, conditions had deteriorated further. The hundred-man *Swan* had joined the *Rose*, so there were more mouths to feed. Now Wallace was sending his sailors on foraging missions to Aquidneck Island, stealing crops and animals. When his supplies got too low, he offered an ultimatum to Newport: send us sufficient provisions or we will bombard you until there is no town left. The Assembly was in a quandary, but commander George Washington advised that Newport do as Wallace demanded, lest the town be destroyed. Wallace was able to buy some produce, and the emergency passed. But people kept leaving in droves. On October 9, 1775, Ezra Stiles entered in his diary: "This day I removed one Load of my Books & Furniture. The Carting of Goods & removing of the pple continued all day yesterday & yet continues. The infernal Wallace with 3 Men o' War, 2 or 3 more armed vessels . . . anchored at Bristol and ordered the Magistrates to come aboard & bring 300 sheep in one hour, else he would fire upon the Town." Next day, Stiles lamented, "How does this Town sit solitary that was once full of People! I am not yet removed, altho' three quarters of my beloved Chh & Congregation are broken up and dispersed. Oh Jesus I commit them & myself to thy holy Keeping."

At the time Stiles wrote those words, war had already broken out in America. The Revolution was a reality. On the night of April 19, 1775, General Gage sent a unit of his men to confiscate the armory at Lexington, Massachusetts. They were engaged by militiamen, Paul Revere made his famous ride, and by morning, after more conflict at Concord, there were 275 British casualties and more than 100 on the American side. Word of the skirmish immediately spread down the coast. Within days, Rhode Island committed 1,000 men to the cause of liberty, but they returned home after the British retreated to Boston. When the General Assembly authorized an army of 1,500 men, Governor Joseph Wanton, Jr.—last of the four Wanton relatives to occupy the chief executive's chair—refused to sign the commission, and was suspended from office by the Assembly for his Tory leanings. He was later stripped of the governorship when he failed to recant; Nicholas Cooke took over in his stead.

Everything was moving at lightning speed. While members of the Continental Congress were contemplating independence, they also authorized Abraham Whipple and Stephen Hopkins's brother Esek to begin sea engagements with the enemy. The Rhode Island General Assembly inaugurated the first navy in the colonies and commissioned two ships, the *Katy* and the *Washington*, to act in defense of Narragansett Bay. The provincial navy got off to a shaky start given the sophistication and might of the British fleet, but some victories were achieved. In mid-June, the Battle of Bunker Hill was waged, and while the Americans were defeated, they suffered fewer casualties than the British. All around, there was a growing air of confidence that the war could, with luck, be won.

Captain Wallace in the *Rose* was making life nearly impossible in Newport. Although it was carrying a completely legal cargo of sugar and rum, Wallace seized William Vernon's ship *Royal Charlotte* and sent it to be condemned in Boston. "Vernon, usually a temperate writer, was furiously agitated. 'The depredations committed by this petty tyrant [Wallace] upon our Trade and the defenceless Town of Newport is shocking to human nature. He is savage beyond belief and description.'" Vernon petitioned for his goods to be returned, and got the message that the British "cannot permit the Property of men in open Rebellion to be disposed of for their benefit." Then Wallace made good on his threats to level Newport. In July 1775, he opened fire on the town. According to the *Mercury*, "this greatly terrified the women and children, especially those women who were with child." He repeated these attacks many times for months to come, creating a tension that many people refused to bear. Confirming Ezra Stiles's observations, the newspaper reported that "a great many of the inhabitants moved part of or all their effects out and many families . . . left town. The carts, chaises, riding chairs and trucks, were so numerous that the streets and roads were almost blocked up with them."

Conditions only got worse. In December, Wallace sent notice that his Christmas present was going to be the destruction of Newport. According to the *Mercury*, the captain announced that inhabitants "should be burnt in their houses if they did not instantly turn out." When they fled, British soldiers plundered townspeople's possessions and set fires when they were resisted. The soldiers were less than polite, because we also learn that "some women were stripped of their clothing." The once-flourishing town of Newport was in complete disarray, its population diminishing daily, its commerce contracted to the point of cessation.

For most of 1776, Newport wilted. Captain Wallace and his flotilla abandoned Newport for fresher kill in March, but by then the damage had been done. Newport was traumatized, inert, its harbor nearly in ruins, its business with the outside world halted. Abraham Whipple had his tiny navy running, but that was no consolation for Newport. For all intents and purposes, it was finished as a capital of commerce. On February 20, Ezra Stiles entered into his diary: "Rode to Dighton, & here hired a House for the Removal of my family in these calamitous & dangerous & distressing Times. All marketing from Narrag. & the northward cut off at Newport by the Fleet—the ferries stopt—no wood Boats—The Town with perhaps a Third of its Inhabitants yet behind suffering greatly for Wood & Provision—especially Wood—Fences and Homes rapaciously pulled down for fewel—the poor & rich in one common Destress. Indeed our greatest Destress for Fewel. Rye & Ind. Meal 5s a bush. Mutton & Beef 4s. All Business stagnated." On March 11, the Rev. Dr. Stiles reported, "Packing up my Things for Removal." Even the most dedicated of Newport lovers had had enough.

For Newport, there was no bright side, no dream of a miracle on the other side of the rainbow. The ravages of war had taken their toll on the town already; Newport was at the mercy of forces it could not any longer control—and it was going to get even worse. But the defiant people still clinging to their property were, for the moment, not about to lose hope in the ultimate goal, the quest for independence. After all, that had been Newport's defining quality since 1639.

On May 4, exactly two months before the Continental Congress issued the Declaration of Independence for the new United States of America, Rhode Island's General Assembly, frustrated over Congress's indecision on the matter, took the initiative and declared their allegiance to the king null and void. Their proclamation established Rhode Island as a free state, the first of the thirteen colonies to so declare. The Assembly asserted:

Whereas, in all States, existing by compact, protection and allegiance are reciprocal, the latter being only due in consequence of the former; and,

Whereas, George the Third, King of Great Britain, forgetting his dignity, regardless of the compact most solemnly entered into, ratified and confirmed to the inhabitants of this colony, by his illustrious ancestors, and, till of late, fully recognized by him,—and entirely departing from the duties and character of a good King, instead of protecting, is endeavoring to destroy the good people of this Colony, and of all the United Colonies, by sending fleets and armies to America, to confiscate our property, and spread fire, sword, and desolation throughout our country, in order to compel us to submit to the most debasing and detestable tyranny; whereby we are obliged by necessity, and it becomes our highest duty, to use every means with which God and nature have furnished us, in support of our invaluable rights and privileges, to oppose that power which is exerted only for our destruction.

Be it therefore enacted by this General Assembly, and by the authority thereof it is enacted, that an act entitled "An act for the more effectually securing to his Majesty the allegiance of his subjects, in this his colony and dominion of Rhode Island and Providence Plantations," BE, AND THE SAME IS HEREBY REPEALED.

In all further civil or judicial proceedings, the name of the king was to be omitted and the name of the governor inserted. All allegiances to the Crown were severed. Governor Cooke forwarded the legislation to General Washington, and copies of it were distributed throughout the new "state." Some historians have asserted that Rhode Island's was not a "true" Declaration of Independence, that the proclamation lacked a decisive statement of freedom. It is difficult, reading the words above, to see the Assembly's action as anything *but* a clear severing of ties with the Crown. In any case, May 4 has long been celebrated throughout Rhode Island as Independence Day.

Word reached Newport a few days after Congress declared independence on the Fourth of July. On the eighteenth, the General Assembly met and voted that they "do approve said resolution, and do most solemnly engage that we will support the said General Congress with our lives and fortunes." Thirteen guns rang out the salute to the new nation, the Declaration was read from the balcony of Colony House (soon to become State House), and those remaining in town celebrated loudly. It was the first outpouring of joy they had been allowed to express since Wallace disturbed the town, and although the residents did not know it, it was going to be their last for a long time. The Assembly then proclaimed that the territory's new name would henceforth be "The State of Rhode Island and Providence Plantations."

A few days before, Ezra Stiles, now in self-exile in Dighton, Massachusetts, entered in his diary:

Mr. Channing returned from Newport & brought the Congresses Declaration of INDEPENDENCY dated at Philadelphia the fourth day of July. This I read at Noon, & for the first time realized Independency. Thus the CONGRESS have tied a Gordian Knot, which the Parliament will find they can neither cut, not untie. The *thirteen united Colonies* now rise into an *Independent Republic* among the Kingdoms, States & Empires on Earth. . . . And have I lived to see such an important & astonishing Revolution? Policy transfused thro' the collective Body of the Ruling Powers in Great Britain; and their violent, oppressive & haughty Measures have weaned & Alienated the affections of three Millions of people & dismembered them from a once beloved Parent State. Cursed be that arbitrary Policy! Let it never poison the United States of America!

Rumors of war swirled around Newport throughout the autumn, and unlike many rumors at the time, these turned out to be true. It is fitting that Ezra Stiles, a man who loved Newport as much as anyone alive, described what happened on December 7, 1776.

This Evening we are alarmed at Dighton, with certain News, that a Fleet of about *Eleven Men o' War & perhaps 70 Transports* arrived at Newport this day about Noon, and anchored under Conanicott between that & Newport, and that the Town is in great Consternation & Distress. This afternoon many Canon were heard here. Many are removing from Newport & Bristol. The good Lord prepare us for, and carry us thro' all the Tribulation in which it may please him that we shall be involved! How soon the aspect of public affairs may be changed? I expect that tomorrow Newport will be in the hands of the Enemy, who doubtless intend to winter there.

They not only stayed the winter. The British army occupied Newport for three years.

A long twilight had begun.

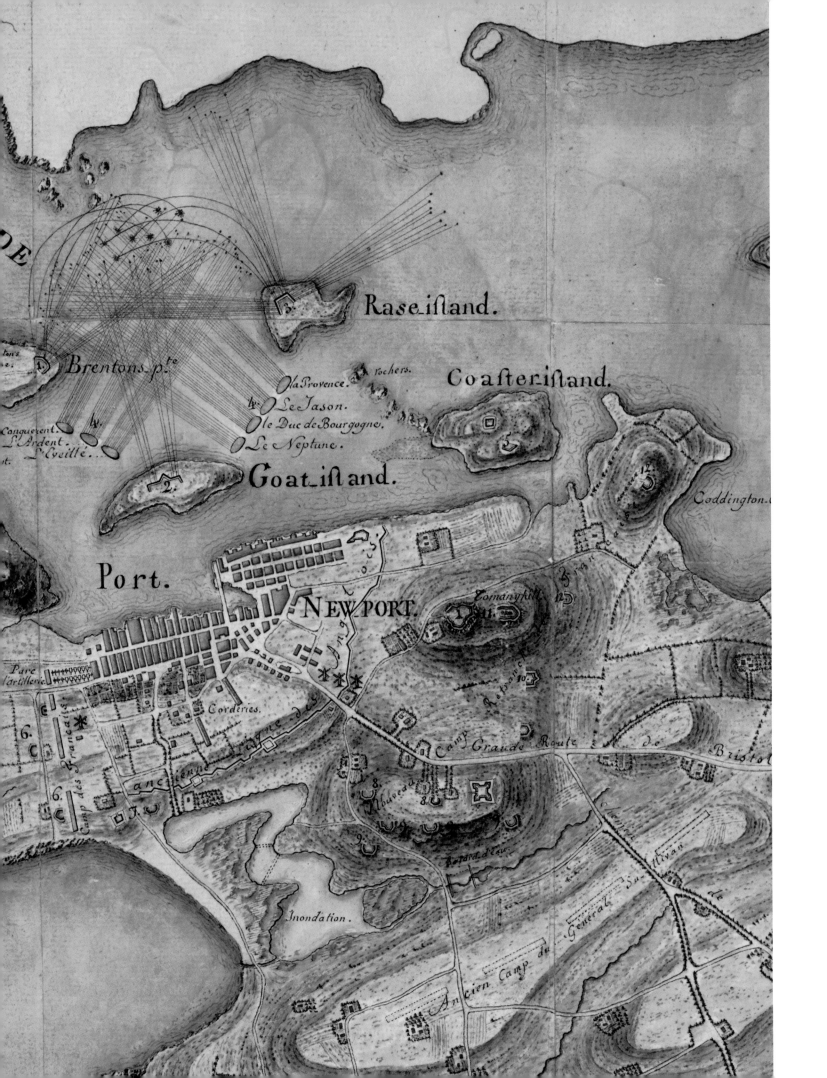

Rase island.

Brentons.p.te

rochers.

Coaster island.

la Provence.

Conquerent.
L'Ardent.
L'Éveillé.

Le Jason.
le Duc de Bourgogne.
Le Neptune.

Goat island.

Coddington.

Port.

NEW PORT.

Tomanyhill.

Parc
d'Artillerie.

Corderies.

Rathsbone

Camp

Grande Route

de

Bristol

Nouveau

Bojard d'Eau.

Inondation.

Ancien Camp du General Sullivan de

Independence and Decline

Newport's Nightmare

Newport's bitter twilight was filled with fog, fulmination, and the stench of smoke. The war had come to roost on its doorstep, ready, like a ticking time bomb, to detonate at any moment from occupation into conflagration, and the populace was seized with uncertainty and fear. No one, not even the enemy, knew how long the invading force would linger. No one, except the British commanders, knew whether their ultimate mission was to use the city as a strategic base of operations or to destroy it completely. As months trickled into years, the constant tension provoked by British soldiers turned from gross inconvenience and insult into nightmare. Newport, again, was an unwilling hostage to the whims of the Crown.

Boston had been occupied by the British army before the Declaration of Independence, but those forces retreated south after the war began in earnest. Philadelphia, Charleston, Savannah, and other American towns all suffered during the Revolutionary War from hostile military presences. Only New York and Aquidneck Island, particularly Newport, suffered the full brunt of the enemy's hostility for so long a time. No other northern seaboard was as vanquished as proud Newport.

Because of the initial British war strategy to isolate New England and cut it off from its allied colonies, in order to destabilize and then defeat the confederation, Newport, with its copious sheltered harbor, was the ideal staging area for the Royal Navy. British Admiral George Rodney reported Narragansett Bay was "the best and noblest harbor in America capable of containing the whole Navy of Britain, and whence they could in all seasons lie in perfect security and from whence squadrons in forty-eight hours could blockade the three capitals of America, namely Boston, New York, and Philadelphia."

Geographically, Newport, the jewel of New England, the Venice of America, was its own natural enemy.

In the summer of 1776, General Sir William Howe, commander-in-chief of the British army in North America, had a dilemma. Along with his brother Admiral Richard, Lord Howe, who commanded the Royal Navy, Sir William had to determine how to quickly defeat the ragtag Continental Army under George Washington and

Plan de la ville, port, et rade de Newport, avec une partie de Rhode-Island occupée par l'armée française aux orders de Mr. Le comte de Rochambeau, et de l'escadre française commandée. par Mr. le Chr. Destouches. (detail), c. 1780
Manuscript, pen-and-ink and watercolor
This detail shows the defended anchorage for the French naval vessels and their placement to complement the shore batteries and to obtain maximum crossfire effect by their placement.
Library of Congress
Washington, D. C.
The Rochambeau
Map Collection, Geography and Map Division

bring the rebelling colonies back into the imperial fold. Howe firmly believed diplomacy and friendship might be the key, and he was loath to launch a big battle that could kill hundreds of colonists, further alienating the provinces. Even though the British had gained experience in America during the protracted French and Indian wars, this contest was different from any other their armed forces had engaged in because they were now fighting their own cousins. And, unlike Europe, where generals could lay siege to a strategic metropolis, defeat it, and claim victory, America was an enormous, sprawling, decentralized territory without an obvious capital (despite Admiral Rodney's claim). But the generals strode in lock-step and planned their American adventure as if they were in Europe, not comprehending that if they conquered one important city, or even an entire colony, the rebels would simply retreat to another area and no lasting damage would be done.

Regardless of Howe's initial inclinations, the British ministry in London under Lord North demanded that the American rebels be destroyed on the battlefield in order to quell the rebellion with dispatch. In August 1776, the 25,000-strong British force had their best opportunity to inflict permanent damage on the Continentals at the Battle of New York. General Washington, elected commander-in-chief of the Continental Army in July 1775, could have (should have) been bottled up on Brooklyn Heights, but British bungles and a heavy fog cover allowed him and his army to escape to Manhattan, and eventually to Westchester County and beyond, keeping the revolution alive. Historians have long debated whether Sir William's heart was really in the total destruction of his enemy, because so many chances for decisive early victory were ignored; some claim that the fact he had American relatives perhaps colored his attitude. Howe's generals, particularly Sir Henry Clinton, seethed at the slipshod, gentlemanly manner in which their commander was prosecuting the war and were vocal in their disregard for a strategy gone awry. Throughout the autumn, the British consolidated their hold on New York City, but they passed up crucial opportunities to annihilate George Washington's demoralized and largely untrained troops.

Then the British command launched another questionable operation, much to the befuddlement of Clinton and others who wanted to strike at the core of the rebel strength. Instead of directing the navy to take on Washington along the Delaware River, where he might have been surrounded by Charles, Earl of Cornwallis's newly arrived brigades and forced to surrender, Howe played it safe and ordered a large contingent of his troops and naval vessels to head north and occupy Newport for the winter. Years later, in his narrative of the war, Sir Henry wrote: "I must confess that I never approved of the Rhode Island expedition, as I looked upon the time of year as more favorable for a move to the southward, which appeared to me of the utmost importance in that early stage of the rebellion, before time had been given to those provinces to strengthen themselves. . . . But I very soon perceived that the plan of possessing Rhode Island had been too strongly determined on to be laid aside. The Admiral wanted a winter station for his large ships, and every other consideration must give way."

Both Admiral Howe and General Howe believed that Newport would offer little resistance and, being an island, would afford the best defense for the admiral's men and safety for the fleet. In this, they calculated correctly. The militia on Aquidneck Island at the time consisted of some seven hundred poorly equipped patriot soldiers, and when General Clinton's squadron appeared off Point Judith on December 7, the Americans, outnumbered ten to one, prudently evacuated to Bristol and Tiverton to await orders from Governor Nicholas Cooke or General Washington. Much of the animal stock was driven off Aquidneck and

Corbutt
General Howe, 1777
Mezzotint
Newport Historical Society
Newport, Rhode Island

Conanicut islands, and many women and children were housed in the interior or ferried to the mainland. Most of the cannon had already been removed from Newport earlier in the year for safekeeping in Providence, and the forts at Brenton's Point (now Fort Adams) and on Goat Island (then called Fort Liberty) were useless to the rebels. Newport lay wide open to the invading British.

Frederick Mackenzie, of Irish and French ancestry, was then a major in the British army, stationed in New York. Throughout his several years in America during the war, he kept a detailed, keenly observed diary, which is one of our best sources of information from the British point of view. He was among those troops that sailed from New York to Newport, and he reported: "When the leading ships had got as far as the N. end of Conanicut Island, they hawled around the point to the Eastward, and steered down the Middle Channel towards Newport on Rhode Island, keeping near the Rhode Island shore. The rest of the fleet followed in order, and about 4 oClock the signal was made to anchor, which was done by the whole fleet at 5 in the afternoon, without the smallest accident, about 4 miles from Newport, between Dyer's Island and Weaver's Cove, half a mile from the Shore."

On December 8, 1776, General Clinton's seven thousand British and Hessian troops under the command of Commodore Sir Peter Parker, supported by fifteen warships and seventy transports, landed in Middletown and, after pillaging houses and farms, marched the few miles south to take over Newport. Not a shot was fired by the rebels. Dr. Ezra Stiles recorded in his diary: "It seems to be our Turn now to taste of the heavy Calamities of the War. May God deliver us in his own Time out of all our Destresses. . . . This afternoon we hear that the Enemy landed yesterday about the Middle of the West Side of the Island, about Three Thousand Men: & Marched into Newport, paraded before the Courthouse & there published the Kings Proclamation, & formally took possession of the Town & erected the Kings Government & Laws."

The invasion of Newport offered an historical irony. In 1676, while Narragansett and Wampanoag Indians rampaged across mainland Rhode Island during King Philip's War, torching towns and spreading mayhem, Newport was spared physical destruction because the island was never attacked. Now, exactly a hundred years later, we see the reverse. Newport was under siege by another enemy while the continental Rhode Island towns remained mostly unscathed.

The early days of the occupation of Newport were marked by confusion on both sides. Transporting and lodging so large a force had its problems. Mackenzie relates what it was like for the invaders: "As the troops could not get their tents on shore from the transports last night, they were obliged to lie without any shelter, on a bleak hill, much exposed to the severity of the weather. . . . Very hard frost last night, and Ice an Inch and half thick this morning. The Hessian Regiment of Du Corps, marched into Newport, where they are to be quartered. Three Battalions of British and 5 of Hessians remain encamped on the height above where the Army landed."

From his safe vantage point in Dighton, Massachusetts, the always well-informed Ezra Stiles described in his journal another kind of hardship that greeted the inhabitants of Newport. On December 11, Colonel William Richmond brought Dr. Stiles a proclamation from General Howe offering pardon for all citizens (subjects no longer) who wished to profess Loyalist sympathies and support the Crown. The paper goes on to describe American atrocities (false) and that "the People of Great Britain are generally & almost universally so incensed against us that they are ready to enlist &c.; this may be true." Stiles finished the day's entry with these words: "About 15 or 20 Persons are imprisoned at Newport by the Regulars chiefly of the lower sort & some that had borne Arms. The Officers were taking up houses for Barracks, & among others have taken my House & Meetinghouse—which last it is said they intend to make an Assembly Room for Balls &c after taking down the Pews. As yet they have put none to the Oath of Allegiance."

Major Mackenzie wrote on December 12, "The Inhabitants of this Island being principally Quakers, are exceedingly alarmed at the appearance of the Hessian troops, and under great dread of them. A Quaker told me today, that as the Rebels were now driven off the Island, he hoped the General would send all the Hessians on board ships again."

That wish was not to be fulfilled. In fact, the destruction of Newport was beginning. Every church building in town except the Anglican Trinity Church would be altered and used in the same fashion as Dr. Stiles's Second Congregational Church: sleeping quarters for troops or for entertainment; one was actually used to stable horses. During the first winter of 1776–1777, there were few deprivations in Newport. Although firewood was becoming scarce, the troops were well victualed from their own provisions, and the weather was relatively mild. Within weeks, almost every private house in town was taken over by officers and men, and a large number of inhabitants were displaced; rich or poor, no one was exempt. Stately mansions owned by the merchant elite along Spring and Thames streets were billeted by superior officers, some of whom were pleasantly surprised by the elegance of their new surroundings. Still, the hope among people backing the revolution was that the enemy was only using Aquidneck Island as a winter respite and would move on to fight elsewhere when the spring campaigns commenced.

Governor Cooke convened the General Assembly in Providence in mid-December and appealed to Massachusetts and Connecticut for aid in men and materiel. The Assembly voted to raise a standing army to be led by General James Mitchell Varnum of East Greenwich, and every man in the new state able to bear arms was to be conscripted. "Liberty or Death" was taken as the motto for their campaign, and the elected

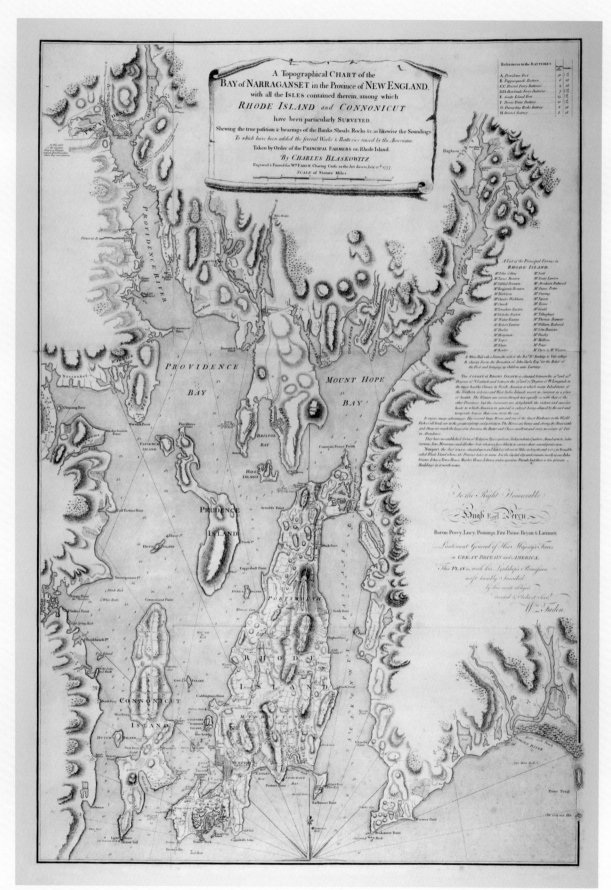

Charles Blascowitz,
cartographer, and
William Faden, engraver
and publisher, London
*A Topographical Chart
of the Bay of
Narragansett*, July 1777
Engraving
Photograph by John Corbett
Newport Historical Society
Newport, Rhode Island

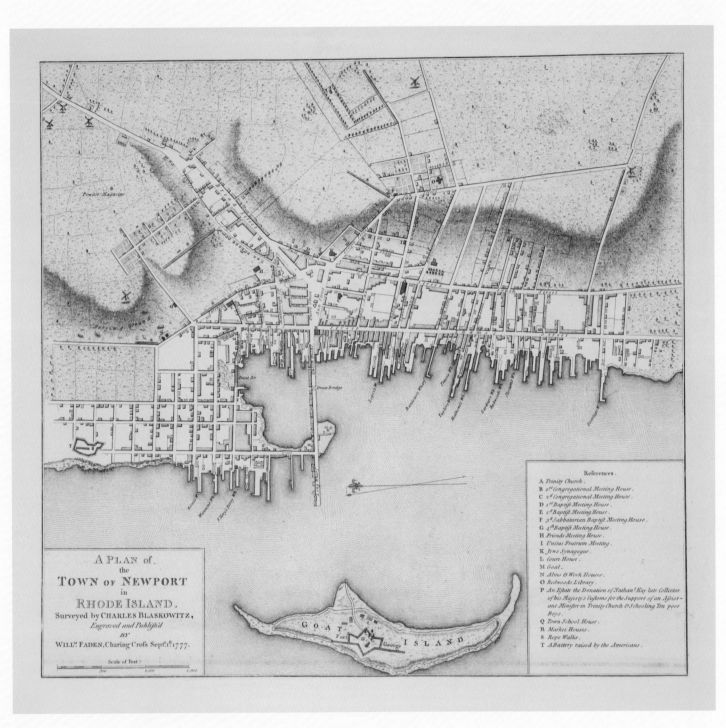

A PLAN of.
the
TOWN OF NEWPORT
in
RHODE ISLAND.
Surveyed by CHARLES BLASKOWITZ,
Engraved and Publish'd
BY
WILL^m FADEN, Charing Crofs Sept^t.1st.1777.

Scale of Feet.

References.
A Trinity Church.
B 1st Congregational Meeting House.
C 2^d Congregational Meeting House.
D 1st Baptist Meeting House.
E 2^d Baptist Meeting House.
F 3^d Sabbatarian Baptist Meeting House.
G 4th Baptist Meeting House.
H Friends Meeting House.
I Unitas Fratrum Meeting.
K Jews Synagogue.
L Court House.
M Goal.
N Alms & Work Houses.
O Redwoods Library.
P An Estate the Donation of Nathan.^l Kay late Collector
of his Majesty's Customs for the Support of an Assist-
ant Minister in Trinity Church & Schooling Ten poor
Boys.
Q Town School House.
R Market Houses.
S Rope Walks.
T A Battery raised by the Americans.

GOAT ISLAND
Fort George

officials were unanimous in their will to fight to the end. A council of war consisting of leaders throughout New England was hastily called, with the eminent Stephen Hopkins as president. This body advised that an American militia of some six thousand be stationed in Rhode Island, either to advance on Newport or to protect Providence in the event that the British force might make a move on Boston. That order was all well and good on paper, but the authorities had great difficulty in raising the allocation. In a letter from Cooke to George Washington in March 1777, the governor lamented, "We have already given every encouragement in our power to men to enlist with the continental battalions; and I am sorry to inform you that there are but 400 enlisted. Nor, in the present state of affairs, do I see any prospect of our being able to complete them . . . the other states always fallen short of their quotas. . . . Your excellency is sensible that near a quarter of the state is in possession of the enemy. . . . I need not add, that this situation creates insuperable difficulties."

In Newport, the stalemate solidified. The two opposing American factions, Tories and patriots, settled in for a long and uncomfortable coexistence. Newport was home to over five hundred Royalists who stayed loyal to the king and Parliament. The majority of them were from a merchant class with direct ties to London, who felt threatened that the rabble might disrupt their business pursuits; politics per se played a lesser role in their fidelity: profits provided them with a reason to want to maintain the status quo. For others, the ideological issue was paramount: they did not believe the Crown had mistreated the colonies and they did not think independence from the mother country was warranted. The iciness between neighbors — once friends, now avowed foes — was palpable as people's social interactions were turned upside down by the daily realities of the occupation. There were few secrets: everyone seemed to know each other's allegiances. Tory Newporters frequently mingled with British officers; they felt protected and secure, certain that their wayward erstwhile friends would, in the end, come around to sanity and drop their ill-advised rebellion. The deposed Tory ex-governor, Joseph Wanton, Jr., dined weekly with his new comrades on the general staff. The far greater number of inhabitants, who backed the Continental Congress and General Washington, on the other hand, could not fathom the blindness of their former friends who were clinging to the *ancien régime* and a way of life that had reached its end. The longer the British remained, the more strained were the tenuous ties between townspeople. When marauding Hessian and British soldiers looted the town and began to tear down the houses of rebels, partly as retribution but mostly for fuel (Stiles reported that 130 homes had already been razed by March 1777), the battle lines were clearly drawn.

For months rumors swirled throughout the new United States that King George III was about to forgive his upstart subjects in America and declare a peace — *if* the provinces would return to British rule. Some welcomed the rumored tender, but most Americans by early 1777 had already firmly chosen independence. In just two years, the psychology of the country had changed from conditioned loyalty to defiance. Even a number of wealthy traders had come to the realization that the days of England's rule were over. Ezra Stiles wrote: "I hear more of the Reconciliation plan circulating. This is doubtless the Olive Leaf; but it comes too late. Such an Offer in Answer to the last Petition of the Congress to the King would have been received with Joy; not so now. I mentioned it to a Merchant of Eminence, who had lost about £3000 sterling by the Enemy & owned a Thous'd more in Houses in Newport. He replied, he had rather lose all the rest & America throw themselves into the hands of France than to return to be under the Dominion of G. Britain." News of like-minded reaction in other colonies fortified Newport's resolve.

FAR LEFT

Charles Blaskowitz, cartographer and William Faden, engraver and publisher, London
A Plan of the Town of Newport in Rhode Island, September 1, 1777
Engraving
Courtesy of
The Preservation Society of Newport County
Newport, Rhode Island
The Collection at Hunter House

Major Mackenzie did not limit his observations merely to military matters. In mid-December, he wrote:

There is a hill about 7 miles from Newport, and on the Eastern side of this Island, Called Quaker Hill, from whence there is a very fine view of all the N. part of the Island, and of the adjacent Islands, and the Continent for many miles. The many fine and well cultivated Islands, and the beautiful bays and inlets, with the distant view of towns, farms, and cultivated lands intermixed with Woods, together with the many views of the adjacent waters, contribute to make this, (even at this bleak season of the year) the finest, most diversified, and extensive prospect I have seen in America. . . . In the beginning of Summer this must be a delightful view, and I should think hardly to be equalled in America, or any other Country.

Throughout the winter and spring of 1777 the situation in Newport continued to deteriorate, physically and financially. Having been harassed repeatedly for their religious beliefs in Europe and deeply suspicious of any military force, the entire Jewish community evacuated to carry on their lives and businesses in safer climes; only a few returned after the hostilities were over. The Royal Navy had brought about an almost total cessation of the once-robust trade in the harbor, with disastrous results not only for the once-busy and wealthy merchants, but also for nearly everyone else in town. The economic losses rippled down the social chain to the point that very few people had any paying work. The initial optimism that the British forces would withdraw come spring was dashed when it became apparent they were in Newport for the long haul. Spirits plunged, more men uprooted themselves and their families and made the difficult decision to head for the mainland. Spermaceti candle factories, warehouses, rum distilleries, ropewalks, and a dozen other enterprises, all closed their doors. Artisans by the hundreds sought out Providence, which, after the war, benefited handsomely from the large influx of skilled workmen. But, in Newport, the longer the British dug in, the more serious were the consequences for Americans in rebellion. From a population of close to 9,200 in 1774, the town had shrunk by more than half, to about 4,000 a mere three years later.

In January 1777, General Clinton returned to England to be replaced by Hugh, Earl Percy, a man more in step with General Howe's sentiments in not wanting to alienate the populace. Clinton had let his troops run free, molesting men and women alike, stealing anything at hand and even ransacking the Redwood Library of many books. Percy put a stop to the vandalism and ordered that the Redwood's volumes be returned (some were, while others were used as fireplace kindling). The townspeople were somewhat relieved, but their good fortune lasted only four months, when Lord Percy was recalled and General Richard Prescott took command of the forces in Rhode Island. Arrogant and malicious, the general allowed the mean tyranny to resume. According to the historian Florence Simister, "Prescott was a petty tyrant and overbearing. In one notable instance he became enraged because Quakers refused to take off their hats in his presence. After that, whenever he met one of them in the street, he knocked the man's hat off or ordered his servants to do so. If he saw more than two men together, he shouted, 'disperse, ye rebels!' " General Prescott would soon pay dearly for his unpopularity.

With the American forces gathered on the mainland and almost nightly shelling enemy forces on Aquidneck, the occupiers erected or built up fortifications within Newport, on Goat Island, at Howland's Ferry in Portsmouth, and at other strategic locations. British officers were in constant readiness, waiting for an American army that would seek to dislodge them from their island sanctuary. But while there was frequent sniping by the rebels from the safety of the mainland, no large assault was in the works: the Americans could not raise a standing army big enough to take on the well-trained and disciplined British and Hessian soldiers supported by a substantial naval presence. The rebels also lacked sufficient arms and powder to wage a genuine battle; their real mission was to be ready to repulse an invasion of Providence, should it come. But a more strategic decision superseded the logistical one. General Washington, while perplexed by Howe's orders to garrison Newport, warmly welcomed his move. General Nathanael Greene, a native Rhode Islander and one of the Continental Army's finest officers (he would distinguish himself throughout the war and rise to become

Valentine Greene
Nathaniel Greene, 1785
Mezzotint
from a painting by
Charles Wilson Peale.
National Archives
Washington, D. C.

Washington's second-in-command), fully agreed with his commander's views. Both men realized that while seven thousand men lay idle in Newport, they could not be used to wage war against Washington's troops in New Jersey and Pennsylvania, nor to aid General John Burgoyne's army engaged in the northern campaign slogging south from Canada. Throughout 1777, Greene lobbied against an attack on Newport: let them sit, he reasoned, while we take on a smaller force. The historian Charles Carroll concluded, "The encampment at Newport was only one of the inexplicable stupidities of a war that indicated little of military genius among the King's forces in America."

British Blunders

On paper, Britain's superior forces ought to have subdued the American Revolution from the outset. They possessed the largest navy on earth and a huge, well-oiled army that had proven its might and effectiveness in battle. They held an overwhelming numerical superiority, better munitions, and a clear political rationale for not letting their American cousins revolt against the king. But wars are not fought on paper, and the fact that the theater of war was so vast, and that the Americans were fighting with so emotional a purpose, tipped the scales early on: independence from tyrannical overlords was a more compelling cause than a police action against rebels. Strategically, the British command made so many harebrained miscalculations that, in retrospect, one might believe they wanted to lose the thirteen colonies. They created many more of their own problems than General Washington's ragged troops did in the beginning, and their eventual defeat can be laid to extraordinarily poor planning, a serious misunderstanding of the enemy, arrogance, plus strained logistics and communications. After 1777, regardless of how long the fighting continued, it was becoming clear to military strategists—English, American, and French—that America would prevail. It was too huge to conquer, particularly by a bumbling British general staff abetted by ill-informed government ministers on the other side of the Atlantic Ocean.

Yet, in the early stages, very little seemed to favor the rebels. Washington's small and poorly outfitted army had been routed in New York and forced to flee across the Hudson River to New Jersey, where the men continued to avoid a large, decisive battle with hostile forces that would have ended in a bloodbath. But General Howe had now divided his army and Washington won two decisive, and morale-boosting, skirmishes at Trenton and Princeton in December 1776 and January 1777. Howe, surprised and spooked by Washington's lightning strikes, evacuated New Jersey and pulled the bulk of his troops back to the safety of New York, and in doing so, lost access to the extensive provisions he needed, and had planned on, to feed his army. From then on, he had to rely on being supplied by the Royal Navy from Britain, three thousand miles distant. Ships originally designated to form a blockade of the American coast to deprive the rebels of much-needed munitions were used in the most ineffective manner. Then Howe, thinking in conventional eighteenth-century military fashion, decided that taking Philadelphia, America's largest metropolis, would strike a decisive blow. He "took" the city but did not hold it, and the occupation didn't hurt anything except American pride. With a large number of troops bottled up in three cities—Philadelphia, New York, and Newport—and his navy scattered, Howe had created his own impasse. Then, in October 1777, the British suffered a major defeat in the northern theater when General Horatio Gates, greatly abetted by Washington's overall strategy and Benedict Arnold's brilliant tactics, forced British General John Burgoyne to surrender his entire army of six thousand men at Saratoga, New York. London was shocked by the unexpected loss, but did little to rectify the situation on the field. The naval authority David Syrett concluded, "The 1777 campaign in America is one of the most appalling examples of strategic planning in British military history."

According to the Brown University historian Gordon S. Wood, "Saratoga was the turning point. It suggested that reconquest of America might be beyond British strength. It brought France openly into the struggle. And it led to a change in the British command and a fundamental alteration in strategy." After the debacle at Saratoga, both Admiral Howe and General Howe submitted their resignations to London; Sir William was replaced by Newport's nemesis General Henry Clinton, now rested after a year in England. But the hawkish Clinton's arrival could not materially change the direction of the war in America because, in 1778, France began to aid the Americans and that led to an about-face in London's prosecution of the war. Now the British had to defend themselves at sea against the powerful French fleet and many in England feared that its arch-enemy, still smarting from defeat in the Seven Years' War, would invade their island. Great Britain was in tumult, its strategies in shambles, and its army in America no better off than on the day it arrived in 1774 to put down the rebellion in Boston. No one, it seemed, was in charge.

In Newport, tensions increased. While townspeople were deprived of the patriot-leaning *Newport Mercury*, which ceased publication during the occupation, Loyalists could follow the progress of the war in the *Newport Gazette*, a Tory broadsheet published by the former Boston printer John Howe that, obviously, took a particularly partisan line on the unfolding drama. In his first printing, Howe addressed General Clinton thus: "May it please Your Excellency: We the freeholders and inhabitants of the town of Newport, penetrated with a truly grateful sense of His Majesty's paternal affection and tenderness for his unhappily deluded American subjects . . . humbly presume to address Your Excellency, most heartily congratulating you upon your arrival among us, sincerely praying that your endeavors for the establishment of peace and good government to this once flourishing, but now distressed town, may be crowned with success." Tories may have enjoyed reading the rag, but the majority of Newporters wouldn't have wrapped their dead fish in it, let alone read it, except for amusement.

With a dearth of trustworthy information, rebels had to rely on rumors to get a sense of what was happening at the front. Those supporting the Revolution who scanned the Tory broadsheet would have seen numerous articles accusing American leaders of self-interest, thievery, double-dealing, and selling out their fellow countrymen for personal profit. The acidic assaults on members of Congress were constant, biting, and absurd. Another staple of the *Gazette* was the weekly "reporting" of desertions in the Continental Army and the inhumane measures taken to enlist recruits. While some of the information was probably close to correct, the exaggerated numbers must have been pure fantasy. Objectivity, on both sides, was absent.

As in other parts of the country, Newport was the target of a persistent propaganda war being waged by both sides. General Howe clearly believed there was a large Tory contingent in America waiting for the rebels to fail, and he wanted to cultivate it and keep it loyal to the Crown. On the other hand, the rebels in Newport had to be content with copies of pro-American pamphlets and newspapers smuggled into town in order to get their side of the story. Because of the volume of naval traffic coming into the harbor, there was no lack of information. As news of various battles filtered into Newport, passions rose and fell. When Washington was victorious at Trenton and Princeton, support for the invaders diminished; when his army was put on the run, some began to waver. After Saratoga, however, there was a precipitous decline in Tory support as those who were torn in their allegiance mostly came over to the patriot point of view. In short, it was a murky, anxious time.

Ever since the occupation began, American militiamen had waged an unrelenting guerrilla campaign against the entrenched British troops, silently rowing men from the mainland at night to conduct raids on specific targets. Major Mackenzie's diary is rife with reports of small-scale incursions that often took the lives of soldiers on both sides: "10 June. About half past ten last night The Rebels made an attack upon the Subaltern's post on the road to Commonfence Neck. They landed about 50 men . . . and advanced very silently towards the advanced Sentries, who, in consequence of the darkness of the night, and their creeping up, did not perceive them, until they were within about 20 yards of them." In the ensuing battle, three British soldiers were killed and one American wounded before the rebels were beaten back to their boats. Even if the commanders on both sides were wary of launching an all-out attack, other American officers were not content to wait patiently for *some* action to commence. For the moment, this was a war of attrition and nerves; the rebels were determined to make the most of it, take the initiative, and harry the invaders who haughtily held their homeland.

But war takes its toll in other ways as well. Mackenzie recorded on July 6: "A soldier of the 43rd Regt. shot himself last night. I cannot help observing here that a soldier of the 22nd Regiment shot himself, and that another soldier of the 43rd cut himself with a razor across the wrists; several soldiers also have deserted, some of them men of good characters who were not suspected of such an act. I am inclined to believe that many of these things proceed from our having remained so long in a state of inactivity. . . . We attempt nothing against the enemy." A Newport patriot named Fleet Greene, son of Samuel Greene, a carpenter who worked on the

Redwood Library when it was being built and a relative of the famous General Nathanael Greene, also kept a running diary during the occupation, not as copious as Mackenzie's but informative nonetheless. Greene, then in his twenties, reports in June that "a Hessian soldier that was sentenced to be whipped drowned himself in a pond near the beach. He was taken up and dismembered as a public example." He also informs us: "Last night a man was beat by the Hessians. It is now dangerous to walk the streets after dark." The German Hessians were particularly reviled by Newport patriots; these mercenaries in the pay of King George III, parading around town in their strange uniforms and speaking little or no English, were believed to be callous killers; most Newporters were frankly much more afraid of them than they were of their English cousins.

One sensational story in 1777 did not have to rely on newspapers to spread rapidly throughout Rhode Island and beyond. General Prescott, commander of British forces in Rhode Island, had his headquarters in Newport at Banister House on Spring and Pelham streets, but during the warm months he was known to ride to Portsmouth and stay at the home of a Mr. Overing, a wealthy Tory sympathizer whose property bordered Abraham Redwood's estate. Rumor has it that it was not only the cool breezes the general was seeking, but also the companionship of a woman. Across the bay at the Yankee militia headquarters, an ambitious young colonel named William Barton heard about the general's nocturnal habits and devised a daring plan. On the night of July 9, a party of forty American soldiers led by Barton, having arrived on Aquidneck in five whaling boats, quietly traversed the mile from the shore to Overing's house, tricked the sentry and overpowered him, and made their way in three columns into the house. There Barton found General Prescott in bed in his nightshirt (alone, alas; no lass), befuddled and enraged. Barton allowed him to put on only his waistcoat and slippers, and the Americans marched the general and two of his men back to the boats without incident, then rowed past numerous ships of the Royal Navy up to Providence with their prize.

Jubilation was the order of the day. Colonel Barton became an overnight hero, rewarded by both the Rhode Island General Assembly and Congress with money, a promotion, and a sword. By evening of July 10, everyone on Aquidneck knew that the general had been successfully kidnapped, to the great chagrin of the British brass. How, they wondered, could they lose their commander to a bunch of ill-equipped Americans? For days, everything in Newport was in chaos until a temporary commander was chosen. A week later, General Sir Robert Pigot arrived from New York to assume leadership in Newport.

Under guard in Providence, the once-pampered pompous general was unhappy, particularly concerning his sartorial conditions. According to S. G. Arnold in his history of Rhode Island, Prescott called for a barber at once to fix his hair. Two days later, a ship arrived from Newport under "a flag of truce bearing the general's entire wardrobe—his purse, his hair powder, and a plentiful supply of perfumery." After a year of incarceration, General Prescott was exchanged for the American General Charles Lee, who had been captured by the British in December 1776.

As bold and ingenious as the Prescott episode was, 1777 brought a disappointing military failure as well. Although General Nathanael Greene lobbied against an incursion in Rhode Island, throughout the summer and into the autumn pressure was brought to bear in Congress to mount an American offensive against the British on Aquidneck Island, to cause a diversion from the campaign in New Jersey and Pennsylvania. Washington had appointed General Joseph Spencer to command his Rhode Island forces, and over a period of several months men from all over New England had gathered along the east bank of the Sakonnet River:

3,000 volunteers from Massachusetts, 1,500 from Connecticut, and the rest from Rhode Island, until Spencer had a force of about 8,000 soldiers ready to invade the island and take on the enemy. At that time, the British ranks had dwindled to about 4,500, so the patriots had the advantage in personnel. Attack was anticipated daily, for weeks, then months, and still Spencer dallied, professing that he did not have sufficient naval support. In the meantime, the British and Hessians were able to strongly fortify their positions along the shore. Frustrated officers and men began to grumble, and in the autumn, they began to desert in droves.

It was in October when Spencer felt ready to launch his waterborne assault, and then the nemesis of any military campaign reared its untimely head—weather. A huge storm, described as a gale but probably a full-fledged hurricane, raged for three days, making the attack unfeasible. More men, by the hundreds, melted away from the patriot encampment, to the point where Spencer had only about five thousand under his command. On October 26, he abandoned the expedition when news reached him of Burgoyne's surrender at Saratoga.

General Spencer was harshly condemned for his failure to act with authority and dispatch, and there arose a clamor among the citizenry for his dismissal and punishment. Yet, after two military courts of inquiry (ordered by Congress) heard his defense, he was cleared of all charges of incompetence and allowed to maintain his position in Rhode Island. While some historians decry his performance and his subsequent acquittal, others see his implementation of the supposed siege as part of a larger agenda worked out by the commander-in-chief. Charles Carroll maintains,

> Neither Washington nor Greene wished the British elsewhere than at Newport in 1777; it is conceivable that Spencer had been instructed to conduct his campaign in such manner as to keep the British army in Rhode Island for the time being. Burgoyne's instructions to Baum [a general on the British staff], who met with disaster at Bennington, were to march across country

to Springfield, where he would meet his majesty's forces from Rhode Island! If Spencer actually aimed to prevent the sending of reinforcements from Newport to Burgoyne's army and to upset the plan for an invasion of central New England, culminating in junction of the British forces in western Massachusetts, he had been eminently successful; and Rhode Island, in enduring the discomfort of British occupation was suffering vicariously for the nation.

The Battle of Rhode Island

Major Mackenzie, in mid-November 1777, entered in his diary: "High wind last night and severe frost. . . . The inhabitants here say we shall have a very severe winter; they have found by experience that when much rain falls in October and November the ground being wet when frost sets in, the winds are much colder than when there has been a dry autumn." Those inhabitants could not have been more correct: the winter of 1777–1778 was extremely harsh, and the suffering was intense among soldiers and civilians alike. But in this case, the Newport citizens had the worst of it. According to the diarist Fleet Greene, throughout the autumn, soldiers and sailors continued to steal potatoes, corn, and other produce from inhabitants. British authorities imprisoned those who congregated in groups larger than two, who refused to work on Sundays, and for a host of other reasons. Clothing was stolen, leaving noncombatants with precious little with which to fend off the freezing temperatures. To make matters more woeful, smallpox broke out in December, frightening everyone.

Newport was slowly spiraling into despair. British vessels sailed south weekly in search of firewood; both Mackenzie and Fleet Greene carefully reported activity in the harbor: ships coming with men, with supplies, with wood, with rumors. In December, when about two thousand more troops arrived in Newport from the summer campaign along the Delaware River to take up their winter quarters, the needs became greater. And the spirits of the patriots descended further. Newport was a busy depot for the invaders. But little of the bounty was shared with the townsfolk.

Throughout the winter, Mackenzie was making entries in his diary like the following from late December: "Heavy rain, hard frost, and very strong cold wind at W. The Rain becomes congealed as soon as it touched anything, so that everything exposed to it is encrusted with Ice. Walking is very dangerous, and the roads are almost impassable for horses and Carriages." A month later: "The greatest part of the wood upon this Island has already been used. A small quantity is procured from Conanicut, but nothing equal to the consumption of the Garrison, which amounts to about 300 Cords per week." This was Fleet Greene in January 1778: "The weather has been so extremely cold that it is said some of the inhabitants have frozen to death in their houses." Edward Field in his history of Rhode Island says, "As the winter advanced, destitution and suffering increased, particularly among the refugees from Newport, of whom there were over 100 in Providence alone. An appeal was made through the press for aid, and the response was prompt and generous." Ambrose Serle, an English private secretary to Lord Howe, accompanied the admiral to Newport in January 1778; among his observations: "Walked this morning to the East Side of the Island opposite the main, from whence the Rebels lately laid their Plan of making an Attack, & passed by a House called Whitehall, formerly the favorite Residence of Bp. Berkeley, whose name is still held in Veneration here. The Country is pleasant, but entirely stripped of its Trees & Fences, wch have been taken for Fuel."

Regardless of the hardships the rebel citizens of Newport were enduring, regardless of the loss of liberties they had become so accustomed to over the previous 125 years, the *spirit* of independence associated with the townspeople was still on open display. General Robert Pigot, in charge of Newport for much of the occupation, wrote to a friend, "This place [Newport] has the most handsome homes, the broadest streets and the most gracious public buildings in all of America. It is populated, unfortunately, by a stubborn breed who refuse to admit defeat." Ambrose Serle, the secretary to Lord Howe, an upper-class English gentleman with the stultified and patronizing mindset to match, made one of the most telling observations about Newporters in March 1778. Of course, it is even more revealing of Mr. Serle himself. It is quite clear, upon reading his diary entry, how alienated the Yankees in Rhode Island had become from the mother country, and why the Revolution, no matter what it took, would succeed.

Nothing can more plainly prove the Force of political Institutions upon the Conduct of a People, than the manners and Temper of the Inhabitants of this Island, wch was governed perhaps in the most truly democratic mode of any in the World. They are vulgar in their Behaviour, yet affect what they think Politeness, which is a sort of Rudeness that suits so ill with it, that they are never more irksome than when they offer to be civil. Generosity of Spirit is certainly not among their Virtues: They don't seem to feel an exalted Sentiment, nor are they troubled with refined Sensibilities. Their Religion is altogether problematical. They have almost every Sect of it here: Nor do they seem to think that Unity & Concord are essential Branches of it. In short, they do not appear to merit Confidence in any Shape. Smuggling, Trade, Republicanism, Dissensions, and Luxury, have spoiled their manners & rendered them Disagreeable Companions for the most part, as well as bad Subjects. As human Nature is the same every where, I can only impute all this to the Errors of their Government, which operates as strongly upon a People as Education upon Individuals.

As spring struggled to make its appearance in 1778, the outcome of the rebellion was looking brighter, regardless of Britain's superiority in the field. By February, Benjamin Franklin, the de facto American ambassador to France, had used his cunning and diplomatic skills to convince King Louis XVI to sign two treaties with Congress that would have enormous implications for the outcome of the struggle. One was a treaty of amity and commerce allowing Americans to trade freely with France. The other was far more important. Franklin persuaded the king to renew hostilities with England and supply military forces for the fight in America. Immediately, Great Britain was on the defensive where it was most vulnerable—the high seas.

The fledgling patriot navy was not yet a factor on the ocean. And although Britain had the larger fleet, its ships were so strung out along the extended American coast that they were highly susceptible to a focused French attack. Parliament, quickly foreseeing the implications of French involvement, launched the Carlisle Commission, which attempted to mend fences by offering Congress a peace treaty with the

VALLEY FORGE

Newport was not alone in its suffering that winter of 1777–1778. General Washington made his winter quarters for the Continental Army from December to May at Valley Forge, Pennsylvania. Cold and snow were severe, the troops lacked adequate food, and clothing was scarce. Many of the soldiers were forced to bandage their feet against the elements for lack of boots. Troops deserted in alarming numbers, discipline was lax in the extreme, and many of the ten thousand soldiers were tempted to mutiny. But Washington—and the cause of freedom—was helped greatly by two experienced soldiers, the Marquis de Lafayette from France (now a major general under Washington) and General Baron von Steuben of Prussia. With his old-school deportment and experience with the British military mind-set, von Steuben drilled the dispirited Americans each day to act and fight as a unified corps, demanding strict organization. By the end of the winter lull, Washington had a credible fighting force at his command.

proviso that the territories would stay dependent. It was insultingly too late for such a proposal; Congress quickly and angrily dismissed the overture and welcomed their new French allies into the fray. From mid-1778 onward, American politicians and soldiers displayed a newfound resolve. Later, when Spain, Holland, and other European nations joined France in the alliance against Great Britain, King George III was precariously, uncomfortably, on his own.

The consequences of the Franco-American partnership were felt in short order. French warships began seizing British ships throughout the West Indies (over 250 in 1778 alone) and increased the flow of badly needed munitions to the American continent. A large number of King George's ships of the line and others were recalled to defend the English Channel, thus depriving British commanders of their use in rebel waters. Britain was being stretched thin. In May, when General Clinton took command of the army, one of his first directives was the evacuation of Philadelphia after the army had held supremacy only eight months there. The occupation had accomplished little, and the slowly retreating army offered Washington a number of tempting targets as the force wended its way back to New York City. The rigorous training initiated by von Steuben paid off: for the first time, the confident Continental Army contested as equals with their surprised British combatants.

But, in Rhode Island, no one was safe from British terrorism. On May 25, a battalion of six hundred men sailed up Narragansett Bay and laid waste to Warren. The soldiers burned houses, pillaged whatever they could find, and brought away a number of prisoners. There had been no direct provocation for the raid, but fear of the French must have been part of their rationale. Fleet Greene reports: the marauders "proceeded thence to Bristol, set fire to the town and then embarked after burning 120 flatboats." The next night in Newport: "The town was alarmed by the cry of fire, which proved to be the house of Mrs. Peleg Anthony, the inhabitants went to the assistance; the general cry amongst the officers and soldiers was that the inhabitants set the house on fire as a signal. The inhabitants, without respect of persons, were greatly abused, knocked down and beat. Wearing apparel of all sorts, necklaces, rings, and paper money, taken as plunder at Bristol and Warren, were offered for sale by the soldiers." The British were getting vicious.

In early July, the real prize of the accord with the French hove into view. Jean-Baptiste, comte d'Estaing, formerly a general in the French army but recently awarded an admiralty and command of the French fleet in America because of his friendship with Marie Antoinette, crossed the Atlantic with eleven ships of the line, a 50-gun ship, and five frigates; the squadron was sighted off Chesapeake Bay. In New York, Lord Howe (not yet relieved of his duties) and General Clinton were in a quandary: where would the French admiral strike first? All the British could do was make wild guesses—and with a sorely depleted Royal Navy, hope and pray. D'Estaing flirted with the idea of an assault on New York harbor and menaced his adversaries there, but being unfamiliar with the tides and having no pilots who knew the waters, demurred. On July 22, the French fleet departed to the south as a ruse, leaving Lord Howe in the dark. Then on July 28, he received intelligence that he dreaded: the target was Newport.

Admiral Howe's fears of a Rhode Island invasion were justified because the French were clearly superior in firepower; a combined campaign employing American land troops and French sea strength could potentially doom the occupation force. While the liberation of Aquidneck Island was a priority for some Americans, it had been impossible with the British fleet in Narragansett Bay. Now with French might and

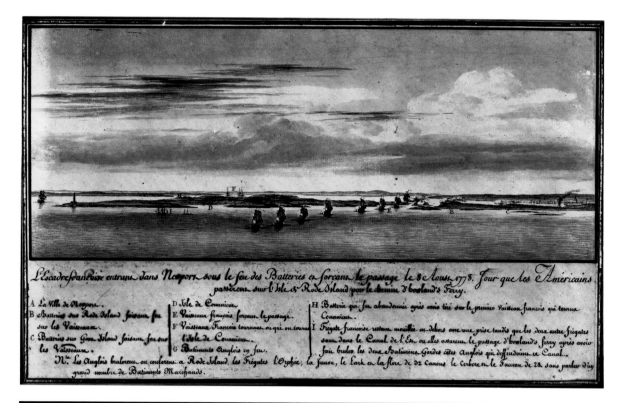

Pierre Ozanne
Le vaisseau le Languedoc dématé par le coup de vent dans le nuit du 12' attaqué par un vaisseau de guerre Anglois l'après midy du 13 Aoust 1778
Pen-and-ink drawing
This drawing shows the French vessel *Languedoc*, D'Estaing's flagship, under attack from the British ship *Renown* commanded by Captain Dawson, who was taking advantage of the fact that the disabled French ship had lost her mast and rudder during strong winds the previous night, August 13, 1778.

Captain James Cook of Great Britain—known
to the world as the man who twice circumnavigated the globe, discovered New Zealand,
charted the transit of Venus, outlined the
Australian coast, discovered the cure for
scurvy, mapped the Pacific Ocean as no one
before, and sought in vain for the Northwest
Passage across North America—has a
direct, though odd, connection to Newport.
His two most renowned ships, the *Resolution*
and the *Endeavour*, both of which had circled
the earth, were taken over, upon retirement
from Cook's command, by the Royal Navy for
use as transport or whaling ships during the
War of Independence. According to the writer
Tony Horwitz, "In a believe-it-or-not twist, marine archeologists have recently discovered
that the two ships, which travelled some
hundred and fifty thousand miles under Cook,
ended their days within hailing distance of
each other. The *Resolution* ran aground in
Newport, Rhode Island, and now lies buried
under landfill. Sunk in the harbor nearby is
a convoy that was scuttled by the British in
1778, a year before Cook's death, to keep
a French fleet from attacking Newport. One
of the ships in the convoy is the *Endeavour*."
Horwitz's claim is impossible to confirm, but
likely.

experience, here was the opportunity to carry the battle to Newport. Lord Howe sailed to Rhode Island as soon as he could to direct the engagement.

On July 29, d'Estaing sailed into Narragansett Bay; he sent two ships of the line to anchor between the mainland and Conanicut Island, which the British evacuated quickly, and directed his frigates to secure the Sakonnet Passage between Newport and the eastern mainland. The British and Hessian forces were ordered from all points of the island to congregate in fortified Newport, awaiting the onslaught. Fleet Greene observed: "The town appears in the greatest confusion," and "All the livestock are brought in from Portsmouth and Middletown, likewise all carriages, wheelbarrows, shovels, pickaxes, &c, are taken from the inhabitants. . . . A number of trees were cut down and put in the road to obstruct the Provincials march. . . . The army continues to lay waste the land, cutting down orchards and laying open fields." Houses outside the military lines were torn or burnt down for defensive reasons.

To appreciate how complicated relationships within Newport had become during this time, when neighbors became estranged because of conflicting allegiances, consider the delicate situation within the Almy family. Benjamin Almy was an ardent patriot who was serving with the Rhode Island militia when the French arrived. His wife Mary, mother of his six children, was devoted in her support of the Crown. While he was in the field preparing to battle the British, she kept a detailed diary, addressed to her husband, which serves as a poignant roadmap to the bitter realities of this particular war.

> All the fleet in motion; everything in consternation; the inhabitants much distressed; the batteries all spirited; all warlike preparation; the streets filled with carts and ordnance stores. . . . Every man ordered to be in readiness; the American troops were landing at Howland's Ferry. Oh! What a sound! When I look over the list of my friends on both sides of the question, my heart shudders at the thought, what numbers must be slain, both so obstinate so determined. Well may we say, what havoc does ambition make. Cursed Frenchmen, they would not have come, had it not been for you.

For days, nothing of substance happened; the authorities were edgy in the extreme and civilians in town were ordered not to leave their houses on fear of death. When a French warship began shelling, Greene wrote, "The harbor is in one continual blaze, the shots fly very thick over the town." Mary Almy wrote, "Heavens! what a scene of wretchedness before this once happy and flourishing island. Cursed ought, and will be, the man who brought all this woe and desolation on a good people. Neither sleep to my eyes, nor slumber to my eyelids, this night." The senior naval officer at Newport, Captain John Brisbane, had gathered his fleet close to town in the harbor. When d'Estaing finally began the amphibious assault on August 8 with ten ships of the line concentrated to the east of Conanicut, Brisbane ordered that the remaining transports be sunk off the North Battery to prevent the French fleet from moving close enough to Newport to bring it under close bombardment from the ships' artillery and cannon. Five venerable warships, all prized frigates, were set afire lest they fall into the hands of the enemy, a move Major Mackenzie thought to be ill-conceived and

Artist unknown
*Major-General
John Sullivan*, 1868
Etching
from Thomas C. Amory,
*The Military Services
and Public Life of
Major-General John
Sullivan* (Boston:
Wiggin and Lunt, 1868).
Newport Historical Society,
Newport, Rhode Island

premature. This was the single largest Royal Navy loss of the War of Independence, and it was brought on by the British themselves.

The Battle of Rhode Island was engaged. The next day, August 9, about six thousand American soldiers under the command of General John Sullivan (who had replaced the now-retired General Spencer), with Lafayette and native-son General Nathanael Greene as seconds-in-command, were ferried from mainland garrisons in eighty-five flatboats to the northern edges of Aquidneck to begin their march to the south and the siege of Newport. Then, that same evening, Lord Howe's fleet from New York, consisting of seven ships of the line, gunships, frigates, and warships, clustered around Point Judith to reconnoiter before moving into action. The first major sea battle of the Revolution was about to commence, and the fate of Newport—and perhaps America—hung in the balance.

As conceived by Washington and Lafayette, the endeavor to liberate Aquidneck from British hands was to be a two-pronged campaign: d'Estaing was to disembark some four thousand French troops near the south end of the island to fight alongside American soldiers and then engage Lord Howe's navy; General Sullivan's men were to march south from shore to shore, lay siege to the British army lodged in Newport, and force them to surrender, or die. The plan, so scrupulously drafted on paper, of course didn't work. Human error, hesitations, exaggerated fears, botched communications, and the vicissitudes of weather all combined to turn the Battle of Rhode Island into a messy, unpredictable, and ultimately disappointing affair. This was the first time the Americans and French had fought together as allies, and they had quite different styles and strategies; in the end, the results did not bode well for the alliance. Too many large egos and commanders with different goals also played a part. And once again, Mother Nature proved to be the biggest spoiler of all.

When Admiral d'Estaing saw Lord Howe's fleet, he had two choices: maintain his position at

Newport and force the British to come after him within the bay, or seek a larger arena in the open ocean in which to do battle. Had he chosen the first option, he might well have been able to force the British garrison to surrender. But, with his training as a land soldier, d'Estaing did not like feeling "trapped" inside Narragansett Bay with his large ships, regardless of how commodious it was. He also had intelligence that British Admiral John Byron (grandfather of the Romantic poet Lord Byron) was on his way to American waters with a fleet; d'Estaing wanted to take on Howe before he was reinforced. So, on August 10, he took his squadron out of the bay and sailed south. Seeing the French coming, Howe formed into a line of battle and retreated, with d'Estaing in pursuit. For the entire next day, both admirals jockeyed for the weather gauge (being windward of the enemy so as to control the fighting) without joining battle. Winds were variable until mid-afternoon, and then the skies turned decidedly foul; both fleets retreated.

In an uncanny repeat of the previous year's campaign being upset because of adverse conditions, in 1778, just at the point when the first significant sea battle of the war was to commence, another storm descended on the northeast Atlantic. This was no burned-out extratropical cyclone—it was a full-fledged hurricane, lasting nearly three days, and as a result of its fury both fleets were widely scattered and severely damaged. Sails were ripped to tatters, rigging was destroyed, men died. The French had two of their largest vessels totally dismasted; not one of their ships was without need of extensive repair. The British suffered

the same pounding. When the tempest blew itself out, Howe was forced to retreat to New York to perform major surgery on his bereft armada. After a week at sea re-forming his crippled fleet, d'Estaing limped back to Newport harbor.

Although the French ships were in obvious poor repair, Americans on shore celebrated d'Estaing's return. With the British fleet gone, they could now press their advantage and take Newport by siege. But the elation was premature. French naval officers unanimously voted to retire to Boston for a detailed overhaul of their battered ships, and no matter how strenuously generals Sullivan and Greene objected, d'Estaing was unmoved. Lafayette also attempted to convince his countryman to stay a few more days so battle could be waged advantageously, but to no avail. As much as the French admirals may have cared about winning a key triumph against their ancient enemy, they were far more protective of the long-term safety of their ships and sailors. Orders from Paris were clear: do what you may to help the rebels, but do not jeopardize the integrity of the fleet. A major opportunity was wasted. After one day, the French departed Newport and headed north for repairs. The Americans felt betrayed by their ally.

The hurricane had left its mark on land as well. While the British were protected in their Newport housing, American troops on the island were totally exposed. Edward Field relates: "The wind blew with great violence, driving a flood of rain before it, accompanied by thunder and lightning; in fact, says an observer, 'it never rained harder since the Flood.' As night came on the tempest increased in fury, leveling tents and so damaging the ammunition in the hands of the troops that the whole army for the time was practically defenseless. Several soldiers died from exposure, and horses, too, succumbed to this notable August storm." The maxim "trust in God and keep your powder dry" was never taken more seriously. Days of consternation followed until fresh munitions arrived and the men could arm themselves again. While the British were certainly compromised by the storm, they suffered nowhere near the damage of the exposed Americans. Why the rebels did not attempt a concentrated attack when they held the advantage remains a mystery. But Sullivan and Greene may have been reluctant to attack the heavily fortified lines surrounding Newport and opted for a battle in the open spaces to the north of town.

Even with the French sea power removed, American ground forces still had a score to settle. But following d'Estaing's departure the camp was overcome with doubts. General Greene related to Washington: "It struck such a panic among the militia and volunteers that they began to desert in shoals. The fleet no sooner set sail than they began to be alarmed for their safety. This misfortune damped the hopes of our army." In fact, several thousand American militiamen, their tour of duty expiring, chose to leave the island. Continental Army officers could do nothing to dissuade them. Now Sullivan and his command were facing the enemy with a drastically reduced force, most of them inexperienced, with no naval backup. And the British held the better position. The American general had to radically alter his original battle plans; with his depleted army he could no longer lay siege to Newport. When Sullivan received word from Washington that General Clinton was returning to Newport apace in Howe's repaired ships, he knew his best opportunity to win the battle had passed. If Howe and Clinton chose, they could trap his entire force on the island. Now all he could do was protect his men, skirmish with the enemy, and make an orderly, safe, retreat from Aquidneck Island.

To accomplish this task, Sullivan ordered his battalions to open fire on the British outworks of Tonomy Hill Fort and Green End Fort north of Newport, to give the appearance of taking the offensive and pressing the siege. Bombardment went on for hours on August 23, and both forces remained stationary for six days of desultory cannonade and artillery pounding. Then, on the evening of August 28, having sent their heavy equipment ahead, the Americans, now numbering only about five thousand troops, began their retreat to the north of the island; there they would await the return of the French fleet, which had been promised by Admiral d'Estaing. Sullivan and Greene believed that if the French could make hasty repairs at Boston, the ships could be employed to continue the assault on Newport. But this was merely wishful thinking. Even though Lafayette would ride seventy miles to Boston in seven hours to implore d'Estaing to return immediately, the admiral again turned a cold shoulder. In fact, d'Estaing would not ever return to Newport, and he would be severely criticized by contemporaries and historians alike for his inaction.

By the middle of the night, the American army (a combination of "regular" Continental troops and militia) had encamped on fortified Butts Hill, which commanded both Bristol and Howland's Ferry, and awaited an attack by General Robert Pigot's emboldened men. Their battle line extended east to west, from shore to shore. The Battle of Rhode Island, the only major battle of the Revolution to take place within the state and one of the largest of the whole war, commenced in earnest on Saturday, August 29. Pigot discovered the American retreat early on that morning and ordered his troops in pursuit; in two columns, they marched north on the East and West Main roads. Sullivan's pickets were posted about three miles ahead of the main force, and were ordered to exchange fire with the British vanguard and slowly lead them on. All morning, the strategy worked, and the British 22nd Regiment marched straight into a trap set by Greene's forces; over a quarter of the men were killed by the patriots. Major Samuel Ward, Jr., commanded a division of black militia who had been promised freedom for enlisting; three times that afternoon they repulsed concentrated attacks by Hessian formations, which suffered heavy losses. More Hessians battled with Sullivan's right flank, bayonet to bayonet, and again the Hessians fell back, defeated. All across the northern tip of the island Americans met their enemy with full force; the air was heavy with the stench of powder from artillery pieces and muskets, a ceaseless rumble of cannon carried across the skies, and the ground was littered with casualties. Regardless of the British and Hessian onslaught, the rebels fought harder. As darkness fell, the British and German troops deserted the field, abandoning their dead and wounded. The Americans had held firm.

Israel Angell, a colonel with the American troops commanding a reduced regiment, was in the thick of the battle. In his diary he reported: "I was ordered with my Regt to a Redoubt on a Small hill which the Enemy was trying for and it was with Difficulty that we got there before the Enemy. I had 3 or 4 men killed and wounded today; at night I was ordered with my Regt to lie on the lines. I had not Slept then in two nights more than two or three hours. The Regt had eaten nothing during the whole Day. This was our situation to on guard, but we marched off Cheerfully and took our post."

From his vantage point in Newport, Fleet Greene wrote of the day: "Early this morning a report prevailed that the Provincials were leaving the island. Immediately the English regiments, with Anspach Chasseurs, and Hyn, regiment of Germans sailed [sallied] from the line and attacked a party of Provincials on the road, but were beaten off with loss. The Provincials halted at Windmill Hill, and were followed by the King's troops, when a smart battle ensued. The 22nd, 43rd, and Anspach and Hyn regiments met with great loss. At 10 o'clock they began to bring the wounded men into town. All carts are taken up to bring them."

General Sullivan's timing proved prescient because Clinton's fleet appeared off Block Island

The SIEGE OF RHODE ISLAND, taken from Mr Brindley's House,
on the 25th of August, 1778.

Artist unknown
*The Siege of
Rhode Island, taken
from Mr. Brindley's
House, on the 25th of
August*, 1778
Engraving
Redwood Library
and Athenæum
Newport, Rhode Island
Gift of Hamilton Fish Webster
and Lina Post Webster
Webster.16

during the afternoon of August 29. Had he not pulled his troops to the northern end of the island, ready for debarkation to the mainland, the whole force would have been trapped. On the morning of August 30, it was agreed by the officers that nothing more could be done, and the withdrawal was put into action. A number of Americans pitched tents within sight of the enemy throughout the day to give the impression that they were digging in for an extended stay, while the remainder of the troops prepared for a night evacuation of stores, equipment, and men at Howland's Ferry. Pickets were placed to protect the action, and with darkness falling, the entire American force began to ferry to the mainland. The British, although quite near, did not discover their movements. The retreat took all night, and according to Sullivan's report to General Washington, "not a man was left behind, nor the smallest article lost. . . . The event has proved how timely my retreat took place, as one hundred sail of the enemy's ships arrived in the harbor the morning after the retreat." Fleet Greene reported: "Last night the Provincials retreated from Windmill Hill to the Main, undiscovered. This morning the ground was taken possession of by the King's troops. Since the retreat of the Provincials, the inhabitants of Portsmouth and Middletown are plundered. Some families are destitute of a bed to lie on."

The battle resulted in heavy casualties on both sides. S. G. Arnold reported that 211 Americans were killed or missing while 1,023 British and Hessian soldiers perished or were taken prisoner. Considering that the enemy troops were more experienced and better armed than the raw American militiamen, their successful repulse of the king's army was laudatory. Whether good leadership, valor on the part of the soldiers, or the willingness to fight harder for one's own soil tipped the balance is unknown. But Marquis de Lafayette was heard to remark that the Battle of Rhode Island "was the best fought action of the war."

Even though Sullivan and his officers failed to achieve their objective on Aquidneck Island and were forced to abandon the field, Congress nonetheless declared the Battle of Rhode Island a victory for the newly allied forces and formally voted thanks to the troops. At the same time, Sir Henry Clinton was highly critical of the way General Pigot prosecuted the war, declaring that the commander might have lost Newport had the Americans counterattacked on the night of August 29. Either way, no one was victorious, and the battle was soon filed away in memory as another missed opportunity to rout the British. Had the rebels won decisively, the War of Independence could have come to an end at Newport. Washington, who needed a miracle to relieve him from his own constant demands on the front, was disappointed: "If the garrison of that place, consisting of nearly 6000 men had been captured, as there was, in appearance at least, a hundred to one in favor of it, it would have given the finishing blow to the British pretensions of sovereignty over this country; and would, I am persuaded, have hastened the departure of the troops in New York as fast as their canvas wings could carry them away."

Weather, d'Estaing's stinginess, and the vagaries of armed conflict all contributed to the ultimate impasse at Newport. Yet the Battle of Rhode Island was significant because it marked the conclusion of any major fighting in the northern states; even though the English were to hold Newport for another year, nothing of value was accomplished and the Americans were able to bottle up British troops that could have been deadly in another arena. While the Continental Army was desperate for another conclusive victory, the political pressure on Clinton and his army for a resolution to the fighting was even more intense. British strategy was in shambles. With stalemate in New England and the mid-Atlantic states, Clinton, and thus Washington, shifted the axis of the Revolutionary War to the southern campaigns, in preparation for what would be the successful culmination achieved at Yorktown in 1781.

Descent to the Doldrums

Poor manhandled Newport, showing daily its decline into poverty and disrepair. Although spared from fiery destruction by the battling naval fleets, the town was fast losing the charm it so proudly displayed during the height of its Golden Age. The silversmiths, glass cutters, furniture makers, carpenters, and rum makers had by now mostly fled to the safety of the mainland. Tories who remained were sheltered by the British army, but were showing a drabber, more threadbare appearance. The majority of townspeople, now thoroughly supporting the cause of rebellion, fared far worse. Their cows were stolen, their houses torn down, their churches desecrated, their firewood denied them. With so many households disrupted, African slaves once sheltered by their masters were objects of British abuse. Anger at their British masters after two years of occupation was manifest, and growing. As they walked through the dilapidated streets of Newport, all they saw was red coats and destruction; their lives were in ruins, their harbor destitute, and their futures were looking bleak indeed. Poor Newport, home to the ravages of war.

After the Battle of Rhode Island, a dull routine set in. As much as the rebels wished their vanquishers away, that was not to be. Fearing an attack by d'Estaing after the repair of his fleet in Boston, the British reinforced Newport, bringing the total to over nine thousand men. Admiral Byron dropped anchor with his ships. General Pigot returned to England only to be replaced by the hated General Prescott, now free again after his dramatic abduction of the previous year. Prescott, it should be noted without surprise, was not fond of Newporters, and made life as hard as he could for them. Soldiers were idle and irksome; garrisons grumbled. Remnants of the Continental Army under General Sullivan still haunted the shores around Tiverton and Bristol, on guard in case of a British assault on Providence. But the energy, on both sides, seemed spent. A sort of melancholy hung in the autumn air, a palpable sense of boredom and frustration as weeks passed into months with little of consequence occurring. The *real* war had passed Newport by.

On October 31, Major Mackenzie recorded in his journal:

We are left at present in a Strange situation: Two of the three passages are entirely open to the Enemy. The winter advancing, & no provision made for the supplying the Garrison with firing. Only two frigates in this Station, so that we are a good deal exposed to the Enemys Naval force, and utterly unable to send a proper convoy with the vessels for wood to Long Island. No barracks provided, no materials to fit up any, nor any Straw for the troops either while in the field, or when they come into

A NEW NAVY

In June 1775, the Rhode Island General Assembly voted to inaugurate the first official navy in the colonies by commissioning two armed vessels, the *Katy* and the *Washington*, to guard against marauding British ships. Command was given to Abraham Whipple, the hero of the *Gaspee* incident. Because Rhode Island was so dependent on the sea, the Assembly next directed its representatives to Congress, Stephen Hopkins and Samuel Ward, to demand the creation of a Continental navy. New Englanders, particularly John Adams of Massachusetts, were heavily in favor of the measure, and in December Congress appointed Esek Hopkins of Providence, Stephen's younger brother, to the post of commodore. Esek took command of eight small ships in January 1776, and the United States Navy was born.

Esek, however, ran afoul of Congress when he countermanded its orders, performed poorly in his first skirmish with a Royal Navy vessel, and proved unpopular with his men. Congress censured him in August, just six weeks after the Declaration of Independence. Unlike his famous and accomplished brother, Esek's fate was star-crossed. Although he was humiliated by Congress, he was left in his post. Ordered to fit out and man two new naval ships in Providence, he was unable to fill his crew because navy wages were paltry compared to what sailors could earn from privateering. He was struggling there when the British invaded Newport in December 1776, thus trapping him and his ships at the northern end of Narragansett Bay. Congress suspended Hopkins in March 1777 and dismissed him from service the next year. Abraham Whipple (who was married to Hopkins's sister) fared better, at least until the end. He procured badly needed munitions in France, seized seven British merchant ships, and brought them to Boston as prizes (greatly enriching himself in the process), but was captured by the enemy in Charleston and spent the remainder of the war in prison. Only Captain John Paul Jones brought lasting fame to the fledgling United States Navy during the Revolution.

quarters. Indeed this Garrison appears on the whole, to have been very much neglected for some time past.

Fleet Greene in November 1778: "The great scarcity of fire-wood forces the people to leave the Island. No wood is allowed to be sold them. . . . The large Baptist meeting house is taken up for the Navy hospital. . . . Several hundred of sick men were this morning brought ashore from Byron's fleet, and carried to the Baptist meeting house. They die very fast. . . . No fire wood is allowed to be brought in from the country for the inhabitants, notwithstanding numbers of families are ready to perish for the want of that article. All the wharves are taken up for the fire-wood for the troops." And in these perilous times, nature refused to cooperate. In December, Arnold reports: "Another terrible storm, more severe than that which had disabled the contending squadrons in August, caused great disaster on sea and shore. The depth of the snow, and the intensity of the cold, was unparalleled in this vicinity. Sentinels were frozen at their posts, or stifled by the whirling snow, and so many Hessians perished for cold and exposure on that dreadful night in Newport, that this gale was long known as 'the Hessian storm.' " Fleet Greene said over fifty people died on one night alone.

On top of those accumulated woes, almost no one had any money: not the state, not the towns, not the common people. Supporting the militia had drained the treasury. Paper currency, issued by the General Assembly and the Continental Congress, had depreciated to virtual worthlessness. Silver coins were becoming a rarity. Rhode Island had the power of taxation, but there was almost nothing to tax any longer. In a plea for aid from the people of Connecticut, Governor William Greene wrote, "The most obdurate heart would relent to see old age and childhood, from comfortable circumstances reduced to the necessity of begging for a morsel of bread." Connecticut refused to help, and the same for Massachusetts, partly out of their own problems at home, partly out of spite for the long-hated Rhode Islanders. Two thousand former inhabitants of Aquidneck Island were scattered on the mainland, homeless and penniless, and the bulk of them had flocked to Providence, straining every inch of the fabric of society. Firewood was selling in Bristol for $40 per cord at a time when the average workman made $80 per month, if he was lucky. Charles Carroll writes: "The people were reduced to desperate straits. When Burgoyne was permitted to pass through Rhode Island to Newport on his way to embarkation [back to England], his route was laid out through open rural sections in order that he might not see the desolation prevailing in Rhode Island communities."

Throughout the winter and spring of 1779, these conditions prevailed and often worsened for

Newport. While its neighbors spurned Rhode Island's cry for help amid ruin, South Carolina delegates to Congress understood its plight and voted to relieve the state, a quarter of which had been under enemy control for over two years, of $50,000 on taxes due—a clear indication that the tiny state had borne more of the war's burden than other territories. General Sullivan was replaced by General Horatio Gates, of Saratoga fame, but the military conditions around Narragansett Bay were not altered. The British continued to embark on small-scale incursions along the coast to steal sheep and cows and lay waste to certain communities with a strong rebel base; American forces also made lightning raids on enemy fortifications and increased their privateering efforts in the bay and beyond Point Judith. In the end, little was accomplished by either side. The deadlock continued.

The Continental Navy, however, was asserting itself on the high seas. After an inauspicious beginning under Esek Hopkins, Congress was able to add a significant number of ships and able captains to its fleet, and the harassing of British merchant vessels soared to the point that London was becoming concerned. The Royal Navy was still spread precariously thin, unable to provide effective protection for the hundreds of supply ships plying the Atlantic and at the same time serve as cover for the land troops in battle. Burgoyne had learned the hard way that if battalions are too far inland and not supported by naval power, they are susceptible to capture. Yet the British now found themselves not even able to protect their garrisons near the ocean. Desperately needed supplies were being captured by the rebels, and English merchants were making their anger known in Parliament.

To make matters worse, the Admiralty had dispatched a new, but second-rate, commander to take charge in North America, while Admiral Byron maintained his position in the West Indies to protect those valuable island possessions, now that Spain had joined France in the fighting. Rear Admiral James Gambier was, in most seamen's opinion, a conventional thinker, unfit for leading his own ship, let alone the entire Royal Navy along the American coast. He was referred to as "an idiot" by a fellow flag officer and detested by his men. And, to add to the problem, Gambier and General Clinton, charged with developing a joint strategy for victory, barely spoke to each other. Later in 1779, when Admiral Marriot Arbuthnot was sent to take over from Gambier, the latter refused to relinquish his authority, thus setting up a power struggle that further compromised British plans. Clinton, stymied over the lack of support from his own navy, could do little but complain to London and throw up his arms in frustration. With the navy and army at loggerheads, almost nothing was accomplished except for the destruction of Castine, Maine, in July, that resulted in the largest naval loss for the Americans in the entire war.

At the same time, General Washington was suffering from mass desertions of his troops, who had not been paid by Congress for months. With his depleted forces, the commander-in-chief was not in any position to take on Clinton's army in the North; instead he had to use his cunning in order to avoid a decisive battle, while begging for more direct assistance from his ally. The French, alas, were far more focused on their sea struggle with Great Britain, and action in the Caribbean was higher on their priority list than abetting the Continental Army. Meanwhile, Savannah and Augusta had fallen to the British as their new strategy began to unfold, and for many months Washington agonized over a plan to liberate the southernmost territories. With the opportunity to end the conflict at Newport gone awry, Washington could envision no short-term solution and was fearful the war would now stagger on indefinitely.

By June 1779 Admiral d'Estaing, after wintering in the West Indies, had reappeared in American waters off Savannah to support troops trying to liberate the city and, again, he failed to deliver. General Clinton sent more troops to the Carolinas over the summer and now the focus of the war was almost completely on this flank, because of the perceived number of Loyalists residing there. Clinton believed that if he could isolate the South and create a firm base, he could then move northward with impunity. What he did not anticipate was the large number of rebel guerrillas who would make that dream impossible. The devotion to the Revolution was in fact far stronger in the South than the British had ever imagined.

At this juncture, Admiral Arbuthnot began to question Clinton about the strategic advantages of leaving so many men idle in Newport when d'Estaing or another French fleet could, with the British navy so strung out along the coast, sail in and take the headquarters in New York City. For Arbuthnot, the usefulness of Newport had reached its end. While the two men seemed to concur on few things, this time Clinton agreed with his obstinate fellow-officer: the town was no longer relevant. The plan to use Newport as a major base for action never really worked because Washington, except for the futile Battle of Rhode Island, was content to let the troops grow rusty there and keep them out of the larger conflict. In the big picture, the occupation of Aquidneck Island was another British blunder. On October 7, 1779, orders were issued jointly by Arbuthnot and Clinton to begin the evacuation of Newport and bring the garrison south.

"The Town is in Ruins"

On October 12, Fleet Greene noted in his diary, "Arrived, the refugee fleet from the eastward. The army and merchants are carrying their baggage as fast as possible. The whole town appears in one general confusion." A squadron of fifty-two transports had been sent into the harbor and for two weeks Newport witnessed the frenzied activity of cannon and stores being loaded on board, barracks cleared out, and wanton destruction of property. In his concluding entry, Greene informs us: "The evacuation of the town took place on the 25th October 1779; when they marched through the town in solid columns, into the Neck, and embarked on board their ships and sailed for New York at 8 o'clock in the evening." Finally, the British were gone. But not before revenge was taken one last time.

Two years and ten and a half months had passed since the imperial invader had descended on Newport. Now the town was a shell. During the two-week packing-up period, General Prescott had turned his nearly six thousand men loose. First, the lighthouse at Beaver Tail on Conanicut was burned, then the wharves in Newport harbor, culminating with the destruction of Long Wharf, the very heart of the town's commerce. Another 160 houses were pulled down and put to the torch. Wells were filled with dirt and debris. Church bells were stolen (except Trinity's). Lastly, barracks at today's Fort Adams were destroyed just before the exodus. Johann Dohla, a Hessian soldier stationed on the island, kept a diary of his adventures. On the day of departure he wrote:

> All troops were hastily embarked. Newport and all of Rhode Island [Aquidneck], and Conanicut, was completely vacated. . . . There were also many merchants and inhabitants from the island, with all their possessions on the ship, who wanted to sail to New York also. Some days before our departure, all garden produce and fruits of the fields were turned in. We therefore received much

fresh meat and on some days had a surplus of food and drink. On our march out of Newport all the houses were locked, and it was on the strictest orders of General Prescott that no inhabitants, and especially no females, permitted themselves to be seen at any window or on the street, and should anyone show themselves, those who were on patrol were ordered to fire at them immediately. Therefore, in Newport it appeared as if the entire city had died.

The Hessian was not far from the truth. Between forty-five and fifty Tory families, mostly wealthy and prominent, left Newport forever along with the stolen town records, which were largely destroyed when the ship carrying them sank off Hell Gate in New York. Six months later, they were retrieved and the remaining documents were returned to Newport years later. Not many of the pages survived their watery grave. Estimates differ, but it is generally agreed that between 300 and 500 houses and public buildings (out of the 1,100 standing before the war) had been reduced to rubble by the British. Not a single tree stood within five miles of the harbor, and precious few were to be found intact anywhere else on the island. Property damage was later set, conservatively, at about $500,000. William Ellery, a signer of the Declaration of Independence, whose properties were confiscated and largely ruined by the British, returned to town and wrote that Newport is "a barren city, with shuttered houses, a pillaged library, books burned, and commerce practically at a standstill."

Months later, the Reverend Ezra Stiles, now President of Yale College, returned to his beloved Newport to view the destruction and visit with members of his old congregation for a few days. In his diary, he committed on May 31, 1780:

> I took a melancholy farewell, & left Newport on return for New Haven. About three hundred Dwellinghouses I judge have been destroyed in Newport. The Town is in Ruins. But with Nehemiah I could prefer the very dust of Zion to the Gardens of Persia, and the broken Walls of Jerusalem to the Palaces of Sushan. I rode over the Isld and found the beautiful Rows of Trees which lined the Roads, with sundry Coppices or Groves & Orchards cut down and lain waste; but the natural Beauties of the Place still remain. And I doubt not the place will be rebuilt & excede its former splendor.

The good Doctor Stiles would, in time, be proven correct.

Within hours of the British evacuation, American soldiers, who had been watching the withdrawal from Little Compton and other points on the mainland, arrived from Tiverton to secure Newport. The army found a populace eager to embrace them, relieved that their plight had eased, but distressed over what their future would hold in their beleaguered, reduced town. With the commercial harbor so badly damaged and filled with the wrecks of the enemy fleet, navigation was nearly impossible for the immediate future. But the more crucial issue was that, even if the docks had been untouched, there was next to nothing—no goods, no animals—to export. Newport was in a subsistence mode: rum making, the engine of the former economy, was only a memory. There was no molasses from the West Indies, nor would there be as long as the war dragged on. There was little furniture making, nothing to send to the ports of the world; nor could the inhabitants resume making the lucrative spermaceti candles because whaling was at a standstill. Some merchants were able to continue business, but at a greatly reduced level. It was as if Newport had reverted to the days of a century before, when it was struggling to make its mark on a wider audience. Only now, that original optimism and commercial drive had vanished along with the wharves.

With the island's trees almost totally destroyed, there was little timber to rebuild the town, nor was there a great impetus given the population depletion. Hundreds of dwellings stood empty, awaiting the return of those who had fled to the mainland. While a good number of people did trickle back and reclaim their former lives, the majority stayed put in their new accommodations. The General Assembly decreed that houses and other property of Tories who embarked with the British forces were to be confiscated by the state and used as compensation for those who had lost the most. In the end, it was of little help. Newport was now eclipsed by Providence, never again to challenge its old rival in the commercial realm. The town had been traumatized in so many ways that a doleful specter pervaded the atmosphere.

Newporters had their freedom, but little else of value. Yet they were stoic and determined to move ahead. After the initial euphoria of being free of oppression, they began to re-establish their lives to fit the prevailing conditions. Ferry service to Jamestown was restored, as well as to the mainland. Some wharves were hastily repaired for unloading much-needed firewood as well as for use by a few privateer vessels. After the long hiatus, town meetings resumed and deputies to the General Assembly elected; known Tories were excluded from taking part in any civic positions. Then the winter of 1779–1780 descended, bringing more desolation and despair. Temperatures dropped to record lows, and for five weeks Narragansett Bay was frozen over with ice thick enough that one could walk from Newport to Conanicut Island, an unheard-of condition. The price of firewood soared, food was scarce and exorbitantly expensive, and the citizens of Newport kept to their frigid houses as activity in town came to a standstill. When would their lives ever return to a semblance of normalcy? When would the bad luck end?

Not before the extended occupation by yet another foreign army.

The French Connection
Throughout the spring of 1780, General Washington, although outwardly calm and dignified, was close to despondency; his soldiers deserted by the hundreds as wages continued to be withheld, because of Congress's inability to collect sufficient taxes from the states, while Clinton's ranks were being reinforced by new men. Then on May 12, Charleston, with a force of 5,500 Americans, was surrounded by Lord Cornwallis and had no option but surrender. It was the most devastating defeat of the war for the Americans. The British now effectively controlled the South. And Congress again cajoled the thirteen states to send more men and materiel to lighten Washington's heavy load.

The Marquis de Lafayette had returned to France after the Battle of Rhode Island to speed up delivery of more men and ships to aid the Americans, whose predicament was magnified by the absence of the forces promised to Benjamin Franklin in 1778. The embarrassment over Admiral d'Estaing's failures spurred him on, and Lafayette returned in early spring with the news that a large contingent of soldiers and a well-equipped fleet were on the way, information that gave Washington heart. Not long after, General Clinton, through his network of spies, learned of the French intentions, although he had no idea where they would strike first upon arriving in America. Ever mindful of his increasingly spread-out position on land, Clinton became alarmed over how exposed he was. The American traitor Benedict Arnold, then in the midst of conspiring to turn West Point over to the enemy, privately informed the English that his sources indicated Newport would be the initial destination, but Clinton for some reason dismissed that intelligence.

In early June 1780, an advance ship from France, *Hermione*, put into Newport after a battle with the British off Point Judith. After tending to the wounded, the crew began preparations for the arrival of the larger force. Congress ordered that food and horses be sent to the town to feed the men, and the French sailors began organizing the harbor, preparing hospitals, and repairing warehouses. Their main task was to raise the many British ships sunk there, so French vessels could safely navigate close to Newport's center. On July 10, 1780, the eagerly anticipated French fleet of seven ships of the line, two frigates, and thirty-five transports commanded by Admiral Chevalier de Ternay appeared off Point Judith. The fleet carried some six thousand soldiers—only half of the number promised because the French Navy could not muster enough transport ships at the time—under the command of the comte de Rochambeau, one of France's most illustrious generals.

Rochambeau would prove to be the linchpin, the savior Washington had been awaiting since the Revolution began. While Lafayette was indispensable to the American general, he was young and did not command the reverence of his war-hardened superior. Jean-Baptiste Donatien de Vimeur, comte de Rochambeau, was born into a noble family in Vendôme, in the rolling Loire Valley. He had distinguished himself repeatedly in France's numerous battles and was a highly respected fifty-five-year-old at the time he landed in Newport. He was famous for his insistence on strict discipline and order among his troops, was considered prudent in the use of his men, and, above all, had grown wise in warfare. He commanded respect and deference throughout the French Army because of his judgment and restraint. Despite the great disappointment in Admiral d'Estaing's actions, or lack thereof, Rochambeau, because of his calm authority, was able to quickly reassure the suspicious American military and populace and take the alliance to a new level of cooperation.

When the French landed at Newport on July 11, no one came out to greet the august general, and a lesser man would have burned at the snub. One reason for the lack of pomp was that the town simply did not expect them; another was the ingrained suspicion of yet *another* foreign army coming into their midst, even if they were to prove to be America's liberators. Newporters were exhausted and traumatized. Rochambeau had troubles too; over nine hundred of his men were suffering from scurvy and he had to get them off his ships and into hospitals. Rochambeau dealt with it all by being gracious and charming to those who eventually emerged from their homes. But it was his unexpected promise to pay rent for all houses occupied, as well as to pay for all provisions—not in nearly worthless paper bills but with silver and gold coin—that won the day. The citizens were at first incredulous that they were to be treated fairly, but when it sunk in that the French might truly be their redeemers, wariness turned to joy. His message delivered, the general retired to his ship for the night.

The next day, the reception of the French was ecstatic. Newport recovered from its lack of hospitality

Attributed to
Jean Baptiste Louis
Le Paon
Comte de Rochambeau,
c. 1785
Oil on canvas
The Anne S. K. Brown
Military Collection
at Brown University
Providence, Rhode Island
Courtesy of the
John Nicholas Brown Center
Providence, Rhode Island

and filled the streets to greet its allies. Although still circumspect, the citizens went to great lengths, even in their strained condition, to demonstrate thanks and support. That night, according to Ezra Stiles, "Newport was beautifully illuminated and 13 grand Rockets were fired in the Front of the State House. . . . The Bell rang at Newport till after Midnight . . . the Whigs put 13 Lights in the Windows, the Tories or doubtfuls 4 or 6." Citizens too poor to burn candles in their windows were provided for by the Town Council. Many Quakers, who had an aversion to greeting any armed force, placed no lights in their windows; in retaliation, other locals threw rocks through their thin glass outlooks. Regardless of its condition, Newport was intent on welcoming the French with a modicum of style and élan.

When the troops disembarked the following morning at what is now King Park along Wellington Avenue after a 13-gun salute from the ships, they were organized and professional. French and American quartermasters set up a billeting arrangement that would bring the least disruption to the town, and, as the weather was good, most of the men lived in tented camps along today's Bellevue Avenue, Ocean Drive, and at Castle Hill during the first few months. Later, they would be moved into houses that had been repaired by locals but paid for by the French. Rochambeau, apart from his military prowess, was also frugal: he determined it would cost far less to fix up the dilapidated houses in Newport, Bristol, and Warren than to build new barracks from wood that had to be transported from afar. As it was, he spent the equivalent of about $80,000 for the billet, a sum that Newport could never have afforded. Thus the French occupation was a boon to the ailing town. Evidence suggests that most officers staying in town did not pay rent, but were guests of the inhabitants; soldiers in the repaired dwellings did render rent money.

The general, accompanied by his son, the vicomte de Rochambeau, chose Vernon House, which stands on the corner of Clarke and Mary streets, as his headquarters. William Vernon, the owner, then serving as the president of the Eastern Navy Board in Boston, was open to Rochambeau's use of his house, and was reimbursed nearly $500 for damages at the end of his visit. At some point, Rochambeau built a large club room, or *salon*, for his officers (often called his ballroom) in the garden of Vernon House. The general's aides-de-camp, almost exclusively from the French nobility, took rooms in nearby dwellings, but they gathered daily with their commander to plot strategy and oversee administration. Admiral de Ternay, already suffering from an illness that would take his life in December, set up his quarters in the house of former deputy governor Joseph Wanton, Jr., now known as the Hunter House, on the Point; he was buried at Trinity Church after a huge funeral procession through town. The Brigadier de Choisy stayed in the home of Jacob Rodriguez Rivera on Bridge Street. Another eminent officer, Major General Chevalier de Chastellux, took over the charming Mawdsley House at 228 Spring Street. Other noble aides were quartered with ranking Newport families such as the Malbones, Wards, Robinsons, Hazards, and Coggeshalls.

So methodical and organized were the French that within days every soldier was secure in a house or tent, his equipment and uniform sparkling clean. After the terror of the rampaging British and Hessians, townspeople could barely believe their eyes. One writer asserted, "Throughout the Newport stay the troops behaved in a remarkably orderly fashion. Visitors to their camp were amazed to note that they did not even pluck the apples hanging over their tents until their officials had bought and paid for them. There were no incidents; no tavern brawls; no girls raped. They were an asset to the community, not a plague." Foraging companies were sent into the wilderness to gather provisions and prepare for winter. To combat boredom and create cohesion, the troops were drilled daily; while not in training, they were rebuilding fortifications, constructing new ones, and mounting guns, because word that another British fleet was on the way to Newport had reached Rochambeau. Ever careful, the general made preparations for nearly every contingency, even though he was operating in a strange and formidable environment.

When a larger British fleet under Admiral Arbuthnot blockaded the French weeks later, Rochambeau feigned nonchalance but for safety's sake urgently requested a reinforcement of 1,500 Rhode Island and Massachusetts militia; his instincts told him the enemy would never dare enter Narragansett Bay to take on his forces. He was worried, but he turned out to be right. After ten days of hovering around Point Judith, the British disappeared. In fact, General Clinton was ready to invade Newport with a formidable army and had his men assembled on Long Island in preparation. But the bungled communications and increasing hostility between him and Arbuthnot created yet another fiasco; Clinton was forced to abandon his plans and return, angrily, to headquarters. When Washington made a small-scale move on New York, Clinton was unprepared, and although no real harm was done, the French now viewed the American general in a more favorable light as a man of action. Clinton rued his missed chance to take on Newport because the French lodgment there created a new psychological advantage for the rebels. Clinton wrote to London, "It has revived a dying cause. Washington has raised an army, and the whole continent seems alive upon it."

Lafayette arrived on July 25 to bring thanks and respects from General Washington, and to arrange for a face-to-face meeting between the two commanders. The French were in America—now what were they to *do*? Washington's army was situated around White Plains and the general badly wanted to launch a full-scale joint attack on the British in New York City. When Rochambeau and Washington met at the Wadsworth House in Hartford in September, the American pled his case to the older and far more experienced French officer. While tempted to wage the battle, Rochambeau demurred, saying that he needed the other six thousand soldiers who were supposedly on their way to Newport in order to prosecute the action successfully. Although Washington was officially commander-in-chief of the combined army and badly in need of a victory to motivate his disheartened troops and prove his leadership to Congress, he reluctantly realized Rochambeau was probably correct in his judgment, and acquiesced. Then news came that Admiral Rodney had blockaded Newport again, and that ended any idea of action for the present time. The two men agreed to use the autumn and winter to plan a concerted spring campaign against Clinton's forces in New York. In the meantime, Rochambeau sent his son back to Paris to speed the arrival of more men and money. He wanted to fight, but he was determined to do the job professionally. For the disappointed Washington, although bolstered by his new allies, another season had come to naught.

In Newport, the presence of the large foreign contingent led to new levels of the town's already well-known tradition of acceptance. The French, of course, were mostly Roman Catholic, a religion vilified and feared in nearly every colony except Maryland since the Pilgrims had landed in 1620. Now the town was teeming with papists, and Newport hardly blinked. The enormous goodwill created by Rochambeau's control of his men was certainly part of the reason the troops were welcomed and feted as they were, but it is difficult to imagine any other New England community (with the exception of Providence) that would have embraced these hated so-called heretics as graciously as Newport did. For the entire year that the French cohabited with the townsfolk, there are only fleeting hints of argument or dissension over religious beliefs.

Newport's tolerance for openness in theology again exhibited the profound and indelible influence of John Clarke's 1663 Charter.

The officers had plenty of time on their hands and indulged in ice skating, sleighing, and fox hunting as diversions. The chevalier de Chastellux, taking over the Mawdsley House, chose to present his *petits soupers* for French and American guests. Ezra Stiles wrote of his experience: "Dined at Gen. de Chastellux in splendid manner on 35 dishes. He is a capital Literary Character, a Member of the French Academy. He is the glory of the Army." The sophistication of the French officers, so accustomed to glittering court life at Versailles or Paris society, astounded Newporters. Their knowledge of classical literature, precision with music, and scientific inquiry rubbed off on many an inhabitant.

Other advantages of the French occupation accrued to the town. Over the autumn and winter months, officers gave a number of balls and dinners and got to know the famous belles of Newport. It is clear from the numerous reminiscences left by these men that they were quite smitten by the young women, and most likely the emotion was returned. These noble gentlemen, in their handsome multi-colored uniforms and cocked hats, displayed a disciplined urbanity and brought a new and welcome gaiety to the town. The names of Polly Lawton, Margaret and Mary Champlin, Mehetable Redwood, the misses Hunter and the misses Ellery, are etched with longing by several of the men who did not forget their encounters with these women years later. One description will suffice. Louis, baron de Closen, one of Rochambeau's aides, was very busy flirting with these women during this period. He reflected,

> The fair sex is really quite extraordinary as to their charm and kindness. Nature has vouchsafed the greatest possible beauty of feature, their complexion is white and clear, their hands and feet are as a rule small, but their teeth are inferior, for which the great amount of tea which they drink may be responsible. One rarely sees a woman with a bad figure. Their style of dress and the way of arranging their hair is quite English. Nevertheless, French fashions are not unknown to them and one feels sure that the visit of the French army will have its good influence upon them in this respect.

Washington in Newport

The winter of 1780–1781 was not a happy time for George Washington. A large portion of his army mutinied and walked out of camps at White Plains, New Jersey, and Pennsylvania. Congress was deeply in debt and could not afford to pay the soldiers, and at the same time was making heavy demands on the general for a victorious engagement against the enemy. Yet inaction and indecision reigned in both the French and American camps. Dispatches and letters went back and forth, strategies were considered and dismissed, possible openings explored. The French navy was still seriously out-gunned and, until another huge gale knocked three British ships of the line out of commission in January, was unable to move out of Newport harbor. Still, nothing could be decided. Finally, it became apparent that another face-to-face meeting was required to break the logjam, and a disheartened Washington rode by horseback to Newport in early March.

Washington and his party were ferried from Conanicut to the flagship *Duc de Bourgogne*, where Rochambeau greeted him and conferred upon him the office of Maréchal de France, an honor that formally made Washington Rochambeau's superior. Then the two generals proceeded into Newport. Louis-Alexandre Berthier, an aide-de-camp to Rochambeau and later a field marshal under Napoleon, was present when the men landed and confided to his journal one of the finest first-hand accounts available.

> All the generals were assembled. He then went ashore where all the general staff of the army received him on the slip to the accompaniment of the noise of cannon from the French batteries. All the troops were under arms, forming a huge parade, lining the route on both sides of the street from the slip to his quarters. Each general saluted him at the head of his division. Similarly, M. le comte de Rochambeau, who preceded him along with his whole staff, saluted him at the head of the senior regiment. The general passed through the massed soldiers where the nobility of his stature and of his face, the imprint of all his virtues, inspired in everyone the affection and the respect due him, increasing, if that were possible, the high opinion which we had of his rare quality.
>
> He dined at General Rochambeau's. That night he was driven through the town which was everywhere illuminated. All the people hurried to march in front of him with torches and with marks of genuine joy.

Washington was Rochambeau's guest at Vernon House, where they spent long hours conferring, laying out plans and various contingencies. Both generals felt enormous pressure to take the war to the British. Lafayette and an American army were fighting in Virginia, and one suggestion was to proceed there immediately. Emotionally, Washington favored the idea because the now-hated American traitor Benedict Arnold was commanding 1,500 British soldiers there, wreaking havoc. Washington felt so utterly betrayed by Arnold that he personally wanted to hunt him down. Now that the French had the momentary ability to freely leave Newport harbor, it was decided to send the fleet to the Chesapeake to aid Lafayette. What to do with the allied armies was a thornier question. While Washington still advocated an attack on Clinton in New York, a possible Virginia operation was a more prudent maneuver—*if* the French navy would cooperate, and that was by no means assured; Rochambeau could lobby the navy, but he could not command it. In the end, no real decisions came out of the Newport meetings other than a temporary fleet movement to Virginia, which proved to be inconclusive.

Some writers have contended that Washington and Rochambeau outlined the Yorktown campaign at Vernon House, but that would have been nearly impossible. First, Lord Cornwallis was still deep in Carolina territory in March, pursued by General Nathanael Greene, and no one knew where he was headed next. Second, Rochambeau's son had not yet returned from Versailles with the devastating news that King Louis XVI would not be sending the promised six thousand additional troops Rochambeau was depending upon; the monarch was offering more money and would make Admiral de Grasse's huge fleet available, but no new men. That information, which the Frenchman received before he met again with Washington in Wethersfield, Connecticut, in May, totally changed his outlook on what options were feasible.

Meanwhile, the merriment continued in Newport among battle preparations. As a Maréchal de France, Washington was now due great respect. Everywhere he went, he was followed by adoring crowds.

GENERAL WASHINGTON *is escorted by the* COUNT *de* ROCHAMBEAU *to the* ALLIED HEADQUARTERS *at the* VERNON HOUSE, NEWPORT, RHODE ISLAND, MARCH 6, 1781.

Never had the young country had such a hero. The night after he arrived, Rochambeau hosted a large dinner ball in the American's honor, most likely at Mrs. Crowley's Assembly Room, which stood at the corner of Church and Thames streets. The many belles of Newport along with the cream of the French officer corps were present. In an oft-told tale, we learn that after supper, Washington, as the guest of honor and ranking soldier, was asked to choose a partner to begin the evening of dancing. Looking around the brilliantly decorated room, he picked Miss Peggy Champlin, a celebrated Newport beauty and a favorite of the Frenchmen. Social custom demanded that she select the opening music, and with her hand in General Washington's, she chose the popular piece, "A Successful Campaign." As the musicians were beginning to play, a number of French officers arose, plucked the instruments from their hands, and accompanied the general and Miss Champlin as they inaugurated the night's festivities.

Washington and his men met with their French counterparts for the next several days to continue military discussions and attend numerous social events and gala dinners. He departed Newport on March 13 for New Windsor with another 13-gun salute from his allies. Rochambeau, as a courtesy, rode with Washington most of the way to Providence. It is clear from personal letters and the journals of others that the two generals enjoyed and respected each other. Rochambeau, older, noble, war-hardened, and sympathetic to the American cause, was a source of strength for Washington; he graciously accepted the superior command position conferred upon Washington and made the task of defeating the British his main priority. In the same vein, Washington was universally beloved by his army and their allies. Regardless of the hardships placed on him since the war's onset, Washington never buckled under the strain; he remained almost regal in his bearing and dealings with others. America desperately needed a man of strength and tact to honor in its time of travail, and in George Washington it found its answer. The prince de Broglie, one of the keenest observers of life and men in America, wrote of the general that "in his private conduct he preserves that polite and attentive good breeding which satisfies everybody and offends no one. He is a foe to ostentation and to vain-glory."

Yorktown

Although no one could have predicted it, the final battle of the American Revolution was only five months away when Washington and Rochambeau met at Wethersfield in late May 1781 to plan the summer campaigns. After so many years of frustration, defeat, waiting, and begging for support, Washington could not have conceived that so swift and decisive a victory might lie so soon in the future. As the two generals laid out strategies, the holding back of two regiments from France appeared to compromise the prospects of future engagements with Clinton's well-fortified army around New York. Rochambeau lobbied for an excursion against Virginia, but could not endorse it unless he had support of the French fleet under Admiral comte de Grasse, then in the West Indies. Spirits were not high when Washington and Rochambeau agreed that, given the current circumstances and without knowledge of when the French fleet might arrive off American waters, New York was the only feasible target for the moment.

Rochambeau returned to Newport and readied his army for departure. While the fleet, under its new commander, Admiral de Barras, was to maintain its position in Newport in readiness to reinforce de Grasse, the army was to join Washington's forces at Dobbs Ferry along the Hudson River. On June 10, after numerous ceremonial dinners and doubtless sad farewells to the beautiful belles of the town, Rochambeau's army broke camp and began the month-long march south. After nearly a year of inactivity, the soldiers were finally on the move, and the town they left behind was in better shape than when they had arrived. Hundreds of houses had been repaired to some extent, fortifications had been improved, and the harbor was now mostly clear of sunken ships. Although it was nowhere near the level it had enjoyed before the British invasion, Newport had begun to see a glimmer of prosperity with the influx of so much French coin.

The allied army was close to ten thousand men, yet when Washington assaulted the defenses around New York, he found them better prepared than his intelligence had suggested. With the British army divided into three major arenas—Carolina, Chesapeake, and New York—Clinton was protecting his headquarters like a cornered man. Without naval backup, Washington was again stymied in launching an all-out siege. There was an air of frustration enveloping the Franco-American camp, a renewed sense that *nothing* would break the deadlock. Then, on August 15, Rochambeau received the dispatch he had been waiting months to receive: Admiral de Grasse's formidable fleet was headed to Chesapeake Bay. The French general sent word to Newport for de Barras's ships to sail as soon as possible. They did not know it, but they were setting off from Narragansett Bay for the decisive engagement of the Revolutionary War, the Battle of the Virginia Capes.

Lord Cornwallis had headed into Virginia with the idea that he could cut off the north-south lines of the Americans by joining up with Benedict Arnold's small but lethal force. The British general reasoned that he would either be successful in his efforts or be evacuated by what he still believed (quite wrongly) to be a superior Royal Navy. He had no idea that de Grasse was on his way, and thus chose probably the worst strategic position possible: a peninsula between the York and James rivers. After harrying Williamsburg and being pursued by Lafayette's regiment, he marched his men farther east to Yorktown and prepared fortifications, firmly believing that Clinton was in the process of reinforcing him from New York. At the same time, the British fleet was then being taken over by Admiral Thomas Graves, reputedly of average ability and intellect—a poor combination of talents for a man about to fight one of the most significant sea battles in history.

By late September, all the Franco-American forces had arrived at Yorktown. Prayer would not save Clinton. On September 5, Admiral Graves, with nineteen ships of the line, went up against the de Grasse fleet of twenty-four ships of the line in the Battle of the Virginia Capes. Neither side could claim total victory, but the French in fact prevailed because they held control of Chesapeake Bay and therefore Graves could not enter to lend aid to Cornwallis. Graves had let several opportunities pass by to slip in and reinforce Cornwallis but, in the words of one naval historian, was "paralyzed by indecision." When Admiral de Barras arrived with his fleet from Newport, Graves knew he was defeated. Once again, terrible communications and timid leadership had sunk British attempts to retain its former colonies. Graves withdrew and returned to New York for repairs and an unpleasant interview with General Clinton who, by then, knew the conflict was as good as over.

The combination of the Rochambeau-Washington battalions, three thousand men from the fleet of the comte de Grasse, and Virginia militia brought the allied force to nearly sixteen thousand. Cornwallis had only half that number. Battle was joined in the first week of October, and it was a classic eighteenth-century-style blockade with heavy cannon. Washington wisely handed over command of the field to Rochambeau, who had vast experience: he had taken part in fourteen sieges in European wars. Although the outcome was never in doubt after the Royal Navy departed, Cornwallis held out for two weeks under blistering attack. On October 17, four years to the day after Burgoyne's defeat at Saratoga, the white flag appeared above Cornwallis's redoubt and the British general asked for terms of capitulation. The next day, military action was suspended, and on October 19, 1781, Cornwallis formally surrendered. For hours, British soldiers emerged from their trenches to stack their firearms in front of French and American officers, accompanied by their band playing the tune "The World Turned Upside Down." In a fine stroke of military decorum, when British General Charles O'Hara attempted to hand over his sword to Rochambeau, the diplomatic French general gestured that it be given to George Washington, standing beside him. Cornwallis had declined to make the surrender in person, so Washington, not wishing to take the sword from an inferior officer, demanded that the instrument of capitulation be given to his second-in-command Major General Benjamin Lincoln. Thus the British gave up the field, but to the upstart rebellious Americans, not their ancient Gallic enemy.

Five years and four months after the Declaration of Independence had been signed by a group of resolute but nervous patriots, the War of Independence had been won.

Picking Up the Pieces

A republic was born. The infant United States of America, free of monarchy and the centuries-old conventions of the Old World, set about to create a literal New World. The country was now a sovereign nation, beholden to no one, open to everyone. At the time of the Treaty of Paris, Enlightenment ideals of equal justice, equal opportunity, and equal responsibility to the government of the people were widely discussed and accepted, and not only by the political and social elite. America conceived of itself as original and innovative; it dared turn conventional wisdom on its head. The struggle against King George III had been more than ridding itself of tyrannical rule and arbitrary governance; it was a triumphal proclamation that personal liberty and religious freedom were the order of the day. America invented the future.

Born in opposition to the English Crown in 1639 and borne by defiance ever since, Newport celebrated the resounding victory at Yorktown with gusto. And two years later, when news of the official birth of the nation was received from Paris, the townspeople took to the streets. The lively experiment in religious freedom that Newporters had struggled for so long to protect and maintain would, in a few short years, become the law of the whole country under the Bill of Rights. Rhode Islanders were vindicated. They had been right, from the beginning, and now the rest of America was catching up. Even the restriction in Rhode Island against Roman Catholics (clearly contravening the dictates of Roger Williams and the 1663 Charter) would be repealed shortly (1783), due mostly to the French role in helping America win the Revolution. Jews and other non-Christians had to wait until 1798 to gain full citizenship.

In the political sphere, Newport and Rhode Island had also been ahead of the curve for nearly a century. Republicanism, with the power of the government vested not in an omnipotent monarch but in the people themselves, was tomorrow's news, the foundation of the emerging nation. Equality (as startling a concept then as religious freedom had been the century before) was the rallying cry. Freedom was the watchword. All of this was familiar to Rhode Island because its inhabitants had been living in the freest, most democratic, most egalitarian of all the colonies. And their very independence and stubbornness would be heartily demonstrated (and not widely appreciated) as the thirteen states spent the next years groping toward a unifying definition of the United States.

For most Americans, the decade between Yorktown and Rhode Island's ratification of the Constitution was an exciting, optimistic, proud era. Free to determine their own future, common people and the perceived elite joined the political debate swirling around them, assuming their responsibilities as citizens. The multitude of voices, opinions, desires, and complaints all added to the crescendo of discourse. Republicanism had never in world history been attempted on a canvas as broad as America and conservatives were doubtful it could ever succeed. But the prevailing voices (Jefferson, Madison, Hamilton) encouraged the attempt, and the country, with little to lose in the radical experiment, eagerly followed suit. Why not, thought the man toiling on his farm or in his shop, aspiring to a better life for himself and his family; why not taste the fruits of freedom and see where it takes us? That attitude was very familiar to Newporters.

Yet, throughout the 1780s, Rhode Island displayed a deep suspicion of *any* outside authority, regardless of how benevolent, and that attitude hampered its relations with its sister states. The basic questions were: How different was Congress going to be from Parliament? Who was to lead this new country? Quick to rebel against anyone wanting to tamper with the Charter privileges of 1663, Rhode Islanders, and particularly those in Newport, saw little advantage in reinventing the wheel. They already lived under unprecedented freedoms and didn't give much thought to the intense debates going on at the Constitutional Convention in Philadelphia. These citizens were different in temperament from their neighbors, and had been since Roger Williams formed the colony. If Rhode Island was divisive and fractious in its party politics, so be it—what they had, in their small geography, was essentially a family feud. So, as all the other states labored to write their separate constitutions for themselves (John Adams wrote a splendid one for Massachusetts; likewise

Benjamin Franklin in Pennsylvania), leaders in Rhode Island were perfectly content to simply strike the word *Charter* from John Clarke's brilliant political document and substitute the word *Constitution*. Why, they reasoned, alter what was near to perfection? In a long-simmering debate over which state had produced the first, or the best, constitution, most people fail to recognize that in spirit if not in fact, Rhode Island predated all the others by nearly 120 years. The liberties granted to Rhode Island by Charles II had not only stood the test of time, they would also lay the foundation for most of the basic privileges afforded Americans under the United States Constitution and the Bill of Rights.

The whinny of a tired horse, the clatter of cartwheels rolling over battered cobblestones, decrepit store signs hanging limp along Thames Street. The nearly empty harbor. Crude graffiti covering the walls of the Redwood Library. The ramshackle State House, the unkempt Parade, and desecrated churches. The remains of Long Wharf being surreptitiously surrendered to the sea. The young mother searching for bread or milk, the former soldier limping on his cane along Water Street. Shattered shops and abandoned homes. Newport, circa 1785—and beyond. For decades.

The town was broken. From being one of the five most vigorous cities of colonial times, it had been brought to the condition of a second-rate enclave, depressed in comparison to its former competitors. The British had devastated Newport, and for nearly fifty years it struggled to redefine itself. Antoinette Downing, in *The Architectural Heritage of Newport, Rhode Island*, carefully recorded the few new buildings erected between 1785 and 1830, and the operative word is *few*. Lacking the essential ingredients for growth—money, materials, and manpower—Newport, proud even in its penury, stagnated and withdrew from the spirit of buoyancy that spread across the United States after the Treaty of Paris. The town was tattered and torn.

Four descriptions, written decades apart, paint a picture of Newport after the Revolution. The first, written by Francisco Miranda, a native of Venezuela (and years later, the first independent leader after its split from Spain) then traveling through America, dates from 1784 when he spent some weeks in town. He describes the natural beauty of Aquidneck Island and the social delights of having teas and suppers with the Misses Peggy Champlin and Nancy Hunter. Interestingly, he also notes the large number of South Carolinians in Newport for health reasons; war changed the architecture of Newport, but not the radiant climate, and Southerners returned to the island immediately after the Treaty of Paris to escape fever. Then Miranda concludes his diary entry:

> The women in their majority are very good looking, affable and civil and dress with good taste; the men boorish, even unsociable, negligent in their dress and manners and generally very uneducated. The buildings and houses of decent appearance I don't think are more than three dozen in all the town, the rest are hovels and small shops. In Main Street [Thames] which is the principal one of the city (it is about a mile long) and in reality there is no other, there are about three stores which deserve the name of such, the rest are small booths; all the goods which they and the stores contain I should say could be bought for 30,000 pesos. It is a pity that such a beautiful location and one so advantageous to commerce should be in such a miserable and decadent state.

The second prospect, written by Brissot de Warville while in exile from his native France, was published in *New Travels in the United States of America, Performed in 1788*:

> Since the peace everything is changed, the reign of solitude is only interrupted by groups of idle men standing with folded arms at the corners of the streets, houses falling to ruin, miserable shops which present nothing but a few coarse stuffs or baskets of apples, and other articles of little value; grass growing in the public square in front of the court of justice, rags stuffed in the windows. . . . Everything announces misery. But in the midst of these disorders you hear nothing of robberies, of murders, or of mendacity, for the poor do not degrade themselves so as to abjure ideas of equity and shame. The Rhode Islander does not beg and he does not steal.

The third was written by another Frenchman, the duc de la Rochefoucauld-Liancourt, a decade later. The duke was disheartened by the scene:

> Before the war there were many opulent inhabitants on Rhode Island, at present only the ruins of their houses, and traces of their former inclosures can be seen. The houses are either desolate or are inhabited by people who, on account of the smallness of their capitals, their dislike to labor, and many other reasons, are much inferior in condition to the people of other parts of New England.

The final portrayal is perhaps the saddest. In a letter from the Newport native Dr. Benjamin Waterhouse to his old friend Thomas Jefferson on September 14, 1822, Waterhouse makes the following lament—but note the date. Thirty-three years had passed since the British evacuated and still:

> I have seen not a little of other countries, but I never saw any Island that unites finer views, rendered pleasant by variety of hill & vale, rocks, reefs, beaches, Islands & perennial ponds than this. . . . Before the discovery of our mineral springs, Rh. Island was in one view the Bath of the American world. . . . This and the Redwood Library gave it both a literary & a genteel air; and rendered it the best bred society in N. England. But—alas!—how changed! The British destroyed, for fuel, about 900 buildings, of [to] be sure the poorer sort; yet it has never recovered the dilapidation. The town of Providence has risen to riches & elegance from the ruins of this once beautiful spot; while Newport resembles an old battered shield—its scars & bruises are deep and indelible. Commerce, & all the Jews are fled. The wharves are deserted & the lamp in the synagogue is extinct; and the people are now so poor, that there are not more than ten, or a dozen people who would have the courage to invite a stranger to his table.

A REPUBLIC

What is a republic? The term has been defined differently throughout history (as has the word *democracy*), but at the core, a republic is simply a state without a king, as Machiavelli stated in 1513. After the execution of King Charles I in England, for only a decade, the Puritan Commonwealth was a republic, but a failed one. Rome, Switzerland, Iceland, and Venice were all republics at various times, and with different degrees of success. John Adams defined a republic as "an empire of laws, not men," but that is not sweeping enough. Franklin wrote that republicanism was "the sovereignty of the people." In *The Federalist Papers*, James Madison, in his passionate argument for a strong, centralized United States government, correctly described a republic as "a government which derives all its powers directly or indirectly from the great body of people; and is administered by persons holding their offices during pleasure, for a limited period."

Constitutional Crisis

With the war won, the great debate of the 1780s was over the kind of government Americans wanted. Millions of words were written on the subject, unending debate ensued, and "the people"—the new sovereigns of the country—were passionately committed to the outcome. After untold proposals and amendments and arguments, in the end the choice came down to two: a weak and beholden central government dominated by the will of the individual states (Articles of Confederation); or a forceful and powerful federal government with unifying leadership, in which the original states retained most of their rights but could be regulated by a bicameral Congress, a strong executive branch, and an independent judiciary (Constitution).

From its inception in 1774, the Continental Congress labored to write the laws that would govern the loose coalition of former colonies and dictate some definition and order as they broke from Britain and conducted the War of Independence. That Congress was under severe strain in every conceivable sense, yet it was able to create the Articles of Confederation and Perpetual Union that were sent to the state legislatures in 1777 and finally ratified by all thirteen states in 1781 as the fighting was drawing to a close. The Rhode Island General Assembly, still controlled by an educated, outward-looking merchant class, had no major issues with the thirteen Articles because they were essentially toothless when it came to impinging on the privileges of the 1663 Charter. In fact, Rhode Island was the first state to sign. Article Two clearly declared that "each state retains its sovereignty, freedom, independence, and every power, jurisdiction and right which is not, by this confederation, expressly delegated to the United States." Thus Rhode Island could not be dictated to by Congress. Or so it thought.

But the Articles of Confederation were, in fact, far too weak to serve as the law of the new country because Congress lacked any authority to regulate coinage, conduct diplomatic initiatives, or, most important, institute taxation. Congress could not command respect either within the United States or abroad. In order to please the strong state legislatures during the hostilities, it had stripped itself of all the essential powers necessary to conduct a viable government. While the Articles were a necessary first step in defining the new nation, most legislators believed they were neither broad nor deep enough to augur well for the future. At the close of the war, America consisted of thirteen separate entities, each with its own constitution, and each going its own way. At a time when foreign diplomatic initiative was urgent for the very existence of the United States, Congress was impotent. In George Washington's words, the Articles of Confederation were "little more than the shadow without the substance."

Rhode Island contributed heavily to the war effort, both in the number of men under arms proportionate to its population and in money spent. But after Yorktown, the General Assembly grew apprehensive and began repudiating the United States because it was perceived as a threat to the Charter. The state began to show its defiance of Congress over the taxation conundrum. Congress desperately needed money to pay for the extraordinary war expenses and it proposed a 5 percent impost tax on all foreign trade and admiralty court prizes. The Rhode Island congressman General James Mitchell Varnum, a decorated and respected soldier, understood the need for national revenue and central authority and lobbied for it at home. He immediately came under fire from those (the majority) who believed that *any* tax, no matter how badly needed by Congress, was illegal and an infringement of the Charter. An ambitious Providence lawyer and philosophy professor at what was to become Brown University, David Howell, began a newspaper campaign against Varnum and the impost. Howell asserted that "Congress may call upon us for money, but cannot prescribe to us the methods of raising it; that is within our sovereignty, and lies solely in the power of our own legislature." Sure enough, Varnum was thrown out of office at the next election, replaced by none other than David Howell.

The historian Edward Field explained the reasoning. "Just as she [Rhode Island] had thus been anxious to resist aggression upon her liberty and welfare, so now she was determined to resist any project whereby her privileges were to be curtailed by her sister states. She had signed the Articles of Confederation with the understanding that she should not be molested in the conducting of her own affairs, and she did not now intend that her power in levying taxes should be interfered with by any other jurisdiction." Another powerful incentive to waylay the proposed tax was that, as a maritime state with little farming capability and no access to western expansion, Rhode Island would pay a disproportionate amount of taxes. Newport merchants opposed the impost tax in the beginning because it represented yet another "foreign" attempt to control their trade.

Howell's stand—and he was strongly supported at home—was a mere prelude to the enormous difficulties that lay ahead for Rhode Island in its relations with the other twelve states. Its unrelenting devotion to the freedoms of the Charter of 1663 were a matter of deepest principle and tradition. No matter how angrily the General Assembly was vilified by others, who never fully understood the Rhode Island Way, its members held out. Thus, even after all the other states voted in favor of the impost, Rhode Island refused. Since all thirteen states had to agree in order to amend the Articles, Rhode Island's intransigence was highly unpopular. Howell was shunned by many of his colleagues and was the victim of an ugly smear campaign against him in Rhode Island, yet he refused to give in. The impost was defeated yearly in Congress until 1785, when Rhode Island merchants finally came around, because their goods were often being taxed twice. In the meantime, Congress had to scramble to find other means of raising money.

America had won the Revolutionary War but was fast losing the peace. The years after Yorktown were punctuated by interstate rivalry, willy-nilly taxation codes, and a sense of waywardness as a "unified" nation. The Continental Congress was less than effective in controlling the future of the supposed United States; in fact, they were anything *but* united as they came to terms with their obligations to act in unison for the better good of all concerned. Making the jump from thirteen separate colonies under the British Empire to a cohesive, rational nation was not an easy task. Regionalism, selfishness, and principle all contributed to the sense of drift.

Within Rhode Island, a growing rift was developing between the merchant class (Newport, Providence, and Bristol), who were largely in favor of a strong central government to regulate trade, and the farmers and small-town residents, who were deeply suspicious of Congress and did not intend to forfeit the liberties they already possessed. The feud was reminiscent of the Ward-Hopkins controversy in that it pitted town against country in the starkest manner. In essence, the Anti-Federalist "Country Party" advocates were angry at the high rate of taxation leveled against them by the General Assembly and by Congress, and angry at the merchants to whom they owed a great deal of money. An economic depression between 1784 and 1786 added fuel to the enmity between the groups. They also chafed under the system of appropriating delegates to the General Assembly: seaboard towns still sent more legislators than rural ones, even though a substantial

Providence Gazette and Country Journal (Providence: John Carter), No. 23 of Vol. XXVII, Saturday, June 5, 1790.

Redwood Library and Athenæum

Newport, Rhode Island

RATIFICATION *of the* CONSTITUTION *of the* UNITED STATES, *by the* CONVENTION *of the State of Rhode-Island and Providence Plantations.*

WE the Delegates of the people of the State of Rhode-Island and Providence Plantations, duly elected and met in Convention, having maturely considered the Constitution for the United States of America, agreed to on the 17th day of September, A. D. 1787, by the Convention then assembled at Philadelphia, in the Commonwealth of Pennsylvania (a copy whereof precedes these presents) and having also seriously and deliberately considered the present situation of this State, DO Declare and Make Known:

1. THAT there are certain natural rights, of which men, when they form a social compact, cannot deprive or divest their posterity—among which are the enjoyment of life and liberty, with the means of acquiring, possessing and protecting property, and pursuing and obtaining happiness and safety.

2. That all power is naturally vested in and consequently derived from the people; that magistrates, therefore, are their trustees and agents, and at all times amenable to them.

3. That the powers of government may be re-assumed by the people, whenever it shall become necessary to their happiness:—That the rights of the States respectively to nominate and appoint all State officers, and every other power, jurisdiction and right, which is not by the said Constitution clearly delegated to the Congress of the United States, or to the departments of government thereof, remain to the people of the several States, or their respective State governments, to whom they may have granted the same;—and that those clauses in the Constitution which declare that Congress shall not have or exercise certain powers, do not imply that Congress is entitled to any powers not given by the said Constitution;—but such clauses are to be construed either as exceptions to certain specified powers, or as inserted merely for greater caution.

4. That religion, or the duty which we owe to our Creator, and the manner of discharging it, can be directed only by reason and conviction, not by force or violence—and therefore all men have an equal, natural and unalienable right to the free exercise of religion, according to the dictates of conscience; and that no particular religion, sect, or society, ought to be favoured or established by law, in preference to others.

5. That the legislative, executive and judiciary powers of government should be separate and distinct; —and that the members of the two first may be restrained from oppression, by feeling and participating the public burthens, they should at fixed periods be reduced to a private station, return into the mass of the people, and the vacancy be supplied by certain and regular elections—in which all or any part of the former members to be eligible or ineligible, as the rules of the Constitution of government and the laws shall direct.

6. That elections of Representatives in the Legislature ought to be free and frequent—and all men having sufficient evidence of permanent common interest with and attachment to the community, ought to have the right of suffrage: And no aid, charge, tax or fee, can be set, rated or levied upon the people, without their own consent, or that of their Representatives so elected;—nor can they be bound by any law to which they have not in like manner assented for the public good.

7. That all power of suspending laws, or the execution of laws, by any authority, without the consent of the Representatives of the people in the Legislature, is injurious to their rights, and ought not to be exercised.

speedy, and of writing and publishing their sentiments:—That the freedom of the press is one of the greatest bulwarks of liberty, and ought not to be violated.

16. That the people have a right peaceably to assemble together, to consult for their common good, or to instruct their Representatives; and that every person has a right to petition, or apply to the legislature, for redress of grievances.

17. That the people have a right to keep and bear arms: That a well-regulated militia, including the body of the people capable of bearing arms, is the proper, natural and safe defence of a free State:—That the militia shall not be subject to martial law, except in time of war, rebellion, or insurrection:—That standing armies in time of peace are dangerous to liberty, and ought not to be kept up, except in cases of necessity; —and that at all times the military should be under strict subordination to the civil power:—That in time of peace no soldier ought to be quartered in any house without the consent of the owner—and in time of war, only by the civil magistrate, in such manner as the law directs.

18. That any person religiously scrupulous of bearing arms ought to be exempted, upon payment of an equivalent to employ another to bear arms in his stead.

UNDER these impressions, and declaring that the rights aforesaid cannot be abridged or violated, and that the explanations aforesaid are consistent with the said Constitution, and in confidence that the amendments hereafter mentioned will receive an early and mature consideration, and conformably to the fifth article of the said Constitution speedily become a part thereof: WE, the said Delegates, in the name and in the behalf of the People of the State of Rhode-Island and Providence Plantations, DO, by these presents, ASSENT TO and RATIFY the said Constitution. In full confidence, nevertheless, that until the amendments hereafter proposed shall be agreed to and ratified, pursuant to the aforesaid fifth article, the militia of this State will not be continued in service out of this State for a longer term than six weeks, without the consent of the Legislature thereof; that the Congress will not make or alter any regulations in this State, respecting the times, places and manner, of holding elections for Senators or Representatives, unless the Legislature of this State shall neglect or refuse to make laws or regulations for the purpose, or from any circumstance be incapable of making the same; and that in those cases such power will only be exercised until the Legislature of this State shall make provision in the premises; that the Congress will not lay direct taxes within this State, but when the monies arising from the impost, tonnage and excise, shall be insufficient for the public exigencies, nor until the Congress shall have first made a requisition upon this State to assess, levy and pay, the amount of such requisition, made agreeably to the census fixed in the said Constitution, in such way and manner as the Legislature of this State shall judge best; and that the Congress will not lay or make any capitation or poll-tax.

DONE in Convention, at Newport, in the State of Rhode-Island and Providence Plantations, the twenty-ninth day of May, in the year of our Lord one thousand seven hundred and ninety, and the fourteenth year of the Independence of the United States of America.

By Order,

DANIEL OWEN, *President.*

Attest. DANIEL UPDIKE, *Secretary.*

AND the Convention do, in the name and behalf of the people of the State of Rhode-Island and Providence Plantations, enjoin it upon the Senators and Representative or Representatives, which may be elect-

Revolutionary debt. . . . Noncompliance with the requisition could, perhaps, offer sufficient pretext for a resort to military force by the United States." One senator quipped of the measure, "It was meant to be used in the same way that a robber does a dagger or a highwayman a pistol, and to obtain the end desired by putting the party in fear."

Appropriately, the ultimate convention meeting was held in Newport, still the official capital of the state, and known to be the most Federal-leaning of all Rhode Island towns. Whether the setting made a difference or the threat to tear the state apart, a number of Anti-Federalist delegates stayed away. When the convention got down to business on May 25, more debate ensued for days. The tide was turning, and the Federalists could sense that the fight had finally gone out of the majority of Country Party delegates. When the ballot was finally taken on Saturday, May 29, at five o'clock, fifteen months after the birth of the American government, ratification of the United States Constitution passed by two votes, 34 to 32. It was the narrowest margin of victory in all the thirteen states.

First in war, last in peace. Rhode Island had joined the Union.

Newport rejoiced.

Union and Survival

6

Brave New World

Although Newport was doing its utmost to reestablish its former glory, the town was being left in the dust, literally and metaphorically. With the coming of Union, a radically new vision began emerging within the American psyche, once the people were unshackled from the constraints imposed by their former overlords. In two critical areas, freedom from the Crown afforded fresh and expanded economic opportunities. Before Independence, Americans had been greatly restricted in what goods they were allowed to manufacture in the colonies because Great Britain was intent on protecting and promoting strictly English products. Likewise, the colonies had been heavily proscribed in their international trading targets; London dictated to them which nations were fair game and which were off limits (not that Newport had paid much attention to those directives). Now, with liberty, both of those limitations were lifted; America could set its own rules, determine its own future. For many people, this meant casting their eyes westward at the great expanse beyond the original thirteen borders. For many people, this meant casting their eyes westward at the great expanse beyond the original thirteen borders. For others, it meant redefining what might be accomplished in their immediate vicinity. The land was finally *theirs*, and ideas about what to do with it were as abundant as robins in springtime. As politicians wrangled in their continuing efforts to create a working, just government, a large number of Americans turned away from the contentious public sphere and focused on personal advancement.

In F. Scott Fitzgerald's novel *The Great Gatsby*, the narrator Nick Carraway warns Jay Gatsby "You can't repeat the past." The protagonist's response of "Can't repeat the past? . . . Why of course you can!" sums up the attitude of many Newporters at that time. They desperately desired to revive their Golden Age of superiority and splendor. But, as if the devastation wrought by the British occupation were not enough, the ambitious maritime economy that existed before the Revolution was now seriously compromised. Many of Newport's traditional markets had been lost to competition from more aggressive ports, and trading was no longer viable as *the* steady seed of growth. Risk capital, which had formed the bedrock of the mercantile system, was dangerously depleted, as was its necessary corollary, the spirit of adventure. Businessmen along Narragansett Bay looked north to Providence for new sources of financing and new trade routes, now that the

Samuel King
A South West View of Newport. Newport, Rhode Island (detail), 1795
Engraving
after a drawing by
L. Allen.
Courtesy of the
Rhode Island Historical Society
Providence, Rhode Island
Graphics Collection: XXB
Prints N5 8
RHi X3 213

West Indies were precarious for American shipping due to British embargoes—but, most of all, they sought out innovative ideas.

Until the Revolutionary War, Newport had been the undisputed spiritual, political, economic, and social capital of Rhode Island and Providence Plantations. The British occupation had stifled creativity and credit; the town was in steep decline when it came to currency and clout. The next fifty years would witness an almost complete reversal in the way Rhode Islanders earned their wages as the state's monetary engine migrated from the sea to inland manufacturing. The new, lucrative industries in textiles as well as base and precious metals required an abundant, reliable supply of rapidly running water to power the machinery—the Blackstone, Woonasquatucket, Pawtuxet, and Moshassuck rivers—and those rivers were all in the north of the state and on the mainland. Aquidneck Island had no powerful streams to aid in its revival: Newport had no rivers at all. What the town had was atrophy.

The Brown brothers of Providence helped spur the rising industrial economy, and hundreds of others in the northern tier followed suit, turning Providence into the de facto hub of the state. With its maritime dominance dwindling, Newport witnessed the seismic shift in the relative power of these towns with an air of inevitability. In 1790, the two rival towns had nearly identical populations: 6,716 people in Newport and 6,380 in Providence. By 1840, Newport had grown to a mere 8,333 while Providence exploded with 23,171 inhabitants. In terms of dollar power based on taxable property, Newport grew from $1,450,000 in 1796 to only $4,247,000 in 1849. Meanwhile, Providence in the former year could boast $2,950,000—but by 1849 the number had soared to $28,407,000. Not until Newport transformed itself into one of America's premier summer resorts for the wealthy would the economic imbalance begin to reverse itself. And even then, the two towns would remain distinctly different in personality and purpose. The contest for power and prestige that had begun in the 1750s with the contentious Ward-Hopkins controversy was essentially over by 1800, and Providence had prevailed. For the moment.

Following ratification of the Constitution at Newport on May 29, 1790, the General Assembly implemented the procedures necessary for actually participating in the Union. In June 1790, Rhode Island became the ninth state to give its blessing to the national Bill of Rights, thereby making it the law of the land (it passed its own state version of the Bill of Rights in 1798). In its August session, the Assembly elected Joseph Stanton, Jr., of Charlestown and Theodore Foster of Providence (also, conveniently, Governor Arthur Fenner's brother-in-law) to the United States Senate. Stanton was a staunch Anti-Federalist and stalwart of the Country Party, while Foster was a Federalist, thus balancing the team. Benjamin Bourne of Bristol, a Harvard graduate who strongly favored Union and had been a leader in the fight for ratification, was chosen as Rhode Island's first Representative to Congress. All members of the Assembly took an oath in support of the Constitution and passed eleven of the twelve amendments that had been proposed by Congress. The state was inching its way toward real confederation with its sister states and learning how to temper its famous rambunctiousness in order to live peacefully within the larger Union. But Rhode Island's innate rebelliousness made that a tall order.

President George Washington, accompanied by Thomas Jefferson, then Secretary of State, and

Governor George Clinton of New York, among others, visited Newport on the morning of August 17, 1790, to welcome Rhode Island, at last, into the United States. Having been snubbed by the president the summer before because of the state's refusal to ratify the Constitution, the town's citizens were delighted by the official attention now paid to them. Arriving by packet ship from New York, the party was greeted at Long Wharf (what was left of it) by a large delegation of citizens eager to see their leader. After being led to their lodgings, the president and his entourage walked around town to survey the damage inflicted by the British and the partial refurbishment by the French, then were feted at a dinner for eighty at the State House, accompanied by thirteen toasts and many speeches. The historian George Woodbridge reports that "according to local tradition, the town, as a result of the misfortunes it suffered during the Revolution and of changing patterns of trade, could not afford silver and good porcelain dishes for such a large dinner but they had all been supplied by many small loans from those citizens who still possessed such things." The party over, Washington continued his walk around Newport to the cheers of the proud and supportive populace.

The president was treated to formal speeches by four different groups during his stay in Newport. First was an official address by the town leaders, then the Christian clergy, followed by King David's Lodge of Masons. The last was a warm welcome and expression of thanks from Moses Seixas, the warden of the Congregation Jeshuat Israel, of what is now known as the Touro Synagogue. Seixas led a small group of Jews who had come to town after the British decamped. Washington's reply, "To the Hebrew Congregation of Newport, Rhode Island," has since become famous for its sentiments of inclusion for Americans of all religions. The president wrote,

> The Citizens of the United States of America have a right to applaud themselves for having given to mankind examples of an enlarged and liberal policy: a policy worthy of imitation. All possess alike liberty of conscience and immunities of citizenship. It is now no more that toleration is spoken of, as if it was by the indulgence of one class of people, that another enjoyed the exercise of their inherent rights. For happily the Government of the United States, which gives bigotry no sanction, to persecution no assistance requires only that they who live under its protection should demean themselves as good citizens. . . . May the Children of the Stock of Abraham, who dwell in this land, continue to merit and enjoy the good will of the other Inhabitants, while every one shall sit in safety under his own vine and fig-tree, and there shall be none to make him afraid.

Appropriately, the president's response citing "liberty of conscience" was addressed to people of the one town in New England, indeed, in all of America, that had always promoted and protected a person's right to worship his or her own God, without fear of reprisal or revenge. And though anti-Catholic sentiments were strong throughout colonial and early statehood years, Newport accepted and entertained Rochambeau's French officers and soldiers, most of whom were Catholic, for nearly a year.

After the brief but psychologically uplifting visit by the first American president, Newport settled into a state of suspended animation. Both the economic and political power bases of Rhode Island were inexorably floating northward up Narragansett Bay to Providence, which was exhibiting a vibrancy and confidence once associated with Newport. One example of the drift: after Governor John Collins sacrificed his career by defying the Country Party leaders and casting the deciding vote in favor of a Constitutional convention, he was hastily replaced by Providence's Arthur Fenner, Jr. Unlike the previous century and a half when Newport practically owned the top position in the state as a birthright, it would be twenty years before another Newport man would occupy the governor's chair.

Just as Samuel Cranston had been elevated to the chief executive post at a turbulent turning point in the state's history nearly one hundred years before, Arthur Fenner took control when Rhode Island was desperate for fair-handed, constructive, and convincing leadership. Fenner was so astute and capable that he was elected for sixteen consecutive terms, from 1790 until his death in 1805, when he was succeeded after two years by his son James Fenner, who served as governor from 1807 to 1811, and again from 1824 until 1831. Another political dynasty had been born. Like Cranston before him, Arthur Fenner, who entered politics after a successful career as a merchant and was elected as a coalition candidate, was able to quickly mend fences and garner respect from both Federalists and Anti-Federalists, thereby infusing Rhode Island politics with a sense of balance and purpose rare for the era. Although firmly in the Country Party camp initially and against the state's ratification of the federal Constitution, Fenner rethought his position, reversed himself, and embraced the new Union upon ascending to the governorship, thus setting an example for other radical party adherents who began to see their resistance to Union as counterproductive. As a result, the Country Party quickly lost its overriding influence and the power vacuum was filled by Fenner himself, despite the relative weakness of the governor's chair. By hewing to the middle course and successfully negotiating between the two opposing parties, Arthur Fenner was able to heal the wounds of the 1780s and set Rhode Island on one of its most peaceful political periods in decades. Too much passion and invective had been spent over the constitutional issue. Under Fenner's skillful stewardship, Rhode Island was settling down and facing the future.

Another Revolution

Since the dawn of its history, Rhode Island had staked its future prosperity and well-being on commerce and oceanic trading. While "Hope" is appropriate as the state's motto, the ship would serve as an apt symbol for the first 150 years of existence. Generation after generation of Newport men depended on the sea for their wealth and social standing. While they had learned the hard way to diversify their investments across a broad range of naval activities—shares in numerous ships, multiple destinations, and extensively varied cargoes—these businessmen were blinded by their early success and rarely sought out other avenues of commerce. The sea was their sole investment, and they would sink or swim on its tides of fortune. In short, the maritime world was all they knew.

But with the coming of Union, that water-bound universe was about to decline—and with the fall came the further eclipse of Newport for nearly a half century.

The Industrial Revolution was on the horizon.

The year 1790 was a watershed not only because of Rhode Island's ratification of the United States Constitution, but also because in December, Moses Brown, the youngest of the famous four Brown brothers of Providence, and his new acquaintance, Samuel Slater, opened the first successful cotton-spinning mill in America at Pawtucket Falls on the surging Blackstone River, just north of Providence. Moses Brown had wide-ranging interests and was not bound to maritime commerce as his sole endeavor. He had attempted

Samuel King
*A South West View of
Newport*. Newport,
Rhode Island, 1795
Engraving
after a drawing by
L. Allen.
Courtesy of the
Rhode Island Historical Society
Providence, Rhode Island
Graphics Collection: XXB
Prints N5 8
RHi X3 213

to build an efficient thread-spinning apparatus twice before, but the efforts had failed because they lacked waterpower for continuous operation. They were too slow, too prone to breakdown. The only workable textile machines were in Britain, and their mechanisms were closely guarded state secrets. But Samuel Slater, an Englishman who had toiled for seven years in the cotton-spinning factories of Derbyshire, had memorized the workings of the ingenious water-driven cotton-spinning equipment engineered by Richard Arkwright and, having emigrated to America against British laws forbidding skilled craftsmen to leave the country, was looking to re-create the famous Arkwright design. He wrote to Moses Brown offering his services, and Brown, being a risk-taker, took him on. The rest, as they say, is history.

Rhode Island pioneered the textile trade in America, cloth created by intricate machines driven by the power of fast-moving rivers. With Brown's investment and Slater's know-how, the two men forged a new industry, one that would eventually govern the state's fiscal structure and would change the entire character of Rhode Island—economically, politically, socially—for the next century and beyond. The land, not the ocean, would dominate the culture. Water would become the crucial element in the coming economy, but now it would be fresh river water, not the saltwater of the sea. With the success of the first textile enterprise (known as the Old Slater Mill), Brown, along with his associate and brother-in-law William Almy, brought Slater aboard as a partner in their firm and they went on to found numerous new mills throughout the northern section of the state. Within a mere two decades, dozens of competitors arose (mostly Providence men), the rivers were dotted with mills, factories, and villages, and the Blackstone and Pawtuxet valleys became synonymous with the fast-growing, thriving, American textile industry. According to Irving B. Richman, "Within thirty miles of Providence in 1805 there were five small cotton factories operating 4000 spindles. In 1815, within the same radius, there were 171 factories employing 26,000 workmen, operating 134,588 spindles, and consuming annually 29,000 bales of cotton in the production of 27,840,000 yards of cloth."

From 1790 until about 1815, the nascent Rhode Island textile industry, producing both cotton and woolen fabrics, absorbed financial as well as human resources. As the state made its recovery from war debts and the paper-money crisis, available capital was ploughed into textile mills, new machinery, and raw materials at an increasing rate. An ambitious marketing plan was implemented to sell the goods throughout America. Return on investment was generally safe and steady, unlike maritime commerce with its incessant natural and political hazards. Now there were new jobs to be had, thousands of them. Blackstone Valley factories employed a large number of women and children, along with men, doing the spinning, weaving, bleaching, and dyeing. They toiled under dreadful working conditions, but there was little complaint at the time; the fact that they had steady employment soothed the drudgery of long hours and brain-numbing routine. New villages sprang up to support the mills, many of them controlled by the factory owner, and more families fled their underperforming farms or static seacoast towns to partake in the Industrial Revolution. With the steady rise of mills and factories, the population distribution (increasingly augmented by new arrivals from Europe and the British Isles) began to shift to greater Providence and the northern counties—a development that would lead to one of Rhode Island's most contentious political and social battles later in the nineteenth century.

While Providence was looking to the future, Newport, unable to join the march toward industrialization because of its geographic isolation and limited natural resources, cast its gaze into the past during the decades following 1790. Maritime commerce was what these men understood, and they re-entered the world of trade believing they could simply pick up from where they had been the day before the British invaded, a decade and a half earlier, and dominate the state's economy. The majority, however, were sadly mistaken. Some merchants, like the family firm of Christopher, George, and Christopher Grant Champlin and the syndicates of Gibbs and Channing or Gardner and Dean, were successful in opening profitable trade relations abroad, often in partnership with Bristol or Providence merchants in order to offset risks. The historian Peter J. Coleman reports: "From the Baltic, especially Denmark, Sweden, and Russia, they obtained naval stores as well as tallow, candles, iron, steel, and glass. England, France, Holland, and the Hanse ports were sources of manufactures, liquor, wines, nuts, cheese, salt, coal, and a variety of Oriental commodities. Southern Europe, particularly Portugal, Spain, and Gibraltar, supplied specie and such Mediterranean specialties as currants, corks, baskets, and merino sheep. In return, Rhode Island merchants shipped staves, provisions, tobacco, sugar, rum, coffee, Oriental goods, and occasionally, manufactures." There was activity again in Newport harbor, but it was paltry in comparison with former times.

South America and Asia were the new targets. Canton had been the destination, in 1787, of one of the first Rhode Island ships to seek that far-away market: the *George Washington* returned to Providence after an eighteen-month voyage, yielding a profit of over $100,000 in continental dollars for members of the Brown family. Some Newport merchants jumped on the Chinese bandwagon and did well, but those trips were infrequent because of the large expense involved with staging such an enterprise, particularly financing the construction of ships large enough to withstand the rigors and duration of the Pacific Ocean voyage. Only the biggest firms could navigate in that arena, and Newport, once the home of dozens of great fleets like those of Malbone, Banister, and Lopez, could no longer boast of such prowess.

Newport trade inched forward, but, aside from the old European haunts, it was mostly along the American coast. Smaller ships continued to work Caribbean waters, but profits were unpredictable and meager because of harsh British restrictions. During the chaos of the French Revolution, beginning in 1789, Newporters were able to take advantage of the lack of authority and trade successfully with French islands. But with their options contracting and purses getting lighter by the year, a number of Rhode Island merchants, particularly from Newport, Bristol, and Providence, plunged back into the trading strategy that had proved to be so lucrative during the Golden Age—shipping slaves from Africa to the American South or the Caribbean. Although risky and unpopular with a growing number of Americans, the profits were such that some Rhode Islanders could not stay away from the Guinea Coast.

The slaving issue was, in this new era, even more complex legally and morally than before the War of Independence. In 1784, the Rhode Island General Assembly had passed an Emancipation Act granting gradual manumission to all children born to slave mothers after March of that year. The act was only a halfway

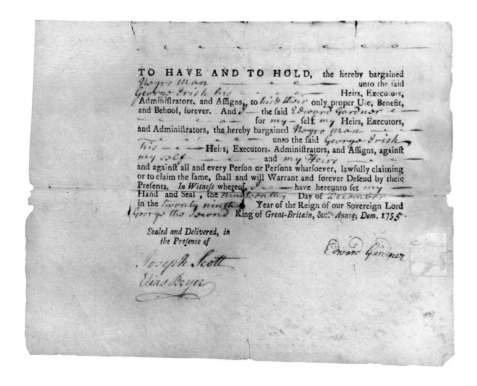

Bill of Sale (in part)
Bill of sale for
Negro man being sold
by Edward Gardner
to George Irish,
December 19, 1755.
Redwood Library
and Athenæum
Newport, Rhode Island
Irish Family Papers

measure because it failed to free all the slaves in the state, but it sent a signal that the old ways were about to come to an end. With legislative sanctions, abolitionists led largely by the Quaker community brought more pressure to bear to obliterate slavery forever. More and more preachers, particularly Samuel Hopkins of Newport, were emboldened to speak out against the trade, and their congregations heeded their words. Thus the General Assembly enacted another law in 1787 that clearly prohibited any Rhode Island citizen from taking part in the African traffic. In 1794, the United States Congress forbade any American from "carrying slaves between foreign ports and made it a federal crime to violate state laws against the slave trade."

None of those sanctions mattered. Regardless of state or federal laws, renegade merchants continued to defy authority in search of profits that would help rebuild the edgy economy. In Bristol, James DeWolf and his family made a fortune off the backs of black Africans. Coleman asserts that "between 1803 and 1807 Newport merchants shipped almost thirty-five hundred slaves to Charleston, about six times the number delivered by either Providence or Warren firms." And in Providence, the Quaker Moses Brown sued his older brother John, then a Representative in Congress, for not only defending the trade, but engaging in it as well. John Brown was acquitted, partly because his leadership during the torching of the *Gaspee* in 1772 was not forgotten by the Providence jury. But Narragansett Bay merchants withdrew from slaving only when profits declined precipitously and public pressure became so intense that it was no longer worth defending. For decades, neither the niceties of the law nor the nefariousness of their mission inhibited these men. It was all about money.

Privateers out of Newport harbor plied the waters, particularly when the United States was in a state of war with Great Britain or at diplomatic odds with France. Some did spectacularly well, but many others failed and disappeared from the historical record. The risks involved kept mounting and ship owners reluctantly realized that the good old days were probably gone forever. Little known is the fact that Newport seamen also took an active part in the reinvigorated whaling industry for decades, but the results, again, were disappointing overall. While Nantucket, Warren, and New Bedford made whaling a profitable way of life for decades, Newport was half-hearted in its efforts. It seemed that wherever Newporters looked for relief from their economic burdens, someone slammed a door in their face. The town was desperate for revitalization and productivity—but it was looking in the wrong direction. Newport's primary asset was its harbor; by the 1830s, that asset was devalued. A whole way of life was slowly, painfully, vanishing. And it wasn't just because of the effects of the British occupation. The town was bringing it upon itself, caught as it was in an economic vicious circle.

One of the most thorough and perceptive studies of Newport's decline during these decades was written by Peter J. Coleman. In *The Transformation of Rhode Island: 1790–1860* (published in 1963), he maintains that a number of converging factors led to the rise of Providence at Newport's expense. Coleman's first assertion is that Providence refused to "rest on its laurels" and eagerly plunged into sophisticated and adventurous maritime trading around the world (China especially), while Newport merchants were more content to revisit known ports. At the same time, Providence was developing its manufacturing and land-transportation infrastructures, thus diversifying its workforce and economic base. In the beginning, Newport never even attempted to enter the developing new world of the factory; when it did, in the 1830s, those efforts failed after two decades.

Over that seventy-year period, Providence's hinterland became the most highly industrialized area in the United States, enriching its investors and creating greater cargoes for its ships. During those same years, Newport failed to adjust. Although Coleman acknowledges that the British occupation "inflicted irreparable damage," he believes the lost momentum was due largely to a "failure of nerve" on the part of its business elite. Gone were the "vigor, opportunism, and resourcefulness of the early days." Entrepreneurial leadership and optimism vanished; the merchants lacked vision; investment opportunities were few. Investors were too cautious, passing up the high-risk enterprises like the China trade that led others to riches (and were once the hallmark of Newport men). Depression became chronic; the town was lethargic, "incapable of rousing itself from torpor." During the War of 1812, "Newport was prostrate with fear of another British invasion, and this led to the second flight of capital and talent." Add to this inventory of woes the unalterable geographic fact that as an island, its "insular location impeded development of turnpikes and railroads."

In the end, everything comes down to people, and for the first time in its history, Newport lacked decisive, creative leadership. Because of a lack of confidence, the town had fashioned its own vacuum from which it was difficult to escape. A long string of bad luck had unnerved the once-adventurous merchant class. Understandably, men who had come of age during the Revolution had turned timid. Coleman, referring to the 1820s, believes that an entire generation passed "before anyone advanced proposals for revitalization." To drive home his point, he reminds us of a famous article from the *Newport Mercury*: "According to tradition, pupils were released from school one day in 1829 to witness the raising of the first house to be built in Newport in fifteen years."

Newport had hit its nadir.

In the early 1820s, an Englishman named Adam Hodgson was making a tour of America and Canada and writing highly descriptive letters home. In January 1821, he visited Newport and reported that he had seldom seen "a more desolate place . . . or one which exhibited more evident symptoms of decay. The wooden houses had either never been painted, or had lost their paint, and were going to ruin. A decent house here and there, seemed to indicate, that some residents of respectability still lingered behind; but the close habitations, with their small windows, and the narrow, dirty, and irregular streets, exhibited no trace of the attractions which once rendered this a summer resort for the planters from the South."

Ironically, it would be this same class of "planters from the South" who would, in the not-so-distant future, rediscover the island's inherent natural charms and form the mainstay of the summer-colony pioneers, leading to the revitalization of Newport's prosperity and pride.

The War of 1812

While Newport brooded, America tested its wings. Peace had prevailed throughout the last decade of the eighteenth century, but with the onset of the Napoleonic Wars in Europe and yet another confrontation between Great Britain and France, the United States was inevitably drawn into the contest, given its growing maritime commerce. Relations with both powers deteriorated because of privateering, embargoes, and impressment of sailors. America's determination to stay neutral was impossible to sustain, regardless of who was president or whether the Federalists or Republicans controlled Congress. Napoleon's bloody march through Europe created a world war, and small as America was at the time, it was destined to become a combatant, if only at sea, initially.

The lead-up to the War of 1812 was long and slow, propelled by a series of events—isolated and insignificant in themselves, but which taken together magnified a growing interference with American sovereignty, primarily by Britain. For over a century, European ship captains had been filling their crews by kidnapping ("impressing") military-age men on shore. Then the British raised the ante and began impressing men off ships captured at sea. Ever since the peace treaty of 1783, the Royal Navy had viewed United States commercial vessels as ripe targets for impressment, which angered the Americans. Merchants were especially upset, because the situation forced them to pay higher salaries, thus reducing profits.

The first tangible incident occurred in Newport in 1794 when the British war sloop *Nautilus* laid anchor and her commander, Captain Boynton, came ashore in search of provisions. Word had reached town that the *Nautilus* was carrying a number of Americans, several of whom had recently been impressed in the West Indies. As it happened, the General Assembly was then in session in Newport for its annual May meeting, and its leaders immediately summoned the English captain to answer charges of kidnapping before the Superior Court. He denied having any illegal seaman on board, and played down the charges. Charles Carroll relates, "As he started to leave the State House, however, and came face to face with the crowd of Newporters who had assembled, he turned back for further conference. By agreement the captain, who remained in the chamber, sent an order to the *Nautilus* to muster the crew for examination by a committee. Six of the crew, who proved American citizenship, were discharged and paid accrued wages, and the incident was closed. Great Britain made no diplomatic representation, in spite of the plain fact that Captain Boynton had been intimidated by the people of Newport."

The competitive situation at sea continued to deteriorate, and many Americans were urging another war with the former mother country. But President Washington insisted that neutrality and peace be maintained, and in 1794 sent Chief Justice John Jay to negotiate a treaty with the British, which satisfied some of the more hawkish politicians, for the moment. The downside of the treaty was the extended rift that emerged in the relationship with France, known as the Quasi-War. The new republican government in Paris was stung that America would not side with it in the battle with Britain, and demonstrated its anger by cutting diplomatic ties with its former ally while increasing French privateering efforts against United States shipping. Year after year, the insult to American free trade kept deepening. The Federalist President John Adams, having taken over from Washington in 1797, attempted to thwart the pro-France stance of his political nemesis Thomas Jefferson, of the Anti-Federalist (Republican) Party, by signing the Alien and Sedition Acts in 1798; this blatantly anti-French set of laws of highly questionable constitutionality that gave the president the power to jail suspected aliens without due process. The acts were so unpopular, because of the suppression of free speech, that they led to Jefferson's election as president in 1800. Federalists were in retreat.

The following decade saw little remission of the tensions with either France or Britain. As a result, the American navy needed reinforcement, Fort Adams in Newport was dedicated for the defense of

Narragansett Bay, and the country went on and off war footing with the frequency of a metronome at low speed. Impressment continued, as well as harassment of American shipping. In 1807, the Royal Navy warship *Leopold* attacked the American frigate *Chesapeake* and hauled four men off the ship as deserters, three of whom were Americans. Since the incursion took place just off the American coast, news spread rapidly and the war cry was raised again. In Newport, Carroll relates, the largest meeting in years denounced the "late insult on our National Flag." Congress authorized the president to call up a hundred thousand militia.

But Jefferson did not want to commit his unprepared country to war, so instead he pushed the Embargo of 1807 through Congress, forbidding all maritime commerce with *any* foreign port, as a way of punishing the miscreants abroad. Britain hardly blinked, France shrugged, but American merchants were severely curtailed. "In Rhode Island, the embargo affected almost the entire population. The losses to merchants and others engaged in commercial occupations was indicated by a decrease of exports from $1,600,000 in 1807 to $240,000 in the following year in Rhode Island alone. It was estimated that $1,000,000,000 worth of produce was held in the United States by the embargo, and deteriorated or became a total loss." In Massachusetts, once proud Salem and Newburyport were completely ruined. Any hopes Newporters had of resuscitating their trading glories were fully dashed by Jefferson's economic boycott of the Continent. It can be argued that the Embargo of 1807 was the most significant blow to Newport's commerce, even larger than the War of 1812 itself. Needless to say, the embargo was wildly unpopular (except with manufacturers who benefited from the dearth of competing European goods); the General Assembly resolved in 1809 that the act was "unjust, oppressive, tyrannical, and unconstitutional." By that time, Jefferson had realized the folly of the suspension of trade, and the embargo was repealed in 1809. Lasting damage to the structure of the economy had been done. War was now all but inevitable.

Jefferson was succeeded by James Madison (also a Republican) in 1809, and in New England, the battle that ensued under his administration was referred to bitterly as Mr. Madison's War. The Northeast, unlike the South which lusted for armed action, was almost uniformly against the onset of hostilities because of the detrimental effect it would have on commerce. In Newport, there was little support for Henry Clay's desire to try to conquer Canada, because of the direct threat of a British attack from the north. Fort Adams, as it was then configured, was serviceable but not anywhere as formidable as it would be decades later. Narragansett Bay, again, lay open to the enemy, should Britain wish to reenact its maneuvers of 1776. For all the talk in Congress over the previous twenty years about the strategic importance of the bay and its towns, no real fortifications had been built there and residents felt abandoned by their national government. Newport was vulnerable, and given its experiences during the Revolution, the town's inhabitants were dead-set against taking on the intimidating Royal Navy.

What Newport thought did not matter in the new federal Capitol building in Washington, D. C. The declaration of war with Great Britain was passed by Congress and signed by the president in June 1812. Now the foreign-policy decisions made by the national government were having a direct effect on Rhode Island affairs, and neither the majority of politicians nor the populace were pleased. Trying to force Great Britain to respect America's maritime rights by going into battle seemed futile and was bound to be highly detrimental to trade. But Madison and the Republicans saw things on a broader canvas and were attempting to draw the nation together by standing up to London.

Rhode Island's response to the War of 1812 was to throw the respected, but Republican, James Fenner out of the governorship and replace him with the Federalist and openly antiwar William Jones, who had been born and raised in Newport but resided in Providence for commercial reasons. Jones had been a captain in the War of Independence, was captured at the siege of Charleston, and thereafter released on parole and not able to fight again for his country. Now, with another war facing him, Governor Jones repeatedly and vigorously protested Madison's actions, to no avail. However, Jones and the General Assembly chose to show their displeasure by withholding Rhode Island's 500-man militia from any fighting unless it occurred on the state's soil, much to the consternation of the war planners and politicians in Washington, D. C. Given their strong antiwar stance, the Federalists were able to maintain control of the General Assembly for years to come, and William Jones was reelected six times.

The War of 1812 was driven by matters on land as well as at sea. Many citizens of southern and mid-Atlantic states were eagerly seeking to expand their borders to the west, but they were effectively blocked by Native American tribes unwilling to be pushed from their ancestral lands once again. Violence escalated between the white pioneers and Indians. It was strongly rumored, and fully believed by the frontier settlers, that Britain, via Canada, was mischievously arming the Native Americans to repel the westward movement of large numbers of Americans and recent immigrants. London was not blind to the fact that, with the vast Louisiana Purchase in hand, a much larger United States might one day be a more dangerous enemy. Henry Clay, Speaker of the House of Representatives from Kentucky, and John Calhoun, senator from South Carolina, believed that the only way for Americans to move into the new territories was to expel the British from Canada and break their relationship with hostile Native Americans. Thus their strong support for confronting the English. In short, Republican land lust was a major motivation for the conflict, more so than the impressment of (mostly) New England seamen.

From a military standpoint, the War of 1812 resembled a badly acted vaudeville sketch more than it did a well-planned campaign. One would think that, since it was America that had initiated the hostilities, America would have been prepared. Such was not the case. President Madison had cajoled the country into war with no idea how woefully insufficient his men or materiel were at the outset. Without a trained, standing army, the United States was forced to depend on its various militias, where discipline was lax and coordination among groups poor. With Canada as the prime target, America attacked the British at Detroit, optimistically believing that the fight would be an easy and glorious victory. That hope was dashed when the American commander, General William Hull, surrendered his superior force to a regiment of Canadians in August 1812. One defeat or disaster followed upon another for the United States on the northern border. Battles along the Niagara and Saint Lawrence rivers brought victories for the English because of their early domination of the strategically crucial Great Lakes. Still locked in their epic struggle against Napoleon on the Continent, the British sent second-rank troops to America, and still they prevailed. The United States Navy began to show its strength with victories by the *Constitution* and other ships, but the British had begun to blockade the Atlantic seaboard, stranding many naval and commercial vessels in their harbors.

Despite its resentment at being coerced into a conflict it deemed detrimental to its future, Newport launched a number of successful privateering and naval missions from the harbor. Driven by patriotism and a well-deserved antipathy for the British, Newport sailors once again drew on their love for the chase. In the autumn of 1813, the *Vigilant*, a schooner built in Newport the year before and in the service of the United States Revenue Cutter Service, went after the British privateer *Dart*, which had already captured more than twenty American ships in Long Island Sound over the summer. Captain John Cahoone persuaded two dozen seamen to augment his regular crew and when the *Dart* appeared off Newport, the *Vigilant* was ready to do battle, even though the enemy ship was better armed. Surprising the *Dart* by sailing directly toward it and opening fire, Cahoone was able to dispatch a boarding party, which quickly overcame any resistance. The prize was brought to Newport and yet another threat to the town was neutralized.

By 1814, despite some American headway and a great naval victory at Lake Erie, the war looked to be a losing proposition. Britain sent more ships and men to the North American theater, increasing the pressure on the United States. By this time, most of New England, and Newport in particular, was steadfast against further engagements. The Royal Navy had appeared off Point Judith in previous years, spreading panic in the town; many people fled to the mainland. Trade had been reduced to nearby coastal expeditions, yielding little profit. Then, in the summer of 1814, the enemy changed its tactics and began assaulting ports along the Atlantic. In August, the British sailed up the Potomac River and torched the poorly defended United States Capitol and the White House as a symbolic display of its supremacy. The humiliated United States government was forced to retreat. Later that month, the British burned large portions of Stonington, Connecticut, so near Rhode Island that Governor Jones called out the militia and enforced Fort Adams. Newport again experienced the fear of invasion. Antiwar sentiment grew apace, and for good reason. According to one recent historian, "The British in fact planned to invade Rhode Island in September, but their military plans changed and the projected invasion never took place."

Then the combat took a sharp turn. The British were checked at the Battle of Fort McHenry near Baltimore and defeated at Plattsburgh, New York. In London, where there had been little enthusiasm for the war in the first place given the extraordinary costs associated with defeating Napoleon on the Continent, ministers looked for a way out. Peace offers were proffered, and President Madison, bewildered by the generally poor performance of his forces and also facing a depleted treasury, signaled his desire to end hostilities. John Quincy Adams, son of former president John Adams and a future chief executive himself, led the American delegation to Ghent, Holland, for months of niggling negotiations, which were finalized on Christmas Eve 1814. But news traveled slowly then, and when Andrew Jackson won a significant victory for America at the Battle of New Orleans in January 1815, after the war had technically ended, the United States felt more empowered and confident.

Diplomatically, the Treaty of Ghent changed almost nothing for either side. Impressment, supposedly the real reason for the war, was not addressed and did not stop; all conquered territories were restored to their former borders. The War of 1812 might be looked on as a fiasco, but in fact, some (questionable) gains were made within the United States: British support of Native Americans came to an end and many tribes were forced to submit to treaties, opening their lands to settlers eager to expand the boundaries of the country. It was an odd war, one that left Rhode Island disillusioned and bitter. Newport had fallen farther behind because of it, while Providence churned ahead with its newfound manufacturing economy. Perhaps the most positive spin on the War of 1812 can be summed up in the words of the historian Harvey Strum: "Although the conflict ended in a stalemate, Republicans considered it a victory, one that redeemed American honor, won the respect of Europe, proved the abilities of the citizen-soldier, and demonstrated that a republic could indeed wage war."

Oliver Hazard Perry and the Battle of Lake Erie

There was, however, one major military campaign during the War of 1812 that made Rhode Islanders—indeed, all Americans—proud. When the Newport resident Oliver Hazard Perry, then a twenty-seven-year-old captain in the United States Navy and commanding a small fleet of ships on Lake Erie, defeated a more formidable and experienced British force in a fierce one-day battle on September 10, 1813, America achieved the most notable victory over the Royal Navy in its history. Perry was catapulted to fame, feted throughout the country, and wined and dined everywhere he went. His bravery and prowess became legend.

Oliver Hazard Perry was born in South Kingston, Rhode Island, in 1785 to Christopher and Sarah Alexander Perry; his younger brother, Matthew C. Perry, would also grow up to figure prominently in American naval history by opening Japan to the West. Oliver was a compact, clever lad, handsome and full of energy. He was educated at home by his reputedly beautiful and strong-willed Irish mother, then the family moved to Newport and Oliver set off to learn about life at sea. There is an interesting parallel between the Perry family of the nineteenth century and the Wantons of the eighteenth. Both families had been staunch pacifist Quakers, yet both produced some of Newport's most illustrious fighters on the sea, two per family. Having rejected the Society of Friends' ban on carrying arms, both the "Fighting Wantons" and the "Fighting Perrys" brought military glory to Newport. Both families migrated to Episcopalian Trinity Church, both were among the town's most prominent citizens, and both have gone down in history for their varied accomplishments.

It is not hard to understand Oliver's love of, and success at, a career as a sailor. His father, Christopher, was an officer in the United States Navy and captain of the 180-man frigate *General Greene*. At the age of thirteen, Oliver Hazard Perry signed on to his father's crew as a midshipman and began to distinguish himself from the start. After initiation in battle against the French off Haiti in 1800, the young Perry was assigned to the *Adams* for service in the Mediterranean Sea against Tripolitan pirates in the Barbary War. Despite his tender age, he quickly rose in rank because of his conspicuous abilities, both as a seaman and a leader of men. By 1805, the navy had awarded Oliver Perry the command of the *Nautilus*, a heavily armed schooner that saw action at the decisive battle of Darnah, off the Libyan coast. And he hadn't yet turned twenty years old.

When commanded to report back to Newport from 1807 to 1809 to construct a fleet of gunboats to help enforce President Jefferson's Embargo Act, the spirited Lieutenant Perry met his match in Miss Elizabeth Champlin Mason, one of Newport's famous beauties and a member of two of the town's most prominent families. The couple courted for four years, married in May 1811, and had four sons and a daughter. In between their meeting and wedding, Perry was given command of the *Revenge*, which, after a successful recapture of an American ship that had fallen into British hands, ran aground off Watch Hill, Rhode Island, in a storm. Perry was exonerated of any blame by a court of enquiry, because the ship was under the command of a pilot at the time of the accident. Still, losing one's ship, regardless of the circumstances, is not a smart move for career advancement in any navy.

Back in Newport at the outbreak of the War of 1812, and concerned about his own future as well as his country's, Perry wrote letters to Washington pleading for a command that would get him back in the

Artist unknown
Oliver Hazard Perry,
c. early 19th century
Oil on canvas
Photograph by Daniel McManus
The State Archives,
the State of Rhode Island and
Providence Plantations
Providence, Rhode Island

FARE REDUCED

BETWEEN

PROVIDENCE, NEWPORT,

AND

NEW-YORK.

CABIN FARE from BOSTON to NEW-YORK, $3 25—DECK DO. $1 88.
Do   Do   PROVIDENCE   Do   2 00— Do Do 1 00.

Cabin Passage $1.—
Deck do _____ 75 cts

THE SPLENDID STEAMBOAT

TELEGRAPH,

CAPTAIN WILLIAM J. WISWALL,

WILL LEAVE INDIA POINT, PROVIDENCE,

On *Saturday Evening* ~~May~~ *June 21st*

At half-past 5 o'clock P. M.

On the arrival of the Mail Train of Cars from Boston.

This Boat has recently been put in the most complete order, and is now as competent to perform her trips as any Steamboat on the Sound.   In order to *insure* safety she carries, in addition to the ordinary Quarter Boats, one of Ingersoll's Patent Life Boats, (capable of supporting 100 persons,) and a powerful Fire Engine, besides Hose Attachments to the Propelling Engine.

All kinds of Freight taken at the lowest rates.   Passengers by this Boat will arrive in New-York in time to take the Morning Boats for the South and West.

Leaves Newport at 8 oclk, PM ___ **C. H. BRAINARD**, 82 Washington Street, or to the Agent on the Wharf.

A. Hanford, Xylographer, 58 Nassau Street, N.Y.

during the summer months, ensuring an easy way for Carolinians to reach Aquidneck Island as the number of Southern visitors blossomed even before the 1830s. But as familiar and reliable as these wind-borne ships were, something new was on the horizon. Several inventors in Europe and America had successfully tinkered with private steam-powered ships, but not until Robert Fulton launched his commercial 150-foot *Clermont* on the Hudson River in 1807 did the general public take real notice. The inaugural voyage from New York to Albany took over thirty hours as the wood-charged paddlewheels worked against the current, but the excitement over the extraordinary evolution from sail to steam was universal. A new age had dawned, one in which the vagaries of weather and wind would no longer have to hold a ship in port. Precise schedules were now possible, and even though the new breed of steamship was smelly, dirty, and noisy, ocean-going passengers were enthralled by the new technology.

In 1817, the steamboat *Firefly* spent the summer in Narragansett Bay, ferrying passengers and freight between Newport and Providence. Although often initially slower than the sloops plying the bay, it must have been clear to most observers that the days of sail would eventually become extinct in the world of commerce. Between 1822 and 1830, steamships provided regular summer service between Providence and New York, with a stop in each direction at Newport. The trip at that time took about thirty hours, cut down later to ten hours, when bigger, more efficient coal-burning engines were invented. There was little room on these early steamers for passengers: because they burned wood and the journeys took so long, practically the entire deck of each vessel was piled high with cords of fuel. But progress in improving the ships was remarkably swift. According to Stuart Hale, an expert on Narragansett Bay history, "The first commercial Bay steamers, the *Fulton* and the *Connecticut*, were relatively slow and relied on sails as well when the wind was favorable, but in 1826 the *Washington* made a round trip to New York in 48 hours, including a nine-hour stopover. The *Chancellor Livingston*, launched in 1828, could make 8 ½ miles an hour and accommodate passengers in its main cabin, where meals prepared by a master chef were served. By 1829, speed had increased amazingly. The *President*, launched that year, was reported capable of 17 miles an hour." By the mid-1830s, steamship companies

ISLAND ISOLATION

Given its isolated geographic locale, Newport was at a disadvantage when it came to easy land travel. All trips to the mainland depended on water-borne routes until 1794, when First Bridge linked northern Aquidneck Island with the eastern mainland at Tiverton. But it wasn't until 1929 that the Mount Hope Bridge was erected, connecting Portsmouth to Bristol. The Pell-Newport Bridge, which changed the chemistry of Newport forever, did not open until 1969. Thus the Newport to Jamestown ferry, which operated from 1675 until 1969, was one of the longest-running public transportation systems in America.

J. P. Newell
Sketches of American Scenery: Steamboat and R. R. Depot at Newport, R. I., 1866
Colored lithograph
Boston, Massachusetts:
L. Prang and Co.
Redwood Library
and Athenæum
Newport, Rhode Island
Gift of Hamilton Fish Webster
and Lina Post Webster
Webster.24

began installing sleeping berths on board, so the trip from New York to Newport could be navigated at night and the pampered passengers would arrive in town refreshed.

Just as the Watt steam engine revolutionized maritime travel, the same phenomenon was occurring with travel on land. For centuries the trusty, docile horse had conveyed humans on its back, pulled carts, carriages, and plows, and proved to be the most reliable of beasts. Horse-drawn stagecoaches had become the staple of travel before the 1830s and the advent of railroads. In earlier times, passengers wishing to go from Newport to New York City by land would begin their journey at the ferry wharf, sail to Wickford, then board a stagecoach for the long ride south. Stagecoach lines all had relationships with taverns and inns along the route so passengers could take a rest and be wined and dined. By the 1820s, ferryboats were large enough to accommodate coaches, horses, and passengers, so one could board a coach in Newport and not be bothered by getting on and off various vehicles. According to one historian, by "about 1825 the horse boat at Slade's Ferry began to carry stage-coaches and Isaac Fish ran coaches from Boston to Bristol and Newport over the ferry. In the rates of ferriage for the Newport horse boat in 1828 the charge for a stage-coach was to be $0.75."

But the stagecoach business quickly faded when railroads began pushing out from New York and Boston in the 1830s, covering the land with thousands of miles of steel track and driving the Industrial Revolution to the frontier. Rail and steam companies conspired to coordinate schedules to make travel in New England as swift and comfortable as possible. By 1838, rail lines stretched from Boston to Stonington, Connecticut, where a steamship would finish the trip to New York City. Still, Newporters were at a disadvantage

for off-island travel because the ferry was the only means to reach rail hubs until the 1860s, when a railroad bridge was constructed connecting Aquidneck Island to Tiverton and points north. Before that bridge, the most efficient way to get to New York after 1845 was via the Fall River Line steamer, which used Newport as its base of operations. In fact, most visitors to Newport from New York or Philadelphia preferred the Fall River Line to the railroads, especially in summer and fall months when the sea voyage was peaceful, relaxing, and less arduous.

Fort Adams and Other Structures

Around Newport, expansion of another variety was taking place. In 1795, French engineer Louis de Tousard was charged by Congress to strengthen the defenses of Narragansett Bay by establishing a new fortification on what was then known as Brenton's Point, now called Fort Adams (the present-day Brenton's Point is a state park at the south end of Aquidneck Island). The United States Military Academy on the Hudson River was just being formed and as yet had not graduated any engineers trained in the science of military defense, so President Adams was forced to seek expertise abroad; the French, as everyone in Europe understood, had the best military siege planners of all. Tousard was asked to help organize a national system of strategic forts to protect the Atlantic seaboard and Gulf of Mexico from enemy attack. As had been bitterly learned in the War of Independence, if Newport and Narragansett Bay were in enemy hands, New York and Boston, indeed all of New England, would be vulnerable.

According to the architect Willard B. Robinson, who acted as technical expert on the restoration of Fort Adams in the early 1970s, "Defense of the Narragansett [Bay] was considered one of the most important objectives of the national system. Tousard had earlier reported that it is 'the best Harbour on the Coast of the United States.' When he was instructed to strengthen defenses of Newport with construction of several batteries on Brenton's Point, his judgment on the importance of the Bay had motivated him to 'request permission for building a small closed Fort and render the works permanent by erecting a wall inside and outside.'" Tousard spent several years in Newport erecting his fortification, and upon completion on the Fourth of July, 1799, he installed a stone tablet above the main gateway inscribed: "Fort Adams. The Rock on Which the Storm Will Beat." It was a good beginning, but by 1820 the fort had been so neglected as to be practically useless against attack by a new class of large naval ships of the line carrying hundreds of guns and cannons. The fort was also too small, as had been learned during the War of 1812 when less than a hundred men were sent to garrison it when the Americans feared another British invasion. Tousard's Fort Adams could only accommodate twelve guns, obviously an insignificant number against an enemy fleet.

So in the early 1820s, the fledgling Army Corps of Engineers began the task of guarding America's coastline with strong fortifications able to withstand sustained nautical attack. Congress was adamant that the ignominy suffered by the British burning of Washington, D. C., during the War of 1812 was *not* to be repeated. Several forts were erected in the South, then the Frenchman Simon Bernard, a military engineer with a degree from the prestigious L'Ecole Polytechnique,

WILLIAM HUNTER

When the esteemed Dr. William Hunter died in Newport in 1777, his son William was only three years old, far too young to be influenced by his father's ardent Tory sympathies. In a fine reversal of fortune, young William grew up to become one of Newport's most honored political figures of the nineteenth century. In 1786, William's Loyalist mother, Deborah Malbone Hunter, in an attempt to persuade the British government to repay her for the family losses during the war and in need of an eye specialist for her ailing daughter Eliza, sailed to London, leaving her twelve-year-old son in the care of Dr. Hunter's apothecary, Charles Feke. She never returned to America. William went to the school of the renowned classicist Robert Rogers (present-day Rogers High School is named for him), who prepared him so well that the boy entered Rhode Island College (later Brown University) and graduated at the age of seventeen, in 1791. William Hunter followed his mother to London later that year, intending to follow his father into medicine, but was more intrigued by a career in law. He prepared at the Inner Temple and studied with some of London's most esteemed scholars and orators. He returned to Newport in 1793, was admitted to the Rhode Island bar in 1795 at age

CONTINUED ON PAGE 272

twenty-one, and four years later won election to the General Assembly, a position he held until 1811 when he was selected by the governor to fill a vacant seat in the United States Senate. Three years later, he was elected for a full six-year term. Hunter was a brilliant speaker, and was highly respected by his peers in the Senate for his moderating politics and fair play.

In 1804, William had married Mary Robinson, a New York Quaker and a descendant of the Wanton family, and a year later they had moved into what we know today as Hunter House on Washington Street, the most celebrated private colonial dwelling in Newport. In 1834, William Hunter was appointed by President Andrew Jackson to be the chargé d'affaires to Brazil, and his relationship with the emperor, Dom Pedro, was so congenial that the ruler asked that Hunter be promoted to the position of minister plenipotentiary, a title he held until being recalled in 1845. The Hunters returned to their house in Newport, where he returned to his writing on religious freedom in Rhode Island. William Hunter died four years later, his book unfinished.

together with the American Joseph Totten, a lieutenant colonel in the army, came to Newport to set about designing and building one of the nation's most secure forts—one that would deny an enemy fleet access to the bay and also withstand an attack on the ground. Apart from Fort Adams, planned to be the jewel in the crown of Narragansett defenses, forts on Conanicut, Goat, and Rose islands were also envisioned, although the work was never fully completed. Beginning in 1824, engineers totally leveled Tousard's old fort and set to work after Congress appropriated $50,000 for the new structure.

Standing on the 52-acre grounds, once a grazing pasture for William Brenton in the 1650s, the new Fort Adams began to rise in 1825; construction went on steadily until the mid-1840s, when the major work was completed and a garrison of artillery troops was stationed there. Final touches went on until 1857 because Joseph Totten, by then chief of the Army Corps of Engineers, used Fort Adams as a training ground for young engineers. By the time he was finished, the total cost was over $3 million, and Totten had created one of the largest and most impenetrable structures in America—a testament to the importance of Narragansett Bay in the eyes of military strategists.

Based on the fortification theories developed by the brilliant Sébastien de Vauban for King Louis XIV in the latter half of the seventeenth century, and improved upon by another French engineer, Marc René, the marquis de Montalembert, a hundred years later, Fort Adams is a pentagonal-shaped giant wedge measuring over 1,740 yards at the perimeter; hovering over the entrance to Narragansett Bay, it denies passage to any enemy vessel intrepid (or imprudent) enough to sally forth across its lines. Built of local shale and huge granite blocks imported from Maine, the edifice also consumed an untold number of bricks produced in and around Newport. Totten advertised regularly in the *Newport Mercury* for supplies and workers. One advertisement in January 1831 states the conditions for a contract for the delivery of "1,000,000 Common Bricks, 8 inches by 4 inches by 2 1-4 inches" that were to be used in shaping the huge three-story gun casements.

And who set those millions of bricks? The construction of Fort Adams ushered in a new era in Newport's expansion and rebirth with the beginning of Irish immigration to Rhode Island, and it was chiefly Irish-born masons who were responsible for the back-breaking part of the fort's creation. Ireland's economy was almost totally dependent on agriculture, yet beginning with the Penal Laws in the seventeenth century, London mandated the consolidation of small farms into vast estates to enrich the mostly Anglo-Irish and Scottish Protestant aristocrats. Disenfranchised tenant farmers were left even more impoverished as their legal rights were severely proscribed, decade after decade, by Parliament. In the 1840s, the country was suffering from massive failures of its staple crop, the potato. Famine was rife, and thousands of people looked to America as an answer to their plight.

The Irish exodus to America was beginning, as was another transformation in Rhode Island's religious profile, since the majority of the newcomers were Roman Catholic. Most of the early Irish settlers were semi-educated farmers, accustomed to hard work, and these were the men who helped build Fort Adams. When later potato crop failures became epidemic, poorer, uneducated subjects began arriving en masse. Some native Yankee Rhode Islanders became alarmed, and agitation against Catholics began in earnest in the 1840s.

Regardless of the nationality of the laborers, they had their work cut out for them by the sheer scale of the fort. The granite perimeter walls are five feet thick, more than enough to withstand bombardment from a passing fleet, which at the same time must be receiving a severe pounding from the fort's 468 cannons, distributed in three tiers and mostly tucked safely away in fortified casements for protection. Fort Adams was state-of-the-art when it was completed, even though artillery advancements had rendered many of its sister forts unsafe in the intervening decades. Since the 1850s, the fort has withstood the vicissitudes of weather and decay, yet still stands proud and untamed against the elements. It has been home to numerous social functions, picnics for officers and their ladies, the famous Newport Jazz and Folk Festivals, countless romances, and nesting owls. The only event Fort Adams has *not* witnessed was the one it was built for—war. After all the money and effort expended to protect the bay, the irony is that once Newport was finally safe from the ravages of a marauding enemy, no naval force ever directly threatened the town again. Had Fort Adams been built before the Revolution, it is doubtful the British would have ventured their assault and occupation of Newport. Timing is everything.

While Fort Adams was the most ambitious structure to proclaim the spirit and determination of Newport during the first half of the nineteenth century, a number of other projects and public buildings, mostly

Artist unknown
Fort Adams,
c. late 19th century
Color lithograph
Redwood Library
and Athenæum
Newport, Rhode Island
Gift of Hamilton Fish Webster
and Lina Post Webster
Webster.74.4

churches, were also being created. In 1800, the former Parade, now renamed Washington Square, was formalized with circular paths and rows of Lombardy poplar trees, a gift from the same Major Tousard who designed the original fort. Between 1806 and 1807, the town's first Methodist Episcopal church—St. Paul's, on Marlborough Street—went into use, but not without controversy. According to a writer in 1882, "When it was noised abroad that a Methodist church had been built in Newport with a steeple and pews, and that it was fitted with ornaments like those of other denominations, there was a decided sensation. Good Bishop Asbury lifted his hands with holy horror when he first saw it and predicted that a church which began with a steeple would end with a choir, and perhaps even with an organ. It is understood that this was the first Methodist church with pews, steeple and bell in America, and probably in the world." For the austere Methodists, this was indeed a departure.

In 1824, the first organized black church was established by the former slave Newport Gardner, a man famous throughout town for his turtle soup. Called the Colored Union Church and consisting of some twenty members, the church was actually an outgrowth of the 1780s-era Free African Union Society, which claimed to be the first African cultural organization in America. The group purchased the Fourth Baptist Church on Division Street and began holding regular services.

Although Roman Catholics with the French army celebrated mass in the Colony House during

Union Congregational Church, 1870

The progenitor of all African-American churches in Newport.

Photographer unknown

Newport Historical Society

Newport, Rhode Island

their year-long stay in Newport in 1780–1781, after their departure, there were few, if any, adherents to that faith. When Irish and European laborers arrived to work on Fort Adams, the Catholic church responded by organizing a parish and purchasing a small building on Barney and Mount Vernon streets for religious services. The number of Catholics increased quickly, so St. Joseph's parish was built in 1837; a decade later, St. Mary's Church was started at Spring Street and what is today Memorial Boulevard to accommodate a larger congregation. (It was at St. Mary's in 1953 that the Massachusetts Senator John F. Kennedy married Jacqueline Bouvier, whose mother lived at Hammersmith Farm.) The other significant religious structure of the period was the Greek Revival Zion Episcopal Church at Touro and Clarke streets, erected in 1834. A good indication of how times change but buildings remain basically the same can be found in the fact that the edifice, which was originally built for the glory of God, in the early twenty-first century served to worship Hollywood—it was a movie theater.

On the domestic front, Newport was changing very little. Most houses retained colonial-style features and remained relatively small. The Historic Hill section, particularly upper John Street, began to be built up on small lots after 1800; in 1835 Alexander McGregor, the chief stonemason on the construction of Fort Adams, built himself a wooden Greek Revival house at 63 John Street, and others followed suit. But there were some exceptions. According to Antoinette Downing,

> the three-story, hip-roofed brick mansion that Samuel Whitehorne, successful merchant and distiller, built on the southeast corner of Thames and Dennison Streets in 1804, equals in charm and handling the best early nineteenth-century houses of Providence and Salem. . . . The front door with its leaded glass sidelights and the elliptical leaded fanlight above, the roundheaded hall windows and the top story's bull's eye windows combine to enhance the early republican character of the style. In the interior, a broad elliptical arch separates the front hall from the back, where the stairway rises in two runs to the second floor. In essence this is the same scheme employed in the Hunter house of 1750, and again, the difference is one of detail and scale . . . Samuel Whitehorne's mansion is one of Newport's finest nineteenth-century houses.

Newport was expanding. Other significant Greek Revival houses were built on Mill and Pelham streets and around Touro Park. But on the whole, until the Kay-Catherine streets neighborhood and later Bellevue Avenue began to be developed, Newport remained a largely colonial town in look and in feeling.

Newport Artists

For hundreds of years, the countryside around Newport has inspired artists because of its abundant natural beauty. Dozens of first-class painters have attempted to capture the charms of the landscape, the gentle roll of the hills, the majesty of the ocean, and the luminous quality of the air.

DR. BENJAMIN WATERHOUSE

One of Newport's most eminent native sons of the era was the irascible Dr. Benjamin Waterhouse, whose life spanned nearly a century. Born in town in 1754, he was a childhood classmate and friend of Gilbert Stuart, who painted the portrait of the twenty-two-year-old Waterhouse that hangs in the Redwood Library. Because of the wealth of medical texts at the Redwood, Waterhouse determined as a young man what his calling would be. He studied with the finest physicians in London for three years, went on for a degree in medicine at Edinburgh, and finished off his education at Leiden, where he roomed with John Adams and his son, John Quincy. He returned to Newport at the end of the Revolutionary War, but because of his superb education, he was soon appointed professor of theory and practice at the new Harvard Medical School in Cambridge, where he had a long and stormy tenure. Waterhouse's fame rests primarily on his battle to introduce the cowpox vaccine in America to battle the dreaded smallpox, a disease that killed approximately 10 percent of the world population in the eighteenth century. Most of Waterhouse's less far-seeing contemporaries were aghast at the idea of inoculation, and fought his efforts. But when he received

CONTINUED ON PAGE 276

some of Edward Jenner's vaccine from London in 1800, he immediately used it on his five-year-old son and other family members. It worked. After Waterhouse successfully lobbied other states to begin systematic inoculations for children, with positive results, others in the medical profession reluctantly came to understand the benefit of vaccinations for saving lives. After being forced to resign his post at Harvard in 1812 because of ongoing feuds with other faculty members, Waterhouse was appointed hospital surgeon for the Eastern Military District by President Madison, and later medical superintendent of New England's army bases. He had wide-ranging interests, was a prolific and successful writer on scientific subjects, and was throughout his life a controversial man. Waterhouse died in Cambridge in 1846, by which time his championing of the smallpox vaccine had saved countless lives in America.

A number of early painters associated with the town concentrated more on people and portraiture, and Newport's reputation of being a haven for artists, fostered in the eighteenth century by the presence of John Smibert, Robert Feke, Samuel King, and Gilbert Stuart, did not vanish with the town's temporarily reduced circumstances. In the early nineteenth century, the men and women who drew their inspiration from the local culture and countryside carried on the fine arts tradition with passion and true talent.

Of the five most prominent artists who had direct connections with Newport in this era—Edward Greene Malbone, Washington Allston, Michele Felice Cornè, Jane Stuart, and Charles Bird King—probably the most historically significant painter was Malbone. Born in Newport in 1777 to John Malbone and his common-law wife, Patience Greene, Edward displayed talent early on and was producing detailed and sophisticated miniature portraits before he even reached his teens. For several generations, the Malbone family had been prosperous, well-respected in town for their military and commercial acumen, and well traveled; thus Edward was encouraged in his pursuit of an artistic career. Malbone's early and devoted friendship with his fellow artist Washington Allston, when the latter was living in Newport for health reasons, undoubtedly fired his enthusiasm for art.

Most biographers of Edward Greene Malbone describe him as essentially self-taught as a painter, although there is evidence that both he and Allston received some training from Samuel King, a fascinating, Newport artist and navigational-instrument maker whose portrait of Abraham Redwood resides, appropriately, in the Redwood Library. King was considered the resident sage because of his many talents, which included dabbling in miniatures, and tradition dictates that he gave Malbone some of his own work to copy. Whatever instruction the young man received, it is evident that he was devoted to painting above all else.

Like many enterprising young men of the time, Malbone set off at the age of seventeen to make his name in more cosmopolitan, and wealthier, environs. Starting in Providence, where he advertised his availability in the local newspapers, Malbone quickly attracted a devoted clientele and remained there for two years painting dozens of miniatures. The art historian Martha Severens explains, "During the early years of the American Republic, miniature portraits were a popular art form, often used to commemorate such important personal events as courtships and marriages. Because of their small size (Malbone's usually measure 2 15/16 inches by 2 5/16 inches), their delicate technique (watercolor on ivory), and their often precious settings (gold lockets, sometimes set with semiprecious stones and accompanied by locks of hair), miniatures were ideal expressions of affection."

Malbone next settled in Boston, where his good friend Washington Allston was completing his education at Harvard, and continued his work with the upper-crust patrons who were eager to pay $50 to $100 for his portraits. Ever peripatetic, Malbone set off to conquer Philadelphia, New York, and Charleston, before he and Allston departed in 1801 for London, then the capital of the art world. Malbone's maturing talent was apparent to everyone, and he rapidly succeeded in capturing the attention of Benjamin West, the president of the Royal Academy, who was enthralled with Malbone's delicate work. For the next six years, Malbone continued his itinerant ways, traveling among Boston, Newport, New York, and cities in the

South, continually being sought out by the best families to have their portraits painted. But Edward Greene Malbone was not destined to live long enough to reap the praise he so obviously deserved. Having contracted tuberculosis, Malbone died in Savannah, Georgia, at the age of twenty-nine, having produced over seven hundred portraits in just twelve years.

Malbone was a gentle man, admired and befriended by many people. As an artist of miniatures, he was considered a genius as a technician, and his work evolved markedly even in such a short time span. Severens remarks,

> Malbone capitalized on the translucency of his medium, creating expansive and airy portraits. The hallmark of his style—something his imitators never fully captured—is a delicate system of hatching and cross-hatching, usually most visible in his backgrounds. . . . Malbone's sitters invariably appear self-assured, well bred, and handsome. More often than not the subjects were young. Malbone is credited with creating pleasing likenesses, as noted by Allston: "He had the happy talent among his excellencies, of elevating the character without impairing the likeness, this was remarkable in the male heads, and no woman ever lost any beauty from his hand, nay, the fair would often become still fairer under his pencil."

some portraits, but somehow the spirit that had sustained him for so long was spent. He toiled away at one large canvas, *Belshazzar's Feast*, for decades without ever finishing it. America caused him to lose his grand vision, even though he was able to assemble an exhibit of forty-seven canvases in Boston in 1839, many of which have been lost. Four years later, Washington Allston was dead. In the opinion of the art historian Kristen Foster,

> In contrast to the attention he received in England, Allston continually found the American public uninterested in romantic idealism. When they did show an interest in art, Americans preferred the political messages embodied in the canvases of neoclassical painters. . . . In the early nineteenth century many critics considered Allston to be one of the greatest painters produced by the United States. Nevertheless, by the end of that century his reputation was in decline, and with the triumph of artistic realism in the twentieth century, many argued that the painter's efforts to bring romantic idealism to America had failed completely. However, scholars have begun to express a new appreciation for the breadth of Allston's vision within the context of America's early republic.

Of lesser note in the pantheon of art history, but an important tale nonetheless, is the colorful calling of the later Newport resident Michele Felice Cornè. Born on the island of Elba in 1752, he rose to the rank of captain in the Neapolitan army, and fought against Napoleon before adventuring to America in 1800 on a ship hailing from Salem, Massachusetts. Cornè landed penniless but possessed ready talent with a brush, so, like many millions of immigrants before and since, he created a new life for himself. Nina Little, an expert on the artist, states, "Apparently Cornè had received training as an ornamental painter before he left Italy, for he seems to have lost no time in entering upon that career in Salem. Within a decade it brought him recognition in many areas of decorative painting, including scenic murals, overmantel pictures, fireboards, and large panoramas. His subjects may be broadly grouped under marines, portraits, and landscapes. They were variously executed in oil, watercolor, and gouache on wood, canvas, and paper."

Cornè moved to Boston around 1812 and stayed for ten years painting frescoes for many houses, as well as tavern signs, lively fireboards, and other architectural pieces. Already known throughout New England for his paintings of ships, his big break came in 1816 when he was commissioned to illustrate the book *The Naval Monument* with twenty-one paintings depicting famous naval engagements during the War of 1812. The book was very popular and eased the artist's monetary worries. In 1822 he visited Newport, liked the slower pace of the town, bought a piece of property at the corner of what are now Mill and Cornè streets, and built a house for himself. In his *Reminiscences of Newport* (published in 1884) George Champlin Mason writes, "There was no employment in Newport for Cornè's pencil—not a picture to paint, not a wall to decorate. In the full vigor of his manhood, when he arrived here, flushed with his recent success, he could hardly content himself to live in idleness." So, Mason goes on, the artist contented himself with painting images on the walls and floors of his new house, a project that took him years.

Cornè was very social and a grand storyteller, regaling his guests with tales of Italian wars in his heavily accented English. According to Mason's memoir, Cornè was famous in town for a reason that had

nothing to do with his art: "He was the first person in Newport to eat tomatoes. Before his advent here those vegetables were looked upon as poisonous." Clearly the tomatoes did more help than harm, because Michele Felice Cornè died in Newport in 1845, at the age of ninety-three.

Nina Little sums up his achievement: "Cornè's work is far from academic, yet his competent, professional style hardly places his land- and seascapes in the category of naïve American Art. He was obviously a talented ornamental painter, although the quality of his work admittedly varied. But his remarkable versatility, picturesque personality, and crisp, colorful technique combined to bring a refreshingly different dimension to early nineteenth-century New England art."

Although largely ignored by art historians today, Jane Stuart deserves mention not only because she was the only child (out of twelve) of Gilbert Stuart's to pursue a career as a painter, but because she had talent. Overshadowed by her difficult father's fame for her entire life, Jane Stuart became a highly proficient copier of his work; some critics believe that she actually painted large portions of Gilbert Stuart's canvases in his later years when he was physically incapacitated. Born in Boston in 1812, Jane Stuart showed an early talent for painting and often sat with her father when he was at work in his studio. He encouraged her proclivities but apparently would not give her serious formal instruction, because he believed that painting could not be taught. Nonetheless, his youngest daughter matured rapidly in her craft. When Gilbert died Jane was only

sixteen; she inherited some of his unfinished work, his easel, and his devotion to portraiture.

Along with her mother and sisters, Jane Stuart moved to Newport in 1831 and, until her death in 1888, became, in the words of Berit Hattendorf, the "most prolific portraitist in Newport during the nineteenth century," dominating the town's artistic and intellectual sphere from her home at 86 Mill Street with her weekly receptions, parties, and teas. Aside from the copies of her father's work, including one of George Washington that hangs in the Redwood Library, Jane Stuart was best known and respected for her loving portraits of children. In an excellent short monograph on Stuart, Hattendorf asserts: "In her own work she had an unusual diversity and, like her father, a keen eye for color. She often painted from daguerreotypes and ambrotypes, allowing her to expand her business successfully to meet a wider range of customers. In doing this, she developed a very individualistic style, but in her copies of her father's work, she became his most successful emulator."

After her death, an obituary writer for the *Newport Mercury* had this to say about Jane Stuart: "She bore a striking likeness to her father in the face and inherited much of his epigrammatic powers of conversation. She was a woman of brilliant wit, quaint powers of satire, with a rare knowledge of the world, and maintained a high social position to the last in spite of poverty and many embarrassments, and her society was much sought by cultured frequenters of Newport."

The last of the quintet of Newport artists who left their mark on early nineteenth-century American culture is Charles Bird King, born in 1785 to Zebulon King and Deborah Bird King, a prosperous couple who had a long association with the town. The elder King had served as a captain in the Continental Army during the Revolution and, as a result, had been awarded a plot of land in Marietta, Ohio, as compensation. Tilling his fields one day four years after the birth of his only son, King was attacked by Native Americans and murdered, and Charles Bird King came into a large inheritance that allowed him to devote his life to pursuing a career as a painter.

Charles Bird King was raised in Newport in his mother's Moravian faith, an upbringing that influenced him for life because he is universally depicted as a gracious, honest, and especially generous man. His good friend and fellow-artist Thomas Sully said of him: "As a man, he is one of the purest in morals and principle. Steady in friendship, and tenderly affectionate . . . without professing to belong to any *particular* set of Christians, he is the best practical Christian I ever was acquainted with. Possessing wealth, a clear conscience, and talent, King lived one of the most serene existences of any artist of his age—perhaps of any age."

Like his friends Edward Greene Malbone and Washington Allston, King also received early training from Samuel King (no relation) during his childhood in Newport. His grandfather Nathaniel Bird, a well-to-do merchant, also painted, and it is likely that the boy enjoyed both instruction and encouragement from

Charles Bird King
Self-Portrait at 30, c. 1815
Oil on canvas
Redwood Library
and Athenæum
Newport, Rhode Island
Bequest of the artist
RLC.PA.060

Bird, who became his surrogate father. But King himself recounted that the biggest influence of his youth was the Redwood Library, where he spent days on end studying literature, the arts, and architecture. So deep and lasting was his affection for the Redwood that he became one of the most active and generous benefactors in the library's history. Along with William Ellery Channing, who also frequented the Redwood in his Newport youth, Charles Bird King was forever transformed by the ability to rummage through the stacks of one of America's finest libraries.

King's real passion, however, was painting, and in 1800 he set off for five years of professional training in New York City from Edward Savage, followed by six years in London at the Royal Academy under the tutelage of his fellow-American Benjamin West, then head of the prestigious institution. Most of King's London paintings are lost to us, but it is reported by Andrew Cosentino, who wrote in his 1977 work on King, that he produced scenes from Shakespeare's plays, mythological renditions, and numerous portraits. Thomas Sully, on King at that time, wrote: "I found him, as a fellow student, the most industrious person I ever met with. He limited his hours of sleep to four—was jealous of the least loss of time—his meals were dispatched in haste, even then (while eating) he read some instructive book. By his unremitting assiduity he has amassed a fund of useful knowledge."

Confident of his skills and not wanting to remain in London while his country was at war with England, King returned to Newport in 1812 with twenty-seven volumes of books, which he presented to the Redwood Library, the first of his many gifts over the next half century. Then he spent a peripatetic six years living in Philadelphia, Baltimore, and Washington, D. C., honing his craft as a portraitist. Witty, urbane, and well-read, King made friends wherever he lived. In 1817, he painted portraits of President James Monroe and Daniel Webster. The active social and diplomatic life in Washington clearly appealed to him, because he chose the capital as his primary residence from 1818 until his death over forty years later. "During his many years in Washington, he was eminently successful both as an artist and as a social figure. As Dunlap noted while in Washington in 1824, King was 'full of business and a great favorite, assiduously employed in his painting room through the day, and in the evening attending the soirées, parties, and balls of ambassadors, secretaries of the cabinet, president or other representatives and servants of the people, and justly esteemed everywhere.'"

But Charles Bird King never lost his love for Newport, and he returned there every summer to his house on Clarke Street, renewing old friendships and meeting visitors from the burgeoning vacation colony. And his close association with the Redwood Library continued without interruption—practically every other year, King gave more books, paintings, and cash to the institution. Yet his relationship with Newport was at times bittersweet. King carried dozens of paintings up from Washington one summer in the early 1850s, built a gallery addition to his house, and let the people of the town know that they were welcome to stop by and partake of his work. Almost no one did, and King sulkily resented the rebuff. From his point of view, Newport just was not sophisticated enough to appreciate his talent.

During his long sojourn in Washington, King spent his time painting diplomats, politicians, and other distinguished visitors. But his real reputation rests on his careful and caring portraits of American Indians painted over the course of thirty years. Whenever a Native American delegation was invited to the capital for the seemingly endless negotiations with Congressional committees on the fate of their futures, King would arrange to paint the most prominent of their leaders, at the behest of the Bureau of Indian

Affairs. In all, he produced about one hundred canvases of these men of various Indian nations, and when gathered together in the new Indian Gallery, the first government-sponsored collection of art in the United States, they were lauded by most observers for their faithfulness and force of character. One critic commented, "It is the only collection of paintings in this city, and though not very extensive, is equal, if not superior to any in this country in beauty of coloring and skillfulness of execution." It is curious to note that the man whose father was scalped by Indians went on to become their most sympathetic portrayer.

A large fire consumed much of the Smithsonian Institution in 1865, devouring the bulk of King's Indian collection. The artist, however, was not around to mourn the loss of so much toil and assiduousness: Charles Bird King had died three years before in Washington and had been laid to rest in Newport. A few years before his death, he had given the Redwood Library 78 paintings, but his bequest in his will was stunning. He made a gift to the library of 395 books, another 75 paintings, $10,000, and 14 volumes of scrapbooks, bound and unbound, of engravings. In all, it is estimated that he gave the Redwood some 215 canvases, and the scrapbooks contain more than 1,100 prints and a scattering of original drawings. When it came to Newport, Charles Bird King was a munificent man.

William Ellery Channing

Since its founding in 1639, Newport had been the cradle of religious tolerance and autonomy in North America, accepting and protecting people of nearly every persuasion. The constant struggle over issues of faith that dominated the seventeenth century grew less contentious in the eighteenth century as political concerns trumped ecclesiastical ones and the Rhode Island Way, an insistence on freedom of choice without persecution, became the creed of the new United States. But in the nineteenth century, just at the time Roman Catholics began arriving in significant numbers from Europe and the British Isles, a deep schism emerged in the once all-powerful branch of Massachusetts Puritanism, the Congregational church. And the man who led the charge in liberalizing that bastion of strict Calvinist teaching—and in doing so, creating a new Christian sect called Unitarianism—was a Newport native, William Ellery Channing.

Channing was more than simply a religious pioneer: his essays and sermons deeply influenced generations of thinkers who put the Unitarian movement on the map in New England, as well as those writers (Ralph Waldo Emerson, Henry David Thoreau, and others) who championed a more radical ideology known as Transcendentalism. William Ellery Channing was the primary force, spiritual and intellectual, behind the rejection of the harsh conservatism of Congregationalism and the subsequent embrace of a faith based on the inherent goodness of mankind, not a theology that stressed human depravity. In short, Channing humanized Protestantism. The historian David Robinson believes, "An essential step in this revolution was a redefinition of the spiritual capacities of human nature in opposition to the inherited doctrines of Calvinism, which made the self a repository of enormous spiritual energy. This complete rethinking of the nature of the self was inevitably more than a theological innovation, for a new sense of the self implied a new sense of all the relations of the self—moral, social and political. When Channing therefore came to define the religious life as a continual pursuit of self-culture, he offered a new way of living religiously, or a new spirituality."

TRANQUIL BEAUTY
William Ellery Channing's love for Newport was lifelong. In numerous letters to friends in America and Europe, he waxed poetic about the charms of Aquidneck. One example: "I write you from our dear native island, a spot which becomes more and more dear to me. Whilst the generation with which I grew up has disappeared, nature is the same; and even when a boy, it seems to me that my chief interest clung to the fields, the ocean, the beach. What I want at this season of the year is repose, and I know no part of our country which has more tranquil beauty than this . . . I believe it is universally acknowledged to be the most beautiful place on our whole range of sea-coast."

William Ellery Channing was born in Newport in 1780 into a prominent political and mercantile family with deep roots in the town. His father was a former attorney general of the state and a federal district attorney; his mother was the daughter of the same William Ellery who signed the Declaration of Independence. So respected was the family that President George Washington dined at their home on one of his visits to Newport. After his father's early death, grandfather Ellery, a highly distinguished figure, became the boy's moral compass. During his school days in Newport, Channing befriended the artists Washington Allston and Edward Greene Malbone, and throughout his life was close to the artistic community in New England. He spent hours each week at the Redwood Library, and in later years wrote fondly of the peaceful Harrison Room that he often had all to himself while systematically working his way through the library's large collection. After graduating first in his class at Harvard and eighteen months tutoring in the South, Channing decided on the ministry, and was chosen to lead the Federal Street Church in Boston in 1803. Although Boston became his professional home for the rest of his life, Channing returned to Aquidneck Island every summer to Oakland, the Portsmouth estate of his wife, a cousin named Ruth Gibbs, who was quite wealthy because of her father's success at the firm Gibbs and Channing. Oakland became Channing's most treasured refuge for his entire adult life.

By 1810, the long-held authority of Boston and other New England Congregational churches was beginning to be seriously challenged by a growing number of pastors who believed the hellfire and brimstone Calvinist orthodoxy was basically corrupt because there was no room in the theology to recognize mankind's innate optimism or potential for good works. A revolution was in the wings. The old guard, unwilling

William Ellery
Channing, 1880
Print
from *Harper's Weekly*,
XXIV (Saturday,
April 17, 1880) 253.
Newport Historical Society
Newport, Rhode Island

to bend or listen, demanded that their more liberal (and mostly younger) colleagues recant or separate. Because of his eloquence and persuasiveness in the pulpit and his widely read essays, William Ellery Channing was acknowledged as the leader of those who chose to fight for their beliefs. When his revolutionary 1819 "Baltimore Sermon" was published under the title *Unitarian Christianity*, it became, in the words of the historian Daniel Howe, "the virtual manifesto of the liberal movement in theology, now explicitly Unitarian." Channing's mission was to reinvent the ways people conceived of God and the Bible, and how they interacted with the divine. By empowering the individual's station in the relationship and denying the straitjacket doctrine of original sin, he believed that a freer, more satisfying spirituality would ensue.

By the late 1820s, Channing's acknowledged leadership of the Unitarian faction was cemented, and he moved beyond theological matters to address national cultural concerns. His writings had made him famous throughout Europe and the United States; many people paid attention to his views on the need to establish a rigorous homegrown culture and reject the established aesthetics of the Continent. Channing's essay, "Remarks on a National Literature," was a clarion call for Americans to break the European mold and create a body of writing that celebrated American values and self-consciousness. This strong appeal to elevate native ideas and ideals led to the formation of the Transcendentalists, a group that favored the divinity of mankind and was fervently Romantic in its outlook. Channing wrote:

> We mean not to be paradoxical, but we believe that it would be better to admit no books from abroad, than to make them substitutes for our own intellectual activity. The more we receive from other countries, the greater the need of an original literature. A people, into whose minds the thoughts of foreigners are poured perpetually, needs an energy within itself to resist, to modify this mighty influence, and, without it, will inevitably sink under the worst bondage, will become intellectually tame and enslaved. . . . It were better to have no literature, than form ourselves unresistingly on a foreign one. The true sovereigns of a country are those who determine its mind, its modes of thinking, its tastes, its principles; and we cannot consent to lodge this sovereignty in the hands of strangers. A country, like an individual, has dignity and power only in proportion as it is self-formed.

William Ellery Channing was a classical humanist, a rationalist who believed in the supernatural and the miraculous and, at the same time, a determined democrat committed to the potential of all Americans. He was staunchly antislavery and antiwar, and alienated some of his parishioners with his outspoken views on those ancient practices. He championed public education for all: while he cared deeply about the soul, he was an avid proponent for using the brain as well. According to Daniel Howe, through his preaching and his books, Channing "influenced such important contemporaries as Charles Sumner, Horace Mann, James Russell Lowell, Henry Wadsworth Longfellow, Lydia Maria Child, and Dorothea Dix. As this list indicates, the characteristic

SCANDAL

Newport was the venue for one of the most spectacular courtroom dramas of the nineteenth century in May 1833, when thirty-seven-year-old Methodist minister Ephraim Avery went on trial for the murder of five-month-pregnant Sarah Cornell, a single twenty-nine-year-old mill worker who had been strangled near Tiverton the previous December. Like later sensational tribunals, the trial became national news, with reporters from major metropolises packed into the State House on Washington Square to witness the month-long proceedings. Publicity had been so intense that lawyers had to dismiss over a hundred potential jurors before empanelling a group of twelve peers.

The story that emerged through the lens of the prosecutors was that Avery, a married man preaching in Bristol, had had an affair with Cornell, got her with child, and murdered her before she could ruin his reputation in the church. Eyewitnesses testified that they had seen a strange tall man near the scene of the crime the day before Cornell had been found. Jeremiah Gifford, the Portsmouth to Bristol ferry pilot on the Aquidneck side told the courtroom (filled with Newporters who couldn't get enough of the sordid story) that Avery had tried to get Gifford to take him to the mainland on the night the woman's death occurred; he refused, and Avery had to sleep in the ferryman's home. The defense contended that Sarah Cornell was a loose woman with a past and had committed suicide; Avery, his lawyer asserted, was nowhere near Tiverton, despite ample evidence to the contrary.

The trial provoked pent-up passions on both sides. Because of shifting social mores due to the rise of industrial towns dependent on female workers, women were gaining new freedoms, causing considerable grumbling among conservative citizens. At the same time, Methodist ministers were perceived by many as freewheeling showmen, no better than carnival barkers, and a threat to traditional Protestants. In the end, Avery's lawyer won the contest, and the jury of twelve men acquitted the preacher of the murder of Sarah Cornell—even though the presiding judge later proclaimed his certainty of Avery's guilt.

New England mixture of individual self-culture and social reform owed much to Channing's precept and example." By the time of his death in 1842, he had become one of the most distinguished moral leaders of the nineteenth century.

The historian Pieter Roos is fond of pointing out that within three theological generations, due to the melting-pot nature of Newport, the town had progressed from the extreme Puritanism of Nathaniel Clap, through the moderating influences of Ezra Stiles, and finally to the radically liberal preaching of William Ellery Channing. The ethos of religious toleration set down by Roger Williams and John Clarke nearly two centuries before found its apogee in Channing's expansive reform principles. A bronze statue in Touro Park is an enduring reminder of the man.

The Dorr Rebellion

By 1840, Rhode Island had changed almost beyond recognition since the state entered the Union fifty years before. If Rip Van Winkle had been a Rhode Islander, he would not have known where he was after awakening from his long slumber. New towns had sprouted up in the northern tier; seacoast communities looked like ghosts of their former selves. In 1790, the state was inhabited by some 69,000 people. A half century later, that figure had ballooned to 110,000, and almost all of the increase was felt in and around Providence as natives and foreigners alike flocked to the area for employment. By 1840, Rhode Island had transformed itself into the most highly industrialized state in America. And as population continued to mushroom, so did economic prosperity in and around Providence. In Newport, maritime trade was all but dead.

In 1827, a lace-manufacturing factory was built in Newport, employing some five hundred female workers; it lasted less than a decade. By 1832, Rhode Island hosted 126 cotton mills, but only one of them could be found in Newport. The state woolen mill industry clustered around Peace Dale in South County and in the north; in 1832, 22 woolen manufacturers were in business, and not one of them was located in Newport. Even after Samuel Slater pioneered the new steam engine in 1827, which ran on coal and not water power, thus freeing plant owners from having to erect their factories right on the banks of rivers, Newport still could boast only a few cotton-milling enterprises, and none of them lasted more than a couple of decades. The later invention of the reciprocating steam engine by George Corliss of Rhode Island, which produced a constant speed and cheaper energy costs, should have made Newport an excellent base for cotton spinning because its high coastal humidity was a benefit: thread that was moist did not break in the high-speed operations that the Corliss provided. It did not happen. Newport was penalized by businessmen who preferred mainland, not island, locations for their new factories. Moreover, the town was stymied, complicit in its own complacency, due to a dearth of far-sighted entrepreneurs willing to take large risks.

But just as industrialization and mechanization were changing the physical landscape of the state, its human profile was inevitably altering as well—and the rapid population growth brought to the forefront a long-simmering debate over how Rhode Island was governed. In short, the venerated Charter of 1663, the very foundation of the state's personality and character, had outlasted its usefulness in republican America of the nineteenth century and was now viewed by Jacksonian reformers as the chief roadblock to an openly democratic and representative state system. What John Clarke achieved in 1663 was radical and forward-looking. But with Union, while other states produced amendable constitutions, Rhode Island chose to adhere to a document that could not be altered—except by an English monarch who no longer ruled them. That fact alone produced one of the most severe and wrenching constitutional crises in United States history, known as the Dorr Rebellion.

The crux of the dilemma lay in two critical areas. Problem number one was the fact that the 1663 Charter set the number of representatives each town could elect to the General Assembly. Newport, the largest and most important metropolis at the time, was awarded six seats; Providence, Portsmouth, and Warwick each had four; and new towns got two votes. That was well and good in colonial days when population shifts were minimal and few new towns took shape. But now Providence was larger than its old rival, the most dominant town in Rhode Island by far, and still it had to live with only four legislators; mill towns in the north were expanding at breakneck pace and had almost no voice at all. Older farm communities, once prosperous but now practically devoid of citizens, retained their two votes. Everything was out of proportion.

The second problem lay in the reality that while the Charter specified no suffrage qualifications, the General Assembly had set the standards in the early eighteenth century when it decreed that only adult white males who owned the equivalent of $134 in property or their firstborn sons could be legal freeholders. And only freeholders could vote. This medieval practice of primogeniture was clearly inconsistent with the current ideals of liberty for every (white) man. Again, in colonial times, most men did own property and thus qualified for inclusion in governmental functions. In Newport in the 1750s, for instance, about 80 percent of the males had voting rights. But the huge upsurge in population by 1830 meant that over 60 percent of the men in the state were disenfranchised because they could not meet those qualifications. The males who filtered into the new northern industrial towns were renters, not owners, and there were thousands who had no empowerment at all. Once the most democratic of colonies, Rhode Island as a state had descended into the least free and open in all of America. The irony is difficult to deny: John Clarke's Charter once guaranteed more freedoms than any other colonial document; now those words were being used by recalcitrant politicians to deny the rights America had fought for in the War of Independence.

Beginning in 1797, literally dozens of attempts had been made to persuade the General Assembly to liberalize the malapportionment and male suffrage inequities. By 1840, the legislators had not budged. Power is difficult to give up: the elite Yankee representatives repeatedly refused to cede authority, regardless of how clear the evidence that their intransigence made them appear more like didactic Roman senators than fair-minded politicians in a democratic country. Native-born, Protestant laborers came to Rhode Island to find work and were shunted aside because they did not own land. Surely the continuing cascade of poor Irish Catholics immigrants into the state played to the General Assembly's prejudices—who wanted to give *them* the vote? Their growing conservatism and nativism swayed their decision to maintain the status quo. The governor had little clout and was consistently ineffective in getting his peers to moderate their stand. So the legislators in the General Assembly acted as if Rhode Island was their own private fiefdom; and to the outside world, that's exactly how it appeared.

The man responsible for provoking Rhode Island into the modern political world was an unlikely candidate for the task. Thomas Wilson Dorr was born in Providence in 1805 to a wealthy and socially

prominent business family. He attended the exclusive Phillips Exeter Academy, then Harvard, and rounded out his patrician education by studying law in New York City. Dorr returned to Providence in 1833 and started his political career by being elected to the General Assembly the following year as a Federalist. By all accounts, Thomas Wilson Dorr at that time was an affable, well-liked, and able legislator of the reform-minded faction—a moderate man who nonetheless was set on an agenda to make the state government more inclusive and fair for all citizens. His moderation, however, was soon to be replaced with a more radical approach to solving the quandary of antirepublicanism.

As the movement to jettison the 1663 Charter in favor of a modern, more liberal constitution picked up momentum during the late 1830s, Dorr became deeply involved. At a time when, throughout America, the focus was on inclusion, not exclusion, Dorr was increasingly troubled by the fact that men in Rhode Island were forced to pay taxes and serve in the militia, yet could not secure the vote because of antiquated laws. In 1840, he was instrumental in forming the Rhode Island Suffrage Association, a group dedicated to achieving voting rights for all white males in the state above the age of twenty-one, regardless of property qualifications. To Dorr, the imbalance between the reality and the ideal was intolerable: under the Charter, it was possible for a mere 1,900 voters to control the fate of a state with 110,000 inhabitants. As agitation mounted and meetings were held throughout Rhode Island, the General Assembly refused to consider any alteration in the laws.

Frustrated at every turn, the Suffrage Association opted to remedy the situation on their own by forming a "People's Party" and calling for a convention in October 1841 in Providence to produce a new, more equitable constitution. Dorr was now the acknowledged leader of the party and, during a three-day convention, he and his colleagues drafted a fair and modern document that allowed voting rights to most adult white males in Rhode Island. In December, defying the sitting authorities, the extralegal People's Constitution was offered for statewide ballot and passed by 14,000 voters, both registered and new; significantly, a majority of *legal* freeholders backed the new form of government, thus sending a clear and troubling message to the General Assembly.

Now the crisis was reaching full boil. The old-guard legislators totally rejected the People's Constitution but also realized that they had to modify their approach to appease angry citizens. So, Governor Samuel Ward King (who favored more moderate laws) and the General Assembly decided to submit *their* version of a new Landholders' Constitution to the legal freemen; this version liberalized (to some extent) male suffrage and, surprisingly, called for adult blacks and working men to be given the vote as well, a step the Dorrites dared not take lest they alienate the conservative bloc. Yet when the Assembly's new document was presented to eligible freemen, it was defeated by a narrow margin because Dorr pleaded with his followers to abstain from voting.

Stalemate. Who was in power? Both Dorr and Governor King petitioned President John Tyler and Congress for support in order to solve the constitutional conundrum. As the historian William G. McLoughlin puts it: "The critical issue was: What constitutes true republicanism, the voice of the people or respect for duly constituted authority? Or, to put it another way, can the principles of natural rights and popular sovereignty justify circumvention (or replacement) of the prevailing, formal institutions of law and order? . . . Led by Dorr, the reformers turned to the radical concept of popular sovereignty, arguing that, where the will of the people was consistently frustrated, they had the power to take matters into their own hands against would-be despots." Faced with a constitutional issue that went beyond Rhode Island's borders, politicians in Washington were loath to get involved in the debacle and gingerly passed responsibility back to the state for resolution.

There was nothing close to resolution; the situation only got murkier. The Dorrites, furious at the General Assembly for not giving up power in the face of an electoral defeat, let their emotions get the better of them and pushed ahead to form their own new regime. In April 1842, they elected Thomas Wilson Dorr as governor. So now the state had two governors and two legislatures because Samuel Ward King was elected in the "legal" election that spring; the opposing governments confronted each other in Newport in May. Tensions ran so high that it was feared that civil war was in the wings. Yet for some unknown reason, the People's Party made no attempt to seize institutional power or government buildings, so the deadlock continued unabated. The State Supreme Court had already declared the People's Party constitution illegal and that all efforts to institute it would be grounds for treason. Governor King, frustrated with the usurpers, appealed to Congress for support again, and this time he got it. Undeterred, Dorr traveled to Washington in person to get President Tyler's backing, which again was not forthcoming. When Dorr arrived home, after a stopover in New York City where he received the blessings of Tammany Hall politicians, he found that his opponent had declared martial law and had imprisoned a large number of his faithful followers. A $5,000 bounty had been put on Dorr's head as well. That prompted him to leave his radical rhetoric behind and take the initiative by trying to defeat the Charter government, because he believed he was the duly elected governor.

In an amateur military action, Dorr and about two hundred of his supporters (many of whom were Irish Catholics) seized two Revolutionary War cannons captured from the British and, on the evening of May 17, planned to lay siege to the arsenal in Providence, also guarded by a force of two hundred men. The cannons were loaded and aimed. Dorr ordered the guns to fire . . . and nothing happened. Over seventy years old, both turned out to be duds. Panic then prevailed, fog descended, and Dorr's forces dispersed without a shot. Knowing he would be arrested shortly, Dorr fled the state. But the arsenal fiasco lost Dorr a large number of moderate, peaceful followers who were appalled at the attempted armed coup. Now only a band of disaffected hooligans associated with the radical labor and political organizer Seth Luther could be called on for support.

In the meantime, rural Democrats and urban Whigs (both conservatives and backers of the Charter government) had banded together to form the Law and Order Party. And, just as the name connotes, they went on a witch hunt to track down and arrest anyone associated with Dorr. When the remnants of his little army massed at Chepachet at the end of July 1842 to force another battle, they were confronted by several thousand Law and Order militia. Realizing the folly of trying to take them on, Dorr disbanded his men and headed for New Hampshire. All hope had been lost, and Dorr had almost no support anywhere in Rhode Island. Hundreds more arrests followed the Chepachet incident as the new rulers made an example of those who might be willing to overthrow a legitimate sitting government. The Dorr Rebellion fizzled.

William McLoughlin explains how the crisis was finally resolved. "In November 1842, the Law and Order party, now under Governor James Fenner, called another constitutional convention. This convention's work closely resembled the defeated Landholders' Constitution . . . [in that it] specifically gave native-born citizens more liberal voting rights than naturalized citizens. Duly ratified by the voters, the new constitution went into effect in 1843, and the old charter was gone forever. In effect, Dorr won his point against the inadequacies of the old charter, though he failed to sustain the popular-sovereignty ideology of 1776 and 1787." The legal scholar Patrick Conley puts Dorr's role in another context. "Some American historians have suggested the name 'Age of Egalitarianism' for the period from the mid-1820s to the mid-1850s, because a passion for equality of opportunity was the overriding theme of the political, social, and economic activists. A more broadly-based [sic] democracy, and assault on neomercantilism and government-granted privilege, and a crusade for a more just, humane, and upwardly mobile social order were hallmarks of the era. This was the first great age of American reform, and Dorr was in the midst of it as an archetypal equal rights proponent."

Thomas Wilson Dorr was a good man who went overboard in his zeal for a more inclusive government. And he suffered the consequences of his rebellion. After a year living in New Hampshire, Dorr returned to Providence of his own free will and was immediately arrested. Tried for treason before the Rhode Island Supreme Court, he was found guilty and sentenced to life imprisonment in solitary confinement and hard labor in 1844. When political sentiments shifted the following year, Dorr was set free. But prison had broken his health and spirit, and he disappeared from the political scene. Thomas Wilson Dorr died in 1854, vanquished but not forgotten. In an odd way, Dorr sacrificed himself but ended up with the victory for the people he fought so hard to enfranchise.

Newport was divided over the Dorr episode. Many of the more liberal stance recognized the unfairness of continuing under the hallowed Charter of 1663, and were eager to see the ugly partisan battles disappear; they sought a higher tone for their political life. Others were against change: they were emotionally drawn to the Charter because of the great protections it had afforded the town for 180 years, and they feared giving it up because inevitably Newport would lose its majority status in the General Assembly when the state was reapportioned (it did). Northern mill towns, teeming with people, gained many more representatives, as they should have, and slowly the state began to right the old imbalance over the next decades.

But, in fact, Newport lost little in giving up some of its old legislative authority. By 1843, it was already a very different town from the days of its colonial preeminence, and now the political power it once possessed was no longer its raison d'être. Something new was blowing on the winds. Signs of reinvigorated life were on the horizon in the form of ships—both steam and sail—arriving in the harbor, carrying a growing number of visitors from afar, their wallets packed with dollars, who were beginning to flock to the town for the summer social season.

Newport's grand revival had begun.

Society Ascendant

7

Strangers Bearing Gifts

Picture the scene that had been playing out yearly since the 1750s: *Dozens of people line up along the long quay in the harbor in Charleston, South Carolina, in early May, waiting for their extensive belongings and their attendant house slaves to be laded onto the ship. The captain strides among the expectant passengers, welcoming those he knows from previous years' voyages, greeting others who are making their first excursion north. Soon the large gangplank is lowered and the well-dressed, well-mannered ladies and gentlemen and their well-behaved children march on board to secure their cabins and stroll along the deck. As the vessel slips its mooring and heads into the Atlantic Ocean, the sense of relief and excitement mounts among the passengers. Behind them, throughout the murky Carolina marshes, lies the pervasive seasonal pestilence they are escaping. Ahead of them, after some eight to twelve days at sea, is their safe haven and salvation: Newport, Rhode Island.*

The Avenue & Ocean House Hotel-Newport Rhode Island (detail), c. 19th century
Color postcard
Redwood Library and Athenæum
Newport, Rhode Island
Gift of Hamilton Fish Webster and Lina Post Webster
Webster.62

Given its abundant natural assets, it is fair to assume that Newport might easily have made the transition to becoming a quintessentially quaint and sleepy New England seaside community that reveled in its past glories while fashioning a future of diminished expectations. Another Nantucket, perhaps. Looking at the previous decades' string of bad luck and reduced influence, town leaders in the 1830s probably didn't dare to envision anything more ambitious than maintaining the shaky status quo and hoping *some* form of endeavor would, to some extent, revive the town's fortunes.

The young United States of America was undergoing astoundingly swift changes as rising native birth rates and foreign immigration began to swell cities on the Eastern seaboard with workers eager to participate in the surging industrial economy. New England farms languished as modern larger factories drew men and women to more dependable employment. The pace of the country was accelerating, with railroads snaking farther west (a migration anticipated by George Berkeley over a century earlier) and steamships conveying people and goods to diverse ports. The democratic impulse created by the Revolution and cemented by the Constitution contributed further to the breaking of the European stranglehold on values and traditions; Americans continued to create their vibrant new world in their own inimitable image. Society itself was embroiled in upheaval as Jacksonian ideals championing a liberal economy and the empowering of the common man penetrated the previous pecking order.

At the beginning of the nineteenth century, what we know today as the leisure industry did not exist: the majority of Americans worked hard, saved their money, and traveled only when necessary. Yet the nation was growing bolder and wealthier as the fruits of modern industrialization ripened. The Erie Canal had opened, linking Atlantic Ocean ports with the vast Middle West. Newly created states joined the Union, and the land rush was on. A sparkling spirit of adventure was in the air, and more people, with more free time, money, and a case of wanderlust, wanted to experience different parts of the United States. The upper classes had always taken for granted the idea of travel for pleasure or edification; now, between 1820 and 1850, that concept began to pervade the burgeoning middle class, giving rise to a fresh phenomenon in America, known as "the resort."

Although the Puritan clutch on American mores had lost much of its stubborn grip, the country still suffered from guilt over the struggle between the claims of labor versus leisure. For most people, hard work was a redeeming social as well as religious ideal, and for many decades following the Revolution, the rich and idle landed aristocracy was held in contempt by the rising multitudes for its decadent "European" ways. That attitude began to dissipate as writers, preachers, and social critics trumpeted the need to celebrate mankind's innate need for relaxation. The "complete" person was no longer viewed as someone who toiled endlessly to gain a foothold at Heaven's gate; a more balanced existence was advocated, as the very concept of "free time" underwent radical revision. Enjoyment of being alive joined hard work as a moral imperative. The commemoration of "the good life" had begun.

Newport historian George G. Herrick writes,

> the search for air and water, for health and pleasure began in the 1820s with the development of resorts at Cape May, Nahant and Saratoga Springs. Perhaps that is what moved William Ellery Channing, the dean of American Unitarianism, to question the orthodox Protestant distrust of play. In 1837 he delivered a speech on temperance in which he held that "man was made to enjoy as well as to labor, and the state of society should be adapted to this principle of human nature." He reminded his audience that God had "implanted a strong desire for recreation after labor." But it took Henry Ward Beecher, the prominent Presbyterian minister in Brooklyn, actually to coin the term "vacation" in the sense that we know it today. This he did in "Farewell to the Country," an essay in September 1853, after an agreeable sojourn in Connecticut. Thereafter, he preached the virtues of summer in the open air. Previously the word "vacation" had meant an interruption in juridical or academic proceedings. The great game could begin.

The timing of this substantial development was ideal for Newport. Over the half century from 1840 to 1890, Newport emerged from its long descent into the doldrums to become, at first, a comfortable summer colony for Southerners and New England intellectuals and artists and, after the Civil War and the virtual disappearance of Confederate visitors, *the* place for lavish palaces built by New York Society's "Four Hundred" and an internationally renowned playground referred to reverently as "The Queen of Resorts." This extraordinary reincarnation was not due to any far-reaching master plan etched out by Newport's politicians or

Chapin, John R.
*View of the
City of Newport,
Rhode Island*, 1852
Engraving
Redwood Library
and Athenæum
Newport, Rhode Island
Gift of Hamilton Fish Webster
and Lina Post Webster
Webster.1

businessmen—no, the resurgence began because South Carolina and Georgia tidewater farmers were forced to abandon their plantations each summer in order to escape the ravages of country fever, better known today as malaria. For hundreds of these cotton and rice farmers, Newport, beginning in earnest around the 1740s, was the ideal destination: it offered a sheltered, healthy environment free of killing disease, allowing parents to watch their children grow another year.

By dint of its island geography, climate, pristine beaches, and openness to newcomers, Newport was able to cast off its drab post–Revolutionary War coloration and morph into a glittering butterfly. Unlike resorts at Cape May, New Jersey, or Coney Island and Saratoga Springs, New York, which, throughout the nineteenth century, catered largely to middle-class patrons, Newport ended up drawing the nation's established and emerging fashion-setting elite, the wealthiest and most influential in the land, and thus ascended to the august position of the undisputed premier watering-spot in America. By the turn of the twentieth century, the mention of "Newport" had become a password throughout Europe and America signifying elegance, exclusion, and luxury, and because of the elaborate "cottages" along Bellevue Avenue, also denoting extravagance and decadence. Newport had more than survived: it had conquered its competitors with sumptuousness and social superiority.

Partly of its own volition, backwater Newport, with its few failing textile factories, had proved to be wholly unprepared to join the steady march toward industrialization and affluence underway in most other urban centers across the land. Now, with a fast-growing number of summer visitors arriving each year, the opportunity to redefine and refashion itself was thrust upon its inhabitants, and enterprising Newporters rose to the challenge. A new economic opportunity was available to the town, quite different from the town's earlier commercial pursuits, but potentially lucrative nonetheless. It may appear ironic that outsiders were the ones to salvage the town and set it on its new career, yet it must be remembered that over the previous two centuries, Newport had always been more open to external influences than any other community in New

England. It never lost its sophistication, its charm, its curiosity. Dr. John Clarke's 1663 Charter promoting freedom of conscience had been replaced by the state's 1843 constitution, but the legacy of an open-minded citizenry was still largely intact. Without that cosmopolitanism and the accepting attitude of its people, Newport could not have attained its status as the most sought-after resort in the country.

Most historians correctly assign the 1830s as the turning point in Newport's fortunes, the period when nearly all vestiges of its former seaborne mercantile superiority sank out of sight to be replaced by tourism and the rise of the hotel culture that would accommodate the influx of thousands of pleasure-seekers. But the fact remains that Carolinians and planters from the West Indies had a long-established tradition of summering in Newport, going back more than a century. According to Carl Bridenbaugh, in 1729, the same year Dean Berkeley arrived in town from England, a number of invalid Antiguans journeyed to Newport to restore their health and escape the summer heat. Then, throughout the 1730s, South Carolinians began to migrate north when the connection between spending summers on lowland plantations and debilitation from country fever became obvious. The trickle of planters turned into a torrent during the decades before the Revolution as word spread of Newport's healthful airs. So many families filtered into Newport before 1776 that it became known as the "Carolina Hospital." After union had been achieved and despite the ravages inflicted on the town, Southerners continued to sail north to seek refuge for the season, often renting simple cottages in the Point section or along Thames Street for the duration.

Of all the places to flee to, why Newport? Aside from its superb geographical assets, the best answer is: relationships. Throughout the colonial era, Newport merchants had supplied Charleston with

Long Wharf, c. 1900
Photographer unknown
Newport Historical Society
Newport, Rhode Island

furniture, rum, slaves, horses, and a host of other products. Long-standing trading ties led to lasting friendships between merchants in both towns, and it is not hard to imagine the glowing reports about Newport's gentle climate that sailors related to their beleaguered brethren. After the first several years of making the trek to Newport, it had become common knowledge throughout the sprawling plantation system and within genteel Charleston that Newport offered a pleasant respite from excessive heat and disease.

The "sickly season" was of serious concern to anyone in the South, especially after the 1790s and the introduction of rice cultivation in the broad river flats. One contemporary local historian, who was also a planter and physician, wrote of the lowlands in 1809, "In it sluggish rivers, stagnant swamps, ponds, and marshes are common; and in or near to them putrefaction is generated. In all these places, and for two or three miles adjacent to them, the seeds of febrile diseases are plentifully sown and from them disseminated." It should be noted that the black slaves were immune to the "miasma or malaria" taking hold in the South because of thousands of years conditioning in Africa. Only whites succumbed to the mosquito-borne pestilence (and, of course, they did not understand that it was spread by the insect; it was then believed that the "bad air" of the swamplands was responsible).

The danger during the summer months was real, and everyone in the Carolinas knew it. The landscape architect Frederick Law Olmsted, in his *Journey in the Seaboard Slave States*, quoted one planter as saying "that he would as soon stand fifty feet from the best Kentucky rifleman as to spend a night on his plantation in summer." Olmsted also reported the fate of a party of six spending the day at a rice plantation. Unable to get back to town before night, they shut themselves in the house and sat around fires waiting for morning. But despite their precautions against the miasma, all were stricken with the fever and four died within a week. So serious were the consequences of remaining on the plantation during the prolonged summer that Charleston emerged as a virtual bedroom community for the farmers; many of the lavish townhouses in the city were built and maintained by plantation owners who needed to escape their land with alarming frequency.

Pre-Revolutionary summer sojourners to Newport (these included a number of Philadelphians and Bostonians as well) were accurately chronicled in the *Newport Mercury* after 1767, when the paper began printing America's first "society page" by listing the names of visitors (even then, prominent people were set off in all-capital letters, starting the dubious tradition of the *boldface* name) debarking their ships at Long Wharf. The *Mercury*'s celebration of the rich and famous was unique in colonial newspapers, and because of the publisher Solomon Southwick's reportorial efforts, Carl Bridenbaugh was able to tabulate that over 260 families arrived from Charleston in an eight-year period before the war, and the names are a virtual who's who of the Carolina elite. Along with Georgians and Caribbean island merchant princes, many of these families made Newport their summer home for generations, creating a tradition among Southerners still prevalent (although Alabamans and Texans are now more numerous than Carolinians).

In 1769, for instance, Henry Middleton and his family, John Izard, and the Hon. Augustus Johnston, Esq., arrived in town for the season on the same ship. They are broadly representative of the

LEISURE AND HEALTH

Southern planters weren't the only ones searching for sanctuary from pestilence. Before the 1820s, the majority of American physicians treated illness by trying to adjust an imbalance of bodily fluids and used bleeding, leeches, and powerful chemicals to (try to) achieve wellness in their patients. Then a new breed of doctor emerged (called "irregulars" at the time) advocating less intrusive measures. Cindy S. Aron, a historian of leisure in the United States, writes, "While still holding to the belief in the importance of maintaining a balance of fluids and conserving 'nervous energy,' irregular doctors also began to discuss the benefits of hygiene, fresh air, vegetarian diets, and exercise." The theory was that a "change of climate could alter the balance of bodily fluids and that mineral waters, operating as powerful diuretics and laxatives, could produce the same effects." Both a change of air and the benign waters of mineral springs or the ocean were, by 1850, viewed as essential for good health and long life. Newport had an abundance of clean air and crystalline waters, one of the main reasons for its early reputation as a desirable destination, particularly among city dwellers who were terrified of outbreaks of cholera and yellow fever as much as plantation owners feared malaria. Taking the waters became the rage. In 1844, Mr. E. Trevett advertised his "Sea Baths on the Long Wharf" in the *Newport Mercury*, claiming "these baths impart agreeable sensations to the mind, keep skin clear and clean, the body healthy and vigorous; removing the dead particles of the cuticula, causing blood to circulate freely, lighting up a fresh and healthy glow in the most sallow countenance."

to loftier ideas for their futures. Watching the town fill up with more and more visitors each summer, in 1842 John Weaver persuaded several of Newport's richest men, including Nathaniel Ruggles and Seth Bateman, to put up $14,000 for the construction of a new hotel. With the early success of the original Ocean House, John was able to help bankroll his brother Joseph's building of Atlantic House. Over the years, both men rose to social prominence and became two of the wealthiest and most influential citizens in town. John and Joseph Weaver each represented Newport in the Rhode Island General Assembly and held important positions in city government. Joseph sold Atlantic House during the economic panic of 1857, but John turned over the proprietorship of Ocean House to his son John B. Weaver, Jr., who held ownership until his death in 1894. Ocean House, the hotel that sparked Newport's real rise from economic malaise, was in the hands of one family for fifty years.

All those hotels and innumerable boarding houses were sorely needed. In the summer of 1847, some two thousand visitors arrived in Newport to partake of the carefree season and the town's fine beaches. Old-time Carolinians who pioneered the town's ascent into the social stratosphere would not have recognized the place at midcentury. With the creation of the hotels came the building of new roads and alleyways, more stables for horses, additional housing for servants and hotel personnel. Dozens of stores sprouted up along the once-moribund Thames Street; other avenues were spruced up and maintained. Taverns abounded, and not only those catering to common seamen; first-class drinking establishments were very popular. When Thomas Hunter, son of William Hunter of Hunter House, returned to Newport after seven years abroad, he noted "new shops, new faces, new signs. . . . The strangers leave an abundance of money and a good portion of it goes into Dry Goods and shoe stores." He also reported that "the hotels and boarding houses are stuffed to the roofs, and hundreds come in the morning, who are obliged to leave in the afternoon for want of rooms." The original Bath Road, now the enlarged Memorial Boulevard, was carved out expressly so hotel guests could have easy access to Easton's Beach for their daily swimming regimen. Still, all the activity was in the "old" part of town. In 1850, beyond Ocean House, Newport was mainly farm and pasture land. That condition was soon to be altered dramatically with the extension of Bellevue Avenue from the hotel all the way south to Bailey's Beach.

More than any community in America at the time, antebellum Newport during the summer season was a veritable melting pot (a term that Israel Zangwill would not invent to describe America until 1908), a vivid potpourri of Southerners, New Englanders, Philadelphians, and New Yorkers—as well as free and enslaved blacks, Irish Catholic laborers, female servants from numerous European countries, and many more. For the fifteen years before the outbreak of the Civil War, they all mingled together in the hotels, at the beaches, and along Newport's streets. More than any other American town, Newport witnessed and promoted the surge within society, sprung from its previous stratification, toward a new definition of what was proper, what was acceptable, and of what was perceived as *fun*. Newport became the testing ground for a portion of the population longing to define its "American-ness," to experiment with unorthodox ways of reordering its cultural hierarchy. The town presented a platform for people eager for advancement up the rough-and-tumble social ladder, to fail or succeed at their quest for prestige. Newport had evolved, very quickly, into a place intent on the pursuit of pleasure, a town dedicated in the summer to dancing, bathing, and riding horses along its broad beaches. From a sleepy refuge for Southern planters, Newport had been turned into a virtual carnival where the hotels provided the stage for the daily drama.

Beginning in the 1850s, society pages in major American newspapers were sprinkled with tidbits from the Newport season. No respectable publication could afford to ignore what was transpiring in the newly minted summer capital. For instance, the *New York Times* dispatched not just one, but several, correspondents to the city during the season for weekly reports. These were not perfunctory recitations of boldface names but long, exhaustive articles noting social nuances and goings-on. In the August 16, 1860, front-page piece we learn that "Last night's ball at the Atlantic was the affair of the season thus far. . . . Mr. and Mrs. DOUGLAS [Stephen Douglas, then running for the presidency against Abraham Lincoln] were present, and entered heartily into the spirit of the occasion. . . . Mr. BELMONT, with his wife and some half dozen ladies of her social court, was also present. The dancing was kept up with great life and spirit until a late hour, and the whole affair passed off delightfully." In the same edition, another writer reports, "The beautiful harbor

of numberless cabs and stages, is more and more ubiquitous with the arrival of every boat; the wagon labelled 'for the fishing ground direct,' takes its place every morning to tempt neophytes with visions of enormous bass and a chowder lunch on some torrid rock. (*Newport Mercury*, July 21, 1855)

The second grand concert and Soiree Dansante by the Germania Musical Society, will take place this evening at Ocean Hall. The season will soon be over now, and the visitors will not have many more opportunities to participate in these kinds of gatherings. Knowing this, we suppose that all who like excellent music as well as those who are fond of dancing, will improve the occasion. The town is now very full of visitors, and we anticipate seeing a brilliant audience assembled this evening. (*Newport Daily News*, August 21, 1851)

We learn that Mr. Henry M. Brownell intends placing bathing-houses on the Beach just South of Lily Pond, this summer, for the accommodation of those who enjoy the salt-water. We consider this pleasanter than the Town Beach, in many respects; and it certainly is more retired, and will be preferred by those who bathe for the purpose of health, or as a quiet luxury. But those who go into the surf every day merely because it is *fashionable*, and remain there so long as to injure their health, will, of course, go where the crowd is, even should it be in the public harbor, if it was filled with vessels which constantly endangered the lives of those in the water. Those who are the chained slaves of Fashion can never regard consequences, however fatal they may be. (*Newport Daily News*, May 16, 1850)

The Season is fast drawing to a close, the last brilliant Ball has been given, the dancers are worn with fatigue, the gay and frivolous are surfeited, and Newport the dashing, fashionable watering place, will soon settle into the quiet, unpretending Newport of other days. (*Newport Mercury*, September 7, 1850)

Numerous visitors left records of their vacations in Newport during "The Season." One of the most playful pictures was offered by a journalist named Hiram Fuller who, under the nom de plume of Belle Brittan, supposedly a young woman of eighteen from Alabama, wrote a series of letters for publication in the *New York Mirror* highlighting "her" summer-long stay in Newport. Our Belle displays a shrewd eye and acerbic wit in describing the goings-on in 1856: she laments the absence of eligible young men, gets excited about the big balls at Ocean, Atlantic, and Fillmore Houses, only to be disappointed that her father would only allow her to dance with her cousin, and offers a running narrative of what resort life was like in those hectic days. The letters are part fact, part fiction, but the mood and bustle of the season are clearly captured.

JULY 16, 1856. Oh, this lovely Newport! It is the heavenliest place in the world. The air is so soft, and moist, and cool, and balmy, that, as Coleridge says, "it is a luxury to be." This morning I took my first bath in the sea and it made the blood tingle from top to toe. What a funny scene—a hundred ladies, more or less, in a costume gayer than the chorus of an Italian opera. To see the belles of the hotels, minus their hoops and other fixings—nobody would have known them, divested of their drawing-room conventionalities, swimming about in white trousers and red frocks. Speaking of hoops, I was under the impression, when I made up my wardrobe in New-York, that the fashion of inflated skirts had somewhat subsided, and governed myself accordingly; but gracious goodness! such balloons as the ladies sail about in here, I never saw before. It is a positive fact, that a lady cannot take a gentleman's arm for a promenade, in consequence of the monstrous bulk of her skirtcoats; and any nearer approach is entirely out of the question. I must confess, I don't like the fashion in its excess.

JULY 21, 1856. We are filling up here fast. A great many new faces have appeared since Saturday; and it will soon be difficult to get rooms at any of the hotels. But it is very singular that all the beaux are either little snips in their teens, or superannuated old coxcombs. Why, there are boys here of sixteen, who smoke, drink &c., and seem to have all the airs and vices of veterans; and there are old fellows in wigs, who ape a frisky freshness that is positively ludicrous.

JULY 29, 1856. But the great event of the day—dinner—is approaching; and as the ladies persist in arraying themselves in all their loveliness for the ceremony, it is time for me to prepare for the event. We have to dress about nine times a day here. First, we have to put on a dress to dress in. Then we are ready for breakfast. After that we dress for the Beach—then for the bath—then for the drive—then for the ball—and then for the bed. If that isn't being put through a regular course of dimity and diamonds, then I am no judge of such performances.

AUGUST 11, 1856. I may write now with entire truth, that Newport is full, crowded, squeezed. Sixty-six arrivals at the "Ocean" yesterday; and the other hotels received accessions proportionably to their capacities. Besides, the resident cottagers are overflowing with visitors. And yet, it is not very gay here. In sporting phrase, we have very few "fast people" among us, although a plenty of fast horses. I do love a handsome horse; and may as well confess the honest truth, that, driving with a pleasant, confidential companion, is to me a much more agreeable amusement than dancing. I never before saw so fine a collection of horses as turn out here of an afternoon.

AUGUST 15, 1856. "That will do," I said to myself, on leaving the ball-room of the "Fillmore" last evening, where there was a perfect Congress of beauty, gathered from all sections of the Union. It was the first really successful and brilliant "Hop" of the season. There were about five hundred persons present; and the ladies "looked their prettiest." The toilettes were magnificent; and several novelties were introduced to grace the occasion. One very stately, graceful, artistic-looking matron from New York, who is always dressed in unimpeachable taste, a perfect "model artiste" in millinery matters, appeared in a voluminous cloud of white muslin flounces, ornamented with bunches of lady-apples, ("as large as life and twice as natural") her arms and neck glittering with diamonds almost as large and as bright as her eyes—a rich, beautiful, and fruity-looking picture. She dances and talks, also, as well as she dresses.

Not everyone, however, was as smitten with Newport as Belle Brittan, in the person of Hiram Fuller. For ample evidence, turn to *A Philadelphia Perspective: The Diary of Sidney George Fisher*. Mr. Fisher was an attorney, poet, and historian who held very firm views on the America he inhabited; his extensive journal is a detailed record of society at midcentury. He was also somewhat of a snob, the stereotype of the Philadelphia lawyer at that time. Fisher started going to Newport almost annually in the late 1830s, and in 1839, the two-hundredth anniversary of the founding of the settlement, describes it as "very dull." His primary companions were the Middletons and other Southern gentlemen, yet he even complains of their company. In 1843, he notes how

> the weather was for the most part oppressively warm, and tho the place was crowded the society was dull and commonplace. . . . Shallow, unintellectual people, their thoughts and conversation related to trifles, to the petty events of their circle & to their own little vanities, and tho they are well bred and were kind & civil to me, they wearied me. . . . There was no beauty, but a good deal of prettiness, nothing distinguished for breeding or style or talent, but the ensemble was very fair & there were few vulgar people present. I found no one I cared to cultivate & the balls I thought very stupid.

Yet, for all his sniping, Sidney Fisher kept returning to Newport. Perhaps his own social insecurities were calmed by mingling with those he found inferior. In 1844, he warms up a bit and reports that "the place was crowded with visitors and the society was very good, the elite indeed of all parts of the country. . . . No other resort could exhibit a crowd so distinguished for refinement, wealth, & fashion." But two years later, he's on the warpath again. "I went at first to the Atlantic, but afterwards to the Ocean House, which has been rebuilt on a larger & improved plan. It is a fine house & was well kept, but was very crowded & noisy. . . . The sociable, easy, quiet society is destroyed by the influx of this immense crowd, chiefly from New York, of ultra fashionable people who live for dissipation & carry the winter habits of the city into the summer & the country." By 1848, Fisher is even harsher in his judgments. "The Ocean House was perfectly detestable, dirty, uncomfortable, ill-kept, and filled with hateful, vulgar people, chiefly New Yorkers of the upstart school."

Finally, by 1855, after many regrettable treks to Newport in season, Fisher comes to admit the resort isn't so bad after all. He visits amiably with his Southern friends, lunches with Henry Wadsworth Longfellow ("He has an agreeable countenance, mild, quiet, cordial manners"), and meets the historian George Bancroft, with whom he is not overly impressed. Away from the boisterous New Yorkers and among more intellectual men and women, Fisher finds his social comfort. "The changes of Newport are wonderful. It is now a great place. Hundreds of beautiful cottages when I knew open fields. A large, refined & rich society living in elegant villas. Climate unequalled."

The Great Building Boom

Seaborne enterprise raised Newport from obscurity in the seventeenth and eighteenth centuries, creating prosperity out of penury and spreading the town's reputation along the Atlantic coast and across oceans. After its long and difficult hiatus, Newport rose to prominence again because of developments on land. By the middle of the nineteenth century, Newport had been discovered by a segment of society seeking pleasure and leisure along its sandy shores. Now the city had to be developed and cultivated, gardened and groomed, to ensure its long-term success as a summer resort. John and Joseph Weaver began that process with their popular hotels. Yet by the 1850s, a number of regular seasonal visitors of wealth were tiring of the crowded hotel culture, but not of Newport. They wanted more privacy, more peace and quiet, more of an enduring identification with the city itself. They wanted to be able to entertain their friends in their own homes, surrounded by their own possessions. The man who answered their dreams, offering them spectacular parcels of land on which to build their cottages, was a savvy speculator with the unassuming name of Alfred Smith.

By almost any definition, Alfred Smith was responsible for the post-colonial Newport we experience today. While previous luminaries like Abraham Redwood, Godfrey Malbone, Aaron Lopez, and William Vernon secured the town's position in the cutthroat international mercantile arena, Smith almost single-handedly made Newport accessible to eager outsiders who wanted to possess a permanent place in the palatial paradise. Very simply, Smith was that new breed of entrepreneur who envisioned a more beautiful city while at the same time enriching himself. He was a far-sighted pioneer, a maverick perfectly suited to his expansive age. In today's parlance, Alfred Smith was a real estate broker.

Smith's origins were inauspicious. He was born in 1809 in Middletown into a financially struggling

A REAL CITY

In May 1853, Newporters voted to adopt a city form of government and accepted a new charter, which created a mayor and city council to govern it. The move from township to city reflected the enormous growth of the previous decade that made its old designation outdated. The police department consisted of six men, many streets were lit with either gas or kerosene lamps, and *real* growth was just beginning in the community now hosting ten thousand inhabitants. As the second mayor, George Calvert announced in October 1853, "The prosperity of Newport is greater now than it has ever been before. The advance in the value of real estate within two years has been immense, and unprecedented. In that short period hundreds of new buildings have been erected by our own people, or by strangers, who are attracted hither by the salubrity and charms of our climate, universally recognized now to be one of the best in the world."

Alfred Smith, c. 1880
Early land speculator in Newport.

Photographer unknown
Newport Historical Society
Newport, Rhode Island

family, had scant schooling, and apprenticed as a cloth cutter in Newport and Providence during his youth. He then moved to New York City to work at one of the foremost tailoring emporiums in the country, Wheeler & Company. Smith was talented, ambitious, and thrifty. Wealthy New Yorkers, such as William Beach Lawrence, a leading statesman, internationally acclaimed lawyer, and later lieutenant governor of Rhode Island, sought out not only his suit-making abilities but also his advice about the land market in Newport. According to the local historian Alan Schumacher, Lawrence bought "Ochre Point Farm of over sixty acres for $12,000 in 1835. This was the first large land purchase by an 'outsider' since the Revolution. Other patrons also began to think of Newport as a sea-accessible summer watering place for their families, and Smith was the fellow to consult for local information." Having saved some $20,000 from his clothing endeavors (he reportedly did a brisk business in custom-ordered suits for his Newport clientele and slept in his office to save rent money), Smith gave up the thread trade in 1839 and moved back to Newport to dabble in land acquisition and promotion. His timing, like his tailoring, was impeccable.

Alfred Smith was operating in an uncharted realm. Until the completion of the Ocean and Atlantic Houses, real estate had little interest beyond its value (very low) as farmland. But Smith saw opportunity and, with two other investors, purchased 300 acres of grazing land south and east of Touro Street, a district now known as the Kay-Catherine-Old Beach Road neighborhood. George Engs, also a lieutenant governor of the state, had begun to lay out this area a decade before, but Smith was the one responsible for dividing the land into small lots for building houses, planning the street grid, and planting hundreds of trees. He was also a talented landscape designer and outstanding gardener, and his emphasis on creating beautiful grounds on the parcels he sold went a long way toward creating the arboreal elegance one witnesses in Newport. Soon estates large and small began emerging, erected by Ralph Izard and Hugh Ball of South Carolina and Samuel Ward, a New York banker and father of Julia Ward Howe, author of "The Battle Hymn of the Republic." Many were simple structures made of wood, but a growing number were huge stone piles, which predate and predict the gigantic "cottages" that would later sprout up along Bellevue Avenue. Smith was also responsible for extending Kay Street north and east, all the way to Rhode Island Avenue, and promoting more and more private buildings. Kay-Catherine then became the most fashionable and sought-after area of the city, the nucleus of a thriving artistic and intellectual community that would have great impact on Newport and the nation. Schumacher reports that by 1853 Alfred Smith was prospering: he was the seventh-richest man in Newport, based on tax assessments.

Newport was burgeoning. Construction workers of all stripes began arriving by the shipload to fill the need created by Smith's prescience. The spigot had been opened and money was flowing into town. The West Broadway section grew quickly and both Thames and Spring streets were extended to accommodate commercial ventures. Once-moribund shops began to flourish. More new roads were cut out of the farmland as demands on the city's infrastructure became more acute: everyone, including Mayor Calvert, understood that future affluence would only be gained by making the city more accessible and agreeable to summer travelers and new citizens. According to Jon Sterngass,

> The mayor of Newport reported in 1854 that "hundreds of acres of land that a few years since were farms, are now town lots with costly mansions on them." As late as October 1851, land in the southern part of the city where Bellevue Avenue terminated sold for $300 an acre; a few years later, speculators unloaded it for somewhere between $2,500 and $5,500 an acre. Newport property valued at $5.8 million in 1854 accrued another $2 million in fewer than ten years. Between 1849 and 1859, personal and real wealth in Newport increased spectacularly from $4.5 million to $10.5 million, mainly as a consequence of the presence of summer guests.

Apart from all his other accomplishments, Alfred Smith is best remembered for the creation of Bellevue Avenue. Before 1852, Bellevue Street (as it was then named; previously the road was called Jew Street, then South Touro Street) ran from Kay Street (site of the Hotel Viking) down almost to Narragansett Avenue, a broad road leading to the water that Smith had also already started to develop. Hotels dominated the Hill, and there were not more than twenty or thirty cottages in the surrounding vicinity. Bellevue was little more than a dirt path leading to the mostly treeless tracts of farmland and sheep-grazing pastures once owned by William Brenton. But Smith had an excellent eye, and as he looked south from the corner that now houses the headquarters of Preservation Society of Newport County, he saw another opportunity to create a neighborhood, and more dollars for himself. One hundred and forty acres, from Narragansett Avenue to the

MATTHEW PERRY

In July 1853, the Newport native son Commodore Matthew Calbraith Perry (1794–1858)—younger brother of Oliver Hazard Perry, the celebrated hero of the War of 1812—sailed into Tokyo Bay (then Edo) to deliver a letter from President Fillmore to the emperor of Japan, demanding that his isolated island nation be "opened" to American vessels and traders. For over two centuries the shoguns had closed Japan to nearly all foreigners for fear of polluting their people with alien beliefs and modernizing influences. Now America was set on prying loose that domination for business and military reasons. Because of his reputation for diplomacy and tact, the United States Navy chose Matthew Perry to head the fleet. A veteran of the recent Mexican War and numerous other missions that brought him distinction, Perry was well suited for dealing with the xenophobic Japanese. Perry's "black ships," large armed steamers the likes of which the natives had never seen, made a startling impression. Perry presented his letters to the emperor's minions, stating that he would negotiate only with the highest officials and would return the following year for an answer, hinting broadly that if his country's requests were not granted, he would lay siege to Tokyo.

CONTINUED ON PAGE 314

Perry returned in February 1854 with a larger armada. After weeks of negotiation, he obtained the Treaty of Kanagawa in March at Yokohama, granting United States vessels access to the ports of Hakodate and Shimoda for refueling and supplies and, even more important, the stationing of an American consul in Japan.

Eventually trade between the two countries opened up, and the United States and Japan began a fruitful but uneasy exchange of goods and culture that benefited both nations until the outbreak of World War II. The diplomatic commodore was accorded a hero's welcome upon his return and, among numerous gifts of gratitude, Rhode Island presented him with a silver salver in recognition of his success in Asia. In Newport, an imposing statue of the second famous Perry brother stands in Touro Park.

ocean, were in the possession of Joseph Bailey, whose family had owned the parcel for decades. Smith convinced Bailey to go into partnership and, after buying up a number of adjacent lots, the two men secured full rights to the extensive property. Bailey, less optimistic than his colleague, at one point reportedly remarked about the $27,000 venture, "All I expect to get out of the bargain is driftwood enough to keep me warm for the winter."

By this time, given the scope of his real estate activities, Smith had cultivated many friends in local government. Newport was just about to make the legal transition from township to city, and the new leaders were eager to increase the coffers through expanded taxation. So, in January 1852, the Town Council voted to approve Smith and Bailey's petition to cut a new, fifty-foot-wide highway through the land all the way to the southern shore. After more purchases to create their domain and surveying the land, Smith's dream street, renamed Bellevue Avenue, was begun. A year later, the one and a half mile straight dirt road, wide and inviting, had been completed. Smith had created what would soon become one of the most famous and sought-after addresses in America.

On May 15, 1852, the *Newport Mercury* reported, "The whole face of that portion of the Neck lying between Spouting Horn Beach [Bailey's] and Easton's Beach has been divided and sub divided into building lots, roads have been opened, tens of thousands of trees have been planted, and fine substantial buildings have gone up as in magic. Great has been the improvement, the work is progressing rapidly, and we may look forward to no distant day when the whole south of Newport will present the most charming appearance, equalling in beauty the far famed Isle of Wight." Two years later, in the same newspaper, we read, "By the sale of the lot of land on South Touro Street [Bellevue Avenue], known as the Dixon Lot, every building site south of the Ocean House and north of the residence of Wm. S. Wetmore, Esq., is taken up. This change in the appearance of the 'South End' is

Château-sur-Mer,
original state, 1851-1853
House of William
Shepard Wetmore;
architect: Seth Bradford.
Remodeled in 1872
when owned by
George Wetmore.
Now operated as a
museum house by the
Preservation Society of
Newport County.
Courtesy of the
Newport Historical Society
Newport, Rhode Island

Easton's Beach, c. 1880
Photographer unknown
Newport Historical Society
Newport, Rhode Island

remarkable to those who were familiar with that portion of Newport a few years ago. In the interval the price of land has been doubled again and again until it has reached almost a fabulous price."

Bellevue Avenue was a success from the beginning. William Wetmore, who had bravely built his residence, Château-sur-Mer, prior to Smith's construction of Bellevue, was now joined by dozens of others seduced by Smith's salesmanship, which was famous and feared. According to one report, "He rode about in a highly polished leather chaise, reins in one hand, a rolled-up map of the city in the other. He was likened to a field marshal, baton in hand. Observers claimed that substantial men of affairs staying at the hotels Smith combed for prospects avoided him as best they could, for once he corralled a potential customer, there was no escape. Smith's technique was simple: after he got a man into the chaise, he would not let his prospect out until a sale had been made." He also maintained a vision of what the neighborhood would and would not become, and was often blatantly exclusive when appraising potential clients. Smith not only created "the Avenue," he handpicked the owners as well. Existing farmhouses were bought for remodeling (John Carter Brown of Providence and New York's Ward McAllister each bought one), and empty lots sold quickly. By guaranteeing new owners access to a bathing pavilion at Bailey's Beach (for a ripe price, of course), Smith fashioned his own private oasis far from the common crowd at Easton's Beach.

By 1860, Alfred Smith was acknowledged as the "real estate king" of Newport and, like most rulers, he was intent on enlarging his realm. With Bellevue Avenue now thriving and making him very wealthy, all Smith had to do was look at his map to see that the new south end of the city needed to be connected to areas farther to the west and north. No such roads existed in those days, but it appears that Smith had envisioned a bold master plan to link his beloved Bellevue with the rest of the city. According to Schumacher, Smith brokered a deal in 1857 for Edward King to purchase what was known as Harrison Farm, a large tract south of the harbor. "King then deeded to the City land on which Wellington and Harrison Avenues were built. Prior to this construction, the road leading to Fort Adams and Castle Hill was ill-defined, becoming a quagmire in rainy weather." That was the first step in achieving his ultimate goal: a thoroughfare along the southern shore that would produce stunning vistas for travelers and open up hundreds more acres for development. This new road would start at the south end of Bellevue Avenue and link up with Harrison Avenue to create a "loop" of the city. Thus Smith conceived of, fought for, and eventually presented to the city the plan for what is now known as Ocean Drive.

The challenges of cutting a road along the rocky shore were daunting. Easements had to be obtained, property owners mollified, bridges built, and cash raised for the building of the road. Smith's plan ran into two major hurdles: one owner (a member of the powerful Hazard family) refused to grant his permission and for years would not budge; the second problem was the onset of the Civil War and the drying up of available funds from the city. So, Smith bided his time "until 1866, when a petition of one hundred twenty-five persons forced action by the Commissioner of Highways. By this time many voters realized that a new road would bring additional prosperity to the city as well as creating a beautiful, scenic pleasure drive. It was observed that summer residents were now paying one-third of city taxes." Smith got his Ocean Drive in 1868, and Newport became even more famous as a world-class, fashionable resort. Within a decade of its opening, Ocean Drive was being toasted in the press as being the most beautiful excursion in America.

Ocean Drive, c. 1880
Looking east towards
Green Bridge and
Goose Neck Cove.
Photograph by Stanhope
Newport Historical Society
Newport, Rhode Island

Until his death in 1886, Alfred Smith continued in his role as super salesman, amassing a fortune of nearly $2 million (worth over fifty times that amount in today's dollar based on purchasing power). Through his efforts, Newport was transformed from a tourist town dependent on hotels catering to a largely southern constituency to a summer-colony community of northern big-city tycoons building and frolicking in mansions along the roads he not only imagined, but brought to reality. With Bellevue Avenue and Ocean Drive, the visionary Mr. Smith created the ideal stomping grounds for America's old and emerging elite.

Antebellum City Life

Alfred Smith laid out the grid and supplied the land for cottages, but it took people of wealth to obtain a building site and erect a house. By the time Bellevue Avenue was ready for development, Newport was home to a number of such men, both native and newcomer. Because of its island locale, the city had always been geographically remote: while this proved to be a disadvantage as rampant industrialization swept across America, this isolation kept intact a social structure that was remarkably resilient and cohesive, particularly among the upper class. More than two hundred years after its founding, one still sees the names of descendants of the founders occupying positions of influence and enjoying the afterglow of sustained respect. Some were doing well economically, some not, but their status in town was secure because of former family fortunes. Coddingtons, Coggeshalls, Clarkes, Cranstons, and Hazards are prominent examples of this long legacy.

Newport was an enclave, and it held onto its past even as the rest of the country sped ahead on the iron horses of progress. Many of its upper-class inhabitants were somewhat aloof, preferring to remain outside the mainstream. This is part of the reason so many visitors found Newport quaint and charming, and why the city succeeded so spectacularly as a summer colony for those who tired of big-city brouhaha. Before the post-Civil War invasion of New Yorkers, Newport society had been dominated by people with familiar names: Champlin, Gibbs, Hunter, Bull, Whitehorne, Sherman, King, Stevens, and Vernon. These families had made their riches in the fading mercantile world but were able to preserve and foster their wealth in succeeding generations by going into banking, retail business, law, and medicine. In the 1850s, they were joined by newcomers who planted their roots in the city. The China trade merchant William Wetmore and the attorney Henry Bedlow, both quite wealthy, moved from New York. From Boston came members of the Bancroft, Ruggles, Parkman, and Sumner families, joining the native elite. Richard Randolph, of the prominent Virginia family, and George Calvert (the second mayor) from one of Maryland's founding families, added luster. Many of these men served on the vestry at Trinity Church and held board positions at the Redwood Library. A number of them helped found the exclusive men's club, the Newport Reading Room, in 1853. Not one of them derived his money from heavy industry. According to Harold Hurst, "These rich families not only brought new business to the city but they provided more tax money for the town hall. Outsiders such as Ezra Bourne, Robert H. Ives, Daniel Parrish, and Charles Russell paid higher taxes than did most of the native elite families." In 1860, Wetmore and the native Edward King (also China trade) were the two richest and dynamic men in town.

By the mid-1850s, Newport was such a popular destination that it attracted its first comprehensive directory. One guidebook, *Handbook of Newport*, by John Ross Dix, had already appeared in 1852, informing

By 1859, Newport had retrieved its self-respect, its economy was humming with tourist dollars, and city elders decided to stage a spectacle to showcase its charms and achievements. Bellevue Avenue was already bustling, the Kay-Catherine neighborhood was being developed with fine Victorian homes, and the hotels held the key to present prosperity. It was time to celebrate and demonstrate to past citizens that the city's rebirth was solid. Someone came up with the idea of hosting a "re-union" for anyone born in Newport, and the idea took on a life of its own. The fete was held in late August 1859 and was deemed a stirring success. In the *New York Times* the following day, the excited correspondent gushed, "The morning broke clear and beautiful, as could be observed even by the multitude of fashionable pleasure seekers who are here. It has been a day's weather and a day's social enjoyment, that has made glad the hearts of ten thousand strangers who were attracted hither by the proposed grand social reunion of the sons and daughters and more distant relations of this fine old town. . . . Full seven thousand excursionists arrived by the Providence and Boston boats; and still, although the numbers were far greater than had been anticipated, the programme was carried out with promptitude that was surprising." A huge parade was held, followed by numerous speeches and an outdoor feast. People of all ages mingled and resurrected friendships that had been interrupted by migration. The mood was joyous. Newport basked in glory once again. The event was deemed so successful that another reunion was held twenty-five years later, in 1884. These homages to the city were unusual in America, but were indicative of the esprit de corps shared by many Newport natives.

travelers of the many blessings bestowed upon the city. A few years later, the New Yorker William Boyd compiled the first *Newport Directory for 1856–1857*, a vivid compendium of data that helps us further define and determine what the town comprised in that era. While natives might have found it useful for the presentation of so many disparate facts and names, visitors found it indispensable for deciphering their new surroundings. The first *Directory* is only four by six inches for easy portability, but it is thick with applicable information. It was so successful that it was updated annually in later years. Alan Schumacher made a thorough study of this guide, and listed below are some of the highlights.

Newport was then a city of some 11,000 (compared to over 50,000 in Providence), over 3,000 of whom are listed in the book; one sees primarily English, Scottish, Irish, or African names. Of current summer-colony landed residents, 83 were New Yorkers, 30 from Philadelphia, and about 20 from the Boston area. Interestingly, very few Georgians or Carolinians make the list, perhaps because they were more comfortable maintaining their hotel life, or because they did not want to invest in Yankee real estate while tensions over states' rights and the slavery issue were clearly on the rise. Some 500 names of professionals, tradespeople, and commercial establishments are cited, many accompanied by advertisements. Of note is the fact that almost all of those included were sole proprietorships; Newport was still too small for partnerships or corporations. "The city had 5 attorneys, 3 dentists, 12 physicians and 8 hairdressers, all of whom were male. The most numerous were carpenters (32) and grocers (79). There were as well 26 washerwomen, 3 gristmillers, 1 intelligence officer (shipping) and 1 dancing teacher. The city was served by 11 hotels, 29 boarding houses, 5 restaurants, 12 private and 17 public schools."

The reader is informed that the post office was open from five in the morning until nine at night, that the city was served by ten fire companies, two bell ringers, an Inspector of Nuisances, and nine separate banks. The Redwood Library and Athenæum then held over eight thousand volumes, and there were three other libraries from which to choose books and magazines. We learn that the Newport Historical Society was formed two years before to begin retrieving and storing pertinent data on the city. Newport hosted twenty-one active churches and one synagogue at the time, providing over 11,800 seats; two of the churches catered to African-Americans. Information about transportation, local entertainments, and beaches could also be gleaned. The *Newport Directory*, along with other guidebooks that were starting to appear before the war (such as Dix's and George Champlin Mason's *Newport Illustrated*, in 1854) are like vivid time-capsules, offering concrete evidence about who was important and what the city was like in the decade before America's national unraveling.

Self-inflicted Wounds: Politics and Civil War

From 1843 and the ratification of the new Rhode Island constitution until the outbreak of the War Between the States in 1861, Newport's role in state politics, which it once almost totally controlled, diminished markedly. The city had two fewer representatives in the General Assembly, Providence had five times the population, and the northern tier had taken over as the power base for legislative initiative. In the meantime, Newport was turning inward, fostering its new role as a prime resort and creating a highly localized economy. It didn't need heavy industry; instead, the city only needed to fill its hotel rooms and sell off its vacant land. For nearly two centuries, Newporters had roamed the world selling their goods. Now the world was flocking to Newport in ever-increasing numbers to escape the hurly-burly of an increasingly complex everyday existence.

This about-face in the city's role had the effect of isolating Newport even more from the affairs of state. Its legislators, once undisputed leaders, often took a back bench as the future of Rhode Island was being negotiated. They still wielded power, however, and because of their patrician backgrounds, received respect. Legislators from other communities had to cope with a new, rising class of industrial entrepreneurs who were vying for power, but in Newport, with no organized group standing to oppose the established elites, influence remained largely in the hands of the old guard. While members of the upper crust ably represented the city—Benjamin Hazard, George King, Henry and Robert Cranston, Nathaniel Ruggles, Seth Bateman, and Thomas Hunter being among the most notable—their clout in the General Assembly was compromised because of their increasingly conservative, old Whig voting records. By and large, Newport's conservative legislators strove to maintain the status quo and oppose anything that impinged on their business interests. Broadening the political mandate to new (that is to say, immigrant) voters held little favor for most of the city's statesmen.

On the national level, throughout the 1850s old party allegiances were cracking under the strain of the accelerating tension between North and South. The rapidly shifting platforms and backhanded compromises caused ongoing chaos as the Whig Party disintegrated after the deaths of Henry Clay and Daniel Webster. Most southern Whigs fled to the Democratic Party while in the North, the Republican Party was born. New battle lines were drawn. The overriding issues, of course, were slavery and sectionalism, and the main struggle was over the extension or prohibition of slavery in the new territories and states in the West. With the rise, and influence, of the abolitionist movement in the North, many southern states grew alarmed that their economic livelihood based on plantation-produced cotton and rice harvested by slave labor, would be curtailed.

During the upheavals of the 1850s, a new profile to a lingering phenomenon appeared: a political coalition based on virulent anti-Catholicism called the Know-Nothing Party. National in scope, these bigoted splinter groups from the Whig Party rose in prominence in Rhode Island in 1854–1855 and hijacked the governorship and most of the General Assembly. Aimed primarily at the thousands of Irish immigrants streaming into the state, the Know-Nothingers had one ultimate goal: the obliteration of Catholicism in America. Other local and national issues were peripheral to their philosophy, but these diehard nativists had an extraordinary fear and hatred of papists from any country who thought they could venture to America and find peace and freedom.

Brown University historian Larry Rand contends, "The rise of the Know-Nothing Party effected a change of major importance in the American political scene. Three forces operating together accounted for the rise of Know-Nothingism: the confusion of party alignments, the slavery controversy, and the growth of sincere nativist sentiment."

Because of the anti-Catholicism still lingering from the disruption of the Dorr Rebellion, the

Know-Nothingers found Rhode Island to be fertile ground for their incendiary message. What is alarming is how successful they were, even though their reign of odium was brief. Spurred on by intolerant editorials in the *Providence Journal* openly appealing to racial and religious prejudice, a state-wide campaign began in 1854. Henry B. Anthony, ultra-conservative state secretary to the Whig Party, had become editor of the *Journal* in 1838 and helped fan the fires of hate during the Dorr Rebellion. Patrick Conley writes of him, "From his accession to his death as United States senator in 1884, Anthony compiled a record nearly unmatched in the annals of American nativism." In the April 1855 election, due largely to the attacks on Catholics in the *Journal* and the utter breakdown of the established political order, Know-Nothingers were voted into power—but only for one year. The Whig Party had been decimated and the "Whig" governor, William Hoppin, was a mere puppet dangled by the Know-Nothingers. The *Providence Tribune*, almost as prejudiced as the *Journal*, editorialized that "*America should be governed by Americans*, and not be under the control of a foreign potentate, or be menaced by the minions of the Pope of Rome in matters of State policy."

Remarkably, the short-lived tenure of the Know-Nothing Party, given their rhetoric, caused no major policy changes in Rhode Island. They weren't in office long enough to enforce their vendetta against Catholics. By 1856, the new Republican Party had gained enough adherents to sweep the Know-Nothing Party from power; their organization fizzled, although their message did not. In fact, the Republicans became so strong that until 1887, they elected every governor and federal senator over that thirty-year span, with only one exception. Larry Rand believes that there was far more driving the political agenda than simple religious bigotry. "It was the inability of the Whigs and the Democrats to treat the temperance and slavery issues openly and effectively that permitted the Know-Nothing Party to find the necessary inroads to political success in the state. It cannot be said that the most tolerant of peoples became intolerant in one year. Instead, it can be seen that intolerance, when mated with political desertion on the part of the major parties, can, and often does, give birth to a mutated offspring."

Another offspring of the political calamities of the 1850s was the Civil War itself. With leadership in Washington sorely lacking, regional extremists took control and the country stumbled into a conflict that many historians believe could have been avoided, or at least minimized. In the end, over six hundred thousand soldiers and civilians died because of the various parties' inability to compromise and negotiate, more casualties than any other war in United States history.

The election of the Republican Abraham Lincoln in 1860 (he carried Rhode Island easily but only eked out victory in Newport with 592 votes compared to 560 for Stephen Douglas) launched the country's descent into the war that forever altered the relationship between the North and South. In Newport, former Whigs divided jaggedly into new Republicans who supported Lincoln and "Unionists" (closet Democrats) who backed Douglas and the young conservative governor, William Sprague. Looking at the voting pattern of the election, Newport's margin for Lincoln was far smaller than any other community in the state, a clear anomaly. Most observers believe that Newport's long and close relationship with so many Southerners skewed their perceptions; no other New England community was as knowledgeable about or sympathetic to the concerns of the planters who had been coming to town for over a century. A good number of Southerners over the years had made Newport their home as well, and although they resided in the heart of Yankee New England, their hearts remained tied to their heritage. Business leaders were fearful that a Lincoln victory would mean an end to lucrative contracts. Harold Hurst observed,

> It was hardly coincidental that Samuel Rodman, the manufacturer of "immense quantities of negro cloth" was the Democratic presidential elector from Newport. Finally, hotel owners, who depended heavily on southern patronage, were also frightened by the prospects of a Republican victory. The *Daily News*, in response to their fears, said in a post-election editorial: "Men and women do not go to watering places to discuss politics and sniff the breezes of demagoguism. . . . But even allowing that a majority of our visitors are southerners, are we to surrender our right to think, to vote, to act, to speak as our judgments are to dictate?"

Later writers would find reasons to contradict that editor's opinion. Before the outbreak of hostilities, many people throughout the country believed that open warfare could be avoided and genuinely doubted that the federal government would militarily oppose the secession of Southern states from the Union. A large portion of people below the Mason-Dixon Line were convinced that leaders in the North didn't have the resolve to fight their own countrymen. A little over a month after Lincoln's inauguration on March 4, 1861, with the Confederacy already composed of seven Southern states led by Jefferson Davis, Louisiana general P. G. T. Beauregard fired on the Union at Fort Sumter in Charleston harbor. President Lincoln immediately called for seventy-five thousand soldiers to form the Union Army, and the battle was joined. Most people in Newport now avidly supported their leader and his decision to save the country from splitting asunder.

Was the South surprised by Lincoln's swift response? George W. Curtis, writing in *Harper's Monthly* in 1880, argued that many Southern aristocrats and politicians saw the whole of the North through the narrow lens of Newport's polite hospitality, and therefore deceived themselves about *real* Northern attitudes.

> Newport had been always a resort for them, and there was a decidedly Southern social atmosphere. . . . Thirty years ago a Newport dinner was ruled by any Southern guest of distinction, and he and his friends not only found Northern opinions to be in apparent accord with their own, but they had perhaps a secret surprise and even contempt at the discovery. They did not sufficiently observe that while politics was a chief interest of "society" in the Southern States, the same society in the Northern States was very little interested in politics. The Southern guests had their own way, therefore, partly from indifference, partly from conservative dislike of agitation and disturbance, partly from sincere sympathy of conviction. The misfortune was that the Georgia or Carolina Senator or leader supposed that in the well-bred, easy, self-indulgent Newport world he saw the "North" . . . Newport with all its charms was not a good place in which

NAVAL ACADEMY AT NEWPORT

With war now a reality, Secretary of the Navy Gideon Welles decided that the precarious position of the United States Naval Academy in Annapolis, Maryland, a border state with clear Southern sympathies, put students and faculty in harm's way. So in May 1861 the USS *Constitution*, known as "Old Ironsides," arrived in Newport harbor with 156 midshipmen, the Academy's library, and other necessary equipment; faculty and families arrived later the same day in another ship. The original plan was to house the men at Fort Adams, but its casements were too damp and cold for habitation, so the students remained quartered on the *Constitution*. Most people in Washington were hoping for a short war and thought the Academy's presence in Newport would only be temporary, but when Confederate forces overran the Union Army at Bull Run in July, reality set in and it was clear that the men would have to stay in town for the duration of hostilities. In September, the Atlantic House, newly renovated and enlarged, was taken over, for $5,800 per year, and became the site of the Naval Academy for the next four years. At first, some citizens feared the midshipmen would have a deleterious effect on the town, but the opposite proved true: the Academy infused youthful enthusiasm and was a boost to the off-season social scene, hosting parties and bringing some needed entertainment for Newport's young ladies. Over the years, students sailed in Narragansett Bay on warships and even had the yacht *America*, winner of the first Hundred Guinea Cup (later called America's Cup) race in 1851, to train on. Town leaders tried hard to have the Academy remain permanently in Newport, but opposition in the Senate killed the initiative. In September 1865, Washington ordered the students and professors back to Annapolis, where the Academy has resided ever since.

per acre before Bellevue Avenue was built, to over $2,500 per acre in 1863. In fact, during the war years, sales of lots accelerated every year, with most of the purchasers being summer residents who had decided to put down roots. This was not caused by wartime escapism but because, year after year, wealthy industrialists viewed Newport as a prudent and proper investment. The *Mercury* reported in January 1863, "The sales of real estate which were made by Alfred Smith, Esq., during 1862 amounted to $300,000, while those of 1861 amounted to $250,000, and of 1860, $500,000. Negotiations are now pending, which will cause large changes in real estate in this vicinity, and those having capital lying idle, see no better way of investing, than by the purchase of property which has some *real*ity in it." Those sales were Smith's alone; the figures don't take into account all the land sales by other agents. Later that year in the same paper, we learn that Mr. George Armstrong "has sold 62,184 feet of land on Bellevue Avenue to Mr. Francis E. Bacon, of Boston, for $12,436."

The Civil War had dampened Newport's spirit and siphoned away its Southern gentry, but did little to interfere with the city's heady ascent to its position as the most august resort in America.

The Other Newport: Writers, Artists, and the Intelligentsia

From the 1840s through the 1880s, Newport harbored a diverse group of people who were not subordinate to the whims of fashion nor slaves to the suffocating social stratification settling in among them. Unbeknownst to the boisterous summer hotel clientele and even to some of the more urbane business magnates beginning to colonize Bellevue Avenue, for decades Newport hosted some of America's leading writers, scientists, and artists. Mostly they stayed aloof from the frantic leisure scene, partook of their own, private Newport, and wrote about the joys of the city as they experienced it; often, they later recorded their disappointments when Newport had turned into a social mecca based not on taste and sophistication but purely upon wealth and perceived status dictated by stultifying New York City standards.

A number of talented men and women who dwelt in Newport and benefited from their experiences achieved international recognition. Henry and William James, Edith Wharton, John La Farge, and William Morris Hunt are but a sampling of the coterie of thinkers who were deeply touched by the beauties of Aquidneck Island and the lasting friendships formed in Newport. When they lived in the city, they were mostly young and unknown to the rest of the world. When they matured and produced the works of art that made them famous, they brought with them their separate Newport experiences and molded them into lasting impressions on the page or canvas. These were people whose lives revolved around imagination and craft, who took what they had lived and remembered and massaged those experiences into enduring literature and art. Newport forever influenced their worldview, their values, their aesthetics. In the midst of unyielding frivolity and escapism resided many of the most original minds of the nineteenth century.

In antebellum Newport, the Kay-Catherine-Old Beach Road area teemed with the literati from Cambridge, Boston, and Philadelphia. They were writers, artists, professors at Harvard or Penn, men and women who had traveled to or lived in Europe for extended periods, connoisseurs of art and music. Newport became their meeting ground, and because so many of them had shared the international experience, their bonds were strong. They liked to talk and exchange ideas on the broad porches of their homes or on walks along the sea. They were a class by themselves; wanderers, seasoned world travelers, and intellectuals, they had chosen Newport because it came closest to the culture they had known in Europe, and perhaps because of its freedom from the obligations and restraints of society at large.

In 1858, Henry James, Sr., brought his family to Newport to live in a rented house on Old Beach Road and Tew's Court. Ever peripatetic (they had already lived in Paris, Geneva, and London), James was seeking a good education for his five children, the eldest of whom were William (age seventeen) and Henry, Jr. (then fifteen), who was known as Harry. The senior James had inherited the fortune his father had accumulated in the dry goods business in Albany, New York, and therefore was free to pursue his own intellectual interests uninhibited. He became deeply involved in the philosophy of Emanuel Swedenborg and was close to Ralph Waldo Emerson, whose liberal theories about the importance of creating a strictly American literature influenced him deeply. He encouraged his children to be inquisitive and open to the world, while at the same time demanding they be rigorous in their education and attention to culture.

Upon arriving in Newport (chosen because orphaned cousins lived in town), the elder brothers soon made the acquaintance of Thomas Sergeant Perry and John La Farge. Perry, known as Sargy, was a grandson of Oliver Hazard Perry, hero of the War of 1812, and great-great-grandson of Benjamin Franklin. Two years younger than Harry, he nonetheless impressed his new friends with his wide-ranging interests; he would later distinguish himself through his writing and teaching at Harvard. La Farge, educated in America and France, worldly, and eight years older than Henry James, was already showing talent in his paintings; he

Jacque-Emile Blanche
Henry James, 1908
Oil on canvas
National Portrait Gallery,
Smithsonian Institution
Washington, D. C.
Bequest of Mrs. Katherine
Dexter McCormick
NPG.68.13

would emerge as one of the most significant artists of his time, famous especially for his works of stained glass. Fast friendships were formed that lasted throughout their lives. The basis of those relationships was a shared artistic vision and a mutual love of Newport.

Henry James went on to become one of the most influential writers of the late nineteenth and early twentieth centuries, while William orchestrated in very canny ways an international reputation in psychology and philosophy (as one of the formulators of pragmatism). Yet the genesis of their illustrious careers can be traced to their Newport years when the brothers, mistakenly, were both seeking an entirely different path. La Farge, who had come to town to study under the artist William Morris Hunt, soon interested William James in joining him. Henry tagged along and did some sketches, but after a year of intense work, he realized painting was not his strong suit. Urged on by La Farge, who clearly had the makings of a first-class artist, Henry James followed his intuition, turned to writing stories, and his life path was settled. William also came to the same conclusion concerning his artistic output, even though Hunt thought William could have made his way as a painter; instead, he decided to pursue a life in science, and went off to study at Harvard. In both brothers' cases, their training under Hunt served them well for the rest of their lives; many characters in Henry's subsequent stories and novels were artists.

Before coming to Newport, Henry had had no formal schooling. Now he was enrolled in the Berkeley Institute on Church Street, along with Sargy Perry. Their friendship blossomed during extended walks around the island and long sessions reading at the Redwood, which James considered the best library he had ever seen. After a year and a half, Henry James, Sr., decided that the family should return to Europe; they were gone for eleven months before returning to town for another three years. But Henry clearly missed Newport. From Switzerland he wrote to Perry: "How you do make me wish to get back to America and Newport especially when you talk of the walks we used to take together! Geneva has endless lovely walks, but I think of Lily Pond, Cherry Grove, Purgatory, Paradise, and Spouting Rock (how I delight to write the names)." In a later letter, Henry asks, "How is the Redwood getting along; I miss it very much for there is no place of the kind here, except a venerable old institution, with none but the oldest of books."

Once back in Newport, the friendships with Perry and La Farge deepened, as did Henry's commitment to becoming a writer. His first stories were penned in town, his reading became wider, and he spent countless hours at the Redwood. The young men swam and ice-skated together and talked endlessly about books and ideas. Henry could have had no better introduction to the world of the artist than John La Farge, a brilliant conversationalist whom Henry referred to as a "genius." He constantly prodded Henry to look more carefully at the world around him and more deeply at the people he observed; he instilled an aesthetic standard that the younger man took to heart. Reading James's novels, it is clear that the message was received and remembered.

Another Newport incident also had a lasting effect on Henry. One night in October 1861, a fire broke out in a stable near the Redwood. Many men rushed to the scene to help put it out (they used water from the library's reservoir) and in the commotion, Henry sustained a wound that he referred to mysteriously for many years. Most students of his life believe it was simply a bad back injury, but James wrote of it as "an obscure hurt" that haunted him for life. Whatever it was, he used the injury as a means of not volunteering in the Civil War, and he felt a sense of guilt for years thereafter.

Believing that the family would make Newport its permanent home, Henry, Sr., bought a house on the corner of Spring and Lee streets in 1862. Yet within months, Henry, Jr., decided that he needed a career that would secure an income while he attempted to become a writer, and in September enrolled in Harvard Law School. After a year, he realized that law was a mistake, like the attempt to become a painter, and quit school. Now even more convinced of his calling, he began a career in journalism while continuing to hone his fiction. In 1864, Henry James, Sr., with both oldest sons in Cambridge and another badly wounded in the Civil War and in need of special medical attention, put the Spring Street house on the market and moved the rest of the family to Boston.

But that did not stop Henry, Jr., from making numerous visits to his favorite American town. He watched it undergo its transformation from the idyll of his youth to a great watering place invaded, particularly after the Civil War, by a society he did not admire. In 1870, after spending two weeks in town during the summer season, he wrote an article for *The Nation* in which he chides the gaiety and vanities of the summer visitors and claims that Newport will always win out against mankind: "The beauty of this landscape is so subtle, so essential, so humble, so much a thing of character and impression, so little a thing of feature and pretension, that it cunningly eludes the grasp of the destroyer or the reformer, and triumphs in impalpable purity even when it seems to condescend." After a drive along Bellevue Avenue, he writes, "The atmospheric tone, the exquisite, rich simplicity of the landscape, gave mild, enchanting sense of positive climate—these are the real charms of Newport, and the secret of her supremacy." He delights in walks around the Point, is unimpressed with the new mansions rising along the new Ocean Drive, and believes that nature's beauty will always prevail regardless how foolishly humans behave.

Henry James soon departed for Europe, which he made home for the rest of his life. There he wrote the masterpieces that have secured his position in American letters. Novels like *The Portrait of a Lady*, *The Ambassadors*, *The Wings of the Dove*, and *The Golden Bowl* are clear evidence of a superior literary power and imagination that began in Newport, matured with his travels, and remain among the most complex and compelling works of fiction in America. He helped invent modernism in literature, cast off the often clumsy omniscient narrator, and introduced the portrayal of psychological motivation for the furthering of plot and action. His insistence on showing realistic characters in moral quandaries harks back to the lessons of John La Farge. His influence on writers as disparate as Marcel Proust, James Joyce, William Faulkner, and T. S. Eliot is an enduring endorsement of his talent as a novelist and critic.

American literature was undergoing a metamorphosis around the midcentury as Transcendentalists like Ralph Waldo Emerson and Henry David Thoreau explored new themes based on a celebration of man and nature. These authors offered optimistic, self-reliant, and robust depictions of the possibilities inherent in life when humankind fully inhabited its physical setting. While greatly influenced by European Romantics, these (mostly) New England writers sought to establish a particularly American voice, one that would be immediately distinguishable from the prevailing French and English manner.

Likewise in the graphic arts, new styles and influences were being introduced in the United States. While it was widely acknowledged that the masters dwelt in Europe, where so many serious American painters and sculptors flocked for training (usually quite rigid and stratified), a few artists were setting up small ateliers in Eastern cities to cultivate and encourage emerging American artists. A shift in focus from portraiture to rendering the dramatic domestic landscape was gaining acceptance, the definition of aesthetics and technique was undergoing substantial alteration (although Old School critics were outraged over the perceived "vulgar" art emanating from both continents), and what we know today as the Hudson River School was all the rage, as witnessed by the wide popularity of Thomas Cole and Frederick E. Church. Aquidneck was a very popular subject because of its wild beauty and translucent light. Maud Howe Elliott once wrote, "Newport has been the painting ground of so many artists of the Hudson River School that if it were attempted to speak of them all, this paper would become like the Catalogue of Don Giovanni, so many of these men loved to paint our island." These many canvases, devoured and admired by a public ravenous for culture, further helped popularize Newport as a vacation destination.

But the arts are always in flux, and one of the chief renegades of the 1850s and 1860s was William Morris Hunt. Born in Vermont in 1824, along with his younger brother Richard Morris Hunt, who would rise to fame as an architect in New York and Newport, William spent several years at Harvard, then traveled to Europe for twelve years to pursue a career as an artist. He studied under various teachers and spent one year in a Düsseldorf academy he found frustratingly strict. In Paris, he happened upon a painting by Thomas Couture and was immediately drawn to the freshness of the imagery and brushstroke. Hunt had found his métier, and his mentor. Studying under Couture, and now free of the academicians who insisted on following the fixed principles of the official Ecole, Hunt blossomed. For two years he worked exclusively under his master, until he came under the sway of a struggling artist named Jean-François Millet in 1850. Millet and a small group of painters, in rebellion against the stultifying constraints of the established academies, formed one of the most influential movements in nineteenth-century French art: the Barbizon School, a prime precursor to Impressionism. Presenting mostly peasant themes instead of urban scenes, Barbizon painters were more romantic, more painterly, in their approach, and this appealed greatly to Hunt, who moved to Barbizon for two years to study with Millet, much to the consternation of Couture.

Hunt returned to America in 1855, married, and came to Newport the following year to paint and open a school for students interested in the newest fashions from Paris. In a letter to his mother, Hunt remarked, "I think the advantages of the right kind of society, climate, and geographical position make this [Newport] the most suitable place for us to choose as a residence. I have bought a house here." The house, called Hill-top, was on Church Street and Bellevue Avenue (today the site of the Hotel Viking), and it became a mecca for young men and women seriously interested in painting. He added a large studio for instruction, and during the period that John La Farge and the James brothers were studying with him, it was one of the liveliest places in Newport.

William Morris Hunt was not enamored of the wild romantic panoramas being created by Hudson River School artists. While he had a fine eye, real talent, and loved his surroundings on Aquidneck, his training at Barbizon taught him to eschew elaborate vistas and concentrate on a humanized landscape. The "sublime vastness of primeval nature," so canonized by the prevailing fashion-setters, seemed counterfeit to Hunt. He once said, "The extraordinary does not come within the province of art. You can't represent the height of the Alps or the Sierras. We must keep ourselves within the limits of possibility." He had broader vision than most of his contemporaries and often urged La Farge: "Strive for simplicity! Not complexity! Keep the impression of your subject as one thing. . . . Keep the masses flat, simple and undisturbed, and spend your care on skillfully joining the edges." Hunt was instrumental in introducing Barbizon techniques and theories in the United States, and his studio in Newport was like a laboratory for innovation. Certainly for John La Farge, studying with Hunt expanded his horizons enormously. Even William James, though he ultimately chose science over art, was a beneficiary of Hunt's instruction. The critic F. O. Matthiessen observed, "One of his greatest assets as a psychologist was that he had mastered the artist's skill of grasping concretely the evanescent moment of experience."

Hunt and his family moved from Newport to Boston in 1862 so he could pursue a career as a portrait painter in a more lucrative market. He sold his house to his brother Richard, who would go on to be one of Newport's most influential architects during the decades that New Yorkers dominated the summer scene. William continued his steady output of landscapes and portraits, exhibited regularly and mostly favorably, and continued to instill Barbizon ideas in younger artists. The devastating Boston fire of 1872 destroyed many of his canvases and those of Millet he had bought while in France. Later, he won a commission to paint two huge murals for the New York State capitol building in Albany. Fêted at the time for their power and elegance, they have vanished now because the material they were painted on slowly disintegrated. He remained active and involved in his career, although depression over family troubles and finances was evident to his friends. William Morris Hunt died, probably a suicide, in New Hampshire in 1879, at the age of fifty-five.

The intersection of talent, even genius, that took place on Church Street in Newport in 1860 and 1861 was a remarkable coincidence of fate, one that had a long-lasting effect on American culture. We have Henry and William James trying their hands at becoming painters under the tutelage of William Morris Hunt, side by side with John La Farge, who was to mature into a true master of the graphic arts, encouraging the James brothers with his advice and innate wisdom. Hunt must have sensed that something extraordinary was taking place in his studio, for he referred to those years often for the rest of his life, as did Henry James and La Farge. Rare are such magical moments, but in retrospect it is evident that Newport played host to just such a situation when these men shared their visions of what the structure and intent of real art was, and could be.

John La Farge was a protean creature, ever curious and inventive. Born in 1835 to French parents in New York City, he began to draw at age six, graduated from a Catholic college in Maryland in 1853, and, at his father's request, began to pursue a career in law, all the while continuing to dabble at his art. Traveling to France to meet relatives, La Farge immersed himself in the cultural scene and, like Hunt before him, spent a few weeks studying with Thomas Couture. He then roamed around Europe, paying special attention to museums and galleries. When his father died in 1858, La Farge inherited enough money to give up law and seriously study painting, which he did by moving to Newport to work with Hunt.

More than brushes and an easel awaited him in Newport. Through the connection with Hunt, La Farge met Henry James's new friend Sargy Perry, whose sister was the beautiful Margaret Mason Perry. La Farge was smitten, but religion became a divisive issue because the staunchly Episcopalian Perry family was against their daughter marrying a Catholic. Nevertheless, they continued to see each other, and after a year's

courtship Margaret accepted his proposal; she then converted to his faith, again over the objections of her family. The couple was married in October 1860, moved into a large house on Kay Street, and began their own family. For the next fourteen years, the Newport area was home, although they were forced to sell the Kay Street residence and rent smaller homes in Middletown for financial reasons.

Even though he spent over two years with William Morris Hunt and learned Barbizon techniques from him, La Farge was essentially self-taught as a painter. He was never formally trained in French formulas and so he was free to innovate. All of his work has a certain eccentricity to it that sets La Farge apart from his contemporaries on either continent. Even before Hunt moved to Boston, La Farge was abandoning the studio to paint and draw landscapes and still lifes from nature in the scenic surroundings of Newport. Together with his friend and neighbor John Chandler Bancroft, son of the famed historian George Bancroft and an artist himself, La Farge began an intense technical study of optics, color, and the play of light. He wanted to render nature as it was and not infuse his work with false narratives or pictorial grandeur. Two canvases, *Paradise Valley* and *Paradise Rocks*, painted between 1866 and 1868, were a culmination of his scientific inquiries and his experiments with depicting nature in a new way. According to an anonymous critic, "The *Paradise Valley* was in advance of its time. French impressionism was yet to make its impact upon American art but in this landscape La Farge, animated by his own inquisitiveness, reveals his own discoveries and anticipates the formula of Monet. 'I wished,' he said, 'to apply principles of light and color. I wished my studies of nature to indicate something of this, to be free from *recipes*, as far as possible, and to indicate very carefully in every part, the exact time of day and circumstance of light.'"

La Farge was exhibiting his work regularly and receiving national and international attention. He was ahead of his time, but many other artists and critics could quickly see his talent and his ambitions. His work was selling well. But, being a polymath, La Farge forayed into other art forms, which stole time from his painting. He began a successful career as a book illustrator, then in the mid-1870s, became heavily involved in the decorative arts, a move that necessitated his relocation to New York City, leaving his wife and family behind in Newport. The decorative arts business went well at first, then foundered spectacularly, driving him into bankruptcy and numerous lawsuits that sapped his strength and wallet. The easel now abandoned, he turned to large-scale mural work for private homes (a Vanderbilt mansion on Fifth Avenue in New York), religious edifices (the Channing Memorial Church on Pelham Street in Newport), and public buildings such as the Minnesota state capitol. As with almost everything he created, these grand-style works were highly regarded at the time, and still are. In addition, he began writing books and giving lectures across America.

John La Farge is probably best remembered for his rediscovery of the use of stained glass in windows (at least in America), in both ecclesiastical and secular buildings. Prior to his development of this medium, almost no artists or architects gave any notice to the beauties of scenes created on stained glass, which had been one of the most respected crafts of the Middle Ages. But the ever-curious La Farge, on his travels in Europe, became fascinated with the form and the effect of light shining through multicolored pieces of glass. Back in New York, he began experimenting with age-old French techniques of preparing glass, but found the results wanting. After years of trial and error, the secret revealed itself. "A colored glass container of tooth powder on his toilet table caught his eye at the moment when light was passing through it. His imagination leapt to the suggestion and shortly afterward, with a Luxembourg glassmaker in Brooklyn for an aid, he had developed 'opalescent glass' on which much of his fame was to rest."

According to James Yarnall, an expert on La Farge, "Using layers of glass, semiprecious stones, and molded glass, La Farge patented in 1880 a method of making windows with opalescent glass that is generally credited as the start of a new stained-glass movement. For his accomplishment, La Farge received the Legion of Honor from the French government in 1889." But the officials weren't the only ones appreciative of La Farge's efforts. At the time of the award, a group of fellow artists paid this tribute to him: "He is the great innovator, the inventor of opaline glass. He has created in all its details an art unknown before, an entirely new industry, and in a country without tradition he will begin one followed by thousands of pupils filled with the same respect for him that we have ourselves for our own masters. To share in this respect is the highest praise that we can give to this great artist." Unfortunately for La Farge, his legal troubles in New York kept him from cashing in on his successes in stained glass. He was outmaneuvered by his rival Louis Tiffany, now the household name associated with masterful glass objects. When it came to business dealings, La Farge was a disaster.

The next phase in the artist's colorful career was the most exotic. Approached in 1886 by his old friend, the historian Henry Adams, about traveling with him to Japan (all expenses paid), La Farge, in the midst of his legal and financial woes, eagerly accepted. Japan, newly "opened" to the West by his wife's great-uncle

Matthew Perry a scant few decades earlier, was becoming the target of travel for New England intellectuals. La Farge had for years been collecting Japanese art, and felt the need for a new source of inspiration. For three months, the two men traipsed around the country, visiting shrines, museums, and temples in Tokyo, Osaka, and Kyoto, and picking up prime porcelain and prints. The trip was emotionally and artistically a triumph for both men. According to the historian Christopher Benfey, "Traveling with La Farge to Japan meant not only leaving the United States in a geographical sense but leaving it in a cultural sense as well. For Henry Adams, La Farge was himself a foreign land. If the United States stood for reason and smoothly running machinery, Adams decided, 'La Farge alone owned a mind complex enough to contrast against the common-places of American uniformity.' Americans were forever proclaiming their freedom and individuality, meanwhile settling for whatever was in fashion. La Farge, without trumpeting the fact, was the real, the wholly original thing." Enjoying each other as much as they did, four years later they spent eighteen months exploring islands in the South Seas.

From these excursions came hundreds of watercolors and several illustrated books that helped refresh La Farge's sagging reputation among collectors. His work was exhibited in major international museums, and in Europe he was afforded great respect. Once again, he was seen as one of the most accomplished artists of the century. John La Farge died in 1910 in a Providence hospital, looked after by his wife of fifty years. The art historian Barbara Bloemink sums up his accomplishments. "La Farge's work is astonishing in its variety of forms, techniques and subject matter. He worked in paintings, sculpture, drawing, watercolor, illustration, architectural design, wood engraving, murals, stained glass, and photography. He is credited . . . with collecting and incorporating motifs and compositional elements from Japanese art prior to his European contemporaries, painting plein-air landscapes before the Impressionists, working in Tahiti and the South Seas a year before Gauguin's arrival, and creating a new form of art criticism using psychology and physiology to analyze meaning."

The Town and Country Crowd

Apart from major talents like the James brothers and John La Farge, Newport was home (either permanent or summer) to a large group of intelligentsia who are loosely referred to as "the Town and Country set" because of their association with the club of that name founded by Julia Ward Howe in 1871. While the beaches filled with pleasure-seekers and more cottages lined Bellevue Avenue, this coterie concerned with affairs of the mind quietly went about their lives out of sight of the revelers.

Remembered chiefly as the author of the anthem "The Battle Hymn of the Republic," Julia Ward Howe, born in 1819, was in fact a multifaceted powerhouse, a pioneer in the women's suffrage movement, ardent abolitionist, crusader for equality, and a ranking member of American high society. A descendant of two colonial governors of Rhode Island, Richard and Samuel Ward, and daughter of Samuel Ward, Jr., who made millions of dollars on Wall Street, Julia grew up pampered in New York City, being educated by governesses and attending private schools; she spoke several foreign languages, and began her writing career at a young age. Julia Ward married Dr. Samuel Gridley Howe, head of the Perkins Institute for the Blind and nearly two decades her senior, in 1843; they had six children. The couple became pillars of Boston society and, although he was a rather stern gentleman of the old school, both were admired. Her real passion was writing,

and over the course of her long life, Julia Ward Howe authored fourteen books (including *Modern Society* and *Is Polite Society Polite?*), ranging from poetry to political essays to reminiscences.

Although Boston was her base, Newport was her real love. Julia Ward spent summers as a young woman at her father's house in town, then the Howes purchased a farm in Lawton's Valley in Portsmouth in 1852 (under great pressure from Alfred Smith), which became the nerve center for intellectual and social gatherings for many years. Practically every writer or artist of note who visited Newport in the second half of the nineteenth century attended one of her social salads at the Howe house as a matter of course. Henry Wadsworth Longfellow (a close friend of Julia's brother), Mark Twain, Oscar Wilde, the historian George Bancroft, Bret Harte, William Cullen Bryant, both Henry Jameses, Thomas Hazard (author of *The Jonny Cake Papers*), the Shakespearean actress and popular singer Charlotte Cushman, Oliver Wendell Holmes, Edgar Allan Poe, the actor Edwin Booth, Colonel Thomas Wentworth Higginson, Clement C. Moore (author of "The Night Before Christmas"), the painter John Singer Sargent, and many more graced her home. She created a culture as close as America could get to a European salon, mixing young and old, known and unknown. Of her efforts she remarked, "I felt the need of upholding the higher social ideals, and of not leaving true culture unrepresented, even in a summer watering place." The historian Mary Murphy-Schlichting observed of Mrs. Howe, "Her circle of acquaintances bridged national boundaries: she visited Dickens, Carlyle, and Wordsworth; named her daughter after friend Florence Nightingale; and was related by marriage to the Astors and the Bonapartes. Her social position, education, and marriage made her singular; her eclectic and warm friendships made her unique."

In other words, this doyenne could do as she pleased, and that was to enjoy life while at the same time exhibit certain standards of taste and erudition. People not only respected Julia Ward Howe (particularly after she became nationally famous because of her 1862 anthem), they also adored her wit and easy charms. As serious as she was about the societal issues swirling through America at that time, she also knew that restrained frivolity was a necessary frosting for the good life. The Town and Country Club, which existed for over thirty years, was more than just a loose association of the literary and scientific set: it elected officials (Mrs. Howe was president), published a pamphlet explaining rules and fees (a limit of fifty families at $2 per year), and religiously met at a member's house once a week during the season. Some sessions were comic, others quite serious, with weighty lectures by experts in a variety of fields.

The inaugural meeting at the Point home of John Bigelow has come to be known as the Mother Goose Commencement, a take-off on a Harvard graduation ceremony, and conducted in six different languages. Mrs. Howe wrote many of the skits, and induced the likes of Henry James, Sr., Bret Harte, Professor William Rogers (founder of the Massachusetts Institute of Technology), and George Bancroft (founder of the U. S. Naval Academy) to supply their own. Others delivered satirical speeches (Colonel Higginson's was titled "How to Sacrifice an Irish Bull to a Greek Goddess"), recited poems, and generally reveled in their self-made merriment. A piece in the *Mercury* on August 24, 1871, reported: "They meet for fun and frolic and are not harassed by fears for their good clothes or by any other trifling matters which disturb fashionable aristocrats of Bellevue when they attempt to picnic. They make puns, propound conundrums and read essays. . . . Whatever they do, they come home full of glee and enjoyment, tired and dusty to be sure, but wearing the happiest faces in town."

One of Newport's leading literary figures during those postwar decades was Thomas Wentworth Higginson. After graduating second in his class from Harvard in 1841, he went to Harvard Divinity School and became a Unitarian clergyman. Staunchly antislavery and an early advocate of women's rights, Higginson was asked to leave his position by the conservative congregation in Newburyport because of his outspoken liberal views. He turned to writing articles for the *Atlantic Monthly*, and in the Civil War became a colonel of the First South Carolina Volunteers, made up of slaves freed by Union forces; after sustaining several wounds and surviving a bout of malaria, Higginson left the army in 1864 and, with his invalid wife, moved to Newport, where he set about to make his reputation as a journalist and novelist (to his great regret, *Malbone, an Oldport Romance* did not sell well). He penned the very successful *Young Folks' History of the United States*, which made him economically secure. Yet it is as a literary critic that Higginson is remembered. In his writing, he strongly advocated that women should be seen more in print. A reclusive poet in Amherst, Massachusetts, named Emily Dickinson, bravely sent Higginson some of her poems; many letters ensued, as well as a few face-to-face meetings, and Higginson went out of his way to encourage her. Thus his championing of one of America's finest poets of the nineteenth century did more for his posthumous reputation than all of his books and magazine pieces printed in his lifetime.

A GROWING LIBRARY

By the 1850s, the Redwood Library was overflowing with books—books everywhere, stacked on shelves and chairs, scattered on the floor. The library board wisely decided an addition was necessary, but Peter Harrison's original Palladian design presented a real challenge: how to expand a masterpiece without ruining it? For a brief time board members toyed with the idea of building an entirely new structure, then came to their senses and voted for an extension. George Snell, a Boston architect, was retained in 1858. His plan for what is now the Reading Room "followed the original design of the early building and thus is an important milestone in early Victorian recognition of and regard for 18th century American colonial architectural modes." Instead of inserting prevailing "modern" fashions and attaching towers or porches, Snell respected Harrison's design and stayed within those antiquarian proportions. The Reading Room was in operation in July 1859.

By 1865, the Redwood possessed over eleven thousand volumes, plus a growing and important art collection. It was back to the drawing board, literally. George Champlin Mason, former artist and editor of the *Newport Mercury* and now practicing architecture, was presented the task of developing plans for another extension that would be harmonious with the edifice. He designed what is now the primary entrance on Redwood Street, the Delivery Room, and the Librarian's office. The new section was opened to the public in December 1875. Other smaller additions followed over the decades, but once again, with over two hundred thousand books and an even larger collection of art, the Redwood conducted extensive alterations and enlargement between 2004 and 2006.

Higginson was a jovial, personable man who loved to socialize and mix with a wide range of people. He was passionate about furthering public education, and he succeeded in abolishing the separate Negro schools in Newport, integrating them into the all-white system. He delighted in literary evenings at his friend Colonel George Waring's (famous for his revolutionary work in sanitary engineering) Catherine Street house, The Hypotenuse, where talk and readings would go on well after midnight. In the mid-1870s, Higginson proclaimed about Newport that "there were more authors habitually grouped in that city than anywhere else in America." For all of his far-flung activities in town, his leadership role in the Town and Country Club brought him the most enjoyment because of the fusion of comedy and serious lectures, the fascinating minds encountered, and the camaraderie. In an August 1875 journal entry, Higginson reports: "The Town and Country Club had yesterday a picnic at Castle Hill on the shore. Alexander Agassiz gave some natural history talks; we then had a picnic tea on the piazza of an unoccupied house, which was lent to us in the face of a beautiful sunset across the bay. Mrs. Howe read some verses on 'Satan and Science'—quite funny, and there were speeches by Mark Twain and Ex-Vice President Colfax, who were there as guests. It was very easy and pleasant."

Another popular regular at the Town and Country gatherings, as witnessed in Higginson's diary, was the scientist Alexander Agassiz, one of the most renowned marine zoologists and biologists of the century and a longtime Newport resident at his home and laboratory at Castle Hill. Born in Switzerland in 1835, he moved to America when he was fourteen to join his father, Louis Agassiz, also a respected naturalist, then teaching zoology and geology at Harvard. Alexander graduated from the same school, then went on to earn an engineering degree, a move that would make him a millionaire later in life. He followed his father's career path and began teaching science in Boston, publishing numerous books and articles on natural history.

During the 1860s, Alexander became involved with a failing copper mine on Lake Superior, first as a director and then president. The changes he initiated were so successful that, under his leadership, he turned the Calumet and Hecla mines into the largest and most efficient copper operation in the world, realizing huge profits for himself and his investors. But the deaths of his father and his own young wife within eight days of each other in 1873 jolted him severely and he withdrew from many of his former endeavors. Seeking seclusion, and now extremely wealthy, in 1874 he bought thirty-two acres at Castle Hill and built not only a mansion for himself and his stepmother (who was an educator and writer and instrumental in founding Radcliffe College), but also a state-of-the-art laboratory for the study of oceanography. Each year, twelve to fifteen Harvard students would study with Professor Agassiz, using Narragansett Bay as their training ground. For a quarter of a century these operations were conducted: the research, fieldwork, and specimen gathering that took place at Castle Hill was the inspiration for the world-renowned Marine Biological Laboratory at Woods Hole, Massachusetts. In 1890, with land donated by Agassiz, the federal government erected a much-needed lighthouse at the foot of Castle Hill near Pirate's Cove.

Alexander Agassiz divided his time between Newport and Boston, where he served as curator of the unfinished Harvard Museum of Comparative Zoology; he developed a fundraising campaign and ultimately donated over a million dollars of his own to bring it to completion. During the summer season at Newport, aside from teaching and giving lectures to the Town and Country Club, he entertained his friends and family with his gourmet meals. He traveled widely, became obsessed with proving his friend Charles

Darwin's theory of evolution wrong (which he obviously failed at), and became a world expert on the formation of coral reefs. After his death in 1910, his son George published his letters and some essays; in those writings his love of Newport and Castle Hill is abundantly evident.

A number of other prominent Americans who were not active members of the Town and Country Club enriched Newport's cultural life in the 1860s and 1870s. Raphael Pumpelly (1837–1923), who is little-known today but was one of the country's foremost archaeologists and geologists, lived as a year-round resident in a large house on Gibbs Avenue for forty-four years with his wife and children. Like Agassiz, he also operated a laboratory on his grounds, but his was set up to examine and classify various ores and metals discovered on his worldwide travels. Trained in Europe, he returned to America to develop silver mines in Arizona, then spent a year in Japan surveying minerals until he was obliged to leave for political reasons. Pumpelly went on to China, investigated the Gobi Desert, trekked through Siberia on horseback, and finally after three years came home. His book *Geological Researches in China, Mongolia, and Japan* in 1867 made his reputation with scientists. He spent more years traveling to various sites, often as a member of the U. S. Geological Survey, but his major contribution, when he was almost seventy, was the excavation of prehistoric sites in Turkmenistan in Central Asia occupied by the Ayrans during the Bronze Age. His team confirmed the existence of several different cultures in the area, and Pumpelly's rigorous discipline in documentation and artifact retrieval set numerous standards for future archaeologists. He died at his Newport home at age eighty-six.

Clarence King was born in Newport in 1842 and spent much of his youth in town. He studied chemistry and geology at Yale, and, like Pumpelly (who was a good friend) spent decades on the road engaged in creating topography maps and land surveys. He was so well respected by his peers that when the federal government established the U. S. Geological Survey, Clarence King was chosen its first leader. He had many powerful friends, and the writer Henry Adams called King "the most remarkable man of our times." He died in 1901 and is buried in Newport.

From the Hotel to the Home

During the Civil War years, Newport managed to sustain its steady pace of summer visitors and foster its roaring hotel culture; and it seemed to many that nothing was going to change. Families would come, spend the summer at the Ocean or the Atlantic House, and return the next year for the same regimen of sun, sea, and parties. In fact, people did keep coming in large numbers, but after the war many of them were seduced into buying house lots from the likes of Alfred Smith or Joseph Bailey. Something elementary was shifting in the psyche of upper-class America: as these men slashed through the competition in the cut-throat jungles of business and industry, they wanted to display their ascendance and status as winners, and, at the same time, carve out some solitude. Ever so quickly, the face of Newport was evolving from a festive city dominated by the public hotel (as in Saratoga and Bar Harbor) to a resort concentrated around the private single-family cottage.

Tastes changed, as tastes tend to do. Money that would have gone into the hotel owner's

IDA LEWIS

One of the most revered figures of the last half of the century was the indefatigable Ida Lewis, keeper of the Lime Rock lighthouse in Newport harbor. Many myths surround Miss Lewis, the foremost being that she was the first female lighthouse keeper in America (writer Brian Stinson asserts that almost one hundred other women preceded her in that role); nonetheless, she was responsible for saving the lives of at least eighteen people from the 1850s until her death in 1911. In 1858, with her father incapacitated by a stroke, sixteen-year-old Ida Lewis single-handedly rescued four teenage boys whose sailboat had capsized in the harbor; one of them was the same Wheatie King who would, four years later, lose his life after wounds sustained at the battle of Bull Run. She made numerous other successful recoveries by rowboat in subsequent years, but in 1869, Ida Lewis was catapulted to national acclaim when (on a slow news day) a New York paper ran a prominent story about her derring-do. Then *Harper's Magazine* ran an even larger story, and she became famous throughout the land. A month after the article, President Ulysses S. Grant was visiting Newport and asked to meet the fearless young woman. Ida Lewis rowed to Long Wharf where the president was waiting; he said, "I am happy to meet you, Miss Lewis, as one of the heroic, noble women of the age." She received many honors and presents throughout her life, stayed ever-vigilant for some fifty-four years, and is still known as the most admired female lighthouse keeper in America. Today, the Ida Lewis Yacht Club inhabits her old home.

pocket in antebellum years now went for building and furnishing homes. As the number of paying visitors fell off, so did the quality of hotel life. Jon Sterngass notes, "Newport hostelries had sometimes been compared to their detriment with those of Saratoga and Niagara, but after the Civil War, vituperative attacks became the norm. 'Degenerated would be a clever word to apply to the hotels in this city,' complained the *New York Times* in 1865. 'Such things as first-class hotels have ceased to exist altogether in Newport. . . . There are no persons of note stopping at any of these houses, although the city is filled with the *crème de la crème.*' " With cash dwindling, owners failed to make repairs and upgrade facilities, and one by one they either went out of business or barely hung on in a dilapidated, threadbare fashion. The once-glamorous formal dances and more democratic "hops" were a thing of the past, and as rapidly as these hotels had arisen to help Newport revive, they were now disappearing. The stately Atlantic House, with its indoor roller-skating room and grand ballroom, closed its doors in the mid-1870s, even though it had been enlarged and renovated a mere decade earlier.

A new Newport was emerging in the former grazing fields of William Brenton and William Coddington. George Noble Jones of Savannah started the trend in 1839 when he hired the architect Richard Upjohn to design a Gothic Revival cottage on what would twenty years later become Bellevue Avenue. Kingscote was finished in 1841, sitting almost alone on the hill. The Joneses loved the house, but fled to Georgia during the war; it was sold to William King in 1863 (hence the name). In the late 1870s, George Champlin Mason designed an addition for David King, a relative who had taken possession of the house after William had a mental breakdown. Then William Wetmore built his Château-sur-Mer in 1852 (enlarged by Richard Morris Hunt in 1872), August Belmont put up his bold manor Bythesea in the early 1860s, and John Griswold constructed a large stick-style mansion, designed by Richard Morris Hunt, which is currently the Newport Art Museum, across from the Redwood Library. Now the newcomers had handsome examples to guide them, and Gothic Revival, or Queen Anne style, became all the rage for two decades. The Kay-Catherine-Old Beach Road neighborhood kept expanding, land prices along Bellevue kept skyrocketing, and by the 1870s, eager New Yorkers and other urbanites (locked weekly into their brick and sandstone grids) were eying the suburban expanses along Ocean Drive as well.

These new buildings were experimental in many cases. A few American architects were venturing beyond Greek Revival, trying to instill the latest English tastes. But not everybody got it right. Out by Castle Hill and the Bateman Hotel, Thomas Winans erected Bleak House in 1865, an effort described by Vincent Scully, Jr., in *The Architectural Heritage of Newport, Rhode Island*: "Totally inappropriate upon its flat and windswept site, it gloried in that inappropriateness, even in its name. A great wooden barn with a high mansard, it was split in half by a mountainous cross volume thrust through the house above its entrance porch, and was without a doubt one of the most awkward structures ever raised by man. Yet despite or because of all that, it had a quality. In a way it was the perfect acme and burlesque of a mansion by the sea, a child's dream of grandeur." Decades later the original house was torn down, replaced by a more conventional and better looking structure. It, too, is now demolished, but portions of the original stone fences form a crumbling barrier on the grounds above Narragansett Bay.

While the look of Newport was evolving with all the new cottages, the very nature of the town was being radically transmuted with the demise of the huge hotel and the corresponding rise of the mammoth mansion. Fewer footloose vacationers arrived on the Fall River Line steamboats, but the permanent population began to grow as more people staked their claim in Newport's future by buying land. Property owners got to know each other in new ways, instead of passing like ships in the night in the vast hotel corridors. As witnessed by the Town and Country Club, the Newport Reading Room, and other associations, a rekindled sense of community arose among the recently arrived, although the division between full-time native and the summer colony crowd was never narrowed and would grow even more pronounced during the decades of the Gilded Age extravagances.

Just as Alfred Smith had spurred development with his far-reaching real estate activities, the Newport native George Champlin Mason was crucial in the town's structural growth during the years before the invasion of the New York elite and its bevy of high-profile architects who preferred building with stone instead of wood. Mason, like so many talented and curious people, worked successfully in a variety of fields. Born in 1820 into a prosperous, old-line Newport family (his grandmother was the same Peggy Champlin who danced with General Washington at the comte de Rochambeau's party during the Revolution), Mason spent two years in European capitals studying architecture and drawing. When he returned to Newport in 1846, he began his career as a landscape painter but found he could not make enough money to raise his family. He went into selling real estate (as Smith's main rival for a time), then turned to journalism when he became editor and publisher of the *Newport Mercury* in 1851. For seven years he produced a steady supply of books and articles extolling the beauties and benefits of his city. In fact, his infectious boosterism was an essential ingredient in the rapid growth of the city as a favored resort. During his lifetime, Mason published twelve popular books, all but two of them celebrations of Newport, and hundreds of newspaper and magazine articles. In addition, he was a director of the Redwood Library, and a founder of the Newport Historical Society (1853) and the Newport Hospital (1873).

In 1858, Mason, along with his son and some assistants, decided to try his hand at architecture

George Champlin Mason, c. 1870
Architect, artist, writer.
Photographer unknown
Newport Historical Society
Newport, Rhode Island

for the growing number of people who were in need of having a house designed (in no small measure due to his previous efforts at promotion). He opened Newport's first architectural firm and, because he was so well known and respected, his client list grew quickly. For over thirty years, he turned out plans for more than 150 houses in town as well as public buildings and, his last commission, the United States Naval War College on Coasters Harbor Island in 1891. In many ways, Mason's Queen Anne-style houses shaped the emerging "look" of Newport, which was augmented in later decades with the glittering palaces along Bellevue Avenue. Vincent Scully, Jr., calls his signature style "rather avowedly Swiss in detail," and Alan Schumacher reminds us that "when one drives about Newport today [he was writing in 1970] and notices a gingerbread Hansel and Gretel type gabled cottage the chances are it is of a Mason design and now around 100 years old."

One of Mason's first efforts was August Belmont's Bythesea (1860), followed by designs for the sprawling Tiffany, Ogden, and Schermerhorn homes along Narragansett Avenue. One architecture critic wrote, "Mason quickly settled upon a relatively standardized set of design formulae. His most common house type was the symmetrical, 3-bay, central-entrance dwelling with a hip or mansard roof, rear or lateral ell, a full-height semi-octagonal bay window on one side, and center-hall plan. Often these houses had projected entrance pavilions crowned by a cross gable or treated as a tower." Large or small, they were all constructed out of wood and were vaguely Tudor in appearance. His clients felt comfortable in his creations because they were not ostentatious or eccentric. Given his heritage, Mason was at ease with even the wealthiest of his customers because, like Richard Morris Hunt, he was not simply patronized by the ruling class, he was of it.

George Champlin Mason died in February 1894, but he has left his indelible mark on the city he so fervently loved and promoted.

By 1880, Newport had fully recovered from its post-Revolution trauma of the previous century. The town had survived its long season of discontent and emerged as the American capital of summer fun and fashion. That winning combination of a glorious natural setting (once so alluring as prime grazing land), an excellent harbor, an efficient transportation system, and a receptive population opened Newport once again to a wider world. The city proved that polluting heavy industry was not the only means of prospering, and as societal adjustments across the land ushered in a new leisure class with substantial incomes, Newport made the most of the opportunity to reinvent itself.

In the decades to follow, with the virtual takeover of Bellevue Avenue and Ocean Drive by a self-selecting patrician clique that measured worth almost solely by the millions of dollars one possessed, Newport would be revamped yet again. The thriving artistic and intellectual center would collapse under the weight of unmitigated conspicuous consumption and "vulgar" (the British diplomat Cecil Spring Rice's characterization) expenditures for dinners, home furnishings, and balls. Like the elegant clipper ship of old, Newport's literary and artistic set seemed to vanish from the scene, dispersing to more comfortable settings as gentility gave way to avarice and brutal social competition and marble replaced wood as the building material of choice. By 1880, Newport was teetering on the cusp of a new form of grandeur. The Queen of Resorts was about to become a place unlike any other the New World had ever witnessed—an American Versailles.

The Queen of Resorts

8

The Midas Touch

Wealth was transforming America after the Civil War at a dizzying pace, and nowhere were the nation's newfound riches displayed with more flair and grandeur than in Newport. New York City showcased its stately townhouses along Fifth Avenue, Long Island offered Oyster Bay, and Boston boasted of its Back Bay, but Newport was the scene for the grand American mansion, the regal home that stood apart amid meticulously groomed grounds, the European castle of yore, the fairytale come true. From 1880 until the outbreak of World War I in 1914, summer colonists in Newport designed one of the most sumptuous surroundings ever witnessed in America or on the Continent. The (mostly) transplanted New Yorkers built their dream houses along Bellevue Avenue, Ochre Point, and Ocean Drive, hosted lavish dinner parties and balls, promenaded their fine horses and equipages in their daily coaching exercises and, in doing so, invited the rest of the world to gape in wonder at the splendor they had spawned.

In 1873, in one of his early efforts, Mark Twain and his friend Charles Dudley Warner published a biting novel titled *The Gilded Age: A Tale of Today*, satirizing the brash business dealings of the emerging rich. The epithet, taken from Shakespeare's *King John* ("To Gild refined gold, to paint the lily . . . Is wasteful and ridiculous excess"), has come to define the era of late nineteenth-century America. "Newport" and "the Gilded Age" have become nearly synonymous over the years, rather like "Currier and Ives" or "Laurel and Hardy": it is difficult to think of one without the other. In that era of intemperance and opulence, Newport was *the* Queen of Resorts, the taste-setter, the arbiter of fashion, the only place in America where a dinner party that cost $100,000 was not a source of scandal. Summer activities of the elite, the games, the lavish balls, the elaborate dress were followed relentlessly in the press, adopted by an increasingly prosperous cohort of businessmen and industrialists (subsequently denigrated as "robber barons") eager to enter the higher reaches of society, and scorned by community critics as being appallingly wasteful, frivolous, and vain.

In short, there was extraordinary tension, quite akin to class warfare, in American life during this expansive era: the rich were becoming more numerous and more ostentatiously visible, striving to emulate Europeans in their outlook, while a huge strata of the poor were clamoring for basic needs that

The Breakers, east façade as viewed through the entrance gates, Ochre Point Avenue. (detail), 1893-1895 House of Cornelius Vanderbilt II and the grandest of Newport's summer "cottages"; architect: Richard Morris Hunt. Now operated as a house museum by the Preservation Society of Newport County. Courtesy of the Preservation Society of Newport County Newport, Rhode Island

only government and private agencies stepped forward, often grudgingly, to meet. City slums churning with millions of immigrants and natives were overcrowded and unsanitary. The wealthy were accused, by reformers like Jacob Riis, of being selfish and uncaring; they in turn responded by citing the recent theories of Charles Darwin and the concepts of natural selection and survival of the fittest to justify their own position at the peak of the social food chain. No one, it seemed, was listening. For the most part, the blue bloods went about their business single-mindedly and unperturbed, protected from an increasingly hostile urban environment. The huddled masses gawked at their imperious ways with anger and jealousy, but also with the notion that the good life might be achieved through hard work and a bit of luck. For the striving lower and middle classes, Benjamin Franklin's maxim was heeded as never before: "The way to wealth, if you desire it, is as plain as the way to market. It depends chiefly on two words INDUSTRY and FRUGALITY. . . . He that gets all he can honestly, and saves all he gets will certainly become RICH." Yet many of the businessmen who attained real affluence in the 1870s and beyond ignored Franklin's advice, particularly in regard to frugality and honesty. They would do whatever was needed to dominate the competition. It was a cutthroat culture, with few laws to regulate commerce, finance, or labor, and fewer still to inhibit freewheeling entrepreneurs from making their own rules.

America had always had a small segment of ultra-rich citizens, but until the Civil War, those families were mostly conservative, reticent about displaying their good fortune. During the Gilded Age, not only did hundreds of men achieve staggering wealth but they and their wives began to parade their financial freedom in order to gain acceptance by an increasingly suspicious old guard. Upward mobility seemed to be on everyone's mind except for those already luxuriating in the aristocratic stratosphere, and many of them did their utmost to hold the striving newcomers at bay. It didn't work. Inching up the social ladder continued to be a national sport, albeit a more treacherous one. Mrs. John King Van Rensselaer, firmly ensconced with her upper-class pedigree, remarked, "All at once, Society was assailed from every side by persons who sought to climb boldly over the walls of social exclusiveness." The historian C. Wright Mills adds, "From the eighteen-seventies until the nineteen-twenties, the struggle of old family with new money occurred on a grandiose national scale. Those families that were old because they had become wealthy prior to the Civil War attempted to close ranks against the post-Civil War rich. They failed primarily because the new wealth was so enormous compared with the old that it simply could not be resisted."

An irreversible imperative was becoming manifest in the United States. Thorstein Veblen, an economic philosopher and penetrating social critic who coined the terms "conspicuous leisure" and "conspicuous consumption" in his 1899 classic *The Theory of the Leisure Class* (Newport was most surely on his mind), passed judgment on the cascading cacophony of excessive display of money among the upper classes. "In order to gain and to hold the esteem of men it is not sufficient merely to possess wealth or power. The wealth or power must be put in evidence, for esteem is awarded only on evidence. And not only does the evidence of wealth serve to impress one's importance on others and to keep their sense of his importance alive and alert, but it is of scarcely less use in building up and preserving one's self-complacency." Veblen was among the first academic economists to plumb the psychology of wealth-formation, and his analysis of nouveau riche Gilded Age behavior is difficult to refute. "The basis on which good repute in any highly organized industrial community ultimately rests is pecuniary strength; and the means of showing pecuniary strength, and so of gaining or retaining a good name, are leisure and a conspicuous consumption of goods." Thus lurks the impetus behind the dubious dictum, "if you've got it, flaunt it."

Where was the avalanche of freshly earned money coming from, all of a sudden? Between approximately 1840 and 1870, the unrelenting growth of railroads fueled the economy and made multimillionaires out of men such as E. H. Harriman, James J. Hill, and Commodore Cornelius Vanderbilt. In 1850, America had some 9,000 miles of track; by 1880, the amount had reached 94,000 miles; by 1900, a network of over 200,000 miles of steel was ready to carry the iron horses to market, more than in all of Europe. Railroads were the mainstay of the infrastructure that allowed economic development to soar. Following the Civil War, industry and manufacturing (particularly in the North) spurred the economy into hyper gear, creating a newly minted class of very rich gentlemen, many of whom were anything but gentle. In *The Growth of the American Republic*, professors Samuel Eliot Morison and Henry Steele Commager assert:

> Industry, transportation, banking, speculation, the exploitation of natural resources and of labor, all contributed to the wealth of the country and, even more largely, to the wealth of individuals. . . . In 1870, for example, the wealth of New York State alone was more than twice as great as the combined wealth of all the ex-Confederate states. . . . Every business grew its own crop of millionaires, and soon the names of Morgan and Cooke, Vanderbilt and Gould, Armour and Swift, McCormick and Pillsbury, came to be as familiar to the average American as the names of statesmen. A new plutocracy emerged from the war and reconstruction, masters of money who were no less self-conscious and far more powerful than the planter aristocracy of the old South. Never before had wealth been more irresponsible: the new rich were interested in government only in so far as government had favors to bestow. . . . The war which had flattened out class distinctions in the South tended to accentuate class distinctions in the North.

Industry was the immense engine. By the first decade of the twentieth century the United States had become the wealthiest nation on earth and was beginning to stretch its powerful wings on the international stage. Corporations and trusts (such as Standard Oil under Rockefeller) became the vehicles for amassing vast sums of money, controlling various industries, and curtailing competition. Markets expanded from regional to national to international, and more goods were needed to meet growing consumer demand. Hundreds of thousands of workers poured into factories to manufacture steel (Carnegie), railway cars (Pullman), home supplies (Procter & Gamble), and foodstuffs (General Mills). Wall Street was on an upward-spiraling spree, and even the Panic of 1893 and the subsequent four-year depression did not dampen investors' ardor. At the same time, hundreds of new inventions that increased productivity and added enjoyment to life came to market. Christopher Sholes's typewriter (1867), Alexander Graham Bell's telephone (1876), Thomas Edison's phonograph (1878) and electric incandescent lightbulb (1879), James Ritty's cash register (1879), George Eastman's roll camera (1888), and the Burroughs adding machine (1888) all changed the way Americans did business or spent their leisure time. The companies that emerged after these innovative products became part of modern life (AT&T, International Harvester, Eastman Kodak, Singer Sewing Machine) all made millions

more for their creators and investors. And the factory workers of 1890, the men and women who toiled ten-hour days to produce the goods that filled the pipeline of commerce, were paid, on average, only about $600 per year.

By 1880, the population of the United States topped 50 million. The typical laborer in the North was no longer an independent farmer or artisan living in a quaint Jeffersonian agrarian society, but an urban factory worker pulling down a low wage, eking out a subsistence existence. Whatever he made, his wife, if she worked, took home about half of his salary. Modernization had stripped them both of individual freedom and set them in an impersonal, corporate hierarchical structure that further alienated them from the owner or boss who held forth from the big house on the hill. With newspapers, magazines, and book publishing enjoying enormous growth during the 1880 to 1900 period, the middle-class worker could not escape the constant coverage of the very rich and how they lived and frolicked. Little wonder then that resentment festered and disappointment filled the polluted air. America's first organized labor strikes took place in an atmosphere of rising militancy over wretched working conditions. For many millions of people the fabled Gilded Age was a numbing existence, a bewildering and nervous time. For those who did manage to break out, untold social and financial opportunity lay ahead.

Newport's second Golden Age was in full flower by 1880. While it may be convenient to refer to the era, with all its financial shenanigans and corruption, using Twain and Dudley's derisive term, the arrival en masse of a new breed of wealthy New Yorkers and other urban moguls set the city on a course that would distinguish it from every other playground in the country. And while it is simple to satirize some of the social conventions among the Newport elite (snobbery, silly parties, sequined sashes), many of these people had refined taste (or hired retainers and advisers who had talent) in architecture, home furnishings, and landscape design. That legacy is quite evident even today. William K. Vanderbilt's Marble House may be seen by some as over-the-top architectural ornamentation; it is also a gem in the French palace-style tradition now standing on American soil and, thanks to the efforts of the Preservation Society of Newport County, open for public viewing. Because of their world travels, the people who built these mansions were highly attuned to the art of landscaping. As a result, Newport showcases a greater collection of exotic species of specimen trees and unusual shrubbery than anywhere else in America. The sports we are so familiar with in the twenty-first century—tennis, golf, polo, yachting, even auto racing—either got their start in Newport or were boosted to national prominence and popularity because of being played there and thus chronicled by the national press.

In 2003, the city had a population around 26,500, but it drew close to three and a half million visitors per year to witness its palatial splendors and colonial gems: these buildings are more than surface phantasmagoria. Newport became the Queen of Resorts because something quite special had been created on the former grazing fields of William Brenton. In all stages of history, aristocratic rulers build shrines (pyramids, Parthenon, Coliseum) as symbols of their superiority and evidence of their achievements. In Newport, these took the form of elaborate private homes, and it is difficult to stroll along the Cliff Walk, down Bellevue Avenue, or meander around Ocean Drive without appreciating many of these monuments. Some look to be uninspired piles of stone and glass, designed by architects out of touch with the vocabulary of grandeur; most of these houses, however, work on the large scale and stand as proclamations of regal intent. The Breakers may appear overly ornate and perhaps its seventy rooms are a bit drafty but, with its 45-foot-high Great Hall and sweeping loggia, the building is a spectacular period piece, a window onto the essence of Newport's nineteenth-century Golden Age and an unmistakable expression of America's self-confident expansiveness and mounting imperial appetite.

From 1880 until the introduction of graduated national income taxes in 1913 and the outbreak of World War I the next year, which thoroughly disrupted international trade and sent the planet into chaos, life in Newport for the well-heeled was an uninterrupted holiday, a time for building "cottages" and yachts, bathing at Bailey's Beach, and being seen at the Casino, at parties, or in carriages on Bellevue Avenue. For those who had "arrived," the era was positively dreamlike, drenched in vivid colors and a seemingly unending series of entertainments. The consolidation of Newport as the most luxurious and stratified resort in America was complete. No other rendezvous could compete in terms of opulence or social cachet. When the carnage in Europe put a halt to the gaiety and the summer crowds gradually dispersed, taking their money with them,

Newport again retreated into a languid stupor, just as it had done at the conclusion of the War of Independence, although not quite so dramatically. Many homeowners still frequented the town, and generations of children would henceforth know Newport as their summer retreat, albeit often in smaller houses. The days of the lavish festival were mostly in the past. Large estates were becoming burdens to their owners and heirs, and the "white elephants" (as Henry James described them in 1906) were increasingly left vacant. With the deaths of the dominant doyennes who had kept society intact, Newport gradually settled into limbo by the onset of the Jazz Age. The party was over; another cycle had come full circle.

But until F. Scott Fitzgerald's generation hijacked the action from Newport to Long Island and post-war Europe, the town wore its reputation as the Queen of Resorts proudly.

Casino Culture

On a warm mid-August afternoon in 1879, a former British Army officer and avid polo player named Henry Augustus Candy was riding his horse down Bellevue Avenue when, as the story goes, on a dare from his friend James Gordon Bennett, Jr., he turned his steed and rode up the steps and onto the front porch of the exclusive Newport Reading Room, startling a number of men who were lounging there. Captain Candy, nicknamed Sugar, who was a temporary member of the Reading Room, soon thereafter received a letter from the club secretary accusing him of conduct unbecoming; his $25 subscription fee for the season was returned. Most local writers then go on to assert that an outraged Bennett resigned from the Reading Room in protest and immediately bought the land for what would become the Newport Casino as an act of revenge. A good story, but untrue on two counts. Captain Candy did ride his horse onto the porch and was punished for his whim. But according to the *Sesquicentennial History* (2003) of the Reading Room, compiled by current members, Bennett could not have resigned because he was never a member, and, more to the point, he had started negotiations for the land purchase many months before the celebrated incident. Nevertheless, the legend persists, and James Gordon Bennett did in fact build the Newport Casino, which became *the* place for society to see and be seen for the next forty years.

James Gordon Bennett, Jr., was the flamboyant owner and publisher of the *New York Herald*, the leading American newspaper of the day. Born in New York in 1842 into a prosperous family, he was educated mostly in Europe, served as a distinguished naval officer in the Civil War, and at the age of twenty-six became editor of the *Herald*, which was owned by his ailing father, James Gordon Bennett, Sr. The young scion was an avid athlete, partially responsible for introducing polo to America (Captain Candy was in Newport on Bennett's invitation); a dedicated yachtsman, he was elected the youngest leader in the New York Yacht Club's history, at age thirty-two, and henceforth became known to the world as Commodore Bennett. He was rich and handsome, with an annual income of over $800,000 (approximately fifteen times that in today's currency), all tax-free. Arrogant and feisty, he did as he liked and normally got his way. He ran the *Herald* as his private fiefdom, hiring and firing editors and reporters abruptly, but in truth he managed it and his other ventures (the Paris *Herald* was his creation) well during his half-century tenure. Bennett loved publicity and pre-dated Joseph Pulitzer and William Randolph Hearst in staging stories to increase readership. His most notorious stunt was sending the ace reporter Henry Stanley scurrying across Africa from 1869 until 1871 in search of the supposedly lost Dr. David Livingstone. Bennett kept the expensive ruse going nonstop, titillating

James Gordon Bennett, Jr., c. 19th century
Photographer unknown
Newport Historical Society
Newport, Rhode Island

his large readership with exotic tales of Africa. Stanley, of course, eventually found his prey and the world was informed with splashy front-page coverage that the good doctor had finally been "found." A perplexed Dr. Livingstone was not amused with the trumped-up publicity because in truth, he had never been at all lost.

Bennett's high-profile personal life was tumultuous at times. Two years before the Sugar Candy fiasco in Newport, a hungover Bennett created a much-followed scandal in New York by relieving himself in the living-room fireplace of his fiancée Edith May's home during a large New Year's Day party. Miss May's brother Fred was furious and demonstrated his displeasure by publicly horsewhipping Bennett two days later as the latter emerged from the Union Club. Chagrined but proud, Bennett challenged his attacker to a duel the next day, but neither of them shed blood. The engagement, needless to say, was off. But the humiliated Bennett thereafter found staying in New York repugnant and spent the next forty-five years living mostly in Paris and Versailles, and visiting Newport during the summer season. By cabling his instructions to his editors, he maintained a firm grip on the *Herald*. During World War I, he personally took charge of the Paris *Herald*, and put out an issue every day of the conflict. After years of complicated love affairs, Bennett finally married four years before his death from a heart attack in Paris, in 1918.

James Gordon Bennett lived and imagined extravagantly. Looking around Newport in 1879, he realized that there was no elegant gathering place for all the summer and year-round residents now that the hotels had declined. The proud old Ocean House was bedraggled and forlorn, its glory days in the dust. When he got word that the Sidney Brooks estate on Bellevue Avenue (now a shopping center at Memorial Boulevard) was on the market, Bennett sprang into action. He bought the cottage, Stone Villa, as his residence, and the land across Bellevue for the Casino. By hiring the up-and-coming New York architect Charles McKim and his new partner Stanford White, then only twenty-six years old, to design his elaborate facility, Bennett would be assured of a quality product.

Along with Richard Morris Hunt, who had already designed the commercial Travers properties adjoining the site of the new Casino, the firm of McKim, Mead & White was the most active in leaving its stamp on Newport during this era. After Bennett formed a joint stock association, headed by August Belmont, to raise money for the construction of the Casino, McKim went to work laying out the exterior while White designed the interiors. Wanting to create a harmonious balance between the fancy shops and the Casino itself, "McKim kept the street façade unobtrusive and simple. Symmetrical and ordered, it is not academic," according to the architectural historian Vincent Scully, Jr. By early 1880, work had commenced, and the 100,000-square-foot structure was, amazingly, finished for its large gala opening on July 26, a mere seven months later. The shingle-style edifice, combined with intricate latticework throughout the interior, was (and still is) elegant and welcoming. Scully continues, "Behind the shops and the clubrooms, and reached through a flat arched passageway, is a courtyard surrounded by piazzas which curve out into an apsidal shape at the rear. This interior court is developed more picturesquely than the street façade. . . . The piazzas themselves are excellent examples of White's real genius at this time. . . . The Newport Casino, consequently, is one of the most distinguished buildings of the early eighties, controlled by a coherent spatial sense and a general sense of order."

The Newport Casino was imagined to be an all-purpose pleasure palace and recreation center, open to two classes of patron: the subscribers and shareholders (who were granted more privileges) and the fee-paying general public. It was a democratic, grand affair, offering court tennis (the centuries-old sport of kings), the newly introduced game of outdoor lawn tennis, orchestral performances, balls, fine dining, private rooms, a bowling alley, billiard room, large theater, and a number of other amenities. The Casino, however, despite its name, prohibited gambling. According to its bylaws, the complex was intended "for enjoying games and sports of every kind and description and for the development and improvement of literary and social intercourse and physical and mental cultivation of its members." The Casino was certainly the playground for the elite summer colony, which supported its events with gusto, but it also went a long way toward bridging the gap between the gentry and less prominent native Newporters. The *New York Times* reported in 1886, "In theory, the poor mechanic and clerk can take his wife and children to the Casino every Sunday night and listen to a capital concert for 25 cents per head." It was the first such public-private establishment in America, and because of Bennett's desire for first-rate quality, a success from its first season.

There was nothing else quite like the Newport Casino. Over the years, numerous traditions associated with it became woven into the daily rhythms of the town. It was a fashionable rendezvous for (mostly) summer colony swells to meet in the outdoor oval ring at eleven each morning (Sundays excepted) to listen to an orchestral serenade for an hour and a half. In the afternoon, the theater was packed with people attending plays and other dramatic offerings. As lawn tennis grew in popularity, the courts at the Casino drew large crowds to witness America's first national championship matches. Weekend nights were popular for dining and musical events that were attended by both the summer colony and year-round residents. In very short order, the Casino emerged exactly as James Gordon Bennett had envisioned: the center-stage enticement for a quickly expanding social set eager to be entertained. The Casino not only offered a large variety of activities, it was also the ideal arena to show off one's finery. For both sexes, dressing to the nines and alighting from one's coach at the entrance of the Casino and then promenading into the open horseshoe garden while being studied (and judged) by one's peers was a stimulating, perhaps nerve-racking, but necessary exercise

in the competition to get accepted, or forge ahead in the intricate dance of destiny. The Casino offered the platform for social engineering at a very refined level.

In her lively but sometimes factually flawed reminiscence *This Was My Newport*, published in 1944 when she was well on in years, Maud Howe Elliott, daughter of Julia Ward Howe, wrote, "With the opening of the Casino at the beginning of the 'eighties', a period of extravagant entertaining began for Newport. The balls grew more elaborate, the hours later. . . . Social life in every way showed increasing formality. The old high teas faded out of the picture, and late, elaborate dinners took their place. Great emphasis was placed on gastronomy. The dinners were endlessly long, the decorations costly."

The esteemed British diplomat Sir Cecil Spring Rice (secretary to the legation in Washington at the time; later he served as ambassador to Berlin, Cairo, and the United States) spent two summers in town. In an 1887 letter to a friend in London, Spring Rice gave a vivid account of the spirit of life at the time:

> I went to Newport, of which you must have heard—the finest watering place in the world. At the bottom of the town lies the old fishing village and harbour, filled now with all sorts of beautiful yachts. Away out on the point are two long rows of cottages—built of wood with double coach-houses and wonderful lawns. There is a walk from garden to garden by the rocks on which the Atlantic breaks. Two or three of the cottages are fine houses; the rest are small but infinitely luxurious. The inhabitants are the richest men and the most beautiful women in the world. Their life is everything that riches and beauty ought to entail. It begins at 11, when all society meets at a place called the Casino, where a band plays and where a rare lawn tennis player appears every now and then. But the chief occupation then and afterwards is talking. One sees there in a horse-shoe cloister crowds of these beautiful and gorgeous creatures (all of whom one soon learns to know by sight) sitting and talking with heroes in white flannel (put on for ornament, not for tennis), white straw hats, and instead of a waistcoat a wondrous coloured sash around the waist.

Three years later, in 1890, after a restful fortnight in town, Sir Cecil reported another aspect of his Newport experience. These views are particularly pertinent and insightful because they come from a notably sophisticated foreigner, rather than a socially smitten American parvenu.

> The people beautifully dressed; their features and figures delicate and refined. They are as hospitable as can be. The sea is splendid—the Atlantic swell rolling in right under the cottage windows. In fact, it is the perfection of watering places; and I suppose there is no place like it in the world where people have put themselves to so much trouble and expense to get the means of happiness.
>
> The universal result is boredom. I don't know why. They don't seem to care for anything in the world. They have nothing to talk about, except each other, and nothing to do except to talk. The whole thing is so unreal. They are all strugglers in society, some of them succeeding, some of them having succeeded. Those that have succeeded look across the water, sighing for new fields. They count up each others advantages, as money, looks, dress. They say that if Washington is the town to study the American eagle, Newport is the place to study the American mocking bird.

Cecil Spring Rice put his finger on the pulse—or lack thereof—of Newport society in the Gilded Age, after the artistic and intellectual community virtually fled the scene. Ennui. Tedium. A primary focus on outside appearances rather than the cultivation of a rigorous inner life. Stultifying social strictures imposed by New York trend-setters. A taboo against public discussion of anything "serious," be it politics, religion, or world affairs. It was a complaint echoed by many observers, Henry James foremost among them, an observation that cannot be ignored. For all the gaiety and display, the parties and refined entertainments, the Queen of Resorts, for many participants, presented a beautiful but vapid experience.

O'er the Ramparts

The assault on the old-guard Protestant patricians of Newport had actually begun two decades before the doors opened at the Casino in 1880. And it came from an unlikely quarter, since the wife in the couple that began the seismic shift from simple summer resort enjoyment to high-powered formal entertaining was, in fact, from one of the town's most venerable families.

In 1849, the international financier August Belmont married Caroline Slidell Perry, daughter of the revered Commodore Matthew C. Perry and niece of Oliver Hazard Perry, hero of the War of 1812. In 1860, because of her long association with Newport, August, Caroline, and their children rented a large house on Bellevue Avenue for the summer. They enjoyed the experience so much that August Belmont bought the adjoining 14-acre parcel and the same year built his handsome and elaborate Bythesea, designed by George Champlin Mason. Belmont, already adroit in the social workings of New York City and thus mindful of the need to display his wealth to his advantage, charged Mason with the task of creating a house large enough for sumptuous entertaining.

Once ensconced, Caroline, backed by her husband's fortune and her own position in society, began to change the rules about what was chic and what was déclassé. Large elaborate dinners were hosted throughout the 1860s and 1870s, and she was among the first of many women who would try to mold the Newport summer colony to her whims. She succeeded. Caroline was respected because of her family connections and well liked by other summer visitors, and her extravagances were duly noted—and copied. Caroline Belmont was the trailblazer on the inexorable path toward the formality and fastidiousness so fashionable by the end of the century. It is ironic that a daughter of the conservative and ultra-correct Perry family would be the one to unlatch the floodgates for the spectacle to come.

August Belmont was a fascinating anomaly of the Gilded Age *haut monde*. He was a staunch Democrat swimming in a sea of Republicans; he was a German Jew (nonpracticing; he later converted to Christianity and joined the Episcopal church) in the midst of a majority of Protestants; he was a diplomat (United States ambassador to the Netherlands from 1853 to 1857) when most of his wealthy cohort eschewed service; and he amassed an important art collection without the aid of advisers. Born in the Rhenish Palatinate in 1816 to a well-off landowning family, August started his career at the age of fourteen by apprenticing with the Frankfurt faction of the House of Rothschild, the largest private bank in the world. He proved so adept at business and finance that his employer sent him first to Italy to negotiate a loan with the Vatican, then to Cuba for sensitive government meetings. While in Havana in 1837, Belmont learned of the dire economic downswing sweeping America and promptly went to New York, where he cabled the

Rothschilds that he would represent them in the United States but that he was establishing his own firm on Wall Street as well.

August Belmont had money to lend in 1837, a commodity sorely lacking after the Panic ruined so many bankers. Backed by the enormous influence of the Rothschild name, Belmont quickly grew independently wealthy, one of the richest and most powerful men in the land. He extended his reach and reputation by becoming a leader in the Democratic Party; by the time he and Caroline descended on Newport in 1860, he was a national figure, the first to engage a French chef in a private home in America. While his religion and political leanings made him suspect within the tight-knit New York oligarchy, in Newport he suffered no such slights. With his wife's numerous and increasingly formal dinner parties, and his own standing for introducing Thoroughbred racing to America (he inaugurated the Belmont Stakes in 1867), practically no other family in Newport could compete with them for years.

The Belmonts wanted attention and had the money to achieve their social aims. Caroline Belmont had engineered their ascent with uncanny instinct. She was well-read, an excellent conversationalist, and neither she nor her husband would have fit into Ambassador Spring Rice's description of the bored, uninterested Newporter. The historian Eric Homberger believes, "From Belmont New York learned that aristocrats entertained largely, and were generous in their hospitality. Few could resist following their example." The same can be said for Newport.

Caroline Belmont stood astride the social scene for fifteen years. Unlike some of the women who followed her as society leaders, she was not feared because she did not use her power to intimidate and isolate others. She certainly *ruled*, yet her benevolence was always noted. But in 1875, her nineteen-year-old daughter died, and Caroline Belmont took the veil and withdrew from public society. Now the battle would be waged in earnest to replace her at the helm of the increasingly competitive hierarchy. At her death in November 1892, the *New York Times* eulogized, "From 1860 to 1875 Mrs. Belmont's beauty, grace, and tactful hospitality rendered her society's undisputed leader. Her entertainments were regal and her drawing rooms formed a *salon* — in the social sense of the term — in which might be seen all the noted men and women of the day."

Yet, even before the Belmonts reached Newport and worked their social magic, the town seemed destined to evolve into a high-society mecca dominated by lavish entertaining. In the summer of 1857, the former China-trade magnate William S. Wetmore invited 2,000 people from around the country to attend an afternoon *fête champêtre* at Château-sur-Mer in honor of his friend George Peabody, and 1,500 people showed up to drink hundreds of magnums of champagne, eat, and dance. Newport had never seen the likes of such a large private party, but it was a harbinger of events to come. Mrs. Belmont's parties were elegant, Mrs. Astor's were correct, but Mr. Wetmore's pioneered the large-scale celebration.

The Belmonts may have begun the social transformation of Newport, but others quickly rushed to join the party. It should be remembered that in the Gilded Age the Newport upper crust was, to a large extent, New York society transported north for the summer. Certainly others were held in high regard in town, such as Edward J. Berwind, the coal magnate born in Philadelphia who built the Elms, the Browns of Providence, the Cushing family from Boston, and the Tiffanys and Winans of Baltimore, but the great majority were from Manhattan's Fifth Avenue. The other names famously associated with Newport at this time—Astor, Vanderbilt, Oelrichs, Whitney, Fish, Stevens, Goelet—all had their roots in New York. Newport became their cherished playground, the place for the women to dominate and shine while their husbands toiled in the city and rode the Fall River Line steamers or their own luxurious yachts up on Friday nights.

From the 1870s through the 1890s, old-guard Knickerbockers were still on guard against the relentless onslaught of upstarts, but year by year their resistance was ebbing. In an effort to create a pedigreed pecking order of prestige in Manhattan, the self-appointed social arbiter Ward McAllister in 1872 organized the Patriarchs, a committee limited to twenty-five men who gave lavish balls during the year. Each man was given the honor and duty of inviting four ladies and five gentlemen of impeccable credentials as a means of introducing "the right sort" to one another. Most of the original Patriarchs were New Yorkers of at least three generations. These men, McAllister (a rank newcomer) proclaimed, "had the right to create and lead Society." Many of them (Astor, Livingston, Van Rensselaer, Schermerhorn) are still familiar names today. August Belmont, as a Jew by birth, was, of course, not among the original members, but by dint of his vast fortune and influence, he was admitted in the 1880s. For a quarter century, the Patriarch Balls determined who "mattered" in society, and nearly every year several "new" men and women would be admitted to the lists, as long as McAllister and Mrs. Astor approved. Young belles were launched into society at these fetes, and the number of marriages emanating from them is incalculable. When McAllister published his notorious list of the Four Hundred in 1892, it was essentially a tallying of the names of those who had attended the various Patriarch Balls (although if one counts the names on the list, they only add up to a little over three hundred).

Customs set by these New York gentry were enforced rigorously in Newport. With hotel life dead or dying, the New Yorkers' emerging Newport society broke with previously established patterns of resort life and withdrew behind the thick doors of their cottages. The town became a refuge for rich people who wanted little more than to escape the rigors of big-city strife. A revised code of conduct was introduced, which, by the 1880s, stressed privacy and self-containment. No more large public dances; now the formal private ball took their place, and no matter how many people attended, the operative word was *private*. With the exception of showing up at the Casino for some public entertainments and tennis matches, the New York set circled their wagons, kept Bailey's Beach ultra-exclusive, and hosted parties primarily for their own clannish clique. Even the sports they pursued—yachting, polo, croquet, tennis, and golf—were perceived as hobbies of the highborn. So, year by year the Bellevue Avenue crowd separated itself from the rest of Newport, wrote its own rulebook, and became more isolated from the rhythms of the workaday world. An ever-fascinated national press continued to write of their high jinks and parties; the more they wrote, the more intense the envy of the average people struggling to survive in their chaotic urban purgatory. In an effort to quell the scrutiny by outsiders, the barriers of exclusion rose even higher. But the cult of celebrity had set in for the long term, and there was no escaping public attention if one's bank account numbered in the millions of dollars or one's closet in the cottage on Ocean Drive was filled with dresses from Paris designed by Charles Worth. Throughout the 1890s, at the height of Mrs. Astor's reign as Queen of Newport, the select had become so remote that they talked mostly among themselves, and often only in French. As Cecil Spring Rice shrewdly observed, they had, wittingly or not, produced a hermetically sealed society.

This state of affairs gave rise to a rich irony. As conformity to set social customs produced predictable modes of behavior and the elite became more exclusionary—and, in fact, reactionary—they began

to resemble seventeenth-century Boston Puritans in their desire to create a closed community dictated by order, decorum, and strict adherence to tribal tyranny. By the turn of the twentieth century Newport (founded by men and women in full flight from the strictures and constraints of monolithic Winthropian Puritanism) had reverted to the same type of stultifying social behavior so prevalent during the height of Puritan orthodoxy and so repugnant to the free-thinkers who had forged the town's destiny, like William Coddington and Dr. John Clarke. But in Gilded Age Newport, for the upper crust, their religion was money, their church, the cottage.

Mrs. Astor and Mr. McAllister

Caroline Perry Belmont may have been the first in a line of influential hostesses tilting Newport toward European sumptuousness and formality, but it was another Caroline—Caroline Webster Schermerhorn Astor—who firmly ruled New York and Newport society for thirty years after Mrs. Belmont's abdication. Standing tall, proud, and bejeweled at the pinnacle of society, Caroline— after appropriating the coveted title from her sister-in-law Mary, Mrs. John Jacob Astor III—was known to the world simply as *the* Mrs. Astor. Even before her ascent to the apex in New York City was secure, she had been influenced by her friend and adviser Ward McAllister to bestow her presence on Newport, thus anointing it as the correct summer colony residence for their set. In 1880, her husband, William Astor, grandson of John Jacob Astor who had founded the dynasty and was the richest man in the United States at his death in 1848, purchased and remodeled Beechwood on Bellevue Avenue, an attractive but not overly elaborate Italianate villa. (A large ballroom was added later by Richard Morris Hunt to accommodate the hundreds she entertained regularly.) At that moment in 1880, Newport, with the august Astors at the helm, set off on its voyage as the undisputed aristocratic American resort.

The second Golden Age had officially begun.

Mrs. Astor was born in 1830 into one of New York's most respected old Dutch families, dating back to the 1640s. Her father, Abraham Schermerhorn, was a successful merchant and real estate holder; her mother was a descendant of the Van Cortlandt clan, and thus Caroline was related to the most prominent families in Knickerbocker aristocracy. She was, like so many girls of her class, educated at home by bilingual governesses, then sent to Paris for "finishing." Back in America, Caroline Schermerhorn married William Backhouse Astor, Jr., in 1853 (he later dropped both the Backhouse and the Junior and was known simply as William Astor). His great wealth (he inherited around $20 million at his father's death) allowed his wife to begin her ascent, but she also had an ample income of her own and a far more perfect pedigree than Astor. Mrs. Caroline Astor bowed to no one.

At the time that Mrs. Belmont withdrew from the apogee of the establishment, Caroline Astor was beginning to be disturbed by the influx of so many newly rich families attempting to assault her well-ordered and conservative New York life. She did not smile upon the changes brought about by the machinations of arrivistes like the Vanderbilts and, like the old guard depicted by Edith Wharton in *The Age of Innocence*, went to great lengths to refuse recognition to this rabble poised to degrade her standards. A few years earlier, she had begun her association with Ward McAllister (he helped her arrange the debuts of her two eldest daughters), leading to the ultimately futile attempt to "define" society through admittance to the Patriarch Balls. Year after year, Mrs. Astor and Mr. McAllister pored over the party lists, striking the names of anyone who was not worthy of belonging to their lofty echelon, yet admitting some families when their stars were rising and the balls were in need of new blood (read: marriageable belles).

The partnership between Mrs. Astor and Ward McAllister was in many ways an odd one. He had little money but grand ambitions and the ability to stage memorable parties. She certainly didn't need his help organizing social sovereignty, yet for twenty years they conspired in their fine-tuning of acceptability. McAllister has been variously described (and debunked) as her lapdog, lackey, and, because of his rather stiff manner, her Machiavelli. Yet she did need a great many things attended to, and particularly needed a man around, a state of affairs increasingly rare since her husband preferred to linger at his Hudson River estate, Ferncliff, in Rhinebeck, New York, and on his yacht in Florida, rather than in New York or Newport. William Astor was like the ghost in *Hamlet*, often referred to but seldom seen. In the end, McAllister was convenient and convivial, the necessary "walker" who took care of Mrs. Astor's need for an escort and confidant.

The most sought-after invitation of the New York social season was to Mrs. Astor's annual ball on the third Monday of January at her Fifth Avenue and Thirty-fourth Street mansion. Whom to invite became the burning question, and it was because of her party that the Four Hundred was born. Starting in the mid-1880s, McAllister, who was constantly talking to reporters as the mouthpiece for Mrs. Astor (who wouldn't have dreamed of talking to a newspaper writer), started to refer to this mythic Four Hundred who made up the *crème de la crème* of New York society. Constantly quizzed about the number, McAllister vaguely asserted that four hundred was the number of people who could be ensconced in Mrs. Astor's ballroom. In his estimation, according to the social historian Jerry E. Patterson, "there were only about four hundred people in New York who would feel comfortable there. 'If you go outside that number,' he said, 'you strike those who are either not at ease in a ballroom or else make other people not at ease.'" All of New York's papers jumped on the quote, clamoring for the identity of these august spirits, but McAllister held the press off for another four years before actually naming names.

Mrs. Astor, referred to in the press as the "Mystic Rose," went to great lengths to hold her finger in the social dike teetering on collapse from the pressure of the sheer number of people wanting in. But some things were beyond even her control. For years she was adamant about not allowing any Vanderbilts into her circle, and certainly not into her home. Regardless of their soaring riches, for Mrs. Astor the whole family represented crass upstarts who should not be rewarded with *her* social recognition. Then in 1883, Mrs. Astor was forced to eat crow. William K. and Alva Vanderbilt (worth close to $100 million) had just finished building their luxurious mansion at 660 Fifth Avenue that year and planned a gala costume party to mark its opening. All of society was a-twitter, and many of the young women who hoped to be invited were rehearsing elaborate quadrilles for the occasion; one of these was Caroline Astor, Mrs. Astor's teenage daughter, who was fully expecting to be asked to the ball for no other reason than that she was an Astor. Alva Vanderbilt boldly put out the word that the Astor daughter could not receive an invitation because her mother had never officially called on Mrs. Vanderbilt "at home" and thus did not "know" her in the proper sense. In the

Central, although Cornelius II was considered the harder worker and the one who directed the family money. Willie K. cared more for his 285-foot yacht, *Alva*, and a life of leisure.

By 1880, with so many New Yorkers in Newport either building cottages of their own or buying or renting existing homes, it was inevitable that Caroline Schermerhorn Astor would make her entrance on the Newport stage in order to assert her authority. John Jacob Astor III and his wife, Mary, had purchased a cottage, later named Beaulieu, on Bellevue Avenue in 1879 and other relatives were longtime visitors; the Schermerhorns (cousins of Caroline's) also had deep roots in the community, having built on Narragansett Avenue in the 1860s. So Caroline Astor's move to Beechwood was a natural evolution in her consolidation of power. Caroline's base in New York was secure since Mary Astor, her superior because of her husband's birthright, chose not to combat her dominating sister-in-law for the title. Now *the* Mrs. Astor—Mrs. William Astor—would conquer the Queen of Resorts, which was entirely appropriate since, in addition to the Mystic Rose, many newspapers later began referring to her as "the Queen."

Just how much Ward McAllister had to do with her decision to establish her beachhead on Bellevue Avenue is unknown, but surely he was able to persuade Mrs. Astor that Newport was the only appropriate summer residence since he was intimately acquainted with the community. It was very much to his advantage that she choose Newport over Long Island or Bar Harbor because her presence magnified his own position. McAllister was born in Savannah in 1827, studied law at Yale, made a good deal of money practicing in California and returned East in 1852 to marry Sarah Gibbons, an heiress from Georgia whose wealth allowed McAllister to concentrate the rest of his life to taming and naming society. In 1858, the family (two sons and a daughter) fell under the spell of real estate maven Alfred Smith and bought a small home in Newport. Because he was a descendant of the famous Rhode Island Wards, a cousin of Julia Ward Howe, and related to a number of other aristocratic Southern families who had been in Newport for generations, McAllister was graciously received. Soon after becoming familiar with the town, McAllister purchased Bayside Farm in Middletown, rented some sheep and cattle from a local farmer, and began to host his popular summer picnics, which he titled *fêtes champêtres*. For over two decades, accompanied by dance bands, guests milled about his lavishly decorated grounds drinking champagne and enjoying McAllister's fine cooking, for which he was celebrated. According to Patterson, "Newport loved the picnics. McAllister had brought some vivacity into a resort then noted for its simplicity and propriety. 'Life, for him to enjoy it,' wrote Mrs. John King Van Rensselaer, who knew him well and was a keen observer of the social scene, 'had to be gilt-edged and multi-colored.' "

Ward McAllister used his reputation in Newport to launch himself in New York, which led to his partnership with Mrs. Astor and also to the disparaging nickname, "Mr. Make-a-Lister."

Over the next two decades Newport would become unrecognizable to anyone who had been away for a period of time. The transformation was from an unpretentious hotel-dominated resort focused on swimming, strolling, and public dancing to the regal, stratified, cottage-oriented mecca perfectly sited and suited for the vast mansions that were rising along the Avenue, Ochre Point, and the Drive. The authority of Mrs. Astor's presence was immense, and her unmitigated control over the community was indisputable. In order to remain worthies in her universe, many other New Yorkers now found it necessary to emulate her actions and find space in town. The families of Hamilton Fish, several Vanderbilts, Ogden Goelet, Hermann Oelrichs, and others descended on Newport with their millions of dollars and their New York architects and began the building boom of palatial mansions that elevated Newport into one of the most majestic municipalities in the world. One-upmanship became the game of the era. Narcissism ruled the realm. European finery was the fashion. Expensive costume balls were weekly events. Mrs. Astor, like a magnet in a metal shop, attracted the players. Now it was show time.

The Invasion of the Villa

Stage left: enter Richard Morris Hunt. Stage right: enter Charles McKim and Stanford White. These three architects, with some help from Horace Trumbauer, John Russell Pope, and the firm of Peabody & Stearns, largely created the palatial environment in Newport that most people still marvel at. Homes designed by these men, mainly at Ochre Point and along Bellevue Avenue, represent the densest clustering of grand residences in America and are a constant reminder of the plutocracy's monuments to themselves. Their clients were demanding, yet altogether prepared to spend millions of dollars on mansions they would occupy about ten weeks out of every year. These three men, highly motivated, talented, and competitive, brought European splendor to the New World and in so doing raised the ante for what was acceptable and desirable in domestic dwellings. The villas these men created, in a roughly three-square-mile area in southern Newport, became models for how the rich would display their ornaments, allowing the residents to show the world they had most definitely arrived. Many of the buildings exist now as heirlooms of a bygone era when object lessons in the art of magnificence were the order of the day.

Between 1860 and 1885, there was a gradual shift from the timber-framed stick-style, Queen Anne, and the elegant shingle-style cottages to those constructed in marble, limestone, and granite. George Champlin Mason persisted in building mostly in wood until his death in 1894. Hunt's first venture in Newport, the Griswold House (1863), is a charming stick-style dwelling far different from the mansions he designed later. The striking William Watts Sherman House (1874), conceived by the architect Henry Hobson Richardson in the shingle-style, is an elegant and supple structure, appropriate in size for the plot of land it inhabits on Shepard Avenue. Likewise the shingle-style Isaac Bell House (1883), designed by McKim, Mead & White (Mead was the firm's engineer, office manager, and construction coordinator) for its Bellevue Avenue plot. It is beautifully proportioned, comfortable, and unmistakably American in its vernacular. The Newport architect Dudley Newton, who worked for a number of years with Mason, created a Swiss chalet treasure with the Swinburne House (1875) on Rhode Island Avenue, as well as numerous other houses in town. The list of stunning shingle-style homes in Newport is quite long, and many of them are still well preserved. With the exception of Richard Morris Hunt's renovation of the granite Château-sur-Mer in the 1870s (he completely redesigned Seth Bradford's Italianate structure and changed it to French Second Empire), nearly everyone was building in wood and creating homes that reflected a growing pride in their American qualities.

Writing about the wooden cottage buildings of the period, Vincent Scully, Jr., asserted, "This is not architecture conceived in an academic fashion, two-dimensionally upon a sheet of drawing paper, but architecture felt in the densities and properties of materials, in the reality of three-dimensional space.

Appropriate to their place and climate and expressive thereof, these houses represent in their time a living architecture of originality and power."

But then tastes changed again. The floodgates opened and anything European became all the rage. American design was simply not regal or majestic enough for the men and women venturing in from New Yorks. They had made the European circuit, had seen the grandeur of its palaces, and now they had the means to create houses that would distinguish themselves from the rest. They were accustomed to erecting their Fifth Avenue mansions out of brick or stone, and when they migrated to Newport, they demanded nothing less. At the same time, the premier architects of the day were also coming under the influence of European tastes. Richard Morris Hunt was the first American to formally graduate from the architectural division of the Académie des Beaux-Arts in Paris, and his imprint on Newport was to become almost legendary. Charles McKim also studied at the Beaux-Arts, starting in 1867; later, McKim and White traveled the Continent and returned with an expanded vocabulary. It was just a matter of time—and money—before the shingle-style home in town simply would not do for a client wanting to make a statement. Baroque was back.

Now there was more at stake than just building a big new house. To impress one's neighbors and gain acceptance, it had to be the *right* big house, it had to stand out and boldly assert its merits (a need that speaks volumes about the anxieties of the owners). The historian Paul R. Baker contends,

> No doubt much of the building of great houses did have behind it a competitive drive to outshine others. With their lack of a firmly established class system and acceptance of the democratic myth of universal equality on the one hand, and their desire for achievement and individual distinction on the other, many Americans have had considerable uncertainty about who they are and where they belong. Although group identity has been fairly well established throughout the history of the nation, individual identity has been less readily fixed upon, and tension has been characteristic, and perhaps even endemic, among Americans, given the conflict between democratic uniformity and social differentiation. An exceptionally large and richly appointed dwelling probably could for some relieve insecurities about social position and satisfy personal ambition and pride. Moreover, Americans had the European tradition to emulate: English and Continental experience suggested that high social position was usually associated with elegant residences.

A harbinger of things to come ran at the bottom of a *New York Times* article about Newport on August 12, 1881. After reporting on the weather, the ebbing hotel life, the upcoming fox hunts, the recent meeting of the Town and Country Club, and the popularity of the Casino, the writer informs us:

> It is said that several prominent gentlemen are negotiating for the purchase of the estate at Ochre Point owned by the late William Beach Lawrence, the eminent international lawyer, of this city, who died in New-York last Spring. Rumor connects with this project the names of Mr. Pierre Lorillard, who already owns a good slice of property and a magnificent villa in that section of the city, and Mr. Cornelius Vanderbilt, who is occupying the Wales cottage. Mr. Lorillard purchased all his real estate here from Mr. Lawrence a few years ago. It is Mr. Vanderbilt's intention to become

The Breakers, east
façade as viewed through
the entrance gates,
Ochre Point Avenue,
1893-1895
House of Cornelius
Vanderbilt II and the
grandest of Newport's
summer "cottages";
architect: Richard Morris
Hunt. Now operated
as a house museum by
the Preservation Society
of Newport County.
Courtesy of the
Preservation Society
of Newport County
Newport, Rhode Island

a cottage-owner, as he seems to be very fond of Newport. The Lawrence villa is not occupied this season.

Lawrence's large estate was one of the last of the prime seaside properties available and the bidding for control of it was intense. Eventually it was subdivided among several buyers who went forward with their building plans. The "magnificent villa" referred to in the *Times* article was the first Breakers, designed in wood by Peabody & Stearns in 1879 and subsequently purchased by Cornelius Vanderbilt II when Lorillard decided to abandon Newport to develop his sportsman's enclave at Tuxedo Park, New York. When the house burned to the ground in 1892, Vanderbilt turned to the trusted Richard Morris Hunt to create a fireproof stone structure on the same site. But before the second Breakers (the one that draws so many visitors) went up, Hunt had more than left his mark on Newport.

Like his older brother, the painter William, Richard Morris Hunt (born October 1827) discovered his artistic inclinations early in life. When their mother, after the death of their father, packed up the family for a long sojourn in Europe, Richard had prudently decided not to compete with his sibling at the easel but fancied architecture as his future. After his rigorous, classical training at the Ecole des Beaux-Arts, Hunt was accepted into the atelier of the highly respected Hector Lefuel and aided him for several years in the design of the new additions to the Louvre and Tuileries. During his nine years of study and apprenticeship, Hunt thoroughly absorbed the language of European grand style and statement, and on his return to America in 1855 was one of the best-trained architects in the country. The fact that his career blossomed immediately upon

setting up a studio in New York City had as much to do with his expansive personality (he seems to have been universally respected and liked) as with his abundant talent. Hunt helped found the American Institute of Architects in 1857, was its first secretary and, because of his reputation, was later elected president. Known as the "dean of American architecture," he helped define professional standards that have lasted into the present century. His primary competitor for status during the last decades of the nineteenth century, Stanford White, said of Richard Morris Hunt, "it was to a certain extent from [Hunt] and through him that the real modern artistic advance in architecture in New York and America can be traced."

For forty years, Hunt continued to design buildings that transformed the look of the United States and ushered in a new sense of imperial splendor just at the time the country was evolving politically and militarily into an international power. Hunt's decorum and scale fit the age. Over the course of his career, he introduced the concept of the respectable, upper-class apartment house to New York; was in the forefront of creating cast-iron commercial buildings; designed the commanding Tribune Building for James Gordon Bennett, the Lenox Library, the imposing main entrance for the Metropolitan Museum of Art on Fifth Avenue, and the base and pedestal for the Statue of Liberty. Toward the end of the 1870s Hunt became the principal architect for the Vanderbilt family, and his chateau-style mansion for William K. and Alva at Fifth and Fifty-second Street was widely held to be the most significant private home in New York. It was the grand ball opening of this house that was responsible for Mrs. Astor's surrender to Alva Vanderbilt. Hunt also designed numerous other mansions in New York that won the praise of critics. His plans for George Vanderbilt's Biltmore House in Asheville, North Carolina, produced the biggest private home in America, and his Administration Building at the 1893 Chicago World Columbian Exposition also exhibited his talent at creating grandiose structures. Mr. Hunt loved the large stage.

But it is with Newport that Richard Morris Hunt will be forever associated, even more than New York. On a visit to his brother William in Newport in 1860, Richard was introduced to Catharine Howland, a lovely young New Yorker spending the season in town. The attraction was swift and mutual, and they married the following April. From then on, the family (they had five children) spent each summer in Newport, first at Hill-top, which was purchased from his brother and enlarged, and later at other residences. Newport was central to Hunt's long-term reputation, but it was also home. When the New York crowd led by Astors and Vanderbilts descended, Richard had already been a familiar sight in town for two decades.

Apart from the wood Griswold House and the extensive renovation of Wetmore's Château-sur-Mer (which was the largest house in town for years), Richard Hunt's real contribution to the fashionable aesthetic of Newport was achieved in the 1880s and 1890s. With his four grand palaces, Hunt set the tone and the standard for the majestic American showplace. Some critics assert that other architects came close to emulating his formula, particularly White and Trumbauer, but none of them quite caught the essence or the magic of Hunt's designs because, with the exception of McKim, they did not have the classical Beaux-Arts education in their bloodstreams. They designed some glorious homes, no doubt, but Hunt gave his clients that certain elegance not found elsewhere. Hunt's four Newport houses of the late period are:

OCHRE COURT. Among the first of the European-style mansions to rise along the southern coast was Ochre Court, built by New York real estate tycoon Ogden Goelet from 1888 to 1891 in Indiana limestone and designed by Hunt to resemble a French Gothic-style chateau. It is a huge, imposing structure, seemingly too large for the small acreage it inhabits, but grand nonetheless with its palatial roofline, turrets, and gargoyles. Supposedly, it cost over $3 million to build, and Ogden embraced the striking French design in an effort to one-up his brother Robert, who had built the more rustic Ochre Point not far away. Whatever his motives, the construction of Ochre Court marked the virtual end of the popularity of the American-influenced shingle-style cottages for the very rich and the beginning of serious European copies that were unconnected from any relationship to the land itself. Hunt had blasted off for fantasyland. Finally he had gained clients so wealthy that he could return to his French training and jettison any inhibitions he may have harbored in the past. He was in his sixties, and embarking on a new course. Today the house is part of Salve Regina University.

MARBLE HOUSE. With the success of William K. and Alva Vanderbilt's superb Fifth Avenue mansion in 1883, it is not surprising that the couple sought out Richard Morris Hunt again to splash their prominence along Bellevue Avenue. Hunt offered pure neoclassicism in his design for Marble House, which was over three years in construction at the cost of $2 million. Decorations and furnishings reputedly ran to another $9 million. Like the Goelet brothers, it is probable that Willie K. (as he liked to be called) was intent on outshining his older brother Cornelius II, who was living in the first Breakers. Shielded from prying eyes by high fences during the building, over four hundred workers, toiled away at its intricate creation. Marble House opened in 1892 (it was a birthday gift to Alva) and was instantly commented on, pro and con, as the most lavish home yet to rise in Newport. Sheathed entirely in gleaming New York State white marble, the house literally sparkles in the morning sun.

While the exterior of this Vanderbilt gem echoes strong Greek and Roman influences and ode to order, the interior is done in high French splendor, with a Louis XIV ballroom and dining room, a rococo

Ochre Court, garden façade, Ochre Point Avenue, 1888-1891 House of Ogden Goelet; architect: Richard Morris Hunt. Now serves as the Administration Building of Salve Regina University.
Newport Historical Society
Newport, Rhode Island

Marble House, Bellevue Avenue, 1888-1892 Summer home of William K. and Alva Vanderbilt; architect: Richard Morris Hunt.
Newport Historical Society
Newport, Rhode Island

library, and a dramatic Gothic drawing room. Each space has its own personality. The use of gold, gilt, and warm colors takes the edge off the coolness of the marble and stone, yet nothing takes away from its elegance and formality. Alva wanted a house in which she could entertain in high style (she once said she wanted a social "weapon"), and Hunt gave that to her gladly in his rendition of the Petit Trianon at Versailles. Marble House is now owned by the Preservation Society of Newport County and open to the public.

BELCOURT. Caroline and August Belmont's youngest son, Oliver H. P. Belmont (born 1858, graduate of the U.S. Naval Academy, retired banker), was a confirmed bachelor when he commissioned Richard Morris Hunt to design a cottage that would appear imposing, yet would also house his beloved horses under the same roof. Like his father, Oliver was completely devoted to Thoroughbred racing and the thought of sheltering his steeds in some distant barn was anathema to him. So Hunt, with a little humor mixed in, modeled the 1892, $3 million, Belcourt after a French hunting lodge and constructed stalls for the horses on the first floor. Many visitors were aghast at his pampering (the horses had their own linens), but Belmont loved the arrangement.

Upstairs, the human habitat was decked out in Gothic Grand, with stained-glass windows, a small dining room, a large banquet hall, great hall, and even a chapel. The house is baronial, masculine, and dark inside, lavished with suits of armor and hunting scenes. When Alva Vanderbilt decided she had little in common with her husband, the future woman's suffrage champion abandoned him and moved out of Marble House, crossed Bellevue Avenue, and married Oliver Belmont in 1896. She must have had a real challenge bringing a more feminine touch to such a bastion of male taste, but Alva loved to entertain at Belcourt, and the house became well known for its fancy parties after her arrival as mistress of the manor.

In many ways, Belcourt seems an oddity for Hunt. It is almost diametrically opposed to the classical Marble House across the avenue: fussy, somewhat claustrophobic despite its large dimensions. The airiness of Marble House was more suited to Hunt's predilection for stateliness; but in the end, the architect must serve his client, and Oliver Belmont got what he wanted, horses and all. Belcourt is open to the public.

THE BREAKERS. Hunt's greatest, and last, creation in Newport was the magnificent Breakers (1892-1895), for Cornelius Vanderbilt II. When the original Breakers burned to the ground in 1892, Cornelius got his opportunity to assert his superiority over younger brother Willie K. (and the rest of the summer community) by commissioning Hunt to design a home that would not be equaled in town. Money, he told the architect, was no object. Hunt chose to model his new mansion on various sixteenth-century Genoese *palazzi* and threw in an amalgam of borrowed conceits. Given Vanderbilt's fear of another disastrous fire, it was built entirely in stone. Originally planned to be a sprawling two-story edifice, Hunt, encouraged by Vanderbilt, kept drawing and expanding the plans until he achieved epic proportions with four stories, seventy rooms (thirty-three for staff alone), and grandiose grounds on the 11-acre plot.

Hunt's Breakers is constructed around the central two-story hall, which served as the main reception area. The ornate dining room, music room, and grand salon are among the most sumptuous chambers to be seen in Newport, or, for that matter, anywhere in America. Marble and alabaster abound. Many of the main floor rooms were created in Europe and reassembled at the Breakers by Paris decorator Jules Allard, while

Belcourt, original entrance façade, Bellevue Avenue, 1891-1894 House of Oliver Hazard Perry Belmont; architect: Richard Morris Hunt. Now operated as a house museum by the Royal Arts Foundation. Montgomery Schuyler, "The Works of Late Richard M. Hunt." *The Architectural Record*, V (October-December) 160, 1895.

Redwood Library and Athenæum Newport, Rhode Island Newport Collection

The Breakers, Cliff Walk façade, Ochre Point Avenue, 1893-1895 House of Cornelius Vanderbilt II; architect: Richard Morris Hunt.

Courtesy of the Preservation Society of Newport County Newport, Rhode Island

a number of the living quarters above were designed and decorated by Ogden Codman, a young Boston architect, who purposefully created a contrast between the "public" rooms and the private ones. Yet, according to Paul Baker, "The dwelling was a summer place, and the loggias, terraces, and arcades for outdoor activities were made an integral part of the plan and the design. Moreover, with the high ceilings, especially that of the two-story dining room and great hall, and the very large rooms, some flowing one into another, the mansion, despite its balanced formality of design, was given an open and airy character, appropriate to summer living and summer weather conditions."

The Breakers is Hunt's final masterpiece, but he was not present for the gala party the Vanderbilts staged to celebrate its opening. Just weeks before the event, Hunt fell ill, disregarded his doctor's suggestion to recuperate in New York, and rushed to Newport to supervise the finishing touches on his magnum opus. Within days, Richard Morris Hunt was dead. His funeral on August 3, 1895, at Newport's Trinity Church, was attended by the cream of American society. His professional rival and friend Charles McKim was a pallbearer; others in attendance were Cornelius Vanderbilt and many others in the family, Perry and Oliver Belmont, George Waring, Mrs. George Tiffany, a number of Cushings, and a host of other notables. He was widely regarded as the most influential building designer of the century. With Hunt's passing, the most lavish period in American architecture was winding to a close.

But his Newport treasures remain.

Seventeenth-century Newport was defined by its insistence on religious freedom, John Clarke's Charter of 1663, and the quest for independence from Puritan oppression. Eighteenth-century Newport was chiefly characterized by its international trading status and its inspirational role in the creation of the United States of America. Nineteenth-century Newport was shaped by its active summer society and the many mansions the plutocrats left behind. Richard Morris Hunt was the most influential architect in town, but the famous firm of McKim, Mead & White was a close second in refining the contours and content of Newport's high-end homes and public spaces. No other architectural alliance in America came close to the authority they wielded, particularly in New York City and Washington, D. C. But their work in Newport was instrumental in spreading the new gospel of classicism and Greco-Roman order to a generation of increasingly sophisticated clients who were eager to employ their money to display their refinement.

Charles McKim was born in Pennsylvania in 1847, attended Harvard briefly and then the Ecole des Beaux-Arts in Paris where, like Richard Morris Hunt before him, he was steeped in European traditions and motifs. After traveling throughout the Continent, McKim returned to America and spent six years in New York working for one of the eminent architects of the period, Henry Hobson Richardson, where he met and befriended his future partners William Mead and Stanford White. Confident of his talents and success, McKim started his firm in 1877; White (born in 1853 in New York), after long travels in Europe to make up for the formal education he lacked (although he had earlier studied painting with John La Farge), joined McKim and Mead in 1879 to work on the Newport Casino. McKim was clearly the driving force in the firm's designs but, as was made obvious in their plans for Bennett's pleasure palace, White was the more flamboyant and artistically inclined of the two and was particularly focused on creating elaborate interiors for their structures.

Like Hunt, Charles McKim was also drawn to Newport during the summer seasons; his first wife's family lived in town and McKim became familiar with colonial precedents through renovation projects for his in-laws on the Point. At the same time, he was grappling with the need to create a truly American architecture. His foray into the shingle-style, as evidenced in Newport by the Casino and the Isaac Bell and Samuel Tilton houses (1882), sufficed for a number of years, but McKim kept searching for other elements that would be more representative of America's growing world stature. According to the McKim expert Richard Guy Wilson, after experiments with various forms, he was still not satisfied. "But by the late 1880s the firm, with McKim in the lead, had settled upon classicism as the basis from which an American architecture could be developed. The result was known as American Renaissance: an attempt to both import and rival Old World culture and artistic standards. McKim's principal contributions were in three areas: the Colonial Revival, a new American classicism, and the promotion of architecture and allied arts."

The firm's international fame rests on their classical masterpieces such as the State Capitol in Providence; Frederick W. Vanderbilt's mansion along the Hudson River in Hyde Park, New York; Columbia University, the Morgan Library, the Harvard Club, and the demolished Pennsylvania Railroad Station in New York City. McKim was personally chosen by President Theodore Roosevelt to remodel the White House in 1902 and further develop the extension of the Mall to incorporate the Lincoln Memorial in Washington. Yet despite the high quality of the hundreds of buildings that were envisioned by them, what most people remember is the spectacular murder of Stanford White at the rooftop theater of Madison Square Garden (which, ironically, White had designed) in 1906 by Harry Thaw, whose wife, the former chorus girl Evelyn Nesbit, had purportedly had an affair with White years earlier and kept reminding her cuckolded husband what a great man Stanford White was. Needless to say, given his celebrity status at the time, White's murder

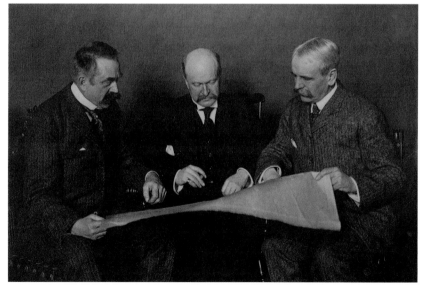

was the talk of the country for years after. But with Stanford White's death, the sparkle went out of the partnership. After Charles McKim's death three years later, the firm was directed by younger associates, but their best work was over.

McKim, Mead & White designed some twenty buildings in Newport in just over two decades. Each has a distinct personality and feel since their clients had differing needs and bank balances. After the Casino, and Robert Goelet's Ochre Point on Narragansett Avenue, the two most significant houses are Beacon Rock on Harrison Avenue for Edward Morgan III (1891) and Rosecliff on Bellevue Avenue for Theresa Fair Oelrichs (1902). In his beautifully illustrated *Newport: An Artist's Impression of Its Architecture and History*, the longtime resident Richard Grosvenor writes that Beacon Rock is a grand example of two different architectural impetuses, the classical and the organic. "The formal entrance is framed by two wings with columns, the design of which stems from a temple on the Acropolis in Athens. A short walk around the house gives a totally different picture, as the symmetrical forms of the front begin to melt into an organic arrangement toward the rear. The material of the house changes from white marble in front to gray slate in back. . . . They were paying homage to the classical tradition; at the same time, they recognized the need to integrate nature into their designs." Landscaping was done by Frederick Law Olmsted. It is a grand, stately palace, yet more understated than most of Richard Hunt's late massive efforts, and perched as it is, high above Brenton Cove, the house is indeed a beacon seen by every boat or ship entering Newport harbor.

The longtime summer resident George Bancroft, whose ten-volume *History of the United States* made him famous (he was also a founder of the U. S. Naval Academy in Annapolis, Secretary of the Navy, and ambassador to Great Britain from 1846 to 1849), had one enduring passion: roses. He gardened and experimented constantly and developed the American Beauty rose on his grounds at the original Rosecliff. After his death in 1891, Tessie Oelrichs bought the property, tore down Bancroft's house, and commissioned McKim, Mead & White to design a home that would rival any other along Bellevue Avenue. The architects succeeded (White performed the lion's share of the work). Using the Grand Trianon at Versailles as the model, White fashioned a stately "H"-shaped mansion sheathed in brilliant white glazed terra-cotta that would be conducive to the large entertainments for which the house quickly became known. With its sweeping Rococo staircase in the white vestibule, the forty-by-eighty-foot ballroom (largest in Newport, where impressive ballrooms were de rigueur among the *haut monde*), expansive salon, and Louis XVI dining room, Rosecliff became one of the most splendid homes in town, even though Bancroft's gardens disappeared during the new construction.

After Rosecliff was completed in 1902, Tessie Oelrichs had the platform from which to launch herself as one of the grande dames of Newport, along with Mamie (Mrs. Stuyvesant) Fish and Alva (Vanderbilt) Belmont, who succeeded Mrs. Astor at the top of the social ladder. While the men of privilege had Wall Street, their clubs, and their yachts, the women took over Newport and ruled Bellevue Avenue at their whim. In the strictly stratified world of a Gilded Age Newport summer season, it was the ladies who set the rules, planned the elaborate balls, spent enormous amounts of money, and dictated who was out and who was in. Tessie

BAL BLANC
From a guidebook to the Preservation Society's cottages we get a sense of Mrs. Oelrichs's flair for drama.

In August 1904 Tessie's celebrated "Bal blanc" highlighted the week of the Astor Cup Race. Everything from the floral decorations to her own magnificent lace dress embroidered with silver mirrored the white motif the hostess had chosen for the ball. Her sister Virginia, who had married William Kissam Vanderbilt II (son of Alva and William K. Vanderbilt of Marble House) in 1899, received with Tessie amid banks of white hydrangeas, roses, orchids, and lilies of the valley. The east lawn fountain was stocked with swans, and a mock fleet of specially constructed white ships floated on the waves at the base of the cliffs.

In a *New York Times* obituary on Tessie Oelrichs in 1926, it was reported that her bal blanc had cost $25,000; other sources claim the number was far higher, probably closer to $100,000 for one evening's entertainment for her four hundred guests.

Rosecliff, Bellevue
Avenue, 1897-1902
House of Hermann and
Theresa Fair Oelrichs;
architect: McKim, Mead
& White. Now operated
as a house museum by
the Preservation Society
of Newport County.
Photograph by Ira Kerns
Courtesy of the
Preservation Society
of Newport County
Newport, Rhode Island

The Elms, garden façade,
Bellevue Avenue,
1899-1902
House of Edward Julius
Berwind; architect:
Horace Trumbauer.
Now operated as a
house museum by the
Preservation Society
of Newport County.
Photograph by John Corbett
Courtesy of the
Preservation Society
of Newport County
Newport, Rhode Island

Oelrichs was in. Born Theresa Alice Fair, she was a daughter of the Nevada Senator James G. Fair, who had made millions as one of the owners of the famous Comstock Lode, the largest silver deposit ever discovered in America. When her mother divorced her father because of his excessive philandering, she was awarded the largest settlement ever granted up until that time: $5,000,000. Tessie made her renowned debut in San Francisco, then made her way East to conquer society. She succeeded quickly. She summered in Newport, met the sporting bachelor Hermann Oelrichs, and married him in 1890 in a wedding that gained national celebrity. Her father's wedding present to her was $1 million, tax free. After her parents died, Tessie and her sister Virginia inherited one of the largest fortunes ever amassed in America. She could do as she liked.

What the vivacious and beautiful Tessie Oelrichs liked was to give parties, big parties: entire operas, ballets, and once even a full-scale circus. Rosecliff was the scene of many of the Gilded Age's most vivid entertainments, rivaled later only by Mamie Fish's more notorious events. McKim, Mead & White had created the perfect theater for her fantasies, almost dreamlike in its perfection.

Rosecliff (now owned by the Preservation Society and open to the public) represented the full flowering of the talents of McKim and White. With their public and private buildings, they set the bar higher for their profession than any other architects working in the period, with the possible exception of Richard Morris Hunt. In a fitting summation of the firm's authority, the critic Leland Roth wrote: "McKim, Mead & White sought an American architecture based on the spirit of the place and its people. For this they embraced classicism, exercising a highly discriminative eclecticism which explored the Georgian and Renaissance sources of the American architectural tradition. McKim's formal training and innate sobriety gave to the firm's work a clarity and judiciousness to which White added richness of texture and plastic ornamentation. Within the context of nineteenth-century idealized formalism and its associational references to the past, the work of McKim, Mead & White represented the most generous realization of commodious planning, sound construction, and visual delight."

The high-end building boom of the 1890s and the first decade of the twentieth century was a nonstop contest to best one's neighbors with the grandest design, the latest technology, and the most opulent interiors. A number of other houses, some of them now open to the public, represent the visions of other prominent architects who accepted the challenge of providing mansions along Bellevue Avenue. Most of them present an aesthetic deeply engrained in the stately, ordered vocabulary of classicism and were built to create the ideal setting for large and lavish parties.

Of the five Newport cottages designed by the Philadelphia architect Horace Trumbauer, The Elms (1902) is the most magnificent; but, because of the seamy Claus von Bulow affair in the 1980s, Clarendon Court (1904) is the most famous (even though it remains in private hands and the gates are always closed). The Elms was built for another Philadelphian, the coal tycoon Edward J. Berwind, whose family had established one of the most prosperous companies in the United States. With railroad and steamship engines needing tons of coal, Berwind rose from middle-class roots to become one of America's richest men. Unlike so many Bellevue mansions, The Elms has sufficient acreage to accommodate the limestone home, which the thirty-one-year-old Trumbauer (who had not yet been to France) modeled on the Château d'Agnès at Asnières;

unlike many of Newport's palaces, it does not look crowded on its site. Later, sweeping terraces and a sunken garden were added to set the house in a proper formal French landscape. One of its many amenities is the basement tunnel that was built to carry the coal to heat the house and run the electricity. Berwind may have made his fortune in the coal business, but he did not want a stockpile visible on his property. The Elms, with its well-maintained grounds and appropriate furnishings, is one of the most superb mansions in Newport and, because it is owned by the Preservation Society, is available for public viewing.

Vernon Court (1901) was designed by A. J. Hastings of the well-known firm Carrère and Hastings, and the architectural historian Vincent Scully, Jr., views this grand house as one of the best later houses on Bellevue Avenue. "Set in its green gardens, the chief one of which is a copy of a garden created by Henry VIII for Anne Boleyn, Vernon Court is a kind of sophisticated essay in esoteric taste. Its white stuccoed walls . . . contrast sharply with the colors of its garden, and the terra-cotta ornament has an appropriately theatrical quality." Recently restored, Vernon Court is now open as the National Museum of American Illustration.

Peabody & Stearns, of Boston, was one of the busiest architectural firms in Newport for over forty years, creating designs for some twenty-five cottages; these ranged from simple shingle-style structures to the original Breakers (1878), the second Ross R. Winans home (1893) near Castle Hill, Vinland, and, its crowning achievement, Rough Point (1891) on Bellevue Avenue for Frederick W. Vanderbilt, which later became the Newport home of the tobacco heiress Doris Duke and is maintained by the Newport Restoration Foundation; it is accessible to the public. Unlike most of the Hunt-inspired classical cottages, Rough Point is best described as English manorial-style; somewhat dark and somber, it is reminiscent of structures one encounters at an Ivy League university or New England prep school. Rough Point is the last of the great houses to be built in a rambling fashion, with casual porches and open spaces. Afterward, society swells migrated to Hunt's or McKim's European grandeur. Its setting at the end of Bellevue Avenue affords one of the most sweeping views of the sea to be found in Newport.

Since the 1880s, a number of well-built houses in the most fashionable areas of town have simply been razed to make room for newer structures. In some cases, they were beyond reasonable repair; in others, it was a matter of wanting to see the demise of an outmoded style. The less drastic measure taken by dozens of homeowners was to make substantial revisions of houses with good bones but not quite right for the period, often altering the original structure in radical fashion. Richard Morris Hunt did that with the Wetmores' Château-sur-Mer in the 1870s, to good effect. When George Peabody Wetmore (a future Rhode Island governor and United States senator) and his young bride returned from their nine-year European honeymoon, they did not recognize the house George had inherited from his father. Likewise at Rough Point: Horace Trumbauer designed major additions in the 1920s and they changed the whole feel of the house.

One of the grandest homes still in private hands as of 2005 is Fairholme, on Ochre Point, owned by Gilbert S. Kahn and John J. Noffo Kahn. The initial 1875 edifice was designed by the noted Philadelphia architect Frank Furness; it was to be his only Newport home. Furness dwelt in the vocabulary of Victorian Gothic, even though he had trained at Richard Morris Hunt's atelier in New York City for years in the 1850s and was well acquainted with the emerging classical order. Fairholme was commissioned by Professor Fairman

Vernon Court, Bellevue Avenue, 1898-1901 House of Mrs. Richard A. Gambrill; architect: Thomas Hastings. Now the home of the National Museum of American Illustration. Photograph by James Yarnell.

Rough Point, Bellevue Avenue, 1887-1891 House of Frederick William Vanderbilt; architect: Peabody & Sterns. Purchased in 1922 by tobacco tycoon James Duke, who had architect Horace Trumbauer greatly enlarge the house. Rough Point was the summer home of Duke's daughter, Doris, who was the founder and patron of the Newport Restoration Foundation. Rough Point is now operated as a house museum by the Newport Restoration Foundation. Courtesy of the Newport Restoration Foundation Newport, Rhode Island

Rogers, also from Philadelphia, as his summer retreat, and Furness furnished him with a large villa perched near the sea on ample grounds. Its large halls and reception rooms were more than suitable for entertaining, although not quite at the lavish scale of Rosecliff or the Breakers.

Remodeling outdated houses is nothing new. But the amplitude on which it was being done in Newport was different. Since 1875, Fairholme has had seven owners, five of whom substantially altered the exterior and interior of the house, continually fine-tuning Furness's vision (and creating new ones to fit the times). The 1875 version, glowingly reviewed in the *Newport Mercury* in May of that year, was clad in wood, in perfect harmony with the aesthetics of that period. According to Bettie Bearden Pardee in her handsomely photographed and informative *Private Newport: At Home and in the Garden*, "Yet much has changed in the house itself. Designed originally as a Queen Anne-style cottage, Fairholme was magically transformed in 1934 with the application of a brick façade, timbers, stucco, gables, towers, and balconies. Every detail and embellishment declared the home's new Tudor presence. . . . The John Drexels remodeled and redecorated the interior during their tenure, 1897 to 1930, adding a ballroom off the main salon for the debut of their daughter, Elizabeth." The next owner, Italian Count Alphonse Villa, made even more alterations and refinements, as have the Kahns. Keeping a seaside mansion fresh and in fashion is a never-ending occupation.

Cliff Walk Controversy

One of the most famous features of Newport, a treasure that has been admired, fought over, and written about for two centuries, is the craggy Cliff Walk along the shore of the Atlantic Ocean. Henry James and dozens of others have extolled its beautiful vistas, its democratic access in the midst of elite exclusivity, its very *being*. The three-and-a-half-mile pedestrian path along the southeastern edge of Newport is a popular destination for residents and visitors alike because it affords some of the finest views of the ocean on one side, and the private property of Bellevue Avenue and Ochre Point mansions on the other. This melding of nature and man-made luxury makes the Cliff Walk, according to Mrs. John King Van Rensselaer a century ago, "the most beautiful and extended walk in the country."

The Cliff Walk has been steeped in controversy for almost as long as it has existed. It probably began as an Indian trail long before the first colonists arrived. Until the 1850s, when it was first referred to in print, the walk would have attracted summer visitors as a pleasant ramble above the sea. But when Alfred Smith pushed Bellevue Avenue to the end of the island and homes began to sprout up like spring daisies, many of the new homeowners were less than pleased that the public could stroll through their grounds at will. The strollers had a different point of view and were adamant about protecting their long-revered rights. In his account of the Cliff Walk, the historian Larry Lowenthal relates,

> In 1852 it was reported that from the southern tip of the island at Coggeshall's Ledge one commanded "an unobstructed horizon, including the town removed into picturesque distance, and the intermediate reach of green fields, sprinkled with occasional groups of trees." The building of new residences and the planting of specimen trees . . . closed those perspectives. Whereas it had been possible to see the ocean from nearly any point along the low ridge that Bellevue Avenue occupies, now one had to go nearly to the water's edge for a view. Whatever ancient right the public possessed to traverse the cliffs became more valuable.

The origin of the right of public access dates back to John Clarke's 1663 Charter. In it, King Charles II mandated that the shorelines of the colony were to be open to all for fishing, the collection of seaweed, as well as other uses (the concept of recreation as we know it did not exist in Clarke's age). Generation after generation respected these rights, and when Rhode Island replaced the Charter with the 1843 Constitution, it too continued to spell out the privileges of the people to enjoy free and open use of the shoreline. As Bellevue Avenue expanded and tourism blossomed, the issue of who owned what intensified. Many of the nearby residents who desired privacy, particularly the Vanderbilts and Belmonts, launched legal challenges to the rights of the public. They lost. Every case brought by private landowners to limit citizens' use of Cliff Walk, all the way up to the Supreme Court, was ruled in favor of the people. Some owners erected walls, fences, and shrubbery to block the walkers' intrusive eyes. Others lowered the grade of the walk in an attempt to make the intruders disappear. For decades there was an uneasy truce between property owners and tourists, but there is no question that the Cliff Walk remains one of Newport's most enduring attractions, open to all.

Cliff Walk begins just above Easton's Beach at Memorial Boulevard and hugs the sea

TRANSFORMATION

Often overlooked in the unending appraisals of the merits or demerits of the cottages on Bellevue Avenue and Ocean Drive is the fact that Newport, once again, was in the vanguard of yet another transformation in American life and culture. These mansions signify a deeper and more profound shift in how citizens viewed their station in the larger world. From 1620 until 1776, the colonies had largely defined themselves as an outpost of Britain and Europe: country cousins breaking ground in the New World, but intrinsically European in their values, politics, and religions. The Revolution altered that mindset. From Yorktown until the Civil War, the Continent was mostly rejected, ignored, and scorned as Americans turned inward and attempted to create a country unlike any they or their ancestors had hailed from. Jeffersonian and Jacksonian ideals prevailed for over half a century, ideals which promoted simplicity, democracy, frugality, and isolationism.

Then came the Industrial Revolution, the rapid rise of the mogul class, the quest for international markets, and an extraordinary expansion of the economy that forever changed the American psyche. With newfound wealth, strength, and a desire to become a major player on the world stage, Americans embraced European styles and values. A *reconnection* was made to a once-spurned legacy. Elegance reemerged, not as a sideshow, but as a necessary ingredient in the upgraded definition of "the good life." Luxury became a valued pursuit for Americans of a certain class who wished to emulate and re-create their European heritage. Newport was at the center of these revitalized ties between the two continents. In Newport, the union was complete. The mansions are but a physical manifestation of a seismic psychological repositioning toward imperialism and power as America entered the twentieth century. Bellevue Avenue broadcasts confidence, grandeur, and a distillation of the growing relationship between the Old and New Worlds. Newport became a microcosm of the emergence, with all its inchoate

CONTINUED ON PAGE 378

rumblings, of the nation that would strut the globe and usher in what Henry Luce once called the "American century."

In 1893, the well-known French writer Paul Bourget was in Newport to do a series of articles for a New York paper. He lunched with Edith Wharton and made an extensive tour of James Van Alen's Wakehurst, Ochre Court, and Marble House, amazed by what he was seeing. "For the last thirty or forty years," he wrote, "thanks to their full purses, [Americans] have laid hands upon the finest pictures, tapestries, carvings, medals, not only of France, England, Holland, Italy, but also of Greece, Egypt, India, Japan. Hence they have in their town and country houses a wealth of masterpieces worthy of a museum."

heights on a rambling course all the way to Bailey's Beach. At the foot of Narragansett Avenue are the Forty Steps leading down to the water. The trail is in disrepair at various points due to erosion, battering winter storms, and simple neglect, but those conditions have not dampened its popularity. The opportunity to get a glimpse of the mansions and grounds of so many celebrated houses remains a quest for hordes of people each year. In 1894, a writer for *Scribner's Magazine*, after describing the beauties of the sea view ("shimmering in the more distant haze the shore of Seconnet [*sic*] and its neighboring rocky islets around which the breakers are flashing in foam"), launches into a panegyric on the views encountered. "On the right of the path, which undulates along its edges and rises and falls with its rolling unevenness, extends that succession of lawns which, more than any other feature perhaps, sets the pitch of Newport's elegance. In these smooth expanses of soft green glowing with unexampled profusion of aristocratic flowers, the art and nature of the place meet in effective fusion. So elegant is it all that one fails to note how high and rugged are the cliffs themselves, the highest on the Atlantic coast from Cape Ann to Yucatan."

Not everyone, however, has reacted positively to the great building boom of the period as seen from the Cliff Walk. While millions of people have gawked at the splendors of the cottages and their gardens, a number of writers have responded with regret that the magnificent scenery had been scarred and cheapened by overreaching architects and their tasteless clients. Newport at the turn of the twentieth century was the object of envy, but it was also the target of numerous journalists who could not control their contempt for many of its mansions and their inhabitants. Some of the charges are valid, some just cheap shots from writers who were jealous of a world they would never enter. A number of well-respected architecture critics have questioned the taste of some of Newport's better-known houses, although often by highly esoteric standards. Place oneself apart from the crowd by too large a distance and it is a sure bet that someone will attempt a low blow.

One such writer was Eliot Gregory who, in a 1901 piece in *Harper's Monthly Magazine*, exclaimed, "Oh! those cliff structures. What monuments to human folly they are! One cannot help wondering what is to become of them in the future, for a fatality seems to pursue the inappropriate piles." His rant continued. "In Paris one feels the sense of artistic satisfaction which comes from harmonious proportions. Until recently the same might have been said of Newport's famous cliffs. The villas on their crests were in keeping with the place and in harmony with the landscape. Unfortunately, the architects of later structures either failed to see this, or wilfully [sic] ignored the subtle laws of proportion, and have marred the fair ocean front with bogus castles and Renaissance pavilions, as out of place on those verdant slopes as a Broad Street office-building would be on the Cours la Reine."

Perhaps the most devastating salvo was fired by Newport's beloved Henry James who, on his return to the city in 1906 to write an article for *Harper's*, let his nostalgia get the best of him. James had been living in Europe for the previous thirty years and, although he had made a few trips to America in the interim, was utterly chagrined by the changes that had taken place in his now wildly rich, and to him, obtrusively naive native land. Newport had always had a special importance for James: a refuge from the world's woes and the place where he discovered his artistic nucleus. Henry James had an abundance of taste, much of it locked in another era. In his long absence from Newport, he romanticized the town of the 1860s, those formative teenage years, building up such a storehouse of memories that only disappointment could await him upon his return. His writing in "The Sense of Newport" (later collected in his book *The American Scene*) is bitter and condescending, the ragings of an older man who felt robbed of his legacy.

James begins his long outcry, "Newport, on my finding myself back there, threatened me sharply, quite at first, with that predicament at which I have glanced in another connection or two—the felt condition of having known it too well and loved it too much for description or definition." After reminiscing about the quaintness of the Point and the glory of Washington Square and the Colony House, he sets his sights on the area of Newport mostly strange to him: Bellevue Avenue and Ocean Drive. He ambles along Cliff Walk, and at the end of his journey, lets go with both barrels to lament the loss of the idyllic landscape of his youth.

> The white elephants, as one may best call them, all cry and no wool, all house and no garden, make now, for three or four miles, a barely interrupted chain, and I dare say I think of them best, and of the distressful, inevitable waste they represent. . . . They look queer and conscious and lumpish— some of them, as with an air of the brandished proboscis, really grotesque—while their averted owners, roused for a witless dream, wonder what in the world is to be done with them. The answer to which, I think, can only be that there is absolutely nothing to be done; nothing but to let them stand there always, vast and blank, for reminder to those concerned of the prohibited degrees of witlessness, and of the peculiarly awkward vengeances of affronted proportion and discretion.

Even for Henry James, this extended tirade is overkill. His pining for the past natural paradise of Aquidneck Island had clouded his usually acute discernment, to say nothing of his vision.

A gentler view of the Bellevue Avenue mansions came in a *New Yorker* profile in 1947 titled "American Town" by the writer Jean Stafford, the first wife of the poet Robert Lowell. After touring Newport and delighting in the Redwood Library and other points of interest, Stafford makes her pilgrimage along Cliff Walk and comments on the panorama.

> In their gargantuan proportions, the coquetry of Swiss chalets and the pomp and ceremony of bogus Trianons made of solemn marble pass beyond vulgarity into something overpoweringly divine and maniac. I know of nothing more magnetically monstrous than these many cottages of Newport, but I also know of nothing so lovely as their expansive lawns that go right down to the ocean, and of nothing so enviable as their windows and back verandas that command a prospect of all this gallant scene of endless breakers and vine-covered promontories and shaggy reefs and violet bays and spinnakers of yachts bellied by a wind that is not felt on land, where the tea is being poured. If I were as rich as could be, I would live in one of these.

How grandly abandoned they must have seemed in 1947. Their glory a thing of the past, and their immense tourist curiosity part of an unimagined future.

Navy, Newport, and Narragansett Bay

High society had become the staple of Newport's existence, fueling the economy with its expensive cottages, dinners, balls, and employment of staff. During August and September, stores along Bellevue and Thames streets did steady, lucrative business. But the season was short, and no matter how much the gentry spent during those months, there was still the rest of the year to survive. The presence of the United States Navy in the region had a profound impact on the town. When summer colonists pulled up stakes and returned to New York, Boston, or Philadelphia to resume their activities, Newport had to make do with diminished income and a depleted workforce. With no full-time industrial base on which to depend, the town's merchants and workers were constantly poised on a precarious teeter-totter, whiplashed between huge summer gains and a moribund, long winter. The navy's various operations on Aquidneck Island had a stabilizing effect on Newport's well-being for over a century.

The American navy got its start in Narragansett Bay during the Revolution; Newport's William Vernon was the equivalent of the first secretary of the navy. Commodore Oliver Hazard Perry and his younger brother, Matthew, brought renown to the service. Steeped in maritime traditions and situated at the entrance to the safe and mostly ice-free bay, Newport was ideal for sea operations, but it had abundant competitors in the race to become a major base of operations. Who got the spoils was a game played out constantly and ruthlessly in Washington, and Rhode Island (until the rise of Senator Nelson W. Aldrich in the 1890s, who, through his cold-blooded use of patronage, was known as "the general manager of the United States") did not possess the power to influence the Congressional committees that determined where military installations were to be placed. When the Naval Academy was moved to Newport during the Civil War, many politicians believed it should stay there when hostilities ended. But again, regional politics came into play and the Academy returned to Annapolis in order to mollify Southerners as the nation attempted to heal its wounds.

But because of the sustained efforts of one determined naval officer, who did duty in town when the Academy was housed at the Atlantic House and understood firsthand the great natural advantages of Narragansett Bay, Newport became home to both the Torpedo Station on Goat Island in 1869 and, in 1884, the Naval War College on Coasters Harbor Island. These two institutions changed the face of Newport and influenced its future by providing a steady stream of employment, a base for technological advancement with torpedo research and manufacturing, and a postgraduate college with a reputation for rigor and first-rate scholarship.

Rear Admiral Stephen B. Luce became Newport's champion within the navy. Born in Albany, New York, in 1827, he was among the first to graduate from the Naval Academy in Annapolis. Following the Civil War, the American navy was in free fall, beset by poor discipline, scant funding, and chaotic administration. Luce's primary concern was the training of officers and seamen, and he wrote a textbook that became required reading for every man in the service, helping to elevate the efficiency of all sailors. Because of his efforts he was promoted to commander of the U. S. Naval Training Station. He may have been a vocal supporter for getting the Torpedo Station located in Newport and was certainly instrumental in establishing the Naval War College in town. Luce found Narragansett Bay to be ideal for training crews and harboring the fleet, and he fought tenaciously for the appropriate recognition of its amenities. He believed strongly in the need for a well-educated service force, particularly among officers, and devoted most of his career to raising the standards of the navy. Without his political acumen and steady persistence, it is doubtful the Naval War College, which was the first institution of its kind in the world, would have existed at all, and certainly not in Newport. The naval historian and War College professor John B. Hattendorf concludes, "Luce was the foremost intellectual leader and the catalyst for the development of professional education, training, and thought in the U. S. Navy from the 1860s to about 1910. He was a key leader during the period of innovation, reform, and revitalization in the 1880s and 1890s." Luce died in Newport in 1917.

The Naval War College was the logical outgrowth of the recruit training program Luce inaugurated in 1875, but at a higher, more sophisticated level. Determined to have Newport as his base, Luce persuaded town leaders to cede Coasters Harbor Island to the federal government specifically for maritime education, thus leading to the creation of the Naval Training Station there. The next step was to get Washington to see the merits of a rigorous postgraduate program for honing the skills of officers headed for senior command and increased responsibilities. Against heavy odds he succeeded, and the Naval War College came haltingly into being, with Luce as its first president. The college took over the old poor house for the deaf and dumb on Coasters Harbor Island and, with a staff of three and with nine first-year students, began its long and illustrious history. Tellingly, seven of the nine men in the first class were later elevated to the rank of Rear Admiral and higher.

The War College offered instruction in the subtleties of advanced command, foreign affairs policy, history, and international law. Two years after its founding, with Luce now back at sea as the head of the Atlantic Fleet, Captain Alfred Thayer Mahan (ironically, a sailor who

From the earliest days of the colony, democratic procedure was taken seriously by the freemen. The General Assembly convened in four towns, with the meeting in Newport in May called 'Lection Day, the opportunity to install the new or reelected governor each year. 'Lection Day was a celebration of political freedom, an opportunity for citizens to party, and it was unique to Newport. After joining the Union in 1790 and throughout the nineteenth century, Rhode Island maintained two capitals, Providence and Newport; the General Assembly shuttled between the sites, even though the real power of the state was vested more and more each year in Providence. Keeping the Newport assembly was a nostalgic nod to the town's colonial power but became an almost empty gesture as the northern town grew so dominant during the upsweep of the Industrial Revolution.

During the 1890s, things began to change. The General Assembly voted to make Providence the sole capital and hired McKim, Mead & White to design an imperial state capitol building. Newport, a political center, was history. As a result of losing its state mantle, the city erected an imposing city hall of gray granite instead; it was dedicated in 1900. Politically, the state was going through upheaval. Rhode Island population in 1870 stood at 218,000; in 1900, it had nearly doubled to 430,000. Much of the increase was due to foreign-born immigration, which bolstered the ranks of the Democratic Party. Reigning Republicans were alarmed that the ethnic surge would topple their hegemony by electing Democratic governors year after year; in 1901, the powerful GOP boss Charles Brayton (called the "kingmaker") rammed legislation through the General Assembly (a mostly Republican body) that stripped the governorship of most of its authority, an act that skewed Rhode Island politics for the rest of the century. The state, already notorious for its political corruption, became even more tainted by bosses, factions, and cronyism. Newport shrugged and went about its business of entertaining the nation's elite.

hated the ocean) arrived to become not only senior lecturer but president as well. It was a propitious appointment because under Mahan's tutelage—and particularly because of the publication of his vastly significant work *The Influence of Sea Power Upon History, 1660–1783* in 1890, a book that caused a major rethinking of the role of naval forces—the Naval War College became an integral component in the future of the United States Navy. Mahan's far-reaching theories on the primacy of sea power in empire-building significantly influenced generations of political leaders eager to justify their desires of expanding American military might around the globe. At the same time, the brilliant strategist William Little was developing his compelling theories on war-gaming and fleet tactics that would transform naval operations throughout the twentieth century and help make the American navy the dominant force it proved to be in two world wars. From its shaky beginnings (few in Washington believed in the need for such a school, at first), the Naval War College has evolved into a world-class institution, and Newport has basked in its glow since 1884.

The development of the ironclad warships *Monitor* and *Merrimack* during the Civil War as well as the navy's general migration from wood to steel hulls greatly changed the needs for new weaponry that would be forceful enough to sink an enemy at sea. Underwater warfare was the wave of the future. The romantic old cannon, fired from the deck of a ship of the line, was no longer adequate for defense, and certainly not effective as an offensive weapon. When the navy took over Goat Island in 1869 and established the Torpedo Station, the move was in response to a transformation in technology that could not be prudently ignored.

Goat Island (now linked to downtown Newport by a causeway) served for centuries as a military installation to defend the town. In colonial days, it was called Fort Anne and later Fort George, in honor of the English monarchs. After the Revolution, it was renamed Fort Liberty, then Fort Washington. In town, however, it was generally referred to simply as Goat Island since, from the early days of the settlement, it was used to graze goats and sheep. The federal government officially took control of the strategically situated island in 1799. When orders to erect the Torpedo Station were issued in 1869, Goat Island was in general disrepair. Seven structures for officer's quarters and a large machine shop were among the first to be erected and the initial workforce consisted of two dozen men. They began building torpedoes to sink hostile ships, but the early devices were crude bombs, more like depth charges, that lacked accurate self-propulsion capabilities. During the 1870s and 1880s, more buildings were added, in particular the laboratory to conduct experiments in electricity to manage torpedo mobility and detonation.

The key figure in this quest was Professor Moses G. Farmer, a tireless tinkerer who, among his numerous contributions to science, was the first person in America to successfully create a reliable incandescent lighting system, beating out Thomas A. Edison by years. In 1859, he lit up a portion of his house in Salem, Massachusetts, with forty lamps. On October 9, 1875, the *Newport Mercury* reported, "Prof. Farmer gave a successful exhibition of his electric lights Thursday night." The press reported that Cottage No. 4 at the Torpedo Station was the first house in the world to be illuminated by electricity. In 1876, Farmer reported to the secretary of the navy on his advances. Edison, by contrast, didn't even begin his research into the lightbulb until 1878, and was successful the following year. Although Farmer was first, he did not pursue his innovative

U. S. Torpedo Station,
Newport, RI, 1876
from sketches by
Theo. R. Davis,
Harper's Weekly, XX
(Saturday, February 5,
1876) 109.
An early view of the
U. S. Naval Torpedo
Station on Goat Island in
the harbor of Newport,
Rhode Island.
Redwood Library
and Athenæum
Newport, Rhode Island
Special Collections

designs but moved on to new challenges. As it turned out, Edison's system was superior for large-scale use, and for that reason he is universally known as the father of the incandescent bulb, even though Moses Farmer was years ahead of the notable maestro from Menlo Park.

Farmer was recruited by Torpedo Station brass in 1872 because of his reputation in electrical experimentation. He intended to stay just six months, but got so involved in various pursuits that he tarried in Newport for nine years. He spent days on end in the electrical laboratory inventing devices that would enable the torpedoes to drive through the water and successfully home in on their prey. Meanwhile, facilities kept growing on the island, with bigger factories, sheds for chemicals, and for machining the torpedoes. By 1900, over 150 men were employed at the station, turning out around fifty torpedoes a year. With the onset of World War I, production jumped substantially, and by the end of hostilities in 1918, Goat Island was rushing through some 350 torpedoes per annum, for both destroyers and submarines.

The Sporting Life

In the last decades of the nineteenth century new outdoor games, either homegrown or imported from Europe, were introduced to American society that brought enjoyment for participants and onlookers alike. As the concept of leisure time matured, taking scenic strolls and swimming at the beach were rivaled by more complex and compelling activities that were controlled by strict rules and gave vent to the competitive spirit so cemented in the emerging American nature. For the most part, these new sports were activities for men and women of wealth, for they had the time to indulge in their creation and to spread them among their peers. Baseball and football were exceptions: their acceptance cut across all class lines. But when one looks at the games that were spawned at a few exclusive clubs in that era—polo, lawn tennis, court tennis, golf, yachting, and automobile races—it is clear that these were competitions between people of means that filtered down the social ladder and became hugely popular national pastimes for the masses. Polo, yacht racing, coaching, and fox hunting remained passions for the upper class largely because of the expense involved in those pursuits. But no one needs to be reminded of how golf and tennis have transformed the American weekend from top to bottom.

Although all of these activities had their origins and were played elsewhere, Maud Howe Elliott was largely correct when she labeled Newport "the cradle of American sports" in her memoir *This Was My Newport*. The attention lavished on the town by the national and international press guaranteed that these new amusements would garner extensive coverage because of their novelty and local popularity. Certainly that was true of the elaborate coaching parades, inaugurated by Colonel Delancy Astor Kane, that invaded Bellevue Avenue almost every summer afternoon. Newspaper and magazine readers were bombarded with pictures and descriptions of the handsome horses, the decked-out equipages of various styles, and the liveried grooms. The vast majority of Americans could come nowhere near displaying that level of wealth, but it did not keep them from ogling the photographs, reading the purple prose in the captions, and dreaming.

Beyond the horse-based activities of polo, coaching, and fox hunting (which was quite widespread on Aquidneck Island in the Gilded Age), Newport's reputation as the "cradle" evolves primarily from the popularity of tennis and golf. When James Gordon Bennett opened the Casino in 1880, it contained not only an indoor court tennis facility (now the oldest in America) but also three outdoor grass courts for the newly introduced game of lawn tennis; within a decade there were twelve well-manicured courts and they were all busy throughout the daylight hours. The new diversion, supposedly invented by British army major Walter Wingfield in 1873, was reportedly brought to America from Bermuda where the young Mary Outerbridge had seen it being played. She brought balls and racquets back to her Staten Island, New York, home, induced a few of her girlfriends to give it a try, and soon her brothers and their friends took it up, albeit much more competitively. Like most nascent games, the rules were haphazard at best, and after tennis had spread to several Eastern clubs, Mary Outerbridge's brother Eugenius called a meeting of other enthusiasts and they formed the United States Lawn Tennis Association (USLTA) to standardize rules, scoring, and court dimensions.

By 1877, a number of Newporters had become enamored of the game of lawn tennis and laid out courts on the grounds of their estates. William Watts Sherman, James Gordon Bennett, Paran

Casino Playground,
c. 1880
Casino outdoor grass
court for lawn tennis.
Photographer unknown
Newport Historical Society
Newport, Rhode Island

Stevens, and Edith Wharton's father, George Jones, all built private courts for family enjoyment. Summer visitors were recruited for play, and when they returned to their native cities, they carried a ready enthusiasm for the new sport. Not as complex as the ancient game of court tennis, lawn tennis appealed to men and women who hungered for a challenging contest played in an outdoor setting.

The first official national championship tennis tournament in America was played at the Newport Casino in August and September of 1881. Enough men had taken up the game with gusto by that time that the championship was able to field twenty-five contenders. The gallery was filled with well-dressed and enthusiastic members of the summer colony and native year-rounders who were impressed with the high level of play, particularly since tennis had entered the country a scant seven years before. The tournament was won by Richard Sears, a nineteen-year-old Harvard student, who was so dominant that he went on to win the Casino's national contest for the next five years, until he retired because of an injury. According to Alan Schumacher, the matches were accompanied by an orchestra playing classical music, and the ladies waved their parasols when pleased with a point. With a good deal of pomp, the Casino governors created a heavily engraved silver vessel and named it the Newport Casino Champion Cup. Thus a number of traditions that mark major tournaments today found their origins in Newport.

With the honor of hosting the national championship, the popularity of the game grew exponentially in Newport. Each year crowds mushroomed to the point that in 1893 a large grandstand had to be erected to hold all the spectators. Crowds still overflowed the Casino grounds. The game matured, the level of play became more sophisticated, and the rest of America was catching tennis fever. Year after year, more national attention was focused on the tournament because the press could cover all the society people at the same time they were writing about the championship players. Tennis Week each August was a real event. Yet in the end, Newport became the victim of politics and a shift in strategy within the USLTA. Schumacher speculates, "A number of factors mitigated [sic] against Newport. The place was remote, the social gallery was too noisy and seating capacity was insufficient for the growing throngs now numbering thousands. Furthermore, USLTA, which shared gate receipts with the Casino, undoubtedly reasoned that greater revenues could be obtained from a community with a larger population." After years of debate, the executive committee of the organization decided to move the national championship to the West Side Tennis Club at Forest Hills, in Queens, New York, in 1915, "thus sadly ending thirty-four years of the National Tournament at Newport . . . [but] the Casino's important role in nurturing the game of lawn tennis in the United States will never be forgotten."

When the New York Yacht Club lost the America's Cup to Australia in 1983 (the races had been sailed off of Brenton Point for over fifty years), there was widespread local anxiety that Newport would be diminished as a yachting center. In fact, the opposite occurred, and in the early 2000s the city held countless regattas and races in season and continued to build on its maritime activities and reputation as a world-class sailing arena. The same fear gripped the Casino governors after the pulling out of the nationals, yet by initiating the amateur Invitation Tournament to be played a week before the more prestigious event, the

Casino continued to play a leading role in American tennis for the next half century. The Invitation was small, but popular, and it drew the biggest names in international tennis year after year, until it was abandoned in 1967 when the game of tennis became overtly professionalized. A number of other tournaments filled the void left by the withdrawal of the nationals and the Casino has remained a vibrant center for the sport, partially because it never succumbed to the temptation to change its thirteen grass courts and cover them with composition material. Newport Casino is one of the rare clubs in the United States to maintain grass courts.

Yet sometimes outdated conventions are meant to be upended, and it took the creativity, persuasive powers, and endurance of the Casino president and longtime Newport resident James H. Van Alen to convince the USTA ("lawn" had been dropped along the way) in the 1960s to alter its scoring system in an effort to speed up play. Before Van Alen's (at first) quixotic and radical break with history, tennis sets would go on until one player reached a two-game advantage. Thus two evenly matched opponents could drag a set out to, say, 18 to 16, exhausting themselves and their audience and making tennis too unpredictable for network television, which has a certain fetish with precise scheduling (baseball being the main exception). Jimmy Van Alen, who came from a long line of Newport nobility, was a maverick, a society heavyweight, and a great booster of tennis who wanted to increase its popularity. Traditionalists, of course, were aghast that anyone would try to tamper with their hallowed game, but in the end, Van Alen's "tie-breaker" scoring formula was reluctantly accepted and it has greatly accelerated the pace of tournament play and enjoyment of the game.

Jimmy Van Alen had tennis in his bloodstream, and was the first American to become captain of the Cambridge (England) tennis team. He was at the forefront of another significant movement in the sport's history when he came up with the idea, in 1952, to create what today is known as the International Tennis Hall of Fame at the Newport Casino. At first conceived of as a national organization complete with a tennis museum, over the ensuing years the idea was expanded to encompass all the world's great players. After a good deal of haggling with the Internal Revenue Service and other government agencies, the Hall of Fame came into existence because of Van Alen's stubborn resolve. Endorsed by the USTA, the International Tennis Hall of Fame is the only official body of its kind in the world. Its place in the Newport Casino is a fitting salute to the fact that the first American national championship was contested within its grounds.

When Captain Sugar Candy made his notorious horseback assault on the veranda of the Newport Reading Room in 1879, he was in town at the behest of James Gordon Bennett in order to teach Americans the art of playing polo. Several years earlier, Bennett had seen a polo match while visiting England and, being an avid sportsman, decided he would introduce the game in his native land. Just as Mary Outerbridge had brought tennis gear from abroad, Bennett purchased mallets, balls, and other equipment, and sponsored the first polo match in America, an indoor contest at a riding academy in New York City in early 1876. By July of that year, Bennett's Westchester Polo Club was playing at a newly laid out field at the southern end of Thames Street owned by Luther Bateman and attracting large audiences, many of whom viewed the games from Deadhead Hill. A number of men, Fairman Rogers, August Belmont, Jr., and George Fearing among them, became enthusiastic about the fast-paced game and set about practicing. By 1879 Newport was home to many excellent players because of Bennett's prodding and Sugar Candy's instruction.

According to most accounts, Western polo began in India in 1862 when British army officers witnessed a group of native horsemen in the Punjab who were riding around a field wielding wooden sticks and taking whacks at a ball made out of willow root. When asked what the ball was called, one of the Indians said, "Pulu." Soon thereafter, some of the officers decided to try the game, and in a short time they had laid out a field with boundary lines and began devising rules. Polo, as it was dubbed, became very popular within the ranks and as the men returned to various parts of Great Britain, they brought the game with them. Polo clubs began sprouting up all over the kingdom, and the level of play that Bennett saw probably would have been quite high.

During the 1880s, polo became all the rage in Newport. Because a player needed numerous "ponies" in order to compete, it was clearly a rich man's sport. But *where* the first matches were played has been a source of controversy for over a century. Many writers contend that Morton Park was the site of the early games, and Maud Howe Elliott in *This Was My Newport* makes that claim. But in 1945, Henry O. Havemeyer, son of Theodore A. Havemeyer who founded the Newport Golf Club, wrote Mrs. Elliott a long letter to correct some of the inaccuracies in her book. Havemeyer contends, "The block in question was never any part of Morton Park. It was owned by Luther Bateman, and for years, it was leased to the Westchester Polo Club. It was to the west of the Morton property and was bounded by Morton Road, Old Fort Road, Bateman's Avenue and Morton Park. The property has since been cut up into small building lots." Havemeyer was a member of the Westchester club for years, so it is probably best to trust his version. Nevertheless, matches were played regularly at this original site, then later out at the Newport Country Club for three years, but the grounds were deemed too wet for safe play, so the club finally moved to the harder grounds at Bateman's Hotel (not to be confused with Luther Bateman's acreage farther in town), near Winans Avenue and Ocean Drive.

Newport became the first American city to host an international polo series when men from Bennett's Westchester Polo Club (Newport was their real home despite the name) challenged England to send over its best players for a best two-out-of-three series. Believing themselves to be sufficiently schooled to take on the mighty Brits of the Hurlingham Club, the Americans lulled themselves into a false sense of superiority. With great fanfare, the match was staged in late August 1886 at the original field and the Yanks took a shellacking. England won the first game by a score of 10 to 4 and the next day dominated the second, winning 14 to 2. The chagrinned Americans presented the British team with the first International Polo Challenge Cup, donated by James Gordon Bennett, and went back to the practice field.

Among a certain set, polo remained popular, but the introduction of tennis in the 1880s and then golf in the 1890s offered a less risky and far less expensive way to spend a Saturday afternoon. The invasion of the automobile also took its toll on the enthusiasts. The number of men who were able and willing to spend the kind of money it took to keep a stable full of horses specially trained to endure the rigors of a polo match was dwindling by the year. In Newport, the weekend contests fell off rapidly after the turn of the century and the sport slowly took on the reputation of being an amusement for the wealthy elite.

_____

When the Stanford University golfer Tiger Woods stepped to the first tee of the Newport Country Club on

_____

August 22, 1995, to defend his title in the United States Amateur Golf tournament, he was not only one of thousands who were commemorating the centennial of that event, but he was standing on the grounds of one of America's first golf courses and the club that had presented the original Amateur in 1895 — the oldest golf championship in United States history. Newport Golf Club (the name was changed in 1917 when it merged with its cousin, the Newport Country Club) had won the honor of hosting the first official amateur tournament because of the indefatigable fervor of its founder, Theodore A. Havemeyer, then president of the American Sugar Refining Company and one of the stalwarts of Newport's summer colony. It took men and women of vision and industry (and money) to pioneer new pastimes in America; Havemeyer possessed all three assets.

In the 1980s, the historian Alan T. Schumacher did extensive research into the club's origins and growth. According to his findings, Theodore Havemeyer was in Pau, France, home to Europe's first golf course outside the British Isles, in the winter of 1889, when he "discovered" the game and fell under its spell. The new aficionado was nearing fifty years of age and wanted to participate in a sport a little less physically grueling than polo. On his return to Newport, he gathered some influential friends and hatched the idea of forming the Newport Golf Club. First, they rented a 40-acre parcel of land at Brenton Point in the spring of 1890 and quickly laid out a crude nine-hole course, using the nearby Bateman's Hotel as a clubhouse. This casual arrangement worked for three years. In March 1893, a corporation named the Newport Country Club was formed with some seventy members. To kick off the season that year, the executive committee threw an elaborate luncheon on the Fourth of July; the *Newport Mercury* reported that 150 vehicles, most of which were owned by the social elite, packed the driveway of Bateman's. Golf fever had definitely taken hold of the Newport community.

To get an idea of the kind of person who went in for golf early on, Newport historian Eileen Warburton relates,

> The friends that the zealous Havemeyer converted reads like a Who's Who of the Gilded Age: three of the Vanderbilt brothers, two of the Goelets, two of the Belmonts. There were Gammells and Brooks, Kings, Burdens, Whartons, Wetmores, and Spencers. E. D. Morgan was one, as was Hermann Oelrichs and John Jacob Astor, James Stillman, Theodore Gibbs, H. A. C. Taylor, and Edward Berwind were all involved. Soon about three-quarters of the industrial wealth of the United States was tramping through these recent pastures in pursuit of the elusive gutta-percha ball, regarding fences, stone walls, marshes, and the occasional sheep as natural obstacles.

In 1894, the membership tried to buy Bateman's Hotel to use as a permanent clubhouse, but the asking price, $240,000, was far too high. So, a syndicate of high-roller members rethought their strategy and decided to buy, for $80,000, the 140-acre Rocky Farm nearby, develop a new course, and build the needed clubhouse. They hired the golf professional W. F. Davis, who went to work designing and laying out not one but two courses: one of nine-hole length for men and serious women golfers, and a shorter six-holer for beginners and children. The ruling committee then hired the young, socially connected New York architect Whitney Warren, Paris-trained at the Ecole des Beaux-Arts, to design the new wooden clubhouse, which was ready

Newport Country Club clubhouse, Harrison Avenue, 1894-1895
Architect:
Whitney Warren.
Photographer unknown
Newport Historical Society
Newport, Rhode Island

for habitation for the Amateur. The stately building, sitting alone on a rise, was beautiful and practical, and still is. Schumacher relates, "When the clubhouse was completed in the summer of 1895 the *New York Times* proclaimed: 'It stood supreme for magnificence among golf clubs, not only in America, but in the world.'" Whitney Warren went on to become one of the country's most distinguished architects, responsible for dozens of public buildings, chief among them New York's Grand Central Station.

Golf was developed in Scotland as early as 1440 and remained primarily a British Isles sport until the 1860s. The most famous golf course in the world, the links course at St. Andrews, Scotland, was open for play by 1551. Newport was not the first American community to indulge in golf mania, although many authorities state that Havemeyer's 1890 creation on Brenton Point was one of the first nine-hole courses in the country. The game (or some likeness to it) is mentioned in numerous other locales, and historians of the game generally agree that the Country Club at Brookline, Massachusetts, was the original American club, dating to 1882, although other clubs claim earlier dates. There is a golf club in Montreal, Canada, that is even older.

By the mid-1890s there were dozens of new clubs and, because rules varied at each one, there were bound to be disputes over who was the better player. Just such a problem arose in 1894 when the leaders of the Newport Golf Club invited the best players in the land to compete for an unofficial national title. The best amateur in America was deemed to be Charles Blair Macdonald of Chicago. When the match was played in September 1894, William G. Lawrence, a member of the Newport club, bested Macdonald by one stroke, but the Chicagoan was furious because of arbitrary rules and complained to anyone who would listen. Theodore Havemeyer, fully aware that an overseeing body must bring order to the fledgling game, called for a meeting of all clubs to form a supervisory organization that would set uniform regulations for American golf. In December 1894, the leaders of five clubs met at the Calumet Club in New York and agreed to form the precursor of the United States Golf Association (USGA), which has monitored the game ever since. Theodore Havemeyer was the first president. The USGA sanctions events, keeps track of ratings, and acts as clearing house for all disputes, from esoteric rule interpretations to changes in equipment.

With Havemeyer serving as leader of the association, the USGA chose Newport as the site for the first *official* U. S. Amateur and U. S. Open Championships to be played in the autumn of 1895. The Open was created to allow for professionals (mostly from Scotland) to compete for a prize. The Amateur was won by Charles Blair Macdonald out of a field of thirty-two players, so in the end he got his revenge. The following day, ten professionals and one amateur competed for the Open title and, to the surprise of many, the tournament was taken by the Newport Golf Club's assistant pro, Horace Rawlins, then just twenty-one years old. Thus two of the most prestigious competitions in American sports got their start in Newport, and one of the champions was a Newport man.

Exactly a century later, defending champion Tiger Woods successfully protected his title at the Newport Country Club. He would go on to win his third amateur championship the following year, then turn professional, to the delight of all duffers, although not necessarily to his new competitors.

Apart from tennis, polo, and golf, Newport was becoming a vast playground for the summer social set, which indulged in almost everything new that came into their sights. Archery was primarily an entertainment for women (consult your Edith Wharton on the importance of flinging arrows amongst the Bellevue Avenue bevy), although many men also took up the bow. Croquet, played on magnificently groomed lawns of grass, was quite popular for years, but suffered a significant decline in players after lawn tennis was introduced. Cricket enjoyed a brief surge in interest, but was judged to be too tedious to catch on in a society that craved instant enjoyment. The Newport Casino offered outdoor bowling, the prestigious Coaching Club, billiards, badminton, indoor court tennis, the annual Newport Horse Show, the Newport Dog Show, and a number of other diversions. Bocce was popular at the Reading Room. Bicycling was viewed as a recreation and a necessary means of transport for negotiating town; Alva Vanderbilt took up the sport and was said to have ridden her bicycle eight miles per day and James Van Alen formed a cycling club that held romantic nighttime lantern rides. Bicycle meets were a regular feature during summer months, and wheelmen, as they were then called, from all over the East Coast assembled to parade down Bellevue Avenue and give special exhibitions of fancy riding on their "bone-shakers."

Lacrosse enjoyed a wave of popularity for over two decades. The Newport Racing Association held regular horse races. In the 1890s, flying box kites off Brenton Point became the rage and continues to be so, although the kites are now far larger and more sophisticated. Rowing in the harbor was fashionable and many races were held to determine the strongest oarsman. Roller skating had become widely popular at the Atlantic Hotel in the 1860s and 1870s; within a decade the Newport Roller Skating Rink was built on Bellevue Avenue and continued to attract large crowds for years. The curious and rare game of roller polo was played on roller rinks; it was a takeoff on polo, but instead of riding horses, the men played on roller skates. In 1883, the Newport roller polo team won the national championship in Boston, but the sport did not attract large audiences and after 1900 it was all but finished as a diversion.

America's emerging national pastime, baseball, was being played at Morton Park as early as

1885 and Newport fielded many teams in the ensuing years. Wellington Park has also long been the site of baseball games, but for most townspeople, the sound of a bat hitting a hardball is associated with Cardines Field on America's Cup Avenue. By 1908 the ballpark was hosting contests, and that same year the city's first league was created, fielding six teams. The Trojans, a local semi-pro team, gained national recognition during the second decade of the century by often playing—and defeating—major league teams. Newport can take pride in the fact that the Trojans beat both the New York Yankees and New York Giants in the same season, although the world champion Boston Braves shellacked the home team in 1916 in front of three thousand spectators. Baseball has long played a significant role in the city's rich sports history and Cardines Field is active today.

The first automobiles to reach America from Europe were expensive trophies, so it stands to reason that wealthy members of Newport's summer colony would have been among the country's original owners. The sporting elite liked new gadgets and challenges, and the fleet horseless carriage was yet another vehicle for them to amass and flaunt in public. In 1897, Oliver H. P. Belmont was the proud possessor of one of the first autos in the land. Not to be one-upped, Harry Paine Whitney promptly went out and bought three "bubbles" of his own. Another car arrival was duly noted in the July 2, 1897, edition of the *Newport Daily News*: a Mr. Eames "who is to use it for pleasure went to the depot, connected the storage battery and rode up Long wharf without creating confusion or doing any damage. The vehicle has a capacity of about twelve miles an hour." The new automobile, whether electric or gasoline powered, created a mild panic in the hearts of horseback riders who were certain their charges would be spooked by the fast-moving contraptions, and a chorus of

Horse racing and horse drawn carriage, c. 1900
Photographer unknown
Newport Historical Society
Newport, Rhode Island

protest emerged throughout Newport to ban automobiles from public streets. Obviously the effort failed, and there were actually few reports of horses bolting at the sight of the strange carriages.

One of the first auto races in America took place in Cranston, Rhode Island, in 1896 (the original contest was in Chicago in 1895); two years later organized races were common at Aquidneck Park in Middletown, with the cars then reaching speeds of over twenty miles per hour, driven mostly by Bellevue Avenue swells who loved nothing more than competing with each other. The *Daily News* reported that over eight thousand people flocked to the park to watch these curious motor contests in September 1900. William K. Vanderbilt, Jr., became so enamored of auto racing that he sponsored a trophy for an annual meet. His passion for the sport led to his being dubbed the "Father of American Automobile Racing." For many years matches were held at Second Beach on the hard sand at low tide, and hundreds of Newporters made their way there to witness these boys-with-toys vie for the glory of being fastest.

One of the most bizarre spectacles in Newport history took place in September 1899 when nineteen of the Bellevue Avenue summer set decided to decorate their autos with over-the-top floral arrangements, compete with each other on an obstacle course on Belmont's property, then drive through town to show off their creations. The *Daily News* reported the following day, "It was the first parade of horseless carriages ever made in this country, and its elaborateness, from the almost unlimited means at the disposal of the participants and the desire among them each to out-do the others, made the display one that will not be likely to be duplicated except under similar circumstances."

The parade was unlike anything the town had seen and the surprised citizens gawked in wonder at the display of conspicuous consumption. To get an idea of the ends to which the participants went to embellish their autos, the newspaper writer proceeded to describe each contestant's efforts. A sampling:

> Mrs. Hermann Oelrichs's carriage was a mass of yellow daisies, with two crossed arches of the same flowers over the top. Wide yellow ribbons tied in huge bows adorned a network of delicate white flowers above. Upon the top were a dozen white doves. . . . Mrs. J. R. Drexel had the wheels of her carriage in white hydrangeas with the hubs in pink. The carriage was covered with a mass of pink hydrangeas tied with pink ribbons. . . . Mr. O. H. P. Belmont's carriage had decorations of yellow daisies on the body, from the four corners of which rose a double arch. The pillars of the arch had bases of blue hydrangeas, with yellow flowers and cat-o'-nine tails above. Surmounting the arch was an eagle with wings outspread. Among the cattails and the body decorations were numerous electric lights. From the pole in front were supported four great sea gulls, as if dragging the vehicle and guided by the eagle with long yellow streamers. Mrs. Stuyvesant Fish rode with Mr. Belmont.

Various sports and outdoor activities took root as national pastimes, and it was inevitable that like-minded people would join together to pursue their pleasures, particularly when large expenditures necessitated the sharing of costs, as in creating a golf course or grass tennis courts. But the concept of the club as a segregated social unit was on the rise in a larger arena in America as well. People wanted to rub shoulders with their peers and enjoy their leisure time together. The local historian George G. Herrick points out that ancient Athenians "had their *symposia*, or friendly meetings, where everyone contributed something to the feast and bore part of its expense." A great variety of associations have ever since been a staple of nearly every society on earth. Herrick continues, "The word club had emerged in seventeenth-century England as a verb meaning to join together to meet the cost of mutual entertainment. Samuel Johnson later defined the word as 'an assembly of good fellows, meeting under certain conditions.'"

Three clubs—one updated, one new, and another the extension of a venerable New York institution—came into existence in Newport. Bailey's Beach, exclusive from the time Alfred Smith colonized it, became even more so after it was incorporated as the Spouting Rock Beach Association in 1897 (largely by the same upper-crust men who were in charge of establishing the Newport Golf Club and Newport Country Club, such as John J. Astor, Oliver H. P. Belmont, Robert M. Cushing, James J. Van Alen, Edith Wharton's husband, Edward, and Cornelius Vanderbilt). The Beach, as it is known, offered swimming, parties, and *the* place to socialize and dine away from the glare of prying journalists and photographers who were, and still are, banned from entering the grounds. The Clambake Club of Newport, founded in 1895 and incorporated in 1897 (actually located at Easton's Point in Middletown), offered trapshooting events, fishing, excellent seafood meals, and another locale (aside from the Reading Room) for husbands to flee the social activities of their wives, although women have always been admitted. The club has been well known for over a century for its regular elaborate clambakes, but also as a site for festive dinner dances and other social functions. Finally, the creation of Station No. 6 of the New York Yacht Club in 1890 brought to Newport a branch of the highly prestigious sailing organization where members and their guests could enjoy meals and cocktails and rest between races. Station No. 6 moved several times over the past century but has found its permanent Newport residence at Harbour Court, the stately former home of Mr. and Mrs. John Nicholas Brown.

America's Yachting Capital

With its commodious, safe harbor, Newport was a natural to become America's foremost yachting center during the last half of the nineteenth century and, because of its long association with the international America's Cup contests throughout most of the twentieth century, the city has often been referred to as the yachting capital of the world. Although pleasure boats had filled Narragansett Bay since at least the 1750s and any old salt could vouch for the primacy of Newport harbor, it was not until a group of wealthy nautically inclined men formed the New York Yacht Club in July 1844 aboard the schooner *Gimcrack*, and made an informal cruise to Newport the following month, that the modern era of yachting began. Every summer thereafter, the annual tours to Newport were part of the club's schedule and the number of vessels participating grew. Following the Civil War and the enormous accumulation of wealth that ensued in the immediate decades, more men began building boats that can only be described as floating palaces. When Newport became the summer center for so many of the New York Yacht Club's members, the boats in the harbor could be seen in ever-increasing numbers. Whether powered by steam or sail, the famous yachts of the Gilded Age were a sight to behold, rivaling some of the best houses on Bellevue Avenue for the splendor of their amenities and the number of servants and staff it took to keep them in top condition.

The emergence of the influential New York Yacht Club in Newport's sailing circles elevated the town from a merely local pleasure center to international renown. Large water-borne contests became increasingly

The Newport Club-House of the New York Yacht Club, 1889 from drawing by Schell and Hogan. Cover of *Harper's Weekly*, XXXIII (Saturday, August 31, 1889) 697, 707. The original two-story clubhouse in Newport of the New York Yacht Club, which was built for $3,000 to provide a satisfactory place for the yachtsmen to land and gather in Newport. The Club leased for five years, with an option to purchase at the end of the lease, a dock adjoining the Commercial Wharf. The upper floor was for use by the ladies, while the lower floor was for use by the ladies and gentlemen.

Redwood Library and Athenæum

Newport, Rhode Island

Special Collections

common on weekends, and lasted long into the autumn months. James Gordon Bennett became Commodore of the New York Yacht Club in 1871 and promptly offered two silver trophies for ocean racing on a course set off of Brenton Reef Lightship, the Cape May and the Brenton Reef Challenge cups, open to boats from around the world. In 1893, the Prince of Wales won the latter cup with the *Britannia*, but, good sport that he was, returned it to the New York Yacht Club four years later with his best wishes. The prestigious Goelet Cup and the Astor Cup races were created soon after Bennett's, and yachtsmen from around the globe congregated at Newport to participate in the many races and regattas the town had to offer.

In 1883, the New York Yacht Club officially placed Newport as a required port-of-call during the annual summer regatta (different from the more informal cruises) and seven years later opened Station No. 6 at the tip of Sayer's Wharf as their Newport clubhouse. Local interest in boating, regardless of the size of the craft, was reflected by the formation of the Newport Yacht Club in 1893 and three decades later the Ida Lewis Yacht Club came into existence. While the America's Cup races themselves did not move to Newport from New York harbor until 1930, the trials that determined which boat would defend the Cup were all raced on the ocean course off Brenton Point until that time. Thus every boat involved in the America's Cup effort for nearly a hundred years was a familiar sight in Newport harbor. There wasn't a sailor worth his deck shoes who did not know of, and rhapsodize about, the splendors of sailing in and around Narragansett Bay.

The Golden Age of sailing in Newport lasted a full century—from the inaugural of the New York Yacht Club's regattas in 1883 until the loss of the America's Cup to Australia in 1983—and some of the boats that dotted the busy harbor during its early decades became legends for their size, craftsmanship, and sumptuousness. The men who commanded these vessels were rich beyond compare, and if a sailboat cost millions of dollars to build and more millions to maintain, so be it. While the women of Bellevue Avenue were burning through their husbands' income with their jewels and dinners and balls, many of the men were content to drift away at sea for weeks on end. In many cases, their boats became floating refuges for friends and mistresses, a chief means of escape from the prying eyes of wives and the ever-curious press in pursuit of scandal. Huge steam-powered sailboats that could span the seven seas became the most popular vessels of the moguls in the 1880s and beyond, as witnessed by James Gordon Bennett's 246-foot *Namouna* (1881), William Astor's 243-foot *Nourmahal* (1884), William K. Vanderbilt's 285-foot *Alva* (1886), and later his 331-foot *Valiant* (1893). Robert Goelet built *Nahma* at 306 feet in 1896, only to be bested by his rather competitive brother Ogden when he launched his *Mayflower* the following year at 320 feet. The money flowed in and the boats got bigger and more decorative. In 1900, when Bennett needed to replace his first yacht, he built *Lysistrata* at 314 feet and used it extensively in his travels to and from France. J. P. Morgan, who often made summer sea treks to Newport aboard one of his three *Corsair*s, did not skimp on service: he employed eighty-seven sailors and servants to help keep his boats seaworthy and shipshape.

Sailing was not the exclusive purview of the super-rich, although their boats certainly

POLICE LOG

Throughout its long existence, the Newport Police Department has kept a running ledger of daily occurrences around town that called for attention. The presiding officer for each eight-hour watch made entries in the large book, generally with impeccable penmanship, tracing the ebb and flow of the city's activities. These logs are mostly mundane, dealing primarily with petty crimes and complaints, but they offer a snapshot of Newport's year-round world and the struggle to maintain an orderly existence in a growing seaport city. For example, the police log from January to September of 1891 chronicles no dastardly acts of murder, no burglaries at homes along Bellevue Avenue, no wanton destruction of private property. Month after month, it is instead a rather dull inventory of petty misdemeanors that appear almost quaint by today's standards. Some illustrations:

"Feb 20. Officer Dewick found the door of the store formaly [sic] occupied by Karl & Anthony open and secured the same. There was considerable many things in there that had not been removed as yet."

"March 7. Officer Tazier reports the sidewalk on William St. around the Bennett estate a glare of ice; he ought to know as he experienced a severe fall this morning."

"June 29. Officer Simpson reports that while he was at the Wickford boat some small boys broke a window in the store at 400 on w St."

"July 21. The people of Burnside Ave. complained to Officer Dugan tonight about men and boys playing ball in the street. They would like to have it stopped."

And finally, probably the most common grumble of the townsfolk is entered as follows:

"Aug. 23. Jeremiah Shea of 37 Denniston St. complains of Mrs. Coffey's place and says she is selling considerable beer, that his boy was in there until 11:30 P.M. and when he went after him he came out and abused him. He also says two empty beer barrels was [sic] taken from there yesterday and thinks two full ones took there [sic] place."

Compared with New York and other larger cities, Newport was a quiet refuge during the latter part of the nineteenth century.

dominated the harbor with their immense proportions. Swift, easily maneuvered catboats abounded around Newport, dozens of classes, shapes, and sizes of vessel were to be seen, and the year-round resident had access to numerous pleasure-sailing opportunities. Crewing on these boats became a rite of passage for an untold number of Newport's young men and women for generations, and throughout the summer months sailing was a passion not to be denied. Newport's connection to the sea has always been a defining feature of its history and legend.

Edith Wharton's Newport

Like her good friend Henry James, Edith Wharton grew up to witness and chronicle the significant shift in society from old-line restraint to uninhibited excess. Perhaps no other writer of the era painted a more complex picture of the clash of cultures being played out in American high society, and in reading her fiction it is not always easy to discern which segment she disliked more. The newly rich are often depicted as crass gate-crashers whose habits and manners are lampooned with Wharton's lacerating dry wit and not-so-subtle innuendoes. On the other hand, the stratified and suffocating moral world of the old rich is impeached for lacking imagination and flexibility. Novels like *The Age of Innocence*, *The House of Mirth*, and *The Custom of the Country* give vent to Wharton's nostalgia for order and decorum, while at the same time damning the headlong rush to demeaning display among the *haute bourgeoisie*. A writer needs conflict in order to tell a good story; Wharton found it all around her, regardless of where she was. While her novels and stories are chiefly set in New York, it is clear that her thirty years of experience in Newport colored her view of the world she lived in—and ultimately escaped.

Edith Newbold Jones was born in New York City in January 1862, into an upper-tier family that counted Rhinelanders and Schermerhorns as relatives; Caroline Astor was a cousin of Edith's mother. The distant last of three children, Edith grew up with governesses for playmates and was instilled with Old New York values of tradition, loyalty to the clan, and integrity. Her father, George Jones, encouraged her to read and take advantage of his large library, while her rather imperious mother, Lucretia, took a dim view throughout her life of her daughter's interest in literature and particularly her pursuit of a writing career. Edith's relationship with her mother was fraught with problems and proved to be a longtime burden. In short, Edith was raised to become very much like a number of characters in her novels.

The Jones family summered for many years in a large, comfortable cottage called Pencraig, on Harrison Avenue and, like Henry James two decades before her, Edith enjoyed an idyllic childhood scampering around Newport and beyond, riding her pony, swimming, and attending low-key but memorable parties. She later recalled, "I enjoyed myself thoroughly that winter, and still more so the following summer, when Pencraig was full of merry young people, and the new game of tennis, played on our lawn by young gentlemen in tail coats and ladies in tight whale-boned dresses, began to supersede the hitherto fashionable archery. Every room in our house was always full in summer, and I remember jolly bathing parties from the floating boat-landing at the foot of the lawn, mackerel-fishing, races in rival 'cat boats,' and an occasional excursion up the bay."

Later in life, those memories of a carefree and beneficent environment would influence her view of Newport when the town turned into a carnival of, in her words, pretentious entertainments. The historian

Mary Murphy-Schlicting writes, "As social constraints multiplied, the complex world of her mother obliterated the pastimes and pleasures of childhood. The simpler charms of Newport were eclipsed by the straightjacket of New York society. When Newport came to mean only the holiday inanities of that limited society, Edith no longer wanted any part of the place, beautiful as it might be."

Edith Jones, whose childhood nickname was Pussy, began writing stories and poetry in her early teens, spending much of her summer days in Newport daydreaming and collecting her thoughts and fantasies on paper. Like most young writers, the work is a product of the limited life she knew, so the characters are by and large society people mired in various romantic dilemmas. Her work held promise, and when she was only sixteen, her family privately printed a collection of her poems in a folio titled *Verses*. The esteemed editor of the *Atlantic Monthly*, William Dean Howells, found merit in Edith's fledgling offerings, and printed one of her poems in his prestigious magazine. A propitious start to a career that would later lead to world renown.

In an effort to speed Edith out of her childhood pursuit of poetry and into the adult world of social responsibility, Lucretia Jones arranged for her daughter's debut a year earlier than usual, an event that took place in the ballroom of Levi Morton's Fifth Avenue mansion in 1879. For the next six years the shy young woman joined the social ranks and participated in the activities of her class, writing occasionally. In April 1885, Edith married Edward Wharton, thirteen years her elder, from Brookline, Massachusetts, a union that was a disaster from the beginning for Edith because not only did Teddy not care about her intellectual cravings, he was a bit mad as well, and became progressively worse as years went on. He loved the social scene in Newport while she began to turn

inexorably against it. Only a later affair opened up her dormant sexuality and gave her the satisfaction her marriage never could.

The new couple took possession of Pencraig Cottage, a guesthouse on the estate across Harrison Avenue, and proceeded to set up house and cultivate a garden. But she was still on her mother's turf. In her memoir, *A Backward Glance*, she admits of this time, "I was never very happy at Newport. The climate did not agree with me, and I did not care for watering-place mundanities, and always longed for the real country." The Henry James scholar Leon Edel believed that this sharp turn in her sentiments toward the town only began after her unhappy liaison with Teddy. Before that, she sang the praises of Newport, and certainly her childhood writings bear that out. The Whartons stayed in Newport from June until February each year, then traveled to Europe, to the delight of Edith because she met friends with whom she could talk literature and ideas and escape the tyranny of dull social gossip.

Upon inheriting a sizable sum of money after the death of an elderly cousin, in 1893 the couple purchased a cottage named Land's End, all the way across town from her mother's property. Finally, she could declare some independence. Wharton later wrote of the experience,

> I had been able to buy a home of our own at Newport. It was an ugly wooden house with half an acre of rock and illimitable miles of Atlantic Ocean; for, as its name, "Land's End," denoted, it stood on the edge of Rhode Island's easternmost cliffs, and our windows looked straight across to the west coast of Ireland. I dislike the relaxing and depressing climate, and the vapid watering-place amusements in which the days were wasted; but I loved Land's End, with its windows framing the endlessly changing moods of the misty Atlantic, and the night-long sound of the surges against the cliffs.

Wharton's love-hate relationship with the town was out in the open. While she and Teddy graced some social functions, she withdrew further to work on making Land's End in her image. The vapid chatter at parties that energized Teddy bored her, the mansions insulted her sense of scale, and the often-wet Newport weather often made her nauseous. She loathed the way the new interlopers in her realm, the fast New York set, were decorating their palaces and she let it be known in private letters to friends: "Teddy hasn't yet rallied from the effects of the Whitney house. It must indeed be a Ghoul's lair. I wish the Vanderbilts didn't retard culture so very thoroughly. They are entrenched in a sort of Thermopylae of bad taste, from which apparently no force on earth can dislodge them."

The exterior of Land's End may have been beyond beautification, but she had ideas about the interior, which were in direct opposition to the prevailing ostentation she found around her. As anyone who has read her fiction knows, Edith Wharton had a very keen eye, and that talent was with her when it came to decorating. She began talking with the young Boston architect Ogden Codman, and he agreed to help her. She wrote that his offer was "a new departure, since the architects of that day looked down on house-decoration as a branch of dress-making, and left the field to the upholsterers, who crammed every room with curtains, lambrequins, jardinières of artificial plants, wobbly velvet-covered tables littered with silver gewgaws, and festoons of lace on mantelpieces and dressing-tables. Codman shared my dislike of these sumptuary excesses, and thought as I did that interior decoration should be simple and architectural; and finding that we had the same views we drifted, I hardly know how, toward the notion of putting them into a book."

The Decoration of Houses was published by Scribner's in 1897. Although a collaborative effort, it marked the official beginning of Edith Wharton's prose career in book form. Everyone was surprised at the volume's instant (and long-lasting) popularity, and its success gave Edith confidence to begin writing full-time. New friendships made at Land's End, such as with the French novelist Paul Bourget, strengthened her commitment to her art. Stories flowed from her pen at a fast pace, and a number were published in national magazines. During the decade that the Whartons owned the Newport house, Edith matured, made her emotional break with her mother (*The Decoration of Houses* was a direct public indictment of Lucretia's style), and came to terms with her deeply troubled, loveless marriage. But more and more each year, Newport was losing any appeal it once had. She was ill too often and had a series of emotional tumults, undoubtedly related to her frozen relationship with Teddy, as well.

By 1899, her good friend Walter Berry was urging Edith to quit Newport for a healthier climate. So in 1901, she and Teddy purchased a 113-acre property in Lenox, Massachusetts, in the Berkshire Mountain region, and built an imposing house named The Mount. By then she had published two collections of short stories and was about to bring out her first novel, *The Valley of Decision*. It was this book that was the catalyst for the friendship between Wharton and Henry James. He wrote her a laudatory letter, she wrote back, and one of the most important relationships in the lives of both authors began in earnest. Many years her senior and by then world famous, James became her mentor. His influence is evident in both the themes of her fiction and the style of her prose, although they had very different sensibilities. Wharton and James often traveled together in Europe and England, visited each other regularly, and, until his death in 1916, were devoted companions.

Because of her yearly trips to the Continent, and her constant travel while there, she began writing magazine articles about the sites she visited, many of which were brought out in book form later. The Wharton expert Judith Funston declared, "Wharton's travel writings are noteworthy on several counts: she was one of the first writers to realize the potential of the automobile to change the face of travel; more important, she demonstrated an ability to capture local atmosphere, an extensive knowledge of history, art, and culture, and an exceptionally sensitive eye for detail and nuance."

The decade after selling Land's End and moving to The Mount was productive and liberating. In 1905, *The House of Mirth* became a best seller and finally made her name. Her two-year affair with the American journalist Morton Fullerton brought her real love for the first time and must have influenced her next masterpiece, *Ethan Frome* (1911), with its dark depiction of frustrated love. Her personal life finally gained some peace after Edith divorced Teddy in 1913, by which time she had made France her home for the rest of her life. More novels appeared and the public was captivated by her tales of morality and manners among the gentry. In 1920, she published what most critics regard as her finest novel, *The Age of Innocence*, for which she won the Pulitzer Prize in 1921, becoming the first woman to do so. Clearly influenced by her Newport experiences, the book harks back to the 1870s and depicts the struggle between social responsibility and personal desire. In hindsight, Wharton is nostalgic for the society of her parents' generation and their high standards, particularly when weighed against the gauche values of the succeeding horde.

Edith Wharton called on Newport memories in her fiction for the rest of her life. Nor had she abandoned the town completely. Her biographer Eleanor Dwight, in the masterly *Edith Wharton: An Extraordinary Life*, writes that she returned several times, and with a fresher attitude and deeper sensibility for having gotten away.

> By the fall of 1902, she was beginning to see the resort as a place whose pastimes and culture could be analyzed objectively. Newport was more than ever the place for gala balls, sports events, and competitive spending sprees, but [in a letter to a friend Wharton wrote] "this life of lazy ladies and gentlemen" would no longer irritate or entrap: "I had a very pleasant week at Newport. Dry, brilliant weather (not a fog), magnificent tennis (I am a devout spectator of that game). . . . It gave me a sense of being at a Greek game—the brilliancy of the scene, the festal dresses, the grace and ease of the two players, & the strange intensity of silence to which the chattering crowd was subdued. It seems to me such a beautiful game—without violence, noise, brutality—quick, graceful, rhythmic, with a setting of turf and sky."

Wharton had left America for France in 1907, returning occasionally for family matters. Her last trip home, in 1923, was to receive an honorary doctorate of letters from Yale, the first woman to receive that distinction. In later years, along with fiction, she penned her memoir *A Backward Glance*. Edith Wharton died at her home Pavillon Colombe, outside Paris, in August 1937, at the age of seventy-five. Leon Edel, in a 1966 address at the Redwood Library reminiscing on the friendship between Henry James and Edith Wharton, noted: "Mrs. Wharton was twenty years younger; and she represents in our literature the novelist who saw, with clear vision, an important moment in the history of certain old families and old ways of life in New York; she recorded the manners, humors, tragedies of that society with unfailing truth and in prose of great lucidity and clarity. . . . Mrs. Wharton represents American prose fiction in its most articulate form; *The House of Mirth* and *The Age of Innocence* written in those beautiful sweeping periodic sentences, stand as the last and among the finest of the novels of the Gilded Age."

Artists at the Bay

Many painters continued to visit Newport to capture the beauty of the landscape and the sea. The allure of the scenery was ever-present, and Aquidneck Island's reputation for luminous light was cause enough to lure a variety of artists over the years. In the waning decades of the nineteenth century, one painter particularly stands out for his depiction of the island's physical charm, but his lasting reputation was made primarily as one of America's first serious seascape artists. William Trost Richards is well known within Rhode Island and beyond; among art historians he is considered to be a pioneer in the genre and one of the leading painters of his day for his realistic renderings of coastal life and the rhythmic, moody movement of the ocean.

William Trost Richards was a Philadelphian by birth (1833) and began his career designing elaborate ornamental metalworks, using his spare time for painting rural landscapes around the city. Like his intricate pieces in metal, Richards's early paintings show a passion for meticulous detail in every scene, an almost religious rigor in the effort to faithfully portray nature's gifts on canvas or paper. Traveling regularly to Europe and the

British Isles, Richards sketched hundreds of locales, later using the rough drafts to create oils and watercolors in his studio. In 1874, along with his wife and children, the artist rented a small house near Easton's Pond for the summer and his love affair with Newport began in earnest. Walking around Aquidneck Island and becoming familiar with the various sea views transformed Richards. Newport was his magnet for the rest of his life. He bought a house on Gibbs Avenue during his first summer in town and until he died made Newport and Jamestown his preferred residences. In a letter to George Whitney, his major patron, Richards wrote: "I have made some new walks and discovered new beauties, and believe that I could from Newport scenery make more charming pictures than I have ever dreamed of before."

The "charming pictures" swirled off of Richards's brushes for decades but they did not lead to the greater fame he sought, primarily because the art-buying trendsetters in American metropolises began to champion the more avant-garde works of European painters, particularly Barbizon and early Impressionist adherents. Richards was cool to the emerging style and was more convinced that his atmospheric, strictly realistic land- and seascapes were the most powerful way to convey nature's true majesty. His paintings and watercolors of the ocean around Newport show a realism then being spurned by a new generation of artists. He admired some of the radical shifts taking place in the art world, notably the expansion of a more robustly colored palette, but chose to go his own way.

Returning to Newport after a lengthy trip abroad, Richards was dismayed by all the new houses that had sprouted up near his Gibbs Avenue home, thus ruining his bucolic views. To get closer to his primary subject, the sea, he and his wife bought land at the Dumplings on the southern tip of Conanicut Island in 1881 and built a shingle-style structure that he named Gray Cliff. From then until 1899, when the United States government condemned the property (against Richards's protests) to make way for military fortifications, the artist painted hundreds of scenes around his home. Writing to George Whitney of the spectacular sweep of Narragansett Bay and the ocean off Brenton's Point, Richards remarked, "You can't realize what a delight it is to have the finest subjects right in one's 'front yard'—and to grow sure that familiarity will not bring contempt. Indeed all this shore grows lovelier day by day, and whether it is fog or sunshine there is equal enjoyment."

Even after the eviction from Gray Cliff and the death of his wife the following year, Richards, who had purchased a house on Arnold Avenue in Newport, kept up a steady output of seascapes, to the delight of his conservative audience. The art historian Linda S. Ferber reminds us that even as new styles were evolving, Richards remained devoted to his vision. "A significant and revealing comparison can be made between the late marines of Richards and those of another near contemporary, Winslow Homer (d. 1910), who was painting at Prout's Neck during those years. Homer's waves, rocks, and sky lock firmly into a pattern on the surface of the canvas, a pattern that is essentially abstract although grounded in a respect for and knowledge of the actual. Richards, possessed of this same respect and knowledge, remained committed to the deep, light-filled space of an earlier romantic realist vision." Richards died in Newport in 1905 at his Arnold Avenue home, at the age of seventy-two.

The town was bustling with people deeply interested in art at the turn of the century and, in 1912, Maud Howe Elliott, her husband John (a serious painter), and a number of others formed the Art Association of Newport with the purpose of mounting regular exhibitions, presenting lectures, and creating an art school. A glaring gap in Newport's cultural life had been closed, and the founders voted to renovate William Morris Hunt's home and studio, Hill-top, on Church Street, turning it into a thriving gallery. Membership grew so quickly that by 1916, with an endowment from Marsden Perry, the officers were able to purchase the handsome Griswold House on Bellevue Avenue to serve as headquarters for the thriving Art Association. Now known as the Newport Art Museum, what began in 1912 with a group of eight dedicated art lovers has grown into one of the town's most popular year-round destinations.

Over the years the museum has held hundreds of exhibitions highlighting the work of national and local artists, devoting considerable space to men like Worthington Whittredge, Winslow Homer, and John Singer Sargent, all of whom created important works while visiting Newport. One name in particular that is closely linked to the Newport Art Museum is Howard Gardiner Cushing, who died in 1916, the year of the move to Griswold House, at the age of forty-seven. Cushing was a distant descendant of Matthew Cushing, who left England for the Massachusetts Bay Colony in 1638 and there sired progeny who would become distinguished jurists: four Cushings would serve as chief justices of the colony's supreme court and one was an associate justice of the original United States Supreme Court. The Cushing family fortune was gained in the China trade of the early nineteenth century, which, from then on, enabled subsequent offspring the freedom to pursue their passions.

Howard Gardiner Cushing was born in Boston in 1869, attended Groton and Harvard, and then spent seven years in Paris studying painting and immersing himself in the swirling art and social scene of the city. When he returned to America, he married the beautiful Ethel Cochrane and set up a studio in New York while summering each year in Newport at the Ledges, the home on Ocean Drive that Howard inherited from his father, Robert Maynard Cushing. He built a studio at the Ledges and for the next twenty years concentrated primarily on portraiture, although he engaged in the decorative arts and large murals as well. His wife became a frequent subject, and his study of her, *Woman in White*, is one of his finest works. Although Cushing is not well known outside of Newport because of his early death, he was recognized by his peers as an important painter, and his work has been collected by the Metropolitan Museum of Art and the Whitney Museum in New York, along with the Isabella Stewart Gardner Museum in Boston. He painted numerous land- and seascapes in Newport; his romantic Chinese panels for Gertrude Vanderbilt Whitney's estate at Westbury, New York, are highly regarded.

Cushing was a popular figure in Newport, and his many friends were saddened by his untimely death. A number of them banded together and, in 1920, provided the money to erect a separate building on the grounds of the Newport Art Museum, designed by William A. Delano, in Howard Cushing's honor. One art historian wrote of Cushing's painting,

His work was distinguished by an exquisite taste in selection, a thorough knowledge of the laws

Benjamin Curtis Porter
*Portrait of
Maud Howe (Elliott)*,
1877
Oil on canvas
Courtesy of the
Newport Art Museum
and Art Association
Newport, Rhode Island
Purchased from the
Museum of Fine Arts, Boston,
1953, through the generosity
of many donors, particularly
R. Campbell James

With so many grand estates dominating the landscape, so many horses and carriages and gardens and broad green lawns to be tended, so much laundry to wash and so many meals to cook and serve, so many floors to scrub and tables to polish, the workforce was a constant issue for the mistresses of the Avenue. The "servant problem" has been around for millennia and has stemmed from a difference in expectations between the servants and the served. In Newport, most of the domestic staff were of European origins, and many of them had come to America to escape domestic service, thus they treated their jobs merely as stepping-stones to better lives. Depending on the size of the cottage, the number of horses kept for coaching, and the refinement of the gardens, summer residents usually employed between ten and sixty men and women to keep the household running. Many of the matrons had full-time staff who would travel to Newport weeks before the arrival of the family to open the houses and make them ready. The head butler, that indispensable majordomo who reported directly to the mistress of the house, would then hire locally the necessary gardeners, laundresses, valets, footmen, cooks, waiters, coachmen, and other help. French chefs became a regular fixture in many cottages, while the Irish maid became a staple of the downstairs crew. When the lady of the house decided to give a dinner party or host a ball, employment agencies would be consulted to supply the necessary extra workers. With a budget of around $300,000 to $500,000 per season, the mistress would marshal her army of mostly white servants and staff like a field general in battle. Household workers wore detailed uniforms to denote their station and duties; if the lady decided at the last minute to change the china pattern for a dinner party, the serving staff would be ordered to adjust their clothes so the livery matched the place settings.

which underlie the conventional presentation of a subject, great beauty of color, and a genius for the invention of variations on conventional modes. On the occasion of a memorial exhibition of his paintings, held at the Century Club in 1923, a critic wrote of Cushing as "A man who was ever a charming and distinguished figure in art circles, who was always the aristocrat in painting, and who by study and consistent development was becoming one of the leading American decorative artists of his time."

Yellow Journalism and the Press

Newport suffered its share of slings and arrows in the press throughout the Gilded Age, given the fact that it presented such a tempting target with the massing of so much wealth and celebrity within such narrow confines. The *New York Times* and Bennett's *New York Herald* covered the social scene in depth each season, as did other major metropolitan dailies. National magazines like *Harper's Monthly* ran long, ruminative articles chronicling how the rich and famous lived and acted, what their cottages were like, and what sports drew their attention; some of these were positive, many decidedly slanted otherwise. Newport was a fishbowl for journalists, a center for gathering gossip and repackaging it as news. It is difficult to judge how much envy and class jealousy played into these contemporary accounts of the town, although many of them read like bad fiction.

But one publication particularly descended to the depths when appraising the goings-on in Newport. For three decades, Colonel William Mann ran the scandal sheet *Town Topics: The Journal of Society* and terrified most of the Eastern elite, either by running or threatening to run salacious stories about their purported deeds and misdeeds. His writers were instructed to be as scurrilous as possible when preparing copy, and Colonel Mann relied on a large network of servants, gardeners, Western Union operators, and others to supply him, for cash, with tasty tidbits that could be blown up and used against the Bellevue Avenue crowd. If a society gentleman got wind of a disreputable article (usually a sexual indiscretion or business setback) about to hit the newsstands, it was well known that a late-night visit to Colonel Mann with an envelope stuffed with cash would usually get the piece killed. *Town Topics* probably raised more money through blackmailing society than through subscriptions to the rag. He was genuinely hated and rightly feared by leading figures all along the Atlantic coast, from Bar Harbor to Palm Beach.

Colonel Mann was a nasty, despicable man. He once confided to a young reporter, "My ambition is to reform the Four Hundred by making them too deeply disgusted with themselves to continue their silly, empty way of life. I am also teaching the great American public not to pay any attention to these silly fools. If I didn't publish *Town Topics*, someone else without moral responsibility would do so. I am really doing it for the sake of the country." The following excerpts from *Town Topics*, chosen at random, give a good idea of how he treated the Newport summer colony and mistreated the integrity of the Fourth Estate.

Thursday, August 11, 1887. "Look at the men at the Casino, and what do you encounter? A parcel of putty-headed young imbeciles, who trade lies about their friends and acquaintances with loose and drunken tongues . . . and finally, men of money only, who look money, think money, talk money, exude an auriferous atmosphere that makes you bilious by reflection. You talk art to them—they are silent; literature—they are dumb; statecraft and politics—they are dazed; you chat about the world and the people in it and they reply in spiritless phrases, culled from the guide books, under whose protection they have travelled." Another, three weeks later. "The Casino Ball produced another turn of the kaleidoscope. The same people attended it and the same general display of lavish bad taste was made. In spite of the fiat against the wearing of diamonds, there were some exhibitions whose vulgar profusion would have been worthy of Long Branch." Unprejudiced, even-handed reporting was out of the question in *Town Topics*. Colonel Mann had his daggers out with a vengeance for anyone with more power or money than himself, but along with his knives he also had his palm out. His judgment of people as morally reprehensible evidently blinded him to his own immorality in blackmailing them.

Last Gasp of the Gilded Age

The solemn extravagance of Newport's cottage culture under Mrs. Astor's control was destined to crumble, and as the Queen aged and lost touch with her minions, a new generation of ambitious women was plotting to seize the reins of society and lay down their more fun-loving rules of behavior. A decade before her death in 1908, Mrs. Astor remarked, "Many women will rise up to fill my place, but I hope my influence will be felt in one thing, and that is in discountenancing the undignified methods employed by certain women to attract a following." That did not happen. In fact, open giddy mayhem was the result, and her supremacy in society was directly challenged by three strong-willed doyennes who, each in her own way, set out to enliven the increasingly leaden atmosphere that developed during the portentous reign of Ward McAllister and Mrs. Astor.

Long before her parting, the Mystic Rose had jettisoned McAllister from her inner circle after he published his pompous and unbearably boring memoir *Society As I Have Found It* in 1890. The Four Hundred, fed up with his rigid and dull rules, followed suit with a sigh of relief. Until his death in 1895, McAllister was on the sidelines, his role of party organizer and top fop taken over by the Baltimore showman Harry Lehr, who, after swaying an amused Mrs. Astor (by daring to insult her jewelry in public saying she looked like a chandelier), went on to court the so-called Great Triumvirate of Mamie Fish, Alva Belmont, and Tessie Oelrichs, each of whom brought a new sense of liveliness and fun to Newport high society. Gone were the ghastly three-hour formal dinners with their absence of interesting talk, whether in French or English. In came Mamie Fish's festive, irreverent themed parties meant to be lighthearted and entertaining— and more American. Now that the upper perch was occupied not by one Olympian goddess but by three highly competitive, earthy women, any diversion that attracted attention and controversy became fair game. Newport became a social amusement park. They loved nothing more than to make fun of their more formal peers, insult one another, and behave in ways that Mrs. Astor would certainly have found demeaning to their class. But that was all part of the exuberance, and in their minds, the stuffy hierarchy that defined them was in need of resolute redefinition.

In a community as small as summer-colony Newport, everything—what one wore, how one behaved, who invited whom to what—was sharply scrutinized. As society let its hair down at the turn of

the century, the women who ruled Bellevue Avenue began to seek out novel, sometimes bizarre, ways of calling attention to themselves, which took imagination, nerve, and a hefty infusion of money. When one hostess threw a particularly dazzling and original ball, she raised the stakes for all the other ladies of the set to come up with a fete even more creative. These entertainments were not limited to weekends: Henry James reported that there could be as many as thirteen dinners on the same evening at the height of the season. One witnessed the same group of people night after night in different gowns and diamond-studded shirts under different roofs, all judging one another. "Women were the core of Newport society and certainly the fiercest competitors in the warfare for supremacy and recognition. As the stakes increased, the rivalry grew mercilessly intense. Women became entrapped within this distorted social reality, where every gesture and change of appearance was publicly scrutinized, and the struggles took their toll on the principal players. 'I know of no profession, art or trade that women are working in today as taxing on mental resource as being a leader of society,' said Alva Vanderbilt."

The pistons of the summer colony pumped with military-like precision and fixed routines were devoutly adhered to. From eleven to one, the elite mixed at the Casino or headed for Bailey's Beach for a dip in the ocean. Luncheons followed, and afternoons were devoted to sports and the never-ending necessity of calling on other members of the cohort, card case clutched in hand, deftly navigating the Avenue to leave as many personals as possible before returning home and changing clothes once again to be ready for the daily coaching spectacle. In *A Backward Glance*, Edith Wharton remembered the ritual.

> The regular afternoon diversion at Newport was a drive. Every day all the elderly ladies, leaning back in victoria or barouche, or the new-fangled *vis-à-vis*, a four-seated carriage with a rumble for the footman, drove down the whole length of Bellevue Avenue, where the most fashionable villas then stood, and around the newly laid-out "Ocean Drive," which skirted for several miles the wild rocky region between Narragansett bay [*sic*] and the Atlantic. For this drive it was customary to dress as elegantly as for a race-meeting at Auteuil or Ascot. A brocaded or satin-striped dress, powerfully whale-boned, a small flower-trimmed bonnet tied with a large tulle bow under chin, a dotted tulle veil and a fringed silk or velvet sunshade, sometimes with a jointed handle of elaborately carved ivory, composed what was thought a suitable toilet for this daily circuit between wilderness and waves.

After yet another change of clothing, the evening entertainments would begin around eight o'clock; many of the balls lasted until dawn, with the hostess serving breakfast before her exhausted guests departed. Then the cycle of events would repeat itself. No wonder the conversation was often insipid. With the relentless pursuit of pleasure and the pressure to be seen everywhere, many in the colony looked forward to the day the season came to an end so they could retreat to a less-hectic pace in the big city. As so many contemporary writers pointed out, these people worked at play with the same vigor and intensity that they brought to competing in games or in business. Fully living the good life in the decades before World War I was not easy.

As America entered the twentieth century, high society was in flux as never before. Change was everywhere, along with growth, and the center could not hold for the simple reason that there were too many people to command. The assault on the bastions of privilege by the swarming, unpedigreed, newly rich created a pulsing dynamic as more people sought status and inclusion in the lofty ranks. For several decades, the moral authority of Mrs. Astor had kept the upper crust intact, but by 1900 the younger generation was rebelling against her outmoded concepts of propriety. Expansion was everywhere. Newport was being challenged for its title of *the* American resort by Southampton, Tuxedo Park, Bar Harbor, and other pleasure centers. People of new wealth, who had either been snubbed in Newport or disliked its stringent value system, created their own meccas and regarded Newport as a decaying dinosaur, out of sync with emerging tastes. As society splintered, diverse groups claimed bragging rights to other spas, and the breakdown of the Knickerbocker aristocracy, in New York and Newport, became a fait accompli. The social compass was askew, its needle bouncing between distant points. The historian Eric Homberger writes, "After a long stay in Paris, Frederick Townsend Martin returned to New York in 1907. He found society greatly changed. It was more selfish, indifferent, bored, and discontented. . . . The pace of change and dissolution had taken on a frightening momentum." The Four Hundred was history, the "list" almost an embarrassment. Authority had vanished. "After Mrs. Astor," Martin remarked, "there was chaos." Mamie Fish, when asked about the successor to Mrs. Astor, boldly stated: "There is no leader of society. It's too large to manage."

Mamie Fish knew of what she spoke. She was a leader in usurping Mrs. Astor's Napoleonic hold on the nobility, and Newport was her battleground as much as New York. Born Marian Anthon in 1853, she was the daughter of a respected attorney in Manhattan and grew up on Irving Place. Not well-educated but intelligent, Mamie was quick and energetic and had the verve to do things her own way. Her marriage to Stuyvesant Fish in 1876 put her in the first rank of New York society because his lineage could be traced back to the Livingston, Schuyler, and Beekman families; his father, Hamilton Fish, was an influential secretary of state under President Ulysses S. Grant. Unlike so many of her peers, Mamie Fish's marriage was a happy one, even though Stuyvesant spent little time in Newport, preferring instead their estate on the Hudson River at Garrison, New York.

His absence, however, didn't hold her back from becoming one of the dominant, and most colorful, hostesses in town. She rented for a number of years, but after building the imposing white-columned Crossways on Ocean Drive in 1898, Mamie Fish went into high gear as a party-giver, and each year she hosted at least one large, memorable fete. With a little help from her amiable court jester Harry Lehr, Mamie Fish presented some of the most outlandish entertainments the town had ever witnessed and surely ones that Mrs. Astor would have frowned upon. But they were irreverent, fun, and people flocked to her parties with anticipation because they were so different from the predictable ball. While her partners in what became known as Newport's "Social Strategy Board," Tessie Oelrichs and Alva Vanderbilt Belmont, gave grand parties themselves, Mamie Fish's were the ones remembered and talked about years afterward. Disdainful of the strict limitations imposed by her class, she invited people from many social strata, including entertainers, actresses, plus other celebrities and notables passing through town, who would probably not have been asked to most Bellevue Avenue homes.

Mamie Fish was a character. She loathed the fact that society had become so hidebound, and she set out to break down the barriers. Wallace Davies writes that "Instead of the customary two- or three-hour dinners, she introduced the fifty-minute dinner, at which footmen served food as if it were a race; a second's pause, and guests found their plates removed. Instead of a different wine for each course, she had champagne served throughout." She delighted in insulting people just for the shock value. One of her favorite lines to her arriving guests was: "Make yourselves at home. And believe me, there's no one who wishes you were there more than I do." According to Cleveland Amory, "With other members of Newport's Great Triumvirate Mrs. Fish feuded with equal aplomb. One day at the Newport Casino Mrs. Belmont swept up to her. 'I have just heard what you said about me at Tessie Oelrichs' last night. You cannot deny it, Mamie, because Tessie told me herself. You told everybody I looked like a frog.' Mrs. Fish was alarmed. 'No, no,' she said. 'Not a frog! A toad, my pet, a *toad.*'" She was a breath of satiric steamy air blowing through an otherwise stuffy setting and, with each prank, she became more notorious, more outrageous, and more adored.

When bored, which was often, Mamie Fish and Harry Lehr lit upon schemes to shock their stodgy companions. Among the more memorable of her parties in Crossways' two ballrooms was a grand celebration for one Prince del Drago. Guests were a-twitter over being able to meet a European dignity, and eagerly anticipated his arrival from the rooms above. What appeared was a monkey in full formal attire, which, after consuming too much of Mrs. Fish's champagne, jumped onto the chandelier and proceeded to pelt the assembled crowd with lightbulbs. Another famous soirée was held to introduce the Grand Duke Boris of Russia to Newport society but, because of a spat with Mrs. Ogden Goelet, who was the duke's host, his eminence would not be able to attend the Fish gathering. Undeterred, Mamie went on with her party for two hundred, letting her surprised company know that the real guest of honor was no less than the czar himself. Anxiously awaiting the big moment, the crowd grew silent. Mrs. Fish bowed regally when the introduction was made. The women began to curtsey as a splendidly dressed gentleman was revealed and took Mrs. Fish's arm. It was Harry Lehr, decked out in Russian finery, and the entire party broke into laughter. Mamie Fish did not need the real duke; she supplied her own tonic. With Lehr again, Mamie concocted the ridiculous Dogs Dinner, where scores of canines, many dressed in proper formal wraps, feasted on liver, rice, and fricassee of bones at a lowered table while the humans looked on with amused, and confused, attention. She hosted an annual Harvest Moon ball, where guests arrived in rustic farmers' outfits. But she is best remembered for her 1913 Mother Goose ball, to which all the company came attired in handmade costumes drawn from characters in nursery rhymes. Mamie herself was fully clad as Mother Goose.

The town had never harbored the likes of her. When she died at Garrison in 1915 at the age of sixty-one, a sorceress of magic was stolen from Newport. Wallace Davies eulogizes her: "To some her death marked the end of an era of elaborate dinner parties and balls in private homes, but more often she was regarded as a disintegrating force who had broken down any lingering tradition of an exclusive 'Four Hundred,' whose antics had made society look absurd, and who therefore prepared the way for the Jazz Age, café society, Elsa Maxwell, and the international jet set."

Mrs. Astor's staid order was breaking down in other ways as well. The third member of the triumvirate was Alva Vanderbilt Belmont, mistress of Marble House and Belcourt. She proved to be one of the more original and colorful leaders in society for half a century. Alva was a trendsetter, a woman who challenged conventions as tenaciously as Mamie Fish. Born Alva Smith in Mobile, Alabama, in 1853, she was familiar with Newport from her childhood days. When she married William K. Vanderbilt in 1875, it was deemed the great social event of the year and she was seen as being just another society lady who would uphold the values of the clan and keep her thoughts to herself. Nothing of the kind materialized. Opinionated and sure of herself, she forced Mrs. Astor to accept her in 1883, rose to prominence for her grand balls, and conquered Newport with the building of Marble House.

But being a society leader did not stop Alva Vanderbilt from committing the gravest transgression of all: after years of bickering and unhappiness, she divorced Willie K. in 1895. It shocked her set. That was simply *not done*. Alva didn't care. She was more concerned with her own well-being than with what others thought of her, and although members of the Vanderbilt family dropped her, the rest of the New York and Newport privileged stayed by her side. She was too powerful to snub. Then she really scandalized the elite when she married Oliver H. P. Belmont in January 1896, closed Marble House, and moved across the street to her new husband's mansion, Belcourt. Five years her junior, Belmont and Alva reportedly sustained a happy marriage until his death in 1908.

Alva Belmont broke the rules, got away with it, and other distressed marriages began to dissolve after her daring breach of decorum. Yet her quest for personal happiness did not stop her from ruining her eldest daughter's desires. Eighteen-year-old Consuelo Vanderbilt was a beauty and had numerous American suitors, one of whom she was deeply in love with. Alva would have none of it because she was determined that

Artist unknown
Alva Vanderbilt,
c. 20th century
Oil on canvas
An unsigned
20th century copy of
a vanished original
attributed to
Benjamin Curtis Porter.
Courtesy of the
Preservation Society
of Newport County
Newport, Rhode Island

Consuelo would marry into the English aristocracy. According to Michael Strange (born Blanche Oelrichs), who was a young woman at the time and later became a famous actress and the wife of John Barrymore, "Newport was becoming the elite hunting ground for titled bachelors in search of a beautiful wife with a fortune, and many attractive gentlemen were to be seen writing their names down at the Casino as soon as it opened, and having their pictures taken in groups on the porches of fashionable boarding houses for wider circulation." Jon Sterngass writes, "At least nine women from Newport society married peers of the British realm, most of whom they had met at Newport summer parties. When Gertrude Vanderbilt actually married the American-born Harry Whitney at the Breakers in 1896, the band excitedly struck up the 'Star-Spangled Banner' after the usual compositions by Wagner and Mendelssohn."

Alva and Consuelo had been introduced to Charles Spencer-Churchill, the ninth Duke of Marlborough, in the spring of 1895 in London and Alva was convinced he was the right match for her daughter. Consuelo wanted nothing to do with the duke; she wanted the young man with whom she was in love. But after a good deal of family wrangling in England, the duke came to America in the summer and was invited to Newport in order to seal a marriage pact. Despite Consuelo's pleas, Alva forced the engagement, which was announced in September at a large ball. The duke, who had negotiated a $10 million dowry with Willie K. the previous evening, looked pleased. Consuelo, who reportedly cried through the night while her father and future husband bandied numbers, looked distraught. It was a business deal, pure and simple. Consuelo endured eleven years of boredom at Blenheim, and then Alva, admitting she had forced her daughter into a dreadful union to satisfy her own lust for aristocratic association, relented and let Consuelo seek an annulment in 1906. She would later divorce the duke and have the freedom to marry a man of her own choosing, the French nobleman Jacques Balsan, and live her remaining years in France.

Throughout the marriage to Belmont, Alva entertained regularly and cemented her position in a society that was changing faster than anyone liked to admit. After Oliver Belmont's death, however, Alva needed new distractions and threw herself into rounds of charity work, which opened her eyes to the need for broad social reform throughout American society. She became deeply involved with the women's suffrage movement for the rest of her life, giving both a good part of her fortune and time to the cause. Militant feminism was just another stage in her life, which was marked by many firsts. In 1909, she opened the doors of Marble House for the first time in years and invited numerous feminist organizations for meetings. In 1921, Mrs. Belmont was elected president of the National Woman's Party and even traveled abroad to represent American women's groups at international gatherings.

Widowed, engaged in social reform, Alva Belmont had retreated from Newport by 1914, but she would never be forgotten. She moved to France, where she died in 1933, feisty and independent to the end.

Newport was physically and culturally transformed by the Gilded Age and, at the same time, the Queen of Resorts left its stamp on the era like no other small community in the country. Newport became the litmus test for defining the period's excesses, its trivialities, its architectural triumphs, and at the same time, it was the stage upon which a large number of the most powerful and influential people in America trod year after year, creating a tableau of the nation's leading players. Presidents, foreign ambassadors by the dozen, and statesmen all mingled with the industrial titans who supplied the muscle and the money that moved America forward. Newport was a laboratory of history, still a lively experiment, a place to work out the kinks of the rising imperialism that defined the nation's role in the twentieth century. In a period of immense change, America emerged as a global power, rich and growing and finally ready to assert its position among nations. When Archduke Francis Ferdinand of Austria was assassinated in Sarajevo on June 18, 1914, by a Serbian nationalist, setting off World War I, America was more than ready militarily to join the conflagration; only its isolationist politicians prevented an early entry. By the end of the Great War, with Europe staggering from destruction, the United States was acknowledged as an equal partner in the international arena, ascendant, purposeful, and more than able to use its strengths to its own advantage.

The nation's might was a direct result of the vast wealth accumulated in the decades between the Civil War and World War I. Although those hundreds of millions of dollars were not made in Newport, they were certainly displayed there, in the cottages, the furnishings, the entertainments, the sports, the yachts, and the jewelry. The press rarely got a glimpse of what upper-crust Fifth Avenue town houses looked like; Newport was what the world got to know about America's powerful leaders: the lawns and gardens along Bellevue Avenue highlighting the enormous mansions set apart by fences and gates. Even the lavish interiors were on display in leading magazines. In the end, Newport was more than just a playground for high society: it was a panoramic picture window onto American fantasies of what was possible, of what could be. That was a big role for such a small city. Jon Sterngass posits, "The trends initiated in Newport at the turn of the century—conspicuous consumption, marriage with titled Europeans, lionization of athletes—made the city a transitional order between the haut monde of the Gilded Age and the twentieth-century cult of personality and spectacle."

Early warning signs of the demise of the Gilded Age are easier to spot now, of course, than they could have been at the time. Even with the deteriorating state relationships in Europe, no one could have guessed of the coming carnage. The tempo of Newport kept pulsing, the festivities went on, even after John Jacob Astor and George D. Widener went down with the *Titanic* in April 1912. That summer, Eleanor Robson Belmont, a beautiful actress (and favorite of George Bernard Shaw) who was married to August Belmont, Jr., staged a lawn party for hundreds that featured the escape artist Ehrich Weiss, better known as Harry Houdini, performing his amazing stunts. His grand finale was freeing himself, after having been tied in ropes, locked in an iron box, and lowered into the sea from Belmont's yacht while J. P. Morgan and the German ambassador to the United States, among others, anxiously looked on. A minute later, he was on the surface, and the party, which was followed by an elaborate dinner at Mamie Fish's, was pronounced a great success. For Newport's privileged class, the world appeared as magical as Houdini's death-defying diversions.

Less than a year after the Belmont party, Morgan was dead. The Age of Indulgence was waning. In 1913, Congress put the final touches on the Sixteenth Amendment, its legislation enacting a national graduated income tax; that law would severely curtail the economic extravagances so prominent throughout the Gilded Age and have a direct and stifling bearing on the future of the owners of Henry James's "white elephants" in Newport. Then came the outbreak of hostilities in Europe. The known world was besieged by loss.

On July 24, 1914, less than a month before Europe became engulfed in mortar fire and the world was pounded into pandemonium by what was naively labeled the War to End All Wars, Mrs. Alva Belmont staged a final going-away party for the Gilded Age, although no one knew the end was so near. Alva, always fascinated with architecture, had built a Chinese teahouse on the grounds of Marble House, designed by Richard Hunt, Jr., the son of Richard Morris Hunt. It was an odd addition to the grounds, but then Alva often did odd things, so few of her friends were surprised.

The *New York Times* correspondent covering the fete described it best.

The Chinese costume ball given at Marble House tonight for the Duchess of Marlborough by her mother, Mrs. Oliver H. P. Belmont, and the dinner before the ball given by Mrs. Stuyvesant Fish at Crossways for Mrs. Belmont, were lavish affairs, and marked the opening of a long list of entertainments. . . . Supper was served under the trees on the north side of the lawn, reached from the terrace [of Marble House] and beneath coverings, where the trees were hung with hundreds of Chinese lanterns and decorated with palms and Chinese flowers. . . . The exterior of the new Chinese teahouse over the cliffs and sea was brilliantly illuminated, electric wires having been connected with the bronze lanterns wrought in China more than a thousand years ago and requiring years to complete the collection of thirty. Electric wires strung through the trees transformed the gravelled walk from Marble House to the Chinese pagoda into a moonlit lane of beauty.

Farewell, epoch of opulence. Adieu, Newport's fabled follies.

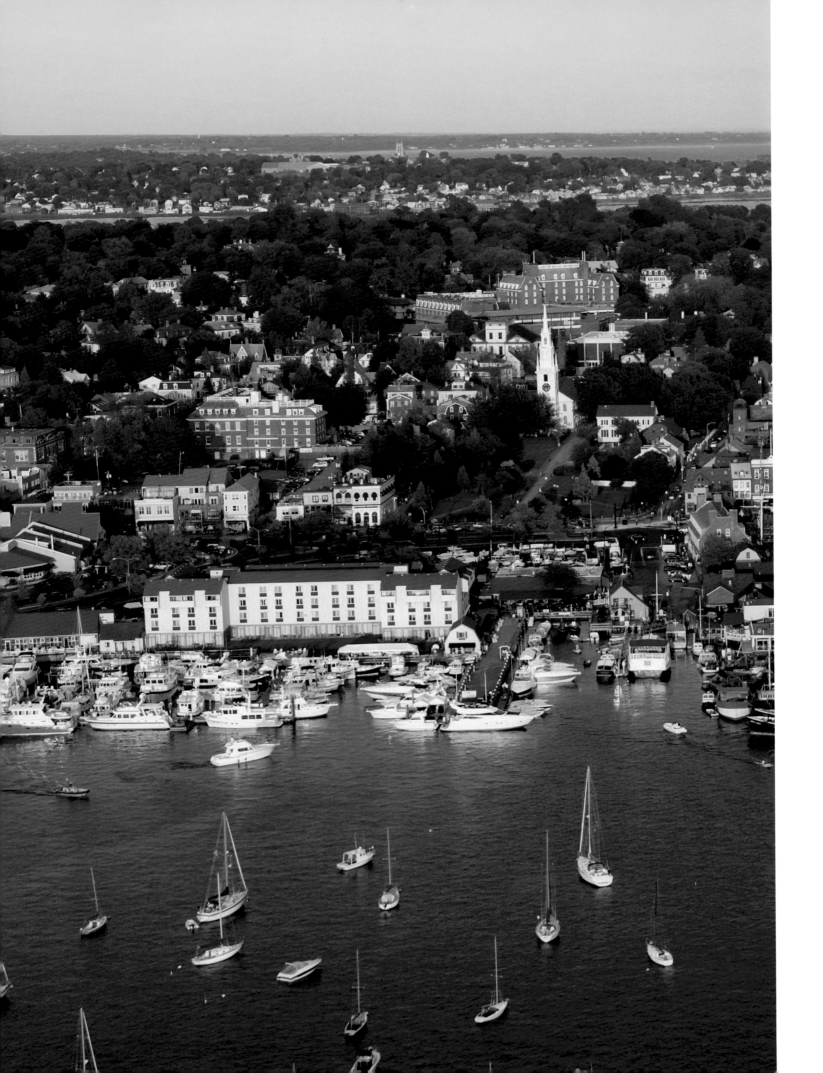

The Grand Revival

9

Facing the Future

Like so many other small cities in America, Newport rode out the roller-coaster twentieth century of devastating world wars, economic depression, and the Cold War with guarded apprehension. It shrank in size, ballooned during years of combat, and found its equilibrium, its roots, when peace prevailed.

Aerial view of Newport harbor (detail), 1994
Photograph by Onne van der Wal Photography Inc.

A new era was dawning in 1914. The town was searching for a new identity after its starring role as Queen of Resorts receded in importance as the Gilded Age ran its course. Newport became more egalitarian, more democratic, as one by one a large number of Bellevue Avenue cottages were shuttered or divided into apartments and the clout of the elite ebbed. Income taxes, the growing expense of keeping all the staff on call, global uncertainty: all contributed to the retreat of the mansion culture. Wars and financial deprivation are enemies of the romantic summer resort, and Newport discovered it needed to find creative ways to redefine itself once again if it were to prosper under rapidly evolving social and economic conditions.

Unlike other small American cities that attempted to reinvent themselves as times and tastes changed, Newport had only to search out its past to discover a path to the future. It had a golden asset. The city possessed a solid core of buildings from the colonial era onward that had survived the ravages of time and the wrecking ball and stood neglected, awaiting care and restoration. During the American Revolution the British tore down hundreds of structures, but the majority of them were shacks and unimportant houses that would have been swept away later. What the invaders left standing was the splendid evidence of a vibrant and wealthy colonial town, and throughout the nineteenth century these buildings held their ground even while deteriorating into eyesores. But the crucial element is this: while countless other municipalities scampered after modernity by sweeping away the past, most of Newport's structures were not razed as the Industrial Revolution swept over the land. *That* transformation largely passed Newport by.

When styles shifted dramatically in the Gilded Age, the influx of great affluence allowed for more lavish displays, and the town's heritage was simply ignored. Did the privileged frolickers, with their focus on sumptuous new castles and comforts, really care about the old colonial culture? No. Somehow, it is difficult to imagine Mrs. Astor wandering around the Point, surrounded by seventeenth- and eighteenth-century houses. One can thank Alfred Smith for opening Bellevue Avenue and Ocean Drive for building cottages;

when someone wanted a new house, he or she didn't have to tear down existing structures in the heart of town but could instead buy an empty lot on the southern tip. At that time, the *absence* of what became known in the mid-twentieth century as urban renewal saved Newport. Thus today the town contains some of the most striking examples of varied architecture found on American soil, a virtual showcase of how the country's aesthetic and domestic tastes matured. All that was needed to bring back Newport's glory was the vision and the will to restore the hundreds of colonial buildings, and some of its Gilded Age treasures, so visitors from around the world could experience a living museum of American architecture. That movement wouldn't begin in earnest until the mid-1940s, but once under way, the original soul of Newport elegantly emerged.

In 1914, however, a different kind of transformation was beginning with the golden shimmering summer all but shattered by the slaughter in Europe. Harbingers of destruction were all around when Germany, under Kaiser Wilhelm II, sided with Austria-Hungary in the Serbian dispute, formed the Central Powers, and declared war on both Russia and France in August 1914. The German army invaded neutral Belgium on its way toward France, and that brought Great Britain into the conflict to counter Wilhelm's aggression. Many observers believed it would be a short and decisive set-to, with the Allies prevailing, and they, of course, were wrong. World War I raged, mostly on French soil, for over four years, leaving between twelve and fourteen million dead, spawning the communist Russian Revolution, and opening the path to Adolf Hitler and Nazism in the following decades. When the United States entered the struggle against Germany on April 6, 1917, after years of guarded isolationism, it did so with reluctance but with the authority of a new industrial and military power in the global arena.

In Newport, the onset of the Great War brought about the virtual suspension of the summer colony's large-scale entertaining. Everything became more subdued as it dawned on citizens that the bloody battles were not going to end soon. But volunteerism among the wealthy began in earnest when the Van Alen family and Mr. and Mrs. William K. Vanderbilt aided the American Field Service by sending ambulances to the front to rescue French and British wounded. Committees helping relief agencies became more popular than the August ball. Throughout America sentiment to remain neutral was strong at first, but with news of trench-warfare stalemates, a majority in Newport openly shifted their sympathies to the Allied cause. And then, less than a year after the war had begun, it abruptly came home to Newport. Alfred G. Vanderbilt, whose sprawling estate at Oakland Farm in Portsmouth was a favorite meeting ground for summer-colony residents, was killed. He drowned when a German submarine sadistically sank the unarmed commercial British ocean liner *Lusitania* off the Irish coast on May 7, 1915, killing nearly 2,000 people, including 128 Americans. Outrage against Germany rose quickly, while Newporters mourned the death of the thirty-eight-year-old horse breeder. He was remembered by the town for his generous financial support in building the YMCA on Mary Street, as well as other philanthropic gestures.

Throughout 1915 and 1916, Newporters read the daily dispatches from the European front with increasing concern. The Marne, Gallipoli, Verdun, the Somme: names soaked in blood. Anti-German sentiments were rampant, particularly in Anglophile Yankee New England. Activity at the Torpedo Station on Goat Island and at the Naval Training Station increased. In Washington, President Woodrow Wilson urged diplomatic solutions to end the hostilities, but the guns in Europe kept unleashing their salvos. It was becoming patently evident that the United States would have to intercede on behalf of the Allies to bring the conflict to an end, yet the antiwar outlook still ran high in the nation.

Then, one peaceful autumn Saturday in 1916, the German submarine *U-53* surfaced in Newport harbor. A front-page article in the *Newport Mercury* on October 14 describes the initial reaction.

> The news of the arrival of the German spread like wildfire about the city, and a large number of shore boats quickly surrounded her. It was at first supposed that she was the Bremen, until her identity was revealed, not as a peaceful merchantman, but as one of the latest and largest type of war submarines. . . . Visitors were allowed on board the vessel as she lay in the harbor, and were shown every courtesy. . . . The submarine remained in the harbor but a little over three hours, getting under way at 5:17. She proceeded at good speed on the surface of the water until off Brenton's Reef lightship when she submerged and was lost to view.

The purported reason for the surprise visit was to mail a letter to the German ambassador in Washington, and while still in the harbor, the U-boat's captain was called on by two United States Navy admirals who were at the War College. Everyone was respectful and ceremonial.

The carnage began soon thereafter. On Sunday morning, reports flooded into the Torpedo Station's wireless that ships had been sunk. *U-53* was stopping merchant vessels, ordering all passengers to take to their lifeboats, then torpedoing the mother ship outside the three-mile territorial boundary just east of the Nantucket Shoals lightship. Four British ships, one Dutch, and one Norwegian met their fate within hours. In Newport, the navy ordered its vessels out to the area to rescue survivors, and for the next twenty-four hours American ships patrolled the waters, eventually picking up over two hundred people, many of them women and children. The *Mercury* article goes on: "The fleet of destroyers that had gone to the rescue began to arrive back in the harbor with the refugees shortly after midnight Sunday night, and every effort was

German Submarine U-53 in Newport harbor on October 7, 1916 which subsequently attacked allied ships off the U. S. east coast.

photographer unknown

U. S. Naval Historical Center

made to care for those who needed shelter. A number of the homes of summer residents were opened to them, including those of Mrs. French Vanderbilt, Mrs. Beeckman and others, while the greater part of the rescued were disposed of at the Government stations."

Since America was still neutral, the navy was hamstrung. "In one instance two destroyers were on hand when a ship was torpedoed by the German but were unable to take any action to prevent it, as the captain was apparently acting strictly in accordance with international law. All that they could do was to stand by and pick up the crew as they took to their boats." After leaving behind its long trail of devastation, *U-53* silently slipped beneath the surface and disappeared.

Newport was outraged by the wanton destruction of Allied property after it had chivalrously received the submarine in the harbor. That act and subsequent ship sinkings just off the East Coast aroused intense hostility toward Germany and were instrumental in President Wilson's decision to demand that Congress declare war the following April, announcing "The world must be made safe for democracy." Newport harbor had been visited by pirate ships, the British and French fleets during the Revolution, and now a marauding and deadly U-boat. For many Newporters, America's challenge in World War I began on that soft sunny Sunday in October 1916.

Throughout 1917 and 1918, the streets of Newport teemed with military personnel on various missions; the pace of the city was so altered that vacationing visitors hardly recognized the place. As the war effort engulfed Newport, the teeter-totter relationship between the Bellevue Avenue beau monde and the rest of town began to shift. The summer colony, which so forcefully ruled throughout the Gilded Age, partly receded from view, while thousands of sailors, soldiers, and laborers surged into town. Because of the extensive presence of the United States Navy, Newport quickly went on war footing after the April 1917 declaration of war. Employment at the Torpedo Station skyrocketed, the Naval Training Station was overwhelmed by volunteers, Fort Adams became packed with Army recruits, and the housing crisis proved so severe that all private residents were asked to take in the young recruits on a provisional basis. Bellevue Avenue mansions became home for scores of men, fields of tents arose at Fort Adams and on Coasters Harbor Island to take care of the overflow, and new barracks were hastily erected on Coddington Point and in Cloyne Field. The patriotic response to President Wilson's call to arms engulfed Newport for two years.

Other activities highlighted the new realities. With the fresh memory of *U-53* surfacing in the harbor, entrances to Narragansett Bay were closed entirely after dark and only the opening to Newport harbor could be used at all because nets had been strung across all other inlets and attack boats patrolled the bay full-time. Over two hundred special policemen, known as the Newport Constabulary, took to the streets. The Red Cross, under the enthusiastic guidance of Mrs. French Vanderbilt, Mrs. Livingston Beeckman, and Mrs. Arthur Curtiss James, greatly increased its ranks with volunteers and prepared for the care of patients at home and on the battlefield. Newport historian Eileen Warburton recounts, "The Civic League, the Ladies Auxiliary of the YMCA, the Girls' Friendly Society, the Girls Patriotic League, and the Charities Organization combined to organize the volunteer-run Home Hospitality, which matched interested servicemen with rooms in town, the various Sunday evening open houses, and the services of the churches, YMCA, and other agencies. The

Presbyterian Church and the parish of Trinity were open for socializing every night of the week, as were the rooms of the two Masonic chapters and the Father Mathew Temperance Society."

In short, Newport became highly focused on the task of defeating the Central Powers. A war of this scope had not been encountered before, yet for all the overcrowding and inconveniences and food shortages, the town absorbed the shock of the modern mechanized world with grace. In the year and a half America was involved in the European engagement, over 75,000 young men received training with the Naval Reserves in Newport. Thousands of them requested immediate duty and were deployed in ships worldwide. Over 2,100 Newporters registered for the army draft and many of them saw action in France after their basic training was completed.

But it was the navy that dominated the town. Because the Germans so effectively employed their submarines to disrupt Allied shipping of manpower and materiel to the front, the role of the Torpedo Station on Goat Island took on real urgency. Construction of new buildings and the manufacturing of torpedoes and particularly depth charges pushed the manpower on the island from about 300 before the war to a height of 3,300 at the time of the Armistice. Working three eight-hour shifts, seven days a week, the Station produced over seventy thousand Mark II depth charges for the navy to deploy against the considerable German threat. Women were particularly important in the bomb-making process because, with their smaller hands, they were quicker and more agile at producing the delicate and intricate timing devices that detonated the charges. The critical role played by the Newport Torpedo Station in the Allied victory cannot be overstated. When the United States entered the war, Britain and France had nearly exhausted their military supplies, to say nothing of their morale. Certainly American soldiers were instrumental in the defeat of Germany, with its vast Ruhr Valley producing weapons nonstop, but it was American guns, ammunition, and industrial muscle that turned the tide and drove the Germans to surrender. All of that hardware had to be shipped across the U-boat infested Atlantic, and without the depth charges, bombs, and torpedoes produced in Newport to counter their offensive, the conflict might have drawn out for a longer time.

Given the danger involved in making all those deadly instruments, it is remarkable that numerous fatal accidents didn't occur at the Torpedo Station. Only one serious incident was recorded during the war years. In late January 1918, twelve men were killed and six seriously injured when they were mixing fulminate of mercury used in loading detonators. Most likely, a spark set the brew off. The explosion occurred in a below-ground, bomb-proof bunker designed to protect the rest of the facility in case of just such an accident. The *Mercury* reported, "To those who did hear [the blast], the noise sounded like the firing of a big gun, but being followed closely by the sounding of the Torpedo Station fire alarm, it was realized that a disaster had occurred. In consequence there was a great flocking of people to the Government Landing, the crowd being composed largely of relatives of men and women employed there, who were naturally very anxious to learn the extent of the disaster and the effect upon their friends there." Even with the threat of another explosion, rescuers rushed to the scene to aid their fellow-workers. It took hours to clear the mangled bodies from the site and restore production. Thus twelve more Newport citizens joined Alfred Vanderbilt as civilian casualties of the war, and now the bodies of Newport's dead soldiers were returning from the front too.

At the time of the Torpedo Station tragedy, Mother Nature was weighing in with the coldest winter on record until that time. Temperatures plunged well below zero for days on end, icing over large

parts of the bay and making shipping nearly impossible. The Jamestown ferries were locked in port, and ice in the harbor was over eight inches thick. By constantly running ships to the Torpedo Station and back to the Government Landing, sailors were able to keep a lane open to transport workers and supplies, but there was widespread anxiety that the Station would become isolated, curtailing the production of the badly needed explosive devices. Coal was scarce since fuel boats couldn't reach Newport, so the city fathers mandated the closing of all retail businesses on Mondays to conserve their modest resources. Military recruits in crude huts and tents had the hardest time of it; newspapers reported on their suffering for days on end. For two months, it was as if Newport had reverted to the days of its occupation by the British army during the Revolution: an uncertain war, bitter cold, fear, and death.

Throughout the remainder of 1918, Newport resembled an armed compound, with fresh recruits filling the town each month, then shipping out for service. Newporters had become so accustomed to the yearly rhythms of the Gilded Age—three months of frenetic summer activity followed by nine months of hibernation—that the constant invasion of so many eager young men changed their patterns as well. Nearly everyone who wanted employment could find it, with munitions workers leading the list. Stores did nonstop business, so owners' ordering routines changed. Although liquor was banned in town by the navy, a steady business in illicit spirits kept a number of Aquidneck Islanders quite busy with their stills and rum running, honing their skills for Prohibition, which was just around the corner. Eating habits also altered. Sugar was scarce for months, and the town instituted beefless and porkless days for the war's duration to save those rations for soldiers overseas. Many things people had become accustomed to in peacetime simply vanished, like the summer colony, during the hostilities. And, as a symbolic sign of the times, Rogers High School ceased teaching German and offered Spanish instead.

Then, at 3:45 a.m. on Monday, November 11, 1918, Newport was flooded with the sound of victory. The *Newport Daily News* ran a banner headline: "ALL NEWPORT CELEBRATES END OF THE GREAT WAR. Whistles Blow, Bells Ring and Crowds Parade the Streets." The reporter began, "Newport celebrated Germany's signing of the armistice terms in royal fashion. It was a spontaneous celebration and thus all the more an expression of the feelings of the community." Mayor Clark Burdick had given the order to the fire department that when news of peace came across the wireless, they were to sound their alarms throughout the city, regardless of the time of day or night. Hearing the clamor, thousands of residents arose, hastily dressed, and headed for the heart of town. The *Mercury* takes up the story: "In almost no time a large throng had assembled on Washington Square and a wild time followed. The Municipal Band was on the job, playing patriotic and popular airs, and the men, women and children joined in marching about the Square. . . . A parade was started down Thames street [*sic*], and practically all the people on the Square of all ages joined in behind the band, giving the serpentine march, and shouting at the tops of their voices, while various noise-making instruments were called into use." School was cancelled, to the delight of the children, and not much work was done once it sunk in that on the eleventh hour of the eleventh day of the eleventh month of 1918, in Compiègne, France, the Germans had finally capitulated to the Allied Forces. Newport was festooned with flags and bunting, people decorated their automobiles, and impromptu parades erupted all over town for the rest of the day. World War I was over. The men and women, soldiers, sailors, nurses, ambulance drivers, were coming home.

But not all of them. Rhode Island contributed some 28,800 to the war effort, and 612 of them were killed in action or by the rampant Spanish influenza that swept through the crowded camps. Newport sacrificed 72 men on the fields of France or at sea, mostly youngsters in their teens or early twenties. A memorial in their honor, a 65-foot fieldstone tower in Miantonomi Park, was dedicated in August 1929.

Prohibition and the Roaring Twenties

World War I was a major milestone in America's maturity into global eminence. Europe was in economic ruins, its authority on the wane; a whole generation of British, French, and German youth had been decimated, and in the end, little had been determined. Continental borders were redrawn, the Ottoman Empire was obliterated with the Middle East cut up into colonial fiefdoms, and all eyes focused on the unfolding drama in Bolshevik Russia. The rise of socialism and communism signaled that another major struggle would be at hand in the not-distant future. Europe was embroiled in a re-run of the French and Indian wars of previous centuries: one conflict leading not to resolution, but to the next conflagration. Only the United States emerged relatively unscathed from the Great War, flexing its newfound muscle at the peace negotiations at Versailles, where President Wilson pushed his Fourteen Points and argued for the creation of the League of Nations as a forum for peace. For a short time, optimism reigned and much of the civilized world wanted to believe, naively, that World War I had brought an end to nationalistic uprisings.

The men and women returning from Europe were greeted with a rapidly evolving America. Peace brought prosperity and proved to be the progenitor for a decade of expansion, speculative spending, rapid stock market growth, and societal experimentation. The giddy Roaring Twenties were at hand, serving up new dances like the Charleston, along with bootleg booze and bathtub gin. The Jazz Age, as chronicled by F. Scott Fitzgerald and his peers, ushered in a new era and marked a further breakdown of staid old societal rules as stylish young women known as flappers bobbed their hair, took to the dance floor, and smoked cigarettes on the street, flaunting their independence.

The United States Congress was mandating substantive revisions in the legal rights of citizens by adopting two amendments to the Constitution that had a direct effect on all Americans. Passage of the Eighteenth Amendment in 1919, known as the Volstead Act, created Prohibition and banned alcoholic beverages in the nation. Until its repeal in 1933, Americans of all segments of society engaged in illicit measures to obtain liquor, and the takeover of the bootlegging industry by the Mafia led to the rise of Al Capone and other shady characters. For most people, Prohibition was a futile experiment in human engineering and was deemed to have been a miserable failure. The other change had longer-lasting consequences. In 1920, after decades of struggle, the Nineteenth Amendment passed Congress, granting nationwide voting rights to women. Alva Vanderbilt Belmont and her fellow crusaders had finally won the battle for full suffrage. According to the *Daily News*, 3,826 Newport women registered to vote that year and most participated in the 1920 presidential election that carried Warren G. Harding to the White House.

In Newport, the greatest transformation was the rapid downsizing of Torpedo Station personnel to less than nine hundred workers. The thousands of military recruits were gone as well and the town settled back into its accustomed rhythms. In the summer of 1919, a large contingent of the summer colony returned, opened their houses, and reignited the social ritual of leaving calling cards and meeting at their old haunts. But much had changed. The daily coaching routine along Bellevue Avenue was gone as automobiles replaced horses for most people. The Casino had lost its cachet. The war and income taxes dampened the spirits of the belle époque: parties were now smaller, quieter, more subdued. There were, however, still over 225 active cottage estates in Newport proper. The majority of them were busy every summer of the 1920s, and society pages across the country still rippled with the names of prominent players and their famous guests.

But with the shuttering of a number of large cottages, there were fewer employment opportunities for the more established Fifth Ward Irish servants and maids, and almost none at all for the newly arrived Greek, Italian, and Portuguese immigrants (most of whom gravitated to fishing, other maritime pursuits, and agriculture). From the earliest times, Newport had been a nucleus for the very rich, and even after the Gilded Age dissolved, the town harbored a large number of wealthy homeowners. Still, the city was slowly shedding some of its exclusive upper-crust credentials and becoming more middle class, more like the rest of the nation. While most Americans still perceived the city as a moneyed man's haven and the press kept spewing forth articles about life on Bellevue Avenue, the reality was becoming something else. The rich paid the highest taxes and continued to lend luster to Newport, but inexorably the town was evolving into a major port-of-call for the United States Navy. For the next half century, the city displayed an almost schizoid persona as more sailors took over the streets while the swell set settled into a more languid lassitude.

The city was also evolving in other directions. Since the 1880s, the West Broadway and Kerry Hill area had been heavily built up with stand-alone wooden frame dwellings that housed hundreds of Irish settlers, new immigrants from Europe, and much of Newport's long-time black community of skilled craftsmen, professionals, and domestics. The Fifth Ward, in the southern district, attracted a large number of newcomers from the British Isles. By the 1920s, the Italian population was swelling rapidly, adding variety to the rich Catholic traditions begun by the Irish in the 1840s. Swedes, French Canadians, and Chinese were moving into various neighborhoods, working in commerce and at the harbor. The Southern Thames Street area in particular attracted a varied working-class mix of arrivals (dominated by the Irish) including French, Germans, Norwegians, Russians, and Arabs. Newport was growing steadily into a diverse city that was decidedly different from its original English bearing.

The decade of the 1920s was a breakout period, a reaction to the horror of World War I. It was time to have fun and revolt against the gentility of previous generations. The Casino Theatre thrived, vaudeville was popular, and other entertainments were a hit at the Opera House. Across America, cities teemed with newcomers from the farm, the tempo of life increased, and Wall Street went into high gear with millions of dollars (many of them borrowed on 10-percent margin) invested in both speculative and sound stocks. America had helped win the war and now strutted proudly with its proven power. In the arts, literature, and music, the country was finding it own new *American* voice, displacing European influences. To a large degree, Mrs. Astor's confined community of mores and values was split asunder, and no one ventured forward to claim the mantle of leadership because society had become so fragmented, just as Mamie Fish had predicted. The country was growing at an unprecedented rate; corporations blossomed with the wealth produced by the stock-market boom. Hopes were high, expectations higher yet. When Charles Lindbergh crossed the Atlantic by airplane in 1927 and symbolically joined North America with Europe, the United States was once again displaying its superiority and technological savvy.

Prohibition defined the Roaring Twenties more than any other communal development. The rise of the speakeasy throughout the country created a social leveler like never before. Rich or poor, black or white, to get a shot of rotgut booze or weak beer, people of all ranks had to rub shoulders at the illegal taverns that sprouted like dandelions after the passage of the Volstead Act in 1919. Certainly there were sedate upper-class clubs with their well-stocked wine cellars in larger cities, but for the most part the speakeasy or the black-and-tan bar were the places to go to drink. A sort of rebelliousness arose from breaking the law and the more the demand for spirits grew, the more the bootleggers increased their volume and profits.

In Newport, small, illegal, mostly private taverns dotted the harbor area to serve thirsty customers. Obtaining the liquor for sale (at prices more than double those of pre-Prohibition) was generally not a problem for speakeasy owners because Narragansett Bay, with its hundreds of coves and hidden inlets, readily lent itself to the steady import of banned booze. The pattern of smuggling was established right after passage of the Volstead Act. All along the Atlantic coast emerged "rum row," a convoy of large ships just beyond the territorial boundary (three miles at first, then moved to twelve miles off shore), filled with cases of liquor from Canada, Bermuda, and beyond. Enterprising smugglers used speedboats, tugs, almost any craft fast enough to elude the Coast Guard, to motor out to the fleet at night, load as many cases as they could carry, then sneak

ADMIRAL WILLIAM SIMS
One of the most renowned heroes of World War I was Admiral William S. Sims (1858– 1936). A tireless reformer, Sims made his initial mark in the navy by campaigning for better guns and sighting apparatus on battleships and more rigorous target training. Regardless of his rank, Sims created a stir in Washington by criticizing the civilian control system, which, he believed, stymied military progress. In early 1917, the then Rear Admiral Sims was awarded the presidency of the Naval War College, but when America declared war, Sims was elevated to full admiral's rank and given command of the Atlantic fleet for two years. In that capacity, Sims performed his greatest contribution to the country. He ordered more destroyers to be built in order to protect the enormous convoy operation he had put into effect, and helped map out the strategy to win the war. It was Sims's dependence on the convoy system that reduced the number of Allied ships being sunk by German U-boats and saved countless lives.

Upon his return to Newport in 1919, to resume his post as president of the War College, Admiral Sims was greeted by the townspeople with an outpouring of appreciation for his role in protecting lives and materiel on the high seas. An arch of triumph was erected at Government Landing and one of the largest parades in Newport history was given in his honor. When he retired from the navy after forty two years of active duty, he and his wife, Anne, stayed on in Newport at their home on Catherine Street. Sims was active with the affairs of Trinity Church, the Newport Art Museum, and the Redwood Library, where he was a board member. He died at age seventy-seven.

back to some inlet around the bay to transfer their cargo to cars or trucks for transport to the speakeasies.

Throughout the Prohibition period, Newport and Narragansett Bay reverted to the days of piracy in the 1700s. Thousands of trips to the rum boats were made by men willing to risk arrest because the profit on the liquor was high: a case of Scotch purchased for $15 at rum row would fetch $35 or more on shore. At first, the Coast Guard was at a disadvantage because its boats were few and slow. As traffic increased, the service upgraded its cutter fleet and began catching the smugglers; they in turn built faster boats that could do up to 50 miles per hour, and the cat-and-mouse game continued apace over fourteen years. Fishing boats were often used to transport the contraband. One local shellfish dealer reportedly made a steady income by filling his hold with bottles of liquor, then covering them with mounds of quahogs and innocently returning to shore.

With so much illicit traffic in the area, Coast Guard and local police were kept quite busy during the 1920s. Scores of arrests were made, but on the whole the rumrunners were more numerous and successful than their pursuers. However, in January 1924, the *Daily News* reported that "the biggest haul of liquor the police have made" came when two officers became suspicious of a Reo truck emerging from Lee's wharf. It was stopped and searched, and patrolman James Lawless discovered eighty-five cases of liquor, "which, conservatively estimated at $50 a case, made a valuation of $4,250." The men were arrested and the spirits emptied down the drain. In August, the newspaper informed its readers that a garage on Coddington wharf was raided and $10,000 worth of fine whiskey was confiscated. Another incident was made public in December 1924 when the Coast Guard seized the fishing boat *Nina* near Brenton Reef; it was stocked with five hundred cases of liquor, but the crew had abandoned ship and disappeared into the night. *Nina* was towed into the harbor, inspected by federal authorities, and the large stash was disposed of. Someone lost a good deal of money. These are but three examples of the kind of lawlessness that prevailed throughout the 1920s in and around Newport, activities that were mirrored in nearly every other town or city in America. As Prohibition dragged on, freelance criminals were usually pushed aside or murdered by the increasingly strong organized-crime syndicates, which then used their clout to venture into other lucrative arenas, setting up a sophisticated and deadly underground that had only been partially checked even to this day.

The most dramatic seizure of the Prohibition era in Newport occurred at the end of December 1929: the notorious 85-foot *Black Duck*, a speedy rumrunner, was spotted in the foggy harbor by the Coast Guard cutter 290 returning from rum row with several hundred cases of contraband booze. The cutter was moored at the Dumplings, awaiting just such a target. Warrant Officer Alexander Cornell turned on his spotlight and called for the *Black Duck* to halt. Instead, it revved its powerful engine and sped away. Cornell ordered a crewman to fire a machine gun across the stern to catch their attention. But the rumrunner swerved sharply and raised waves that rocked the cutter; when the machine gunner opened fire, a fusillade of over twenty bullets hit the pilot house instead, instantly killing three men inside and wounding a fourth in the hand. The survivor turned the boat around and returned to the cutter to surrender. Later, the *Black Duck* was taken over by the Coast Guard and became a well-known patrol boat in Narragansett Bay.

The Great Depression

The nation seemed to be strong and vibrant. Optimism was rife, stocks were high, peace prevailed, and

America looked to the future with lofty expectations. But, turning T. S. Eliot's lines from "The Hollow Men" on their heads, the Roaring Twenties ended with a decisive bang, not a whimper, on Tuesday, October 29, 1929. That was the defining date, the day America hit the brakes and skidded out of control, into a decade of despair. The economist John Kenneth Galbraith wrote of the event, "Some years, like some poets and politicians and some lovely women, are singled out for fame far beyond the common lot, and 1929 was clearly such a year. Like 1066, 1776, and 1914, it is a year that everyone remembers."

The Wall Street crash of 1929 sobered up the country even before the repeal of Prohibition knocked bootleg Scotch off the shelves. On Black Thursday, October 24, 12,900,000 shares traded (twice the normal daily volume), but not all of them had buyers, even at deeply discounted prices. That was new, and that's when reality set in, signaling the end of the bull market. On Black Tuesday, October 29, the Dow closed at 230, down 128 points from its October 11 high of 358. The volume that day was an unprecedented 16,410,000 shares. Bankers and brokers bore their solemn faces and tried to reassure a panicked public with soothing words that the market was fundamentally sound. The tactic didn't work. Prices continued to erode until the Dow bottomed out at 42 on June 30, 1930. General Electric, one of the nation's leading corporations, saw its stock fall from a 1929 high of 403 to 168 at year's end, even though there was nothing essentially wrong with the company itself; it kept plunging the following two years.

The Roaring Twenties, with all the robust speculation and indiscriminate borrowing on behalf of hundreds of thousands of people, had run its course; for the next decade, until the build-up for World War II kick-started the economy, America lived on the edge and on the dole. Soup kitchens, bread lines, and men selling apples on the streets to survive: those are the prominent scenes from the Great Depression. That was how far the mighty United States had fallen. Summing up, the historian Samuel Eliot Morison commented, "The stock market crash of October 1929 was a natural consequence of the greatest orgy of speculation and over-optimism since the South Sea Bubble of 1720."

Economists and historians have been searching for the root causes of the Depression ever since it gripped the nation, and there is still much disagreement among them. It may be safe to venture that human greed, folly, investments made on absurdly high margins of credit, poor governmental oversight at all levels, runaway corporate maneuvering with few checks and balances, a speculative construction boom, pyramid schemes, and the impotence of the Federal Reserve Board all added to the long downturn. Banks failed for the simple reason that they had loans on their books that were impossible to liquidate because of existing laws. The federal government was unable or unwilling to pump large amounts of money into public-works programs, allowing the crisis to fester. Finally, there was a dearth of ideas and innovative products or technologies that might have spurred private investment and rallied markets and the country. Not everyone went broke in the Great Depression. There was venture capital available, but it was sitting smartly on the sidelines.

During the 1930s, the national economy was still deteriorating and consumer spending

The Roaring Twenties were experienced in numerous ways in Newport. Up until the onset of the Great Depression in 1929, the town continued to expand and flourish with so much navy activity. In 1923, the Navy Department officially designated Narragansett Bay as one of four principal fleet bases in the country. Later that year, the largest dirigible airship in the world, USS *Shenandoah*, made a surprise visit. Activity increased throughout the harbor when, in May 1927, the U. S. fleet arrived after maneuvers in the Atlantic. The *Daily News* reported that it was the greatest naval armada ever assembled by America. Schools closed and a record one hundred thousand visitors from all over New England flocked to Ocean Drive and other vantage points to get a glimpse of the 125 ships. Sailors were feted in town for days. It was obvious, after that spectacle, that Newport was a true blue navy town.

Other events of significance during the decade were the partial destruction of City Hall by fire in March 1925; the rise of commercial flying for passengers; the advent of the radio; the 175th birthday of the Redwood Library; the opening of the new Hotel Viking on Bellevue Avenue in 1926; and the opening of the Mount Hope Bridge in Portsmouth, thus finally linking Aquidneck Island with Bristol and the western mainland for automobiles that would markedly alter traffic patterns in Newport from then on. At the opening ceremony, a man dressed as Roger Williams walked from the mainland side to greet another dressed as Dr. John Clarke, who came from Aquidneck Island; in an apt display of symbolism, they met at the middle and shook hands. Ironically, the span was dedicated on October 24, 1929, the same day Wall Street experienced the major decline called "Black Thursday" and set the scene for the catastrophic crash the following Monday and Tuesday.

nose-dived sharply; nearly everyone was nervous. That contraction caused a huge ripple effect as businesses began to lay off workers who were mostly unable to secure new employment. People called on the charity of others, but that often lasted a short time. Practically everyone in the middle and lower classes was feeling the pinch in one way or another, or was watching an unlucky neighbor trying to sell his or her house. Morison points out,

> America, unlike Britain, then had neither social security nor unemployment insurance. This tailspin of the economy went on until mid-1932 when around 12 million people, about 25 per cent of the normal labor force, were unemployed. . . . Small towns in the farm belt were almost deserted of their inhabitants. On the higher level, New York apartment houses offered five-year leases on one year's rent, entire Pullman trains rolled along without a single passenger, hotels and resorts like Miami Beach were empty. For a prize understatement we nominate ex-President Coolidge's 'The country is not in good condition,' in his syndicated press column on 20 January 1931.

In Newport, the market meltdown was initially met with a collective shrug of official shoulders. Summer-colony residents were certainly being hit hard, and it must have been clear that the tax base would fall, but the politicians were looking in the wrong direction. Not having an industrial-based economy, city fathers believed they could escape the misery being witnessed in Providence and other larger manufacturing centers in New England, where some 70 percent of the cotton mills were closed. They were mistaken, and slowly came to understand that the collapse of the nation's economic system was going to affect the city directly and adversely. The local historian Daniel Snydacker posits, "From the beginning, the city of Newport felt it would be immune from any effects of the crash. Part of this attitude was mere ignorance." As the local economy stalled and layoffs began, leaders woke up to reality. There was "a very sharp and serious jump in unemployment. By 25 July 1930, City Hall reported a 20.4% increase in unemployment, and the problem continued to grow for the next four years." The sudden lack of discretionary income affected nearly every merchant in town, leading to curtailment of expansion plans on the table just months before and putting a damper on any forward thinking. The Depression was psychological as well as monetary: it was impossible to escape the ravages, especially in a small community like Newport.

Fixing the shattered economy had to be a national effort, with leadership coming from the White House. When Franklin D. Roosevelt replaced Herbert Hoover as president in 1933 and inaugurated the New Deal with its alphabet soup of recovery agencies, federal initiative was begun. On the local level, a number of charitable organizations rose up to help the neediest, while City Hall started searching for solutions. The monetary impact of the old summer colony was in serious decline, but with the opening of the Mount Hope Bridge allowing easy auto access to the island from all over New England, officials turned their attention to attracting a different sort of vacationer. The day-trippers or middle-class weekenders, who might have been intimidated by Newport during the Gilded Age, now became the target, visitors who would venture to Newport to enjoy what so many people had for two centuries: the natural treasures, scenic drives, and beaches. Seasonal boarding houses were spruced up, and the new Hotel Viking on Bellevue Avenue was an inviting destination. People began to arrive, and although less wealthy than the Bellevue Avenue cottage

owners, at least they brought some respite during hard times.

Unemployment, however, touched every level of society in the city. One local volunteer agency reported that in the autumn of 1931 there were 192 active estates in Newport that had employed 1,882 men and women, only 704 of whom were city residents, and only 202 of them were full-time employees. In contrast, at the height of the Gilded Age, close to 3,000 residents would have found employment at the mansions. By 1934, some 2,000 men and women, mostly laborers, were without work. When Roosevelt's numerous relief agencies began offering cash and opportunities, those numbers fell. Again, the presence of the navy was instrumental in alleviating major pain because by 1935 Washington was pumping in millions of dollars for housing construction. A Works Progress Administration (WPA) survey of Newport, published in 1937, reported: "Since 1918 the great expansion in the United States naval base has brought about a decided change in the character of Newport. Many natives who formerly worked on the large estates during the summer months, and were unemployed in the winter, found year-round employment in the naval units. During the year 1936 the naval stations expended $7,500,000 and employed over 3500 civilians, of which about 75 per cent reside in Newport and about 50 per cent are homeowners. The Navy has more than counteracted the decline in the very wealthy summer trade."

The Bellevue Avenue summer colony was hit hard by the Depression. While many retained their wealth, others were not so lucky. Dozens of estates were auctioned off for back taxes. Times had changed so greatly that many of the owners, even if they could afford their mansions, chose to abandon Newport for other less expensive spots, or none at all. The cachet was almost gone from town. The Four Hundred was decidedly dead. One of the most dramatic and illustrative examples of the plunge in value was seen at Marble House, the magnificent palace built for $2 million and furnished for some $9 million less than four decades before. In 1933 the Vanderbilt family, which could have kept it had they wanted to, sold the house to Frederick Prince for only $100,000. There are many similar stories throughout the 1930s. While the Point and north end of town were bustling with navy activity and the largess from Washington's work programs, the high-end southern tip was largely dormant.

In the end, Newport weathered the Great Depression better than most American cities, partly because of its lack of an industrial infrastructure that dragged so many other communities to the depths. Providence, with its crumbling textile and jewelry empires, fared far worse. One clear indication of Newport's underlying economic health is that not one of its several banks failed in the turbulent 1930s. Daniel Snydacker concluded that four distinct elements saved Newport from disaster during the period. "These were the Torpedo Station, the New England Steamship Company [Fall River Line], the continued operation of the Viking Hotel, and the convention trade. Together they provided enough employment and generated enough income to prevent the kind of catastrophic collapse that happened in other cities." The Torpedo Station was the key to Newport's survival, but the thousands employed by the Fall River Line repair shops on Long Wharf were also a crucial buttress against calamity. The Hotel Viking remained busy throughout the Depression because people felt the need to get away from problems at home. And because of the Viking's large capacity, many conventions chose scenic Newport as a prime destination. "On Friday night, 15 September 1933, registration for the American Legion convention that was in town broke all local records and was not equalled again until the Sheraton-Islander was built after World War II."

Those were troubling times, but in true Yankee spirit Newport survived and had even begun to prosper as Europe once again found itself on the brink of open hostilities. The town remained, as it had in almost every era, a resilient community. But in between, another disaster was in the offing for Newport, an act of nature so powerful it took the city's breath away.

The Hurricane of 1938

After an unusually wet summer of missed beach days and children cranky at having to be inside, the dawn of Wednesday, September 21, 1938, brought golden sunshine, beckoning breezes, and hopes for the kind of gentle day Newport was famous for. But that beauty would prove to be transient. Anyone picking up a copy of the *Daily News* that morning would have found the weather prediction, which read, "Washington, Sept. 21—Forecast for Rhode Island—Rain this afternoon and tonight; cooler tonight. Thursday, fair and cooler." The brief article also mentions a low-pressure front and a storm "moving rapidly northeastward off the coast. . . . The center will probably pass considerably to the southward of Nantucket." Not one word about a gale raging in the Atlantic. Not one word of warning that the most destructive hurricane in New England history was picking up speed and energy and barreling straight for Rhode Island.

Weather prediction in 1938 was still a primitive science, but trackers in Florida had, over the previous days, been watching and warning of a mighty hurricane lingering in the Caribbean. When it blew by the Sunshine State on its speedy path up the coast, the responsibility to keep a close eye on the disturbance passed to the Washington office of the Weather Bureau, and that's where the tragedy began. Although one relatively young forecaster read the atmospheric maps correctly, saw the possible consequences, and urged that a severe storm warning be issued immediately, his older and seemingly more experienced colleagues brushed his concerns aside and divined that the gale would take the predictable eastward surge and head out to sea to die in the frigid northern waters.

There was no warning, not a hint, not a clue. Anyone in Newport making plans to go see *In Old Chicago*, starring Tyrone Power, at Shea's Paramount Theatre or perhaps catch the matinee of *Blondes at Work*, featuring Glenda Farrell, at Loew's Colonial, would have believed that the brilliant morning sunshine would again be cancelled by a little rain and nothing more. Yet farther south, the storm was becoming more intense and menacing, more deadly with each passing hour. New York City experienced gale-force winds just after noon, even though there were still clear skies over Easton's Beach in Newport. When the seas began to get stirred and heavy chops appeared, anyone at the shore would have easily written off the signs and believed that the deteriorating conditions were due to the autumn equinox when tides are highest, not the forerunner to the most violent disruption of nature and human life Rhode Island had ever encountered, more destructive and deadly than the Great Gale of 1815.

Long Island, New York, was the first victim of the storm's rage, but its visit over land did not decrease its intensity. Instead, it made a beeline for Connecticut, Rhode Island, and the rest of New England. R. A. Scotti's chilling account of the hurricane, *Sudden Sea*, reads like a novel.

> As swift and sure as a Joe Lewis [*sic*] punch, the hurricane darted up the Atlantic coast at fifty, sixty, and seventy miles an hour, faster than most cars could travel in 1938. No hurricane had ever raced as fast. It arrived unannounced. It struck without warning, and it showed no mercy. Entire beach communities that seemed secure at lunchtime were wiped off the map by supper. At 3:30 p.m. on Napatree [near Watch Hill, Rhode Island], the Moores were battening the hatches and marveling at the spectacle of rolling breakers. Fifteen minutes later, at 3:45 p.m., vertical walls of water, two and three stories high, were plowing through the cement seawall as if it were transparent.

The speed, power, and fury of the 130-mile-an-hour winds of the nameless gale were beyond anyone's experience, almost beyond comprehension. When the most lethal stage of the storm made landfall on Rhode Island's South County, the entire shoreline and countryside were leveled. And no one knew about the monster cyclone until it was upon them. Scotti continues,

> Town by town, the Northeast darkened and was silenced. The brilliant inventions of modern life were knocked out. Phones failed. Lights failed. Cars flooded. Buses and trolleys stalled. Trains derailed. Long Island could not alert Connecticut. Connecticut could not warn Rhode Island. Each community stood alone, isolated against the onslaught. What had been assumed permanent was lost, and the familiar was made strange. Houses went to sea, boats came ashore, and ordinary objects became recast. A safe harbor became a cemetery; the family car, a tomb. Rooftops were rafts. A shingle became a deadly projectile. . . . Salvation and destruction, redemption and death were as random as the flip of a coin, and the air was so thick with salt and murky spray that day was as blind as night.

When the storm hit Newport around 4 p.m., it was as if a giant light had been switched off. First the winds, then the water. People on streets were unable to walk, given the ferocity of the gusts; trying to hold on to a lamppost was futile because in all likelihood, the post was about to be toppled. By five o'clock, right at the worst time of high tide, the heart of the hurricane hit Narragansett Bay, pushing a gigantic tidal wall of water onto the town and farther up to Providence. Long Wharf was ruined. Water covered everything and Thames

Street was a waist-high raging river. Roofs, poles, ancient trees, everything was being uprooted from the waterlogged soil. The elegant bell spires of the First Baptist Church and the Second Congregational Church were blown off. Streets were blocked by hundreds of fallen trees, hampering rescue operations; scores of boats from the harbor were found blocks away the next day. Dozens upon dozens of seaside grand cottages were extensively damaged and whether they were repaired or abandoned, property values plunged for decades following September 21. Bailey's Beach and nearby Viking Beach (now Hazard's) were obliterated, all cabanas lost. Most of Ocean Drive was impassable for days. There was nothing save chaos and destruction for about three long hours, and in that time, the face of Newport changed beyond recognition.

The next day, September 22, the *Newport Daily News* ran extensive coverage of the disaster (how they managed to get the edition out is remarkable). On the front page, next to a banner headline reading "CHAMBERLAIN AND HITLER CONFER," we read "NEW ENGLAND HAS 150 KNOWN DEAD."

That was just the beginning; in the end, it is estimated that over 680 in New England lost their lives. The majority, 420 people, were from Rhode Island, which received the brunt of the storm because the so-called dangerous semicircle of the hurricane, the side carrying the most wallop, drove into Rhode Island with such force. Over forty people in Newport County lost their lives. Seven children were killed when a giant wave swept over their school bus at Mackerel Cove in Jamestown. Many drowned in cars, on the streets, in their homes; others were hit by flying debris. Property-damage estimates accelerated as days passed. The first figure was a million dollars in losses in Newport alone; four days later, the figure had jumped to $5 million, and kept climbing. Most of the paper's coverage was of the damages sustained by the city. One example:

Flooding in Washington Square following the 1938 Hurricane
Photographer unknown
Newport Historical Society
Newport, Rhode Island

"Mountainous seas engulfed Newport Beach and gave hundreds of awe-stricken Newporters one of the most terrifying sights they had ever seen. Waves that seemed to be sky high crashed over the sea wall and through the buildings, smashing everything in front of it [*sic*] like so much wallpaper, and dashing across the roadway to Easton's pond, which resembled an ocean itself, with whitecaps riding roughly towards the northern shore under the impulse of the storm." The popular roller coaster was found the next day a half mile away, mangled almost beyond recognition.

On Friday, September 23, the city went on assessing damages; the *Daily News* reported that the waterfront damage was the worst ever sustained and would require at least $1 million to repair, and that figure was just for shipping and wharves, not personal property, which was mostly uninsured. Almost nothing was spared anywhere near the shore. About the only ship to survive without some damage was the historic frigate *Constellation*, moored at the Naval Training Station. On land, large parts of Ocean Drive simply disappeared. Out by what is now Brenton Point State Park, the five-foot-deep roadbed was carried off by the strength of the storm and had to be totally rebuilt, a process that took ten months. The links at the Newport Country Club were covered in so much salt water that they appeared as lakes, and the greens and fairways were ruined. Hundreds of homes were completely destroyed and thousands were damaged. Almost any dwelling close to the shore was rendered a disaster area.

The list of damages could cover pages, and it took many people years to repair what one three-hour hurricane tore apart. But Newport began cleaning up its mess immediately. With the help of hundreds of workers hired by the WPA, roads were cleared of fallen trees, electricity and telephone service were restored, the waterfront began its renewal. Many relief agencies sent in volunteers to help townspeople recover, and the National Guard was on hand to help. But the storm's blow to the fishing industry was severe since so many craft had been lost, and it took years for Newport's fleet to be built back to pre-hurricane numbers. Throughout Rhode Island, tree damage alone was so extensive that the state's entire lumber industry was gone in one day. In South County, R. A. Scotti asserts that 99 percent of shoreline property over a seven-mile distance was totally demolished. In addition, "Some four hundred cottages at Misquamicut and almost two hundred on Charlestown Beach washed away. Charlestown Pond and Charlestown by the Sea lost another hundred homes, and Napatree was wiped off the map."

Disaster of that magnitude is disquieting. The Hurricane of 1938 left wounds that went far beyond the physical. Those who survived the storm never forgot the experience of the horror carried on those winds and waves. It came so fast, so unexpectedly, with no time to prepare, that it simply stunned people for years. Like Pearl Harbor, the assassination of President John F. Kennedy, and the September 11, 2001, attacks on the World Trade Center and Pentagon, the hurricane devastated the status quo and underlined how random events can recast our lives. After the storm, some people with dark hair awoke the next morning with their hair turned a brilliant white. In subsequent years, Newporters who heard that another big storm was on the way braced themselves, a little more anxiously, a little more carefully. After almost a decade of dealing with the Great Depression, Newporters, indeed all New Englanders, were feeling less confident, less able to cope with life's vagaries. Psychologically, the Hurricane of 1938 came at a low point in many people's lives and the impact of its swiftness and fury was deeply felt. Something was lost in the storm, never to be fully regained. A sense of security, of control, had suddenly been swept away.

Politics, Past and Present

Throughout the colonial era, Newport was the seat of influence in Rhode Island and Providence Plantations. In the early years of the United States, George Washington and Thomas Jefferson visited leaders in town and from then on many presidents were drawn to Newport for official or social occasions. From James Monroe and John Quincy Adams to Theodore and Franklin Roosevelt and beyond, Newport was a magnet for the high-level rendezvous. Dwight Eisenhower and John Kennedy each made Newport the summer White House in the 1950s and 1960s. During the Gilded Age, nearly every summer witnessed not only United States presidents but also European royalty, foreign ambassadors, and diplomats like Britain's Cecil Spring Rice carrying out behind-the-scenes negotiations while away from their legations in Washington, and, of course, the upper crust of industrial and financial America conducting business on their yachts or in their cottages. In short, Newport was a real power hub as the country moved from infancy to the center of world attention. Until World War I, the more America mattered in international affairs, the more Newport played its part in bringing players together.

There is a decided irony in this situation: as the town garnered prestige and authority beyond the state borders, it lost clout within them. Throughout the nineteenth and twentieth centuries, Newport's influence in Rhode Island politics diminished to the degree that it was overlooked at nearly every turn. Power resided in the north, particularly in Providence, and for the most part that power was wielded by a few spectacularly corrupt Republican Party bosses. Going back to Henry B. Anthony in 1858, old-line Yankee conservatives fought for the next seventy years to consolidate their hold over government and deny the vote to the increasingly large number of European immigrants. After Anthony, the scandal-plagued Charles R. Brayton picked up the exclusionist mantle, championing a crooked rule of the few, and openly bragging about how many votes he was able to buy for his hand-picked candidates at each election. As the Republican Party boss, Brayton held near dictatorial sway for over thirty years. Next in line for the dubious distinction of petty dictator was Nelson W. Aldrich, the Republican senator from 1881 (he replaced the controversial Civil War general Ambrose Burnside at his death) until 1911, who ruled Rhode Island politics with cunning and an iron fist. Aldrich was able to consolidate so much control in the Senate that he gained the unflattering title of "General Manager of the United States," because of his back-room maneuverings on trade, tariff, and banking issues. Together with the Providence utility tycoon Marsden J. Perry (who had a summer cottage, Bleak House, on Ocean Drive near Castle Hill), Nelson Aldrich controlled Rhode Island like no one else in the state's history. In a 1905 article in *McClure's Magazine*, the muckraking journalist Lincoln Steffens wrote a prominent article titled "Rhode Island: A State For Sale," detailing the numerous self-serving deals that were pushed through the legislature to the benefit of the bosses. Aldrich had dynastic aspirations as well, and when his daughter Abby married John D. Rockefeller, Jr., he achieved them. Abby was mother of six children, one of whom, Nelson, would briefly serve as Vice President of the United States. After Aldrich's death in 1915, a power vacuum developed, although Republicans still commanded the General Assembly.

Then Rhode Island did a flip-flop. When the Providence Democrat Theodore Francis Green won the 1932 governor's race, those seventy years of Republican domination ended. During his two terms in office, Green and his congressional allies swept away decades of laws favoring the old rural-dominated oligarchy in what has come to be known as "the Bloodless Revolution of 1935," setting the stage for twenty years of

*President Dwight D.
Eisenhower enjoying
a round of golf at the
Newport Country Club,*
1957
Photograph by
Grey Villet/Time &
Life Pictures/Getty Images

Democratic control and support for presidents Roosevelt and Truman's New Deal and Fair Deal. He concentrated on welfare and economic relief for the unemployed and recognized the importance of the state's immigrant population. For the first time in the century, the overwhelmingly Democratic urban citizens had a voice in their government. Theodore F. Green was elected to the United States Senate in 1936 and was an influential liberal leader in foreign and domestic affairs for twenty-four years, retiring at age ninety-three only because of failing eyesight.

Newport finally regained the political stature that had been absent for more than a century in 1960 when Claiborne Pell was elected to fill Green's Senate seat. Born in New York in 1918, Claiborne Pell was the son of the distinguished diplomat Herbert C. Pell, ally of Franklin Roosevelt and Minister to Portugal and Hungary in the 1930s and 1940s. Aristocratic, wealthy, and fervently liberal, Herbert Pell moved his family to Newport from New York and Tuxedo Park in the late 1920s, and Claiborne attended St. George's School in Middletown before going to Princeton. The elder Pell's support for Roosevelt put him at odds with the majority of the nation's elite who attacked the president as "a traitor to his class." One story indicative of Herbert Pell's independence from his cohorts took place in November 1936.

Pell celebrated the Democratic triumph by ridiculing his fellow patricians. On election night he attended a gathering at Newport's Clambake Club. Earlier that spring Pell had instructed his gardener to plant some sunflowers; by election eve, the sunflowers—now the symbol of the Republican candidate, Governor Alfred M. Landon—had dried up, and birds had eaten their seeds. On election evening as Newport society sat stunned at the Republican debacle, Pell walked from table to table in the club's main dining room, and deposited one withered sunflower on each table. At the end of the presentation, he bowed gravely and withdrew.

In 1960, Claiborne Pell was a political unknown and did not even have the Democratic Party endorsement. Nonetheless, he won the primary and went on to rack up the largest victory plurality in state history until that time in the November election, riding the coattails of his Massachusetts neighbor, John F. Kennedy. Claiborne Pell did his job well. He went on to spend thirty-six years representing Rhode Island in the Senate, retiring to Newport in 1996. For many years Pell was chairman of the Senate Foreign Relations Committee, one of the most distinguished posts in that body. Known as a cerebral, patient politician who championed educational, environmental, and cultural legislation, Pell was on good terms with Democrats and Republicans alike. Two of his finest, and long-lasting, achievements were the creation of the Pell Grants, which have provided financial assistance to millions of needy American college students, and his leadership in the legislation that ushered in the National Endowment for the Arts and the National Endowment for the Humanities.

Claiborne Pell's partner in the Senate from 1976 onward was the Republican John Chafee, ironically another blue-blood representing a blue-collar constituency. Like Pell, Chafee was moderate, well respected, and productive on behalf of his native state. Before his Senate bid, Providence-born Chafee (1922) attended Harvard Law School and then went on to become governor of Rhode Island from 1963 to 1969 and Secretary of the Navy from 1969 to 1972. He was especially active on behalf of environmental legislation, and the Clean Air Act was one of his major achievements. Because of his easy and noncombative style, John Chafee was well respected by Democrats and often served as a liaison between the two parties during tense times. Planning to retire in 2000, Senator Chafee died in office in October 1999. His son, Lincoln Chafee, was chosen to replace him, and then won election to the seat in his own right in 2000.

300 Years of Newport

The Great Depression, the Hurricane of 1938, Adolf Hitler threatening Europe with his Panzer divisions, territorial incursions, and the threat of global war. There seemed to be little joy in a world gone awry in 1939. Yet that year, Newport staged a celebration the likes of which had rarely been witnessed before, a 300th birthday party that lasted for months and involved the entire city. Other communities offered small commemorations honoring their heritage, but nowhere else in America was the spirit of the past so ardently on display, and for so long. Newport sponsored a city-wide revelry complete with parades and pageants. The tercentenary festivities harked back to the city's roots in 1639 and the major events that ensued thereafter, and in so doing, relived a rich and dramatic legacy. It celebrated Newport's solid commitment to religious and political freedom, and it ritualized another tradition dear to every citizen's heart: having fun.

The party began in May on 'Lection Day when the governor of Rhode Island, Portsmouth resident William H. Vanderbilt, gave a welcoming speech from the balcony of Colony House, the site of so many historic pronouncements. A large parade followed, with many people dressed in colonial and other period dress for the occasion. Eileen Warburton describes the scene.

> There were 2,000 members of Colonial-chartered military companies in New England as well as the Newport Artillery. A thousand members of the Machinists Union marched from the Torpedo Station and, weapons flashing in the sunlight, units from the Navy, from Fort Adams, and from the Training Station. The summer colony loaned or actually rode in their choicest remaining vehicles,

costumed in the elaborate dress of the Gilded Age. . . . They all wound down Washington Square and Thames, up Young and Bowery Streets, then down Bellevue Avenue. . . . The costumed spectators, 10,000 of them, continued with a block party in Washington Square that night, where they danced in a light rain to music from the local musicians union.

That parade was just the beginning. All summer long the treat continued.

Precursors of the tercentenary had been taking place since the mid-1920s, when the Point section began commemorating Oldport Days on Washington Street. Local residents would dress in colonial garb and many of the grand old houses and gardens would be opened to the public. But those were generally one-day affairs. In 1939, a huge three-day fair was staged and the festivities drew thousands of curious onlookers. All segments of Newport society took part that year: the townspeople, the summer colony, and the navy were all represented. The *Mercury* covered the event extensively. "Opening of various houses, booths, performances, games, sailing and whaling races, an Indian encampment, attractions for children, and many other events have been arranged for the three-day feature that makes possible a real glimpse of the past in houses that were part of Newport's golden days of commerce when it exceeded New York." The reporter goes on to name many of the people involved in presenting the various entertainments. We learn, for instance, that "Mrs. LeBrun Rhinelander, in charge of the flower booth, was aided by the Honorable Nadine and Noreen Stonor, daughters of Lady Camoys." "On the lawns of the several estates there were exhibits, and an original colonial note was introduced at the Robinson house, where Princess Redwing and her Narragansett Indian followers had pitched their tents for the three-day period. There were 50 in the group and they will put on a pageant showing episodes in Indian life." "Another feature this afternoon was the revival of the 'Town and Country Club,' a famous literary group of old Newport by Mrs. Maud Howe Elliott, who with several of her friends were in costume. This scene proved of great interest."

The pièce de résistance of the tercentenary extravaganza came at the end of August, during Old Home Week, when the "Epic of Newport" was staged on a 500-foot stage at an outdoor theater in Freebody Park over a six-day period. Bleachers to hold five thousand people were erected and a cast of eight hundred residents presented a stirring re-creation of Newport history in nineteen episodes: it started with a prologue of settlers and Indians, then moved on to, among other chapters, the first town meeting in 1639, Dr. John Clarke at the court of King Charles II to obtain the Charter of 1663, the arrival of the Charter in Newport later that year, pirates in town, Dean Berkeley's arrival, the burning of the British ship *Liberty* at the onset of the Revolution, the capture of General Prescott, Commodore Perry at Lake Erie, the Civil War, and the Gay Nineties of the Gilded Age. It was an incredibly ambitious program, and on each of the four nights it was enacted, the show went on without a hitch (except for the nor'easter that interrupted the schedule for three days). "Epic of Newport" was a fitting ode to the city's long history, and decades later, some of the ten thousand people who witnessed the spectacle could still describe the show in great detail.

The finale of the festivities fell on Labor Day weekend, featuring yet another large parade filled with dozens of floats, and an outdoor party for thousands of people. Newporters couldn't get enough of the revelry. Yet at that very time, Europe was descending into chaos once again. As one searches the newspaper record for Saturday, September 2, 1939, there looms the bizarre juxtaposition of headlines in the *Daily News*.

A boldface banner headline reads "NAZI TROOPS DRIVE ON POLAND" while just below we learn "Block Party Tonight on Washington Square" and "Crowds Throng to See City's Float Parade." World War II was beginning on the same day the city celebrated three hundred years of growth, success, and liberty of conscience.

With the coming of combat on the Continent, Newport would be transformed once again, even before Pearl Harbor.

World War II in Narragansett Bay

Nazi Germany invaded France in May 1940. Winston Churchill became British prime minister two days before the Third Reich's offensive. Again, Europe was engulfed in battle and again the United States kept to the sidelines, although the overwhelming majority sentiment in the country favored the Allied forces. Given the scope of the aggression on the Continent, it was evident to most leaders in Washington that it would only be a matter of time before America would be forced to take a stand against Adolf Hitler. Within months of the onset of hostilities, President Franklin D. Roosevelt, who had served as assistant secretary of the navy from 1913 to 1920 and had long taken a special interest in naval affairs, ordered the armed services to begin preparations for the inevitable. Recalling the success of the German U-boat assaults in the previous war, Roosevelt and the military were fully aware of the need for vigilance on the seas.

Domestically, the United States also had to plan for the huge influx at military hubs of young men and women who would fight the war. With vivid memories of the housing shortage in Newport in 1917, Washington authorities went into action by buying large tracts of land in and around the city. It became clear that Newport was to play a significant role in the coming events. In early August 1940, the Philip Caswell property at Hillside Avenue and Beacon Street opposite Miantonomi Park was purchased for the construction of 262 new houses for military personnel. On August 12, President Roosevelt, accompanied by Governor William H. Vanderbilt and Senator Theodore F. Green, visited Newport to inspect the Naval Torpedo Station and Training Station and lay the groundwork for future development of all facilities. The president told reporters that he was pleased with the progress in naval defenses around Narragansett Bay and promised that extensive new barracks construction would begin shortly. Only a month later, estimates for manpower needs in the city were revised upward and the federal government bought more acreage in Middletown for an additional 600 units for enlisted personnel. The Depression-era work shortage was most definitely over.

Newport vibrated with the sound of hammers and saws in 1940. On President Roosevelt's orders, the Torpedo Station was significantly expanded with new housing and manufacturing facilities; its annual budget soared to $7.5 million, ten times its level just five years before. The workforce increased by 20 percent to 4,700. On Coddington Cove more new barracks were built to accommodate 2,500 men. Several millions of government dollars were flowing into the area. On Conanicut Island, Forts Wetherall and Getty were enlarged; Fort Adams was refurbished and now housed 3,000 soldiers. At the same time, the Jamestown Bridge opened, linking the island to the western mainland and greatly speeding up the delivery of men and materiel.

In 1940, Newport's population stood at 30,400, and the city was filling up fast. President Roosevelt had instituted the draft and men flocked to recruiting stations around the country to sign up and receive basic training. Newport, again, began to resemble an armed camp, and the United States was not even at war. The

Daily News reported that during the last six months of 1940, the Naval Training Station "sent out a total of 6,951 recruits to sea or to trade schools. It was the busiest peacetime year in history for the station, as this large total of recruits indicates." The training period was reduced from twelve to seven weeks duration in order to accommodate the mass of men seeking sea duty.

Throughout the first eleven months of 1941, the pace of everything accelerated in Newport. Defense preparations continued practically nonstop, more housing was constructed, more men landed in town. In April, Washington announced that Narragansett Bay would become the operating base for the Atlantic Fleet under the command of Admiral Ernest J. King; Rear Admiral Edward C. Kalbfus would head up land operations and serve as president of the Naval War College. Stationing the fleet at Newport elevated the city's status as a crucial hub in America's military machine while at the same time, the move increased the potential of enemy retaliation should war come. Within weeks, ships of all shapes and sizes began appearing in Newport and expectations rose sharply that the fleet would soon be in service against Germany. In September, the defense housing project called The Anchorage opened, and in late November the Tonomy Hill units were ready for occupants. Just in time. Japan attacked Pearl Harbor on December 7. America was at war.

Overnight, Newport mushroomed into a full-scale military camp. Over the following three and a half years of war against the Axis powers, the Torpedo Station would employ, at its height of activity, 13,000 men and women working around the clock to fabricate some twenty thousand torpedoes (approximately one third of America's production) and other munitions. It was Rhode Island's largest industrial employer in 1944. With all the recruits arriving for enlistment at the Naval Training Station, another housing crunch developed, despite all the new construction over the previous years, and private citizens were again called on to take in the young men. Federal monies were heaped on the area to extend Coddington Point, build factories on Gould Island, expand the Melville Fuel Depot, commission Quonset Point Naval Air Station, and construct new highways. Between all these activities and the constant rotation of naval trainees, Newport was in constant motion. It is estimated that Washington lavished upward of $85,000,000 on Narragansett Bay during World War II.

Life in the city was transformed after Pearl Harbor. Within days of the attack, reports of enemy aircraft in the vicinity mobilized both military and civilian patrols; alerts became regular events with Newport hosting the huge Atlantic Fleet. Women and children were often banned from the highways and school was cancelled when danger was suspected. After becoming accustomed to being on war footing, the community settled down but then had to absorb new realities. War Books, which rationed gasoline and food, were carried by everyone. Scrap metal drives became the norm. Social events were put on hold and the summer-colony activities diminished. Dusk to dawn blackouts were instituted for the entire community, lifted only after D-Day in June 1944. A large anti-aircraft installation was erected at Price's Neck to train sailors and soldiers. The navy also moved swiftly to secure the bay from enemy attack by building antiboat booms between Fort Kearney on Aquidneck Island and Fort Getty on Conanicut. Two submarine detector loops made

ARTHUR CURTISS JAMES

Unlike many Astors, Whitneys, and Vanderbilts of Gilded Age notoriety, the next generation of the Newport elite generally sought a lower profile. Among the leaders of the post-World War I summer community was railroad titan Arthur Curtiss James, one of the wealthiest magnates in the world, yet a man whom *Fortune* magazine described in 1930 as "unknown" to the public. James, born in New York City in 1867, was the grandson of a founding partner in the vast Phelps, Dodge copper mining and railroad empire, which was later controlled by his father; upon his father's death, Arthur Curtiss James inherited $25 million and became the financial brains behind the firm's steady growth, mostly in the West. Although he had numerous interests and sat on the board of dozens of public companies, James accumulated most of his wealth, and his reputation as a shrewd investor, in railroads. At one point, he either controlled or had a major stake in the Northern Pacific, the Great Northern, and the Western Pacific railroads, among others. At the height of his business career, James laid claim to some forty thousand miles of American railroad tracks, one-seventh of the nation's total. He was bigger than James J. Hill and other previous barons, yet almost no one in the country knew anything about him.

In Newport, however, Arthur Curtiss James was well known as a philanthropist and owner of the 125-acre Beacon Hill House estate on top of Telegraph Hill off Harrison Avenue, where he created Swiss Village, complete with prize livestock. Each summer, James opened Swiss Village to the public and thousands of people drove slowly around the grounds to view the splendor he had created. He and his wife, Harriet, also built a number of magnificent gardens at Beacon Hill House; one called the Blue Garden was especially grand. For many years, James was Newport's largest landowner and taxpayer. In yachting circles, James was known as an avid sailor, and his three-masted, 165-foot bark Aloha, which he sailed around the world three times, was the largest of its kind in its class, and familiar to all in Newport. From 1909

CONTINUED ON PAGE 438

to 1910, he served as commodore of the New York Yacht Club.Outgoing and popular in town, James was an imposing figure, tall and full-bearded in an age when most men were clean-shaven. He belonged to all of the Newport clubs and for four decades was active in sports. Arthur Curtiss James died in June 1941, three weeks after his wife of fifty-one years had passed away. Beacon Hill House was vandalized for years and finally succumbed to arson in 1967. After falling into disrepair for decades, James's Swiss Village has undergone a thorough restoration orchestrated by its new owner, a foundation headed by Mrs. Samuel M. V. Hamilton of Philadelphia and Newport.

of ninety thousand feet of magnetic cable were laid in the harbor. U-boat nets were played out across the East and West Passages, and naval vessels patrolled the waters twenty-four hours a day. The navy, knowing full well from its previous experiences with the German U-boat, desperately needed mass production of torpedoes for the protection of the fleet. The workforce ballooned to over five thousand people who worked three eight-hour shifts per day, seven days a week.

Other changes were witnessed. With so many men being drafted or volunteering for service, job shortages became acute across America; Newport was no exception. As the war progressed, more and more women entered the workforce. The Torpedo Station, for instance, employed several thousand women. Many of them lived at the government's women-only facilities at the Perry Mill building. Charitable organizations such as the Red Cross were headed mostly by women; they conducted large fundraising drives and contributed heavily to the war effort. The population of Newport doubled to nearly 60,000, almost entirely because of naval personnel. With so many people in town, a fresh-water shortage became so severe that a reservoir had to be hastily built at Lawton's Valley. But that wasn't sufficient, so the government began piping water from Tiverton. The summer garden tour and tennis tournaments at the Casino were cancelled. The majestic Breakers was turned into a public air-raid shelter. And just to indicate how far the glittering Gilded Age had drifted into memory, the *Daily News* reported that in July 1941, "Rosecliff, the Hermann Oelrichs property, was sold to Mrs. Greta Niessen for $21,000, after the furnishings had brought an estimated $75,000." The house had cost millions to build less than fifty years before.

After D-Day and the Allied march across France to the German border and beyond, many of the restrictions in Newport were lifted. Submarine nets were taken up and the harbor began to get back to normal, even with the considerable navy presence. The Torpedo Station started to cut back on production and instituted two thousand layoffs, with many more promised. The town, which had graciously adjusted to the war and overcrowding, began looking to a future and to the return of peace. Yet some things will never change: on September 14, 1944, another powerful hurricane struck Newport, causing millions of dollars in damages and another wipe-out of all the beach clubs. Hundreds more trees were uprooted. But unlike 1938, this time the town had ample warning and there was no loss of life. Again, the community picked itself up and recovered.

In May 1945 Adolf Hitler committed suicide and Nazi Germany surrendered. Newporters were relieved and happy, but there were no large outpourings of glee or parades. Merriment was premature. Throughout the summer, as layoffs at the Torpedo Station gathered momentum and the Training Station seemed almost empty, citizens waited warily for the endgame in the Pacific theater. Then came the dropping of the American atomic bombs on Hiroshima and Nagasaki in early August, surrender a week later, and the full capitulation by Japan on September 2 aboard the battleship *Missouri*. World War II was over, and now Newporters took to the streets by the thousands. The *Daily News* reported,

Victory over Japan was celebrated in Newport Tuesday with the greatest demonstration of popular feeling that the city has known in its three century odd years of existence. Newport cast restraint and dignity to the winds to celebrate the triumph. . . . Thousands of people jammed their way into the Washington Square and Thames Street areas. The streets ran riot with a flood of humanity eager to express in some way pentup [*sic*] emotions after almost four years of total war. They walked, they sang, they paraded, they danced, but at all times they were good-natured. It was a joyous time. One of the happiest in the city's history. More than once the expression on a woman's lips was: "Thank God, my boy is safe."

More than ten thousand people attended the gathering and subsequent parade, and it was noticed that not much work was accomplished the following day.

Newport had done its duty in World War II. Nearly 180 young men from the city gave their lives in defense of America. Another casualty was the Torpedo Station, which cut its workforce from 9,000 in August 1945 to just 2,300 by December. The following year, the navy decided to move torpedo manufacturing to Illinois, further reducing Newport's war role and leaving even more unemployment behind. What remained was the contribution the Torpedo Station had made. The historian Evelyn M. Cherpak contends that a third of all torpedoes fired during World War II, some forty-five thousand of them, were engineered in Newport. Nevertheless, like so many other munitions centers around the country, Newport had to adjust to a peacetime economy. But the city could be proud of its war record. In October 1945, the navy reported that almost three hundred thousand officers and enlisted men had received instruction at the Naval Training Station during the war. Newport greeted them, housed them, and made them feel at home. Hundreds of ships had a portion of their crews trained at Newport, including battleships, cruisers, destroyers, and hospital ships. By the time of Japan's capitulation, Newport had truly become a "Navy Town" and the men and women from all over the country who remained with the Atlantic Fleet became part of its ongoing history.

Newport had proved to be amenable to naval operations during two wars, so when military planners in Washington began to consolidate the various East Coast bases after the cessation of world hostilities, Newport was the beneficiary. Throughout 1946 more ships and men arrived in town. In early 1947, the navy announced that Newport would become a permanent fleet base for nearly one hundred warships headed by four carriers and 23,500 men. Along with Norfolk, Virginia, Newport was to be elevated to the status of Naval Base. Another housing shortage ensued and Middletown again expanded. More officers moved into Newport. Reflecting Newport's importance as a military education center, the Naval War College resumed its full-year schedule in 1947 and a General Line Officers school for 500 men was established for strategic training purposes. All through the late 1940s, 1950s, and 1960s, the navy dominated the social, economic, and academic life in Newport, altering the physical environment with ongoing construction and setting the tone for the tenor of the town. Sailors were seen everywhere on the streets, in the bars, in tattoo parlors, and all along the harbor.

But in the mid-1960s, the Torpedo Station was torn down and over the coming years, Goat Island was turned into a resort center, home to expensive seaside condominiums and a hotel. Torpedo production was finished, but the sprawling presence of numerous navy facilities (a large hospital, the Surface Warfare and Justice schools, the Underwater Weapons Research and Engineering stations) along the west coast of Aquidneck Island on Narragansett Bay was a boon to the local economy and a source of pride within the community. For decades, a substantial portion of the Atlantic fleet called Newport its home port; many

The renaissance of Newport was not to be an easy accomplishment. Community resistance, worries about funding, and a host of other obstacles had to be overcome. Yet the founders of the Preservation Society were determined to proceed with their mission. In March 1947, the Society invited Kenneth Chorley, president of Colonial Williamsburg in Virginia, to give a speech to the Newport community about the benefits of reclaiming its rich heritage. After recapping what had been done in Williamsburg over the previous twenty-five years and how those efforts had not only saved the past from obliteration but also served as a broad educational forum, Chorley told his audience,

In my lifetime, I expect to see Newport born again. I expect to see the eighteenth-century homes and buildings here carefully restored to the beauty which even their present-day shabbiness cannot conceal. I expect to see Newport a city of lovely doorways, gleaming brass knockers, and well-painted houses. I expect to be among the thousands who will come to Newport to enjoy the lovely music festivals, to review its panorama of architecture, to enjoy its fascinating colonial taverns and to explore its delightfully different shops. Above all, I expect to thrill at the recaptured spirit of the city of that far-off time when a forest of tall masts grew in the harbor, and to delight in the quaintness and charm of its unique waterfront—a memorial which will be fitting indeed for those men of the sea of another century who first made Newport great and who carried the city's fame to the most distant places on earth.

dozens of ships were berthed along the bay until 1973–1974 when President Richard Nixon nixed Newport (reportedly out of a fit of political pique over liberal New England voting trends) and ordered the majority of the fleet to make Norfolk, Virginia, its new rendezvous. Many residents still believe that the mastermind of Watergate pilfered a large portion of Newport's centuries-old naval legacy in an act of petty revenge, but it is more likely that planners in the Pentagon endorsed the move for budgetary purposes.

The Race to Restoration

At the end of World War II, Newport was once again facing an identity crisis. Population declined with the departure of naval trainees and curtailment of torpedo manufacturing, yet the presence of a portion of the Atlantic Fleet created a permanent base for sailors and their families throughout the area. Inexorably, the city was being molded by the large navy contingent, and the economy was highly dependent on federal dollars and whatever spending service personnel could manage. Gilded Age glories were reduced, industry still had made no inroads on the southern part of the island, and in 1945, civic leaders had to come to grips with Newport's future. What kind of community was it to become and who would shape its destiny? Many citizens worried that a virtual takeover by the navy would make the city too dependent on one employer (they were correct), and even with thousands of men in town spending their salaries, sailors were not well paid.

Throughout the long colonial period, Newporters were largely in control of determining the kind of environment they lived in. But the town learned a difficult lesson when the British army took away that jurisdiction at the time of the Revolution. During the nearly half century following 1780, the town was in deep decline, almost paralyzed, as it watched Providence and other northern towns industrialize and modernize. The influx of tourists and great wealth from 1830 to 1914 transformed the town once again—and again, these were primarily outsiders who were in charge of Newport's growth as Queen of Resorts. Then, with the build-up of the navy in Narragansett Bay during the two world wars, Newport's destiny was being forged as much by decisions made in Washington as it was by leaders in City Hall. To a large degree, the town's future was in the hands of the Department of the Navy. Newport was the yo-yo at the end of a long string since it had little to say about development, planning, or the size of its tax rolls.

But 1945 turned out to be a critical year in the city's long history. Newport began to map out its future, even if very few understood the ramifications at the time.

With the founding of the Preservation Society of Newport County, the road to restoration of the city's great legacies was begun in earnest and interest in preservation of the past became widespread. Finally, the answer to the question of what kind of community Newport was to become was found right at home. The city would re-create itself and show the world what over three centuries of American life was really like. Over the half century from 1945 Newport would take control from within, form numerous organizations dedicated to saving its architectural heritage, and emerge as one of the most popular tourist destinations in New England. With groups such as the Newport Restoration Foundation reclaiming the rich store of the city's colonial buildings and the Preservation Society concentrating primarily on nineteenth-century gems, Newport became a showcase of American history. Preservation became an ethic, a new twentieth-century industry that radiated Newport's fame for visitors and citizens alike.

St. Joseph's Roman Catholic Church of Newport owned the 1748 Nicholas-Wanton-Hunter House on Washington Street and used it to board a number of nuns. In 1945, the parish was planning to sell the house's paneled interiors to the Metropolitan Museum of Art in New York. One of the great homes of the colonial era was going to disappear and many people were aghast at the idea. Inspired in part by the numerous restoration projects overseen by the architect Norman M. Isham in previous decades, on August 9, 1945, Katherine Warren and her husband, George Henry Warren, held a meeting at their home on Mill Street to discuss alternatives, and the eleven people present (Mrs. John Nicholas Brown, Maxim Karolik, Maud and Edith Wetmore, among others) decided that they would form an organization and buy the Nicholas-Wanton-Hunter House for $16,000 in order to save it.

But their conversation ranged further, to encompass the idea of preserving other parts of the city threatened by neglect or zealous exploitation by real estate developers. Bellevue Avenue, where great estates were being sold for a fraction of their value, was a prime focus of discussion. (One example, and there are dozens of others: the Bradley-Shipman estate at Ruggles Avenue, now known as the Carey House owned by Salve Regina University, built around 1925 for over $1,000,000, was purchased in 1949 for $8,000 by a developer.) Most of the people at the initial meeting were summer-colony residents who had the imagination to envision what might lay ahead if no action were taken, and the means to stanch the slide of Newport into an urban mediocrity. They formed the Preservation Society of Newport County as a not-for-profit educational organization and began to work together to save important architectural specimens from obliteration.

A movement was born that day, one that gradually led people to understand that the real economic future of Newport lay in the preservation of three centuries of American buildings. The presentation of the country's history through its preserved buildings would lead to tourism and bring new visitors into the city each year to revel in art and music festivals at the same time they were discovering the past. A group of Newporters took control and opened a new destiny for the struggling city. It was neither easy nor self-evident at first that they would succeed. But after years of barely getting by, while remaining steadfastly focused on amassing a collection of priceless heirlooms, the Preservation Society not only endured and prospered, but it also became a model for other cities. Indeed, it served to make the preservation movement more widespread and effective. Katherine Warren's vision and industry saved Newport as a resort and eventually turned it into an international attraction.

There was much to be accomplished. Year by year valuable structures were falling in front of the wrecking ball. After purchasing Hunter House in 1946 and beginning its restoration, the board of the Preservation Society determined that a full-scale survey of Newport architecture was needed so important pieces of the city's history could be identified. Mrs. Michael M. van Beuren provided the necessary funds and the Society commissioned the architectural historian Antoinette Downing and the Yale architecture professor Vincent Scully, Jr., to proceed with the study. In 1952, their findings were published in *The Architectural*

Heritage of Newport, Rhode Island, 1640–1915. The heavily illustrated book became the touchstone for the expanding restoration movement.

The real coup during the early years was the agreement between the Society and Countess László Széchényi to lease The Breakers for one dollar per year and open the house to paying visitors. The countess was the daughter of Cornelius Vanderbilt II who had built the mansion. The Society purchased the home outright in 1972. The influx of tourists wanting to view the house was impressive from the beginning, and proved that Mrs. Warren's prescience was on target. If The Breakers could draw thousands, the reasoning went, then other "cottages" could probably do the same brisk business.

When Hunter House was restored and opened to the public in 1953, it featured a major loan exhibition of eighteenth-century local furniture, silver, and paintings that attracted national media attention and created a lasting reputation for the building. Paul Miller, chief curator of the Preservation Society wrote, "the two halls and nine rooms were completely furnished with outstanding examples of Newport cabinetmakers' art. Many of the pieces were by the Goddards and Townsends, whose shops were originally located not more than a 'stone's throw' from Hunter House."

The City of Newport began a national advertising campaign, and in 1950 claimed that its publicity of Newport as a family resort was seen by some sixty million people. Major magazines once again featured articles about the city's charms and houses and buildings open to the public. Touro Synagogue underwent substantial restoration under the auspices of the National Park Service because the nation's oldest Jewish house of worship was in need of restoration.

Throughout the 1950s the Society kept growing and adding properties to its management. Mr. Archbold van Beuren made it possible for the Society to purchase and restore the White Horse Tavern, dating back to 1673. Today, it is a privately owned restaurant. Under Mrs. Warren's leadership, the Society also hosted a number of large fundraising balls that were reminiscent of Gilded Age glories: the international Washington-Rochambeau gala at The Breakers in the summer of 1955, an event celebrating the 175th anniversary of the French army's arrival in Newport in 1780; the fashionable Tiffany's ball in 1957; and the famous Silver ball of 1959.

Large-scale preservation was catching on. In 1965, the Historic District was established by the City of Newport. More families and individuals were developing a mindset that donating treasured properties or selling them to the Society at below-market prices was a civic duty and good for the future of the community. Some developers bought large cottages and turned them into condominiums in order to save them. During the 1960s the Society continued its progress, acquiring E. J. Berwind's The Elms in 1962 with funds contributed by major donors. The following year, Marble House was obtained from Harold S. Vanderbilt and its original furnishings were given by the Frederick H. Prince Trust. In 1969 the Wetmore estate, Château-sur-Mer, was purchased; two years later, Rosecliff was given to the Society. Later acquisitions and restorations included Kingscote, the topiary garden called Green Animals in Portsmouth, the Marble House Tea House, Malbone (from Alletta Morris McBean), Hopedene (from Mrs. Charles Patterson),

Katherine Warren, 1905
Photographed by John Hopf
Courtesy of the
Preservation Society
of Newport County
Newport, Rhode Island

Chepstow (from Peter McBean), the former Pell house on Bellevue and Narragansett avenues, which housed the Preservation Society's staff, and the Isaac Bell House. Many people made significant gifts to the Society to purchase or help restore these buildings. By the turn of the twenty-first century, the Society controlled a majority of the Gilded Age's most significant structures, and millions of people from all over the world were coming to see them and partake of Newport's many other diversions. According to the Preservation Society, approximately 950,000 tickets were sold each year (2003 figures), making the Society's houses the most visited cultural attraction in Rhode Island and one of the top four historic sites in New England.

Leadership, perseverance, and good community relations were major sources of the Society's success. After nearly thirty years as president, Katherine Warren stepped down in 1975. Born in Oakland, California, in 1897, Mrs. Warren had also been a trustee of the Museum of Modern Art in New York and a member of Mrs. Jacqueline Kennedy's committee to restore the White House. Her vision to make Newport a preferred destination for people curious about the arts, music, and architecture was well on its way at the time of her death in April 1976. John G. Winslow was the next important leader at the helm of the Society, followed by John J. Slocum, Jr., and Armin B. Allen. All three presidents were instrumental in carrying on Katherine Warren's legacy, bringing order and imagination and guiding the organization into maturity. The Preservation Society transformed Newport once again and helped bring it back to its roots using local talent and resourcefulness. A vibrant portion of the city was proudly reclaimed.

While the Preservation Society would mobilize the rescue of some of the architectural treasures on Bellevue Avenue, it was evident to many in town that *something* had to be done about salvaging the terribly rundown colonial core of buildings around the Point area and along Thames Street. There were a number of precedents for the conservation of Newport's oldest homes: Norman M. Isham had carefully restored the

Wanton-Lyman-Hazard House in the 1930s, the original Oldport Association was responsible for relocating two eighteenth-century houses slated for destruction (also in the 1930s), and over the ensuing years many individuals began to renovate their properties. But there was no single organization responsible for saving the colonial-era buildings, and the helter-skelter approach was not yielding the kind of solution necessary for systematic redemption. As navy personnel began moving to base housing in the 1950s, more of the old buildings they had inhabited became vacant. Newport could offer itself to the world as a showcase for three centuries of American architectural tradition only if the dilapidated rooming houses and cold-water flats were restored and returned to single-family occupancy, where pride of ownership would act as a corrective against further decline.

Over the winter of 1963–1964, Operation Clapboard came into existence when a small group of Newport citizens, led by Nadine Pepys, Thomas Benson, and his mother, Esther F. Benson, decided to take action in the Point section. They formed a for-profit corporation, raised funds, identified likely targets for renovation, secured 90- to 120-day options on the houses, and then found buyers who had the vision to imagine what the house would look like after being restored. Operation Clapboard succeeded because the group not only did an excellent job of turning the buildings around, but also of finding people from outside Newport who wanted to move to town and be part of the experiment. Within two years, some thirty houses had been placed with new owners. Many streets on the Point began to look decidedly different, as house after house bore a fresh coat of exterior paint and interiors were brought back to eighteenth-century standards. The dream of returning the neighborhood to its former appearance was being slowly achieved.

But there were growing differences within Operation Clapboard: many of its members wanted to retain the status quo while a growing number wanted to shift to a not-for-profit profile, which would allow the group to receive tax-free gifts and organize educational programs. The rift could not be healed, so in the autumn of 1965, the Oldport Association was founded to pursue the same goals, but as a not-for-profit corporation. The two groups were careful not to compete with each other and did join together for some educational activities and tours, but the splintering damaged the overall movement. Clapboard remained dedicated to saving colonial homes, while Oldport started looking at preserving whole neighborhoods, regardless of the age or style. The latter group was responsible for relocating a number of houses that were targeted for demolition as well as renovating others. Clapboard, on the other hand, began to concentrate on lower Thames Street. Newport was beginning to undertake an extensive urban renovation at the time, and the downtown was in the throes of major change.

Both organizations were faced with rapidly rising home prices by the end of the 1960s and limited funds for development. At the same time, Doris Duke had incorporated the Newport Restoration Foundation to do essentially the same work as Clapboard and Oldport, but with far deeper pockets and an expanded agenda. After salvaging more colonial homes, Operation Clapboard quietly went out of existence in the early 1970s and Oldport was taken over as a division of the Newport Historical Society. They had done their job, however. Executive Director Pieter Roos of the Restoration Foundation maintains, "In its brief history Clapboard provided an invaluable service to preservation in Newport. Although it never owned a house, it was responsible for saving 43 historic buildings and perhaps more importantly, it started something that encouraged what has become one of the most resoundingly successful preservation efforts on the East Coast."

Two active grassroots community groups, the Top of the Hill Association and the Point Association, were continuing the legacy of Oldport and Clapboard by closely monitoring their neighborhoods and calling for block-by-block restoration when necessary.

Like Katherine Warren's efforts to reinvigorate the Bellevue Avenue area, Doris Duke's role in saving colonial Newport cannot be overemphasized or lauded enough. Together, these two determined women were at the center of gathering major decision-making authority under the control of the local community, not New York or Washington. Separately, through the organizations they led, they changed the face and future of Newport. Not only did their decades-long campaigns preserve the past, they also turned the city into a tourist destination for millions of people each year.

Doris Duke founded the Newport Restoration Foundation in 1968 because she was deeply concerned about the continued decay of the colonial-era buildings in and around the city. Miss Duke, as

Doris Duke, c. 1947
Portrait of American tobacco heiress and socialite Doris Duke (1912-1993), around the time of her second marriage to Porfiro Rubirosa, a Latin-American diplomat. Duke's first husband was socialite James Cromwell.
Photograph by New York Times Co./ Hutton Archive/Getty Images

she preferred to be called, had a long association with Newport, made her debut there in 1930, and stayed at her Rough Point estate nearly a third of each year. Born in November 1912, the only child of the tobacco tycoon James B. Duke, Doris inherited over $80 million when he died in 1925. The shy twelve-year-old daughter was quickly pigeonholed as "the Million Dollar Baby" and the "Richest Girl in the World" by the press, and spent the rest of her life trying to dodge a legion of hounding reporters who chronicled her often turbulent relationships. Twice married and divorced, Miss Duke's reputation too often rested on her public escapades and the billion-dollar estate she left when she died in 1993. What the media missed was her talent for amassing an extraordinary art and objects collection as well as her devotion to historic preservation. Her close involvement with the Restoration Foundation, and the amount of money she dedicated to saving colonial and Federal Newport (perhaps as much as $50 million), is a telling tribute to the degree of her care.

Miss Duke's timing was perfect. By 1968, Operation Clapboard and the Oldport Association were running out of options. When she stepped in to take up the cause, public redevelopment agencies were transforming downtown Newport in their headlong quest to modernize the city's infrastructure to accommodate tourism, often with little regard to the fact that they were bulldozing significant historic buildings. In her extensive survey, Antoinette Downing had ascertained that the city contained about four hundred eighteenth-century structures, of which roughly fifty had been targets for previous restoration. Miss Duke had a plan. The Foundation would purchase a house for somewhere between $5,000 and $20,000, then spend an additional $70,000 to $80,000 doing a total restoration. Yet in the 1970s, those completed houses only had a market value of about $50,000 each. Miss Duke's strategy was for the Foundation to retain ownership of all houses while renting or leasing them at prevailing market prices to dedicated tenants. That way, a first-class renovation was possible without concern about the economics. Newport benefited as whole streets became showcases for colonial homes inhabited by families who would maintain the residences, and families benefited by being able to live in an authentic setting at a reasonable price.

The Newport Restoration Foundation has rescued some eighty-five properties on Aquidneck Island, seventy in Newport alone. As wrecking balls were threatening many houses during the heyday of redevelopment in the 1970s, some houses were moved to appropriate vacant lots so they could be saved. In one case, the Foundation dismantled a house in just six days in order to keep it from being razed. The Foundation was also instrumental in the creation (1976 to 1978) of Queen Anne Square in front of Trinity Church, as well as other large-scale projects. Miss Duke was personally involved in all of these operations and enjoyed working with wood and ceramics. Rich as she was and contrary to her image in the press as a snobbish high-lifer, she was often more at home with the scores of carpenters and architects in Newport than she was with the international jet set. At the same time she was saving all those houses from destruction, she managed to assemble a first-rate collection of eighteenth-century Newport furniture and other objects that can be viewed at the restored Whitehorne House on Thames Street.

For nearly a quarter century, Doris Duke committed herself and her fortune to reviving the city she clearly loved. After her death, Mrs. Robert H. (Oatsie) Charles became president of the Board of Trustees of the Newport Restoration Foundation and soon thereafter brought in Pieter Roos as executive director. Together they, the board, and the staff continued the upkeep on all Foundation properties to make certain there was no deterioration of Miss Duke's high standards. The Foundation also maintains the majestic Rough Point, which is open as a museum for the public to view the sumptuous and varied collections created over a lifetime by Doris Duke. Because of her munificence and commitment to Newport, the nation as a whole is richer.

It might have turned out differently. The city could have turned a deaf ear to restoration and preservation and continued to slide into decline. Dominated as it was for so many decades by the United States Navy, many people might have been lulled into a false sense of security by its large presence and simply believed that it was the ticket to the future. Had not Katherine Warren,

THE STEVENS SHOP

One of the most remarkable examples of American career continuity can be found in Newport at 29 Thames Street, site of the John Stevens Shop. The first John Stevens moved to the small, low-ceilinged storefront in 1705 as a stone carver, producing cemetery headstones and designing letters for wood or stone, and dabbling in other building trades. His first headstones were crude, but he improved steadily over the years. His son, John II, followed into the field and his carvings were far superior to his father's. His headstones were adorned with similar borders and smiling cherubs and are easily identified in the Common Burying Ground along Farewell Street. John II was prolific; his gravestones can be seen throughout New England. John III was a young patriot at the time of the Revolution. He left Newport for a few years but returned after the British decamped to resume the family tradition. His ledgers and advertisements in the *Newport Mercury* (1781) fill in the details of the life of a prosperous eighteenth-century stonecutter.

Flash-forward to 1927 when John Howard Benson rented the Stevens Shop and began his career of cutting and engraving on stone (he bought and renovated the property

CONTINUED ON PAGE 448

Doris Duke, and a few other pioneers boldly called for a resuscitation of Newport's treasures (Brick Market, the Redwood Library, Trinity Church, Colony House, among others), laying the foundation for a more varied and vibrant economic base, the city would have been paralyzed when the navy was abruptly pulled from Narragansett Bay in 1973-74. As it is, the Newport that drew millions of visitors each year was healthy financially and offered a multitude of attractions. Nowhere else in America could one feast on so many significant historical buildings that had been so well preserved. Richard Moe, President of the National Trust for Historic Preservation, asserted in 2003, "Charleston and Newport are the bookends of preservation in America."

Urban Decay, Urban Renewal

The efforts of the Preservation Society, the Newport Restoration Foundation, and their sister organizations were tightly focused and, in terms of the community as a whole, small in scope. While their efforts were going on, there was little doubt that the city as a whole was deteriorating in the post–World War II years, and without a comprehensive plan to attack blight and regenerate large areas, Newport would lag behind in its efforts to attract sufficient tourist trade to stimulate the economy. It was a typical midcentury problem faced by scores of American cities: lack of infrastructure maintenance during the war years, economic setbacks, continued ravages from hurricanes (Carol and Edna caused extensive damage in town in 1954), and simple lack of care. When attitudes about what was an "acceptable" urban setting underwent substantial change in the postwar years, local governments were forced to respond. Some communities did a first-rate job of redevelopment. In 2006, the jury was still out on whether Newport's public agencies had achieved as much.

Regardless of the steps taken by private groups, signs of decay could be found in many parts of Newport. Whole lower- and middle-class neighborhoods were standing still or falling on hard times. Even vaunted Bellevue Avenue was being transformed again as a number of private mansions were being converted into schools. Catholic girls' college Salve Regina relocated to Newport in 1947 when Robert Goelet made a gift of his Ochre Court home to the Sisters of Mercy; the institution expanded on Ochre Point and became a fully accredited coed university. That was good for education but not for City Hall as one after another these donated cottages fell off the tax rolls, undercutting the leaders' ability to finance the city's future.

In December 1949, Mayor Edmund W. Pardee formed the Newport Redevelopment Agency, headed by M. Thomas Perrotti, to meet the challenges of the city's plight. After years of fighting neighborhood resistance, the agency began a large-scale clean-up of the West Broadway area, a move that brought balance back to the neighborhood but eventually displaced dozens of lower-income families and led to the development projects that proved to be a disaster in healthy city planning. Interaction with Washington's bureaucracy over federal government funding further delayed coherent progress.

There were a number of factors contributing to the stasis in Newport in the 1950s and 1960s. Eileen Warburton recounts,

While plans languished, the decay of the downtown was greatly accelerated by the ongoing search of over 30,000 sailors for some off-duty entertainment. Little by little, the waterfront district and Thames Street in particular was given over to saloons, bars, and dance halls like the old "Blue Moon Gardens." City government, already saturated with tavern, restaurant, and club liquor licenses, received constant application for more. Prostitution flourished, as did illegal gambling, and the pinball racket was a source of constant controversy until the city banned it altogether in 1958. So rough did the area become that the wharfside section of Pelham Street earned the well-known nickname "Blood Alley."

Up until the 1970s, parents would not let their children walk many downtown streets because they were so unsafe.

The Newport Redevelopment Agency struggled throughout the 1950s to come up with plans, and money, to resurrect the downtown district. Nothing seemed to meet the public's approval. The obstacles were enormous, arguments bitter, and the heaviest decisions concerned the condemning of properties in order to create a viable commercial center and an arterial road that

PRESIDENTS IN NEWPORT
During a seven-year period, beginning in 1957, Newport was the site of the Summer White House for presidents Dwight D. Eisenhower and John F. Kennedy. For both men, Newport was a refuge from the strains of Washington politics, a place to enjoy family and bask in the welcoming climate. Ike spent most mornings of his three month-long visits on the grounds of the Newport Country Club playing golf with the club president Howard G. Cushing and others. Crowds lined Harrison Avenue to get a glimpse of him and, because of the wide-open setting, the Secret Service was on high alert. Eisenhower and his wife, Mamie, spent time on the yacht *Barbara Anne*, went sightseeing in town, and were greeted warmly by citizens. They repeated their vacation, living on the grounds of Fort Adams in what is now aptly known as the Eisenhower House, in 1958 and 1960, the last year of his two-term presidency.

Jack Kennedy's relationship with Newport was deep. He married Jacqueline Bouvier in 1953 at St. Mary's Church on Spring Street; the reception was held at Jackie's mother's home, Hammersmith Farm, on Harrison Avenue. Oatsie Charles, long-time Newport and Washington resident, tells a story of her good friend before his election to the White House. One summer, Senator Kennedy retreated to Hammersmith Farm to recuperate from an illness. Soon Oatsie's phone rang and Kennedy said, "Oats, there aren't any good books over here. Could you bring me something?" Mrs. Charles was also a friend of the British author Ian Fleming, then virtually unknown in America. She gave Kennedy her copy of *Casino Royale* to read. When he became president a reporter asked him about his favorite authors and JFK extolled the virtues of Fleming's Agent 007. The public rushed to discover Fleming and soon he was a regular on the best-seller list. Thus we have Oatsie Charles to thank for four decades of James Bond movies and countless hours of escapism.

In September 1961, the Kennedy family traveled to Hammersmith Farm to rest and sail on his yacht *Honey Fitz*. Occasionally,

CONTINUED ON PAGE 450

PREVIOUS PAGE
*Jacqueline Bouvier
with her husband
Sen. John F. Kennedy,*
as they stand in from
of St. Mary's Church,
Spring Street, after their
wedding ceremony
on September 12, 1953.
Photograph by
Lisa Larsen/Time &
Life Pictures/Getty Images

would cut through the area allowing for easy auto access to other parts of town. In 1962, a plan was finally adopted and passed by voters, and for the rest of the decade, the downtown resembled a war zone with so much demolition and new building. "In 1966 the digging up of Newport's downtown began. Dilapidated wooden houses and sturdy brick warehouses, thriving shops and abandoned businesses, navy bars and coal yards, Blood Alley and Market Square, the Government Landing and the police station, all alike fell before the wrecking ball and the bulldozers. By 1967 the 22 acre waterfront strip below Thames Street between Market Square and Long Wharf was practically denuded." In 1966, all the government buildings on Goat Island were razed to make room for private expansion, and in 1968, a causeway linking the island to Newport was completed. The city had changed greatly.

All of the dislocation and reconstruction were in anticipation of the proposed Newport Bridge, then in the planning stages. As a result, the designers created America's Cup Avenue as the central roadway through the lower city, effectively bisecting the waterfront from easy pedestrian traffic access and marring the very heart of the area. What had for centuries been a community that lived by and for the sea was now cut off from its roots by a four-lane thoroughfare that would funnel increased traffic into the center of town and its small streets. In the 1960s, that was seen as a step forward: more cars, more people, more money in the hands of merchants. By the end of the century that strategy had become discredited as large summer traffic jams became the norm. How could an old city, laid out on a scale to accommodate horses and carriages, deal with the millions of people who ventured there each year in automobiles? While positive in many ways, the massive redevelopment of the midcentury lacked farsightedness, reduced to rubble some significant structures like the Water Works and Ley's Department Store, and forced Newport citizens and visitors alike to rely on their wheels instead of their feet to navigate the city. In the twenty-first century, rethinking and redesigning downtown Newport has become a priority. The well-meaning urban planners of the 1960s and 1970s removed remnants of a discarded past, but they also bored a hole in the soul of the city.

The America's Cup in Newport

Newport is recognized throughout the world for its mansions and music festivals, but for many people the most frequent association is with the thirteen America's Cup yacht races that were held off Brenton Point from 1930 until 1983. When the Cup competitions first moved to Newport from New York harbor, the general public had scant interest in the contests, largely because yachting was viewed as a rich man's sport that was dull to watch. (Competing at that level was, and is, the domain of the wealthy, but the races were hardly dull.) Then, at the very time that the mansions and colonial homes of Newport were being restored, the rest of the world began to notice that America had an unprecedented winning streak at stake. By the 1970s, the international press was covering the event with gusto, and Newport itself was as much a part of the reporting as the battles on sea. During the summer months, when yacht clubs from various nations were in town contending to determine who would challenge the United States in the September finale, nightlife was vigorous, the waterfront was filled with craft, and the bars along the harbor were filled to capacity. When the Cup's longtime proprietor, the New York Yacht Club, lost the trophy to Australia in 1983, the world's attention was focused on the City by the Sea. "Newport" and the "America's Cup" had been synonymous for so long that the shock of losing the prize took a long time to abate.

Why did the New York Yacht Club move the America's Cup trials and races to Newport in 1930? All of the significant members of the club were familiar with Newport, which was a veritable second home for them. The town had been a sailing center for centuries, and all the necessary nautical facilities could be found nearby. New York harbor was getting more congested with commercial shipping, more polluted, and it was becoming more difficult for the spectator fleet to observe the races off Sandy Hook unimpeded. (The Race Committee wanted to switch the competition to Newport in 1920, but the idea was vetoed by Sir Thomas Lipton for a decade.) As any old salt knows, the intensity and direction of the wind are crucial factors in a race, and because the waters off Brenton Point were well known for their light and normally regular breezes in September, it was deemed the superior location. For fifty-three years Newport was the yachting capital of the world, and even after the loss of the Cup, many sailors still consider it to be so.

In 1851, Britain's Royal Yacht Squadron invited other nations to compete in a race off the Isle of Wight. Six members of the recently created New York Yacht Club formed a syndicate that built the schooner *America* and sent her across the sea. *America* was up against fourteen supposedly superior vessels and in unknown waters, yet she won handily, taking home what was known then as the "Hundred Guinea Cup." The first America's Cup races were held in 1857 when the cup was formally transferred to the Yacht Club on the condition that it be placed forever in competition in accordance with the deed of the gift; its name was changed then to the America's Cup. From that time on, the Cup has tempted dozens of men from as many nations to spend untold millions of dollars in pursuit of what became known as the Holy Grail of yachting. Schooners were the early boat of choice, but as designs became more sophisticated, huge gaff-rigged sloops became popular. Every time nations entered the competition to wrest the Cup away from America, boat design was improved. By the time the races moved to Newport, the glorious J-Class yachts were in

America
from *America and English Yachts*
with *A Treatise upon Yachts and Yachting*
by Edward Burgess
Illustrated by the photogravure process from the original negatives of N. L. Stebbins (New York: Charles Scribner's Sons, 1887) Plate XXVII. Winner of the 1851 "Hundred Guinea Cup."
Redwood Library and Athenæum
Newport, Rhode Island

vogue, and many of the American contenders were constructed in Bristol, Rhode Island, at the renowned Herreshoff boatyard.

Given its longevity, the America's Cup rivalries are drenched in lore. Although American boats proved to be superior time after time, many of the matches produced white-knuckle finishes, and every time an improved technology or new boat design was introduced, speculation abounded that the United States would finally be defeated. It took 132 years for that to happen, and the New York Yacht Club's hold on the Cup is still the longest sustained winning record in any sport. But England's Sir Thomas J. Lipton, who made his fortune in tea, tried five times, from 1899 to 1930, in five different boats, each named *Shamrock*, to win the Cup. He was always a gracious loser. In 1934 and 1937, the Englishman Thomas Sopwith challenged, but the American skipper Harold S. Vanderbilt proved superior in Newport waters on *Rainbow* in 1934 and on *Ranger* in 1937. *Ranger* represented the biggest advance in yacht design in fifty years and proved unbeatable. President Franklin D. Roosevelt attended one of the contests aboard the Astor yacht *Nourmahal*. After the 1937 races, because of world events, all competitions were cancelled until a challenge was made by Britain in 1957. Since J-Class boats were enormously expensive to construct, the British stipulated that their offer was valid only if both countries shifted to the new, smaller, 12-Metre class. The New York Yacht Club accepted, and went on to win the 1958 Cup races in the new *Columbia* by a wide margin over *Sceptre*.

Competitors were wondering whether anyone would ever be able to break America's stranglehold on the venerable Cup. Were Newport's waters a jinx on the rest of the world? Other countries were introducing superior designs and sails, and still the Americans managed to dominate. Some observers posited that the American crews were better trained and that was the reason for such a long streak of victories. Still, the challenges kept coming. Millionaires around the globe were obsessed by the fantasy of finally breaking the spell and dethroning the Yanks. In 1962 the Australians entered the fray with the sleek *Gretel*, but captain Emil (Bus) Mosbacher in *Weatherly* trounced the boat from Down Under. When asked by a reporter why he had decided to take on the mighty New York Yacht Club, the Australian syndicate head Sir Frank Packer replied, "Alcohol and delusions of grandeur." President John F. Kennedy not only attended the

America's Cup Ball at The Breakers that September but also watched a portion of the races from the destroyer *Joseph P. Kennedy Jr.*

The next challenge came in 1964 when Britain brought *Sovereign* across the seas. Over the summer four United States boats competed for the glory of defending the Cup, and those races were far more exciting than the actual Cup contests. The famous boat-design firm of Sparkman and Stephens had produced the state-of-the-art 12-Metre *Constellation*, which easily defeated *Sovereign* four races to zero. The identical scenario occurred in 1967 when Bus Mosbacher on *Intrepid* whipped another Australian contender, *Dame Pattie*, in four straight races. American yachtsmen were seemingly invincible, yet again competitors went back to their drawing boards and test tanks to try to find the key to breaking the American domination. But 1970 brought the predictable results: *Intrepid* out sailed and outmaneuvered Australia's *Gretel II* by a large margin. The same for 1974, when the first aluminum "twelve," *Courageous*, defeated Australia's *Southern Cross* easily. The frustration was growing and the cost of mounting a campaign kept rising.

In the 1977 Cup challenge, a new element of drama was introduced in the person of Ted Turner, famously called "the Mouth of the South," for his often outlandish pronouncements on just about anything on his mind. A brash, rich newsman, Turner was a twentieth-century throwback to the great James Gordon Bennett. The colorful and talented Turner took the helm of *Courageous*, while the sailmaker Ted Hood piloted *Independence*, at first thought to be the faster of the boats. But Turner proved to be the better skipper and won

The Schooners Adix and Adela under sail, 1997
Photograph by Onne van der Wal Photography Inc.

the right to defend the Cup, which he did successfully, beating *Australia*. Three years later, Dennis Connor, one of the most dominant sailors of his generation, entered the scene in *Freedom* and thoroughly trounced his countrymen in the summer trials, winning forty-two of forty-seven matches. Connor instituted long training programs and was extremely competitive, driving his crews to near perfection. Even though America still remained undefeated, Connor knew that other nations were closing the technology gap. *Australia* again won the right to challenge Connor, but 1980 would not be the year to dethrone America: *Freedom* won, four races to one.

Cup fever heated up in 1983, when seven foreign challengers invaded Newport for most of the summer to decide which boat would go up against Dennis Connor and the New York Yacht Club. The trials were close, but one boat stood out, and that was *Australia II*. Rumors swirled around the harbor that the boat had some kind of break-through design, and those stories were flamed by the fact that whenever *Australia II* was hoisted out of the water for repair or maintenance, her keel was always shrouded with a skirt. The boat won the challenge trials and in September took on Connor on *Liberty*. The press presence was the most intense ever, with live television coverage of the contests beamed around the world. America had never been challenged that closely before, and with the races tied at three-all in the best-of-seven match, the entire yachting world was watching on September 26 to see the outcome of the most exciting Cup match ever, one now dubbed "the race of the century."

The streak, of course, couldn't go on forever. Connor took the lead at the starting gun, but on the final leg, *Australia II* overtook *Liberty* and cruised to the finish line with a 41-second conquest. Australia 4, America 3. The Cup was finally lost, and in Newport that day is still referred to as "Black Monday." The city was stunned. After an initial celebration, later that evening the Australians hauled their boat out of the water and displayed their ultimate weapon: an innovative and dynamic winged keel that turned out to be the margin of victory. The next day, after the America's Cup had been unbolted from its display case in the New York Yacht Club's Forty-fourth Street headquarters in Manhattan and driven to Newport in an armored truck, the "Auld Mug" was formally presented to the Australian team at Marble House. America's long reign had ended.

But Newport's had not. The city was world famous for hosting the matches for over half a century, and many local sailors, after their initial disbelief that the races would be held elsewhere, went into action and created Sail Newport in 1985 to attract amateurs to their sport. The effort proved very successful, and, in 2005, twenty-two years after the Cup departed, there was more sailing in Narragansett Bay than during the Cup's heyday. Close to fifty different sailing events took place around Newport every year, led by the Sail Newport Regatta. The city's nautical reputation was intact. Since 1936, the popular bi-annual 635-mile Newport to Bermuda race has attracted international participants. In 1976, the Tall Ships from around the world honored Newport by first gathering in Narragansett Bay before departing for New York to celebrate America's Bicentennial. And Newport harbor remained home to a number of restored 12-Metre yachts that once contended for the America's Cup. Each summer, they could be seen gliding through the harbor and if you squinted your eyes, you could imagine them on the course off Brenton Point. So in a way, the spirit of the grand days of Cup competition was not gone at all.

Music, Music, Music

Katherine Warren's vision of Newport becoming a mecca for the arts was partially fulfilled in 1954 when two summer-colony stalwarts, Louis and Elaine Lorillard, staged the first Newport Jazz Festival concerts with help from the impresario George Wein. The Lorillards had conceived the idea to bring top-name, serious jazz musicians to the city on an annual basis, and they succeeded beyond anyone's expectations. Although occasionally beset by assorted disturbances, the Newport Jazz Festival is still regarded as one of the premier musical venues in the world. Nearly every significant jazz player has appeared in Newport and numerous careers have been made or resuscitated because of being seen and heard at the festival. The opening night at the Casino on July 17, 1954, is a good example. Among the performers were Dizzy Gillespie, Billie Holiday, Dave Brubeck, and Ella Fitzgerald. Year after year, regardless of the location of the concerts, the world's greatest jazz artists graced the stage and treated audiences to some of the best performances of their lives.

Throughout the 1950s and 1960s the Jazz Festival's reputation continued to grow—along with the crowds. Fans flocked to Newport by the thousands to hear Louis Armstrong, Miles Davis, Duke Ellington, Count Basie, Thelonious Monk, Gene Krupa, and other stars. Many of the concerts were aired on Voice of America, heard by millions of Europeans and Asians, further spreading the popularity of this made-in-America art form. The festival has been located at Freebody Park, Festival Field off Connell Highway, and for over two decades at Fort Adams, allowing for stricter crowd control. Every summer Newport was invaded by young men and women who, finding no hotel space, slept in parks and on beaches. Riots by spectators in 1960 and 1971 marred the event, and from 1971 to 1981, George Wein moved the concerts from Newport to

Aerial view of
Fort Adams and
Newport harbor, c. 1960
Photograph by John T. Hopf
Newport Historical Society
Newport, Rhode Island

Ray Charles performing at the 1958 JVC Newport Jazz Festival.
Founded in 1954, the Newport Jazz Festival was the world's first outdoor festival devoted entirely to jazz.
Photograph by John Corbett
Newport Historical Society
Newport, Rhode Island

New York City. Since returning to Newport, the music at the Jazz Festival has retained its high standards and the crowds have been more orderly than in earlier years.

With the sustained success of the Jazz Festival, Wein launched the Newport Folk Festival in 1959 (without the Lorillards, with whom he had split). His timing was excellent. Folk coffeehouses had become popular all over America and throughout the 1960s the folk scene was at the heart of antiwar protest songs. With America's commitment in Vietnam escalating, the Newport Folk Festival became the place to launch new material and reprise classics. Joan Baez got her first national exposure at Newport, as did Arlo Guthrie and numerous other artists. It became so fashionable that for years attendance at the Folk Festival was greater than for the Jazz Festival. Newport had a solid international reputation as a music oasis.

The most notorious moment in Folk Festival history occurred on July 25, 1965, when the brightest star in the folk firmament made his pact with the devil and went electric. Bob Dylan was supposed to be the next Woody Guthrie and the folkie world was in awe of his songwriting talents (the voice took some getting used to). In front of a filled-to-capacity crowd, Dylan began his set by strumming a battered acoustic guitar, giving his fans what they had come to hear. But after a brief break, Dylan reappeared on stage with a backup band and, to the horror of orthodox purists, holding an amplified Fender Stratocaster guitar. As he ripped into his amped set of rock music, the stunned audience broke into two distinct camps: those who booed Dylan as a traitor to the cause and those who applauded him because they believed an artist was allowed to switch horses midstream if that's where his talent took him. It was a decisive moment in both the folk-music world and the larger entertainment industry arena. Dylan's betrayal of pure folk music, of course, never hurt his career. In fact, his performance at the Newport Folk Festival of 1965 gave birth to a new genre: folk-rock.

In the following years (the concerts were cancelled from 1971 to 1985 because of the riots at the Jazz Festival in 1971), as tastes changed and creative new artists entered the scene, the Folk Festival became more accepting of different modes of expression. Like jazz, which is in constant flux, with few fixed rules about what constitutes purity, American folk music has evolved since Dylan began to redefine what was permissible. For decades, the Newport Folk Festival has been the leader in introducing new stars and new styles.

The third significant concert series held each summer in the city is the two-week-long Newport Music Festival, featuring classical musicians from around the globe. Since becoming artistic director in 1975 (the festival began in 1969, under the direction of Mrs. Verner Z. Reed), Mark P. Malkovich III has created a world-class event that draws a large international patronage because of the consistent high quality of the musicians and the variety of composers presented. The Newport Music Festival is different from the jazz or folk offerings because Malkovich chooses a variety of venues for the concerts. In the mansions along Bellevue Avenue, at beaches, at Salve Regina University, on cruise ships in the harbor, or at an assortment of other settings, morning, afternoon, and evening, some sixty-five to seventy separate events are staged every year.

Every year brings a new theme or a celebration of a particular composer's work. Malkovich strives to present music never heard before in America, and spends much of each year searching for rare and overlooked compositions. Then he matches new performers to the music and *voilà*, the magic begins. Since the 1970s he has discovered scores of young performers who, after their debut at Newport, have gone on to establish solid reputations. Because of his longtime relationships with these musicians, Malkovich has been able to lure many of them back to the city at greatly reduced fees after they have achieved fame. The performers benefit from the exposure, and Newport benefits from being able to make a claim for the title of the Number One classical festival in America.

Bridging the Gap

Some transformations take a long time. In Newport, with its venerable maritime traditions, the concept of altering the island identity was slow to surface. Geography had dictated the town's destiny since 1639. Thus the act of building a bridge that would connect Newport to the mainland (via the Jamestown Bridge)

J/24's racing under the Senator Claiborne Pell Bridge in Newport harbor, 1998
Photograph by Onne van der Wal Photography Inc.

took 330 years. Most people say it was worth the wait, while others still lament the end of the town's island insularity. The opening of the Newport Bridge (officially the Claiborne Pell Bridge) in 1969 redefined Newport profoundly—and forever. No longer dependent on ferries and other craft, now open to the rest of the country by automobile, the city's crucial chemistry was altered when the bridge went into operation. Physically and psychologically, Newport underwent a metamorphosis. For those 330 years, the harbor had been the heart of the town because the only way on or off the southern part of Aquidneck Island had been by boat. The Mount Hope Bridge of 1929 eased passage for cars coming from the north, but in Newport, the sea offered the only escape. As Americans relied more and more on their cars after World War II, the disadvantage of a ferry-based transportation system became evident. Waiting time at the ferry slips grew longer each year, and disgorging a boatload of cars into the heart of downtown Newport at Ferry Landing caused larger traffic jams. As private and public leaders of Newport looked to a future based on tourism, the arts, and historic preservation, it was difficult to envision how the city could entice visitors unless a major bridge was built.

The idea was not a new one. In August 1945, the Newport-Jamestown Bridge Commission got permission from the United States Navy to construct a two-part span across the East Passage of Narragansett Bay. The plan was to raise one section from Coddington Cove to Gould Island, with a second leg over to Jamestown. Nothing came of this scheme for the usual reason: lack of funding. The commission dissolved, but the dream didn't die. Beginning in the 1950s, when urban renewal designs were dripping off architects' drafting tables, the necessity to bridge the gap across the bay to allow for unfettered access to town was a given in the eyes of most city planners. In theory, a bridge was the path to the future, but yet again, the reality of economics became the greatest obstacle. After years of wrangling, in 1964 state voters approved the Rhode Island Turnpike and Bridge Authority's use of tolls from the Jamestown and Mount Hope bridges to finance the Newport Bridge; a $17.5 million bond was also passed. The location of the bridge was a long-simmering issue as well. Early plans had its terminus in Middletown, but Newport merchants successfully lobbied for a more southerly access to boost their businesses, and in the end they prevailed. As years went by, estimates of the cost skyrocketed from the initial $31 million to the final figure of $61 million.

With funding in hand, the Turnpike and Bridge Authority, under the guidance of Newporter Francis Dwyer, began construction in January 1966 and over a three and a half year period, the job employed thousands of people, hundreds of them locals. The two central towers, 400 feet above the water, were in place by 1967, and the 2.2-mile span—the largest suspension bridge in New England—was due to open in 1968, but bad weather and an ironworkers' strike delayed completion for a year. At the same time, access roads and numerous other bridge-related projects were being undertaken. The Newport Bridge had to be high enough (215 feet) to allow for navy aircraft carriers to pass freely, and if laid end to end, the suspension cables supporting the structure would stretch over 4,000 miles. It was Rhode Island's largest and most costly public works project until that time.

On June 28, 1969, Senator Claiborne Pell and a number of other dignitaries rode in the first vehicle to officially cross the four-lane bridge. The dedication ceremony included many speeches, followed by a parade across the expanse. Newport was now open to the world, and the world flocked to its doorstep. Average daily trips were recorded at 6,580 in 1970 and jumped to 18,400 by 1998. "By 1979, the annual traffic flow had exceeded 3.06 million, and it has gone up consistently ever since: 4.8 million in 1984; 6.4 million in 1989; 6.7 million in 1994; 8.4 million in 1997." During summer months, and particularly at Jazz and Folk Festival weekends, over 36,000 cars pass over the bridge daily.

The coming of the bridge meant that new trade-offs had to be confronted. More traffic in town from tourism brought in more dollars, but with them came severe congestion on summer weekends. Travel to points south was made easier, but some of Newport's romance and mystery were swept away by being linked to the rest of the nation. For many people, the island *psychology* vanished when the city became readily available by car. The venerable Jamestown Ferry went out of business the same day the bridge became useable. Foremost, the look and character of Newport had been forever changed by the opening of the Pell Bridge, but the city's future prosperity had been secured. When the navy fleet departed in 1973, instead of being economically devastated, Newport rallied, promoted year-round tourism more actively, and succeeded in becoming one of the most sought-after destinations in New England.

Three hundred and sixty years after Dr. John Clarke, William Coddington, and their fellow founders made their way to the harbor and laid claim to the land, the city inaugurated its larger lifeline to the world and was no longer isolated in its island setting.

Newport beckons, open to all.

Epilogue

Newport in the early twenty-first century is an international city, visited yearly by some three million visitors, descended upon by sailing aficionados, music lovers, students of architecture, and people intent on witnessing what over three centuries of American heritage looks and feels like. Newport offers living history, encapsulating every phase of America's growth, and in that presentation it is unlike any other city in the nation.

Since its inception in 1639, Newport has been transformed by the events that touched it—reinventing itself when necessary, retaining its treasures when possible. The city's story is one of cycles of prosperity and reversals of fortune rather than one of steady expansion and progress along an inevitable path. Newport proved to be a leader in the transformation of America from its colonial beginnings, throughout its development, up until the present time. Some of the contributions were subtle, a setting of style or nuance; others were fundamental initiatives of lasting importance that pointed America in new, more democratic or artistic directions.

With the King Charles II Charter of 1663, Newport led the colonies in the acceptance of religious freedom for its subjects, a notion still blasphemous at that time in Boston and other towns. Yet it was the Newport model that ultimately prevailed in the nation, and today America is a country renowned for its guarantee of the right to personal belief. Newport was the first colonial town to break with Great Britain in 1776, sending a message to King George III two months before publication of the Declaration of Independence that Americans were ready to openly rebel against his rule.

After the Revolution and the long period of stagnation which followed, Newport became one of the most sought-after destinations for leisure and entertainment in nineteenth-century America: the Queen of Resorts during a period when the nation was radically redefining itself and beginning to present itself on the world stage. Much of the activity of the Gilded Age in Newport might be cast off as frivolous or inane or worse, but that is missing the larger point. The Duke of Wellington famously asserted that the Battle of Waterloo had been won on the playing fields of Eton. Likewise, at a time when America was coming of age socially and culturally, the broad social norms established by the country's elite in Newport set the tone for the imperial and powerful America that evolved between the Civil War and World War I. As the country grew into one of the dominant political and military forces of the twentieth century, its debt to activities that took place in Newport became more evident. The town's grand architecture along Bellevue Avenue from this period alone symbolizes America's growing wealth, influence, and global aspirations.

In the twentieth century, Newport played host to the United States Navy during two world wars. Then, rediscovering its roots, it became one of the leaders in historic preservation and restoration of its architectural assets of three hundred-plus years. No other city in America possesses a collection of period pieces so vast and important, and Newport continues to refurbish its gifts from earlier years. People from around the globe visit Newport to discover a collection of art, artifacts, and architecture that vividly portray all stages of United States history. It is a city alive in promise, alive in the past, and vibrant in the present.

What has placed Newport apart from other American cities over the centuries? It should be remembered that four of the nine founders in 1639 were men of wealth and advanced education. They set the tone for the evolving enclave, demanding toleration in religious realms and freedom for their mercantile pursuits. They had a vision. The town prospered, artisans thrived, and the Redwood Library provided a home for intellectual advancement. Even after the ravages of the Revolution and the ensuing half century, Newporters remembered their special heritage. Thus it should come as no surprise that a spirit of place, a spirit of independence, has always resided in Newport citizens.

The prescient William Hunter (of Hunter House) understood the potential for the city he loved. In 1835, even though Newport was struggling to survive, Hunter looked to the future. In a letter from Rio de Janeiro, where he was serving as America's first Minister to Brazil, Hunter wrote: "I find I love poor, dear, old Newport—and most that inhabit it—I calmly think, even at this distance, and away from the misguiding prejudices and affections of mere locality, that its time of renovation and comparative prosperity is near at hand. I predict this . . . from the natural effects of time and the inevitable progress of national prosperity. . . . People who have money will come there, at least in summer to enjoy it—those who are high in what is deemed rank and are safe in hereditary wealth, because they can show their ranks and wealth advantageously—those who have acquired it by hard knocks because they can elegantly repose from their labors—and those who have clinched it by the little turns and tricks of trade because they hope they may be forgotten at a distance and the glittering butterfly never suspected of having been a grub."

Hunter, of course, was on target with his prediction. Fifty years after he wrote those words, Newport had become the flame that drew the butterfly and the Brahmin alike, the brightest beacon during America's age of expansion. That flame still flickers. Today, people flock to Newport to experience its culture and entertainment, but increasingly more so to savor the rich remains of its two vibrant periods—the colonial Golden Age and the republican Gilded Age. Visitors from around the world want to connect with American heritage, to feel it and see it firsthand. Newport offers that opportunity because, throughout its long and colorful history, a sense of destiny has prevailed in the town. Newport has lived up to Dr. John Clarke's revolutionary vision. It has been a lively experiment indeed.

Acknowledgments

The impetus behind this book was twofold. At a meeting of the Board of Directors of the Doris Duke Charitable Foundation in the late 1990s, Mrs. Robert Charles, known as Oatsie, was asked by a fellow board member if he could read a history of Newport to better understand Miss Duke's contributions to the city. Oatsie replied that no such book existed. At the same time, Ralph Carpenter, who had been involved in many of Newport's restoration projects, had the idea to have a comprehensive volume devoted to Newport history written. Oatsie and Ralph discussed the project, and in late 2001 they asked me to write the book after I had prepared an outline detailing how I proposed to proceed. The plan was to have the book published by the Redwood Library and Athenæum of Newport, the oldest circulating library in America still in its original building.

Ralph Carpenter approached Gilbert S. Kahn and John J. Noffo Kahn about donating the seed money to begin work. After reading the proposal, the Kahns determined that they would donate all of the money for the project through Gilbert's mother's foundation, The Janet A. Hooker Charitable Trust, and full-time work began in early 2002. Gilbert and John's generous gift gave life to a project long overdue.

In any project of this scope, the author becomes indebted to a large number of people who help in a variety of ways. In some cases, encouragement and friendship were offered and accepted; in others, concrete contributions have been graciously given. To begin, had it not been for Betsy and Frank Ray and Lisette Prince, who alerted Ralph that I was available to work on the project, I would not have been offered the opportunity to write this book. Without encouragement from Cheryl Helms, Director of the Redwood Library, the process would have been far harder. She has shepherded all the people involved through every stage of the book's creation, coordinated schedules, and has been the mainstay of the project. Cheryl, along with Ralph Carpenter, George Herrick, and Newport Restoration Foundation Executive Director Pieter Roos, read each chapter, caught my errors in grammar or fact, and offered valuable suggestions along the way. Pulitzer Prize-winning Professor Gordon S. Wood, of Brown University, reviewed some early chapters and rapped my knuckles for my initial lack of appreciation for the nuances of the Puritan movement.

I am grateful for the efforts of Brian Stinson, who produced the greatest share of the research needed to complete the book. His untiring work over two and a half years saved me untold hours because he was able to provide me with the right materials at the right time. His knowledge of Newport and the many libraries he consulted to find the research greatly reduced the production time of this book. Instead of having a project that would last four years or more, I was able, through Brian's efforts, to complete the manuscript in two years and two months. Others who helped in researching materials were Holly Snyder and Celeste Calderón. I would also like to thank the staff of the Redwood Library for their support: Lynda Bronaugh, Wendy Kieron-Sanchez, Lisa Long, Nancy Hackett, Laurel DeStefano, Tony Keys, Marianne Shattuck, Stacey Lyon, Jaclyn Morrell, and Elaine Bunnell made my life more productive and pleasant during the writing stage.

Newport: A Lively Experiment was produced by Poulin + Morris Inc., a highly respected design firm in New York City. L. Richard Poulin played the principal role in bringing this volume to life, aided by Anna Crider and Moonsun Kim. Their sense of style, design, materials, and layout—to say nothing of their expertise in book design and production—has enabled the Redwood Library to publish a book that can be appreciated for years to come.

Others who have given aid and comfort over the writing and editing phases include Stephen Walk, Susan Watts, and Brendan Kelley. Jane Carey has done a fine job as illustrations researcher. Friends such as Patricia Beard, Angela and Garry Fischer, Audrey Oswald, Larry and Betty Lou Sheerin, Jonathan and Bettie Pardee, Ronnie and Lilly Dick, Bill and Janet Russo Jacklin, Ken and Catharine Taylor, Ross and Leah Cann all contributed comments and observations that have made this a richer study of a city they all love. Bill and Allison Vareika, Hon. William Middendorf, Thomas Michie, and Roger and Sandra King helped with the sections on Newport artists. Hon. Esmond Harmsworth, Robert Severud, and Dana Cole provided valuable knowledge of the publishing and printing worlds.

Aside from the Redwood Library, several other cultural institutions in Newport provided materials that have enriched this book. My thanks to Armin Allen, Trudy Coxe, Paul Miller, Charles Burns, and John Tschirch of the Preservation Society of Newport County for their help in a variety of areas. At the Newport Historical Society, Daniel Snydaker, Joan Youngken, and librarian Bert Lippincott III all made my task more enjoyable. Not only has the Historical Society published scores of articles that I used as references in this book, its vast collection of illustrations helps enhance this volume. At the Newport Restoration Foundation, Oatsie Charles and Pieter Roos have been extraordinarily helpful, offering advice and helping me put certain events into perspective.

A number of people read various sections of the manuscript; I am grateful for their insights. Constructive comments were offered by Kenneth Carlson, Michael J. Crawford, Norman Fiering, Wendell Garrett, Hon. Desmond Guiness, Robin Kaufman, Charles Noyes, Walter Patten, Keith Stokes, Olin Stephens, and John Toll. To others who contributed their knowledge, my thanks.

The nuts and bolts of bringing out a book come easily if an established publishing house is the producer. In our case, we have had to learn every aspect of the process. It has never been dull. One of our most important participants has been the publicity firm of Goldberg McDuffie Communications, and particularly Lynn Goldberg and Angela Baggetta Hayes. Together they have given the Redwood Library crucial advice about how to proceed in today's overcrowded and highly competitive book world. To my copyeditor, Jason Weiss, I extend my gratitude for the care and handling of an often unruly text that, through his efforts, is now tamed. If there are errors in the book (and of course there probably are) the blame is the author's, not the researchers' or copyeditor's.

Finally, my thanks to my wife Patricia for putting up with my long absences and almost total inattention to anything not related to the book over the past several years. Along with the almost impossibly erudite George Herrick, Pat has been my best and closest reader, and the history of Newport has been enhanced by her intelligence and sense of style.

Rockwell Stensrud
Newport, Rhode Island
May, 2006

Source Notes

page   *chapter*

PROLOGUE
x   "It is well known": Bridenbaugh, *Fat Mutton*, 5.

THE BIRTH OF NEWPORT · 1639–1655
4-5   Nine Newport founders: Richman, *Making & Meaning*, 157-160.
4-5   Nine Newport founders: Bridenbaugh, *Fat Mutton*, Appendix I, 133.
5   "Many of these settlers": Downing, 15.
5-6   "fronting on the harbor": Field, I, 48.
6   "the Plantation now begun": Ibid., 49.
6   "the Towne shall be built": Ibid., 49.
6   "With the early summer weather": Robson, IV, 140.
6   "The character of the boxlike": Downing, 22.
7-8   Founders' land: Robson, IV.
8   "The sulphurous path leading": Fraser, 17.
9   "They wanted to reduce": Fisher, *Colonial Times*, I, 125.
9   "Instead of men": Ibid., I, 117-118.
9   "Not only were the founders": Schlesinger, 129.
9   "meere Democracie": Winthrop, IV, 383.
10   Massachusetts churches "did not restrict": Field, I, 16.
10   "Puritans, it seems": Foster, 75.
10   "There is no question": Fisher, I, 148.
11   "Williams, having lost faith": Ibid., 304.
12   "American Jezebel" & rival camps: James, *John Clarke*, 4-12.
13   "Were united by a belief": Gura, 50.
13   "Many members of the local": Battis, II, 246.
13   "these ecclesiastical dictators": Field, 42.
14   In November 1637: James, *John Clarke*, 3-11.
14   "By labeling her": McLoughlin, "Hutchinson Reconsidered," 13.
14   "She had very nearly cleared": Battis, 247.
14   "I do not for my own part": Field, 43-44.
15, 17   "concerning Mr. Weelewrights": Winthrop, IV, 278.

17 "The migration of Anne Hutchinson": Bridenbaugh, *Mutton*, 21.

17 "by whom we were courteously": Clarke, *Ill-Newes*, unpaginated.

17 "that if the provident": Ibid.

17-18 "We whose names" & "We that are Freemen,": Robson, III, 94.

18 "have sold unto Mr. Coddington": Ibid., 95.

18 "It was no price or money": Field, 45.

18 "a thousand fathom": Robson, III, 103.

18-19 "buffer zone by selling territories": James, *Colonial*, 8.

19 "Coddington, as we shall see": Field, 47.

19 "He had freed himself": Fisher, I, 304.

20 "Mr. Coddington": Chapin, *Documentary History*, II, 33.

20 "that the Town shall be builded": Ibid, 35.

20 "there came over this summer": Robson, V, 16.

21 "Gorton's extremely liberal": Chapin, II, 47.

21 "the coup d'etat of 1639": Ibid., 56.

21-22 "At Aquiday the people": Ibid., 57.

22 "It is Agreed By us": Ibid., 57.

22 We frequently went five: Wroth, 137-140.

24 1639. . . . In the beginning: Peter Easton's note in *Morton's New England Memorial*, 112-113.

24 "The coast of this island": Wroth, 137-140.

25 Then, in Pocasset: Bridenbaugh, *Mutton*, 12-22.

25 "Our Indians are peaceable": Robson, IV, 144.

25 "sell, give, deliver": Ibid., V, 27.

26 "they are . . . free of": Wroth, 137.

26 "that no man shall go": Chapin, II, 69.

27 "In the fourteenth yeare": Ibid., 82.

28 "of the state of things here": Field, 73.

28 "presenting themselves": Ibid., 76.

28 "It is ordered" & "that none": Carroll, I, 76.

29 "that the law": Ibid., 76.

29 "These laws, so contrary": Field, 53.

29 "attempt to invent": Bozeman, "Religious Liberty," 19.

29 "The prime fact about religion": Bridenbaugh, *Mutton*, 8.

30 "gathered a church": Winthrop, IV, 297.

30 "At the Island called Aquedney": Chapin, II, 116.

30 When the split came: James, *John Clarke*, 26-41.

31 "Historians agree that": Carroll, I, 78.

32 "winning commendation from the Board": Richman, 173.

32-33 Quotes from patent: Bartlett, *Records of the Colony*.

33 "While the words 'civil government' ": Carroll, I, 79.

34 "For Gorton as he came": Winthrop, IV, 490.

35 "that did not even recognize": Field, 82.

35 "They came on foot": Robson, VI, 73.

36 "The form of government established": Bartlett, 202.

36 "These are the laws": Carroll, I, 85.

37 "Sir, this bearer": Winthrop, V, 224.

37 "Our poor colony": Ibid., 298.

37 "That we, the islanders": Carroll, I, 87.

38 "Mr. Coddington went": Winthrop, V, 329.

39   "there is not the slightest doubt": Field, 90.

39   "very fruitfull and plentifully": Winslow, unpaginated.

39-40   "Two of these farms": Richman, 268-270.

41   "No sooner did it become": Ibid., 227.

41   "address unto the parliament": Robson, VII, 117.

42   "there was an agreement": Ibid., 123-124.

42   "The honour of this Collonie" & "How is it": Bozeman, 27.

43   "I, William Coddington": Richman, 305.

SIDEBARS

15   "the Lord hath let me see": Winthrop, IV, 393.

19   Wampum: Field, 13.

25   "Received from Mr. William Coddington": Chapin, II, 73.

27   "John Bartlett and John Huston": Chapin, II, 79.

27   "It is ordered": Chapin, II, 80.

29   "Notwithstanding the different": Clarke, *Ill-Newes*, unpaginated.

30   "Cultural diversity management": Shorto, 274.

33   "Puritanism was above all else": Foster, 5.

34   "And August 20, Mr. Lenthal": Chapin, II, 105.

36   "The Indians . . . began to set": Ibid., 127.

36   "Until recently": Huber, 595.

37   "Aquedneck, called by us Rhode Island": Field, 50.

41   "Just-asses": Winslow, unpaginated.

42   "Sir, I have . . . sent you but ten ewes": Winthrop, V, 428.

THE CHARTER OF 1663 · 1655–1698

46   A John Clarke of England: Bicknell, 6-2

46   In 1634 he married: James, *John Clarke and His Legacies*, 1-4

48   "certain erronious persons": Clarke, *Ill-Newes*, unpaginated.

48   "when Williams had gone": James, *Clarke*, 53.

49   Clarke acted as the official: Ibid., 59-83.

50   "Our trusty" and "unlawful usepations": Carroll, I, 96.

50-51   That was a tall order: James, *Clarke*, 59-83.

51   "If it please God": Fraser, 120.

51   Still, the challenges: James, *Clarke*, 59-83.

52   "were necessitated long since": Carroll, I, 96.

52   "bolstered this plea": James, *Clarke*, 63.

52   "have it much in their hearts": Clarke, 1663 Charter.

53   "The Founding Fathers were": Conley, *Liberty and Justice*, 182.

53-54   He spoke for a unique: James, *Clarke*, 69.

54   "discovered that all this": Richman, *Making and Its Meaning*, 74.

54   "base treacherous": James, *Clarke*, 73.

54-55   "the cruel deceitful": Ibid., 74.

55   "to transport goods": Ibid., 80.

55   "created a corporation": James, *Colonial Metamorphosis*, 49.

57   "This his Majesty's grant": Field, 104.

57   "the first commonwealth": Conley, 181.

57   "At a very great meeting": Robson, "Newport Begins," IX, 79.

58   Houses were being built: Stachiw, 28-40.

58   "This was no accident": Bridenbaugh, *Fat Mutton*, 27.

59   The Narragansett Bay: Chapin, *Documentary History*, II, 103.

59   "coming into this jurisdiction": Richman, 133.

59   "The Society of Friends": Armstrong, 77.

60   "divers Quakers are arrived": Hull, 37.

60   "from whence they may have": *Records of New Plymouth*, II, 180.

60   "as concerning those quakers": Jones, 21.

60   "that we may not be": Callender, 100.

61   "It is a sad condition": Dyer, *The Nation*, 39.

62   "rebellion, sedition, & presumptuous": Robson, IX, 100.

62   "With wicked Hands": Ibid., 101.

62   "I only say this yourselves": Ibid., 101.

63   "In the spring of 1658": Peterson, 180.

63   "In answer to the petition": Robson, IX, 103.

64   "After 1650 a new group": Bridenbaugh, *Wilderness*, 39.

64   The Newport Quaker merchants knew: Bailyn, *New England Merchants*, 201-210.

65   Sanford's letters attest: Bridenbaugh, *Wilderness*, 56.

65   "Loving Cousin, after due Respects": Sanford, P., 8.

65   "Credit then I would desire": Ibid., 14.

65-66   "Loving Brother yours": Ibid., 26.

66   "Sir I have given order": Ibid., 45.

66   "Mr William Pate": Ibid., 46.

68   Too often, in an attempt: Bridenbaugh, *Fat Mutton*, 85-99.

68   "Land lust, just as it": James, *Colonial Rhode Island*, 87.

68   "ordered that masters": Bridenbaugh, *Fat Mutton*, 102.

69   Both Warwick and Providence: Drake, 15-30.

70   "all the fine works": Richman, 436.

70   "Major Peleg Sanford": Ibid., 441.

70   "repair to this island": Leach, 140-162.

70   "use his utmost endeavor": Richman, 447.

71   two "Jewells": LaFantasie, *Correspondence of Roger Williams*, 242.

71   White Horse Tavern: Downing, 8 & 23.

71-72   Wanton-Lyman-Hazard House: Downing, 30-31, 51-53.

72   Mawdsley House: Downing, 89-90.

73   Quaker Meeting House: Downing, 24-25; Stachiw, 30-55.

73   Old Stone Mill: *A Finding Aid*, Redwood Library.

75   "I called upon Dr Moffat": Bowen, 39.

76   "To the seventh we answer": Arnold, 489.

77   Andros came to Clarke's: Field, 156.

78   "That he & a few": *Mass. Historical Society*, VIII, 307.

SIDEBARS

50   "Now let me say these": LaFantasie, *Correspondence*, I, 240.

57   "Rhode Island's early strategies": Irwin, 203.

62   "there is a vein of innocent": Russell, 67.

63   "The surviving fashion": Fraser, 164.

75   "undoubtedly the leading": Bridenbaugh, *Fat Mutton*, 77.

78   "In the weakness of authority": Carroll, I, 192.

82 After more than a half century: James, "From Classical Democracy."

83 "But what do we mean": *Dictionary of American Quotations*, 41.

83 It was a radical departure: Wood, *Radicalism of the American Revolution*.

84 "Governor Samuel Cranston presided": James, *Colonial Rhode Island*, 119.

84 "It is related by Bull": *Biographical Cyclopedia*, 48.

85 "their favoring of pirates": Carroll, I, 173.

85 "the generality of the people": Ibid., 173.

85 "Lordship has taken": Field, 158.

85 "The title gentleman": Wood, 26.

86 "and recommended that it": Field, 159.

88 "My Lords, I am humbly": Ibid., 162.

89 then the lawyers for: Carroll, I, 176.

89 "unpopular trade laws": Roberts, xii.

89-90 "for most American colonies": Hawes, 17.

90 Thus it came to pass: Richman, *Study in Separatism*, 86.

90 The adventure of Bankes: Hawes, 20-40.

91 "shape a course": Ibid., 27.

91 "Just as they were entering": Dow, 89.

91 "was suddenly the cynosure": Botting, 67.

91 "great was the Comotion": Hawes, 28.

92 Our fleet of pirates: Ibid., 33.

92 After a lucky shot: Ibid., 33.

92 "Alas, Mother!": "Edward Wanton," *Biographical Cyclopedia*, 77.

93 "Ruth, let us break": "William Wanton," Ibid., 78.

93-94 "Her men at once sprang": Bartlett, *History of the Wanton Family*, 26.

94 "It would be a grief": Bartlett, Ibid., 29.

94 This episode with Wanton's: Chapin, *Privateers, Ships and Sailors*, 174.

94 "Their portraits were painted": Bartlett, 30.

95 Only as they drew closer: Peterson, 64.

96 A large gallows: Dow, 307.

96 "Indeed, without the internal": James, *Colonial*, 134.

96 In 1710, the town's: Bridenbaugh, *Wilderness*, 143.

97 "To accomplish this business": James, *Colonial*, 134.

98 "The last war of religious": Arnold, 47.

100 Even amidst this turmoil: Field, 169.

100 "The disadvantage to the merchant": James, *Colonial*, 171.

101 "whether an act passed": Field, 176.

101 "In this Charter": Carroll, I, 181.

101 "By 1740, about £340,000": Withey, 25.

101 "Those who were committed": Field, 170.

103-104 "By 1720, trade": Withey, 20.

104-105 That route went from Newport: Richman, *Separatism*, 113.

105 "The general dislike": Arnold, 202.

105 "drove out most": Coulombe, 61.

105 "From 1701 to 1810": Coughtry, 6.

105 "The colony's growing": Ibid., 12.

106 In 1726, Rhode Island: Hawes, 140-170.

106 "Although the trade": Coughtry, 8.

106 "An Engine in the hands": Ibid., 13.

106 Aaron Lopez, a Jew: Hawes, 150-162.

106   Unlike slaves in the South: Youngken, 11.

107   "The nefarious traffic": Conley, *Liberty and Justice*, 200.

108   "He was everywhere": James, *Colonial*, 121.

108   "The death of Samuel Cranston": Arnold, 83.

108   "when he was elected": Mohr, 156.

109-110   "And 'tis very wonderful": Carroll, I, 178-179.

111   "Richard Partridge, agent for Rhode Island": Carroll, I, 185.

114   "This island is pleasantly": Gaustad, 16.

114   "Westward the Course", Berman, 115.

114   "We have been preparing": Gaustad, 22.

114   "that noblest, grandest": Berman, 115.

115   "converse about and debate": Mason, 13.

116   "This remarkable, artful": Gaustad, 22.

116   "If you put this question": Berman, 103.

116   Rev. James Honyman: Hattendorf, *Semper Eadem*, 71.

116-117   "So much understanding": Curtis, "Newport: Historical and Social," 293.

117   "a wickedness never parallel'd": Kenny, 98.

118   "There are days": Schumacher, "Literature and Painting," 49.

118-119   Franklin also commented: Kenny, 99-105.

119   "little is known": James, *Colonial*, 248.

119   "Unfortunately, there is little": James, Ibid., 245.

120   "Ironically, the novelties": James, Ibid., 188.

120   "more learned preachers": James, Ibid., 188.

121   At one point Honyman: Hattendorf, *Semper Eadem*, 53.

122   "a Puritan": James, *Colonial*, 198.

122-123   "ardent desire to promote": Peterson, 320.

123   "Before I saw": Peterson, 322.

SIDEBARS

89   "the charter became an object": James, "Classical Democracy," 119.

92   "Captain Peter Lawrence": Tilley, 19.

94   In a 1708 letter: Arnold, 35.

116   "became a pilgrimage site": "John Smibert." Kalfatovic, 119.

121   "Here are four sorts": Richman, *Separatism*, 134.

THE ROAD TO REVOLUTION · 1740-1776

126   Given its independent spirit: Bridenbaugh, *Wilderness*, 391.

129   "Underneath the apparent calm": Bridenbaugh, *Revolt*, 143.

130   "the Leonardo de Medici": Richman, *Making and Meaning*, 120.

130   Born in 1699, Henry Collins: Nord, 33.

131   Henry Collins was an aesthete: Ibid., 45.

132   "Dr Moffat [*sic*] took me out": Bridenbaugh, *Gentleman's Progress*, 151.

132   "At eight o'clock": Ibid., 155.

132-133   "They are not": Ibid., 157.

136   "You do not remember": Bolhouse, 36.

137   "The most distinctly American": Bridenbaugh, *Colonial Craftsmen*, 82.

137   "the pinnacle of taste": Moses, 5.

138   "From 1740 to the Revolution": Moore, 36.

138	"many, probably the great majority": Carpenter, 7.
139	"unique interpretation" and "an obsession": Moses, 10.
139	"This was a Newport invention": Hughes, 53.
141	William Claggett excelled: Champlin, "High Time," 157.
141	believed that Claggett's knowledge: Ibid., 162.
142	"It is written that": Partridge, 113.
142	"March 3, 1746. Boston": Ibid., 113.
142	"December 29, 1746": Ibid., 113.
142-143	"August 24, 1747": Ibid., 113.
145	Samuel Vernon was a careful: Carpenter, 155-157.
145	Trinity Church possesses: Hattendorf, *Semper Eadem*, 49, 57-59, 73.
146	"had outfitted a third": Purvis, 99.
147	"A three- or four-hundred ton": Bridenbaugh, *Colonial Craftsmen*, 92.
148	In 1729, Newport employed: Champlin, "Art of the Ropemaker," 82.
148	"Once he had three": Ibid., 83.
148	Most colonial shipbuilding centers: Ibid., 81.
149	"in 1770 William Vernon": Ibid., 85.
150	"Sixty to 75 percent of Newport's": Withey, 29.
151	"Thus with the money": Bridenbaugh, *Revolt*, 47.
152	Prices stabilized and production: Clark, 184.
153	"The decision in the case": Arnold, I, 494.
153	"While his credentials": Skemp, "Aaron Lopez," 908.
153	"in Jamaica, Hispaniola": Hawes, 161.
154	"He was a merchant": Levinger, 79.
155	Richard Munday had been voted: Hattendorf, *Semper Eadem*, 55.
157	"Some of the most stirring scenes": Downing, 56.
158	Harrison not only saw: Bridenbaugh, *Harrison*, 43.
160	"By returning to": Ibid., 50.
160	"was perhaps the most important": Sterngass, 41.
160	"206 folio, 128 quarto": Bridenbaugh, *Harrison*, 62.
160	"At a time when Newport": Richman, *Separatism*, 143.
161	"with Advantage for": Jordy, 35.
162	"The scheme he selected": Downing, 83.
164	"next to Abraham Redwood": McLanathan, 17.
164	"he resolved to help": Flexner, 15.
165	But Stuart angered some people: Mount, 35.
167	Stuart was popular: Meschutt, 70.
168	He also made a nostalgic: Channing, *Early Recollections*, 211.
168	"Often underrated because": Meschutt, 72.
169	But when the invaders departed: Porter, 5-22.
172	But Hull's success was unusual: Field, 185.
173	Dennis then refitted her: Hawes, 82.
173	"Then this reputedly wise": Ibid., 83.
173	She had admirable success: Chapin, *The Tartar*, 66.
174	"though he was a Quaker": Bartlett, 209.
175	Tradition holds that a young: Field, 196.
175	"The firing of a gun": Field, 196.
176	"from 90 to 100 vessels" and "merchants of the town": Ibid., 206.
179	"The opposing parties waged": James, *Colonial*, 310.
180	"Party virulence had been increasing": Field, 207.
180	The longtime foes road together: Millar, 27.

180   "powder and ball will decide": Brown, unpaginated.

181   As his colleagues approached: Ibid., unpaginated.

182   "Upward of thirty distill houses": Field, 215.

182-183   "The colonists could see": Morgan, *Birth of the Republic*, 19.

183   "These Americans, our own children": Peterson, 197.

183   "The sun of liberty is set": Ibid., 197.

184   "It is for liberty": Ibid., 202.

185   "licentious, sordid, and incompetent": Snydacker, "Martin Howard," 11.

185   Having taken refuge on the British: Ibid., 15.

187   "it was a demonstration in arms": Carroll, I, 257.

187-188   "a schooner, which for some time" and "Please be informed": Ibid., 255.

188   When the crown threatened: DeVaro, 121.

190   "This day I removed one": Stiles, I, 623.

191   "Vernon, usually a temperate writer": Crane, 121.

191   "should be burnt in their house": Ibid., 123.

191   "Rode to Dighton": Stiles, I, 662.

192   "Whereas, in all States": Carroll, I, 269.

192   "do approve said resolution": Arnold, I, 381.

192-193   "Mr. Channing returned from Newport": Stiles, II, 21.

193   "This evening we are alarmed": Ibid., 93.

SIDEBARS

132   "the largest and most magnificent": Bridenbaugh, *Revolt*, 372.

132   "Romance now takes up": Curtis, "Historical and Social," 298.

136   "a painter, the most extraordinary": Foote, 59.

147   Putting up a colonial house: Bridenbaugh, *Colonial Craftsmen*, 94.

149   "The act against swearing" & etc.: Arnold, I, II, 55-320.

154   "that all men professing": Bartlett, 36.

156   They met each Wednesday: Levitan, 24.

160   "It is fitting that Trinity": Downing, 56.

180   "The whole bay is an excellent": Bartlett, 78.

INDEPENDENCE AND DECLINE · 1776–1790

195   "the best and noblest harbor": Walker, 36.

196   "I must confess that": Clinton, 54.

197   "When the leading ships": Mackenzie, 122.

197   "It seems to be our Turn": Stiles, II, 95.

198   "As the troops could not": Mackenzie, 123.

198   "the People of Great Britain": Stiles, II, 96.

198   "The Inhabitants of this Island": Mackenzie, 126.

201   "We have already given": Carroll, I, 314.

201   "I hear more of the Reconciliation": Stiles, II, 103.

202   "Prescott was a petty tyrant": Simister, 114.

203   "The encampment at Newport": Carroll, I, 313.

204   "The 1777 campaign": Syrett, 72.

204   "Saratoga was the turning point": Wood, *American Revolution*, 81.

204-205   "May it please your Excellency": Abstracts, Newport *Gazette*, unpaginated.

205   "10 June": Mackenzie, 138.

205 "A soldier in the 43rd": Ibid., 145.

206 "A Hessian soldier": Greene, unpaginated.

206 "a flag of truce": Arnold, 226.

207 It was in October: Carroll, I, 316.

207-208 "Neither Washington nor Greene": Ibid., 317.

208 "High wind last night": Mackenzie, 213.

208 "Heavy rain, hard frost": Ibid., 227.

208 "The weather has been": Greene, unpaginated.

208 "As the winter advanced": Field, 238.

208 "Walked this morning": Serle, 273.

209 "This place [Newport]": Vaughn, frontpiece.

209 "Nothing can more plainly": Serle, 279.

210 "proceeded thence to Bristol": Greene, unpaginated.

212 "The town appears": Ibid.

212 "All the fleet in motion": Almy, 17.

212 "The harbor is in one": Greene, unpaginated.

212 "Heavens! what a scene": Almy, 23.

212-213 Five venerable warships: Syrett, 99.

213-214 When Admiral d'Estaing: Ibid., 107.

215 "The wind blew": Field, 493.

215 "It struck such a panic": Dearden, 28.

216 "I was ordered": Angell, 9.

216 "Early this morning": Greene, unpaginated.

217 "Not a man was left": Carroll, I, 329.

217 "Last night the Provincials": Greene, unpaginated.

218 S.G. Arnold reported: Arnold, 430.

218 "If the garrison": Carroll, I, 329.

219-220 "We are left at present": Mackenzie, 414.

220 "The great scarcity": Greene, unpaginated.

220 "Another terrible storm": Arnold, 434.

220 "The most obdurate heart": Ibid., 436.

220 "The people were reduced": Carroll, I, 388.

221 To make matters worse: Syrett, 120-126.

222 "Arrived, the refugee fleet": Greene, unpaginated.

222-223 "All the troops": Dohla, 113.

223 "a barren city": Simister, 155.

223 "I took a melancholy": Stiles, II, 427.

227 "Newport was beautifully": Ibid., II, 454.

227 The general, accompanied by his son: Simpson, 37.

227 "Throughout the Newport stay": Woodbridge, 13.

228 "It has revived": Kennett, 51.

230 The Chevalier de Chastellux: Downing, 96.

230 "Dined at Gen. de Chastellux": Downing, 96.

230 "The fair sex": Forbes, II, 44.

231 "All the generals were assembled": Berthier, 83.

231 Meanwhile, the merriment: Forbes, II, 57.

232 "in his private conduct": Ibid., II, 58.

234 "paralyzed by indecision": Syrett, 201.

236 "The women in their majority": Miranda, 15.

237 "Since the peace": Sheffield, 46.

237 "Before the war": Downing, 101.

237   "I have seen not a little": Richman, *Separatism*, 259.

238   "little more than a shadow": Draper, 407.

239   "Congress may call": Field, 249.

239   "Just as she [Rhode Island]": Ibid., 249.

240   "lost no time": Ibid., 258.

241   "Nothing can exceed": Ibid., 261.

243   At the January session: Carroll, I, 374-378.

243   "Rhode Island was the closest": Bishop, 117.

243, 245   "a two-point program": Conley, *Democracy in Decline*, 136.

S I D E B A R S

202   "There is a hill": Mackenzie, 127.

212   "In a believe-it-or-not": Horowitz, 439.

237   What is a republic?: Everdell, 188.

U N I O N   A N D   S U R V I V A L   ·   1 7 9 0 – 1 8 4 3

247   "You can't repeat the past": Fitzgerald, *The Great Gatsby*, 111.

248   In 1790, the two rival: Conley, *Democracy in Decline*, 161.

249   "according to local tradition": Woodbridge, 128.

249   "The Citizens of the United States": Gutstein, 117.

250   The year 1790: McLoughlin, 112-118.

252   "Within thirty miles of Providence": Richman, *Making and Meaning*, 278.

252   "From the Baltic": Coleman, 39.

254   "carrying slaves between foreign ports": Ibid., 54.

254   "between 1803 and 1807": Ibid., 54.

254   Coleman's first assertion: Ibid., 66.

255   Although Coleman acknowledges: Ibid, 65-71.

255   Understandably, men who had come: Ibid., 67.

255   "a more desolate place": Ibid., 69.

256   "As he started to leave": Carroll, I, 443.

257   "late insult": Ibid., 447.

257   "In Rhode Island, the embargo": Ibid., 447.

257   "unjust, oppressive": Ibid., 448.

258-259   In the autumn of 1813: Mooney, 517.

259   "The British in fact": Strum, 28.

259-260   "Although the conflict ended": Ibid., 30.

260   By 1805, the navy: Copes, 58,

262   Perry arrived in Presque Isle: Altoff, 12-20.

262   "shortage of nearly everything": Copes, 59.

263   "The first attempt": Altoff, 8.

263   Perry quickly mustered: Ibid., 20-30.

264   "was a floating, helpless": Ibid., 29.

265   In the meantime, Elliot: Baker, 370.

265   By 3:00, the Battle: Ibid., 371.

265   Newport proudly presented Perry: Stinson, "Newport Notables."

266   Perry only resided: Ibid.

266   Timothy Dwight: Dwight, III, 57.

266   "The well-bred people": Ibid., 54.

267 "the agricultural interests": Rhode Island *Gazetteer*, 44-45.

269 "The first commercial Bay": Hale, 61.

270 "about 1825 the horse boat": Augusta, 55.

271 "Defense of the Narragansett": Robinson, 78.

272 Based on the fortification theories: Gatchel, 14-16.

273 The granite perimeter walls: Ibid., 18.

274 "When it was noised abroad": Davis, 38.

275 "the three-story, hip-roofed": Downing, 112.

276 King was considered: Zukowski, 114.

276 "During the early years": Severens, 357.

277 "Malbone capitalized": Ibid., 357.

278-279 "I had, in my school days": Dunlap, 154.

279 His paintings became larger: Foster, A. K., 373.

279 Honored in London: Ibid., 374.

280 "In contrast to the attention": Ibid., 374.

280 "Apparently Cornè had received": Little, 262.

280 "There was no employment": Mason, *Reminiscences*, 339.

281 "He was the first person": Ibid., 339.

281 "Cornè's work is far": Little, 269.

282 Along with her mother: B. Hattendorf, 152.

282 "In her own work": Ibid., 161.

282 "She bore a striking": *Mercury*, May 5, 1888.

283 "As a man": Cosentino, 11.

284 King's real passion: Ibid., 12-20.

284 "I found him, as a fellow-student": Dunlap, 261.

284 Witty, urbane, and well read: Meschutt, 688-690.

284 "During his many years": Cosentino, 41.

285 "It is the only collection": Ibid., 42.

285 A few years before his death: Redwood Library, *Hidden Treasures*, 6- 7.

285 "An essential step": W. E. Channing, 6.

287 "the virtual manifesto": D. W. Howe, 681.

287 "We mean not to be paradoxical": Channing, 179.

287-288 "influenced such important contemporaries": Howe, 681.

288 In 1790, the state: Coleman, 220.

288 It did not happen: Ibid., 222-228.

291 "The critical issue was": McLoughlin, 135.

292 "Some American historians": Conley, "Dorr," *American National Bio.*, 780.

SIDEBARS

265 "The gale struck Newport": *Mercury*, Sept. 29, 1815.

272 In 1804, William had married: Porter, 4-10.

285 "I write you from our dear": Channing, 634.

SOCIETY ASCENDANT · 1843–1880

296 "the search for air and water": Herrick, "Some Americans," 19.

298 According to Carl Bridenbaugh: Bridenbaugh, "Colonial Newport," 2.

299 "In its sluggish rivers": Brewster, 4.

299 "that he would as soon stand": Ibid., 6.

300 "As compared with Boston": Bridenbaugh, "Colonial Newport," 11.

300 "Visitors from the South": *Mercury*, August 5, 1826.

300 "It is said to have the finest air": Royall, 101.

301 "When I first knew Newport": Curtis, *Lotus-Eaters*, 52.

301 "Newport is now quite crowded": Brewster, 35.

302 "If the planter's patriotism": Ibid., 35.

302 "This ancient and pleasantly": Sherman, 15.

302 "situated on the hill": Tungett, 17.

303 "On dance nights": Sterngass, 46.

305 "new shops, new faces": Ibid., 45, 50.

305-306 "Last night's ball at the Atlantic": *New York Times*, August 16, 1860.

307 "Newport is pre-eminently": Curtis, "Historical and Social," 316.

307 "The ancient city of Newport": Richards, 337.

307 "We are now in the midst": *Mercury*, July 16, 1851.

307 "It is now the season": *Mercury*, August 14, 1852.

307-308 "The arrival of the Germanians": *Mercury*, July 21, 1855.

308 "The second grand concert": *Daily News*, August 21, 1851.

308 "We learn that Mr. Henry M. Brownell": *Daily News*, May 16, 1850.

308 "The Season is fast drawing": *Mercury*, September 7, 1850.

308-309 "Oh, this lovely Newport!": Fuller, July 16, 1856.

309 "We are now filling up here fast": Ibid., July 21, 1856.

309 "But the great event": Ibid., July 29, 1856.

309 "I may write now": Ibid., August 11, 1856.

309-310 "That will do": Ibid., August 15, 1856.

310 Fisher started going to Newport: Fisher, *Diary*, 140.

310 "the weather was": Fisher, *Diary*, 140.

310 "The place was crowded" and etc.: Ibid., 238-250.

312 "Ochre Point Farm": Schumacher, "Real Estate King," 37.

313 "The mayor of Newport reported": Sterngass, 51.

314 "All I expect to get": Schumacher, "Real Estate King," 45.

314 "The whole face of that portion": *Mercury*, October 14, 1854.

315 "He rode about": "Kay-Catharine-Old Beach," 21.

315 "Smith not only created": Schumacher, "Real Estate King," 44.

316 "King then deeded the city": Ibid., 47.

316 "until 1866, when a petition": Ibid., 47.

317 "These rich families": Hurst, 19.

318 Of note is the fact: Schumacher, "First Directory," 79.

319 "The rise of the Know-Nothing": Rand, 105.

320 "From his accession to his death": Conley, "Catholicism," 42.

320 The Whig Party had been decimated": Rand, 114.

320 "It was the inability": Ibid., 116.

321 "It was hardly coincident": Hurst, 111.

321-322 "Newport had been always a resort": Robson, "One Hundred," 6.

322 "three cannon shots boomed": Ibid., 8.

322 "directly in my rear I heard": Smith, 25.

322 "We learn that Dr. David King": *Mercury*, January 4, 1862.

323 "The sales of real estate": *Mercury*, January 13, 1863.

326 "How you do make me wish": Harlow, 13.

326 Most students of his life: Kaplan, 55.

327 "The beauty of this landscape": Murphy-Schlicting, 179.

327 "The atmospheric tone": Ibid., 179.

328   "Newport has been the painting": "Reflections Newport Artists," 20.

328   "I think the advantages": Danes, 145.

328, 329   "sublime vastness" & "One of his greatest": Ibid., 147.

329   More than brushes: Yarnall, *Watercolors & Drawings*, 6.

330-331   "The *Paradise Valley* was": *Dict. of Am. Biography*, 532.

331   "A colored glass container": Ibid., 534.

331   "Using layers of glass": Yarnal, *Am. Nat. Biography*, 33.

331   "He is the great innovator": *Dict. of Am. Biography*, 533.

333   "Traveling with La Farge to Japan": Benfey, 130.

333   "La Farge's work is astonishing": Yarnall, *Watercolors & Drawings*, 8.

334   "I felt the need of upholding": Murphy-Schlicting, 53.

335   "They meet for fun and frolic": Ibid., 26.

336   "The Town and Country Club had yesterday": Ibid., 32.

337   Pumpelly went on to China: Champlin, *Am. Nat. Bio.*, 938.

337   Clarence King was born in Newport: Wilkins, *Am. Nat. Bio.*, 691.

338   "Newport hostelries had sometimes": Sterngass, 191.

338   "Totally inappropriate upon its flat": Downing, 141.

339   He went into selling real estate: Schumacher, "Mason," 24.

340   "rather avowedly Swiss": Ibid., 22.

340   "Mason quickly settled upon": Jordy, 223.

SIDEBARS

299   "While still holding": Aron, 18.

299   "these baths impart": Trevett, *Mercury*, July 1, 1844.

307   "the finest vessels of their class": McAdam, 20.

311   "The prosperity of Newport": Schumacher, "Real Estate King," 93.

313   In July 1853: Perry, 45-220.

318   "The morning broke clear": *New York Times*, August 24, 1859.

335   By 1865, the Redwood: Howland, 100.

337   "I am happy to meet you": Stinson, "Lime Rock," 18.

THE QUEEN OF RESORTS · 1880–1914

344   "The way to wealth": Franklin, 187.

344   "All at once": Rensselaer, *Social Ladder*, 30.

344   "From the eighteen-seventies": Mills, 49.

344-345   "In order to gain" & "The basis on which": Veblen, 36.

345   "Industry, transportation, banking": Morison, *American Republic*, 11.

348   Most local writers: *Sesquicentennial History*, 35.

349   Bennett's high-profile: *Dict. of Am. Biography*, 200.

350   "McKim kept the street façade": Downing, 162.

350   "Behind the shops": Ibid., 162.

350   "for enjoying games": Schumacher, "Newport Casino," 51.

350   "In theory, the poor mechanic": "Business of Leisure," 117.

352   "With the opening of the Casino": Elliott, *My Newport*, 186.

352   "I went to Newport": Spring Rice, I, 119.

352   "The people beautifully dressed": Ibid., I, 243.

354   "From Belmont New York learned": Homberger, 176.

354   "From 1860 to 1875": *New York Times*, November 6, 1892.

355   "had the right to create": McAllister, 77.

355   Young belles were launched: Mills, 54.

357   "there were only about four hundred": Patterson, 83.

360   "Newport loved the picnics": Ibid., 74.

361   Hunt's first venture: Grosvenor, 45.

361-362 "This is not architecture": Downing, 164.

362   "No doubt much of the building": Baker, *Richard Morris Hunt*, 334.

362-363 "It is said that several": *New York Times*, August 12, 1881.

364   "it was to a certain extent": Baker, *Architecture of R. M. Hunt*, 3.

369   "The dwelling was a summer place": Baker, *Richard Morris Hunt*, 336.

370   "But by the late 1880s": Wilson, 114.

371   "The formal entrance is framed": Grosvenor, 127.

373   When her mother divorced: Benway, 71.

373   "McKim, Mead & White": Roth, 208.

374   "Set in its green gardens": Downing, 174.

376   "Yet much has changed": Pardee, 93.

377   "the most beautiful": Rensselaer, *Our Social Capital*, 55.

377   "In 1852 it was reported": Lowenthal, 118.

378   "shimmering in the more distant": Brownell, 150.

379   "Oh! those cliff structures": Gregory, 170.

379   "Newport, on my finding myself": James, "Sense of Newport," 96.

379   "The white elephants": James, "Sense of Newport," 354.

380   "In their gargantuan proportions": Stafford, 35.

381   "Luce was the foremost": J. Hattendorf, *Am. Nat. Biography*, 95.

382   "Prof. Farmer gave": *Mercury*, October 9, 1875.

384   Like most nascent games: Menke, 936.

385   According to Alan Schumacher: Schumacher, "The Newport Casino," 65.

385   "A number of factors": Ibid., 68.

387   According to most accounts: Menke, 809.

387   "The block in question": Havemeyer, private letter, 1945.

388   In the 1980s: Schumacher, "Newport Country Club," 13.

388   "The friends that": Warburton, *1995 Centennial*, 24.

389   "When the clubhouse": Schumacher, "Country Club," 31.

391   "who is to use it for pleasure": *Daily News*, July 2, 1897.

392   "It was the first parade": Ibid., September 8, 1899.

392   "Mrs. Herman Oelrich's": Ibid., September 8, 1899.

393   "had their *symposia*": Herrick, *Social Club in America*, 2.

396   "I enjoyed myself thoroughly": Edel, 18.

397   "As social constraints multiplied": Murphy-Schlicting, 219.

398   "I was never very happy": Wharton, *Backward Glance*, 90.

398   "I had been able to buy": E. Dwight, 106.

398   "Teddy hasn't yet rallied": Ibid., 52.

398-399 "A new departure": Wharton, *Backward Glance*, 107.

399   "Wharton's travel writings": Funston, 110.

400   "By the fall of 1902": E. Dwight, 68.

400   "Mrs. Wharton was twenty years younger": Edel, 26.

401   "I have made some new": Ferber, "Richards at Newport," 3.

401-402 "You can't realize what a delight": Ibid., 11.

402   "A significant and revealing": Ferber, *Landscape & Marine*, 38.

403-404 "His work was distinguished": *Nat. Cyclopedia of Am. Bio.*, XXIV, 165.

404   "My ambition is to reform": O'Connor, 319.

404-405 "Look at the men": *Town Topics*, August 11, 1887.

405 "The Casino Ball": Ibid., August, 1887.

405 "Many women will rise up": O'Connor, 65.

407 "Women were the core of Newport": Schreier, 23.

407 "The regular afternoon diversion": Wharton, *Backward Glance*, 82.

408 "After a long stay in Paris": Homberger, 274-75.

409 "Instead of the customary": Davies, 621.

409 "With other members": Amory, 217.

409 "To some her death marked": Davies, 621.

411 "Newport was becoming the elite": Strange, 25.

411 "At least nine women": Sterngass, 222.

412 "The trends initiated": Ibid., 227.

413 "The Chinese costume ball": *New York Times*, July 25, 1914.

SIDEBARS

371 "In August 1904 Tessie's": Benway, 79.

378 "For the last thirty or forty": E. Dwight, 69.

385 "The tendency of the rich": Mrozek, 123.

395 For example, the police log: Police Log of Newport, 1891.

THE GRAND REVIVAL · 1914–1969

417 "The news of the arrival": *Mercury*, October 14, 1916.

417-418 "The fleet of destroyers": Ibid.

418 "In one instance two destroyers": Ibid.

418-419 "The Civic League": Warburton, *Living Memory*, 58.

419 "To those who did hear": *Mercury*, February 2. 1918.

421 "ALL NEWPORT CELEBRATES": *Daily News*, November 11, 1918.

421 "In almost no time": *Mercury*, November 16, 1918.

422 3,826 women registered to vote: *Daily News*, December 1, 1920.

422 The city was also evolving in other directions: *Between Golden & Gilded*, 22.

424 Throughout the Prohibition period: Hale, 85.

424 "the biggest haul of liquor": *Daily News*, January 14, 1924.

424 The most dramatic seizure: *Daily News*, December 30, 1929.

425 "Some years, like some poets": Galbraith, 1.

425 "The stock market crash": Morison, *Oxford History*, 936.

426 "America, unlike Britain": Ibid., 944.

426 "From the beginning": Snydacker, "The Great Depression in Newport," 42-43.

427 Unemployment, however: Ibid., 49.

427 "Since 1918 the great": *Guide to Smallest State*. 216.

428 "These were the Torpedo Station": Snydacker, "The Great Depression in Newport," 46.

428 "On Friday night": Snydacker, Ibid., 48.

428 "Washington, Sept. 21": *Daily News*, September 21, 1938.

429 "As swift and sure": Scotti, 94.

429 "Town by town": Ibid., 95.

430 "CHAMBERLAIN AND HITLER": *Daily News*, September 22, 1938.

431 "Some four hundred cottages": Scotti, 227.

433 "Pell celebrated the Democratic": Blayney, 100.

434-435 "There were 2,000 members": Warburton, 91.

435 "Opening of various houses": *Mercury*, July 28, 1939.

436 On August 12, President Roosevelt: *Daily News*, August 12, 1940.

437   "sent out a total of 6,952": *Daily News*, January 3, 1941.

437   A large anti-aircraft: Schroder, 58.

438   "Rosecliff, the Hermann Oelrichs": *Daily News*, January 2, 1942.

438-439   "Victory over Japan was celebrated": *Daily News*, August 17, 1945.

439   contends that a third of all torpedoes: Cherpak, 149.

442   "the two halls and nine rooms": Miller, 6-7.

442   The City of Newport: *Daily News*, December 30, 1950.

442   The following years Marble House: Miller, 7.

444   Over the winter of 1963-1964: Benson, 45.

444   "In its brief history Clapboard": Roos, interview with author, 2004.

447   The Newport Restoration Foundation: Roos, interview, 2004.

448   "Charleston and Newport": Moe, private conversation.

448   In December 1949: *Mercury*, December 13, 1949.

449   "While plans languished": Warburton, 119.

450   "In 1966 the digging up": Ibid., 136.

452   When asked by a reporter: Marshall, 13.

453   The next challenge came in 1964: Stephens, 163.

459   The idea was not a new one: *Daily News*, December 31, 1964.

459-460   "By 1979, the annual traffic": Pantalone, 59.

SIDEBARS

437   In Newport, however: Stinson, "Paradise Lost," 30.

440   "In my lifetime": Chorley, 22.

442   "With his monstrous *élan*": O'Doherty, unpaginated.

447   One of the most remarkable: F. Benson, 5-30.

Bibliography

REFERENCE WORKS

American National Biography. 24 vols. Edited by John A. Garraty and Mark C. Carnes. New York: Oxford University Press; American Council of Learned Societies, 1999.

The Biographical Cyclopedia of Representative Men of Rhode Island. Edited by L. E. Rogers. Providence: National Biographical Publishing Co., 1881.

Dictionary of American Biography. 20 vols. with 10 supplements. New York: Charles Scribner's Sons, 1928–1995. Published under the auspices of the American Council of Learned Societies.

Menke, Frank G. *The Encyclopedia of Sports*. 5th ed. Revised by Suzanne Treat. South Brunswick, N.J.: A. S. Barnes, 1975.

Dictionary of American Naval Fighting Ships. 8 vols. Vol. 8 edited by James Mooney. Washington, D.C.: Naval Historical Division, Department of the Navy, 1959–1981.

The National Cyclopedia of American Biography. Vols. 1–N-63. New York: James T. White, 1898–1984.

Notable American Women 1607–1950: A Biographical Dictionary. Edited by Edward T. James, Janet Wilson, and Paul Boyer. 3 vols. Cambridge, Mass.: Harvard University Press, Belknap Press, 1971.

Pease, John C. *A Gazetteer of the States of Connecticut and Rhode-Island*. Hartford: William S. Marsh, 1819.

ABSTRACTED AND COMPILED RECORDS

"Abstracts from the Newport Gazette, Published at Newport, R.I., during the Occupation of the Town by the British" *Newport Historical Magazine* 4 (October 1883): 103–111.

Bartlett, John Russell, ed. *Records of the Colony of Rhode Island and Providence Plantations*, 1636–1792. 10 vols. Providence: A. Crawford Greene, 1856–1865.

Chapin, Howard M., ed. *Documentary History of Rhode Island*. 2 vols. Providence: Preston and Rounds, 1916–1919.

Collections of the Massachusetts Historical Society. Vol. 8. 1802. Reprint, Boston, 1856.

Police Log of Newport. Newport: Police Department, 1891.

Pulsifer, David, ed. *Records of the Colony of New Plymouth in New England*, 1653–1679. Vol. 2. Boston: William White, 1859.

Abstracted and Compiled Records continued

Staples, William R. *The Documentary History of the Destruction of the Gaspee*. Providence: Rhode
      Island Publications Society, Rhode Island Bicentennial Foundation, Rhode Island
      Supreme Court Historical Society, 1990.

Tilley, Edith May. "Items of Newport Interest in Early Boston Newspapers." *Bulletin of the Newport
      Historical Society* 69 (April 1929): 1–15.

COMMUNICATIONS, MEMOIRS, AND PERSONAL PAPERS

Almy, Mary. "Mrs. Almy's Journal: Siege of Newport, August 1778." *Newport Historical Magazine* 1
      (July 1880): 17–36.

Angell, Israel. *Diary of Colonel Israel Angell Commanding the Second Rhode Island Continental
      Regiment, 1778–1781*. Transcribed by Edward Field. Providence: Preston and Rounds,
      1899.

Berthier, Alexandre. "Alexandre Berthier's Journal of the American Campaign." *Rhode Island History*
      24 (July 1965): 77–88.

Bridenbaugh, Carl, ed. *Gentleman's Progress: The Itinerarium of Dr. Alexander Hamilton*. Chapel
      Hill: University of North Carolina Press, 1948.

Channing, George G. *Early Recollections of Newport, R.I.—from the Year 1793 to 1811*. Newport: A.
      J. Ward, C. E. Hammett Jr., 1868.

Channing, William Ellery. *William Ellery Channing: Selected Writings*. Edited by David Robinson.
      New York: Paulist Press, 1985.

Clarke, John. *Ill Newes from New-England*. London, 1652. Ann Arbor, Mich.: University Microfilms,
      1962.

——. *The Charter, Granted by King Charles II, July 8, 1663*. London, 1663. In *The Rhode Island
      Government Owner's Manual 2003–2004*, 271–276. Providence: Office of the Secretary
      of State Matthew A. Brown.

Clinton, Henry. *The American Rebellion: Sir Henry Clinton's Narrative of His Campaigns, 1775–
      1782*. New Haven: Yale University Press, 1954.

Döhla, Johann Conrad. *A Hessian Diary of the American Revolution*. Edited by Bruce E. Burgoyne.
      Norman: University of Oklahoma Press, 1990.

Dyer, William. *Letter to the Massachusetts General Court: Newport* [1659]. *The Nation* 74, no. 1926,
      May 29, 1902.

Elliott, Maud Howe. "Some Reflections of Newport Artists." *Bulletin of the Newport Historical
      Society* 35 (January 1921): 1–35.

——. *This Was My Newport*. Cambridge, Mass.: Mythology, 1944.

Fisher, Sidney George. *A Philadelphia Perspective: The Diary of Sidney George Fisher Covering the
      Years 1834–1871*. Edited by Nicholas B. Wainwright. Philadelphia: Historical Society of
      Pennsylvania, 1967.

Franklin, Benjamin. *The Autobiography and Other Writings*. New York: New American Library,
      1961.

Greene, Fleet. "Journal of Fleet Greene: 1777–1779." *Newport Mercury*, November 30, 1861–April 5,
      1862.

Greene, Nathanael. *The Papers of Nathanael Greene: 1766–1778*. Edited by Richard K. Showman.
      Chapel Hill: University of North Carolina Press, 1976. Published for the Rhode Island
      Historical Society.

Hagist, Don N. *General Orders, Rhode Island: December 1776–January 1778*. Bowie, Md: Heritage
      Books, 2001.

Kimball, Gertrude Selwyn, ed. *The Correspondence of the Colonial Governors of Rhode Island, 1723–
      1775*. 2 vols. Boston: Houghton, Mifflin, 1902–1903.

Lechford, Thomas. *Plain Dealing, or, Newes From New-England*. London: Nath. Butter, 1642.

Mackenzie, Frederick. *Diary of Frederick Mackenzie: 1775–1781*. 2 vols. Cambridge, Mass.: Harvard University Press, 1930.

Mason, George Champlin. *Reminiscences of Newport*. Newport: Charles E. Hammett, 1884.

McAllister, Ward. *Society As I Have Found It*. New York: Cassell, 1890.

Perry, Matthew C. *The Japanese Expedition 1852–1854: The Personal Journal of Commodore Matthew C. Perry*. Edited by Roger Pineau. Introduction by Samuel Eliot Morison. Washington, D.C.: Smithsonian Institution Press, 1968.

Rice, Cecil Spring. *The Letters and Friendships of Sir Cecil Spring Rice; A Record*. Edited Stephen Lucius Gwynn. Freeport, N.Y.: Books for Libraries Press, 1929.

Royall, Anne. *Black Book; or a Continuation of Travels in the United States*. Washington, D.C.: Privately printed, 1828.

Sanford, Peleg. *The Letter Book of Peleg Sanford of Newport, Merchant (Later Governour of Rhode Island), 1666–1668*. Transcribed by Howard M. Chapin, with notes by G. Andrews Moriarty Jr. Providence: Rhode Island Historical Society, 1928.

Sheffield, William P. *Historical Address of the City of Newport, July 4, 1876: With an Appendix*. Newport: J. P. Sanborn, 1876.

Stiles, Ezra. *The Literary Diary of Ezra Stiles*. 3 vols. Edited by Franklin Bowditch Dexter. New York: Charles Scribner's Sons, 1901.

Walpole, Horace. *Horace Walpole's England As His Letters Picture It*. Boston: Houghton, Mifflin, 1930.

Williams, Roger. *The Correspondence of Roger Williams*. Edited by Glenn W. LaFantasie et al. from an unpublished manuscript by Bradford F. Swan. Hanover, N.H.: University Press of New England / Brown University, 1988. Published for the Rhode Island Historical Society.

Winslow, Edward. *Hypocrisie Unmasked*. London: Richard Cotes, for John Bellamy, 1646.

Winthrop, John. *Winthrop Papers*. 5 vols. Boston: Massachusetts Historical Society, 1929–1947.

ARTICLES, BOOKS, MONOGRAPHS

Adelman, David C. "Strangers: Civil Rights of Jews in the Colony of Rhode Island." *Rhode Island History* 13 (July 1954): 65–77.

Altoff, Gerry. *Oliver Hazard Perry and the Battle of Lake Erie*. Put-in-Bay, Ohio: Perry Group, 1990.

Amory, Cleveland. *The Last Resorts*. New York: Harper and Brothers, 1952.

Anderson, Fred. *Crucible of War: The Seven Years' War and the Fate of Empire in British North America*. New York: Alfred A. Knopf, 2000.

Armstead, Myra B. Young. *"Lord, Please Don't Take Me in August" African Americans in Newport and Saratoga Springs, 1870–1930*. Urbana: University of Illinois Press, 1999.

Armstrong, Karen. *The Battle for God*. New York: Alfred A. Knopf, 2000.

Arnold, Samuel Greene. *History of the State of Rhode Island and Providence Plantations*. 2 vols. 3rd ed. New York: D. Appleton, 1878.

Aron, Cindy S. *Working at Play: A History of Vacations in the United States*. New York: Oxford University Press, 1999.

Asher, Louis Franklin. *John Clarke (1609–1676): Pioneer in American Medicine, Democratic Ideals, and Champion of Religious Liberty*. Pittsburgh: Dorrance, 1997.

Bailyn, Bernard. *The New England Merchants in the Seventeenth Century*. Cambridge, Mass.: Harvard University Press, 1955.

———. *The Ideological Origins of the American Revolution*. Cambridge, Mass.: Harvard University Press, Belknap Press, 1967.

Articles, Books, Monographs continued

——. *Faces of Revolution: Personalities and Themes in the Struggle for American Independence*. New York: Alfred A. Knopf, 1990.

——. *To Begin the World Anew: The Genius and Ambiguities of the American Founders*. New York: Alfred A. Knopf, 2003.

Baker, Paul R. *Richard Morris Hunt*. Cambridge, Mass.: MIT Press, 1980.

Baker, Robert. "Oliver Hazard Perry." *American National Biography*, 17:369–371.

Baltzell, E. Digby. *Sporting Gentlemen: Men's Tennis from the Age of Honor to the Cult of the Superstar*. New York: Free Press, 1995.

Barratt, Carrie Rebora, and Ellen Gross Miles. *Gilbert Stuart*. New York and New Haven: Metropolitan Museum of Art, Yale University Press, 2004.

Barrett, Richmond. *Good Old Summer Days*. New York: D. Appleton-Century, 1941.

Bartlett, John Russell. *History of the Wanton Family of Newport, Rhode Island*. Providence: Sidney S. Rider, 1878.

Bates, Frank Greene. *Rhode Island and the Formation of the Union*. New York: Macmillian, 1898. Published for Columbia University.

Battis, Emery. "Anne Hutchinson." *Notable American Women 1607–1950*, 2:245–247.

Bayles, Richard M, ed. *History of Newport County, Rhode Island*. New York: L. E. Preston, 1888.

Beals, Carleton. *Colonial Rhode Island*. Camden, N.J.: Thomas Nelson, 1970.

Benfey, Christopher. *The Great Wave: Gilded Age Misfits, Japanese Eccentrics and the Opening of Old Japan*. New York: Random House, 2003.

Benson, Esther Fisher. "John Howard Benson and The John Stevens Shop." *Newport History* 213 (Winter 1989): 5–31.

——. "The Restoration Movement in Newport, RI, from 1963 to 1976." *Newport History* 194 (Spring 1984): 38–52.

Benway, Ann. *A Guidebook to Newport Mansions of the Preservation Society of Newport County*. Newport: Preservation Society of Newport County, 1984.

Berman, David. *George Berkeley: Idealism and the Man*. Oxford: Clarendon Press, 1994.

Bicknell, Thomas W. *Story of Dr. John Clarke*. Providence: Privately published, 1915.

Bishop, Hillman M. "Why Rhode Island Opposed the Federal Constitution." *Rhode Island History* 8 (January 1949): 1–10.

Bjerkoe, Ethel Hall. *The Cabinetmakers of America*. Garden City, N.Y.: Doubleday, 1957.

Blayney, Michael Stewart. "Honor Among Gentlemen: Herbert Pell, Franklin Roosevelt, and the Campaign of 1936." *Rhode Island History* 39 (August 1980): 95–102.

Bolhouse, Gladys E. "Abraham Redwood: Reluctant Quaker, Philanthropist, Botanist." *Newport History* 146 (Spring 1972): 17–35.

Bonwick, Colin. *The American Revolution*. Charlottesville: University Press of Virginia, 1991.

Botting, Douglas. *The Pirates*. Alexandria, Va.: Time-Life Books, 1978.

Bowen, Richard Le Baron. "Godfrey Malbone's Armorial Silver." *Rhode Island History* 9 (April 1950): 37–51.

Bozeman, Theodore Dwight. "Religious Liberty and the Problem of Order in Early Rhode Island." *New England Quarterly* 45 (March, 1972): 44–64.

Braithwaite, William C. *The Beginnings of Quakerism*. 2nd ed. Cambridge: Cambridge University Press, 1955.

Brewster, Lawrence Fay. *Summer Migrations and Resorts of South Carolina Low-Country Planters*. Durham, N.C.: Duke University Press, 1947.

Bridenbaugh, Carl. *Cities in Revolt: Urban Life in America, 1743–1776*. New York: Alfred A. Knopf, 1955.

——. *Cities in the Wilderness: The First Century of Urban Life in America, 1625–1742*. New York: Oxford University Press, 1938.

——. "Colonial Newport as a Summer Resort." *Rhode Island Historical Society Collections* 26 (January 1933): 1–23.

——. *The Colonial Craftsman*. New York: New York University Press, 1950.

——. *Fat Mutton and Liberty of Conscience: Society in Rhode Island, 1636–1690*. Providence: Brown University Press, 1974.

——. *Mitre and Sceptre: Transatlantic Faiths, Ideas, Personalities, and Politics, 1689–1775*. New York: Oxford University Press, 1962.

——. *Peter Harrison: First American Architect*. Chapel Hill: University of North Carolina Press, 1949.

Brigham, Clarence S. "James Franklin and the Beginnings of Printing in Rhode Island." *Massachusetts Historical Society Proceedings* 65 (1936): 536–544.

Brown, Robert Perkins, and Henry Robinson Palmer. *The Rhode Island Signers of the Declaration of Independence*. Providence: Rhode Island Society of the Sons of the American Revolution, 1913.

Brownell, William C. "Newport." *Scribner's Magazine*, August 1894, 135–156.

Callender, John. *An Historical Discourse, on the Civil and Religious Affairs of the Colony of Rhode-Island*. 2nd ed. Providence: Knowles, Vose, 1838.

Carpenter, Ralph E., Jr. *The Arts and Crafts of Newport, Rhode Island, 1640–1820*. Newport: Preservation Society of Newport County, 1954.

Carroll, Charles. *Rhode Island: Three Centuries of Democracy*. 4 vols. New York: Lewis Historical Publishing Company, 1932.

Casey, Dorothy Needham. "Rhode Island Silversmiths." *Rhode Island Historical Society Collections* 33 (July 1940): 49–64.

Champlin, Margaret. "Raphael Pumpelly." *American National Biography*, 17:938–940.

Champlin, Richard L. "The Art, Trade, or Mystery of the Ropemaker." *Newport History* 149 (Fall 1973): 81–93.

——. "High Time: William Claggett and His Clockmaking Family." *Newport History* 155 (Summer 1974): 157–185.

Champney, Elizabeth W. "Newport Society in the Last Century." *Harper's New Monthly Magazine*, September 1879, 497–505.

Channing, William Henry. *The Life of William Ellery Channing*. Boston: American Unitarian Association, 1880.

Chapin, Anna A., and Charles V Chapin. *A History of Rhode Island Ferries: 1640–1923*. Providence: Oxford Press, 1925.

Chapin, Howard M. *Privateer Ships and Sailors: The First Century of American Colonial Privateering, 1625–1725*. Toulon: G. Mouton, 1926.

——. *Rhode Island Privateers in King George's War: 1739–1748*. Providence: Rhode Island Historical Society, 1926.

——. *The Tartar: The Armed Sloop of Rhode Island in King George's War*. Providence: Society of Colonial Wars in the State of Rhode Island and Providence Plantations, 1922.

Cherpak, Evelyn M. "Chester T. Minkler and the Development of Naval Underwater Ordnance." *Newport History* 204 (Fall 1986): 155–171.

Chorley, Kenneth. *Only Tomorrow*. Newport: Preservation Society of Newport County, 1947.

Chyet, Stanley F. *Lopez of Newport: Colonial American Merchant Prince*. Detroit, Mich.: Wayne State University Press, 1970.

Clark, Victor S. *History of Manufactures in the United States, 1607–1860*. 3 vols. Washington, D.C.: Carnegie Institute, 1916.

Coleman, Peter J. *The Transformation of Rhode Island: 1790–1860*. Providence: Brown University Press, 1963.

Coleman, R. V. *Liberty and Property*. New York: Charles Scribner, 1951.

Conley, Patrick T. *An Album of Rhode Island History, 1636–1986*. Virginia Beach, Va.: Donning, 1986.

——. *Catholicism in Rhode Island: The Formative Era*. Providence: Diocese of Providence, 1976.

——. *Democracy in Decline: Rhode Island's Constitutional Development, 1776–1841*. Providence: Rhode Island Historical Society, 1977.

——. *Liberty and Justice: A History of Law and Lawyers in Rhode Island, 1636–1998*. East Providence, Rhode Island: Rhode Island Publications Society, 1998.

——. "Thomas Wilson Dorr." *American National Biography*, 6:759–761.

Conley, Patrick T., and John P. Kaminski, eds. *The Bill of Rights and the States: The Colonial and Revolutionary Origins of American Liberties*. Madison, Wis.: Madison House, 1992.

Cooper, James Fenimore. *The Red Rover: A Tale*. New York: Appleton, 1850.

Copes, Jan M. "The Perry Family: A Newport Naval Dynasty of the Early Republic." *Newport History* 227 (Fall 1994): 49–77.

Cortissoz, Royal. "John La Farge." *Dictionary of American Biography*, 10:530–535.

Cosentino, Andrew J. *The Paintings of Charles Bird King (1785–1862)*. Washington, D.C.: Smithsonian Institution Press, 1977.

Coughtry, Jay. *The Notorious Triangle: Rhode Island and the African Slave Trade 1700–1807*. Philadelphia: Temple University Press, 1981.

Coulombe, Charles A. *Rum: The Epic Story of the Drink That Conquered the World*. New York: Citadel Press, 2004.

Cowell, Benjamin. *Spirit of '76 in Rhode Island*. Boston, 1850. Reprint, Salem, Mass.: Higginson Book Company, 1996.

Crane, Elaine Forman. *A Dependent People: Newport, Rhode Island in the Revolutionary Era*. New York: Fordham University Press, 1985.

"Cranston, Samuel." Biographical *Cyclopedia of Representative Men of Rhode Island*, 48–49.

Curtis, George William. *Lotus-Eating: A Summer Book*. New York: Harper and Brothers, 1852.

——. "Newport—Historical and Social." *Harper's New Monthly Magazine*, August 1854, 289–317.

"Cushing, Howard Gardiner." *National Cyclopedia of American Biography*, 24:165–166.

Danes, Gibson. "William Morris Hunt and His Newport Circle." *Magazine of Art* 43 (April 1950): 144–150.

Daniels, Bruce C. *Dissent and Conformity on Narragansett Bay: The Colonial Rhode Island Town*. Middletown, Conn.: Wesleyan University Press, 1983.

Davies, Evan Wallace. "Mamie Fish." *Notable American Women 1607–1950*, 1:620–621.

Davis, Lucius. *History of the Methodist Episcopal Church in Newport, R.I.* Newport: Davis and Pitman, 1882.

Dearden, Paul F. "The Siege of Newport: Inauspicious Dawn of Alliance." *Rhode Island Historical Society Collections* 29 (February and May 1970): 17–35.

DeVaro, Lawrence J., Jr. "The Gaspee Affair as Conspiracy." *Rhode Island History* 32 (November 1973): 107–121.

Dow, George F., and John Henry. *The Pirates of the New England Coast*. Salem, Mass.: Marine Research Society, 1923.

Downing, Antoinette F., and Vincent J. Scully. *The Architectural Heritage of Newport Rhode Island, 1640–1915*. 2nd ed. New York: Bramhall House, 1967.

Drake, James D. *King Philip's War: Civil War in New England, 1675–1676*. Amherst, Mass.: University of Massachusetts Press, 1999.

Drake, Samuel Adams. *The Border Wars of New England: Commonly Called King William's and Queen Anne's Wars*. Williamstown, Mass.: Corner House, 1973.

Draper, Theodore. *A Struggle for Power: The American Revolution*. New York: Times Books, 1996.

Dunlap, William. *The Arts of Design in the United States*. New York: Dover, 1834.

Dwight, Eleanor. *Edith Wharton: An Extraordinary Life*. New York: Harry Abrams, 1994.

Dwight, Timothy. *Travels in New-England and New-York*. 4 vols. New Haven: Timothy Dwight, 1822.

Edel, Leon. *Henry James, Edith Wharton, and Newport: An Address Delivered by Leon Edel at the Opening of the Exhibition Held at the Redwood Library and Athenæum, Newport, Rhode Island, July and August, 1966*. Newport: Redwood Library, 1966.

[Elliott, Maude Howe]. *A Newport Aquarelle*. Boston: Roberts Brothers, 1883.

Everdell, William R. *The End of Kings: A History of Republics and Republicans*. Chicago: University of Chicago Press, 2000.

Ferber, Linda S. *William Trost Richards: American Landscape & Marine Painter, 1833–1905*. New York: Brooklyn Museum, 1973.

———. "William Trost Richards at Newport." *Newport History* 169 (Winter 1978): 1–15.

Field, Edward, ed. *State of Rhode Island and Providence Plantations at the End of the Century*. 3 vols. Boston: Mason, 1902.

Fisher, Sydney George. *Men, Women & Manners in Colonial Times*. 2 vols. 3rd ed. Philadelphia: J. B. Lippincott, 1900.

Flexner, James Thomas. *Gilbert Stuart: A Great Life in Brief*. New York: Alfred A. Knopf, 1955.

Foote, Henry Wilder. *Robert Feke: Colonial Portrait Painter*. Cambridge, Mass.: Harvard University Press, 1930.

Forbes, Allan. *France and New England*. 2 vols. Boston: State Street Trust Company, 1925–1927.

Foster, A. Kristen. "Washington Allston." *American National Biography*, 1:372–374.

Foster, Stephen. *The Long Argument: English Puritanism and the Shaping of New England Culture, 1570–1700*. Chapel Hill: University of North Carolina Press, 1991.

Frank, Robin Jaffee. *Love and Loss: American Portrait and Mourning Miniatures*. New Haven: Yale University Art Gallery, 2000.

Fraser, Antonia. *King Charles II*. London: Weidenfeld and Nicolson, 1979.

Fuller, Hiram. *Belle Brittan On a Tour at Newport, and Here and There*. New York: Derby and Jackson, 1858.

Funston, Judith E. "Edith Wharton." *American National Biography*, 23:110–112.

Galbraith, John Kenneth. *The Great Crash: 1929*. Boston: Houghton, Mifflin, 1955.

Gatchel, Theodore L. "The Rock on Which the Storm will Beat: Fort Adams and the Defenses of Narragansett Bay." *Newport History* 230 (Summer 1995): 1–35.

Gaustad, Edwin S. *George Berkeley in America*. New Haven: Yale University Press, 1979.

Goodwin, Jason. *Greenback: The Almighty Dollar and the Invention of America*. New York: Henry Holt, 2003.

Gregg, Edward. *Queen Anne*. London: Routledge and Kegan Paul, 1980.

Gregory, Eliot. "Newport in Summer." *Harper's Monthly*, July 1901, 165–175.

Grosvenor, Richard. *Newport: An Artist's Impression of Its Architecture and History*. Beverly, Mass.: Commonwealth Editions, 2002.

Guinness, Desmond, and Julius Trousdale Sadler Jr. *Newport Preserv'd: Architecture of the 18th Century*. New York: Viking Press, 1982.

Gura, Philip F. *A Glimpse of Sion's Glory: Puritan Radicalism in New England, 1620–1660*. Middletown, Conn.: Wesleyan University Press, 1984.

Gutstein, Morris. *Aaron Lopez and Judah Touro: A Refugee and a Son of a Refugee*. New York: Behrman's Jewish Book House, 1939.

Articles, Books, Monographs continued

Hale, Stuart O. *Narragansett Bay: A Friend's Perspective*. Narragansett, R.I.: Marine Advisory
        Service, University of Rhode Island, 1980.

Harlow, Virginia. *Thomas Sergeant Perry: A Biography*. Durham, N.C.: Duke University Press,
        1950.

Hattendorf, Berit M. "Newport's First Woman Portraitist: Jane Stuart." *Newport History* 232 (Winter
        1996): 145–169.

Hattendorf, Ingrid M. *The Old Stone Mill: A Finding Guide*. Newport: Redwood Library and
        Athenæum, 1998.

Hattendorf, John B. *Semper Eadem: A History of Trinity Church in Newport, 1698–2000*. Newport:
        Trinity Church, 2001.

——. "Stephen B. Luce." *American National Biography*, 14:94–96.

Hatton, Ragnhild. *George I: Elector and King*. London: Thames and Hudson, 1978.

Hawes, Alexander Boyd. *Off Soundings: Aspects of the Maritime History of Rhode Island*. Chevy
        Chase, Md.: Posterity Press, 1999.

Heckscher, Morrison. *John Townsend: Newport Cabinetmaker*. New York: Metropolitan Museum of
        Art; New Haven: Yale University Press, 2005.

Hedges, James B. *The Browns of Providence Plantations*. Vol. 1, Colonial Years. Cambridge, Mass.:
        Harvard University Press, 1952.

Herrick, George G. *Newport This Week*. "Some Americans Had to Work at Play." June 1–7, 2000.

——. *The Origins of Croquet in America, 1859–1873*. Washington: Privately published, 2001.

——. *The Origins of the Social Club in America*. Newport: Privately published, 2004.

Homberger, Eric. *Mrs. Astor's New York: Money and Social Power in a Gilded Age*. New Haven:
        Yale University Press, 2002.

Hopkins, Stephen. *The Rights of Colonies Examined*. Providence: William Goddard, 1765.

Horle, Craig W. *The Quakers and the English Legal System, 1660–1688*. Philadelphia: University of
        Pennsylvania Press, 1988.

Horwitz, Tony. *Blue Latitudes: Going Boldly Where Captain Cook Has Gone Before*. New York:
        Picador, 2002.

Houston, Alan Craig. *Algernon Sidney and the Republican Heritage in England and America*.
        Princeton: Princeton University Press, 1991.

Howe, Daniel W. "William Ellery Channing." *American National Biography*, 4:680–681.

Howland, Richard Hubbard. "Architecture: The Library's XIXth-Century Architecture." In *Redwood
        Papers: A Bicentennial Collection*, edited by Lorraine Dexter and Alan Pryce-Jones,
        98–110. Newport: Redwood Library and Athenæum, 1976.

Huber, Elaine C. "Anne Hutchinson." *American National Biography*, 11:595–596.

Hughes, Robert. "Claw Daddy: John Townsend's Reputation as America's First True Artist is Set in
        Wood." *New York Times Magazine*, May 29, 2005.

Hull, William I. "The Early History of the Friends in Newport." In *Early Religious Leaders of
        Newport, Rhode Island*, 21–50. Newport: Mercury Publishing Co., 1918.

Hurst, Harold. "The Elite Class of Newport, Rhode Island, 1830–1860." Ph.D. diss., New York
        University, 1975.

Irwin, Raymond D. "Saints, Sinners, and Subjects: Rhode Island and Providence Plantations in
        Transatlantic Perspective, 1636–1665." Ph.D. diss., Ohio State University, 1996.

Isham, Norman M. *Early American Houses*. Topsfield, Mass.: Walpole Society, 1928.

James, Henry. "The Sense of Newport." *Harper's Monthly*, August 1906, 343–354.

James, Sydney V. *The Colonial Metamorphoses in Rhode Island: A Study of Institutions in Change*.
        Hanover, N.H.: University Press of New England, 2000.

———. *Colonial Rhode Island: A History*. New York: Charles Scribner's Sons, 1975.

———. *John Clarke and His Legacies: Religion and Law in Colonial Rhode Island 1638–1750*. University Park, PA: Pennsylvania State University Press, 1999.

———. "Rhode Island: From Classical Democracy to British Province." *Rhode Island History* 43 (November 1984): 119–135.

———. "Where People Thought Otherwise: Rhode Island Before 1776." *Newport History* 196 (Fall 1984): 97–121.

Jefferys, C. P. B. *Newport: 1639–1976: An Historical Sketch*. Newport: Newport Historical Society, 1976.

Jones, Rufus M. *The Quakers in the American Colonies*. London: Macmillan, 1911.

Jordy, William H. and Christopher P. Monkhouse. *Buildings on Paper: Rhode Island Architectural Drawings 1825–1945*. Providence: Brown University, Rhode Island Historical Society, Rhode Island School of Design, 1982.

Kalfatovic, Martin. "John Smibert." *American National Biography*, 20:118–120.

Kaplan, Fred. *Henry James: The Imagination of Genius: A Biography*. New York: William Morrow, 1992.

The Kay–Catherine–Old Beach Road Neighborhood in Newport. Providence: Rhode Island Historical Preservation Commission, 1974.

Kennett, Lee. *The French Forces in America, 1780–1783*. Westport, Conn.: Greenwood Press, 1997.

Kenny, Robert W. "The Rhode Island Gazette of 1732." *Rhode Island Historical Society Collections* 25 (October 1932): 97–107.

Langguth, A. J. *Patriots: The Men Who Started the American Revolution*. New York: Simon and Schuster, 1988.

LaPlante, Eve. *American Jezebel: The Uncommon Life of Anne Hutchinson, the Woman Who Defied the Puritans*. San Francisco: Harper, 2003.

Lathrop, George Parsons. *Newport*. New York: Charles Scribner's Sons, 1884.

Leach, Douglas Edward. *Flintlock and Tomahawk: New England in King Philip's War*. New York: Macmillian, 1958.

Levinger, Rabbi Lee J. *A History of the Jews in the United States*. New York: Union of American Hebrew Congregations, 1930.

Levitan, Tina. *The Firsts of American Jewish History, 1492–1951*. Brooklyn, N.Y.: Charuth Press, 1952.

Lewis, Michael J. *Frank Furness: Architecture and the Violent Mind*. New York: W. W. Norton, 2001.

Little, Nina Fletcher. "Michele Felice Corne, 1752–1845." *Antiques* 102 (August 1972): 262–269.

Lovejoy, David S. *Rhode Island Politics and the American Revolution, 1760–1776*. Providence: Brown University Press, 1958.

Lowenthal, Larry. "The Cliff Walk at Newport." *Newport History* 212 (Fall 1988): 110–143.

MacCulloch, Diarmaid. *The Reformation: A History*. New York: Viking, 2004.

Maier, Pauline. *American Scripture: Making the Declaration of Independence*. New York: Alfred A. Knopf, 1997.

Marshall, Roger. "The Twelves." In "City Guide," special issue, *Newport Life* 9 (Spring 2001): 12–20.

Mason, George Champlin. *Annals of Trinity Church, Newport, Rhode Island*. Philadelphia: Evans Printing House, 1890.

———. *Annals of the Redwood Library and Athenæum*, Newport, Rhode Island. Newport: Redwood Library, 1891.

Massey, J. Earl. *America's Money: The Story of Our Coins and Currency*. New York: Thomas Y. Crowell, 1968.

Articles, Books, Monographs continued

McAdam, Roger. *Floating Palaces: New England to New York on the Old Fall River Line*. Providence: Mowbray, 1972.

McLanathan, Richard. *Gilbert Stuart*. Norwalk, Conn.: Easton Press, 1986.

McLoughlin, William G. "Anne Hutchinson Reconsidered." *Rhode Island History* 49 (February 1991): 13–25.

——. *Rhode Island: A Bicentennial History*. New York: W. W. Norton, 1978.

Menzies, Gavin. *1421: The Year China Discovered America*. New York: William Morrow, 2002.

Meschutt, David. "Charles Bird King." *American National Biography*, 12:688–690.

——. "Gilbert Stuart." *American National Biography*, 21:69–72.

Middlekauff, Robert. *The Glorious Cause: The American Revolution, 1763–1789*. New York: Oxford University Press, 1982.

Millar, John F. "Stephen Hopkins, an Architect of Independence, 1707–1785." *Newport History* 177 (Winter 1980): 24–36.

Miller, John. *The Life and Times of William and Mary*. London: Weidenfeld and Nicolson, 1974.

Miller, Perry. *The New England Mind: The Seventeenth Century*. Cambridge, Mass.: Harvard University Press, 1954.

Miller, Paul F. "The Preservation Society of Newport County: A Brief History." Unpublished manuscript. Newport: Preservation Society of Newport County, 2003.

Mills, C. Wright. *The Power Elite*. New York: Oxford University Press, 1956.

Miranda, Francisco. Translated by Don Juan de Ria_o. "A Spaniard's Visit to Newport in 1784." *Bulletin of the Newport Historical Society* 85 (October 1932): 3–15.

Mohr, Ralph S. *Governors for Three Hundred Years: 1638–1959; Rhode Island and Providence Plantations*. Rev. ed. Providence: Oxford Press, 1959.

Mooney, Barbara B. "Richard Munday." *American National Biography*, 16:90–91.

Moore, Charles J. "The Blockfront Furniture of New England: Boston and Newport Compared." Unpublished paper. Newport, 1993.

Morgan, Edmund Sears. *The Birth of the Republic: 1763–1789*. Chicago: University of Chicago Press, 1977.

——. *The Gentle Puritan: A Life of Ezra Stiles, 1727–1795*. New Haven: Yale University Press, 1962.

——. *Roger Williams: The Church and the State*. New York: Harcourt, Brace and World, 1967.

Morison, Samuel Eliot. *The Growth of the American Republic*. New York: Oxford University Press, 1942.

——. *The Intellectual Life of Colonial New England*. New York: New York University Press, 1956.

——. *The Oxford History of the American People*. New York: Oxford University Press, 1965.

Moses, Michael. *Master Craftsmen of Newport: The Townsends and Goddards*. Tenafly, N.J.: MMI Americana Press, 1984.

Mount, Charles Merrill. *Gilbert Stuart: A Biography*. New York: W. W. Norton, 1964.

Mrozek, Donald J. *Sport and the American Mentality, 1880–1910*. Knoxville: University of Tennessee Press, 1983.

Murphy-Schlicting, Mary. "A Summer Salon: Literary and Cultural Circles in Newport, Rhode Island, 1850–1890." Ph.D. diss., New York University, 1992.

Nash, Gary B. *The Unknown American Revolution: The Unruly Birth of Democracy and the Struggle to Create America*. New York: Viking, 2005.

Nettels, Curtis P. *The Money Supply of the American Colonies before 1720*. Madison: University of Wisconsin Press, 1934.

Nevins, Allan. "James Gordon Bennett." *Dictionary of American Biography*, 2:199–202.

"Newport Casino." *Town Topics: A Journal of Society*, New York, August 1887.

Newport Daily News, "All Newport Celebrates End of the Great War," November 11, 1918.

———, "Bay Bridge Vote Tops City's 1964 News," December 31, 1964.

———, "Big Haul Made," January 14, 1924.

———, "City Recovers From Hurricane," September 22, 1938.

———, "City's Publicity Reaches 60,000,000," December 30, 1950.

———, "Coast Guard Kills Three Rum Runners," December 30, 1929.

———, "Defense Preparations Led Newport Activities in 1941," January 2, 1942.

———, "A Floral Procession," September 8, 1899.

———, "Newport Naval Expansion Considered," August 12, 1940.

———, "The Motor Carriage Here," July 2, 1897.

———, "Training Station Ends Busiest Peace Year," January 3, 1941.

———, "Victory Celebration Breaks All Records," August 17, 1945.

———, "The Weather," September 21, 1938.

Newport Mercury, "Awful and Destructive Storm," September 30, 1815.

———, "Bridge Body Commends Objection Withdrawn," August 31, 1945.

———, "Costumes Add to Colorful Scenes on Washington Street," July 28, 1939.

———, "Day of Jubilation," November 16, 1918.

———, "Examinations at the Torpedo Station," October 9, 1875.

———, "German War Submarine Here," October 14, 1916.

———, "Jane Stuart," May 5, 1888.

———, "Land Sales on Bellevue Avenue," October 14, 1854.

———, "Newport's Great Disaster," February 2, 1918.

———, "Redevelopment Body Names Its Chairman," December 30, 1949.

———, "Sea Baths on the Long Wharf," 1844.

———, "Summer Visitors," August 5, 1826.

———, "Theodore W. King," January 4, 1862.

New York Times, "Guests as Chinese at Belmont Ball," July 25, 1914.

———, "Mrs. August Belmont Dead," November 15, 1892.

———, "The Newport Demonstration," August 24, 1859.

———, "Ochre Point," August 12, 1881.

Nimmo, Eileen G. *"The Point" of Newport, RI*. Newport: J & E Publishing, 2001.

Nord, Barbara K. *The Flagg Family in New England: The Ancestry of Dr. Henry Collins Flagg*. Austin, Texas: Peripatetic Press, 1988.

O'Connor, Richard. *The Golden Summers: An Antic History of Newport*. New York: G. P. Putnam's Sons, 1974.

O'Doherty, Brian. *Maxim Karolik*. Boston: Museum of Fine Arts, 1964.

Pantalone, John. "30 Year Span." *Newport Life* 6 (Spring 1999): 16–19, 58, 59.

Pardee, Bettie Breaden. *Private Newport: At Home and in the Garden*. New York: Bulfinch Press, 2004.

Partridge, Albert L. "William Claggett, of Newport, Rhode Island, Clockmaker." *Old-Time New England* 27 (January 1937): 110–115.

Patterson, Jerry E. *The First Four Hundred: Mrs. Astor's New York in the Gilded Age*. New York: Rizzoli, 2000.

Peckham, Howard H. *The Colonial Wars: 1689–1762*. Chicago: University of Chicago Press, 1964.

Peterson, Rev. Edward. *History of Rhode Island and Newport*. New York: John S. Taylor, 1853.

Plumb, J. H. *The First Four Georges*. London: Hamlyn Publishing Group, 1956.

Polishook, Irwin H. *Rhode Island and the Union: 1774–1795*. Evanston, Ill.: Northwestern University Press, 1969.

Porter, Daniel R. *The Hunter House: "Mansion of Hospitality."* Newport: Preservation Society of Newport County, 1976.

"To Preserve Hidden Treasures: From the Scrapbooks of Charles Bird King." Edited by Stephen J. Zietz. Newport: Redwood Library and Athenæum, 1997. Published on the occasion of an Exhibition, May 19–August 24, 1996.

Purvis, Thomas L. *Colonial America to 1763*. New York: Facts on File, 1999.

Rand, Larry Anthony. "The Know-Nothing Party in Rhode Island." *Rhode Island History* 23 (October 1964): 102–116.

Van Rensselaer, Mrs. John King . *Newport: Our Social Capital*. Philadelphia: J. B. Lippincott, 1905.

——. *The Social Ladder*. New York: Henry Holt, 1924.

Rhode Island: A Guide to the Smallest State. Boston: Houghton, Mifflin, 1937.

Rice, Howard C., Jr., and Anne S. K. Brown, translators. *The American Campaigns of Rochambeau's Army, 1780, 1781, 1782, 1783*. Princeton and Providence: Princeton University Press and Brown University Press, 1972.

Richards, T. Addison. "Newport." *The Knickerbocker* 54 (October 1859): 337–352.

Richman, Irving Berdine. *Rhode Island: Its Making and Its Meaning*. New York: G. P. Putnam's Sons, 1908.

——. *Rhode Island: A Study in Separatism*. Boston: Houghton, Mifflin, 1905.

Roberts, Nancy. *Blackbeard and Other Pirates of the Atlantic Coast*. Winston-Salem, N.C.: John F. Blair, 1993.

Robinson, Willard B. "Fort Adams—American Example of French Military Architecture." *Rhode Island History* 34 (August 1975): 77–96.

Robson, Lloyd A. "Newport Begins." *Newport History* 116 (October 1964): 133–153.

——. "Newport, One Hundred Years Ago." *Bulletin of the Newport Historical Society* 106 (July 1961): 3–18.

Rossiter, Clinton. *Seedtime of the Republic: The Origin of the American Tradition of Political Liberty*. New York: Harcourt, Brace, 1953.

Roth, Leland M. "McKim, Mead & White, Architects." In *Who's Who in Architecture from 1400 to the Present Day*, edited by J. M. Richard. London: Weidenfeld and Nicolson, 1977.

Russell, Elbert. *The History of Quakerism*. New York: Macmillan, 1942.

Sanford, Elias B. *A History of Connecticut*. Hartford: S. S. Scranton, 1922.

Schlesinger, Arthur M. *The Birth of the Nation: A Portrait of the American People on the Eve of Independence*. New York: Alfred A. Knopf, 1968.

Schreier, Barbara A. "The Resort of Pure Fashion: Newport, Rhode Island, 1890–1914." *Rhode Island History* 47 (February 1989): 22–34.

Schroder, Walter K. *Defenses of Narragansett Bay in World War II*. Providence: Rhode Island Bicentennial Foundation, 1980.

Schumacher, Alan T. "George Champlin Mason: Architect, Artist, Author." *Newport History* 138 (Spring 1970): 21–29.

——. "The Newport Casino: Its History." *Newport History* 206 (Spring 1987): 45–106.

——. "The Newport Country Club: Its Curious History." *Newport History* 202 (Spring 1986): 47–105.

——. "Newport's First Directory." *Newport History* 144 (Fall 1971): 93–105.

——. "Newport's Real Estate King." *Newport History* 209 (Spring 1988): 36–51.

——. "Newport—Literature and Printing, 1700–1850." *Newport History* 167 (Summer 1977): 45–64.

Scotti, R. A. *Sudden Sea: The Great Hurricane of 1938*. Boston: Little, Brown, 2003.

Serle, Ambrose. *The American Journal of Ambrose Serle, Secretary to Lord Howe: 1776–1778*. San Marino, CA: Huntington Library, 1940.

Sesquicentennial History 2003. Newport: Newport Reading Room, 2003.

Severens, Martha R. "Edward Greene Malbone." *American National Biography*, 14:356–357.

Sherman, Archibald C. *Newport and the Savings Bank*. Newport: Hartley G. Ward, 1944.

Shorto, Russell. *The Island at the Center of the World*. New York: Doubleday, 2004.

Simister, Florence Parker. *The Fire's Center: Rhode Island in the Revolutionary Era, 1763–1790*. Providence: Rhode Island Bicentennial Foundation, 1979.

Simpson, Alan, and Mary M. Simpson. "A New Look at How Rochambeau Quartered His Army in Newport (1780–1781)." *Newport History* 190 (Spring 1983): 30–67.

Skemp, Sheila L. "Aaron Lopez." *American National Biography*, 13:908–909.

———. "George Berkeley's Newport Experience." *Rhode Island History* 37 (May 1978): 53–63.

———. "A Social and Cultural History of Newport, RI, 1720–1765." Ph.D. diss., University of Iowa, 1974.

Smith, George B. "Formation and Service of the First Regiment Rhode Island Detached Militia." *Newport History* 58 (July 1926). 14–29.

Snydacker, Daniel, Jr. "The Great Depression in Newport." *Newport History* 198 (Spring 1985): 42–55.

———. "The Remarkable Career of Martin Howard, Jr." *Newport History* 208 (Winter 1988): 2–16.

Snydacker, Daniel, Jr., Michelle Christiansen, Deborah Walker, and Elliott Caldwell. "The Business of Leisure: The Gilded Age in Newport." *Newport History* 215 (Summer 1989): 97–126.

Stachiw, Myron O. *The Early Architecture and Landscapes of the Narragansett Basin*. 2 vols. Newport, Rhode Island: The Vernacular Architecture Forum, 2001.

Stafford, Jean. "American Town." *New Yorker*, August 28, 1948.

Stein, Susan, ed. *The Architecture of Richard Morris Hunt*. Chicago: University of Chicago Press, 1986.

Stephens, Olin J. *All This and Sailing, Too: An Autobiography*. Mystic, CT: Mystic Seaport Museum, 1999.

Sterngass, Jon. *First Resorts: Pursuing Pleasure at Saratoga Springs, Newport & Coney Island*. Baltimore: Johns Hopkins University Press, 2001.

Stinson, Brian. "The Heroine of Lime Rock." *Newport Life* 7 (Summer 2000): 18–21.

———. "Oliver Hazard Perry." Newport Notables. Redwood Library and Athenæum. http://www. redwoodlibrary.org/notables/oh_perry.htm.

———. "Paradise Lost." *Newport Life* 9 (Fall 2002): 30–33, 41.

Strange, Michael. *Who Tells Me True*. New York: Charles Scribner's Sons, 1940.

Strum, Harvey. "Rhode Island and the War of 1812." *Rhode Island History* 50 (February 1992): 23–32.

Sweet, John Wood. *Bodies Politic: Negotiating Race in the American North, 1730–1830*. Baltimore, MD: Johns Hopkins University Press, 2003.

Syrett, David. *The Royal Navy in American Waters: 1775–1783*. Aldershot, England: Scolar Press, 1989.

Taylor, Alan. *American Colonies*. New York: Viking, 2001.

Tilley, John Henry. *Newport from 1700 to 1775*. Newport, 1896.

Tungett, Lynne. "Weren't They Grand? The Lost Era of Newport's Grand Hotels." *Newport Life* 7 (Winter 2000): 13–17.

Vaughan, Carter. *Dragon Cove*. Garden City, N.Y.: Doubleday, 1964.

Veblen, Thorstein. *The Theory of the Leisure Class: An Economic Study of Institutions*. New York: Macmillan, 1899.

Walker, Anthony. "Death of a Regiment." *Newport History* 208 (Fall 1987): 166–172.

"Wanton, Edward." *Biographical Cyclopedia of Representative Men of Rhode Island*, 77.

"Wanton, Governor John." *Biographical Cyclopedia of Representative Men of Rhode Island*, 78–79.

"Wanton, William." *Biographical Cyclopedia of Representative Men of Rhode Island*, 78.

Warburton, Eileen. *In Living Memory: A Chronicle of Newport, RI, 1888–1988*. Newport: Newport Savings and Loan Association, Island Trust Co., 1988.

———. "Newport Country Club: That Championship Century." *1995 Centennial U.S. Amateur Championship*, August 1995.

Weeden, William B. *Economic and Social History of New England, 1620–1789*. 2 vols. Boston: Houghton, Mifflin, 1890.

Wharton, Edith. *The Age of Innocence*. New York: D. Appleton, 1920.

———. *A Backward Glance*. New York: Curtis, 1933.

Wharton, Edith, and Ogden Codman, Jr. *The Decoration of Houses*. New York: C. Scribner's Sons, 1897.

Wilkins, Thurman. "Clarence Rivers King." *American National Biography*, 12:691–693.

Wilson, Richard Guy. "Charles Follen McKim." *American National Biography*, 15:113–115.

Withey, Lynne. *Urban Growth in Colonial Rhode Island: Newport and Providence in the Eighteenth Century*. Albany: State University of New York Press, 1984.

Wood, Gordon S. *The American Revolution: A History*. New York: Modern Library, 2002.

———. *The Creation of the American Republic: 1776–1787*. Chapel Hill: University of North Carolina Press, 1969.

———. *The Radicalism of the American Revolution*. New York: Alfred A. Knopf, 1992.

Woodbridge, George. "George Washington and Newport." *Newport History* 220 (Summer 1991): 109–133.

———. "Rochambeau: Two Hundred Years Later." *Newport History* 177 (Winter 1980): 5–21.

Wright, Louis B. *The Cultural Life of the American Colonies: 1607–1763*. New York: Harper and Row, 1957.

Wroth, Lawrence C. *The Voyages of Giovanni da Verrazzano: 1524–1528*. New Haven: Yale University Press, 1970.

Yarnall, James L. "John La Farge." *American National Biography*, 13:31–34.

———. *John La Farge: Watercolors and Drawings*. Yonkers, N.Y.: Hudson River Museum of Westchester, 1990.

Youngken, Richard C. *An Introduction to the Heritage of African Americans in Newport, Rhode Island, 1700–1945*. Providence: Rhode Island Historical Preservation and Heritage Commission, Rhode Island Black Heritage Society, 1995.

Zipf, Catherine W. *Between the Golden Age and the Gilded Age: A History of the Southern Thames Street Neighborhood*. Newport: Cultural and Historic Preservation Program, Salve Regina University, 2004.

Zukowski, Karen. "Artists in Newport." *Newport History* 203 (Summer 1986): 112–131.

Index

Lowercase s appended to page numbers indicates that the subjects are found in sidebars.

A

Acts of Settlement, 97s

USS *Adams*, 260

Adams, Abigail, 119

Adams, Henry, 331, 333, 337

Adams, John, 83, 119, 168, 177s, 181, 219s, 234s, 235, 237s, 241, 242, 271, 275s

Adams, John Quincy, 168, 259, 275s, 432

Addison, Joseph, 86s, 111

Adela (ship), picture of, 453

Adix (ship), picture of, 453

Agassiz, Alexander, 336–337

Agassiz, George, 337

The Age of Innocence (Wharton), 396, 399

Ahlstrom, Sydney, 57

Albany, New York, 269

Albany Conference, 176, 178, 185

Alciphron: or, the Minute Philosopher (Berkeley), 115

Aldrich, Nelson W., 380, 432

Alexander, Cosmo, 164

Allard, Jules, 367

Allston, Ann (Channing), 279

Allston, Washington, 276, 278–280, 283, 286

Almy, Benjamin, 212

Almy, Mary, 212

Almy, William, 251

Almy's Pond, Newport (Richards), 401

Althoff, Gerry, 263

Alva (ship), 360, 395

American Field Service, 416

American Institute of Architects, 364

The American Scene (James), 379

America's Cup, 321s, 385, 393, 395, 450–454

America (ship), 321s, 451

Amity (ship), 91–92

Amory, Cleveland, 409

Andros, Edmund, 64, 68, 77–78, 82, 88

Angell, Israel, 216

Anglicanism. *See* Church of England

Anne, Queen of England, 86s, 87, 89, 94, 97s; portrait of, 86

Anthony, Elizabeth, 163

Anthony, Henry B., 320, 432

Anthony, Peleg, 210

Antinomian Crisis, 12–14, 17, 19, 60

Aquidneck Compact, 17, 19, 37

Aquidneck Island, 3–4, 12, 17, 19–21, 22, 25, 28–29, 36, 37, 38–39, 42–43, 75, 195, 196, 269s

Aquidneck Island General Court, 27–29, 31, 37s, 45

Arbuthnot, Marriot, 221, 222, 228

The Architectural Heritage of Newport (Downing), 236, 442

The Architectural Heritage of Newport (Scully), 338

Arkwright, Richard, 251

Armstrong, George, 324

Armstrong, Louis, 455

Army Corps of Engineers, 271–272

Arnold, Benedict, 60, 64, 67, 68, 74, 75, 75s, 149, 159

Arnold, Benedict (general), 204, 231, 233

Arnold, S. G., 153, 206, 218

Arnold, Samuel, 98, 108, 149s

Arnold, Thomas, 145

Aron, Cindy S., 299s

art and artists, 275–285, 400–404. *See also specific names*

Art Association of Newport, 402

Articles of Confederation, 180, 238–239, 241

Astor, Caroline Webster Schermerhorn, 354, 355, 356–358, 360, 364, 396, 403, 405, 408, 415

Astor, John Jacob, 356, 359, 388, 393, 412

Astor, John Jacob III, 360

Astor, Mary, 360

Astor, William, 395

Astor, William Backhouse, Jr., 356, 357

Astor Cup, 395

Atherton Company, 55, 68

Atlantic Fleet, 423s, 437, 439–440

Atlantic House, 302–303, 304, 307, 308, 310, 312, 321s, 338, 381

Atlantic Monthly, 335, 397

AT&T, 345

Atterbury, Bishop, 116

Augusta, Georgia, 221

Austin, Ann, 59

Australia (ship), 454

Australia II (ship), 454

auto racing, 392

Avery, Ephraim, 287s

Ayrault, Daniel, 103, 133, 155

Ayrault, Stephen, 103, 133, 138, 156

B

A Backward Glance (Wharton), 398, 400, 407

Bacon, Francis E., 324

Baez, Joan, 456

Bailey, Joseph, 314

Bailyn, Bernard, 64

Baker, Benjamin, 143

Baker, Paul R., 362, 369

Ball, Hugh, 301, 313

Balsan, Jacques, 411

Balston, William, 20

Bancroft, George, 310, 330, 335, 371

Bancroft, John Chandler, 330

Banister, Christian; portrait of, 165

Banister, Hermione (Pelham), 149

Banister, John, 147, 149–151, 159, 164, 172; portrait of, 165

Banister, John, Jr., 149

Bankes, John, 90–92

banking, 267

Baptists, 31, 33s, 46, 48, 59, 119–120

Barbados, 58–59, 65

Barbara Ann (ship), 449s

Barbary War, 260

Barclay, Robert, 262–265

Barras, Admiral de, 233, 234

Barre, Colonel, 183

Bartlett, John, 93

Barton, William, 206

baseball, 390–391

Basie, Count, 455

Basto (brig), 184

Bateman, Luther, 387

Bateman, Seth, 319

Bateman Hotel, 303, 307, 338, 388

Battis, Emery, 13

Baulstone, William, 37

Baxter, George, 57

Bay Colony. *See* Massachusetts Bay Colony

Bayside Farm, 360

Beacon Hill House, 437s–438s

Beaulieu, 360

Beauregard, P. G. T., 321

Bedlow, Henry, 317

Beechwood, 356, 360

Beeckman, Mrs. Livingston, 418

Belcourt, 366, 409, 410; picture of, 368

Bell, Alexander Graham, 345

Bellevue (hotel), 300

Belmont, Alva (Vanderbilt) (Smith), 357–358, 364, 365, 367, 371, 405, 407, 408–411, 412–413, 416, 422; portrait of, 410

Belmont, August, 338, 350, 353–354, 355, 367

Belmont, Caroline Slidell (Perry), 353–354, 356

Belmont, Eleanor Robson, 412

Belmont, Mr., 305

Belmont, Oliver Hazard Perry, 367, 369, 391, 392, 393, 410, 411

Belmont, Perry, 369

Belmont Stakes, 354

Belshazzar's Feast (Allston), 280

Benfrey, Christopher, 333

Bennett, James Gordon, Jr., 348–350, 364, 369, 384, 386–387, 395; portrait of, 349

Bennett, James Gordon, Sr., 348

Benson, Esther F., 444

Benson, John ("Fud"), 448s

Benson, John Howard, 447s–448s

Benson, Nicholas, 448s

Benson, Thomas, 444

Berkeley, Anne, 113

Berkeley, George, 109, 111, 113–117, 121, 123, 130, 141, 156; portrait of, 112

Berkeley, Henry, 113

Berkeley Institute, 326

Bernard, Simon, 271–272

Berry, Walter, 399

Berthier, Louis-Alexandre, 231

Berwind, Edward J., 354, 373–374, 388, 442

Bigelow, John, 335

Bill of Rights, 248

Biltmore House, 364

Bird, Nathaniel, 283–284

Bishop, Hillman, 243

Black Duck (ship), 424

Bleak House, 338, 432

Block Island, 37s

Bloemink, Barbara, 333

Blue Garden, 437s

Board of Trade, 32, 75, 82, 85, 86, 88, 97, 105, 109, 110

Bonaparte, Napoleon, 255–256, 255s, 258, 259, 280

Booth, Edwin, 334

Boston, Massachusetts, 4, 10, 12, 17, 19, 27, 33, 34, 35, 39, 42, 46, 60, 62, 78, 101, 104, 126, 137–138, 141, 146, 156, 174, 195, 329, 333

Boston Gazette, 117

Boston News Letter, 92s

Boston Tea Party, 187

Bourget, Paul, 378s, 399

Bourne, Benjamin, 248

Bourne, Ezra, 317

Bours, Peter, 115

Bouvier, Jacqueline, 275, 443, 449s–450s; photograph of, 449

Bowen, Jeremiah, 68

Boynton, Captain, 256

Braddock, Edward, 176

Bradford, Seth, 361

Braintree, Massachusetts, 15

Brayton, Charles, 381s, 432

Brazil, 63, 462

The Breakers, 347, 363, 365, 367, 369, 376, 411, 442, 453; picture of, 342, 363, 368

Brenton, Jahleel, 73

Brenton, Sarah, 169

Brenton, William, 5, 7, 13, 17, 21, 25, 31, 37, 39–40, 65, 73, 75s, 145, 272, 313, 338, 347

Brenton Point State Park, 431

Brett, John, 184s

Brick Market, 162; picture of, 163

Bridenbaugh, Carl, 17, 58, 129, 137, 147, 147s, 159–160, 298, 299

bridges, 269s, 271, 457–460

Bridges, Robert, 48

Brinley, Anne, 39

Brinley, Francis, 85, 121, 149

Brinley House, 301

Brisbane, John, 212

Bristol, Rhode Island, 70, 175, 196, 219

Britannia (ship), 395

British Acts of Trade. *See* Navigation Acts

Brookline, Massachusetts, 389

Brown, David, 63

Brown, John, 133, 152, 178, 181, 188

Brown, John Carter, 315

Brown, John Nicholas, 393

Brown, Joseph, 152, 178, 181

Brown, Moses, 106, 152, 178, 181, 250

Brown, Mrs. Nicholas Brown, 441

Brown, Nicholas, 136–137, 138, 151, 152, 178, 181

Brown, Obadiah, 152

Brown, Peleg, 133

Brownell, Henry M., 308

Brown University, 136, 181, 238, 271s

Brubeck, Dave, 455

Bryant, Ruth, 93

Bull, Henry, 5–6, 8, 17, 26, 59; house, picture of, 7

Bull, Jireh, 73

Bulow, Claus von, 373

Bunker Hill, Battle of, 190

Burdick, Clark, 421

Bureau of Indian Affairs, 284–285

Burgoyne, John, 203, 207–208, 220

Burke, Edmund, 177s, 183, 189

Burnside, Ambrose, 322, 432

Byron, George Gordon, 279

Byron, John, 214, 219, 221

Bythesea, 338, 353

C

Cahoone, John, 259

Calhoun, John C., 258, 300

Callender, John, 123, 130, 136s

Calumet Club, New York, 389

Calvert, George, 311s, 317

Calvin, John, 9

Calvinism, 8, 9, 10

Cambridge, Massachuestts, 14

Cambridge University, 46

Campannall, Mordecai, 63

Canada, 87, 258

candle making, 151–153

Candy, Henry Augustus, 348, 386

Canonchet (Narragansett sachem), 70

Canonicus (Narragansett sachem), 11, 18

Cape Cod, Massachusetts, 9

Cape May, New Jersey, 296, 297

Capone, Al, 422

Carey House (Bradley-Shipman estate), 441

Carlisle Commission, 209

Caroline, Queen of England, 109s

Carpenter, Ralph, 139–140, 170

Carr, Caleb, 64, 67

Carrère and Hastings: 374

Carroll, Charles, 78s, 207, 220, 256–257

Caswell, Philip, 436

Catholics, 228, 235, 272–273, 274–275. *See also* Know-Nothing Party

Chafee, John, 434

Chafee, Lincoln, 434

Champlin, Christopher, 106, 149, 252

Champlin, Christopher Grant, 252

Champlin, George, 252

Champlin, Margaret, 230

Champlin, Mary, 230

Champlin, Peggy, 232, 236

Champlin, Richard L., 141, 149

Chancellor Livingston (steamboat), 269

Channing, Ann, 279

Channing, John, 133

Channing, William Ellery, 279, 284, 285–288, 285s, 296; portrait of, 286

Channing Memorial Church, Newport, Baker memorial window, 332

Chapin, Howard M., 21, 30

Charles, Oatsie, 449s

Charles, Ray, picture of, 456

Charles I, King of England, 3, 5, 9, 26, 32, 38

Charles II, King of England, 4, 45–46, 49–51, 52, 59, 62s, 66–67, 76, 82, 83, 377, 461; portrait (Lely), 51

Charleston, South Carolina, 101, 126, 195, 219s, 224, 267, 295, 300, 302, 321. *See also* southern planters and tourists

Charter of 1663. *See* Royal Charter of 1663

Chastellux, Chevalier de, 73, 227, 230

Château-d'Agnès, 373

Château-sur-Mer, 315, 338, 354, 361, 365, 374, 442; picture of, 314

Chaucey, Isaac, 262–263

Chepstow, 443

USS *Chesapeake*, 256, 257

Chicago, Illinois, 392

Child, Lydia Maria, 287

China trade, 252–253

Chorley, Kenneth, 440s

Church, Benjamin, 70

Church, Frederick E., 328

Churchill, Winston, 436

Church of England, 113, 120–121, 144

Civic League, 418

civil order, 27s

Civil War, 320–324

Claggett, Thomas, 143

Claggett, William, 141–143

Claggett, William, Jr., 141, 143

Clambake Club of Newport, 393, 433

Clap, Nathaniel, 122–123, 130, 288

Clarendon Code, 52, 62, 76

Clarendon Court, 373–374

Clark, Elizabeth (Harges), 46, 57

Clarke, Jeremy, 5, 7, 26, 35–36, 37, 77, 84

Clarke, John, 4–5, 7–8, 14, 17, 19, 27, 29, 30–31, 33–34, 35, 36, 37, 41, 45–46, 48–55, 51s, 57–59, 59, 60, 68, 75s, 83, 84, 99, 120, 121, 175, 288; portrait of, 44, 47

Clarke, Jonathan, 145

Clarke, Mary, 84

Clarke, Walter, 67, 70, 77, 82, 85

Clay, Henry, 257, 258, 319

Clean Air Act, 434

Clerk, Miss, 132

Clermont (steamboat), 269

Cliff House, 302

Cliff Walk, 376–380

Clinton, George, 248

Clinton, Henry, 196–197, 202, 204, 210, 215, 216, 218–219, 221, 222, 224–225, 231, 233–234, 234s

Closen, Louis, baron de, 230

Coates, Charlotte, 167

Coddington, Nathaniel, 85, 91

Coddington, William, 3–8, 13, 14–15, 17–22, 25, 26–28, 30–31, 34–43, 46, 48, 59, 65, 67, 68s, 70, 71, 75s, 84, 98–99, 121, 155, 338

Coddington, William, Jr., 39, 67, 78

Codman, Martha, 442s

Codman, Ogden, 369, 398–399, 442s

Coercive Acts, 189

Coggeshall, John, 5, 7, 8, 13, 17, 21, 25, 31, 35, 36, 59

Coggeshall, Martha, 135

Cole, Thomas, 328

Coleman, Peter J., 252, 254–255

Coleridge, Samuel Taylor, 279

Collins, Arnold, 130, 145

Collins, Henry, 111, 115, 116s, 130–131, 133, 145, 159, 176, 185; portrait of, 131

Collins, John, 240, 243, 249

colonies, governance frameworks of, 173s

Colony House, 71, 138, 156–157, 167, 184s, 192, 249, 274, 434, 448; picture of, 157

Columbia (ship), 452; picture of, 453

Columbia University, 370

Commonwealth, English, 38

Company of the Redwood Library, 109, 115, 151, 159

Comstock Lode, 373

Concord, Massachusetts, 190

Coney Island, New York, 297

Congregationalism, 120, 122, 285

Congregation Jeshuat Israel. *See* Touro Synagogue

Congress of the United States, 235, 242–243, 254, 257, 271, 272, 272s, 291, 422

Conley, Patrick T., 53, 107, 292, 320

Connecticut, colony of, 26, 30, 31, 32, 34, 35, 50, 52, 54–55, 59, 67, 68, 96–97

Connecticut (steamboat), 269

Connor, Dennis, 454

Constellation (ship), 453

USS *Constitution*, 258

Constitutional Convention, Philadelphia, 235, 240–241

Constitution of the United States of America, 53, 240–245, 241s, 248–249

Continental Army, 196, 210, 221

Continental army and navy, preparations for, 180

Continental Congress, 180, 189–190, 191, 201, 206, 207, 209–210, 220, 221, 230, 238–239

Continental Navy, 221

Cook, James, 177s

Cooke, Nicholas, 190, 192, 196, 198, 201

Coolidge, Calvin, 426

Coote, Richard, 85–88

Corliss, George, 288

Cornè, Michele Felice, 276, 280–281; self-portrait, 281

Cornell, Alexander, 424

Cornell, Sarah, 287s

Cornwallis, Charles, 196, 231, 233

Corsair (ship), 395

Corte-Real, Miguel, 75

Cosentino, Andrew, 284

Cotton, John, 13–15, 18, 45

Coughtry, Jay, 105

Council of State, 38

Council on Foreign Plantations, 55

Country Party, 239–243, 248, 250

Courageous (ship), 453

Couture, Thomas, 328, 329

Cozzens, Eleanor, 136s

Crandall, John, 46, 48

Cranston, Henry, 319

Cranston, John, 67, 70, 75s, 78, 84

Cranston, Mary (Hart), 84

Cranston, Rhode Island, 392

Cranston, Robert, 319

Cranston, Samuel, 78, 81–82, 84–88, 89s, 94, 95, 96–97, 99, 105, 108, 117, 121, 123, 250

Criminal Court, 71

Cromwell, Oliver, 3, 13, 32, 38, 42, 49, 51

Cromwell, Richard, 49

Crossways, 408, 409

Cumberland, Rhode Island, 175

currency, 19s, 64, 98–101, 126, 143, 177, 179, 220, 240–241, 267

Curtis, George William, 301, 307, 321

Cushing, Howard Gardiner, 402–404, 449s

Cushing, Matthew, 402

Cushing, Robert M., 393, 402

Cushman, Charlotte, 334

The Custom of the Country (Wharton), 396

HMS *Cygnet*, 185

D

Dame Pattie (ship), 453

Dart (ship), 259

Darwin, Charles, 336–337, 344

David, Jacques-Louis, 279

Davies, Wallace, 409

Davis, Jefferson, 321

Davis, Miles, 455

Davis, W. F., 388

Dead Man Revived (Allston), 279

Deane, Richard, 50

Declaration of Breda, 51–52

Declaration of Independence, 83, 180–181, 191

Declaration of Rights and Grievances, 184

The Decoration of Houses (Codman and Wharton), 399

Defiance (ship), 173

Delano, William A., 403

Dennis, John, 173

Designs of Inigo Jones (Kent), 159, 162

HMS *Detroit*, 264–265

Dighton, Massachusetts, 192, 193

Dix, Dorothea, 287

Dix, John Ross, 317, 318

Dohla, Johann, 222–223

Dominion of New England, 77–78

Dorr, Thomas Wilson, 289–292; portrait of, 290

Douglas, Stephen, 305, 320

Downing, Antoinette, 5, 6, 73, 157, 162, 236, 275, 441, 447

Downing, George T., 303

Drexel, John, 376

Drexel, Mrs. J. R., 392

Duc de Bourgogne (ship), 230

Dudingston, William, 188

Dudley, Joseph, 88–89, 94, 95, 117

Duke, Doris, 444, 446–448; 374; portrait of, 445

Duke, James B., 446

Duke of Cumberland (ship), 173

Duke of Marlborough, 86s

Dummer, William, 95

Dunham, Charles, 135

Dutch West Indian Company, 63

Dwight, Timothy, 266–267

Dwyer, Francis, 459

Dyer, Mary, 10, 46, 60–62, 92, 111

Dyer, William, 5, 7, 35, 37, 41, 60–62

Dyer, William, [Jr.], 62

Dylan, Bob, 456

E

Earl of Clarendon, 55, 57, 77

Eastman Kodak, 345

Easton, John, 22, 78, 91

Easton, Nicholas, 5–7, 8, 20, 21, 25, 27, 28, 31, 37, 59, 67

Easton, Peter, 22, 24, 78; autograph annotations, 16

Easton's Beach, 6

Edel, Leon, 398, 400

Edison, Thomas, 345, 382–383

Eisenhower, Dwight D., 432, 449s

electrical experiments, 141–143

Elements of Lettering (Benson), 448s

Elijah in the Desert (Allston), 279

Eliot, T. S., 327, 425

Ellery, Benjamin, 103

Ellery, William, 100, 111, 133, 180–181, 185, 223, 242, 243, 286

Ellery, William, Sr., 106

Ellery, William (signer), 106

Ellington, Duke, 455

Elliot, Jesse, 263–265

Elliott, John, 402

Elliott, Maud Howe, 328, 352, 384, 387, 402, 435; portrait of, 402

The Elms, 373–374; picture of, 372

Emancipation Act, 253

Embargo of 1807, 257, 260, 266

Emerson, Ralph Waldo, 285, 325, 327

Endicott, John, 48

English Civil War, 3, 8, 32, 38

English Interregnum, 38

English law, 21, 26, 27, 28, 33, 38, 53

Engs, George, 312

Enlightenment, 130

Erie Canal, 296

Estaing, Jean-Baptiste, comte d', 210, 212–216, 218, 219, 222, 224, 234s

Ethan Frome (Wharton), 399

Every, Henry, 92

F

Fair, James G., 373

Fairholme, 374; picture of, 376

Fall River, Massachusetts, 307s

Fall River Line, 271, 307s, 339, 355, 428

Fancy (ship), 92

Farmer, Moses G., 382–383

Father Mathew Temperance Society, 419

Faulkner, William, 327

Federalist Papers, 242

Federal Street Church, Boston, 286

Feke, Charles, 271s

Feke, Eleanor (Cozzens), 136s

Feke, Philadelphia, 140

Feke, Robert, 130, 136s, 276; portrait by, 131

Fenner, Arthur, 243, 248

Fenner, Arthur, Jr., 250

Fenner, James, 250, 258, 292

Ferdinand, King of Spain, 63

Ferncliff, 357

Festival Field, 455

Field, Edward, 29, 39, 208, 215, 239, 240

Fielding, Henry, 109s

Fifth Monarchists, 50

Fillmore, Millard, 302, 313s

Fillmore House, 308, 309

Firefly (steamboat), 269

First Baptist Church, Newport, 430

First Bridge, 269s

First South Carolina Volunteers, 335

Fish, Hamilton, 361, 408

Fish, Isaac, 270

Fish, Marian ("Mamie") (Anthon), 371, 373, 405, 408–409, 410, 412, 413

Fish, Mrs. Stuyvesant, 392

Fish, Stuyvesant, 408

Fisher, Mary, 59

Fisher, Sidney George, 310

Fitzgerald, Ella, 455

Fitzgerald, F. Scott, 132s, 247, 348

Flagg, Ebenezer, 131, 136s

Flagg, Henry Collins, 278

Flagg, Rachel Moore Allston, portrait of, 278

Fleming, Ian, 449s

Fletcher, Benjamin, 91

Florida, 87

Fort Adams, 197, 222, 256–257, 259, 271–273, 418, 434, 436, 455; picture of, 273, 455

Fort Anne, 382

Fort Duquesne, 175, 176

Fort George, 262, 382

Fort Getty, 436, 437

Fort Kearney, 437

Fort Liberty, 197, 382

Fort Louisburg, 173–174, 176

Fort McHenry, 259

Fortune (ship), 95

Fort Washington, 382

Fort Wetherall, 436

Foster, Kristen, 280

Foster, Stephen, 10, 33s

Foster, Theodore, 248

Four Hundred, 355, 357, 404, 408, 409, 427

Fox, George, 59, 60s, 68s

France, 67, 87

Francis Ferdinand, Archduke of Austria, 412

François I, King of France, 22

Franklin, Anne, 117, 119

Franklin, Benjamin, 117–119, 177s, 178, 183, 190s, 209, 224, 234s, 236, 325

Franklin, James, 117–119, 141

Franklin, James, Jr., 119

Frederick H. Prince Trust, 442

Freebody, Samuel, 133

Freebody Park, 435, 455

Freedom (ship), 454

French and Indian War, 87, 131, 151, 175–176, 178, 184s

French Revolution, 253

Fuller, Hiram [pseud. Belle Brittan], 308–310

Fullerton, Morton, 399

Fulton, Robert, 269

Fulton (steamboat), 269

Funston, Judith, 399

Furness, Frank, 374, 376

furniture makers and styles, 86s, 129, 136–141, 143

G

Gage, Thomas, 189, 190

Galbraith, John Kenneth, 425

Gambier, James, 221

Gardner and Dean, 252

gas lighting, 267

HMS *Gaspee*, 185, 187–189, 219s, 254

Gates, Horatio, 204, 221

Gay, John, 109s

Gazetteer of Rhode Island (Dwight), 267

General Assembly of Rhode Island, 42, 63, 68, 70, 71, 82, 88, 95, 97, 98, 99, 101, 108, 119, 121, 136, 145, 149s, 156–157, 169, 173, 177–178, 180, 182, 189, 190, 191–192, 198, 206, 220, 238–240, 249, 253, 254, 256, 257, 258, 272s, 289, 290, 291, 293, 304, 318–319, 356s, 432

General Court of Elections of Rhode Island, 35, 36

General Court of the Massachusetts Bay Colony, 14–15, 17, 62

General Electric, 425

USS *General Greene*, 260

General Mills, 345

Geological Researches in China, Mongolia, and

Japan (Pumpelly), 337

George Fox Digg'd Out of His Burrowes (Williams), 68s

George I, King of England, 97s

George II, King of England, 97s, 109s, 171, 173, 176, 177s

George III, King of England, 177, 179, 181, 201, 210, 461

Georges II, King of England, 100–101

George Washington (ship), 253

Germania Society, 307, 308

Gibbons, Sarah, 360

Gibbs, Theodore, 388

Gibbs and Channing, 252

Gibson, Edmund, 116

Gifford, Jeremiah, 287s

The Gilded Age (Warner), 343

Gillespie, Dizzy, 455

Girls Patriotic League, 418

The Glen, 307

Goat Island, 172, 184, 197, 202

Goddard, James, 140

Goddard, John, 137–141

Goelet, Mrs. Ogden, 409

Goelet, Ogden, 361, 365, 395

Goelet, Robert, 365, 371, 395, 448

Goelet Cup, 395

golf, 387–390, 392

Gorton, Samuel, 19, 21–22, 26, 28, 30, 34–35, 36s, 37, 41s, 42, 75s, 90–91

government. *See* New England colonies, governance in; Rhode Island; *specific legislative bodies*

Grand Central Station, New York, 389

Grant, Sueton, 133

Grant, Ulysses S., 323, 337s, 408

Grasse, Admiral comte de, 231, 233, 234, 234s

Graves, Thomas, 233–234

gravestone carving, 447s–448s

Gray Cliff, 401–402

Great Awakening, 121

Great Depression, 425–428

Great Gale of 1815, 266, 429

Great Migration, 9

Great Swamp Fight, 70

Green, Theodore Francis, 432–433

Green Animals, 442

Greene, Fleet, 205–206, 208, 212, 216, 217, 220, 222

Greene, John, 90

Greene, Nathanael, 202, 206–207, 213, 215, 216, 231, 278; picture of, 203
Greene, Patience, 276
Greene, Samuel, 205
Greene, William, 174, 177, 220
Gregory, Eliot, 378
Grenville, George, 181–182
Gretel (ship), 452
Gretel II (ship), 453
HMS *Greyhound*, 95
Grimcrack (ship), 393
Griswold, John, 338
Griswold House, 361, 365, 402
Grosvenor, Richard, 371
Gunsway (ship), 92
Guthrie, Woody, 456

H

Hale, Stuart, 269
Halliburton, John, 184s
Hamilton, Alexander, 131–133, 132s, 136s, 235, 242
Hammersmith, 40, 73, 75s, 275, 449s
Hannah (ship), 188
Harbour Court, 393
Harges, Elizabeth, 46, 57
Harper's Monthly, 404
Harriman, E. H., 345
Harris, Charles, 95
Harrison, Elizabeth (Pelham), 159
Harrison, Joseph, 158
Harrison, Peter, 24, 136, 147s, 156s, 158–163, 185, 335s; picture of, 158
Harrison, William Henry, 263, 265
Hart, Mary, 84
Harte, Bret, 335
Harvard Club, New York, 370
Harvard College, 115, 116, 149, 180, 276, 278, 286, 290, 325, 335, 336, 402
Harvard Divinity School, 335
Harvard Law School, 434
Harvard Medical School, 275s–276s
Harvard Museum of Comparative Zoology, 336
Hastings, A. J., 374, 376
Hattendorf, Berit, 282
Hattendorf, John B., 381
Havemeyer, Henry O., 387
Havemeyer, Theodore, 389–390
Hawes, A. B., 89
Hazard, Benjamin, 319
Hazard, Thomas, 5, 8, 334
Hazard House, 73

Hearst, William Randolph, 348
Heathcote, Caleb, 109
Heckscher, Morrison, 139
Hemingway, Ernest, 132s
Herald (Paris), 348–349
Hermione (ship), 225
Herrick, George G., 296, 392–393
Higginson, Thomas Wentworth, 334, 335–336
Hill, James J., 345
Hill, Thomas, 184
Hiscox, Thomas, 136s
Historical Discourse (Callender), 123
Historic Hill, 275
History of the United States (Bancroft), 371
Hitler, Adolf, 416, 434, 436, 438
Hodgson, Adam, 255
Hogarth, William, 109s
Holiday, Billie, 455
Holland, 8, 67, 77
Holmes, Obadiah, 46, 48
Holmes, Oliver Wendell, 334
Homberger, Eric, 354, 408
Home Hospitality, 418
Homer, Winslow, 402
Honyman, Abigail, 169
Honyman, James, 115, 116, 121, 155; portrait of, 122
Honyman, James, Jr., 115
Hood, Ted, 453
Hoover, Herbert, 426
Hopedence, 442
Hopkins, Esek, 190, 219s, 221
Hopkins, Samuel, 107, 254
Hopkins, Stephen, 115, 138, 153, 176, 177–181, 182, 184, 190, 201, 219s
Hoppus, Edward, 136, 159
Hotel Viking, 426, 428
Houdini, Harry (Ehrich Weiss), 412
The House of Mirth (Wharton), 396, 399, 400
House of Rothschild, 353–354
Howard, Martin, Jr., 176, 185
Howe, David, 287
Howe, John, 204
Howe, Julia Ward, 313, 333–335, 352, 360
Howe, Richard, 195, 196, 204, 208–209
Howe, Samuel Gridley, 333
Howe, William, 195–196, 198, 202, 204, 205, 210, 212, 213–215; portrait of, 197
Howell, David, 238–239
Howells, William Dean, 397
Howland, Catharine, 364
Huddleston, John, 51

Hughes, Robert, 139
Hull, Captain, 172
Hull, William, 258, 262
Hume, David, 53
Hundred Guinea Cup. *See* America's Cup
Hunt, Catharine (Howland), 364
Hunt, Richard, Jr., 413
Hunt, Richard Morris, 328, 338, 340, 349, 356, 361, 362–363, 365, 367, 369, 373, 413; 374; portrait of, 364
Hunt, William Morris, 324, 326, 328–329, 330, 363, 364, 402
Hunter, Deborah (Malbone), 271s
Hunter, Eliza, 271s
Hunter, Nancy, 236
Hunter, Thomas, 305, 319
Hunter, William, Dr., 164, 184s, 271s
Hunter, William, Esq., 168–169, 184s, 271s–272s, 305, 462
Hunter House, 164, 168–170, 227, 275, 441, 442; picture of, 169
Hurlingham Club, 387
Hurricane Carol, 448
Hurricane Edna, 448
Hurricane of 1938, 428–431
Hurricane of 1944, 438
Hurst, Harold, 317, 321
Hutchinson, Anne, 12–17, 19–22, 26, 28, 30, 32, 36s, 48, 54, 60, 65, 145; picture of, 36
Hutchinson, William, 12, 21–22, 36s
Hyde, Anne, 86s

I

Ida Lewis Yacht Club, 395
Ill Newes from New-England (Clarke), 29s, 45, 46, 48–49, 52
immigrant labor, 272–273, 289, 305, 422–423
Independence (ship), 453
Indians, 34; helping colonists survive, 9, 25; land transactions, 6, 11, 18–19, 41s, 50, 68; legislation against, 25; painted by Charles Bird King, 284–285; relationships with colonists, 11, 18, 25, 36s; slaves, 128; wars and skirmishes, 11, 25, 36s, 67, 69–71, 75s, 197–198, 258 (*see also* French and Indian War)
Industrial Revolution, 103, 177s, 250–252, 381s
The Influence of Sea Power (Mahan), 382
International Havester, 345
International Polo Challenge Cup, 387
International Tennis Hall of Fame, 386
Intolerable Acts, 180

Intrepid (ship), 453
Invitation Tournament, 385–386
Irving, Washington, 279
Irwin, Ray, 57s
Isaac Bell House, 361, 370, 443
Isabella, Queen of Spain, 63
Isabella Stewart Gardner Museum, Boston, 403
Isham, Norman M., 441, 443–444
Is Polite Society Polite? (Howe), 334
The Itinerarium of Dr. Alexander Hamilton, 131–133
Ives, Robert H., 317
Izard, John, 299–300
Izard, Ralph, 313

J

Jackson, Andrew, 259, 272s
Jacobites, 97s, 109s
James, Arthur Curtiss, 437s–438s
James, Henry, 324, 325–327, 329, 334, 348, 353, 376, 379, 396, 398, 399, 400, 407, 412
James, Henry, Sr., 325–327, 334, 335; picture of, 325
James, Mrs. Arthur Curtiss, 418
James, Sydney V., 46, 48, 52–54, 68, 84, 97, 119, 122, 179
James, William, 324, 325, 329; portrait of, 330
James II, King of England, 76–77, 82, 86s
Jamestown, Rhode Island, 224, 401
Jamestown, Virginia, 8–9
Jamestown Bridge, 457, 459
Japan, 313s–314s, 331, 333
Jay, John, 167, 177s, 234s, 242, 256
Jefferson, Thomas, 46, 53, 83, 158, 167, 180, 235, 237, 248, 255s, 256–257, 432
Jenckes, Joseph, 100–101, 105, 108
Jenkens, Robert, 171–172
Jenner, Edward, 276s
Jews and Jewish community, 59, 63, 126, 151, 153, 156s, 161–162, 202, 235, 237, 249, 353
Jireh Bull/Mawdsley House, 73; photograph, 72
USS *John Adams*, 265
Johnson, Samuel, 109s, 115
John Stevens Shop, 447s–448s
Johnston, Augustus, 185, 299–300
Jonathan Nichols House. *See* White Horse Tavern
Jones, Edith Newbold. *See* Wharton, Edith
Jones, George, 385, 396
Jones, George Noble, 338
Jones, Inigo, 136, 154

Jones, John Paul, 219s
Jones, Lucretia, 396–397, 399
Jones, William, 258, 259
Joseph P. Kennedy Jr. (ship), 453
Joyce, James, 327
Justice School, 439

K

Kahn, Gilbert S., 374
Kahn, John J. Noffo, 374, 376
Kalbfus, Edward C., 437
Kalfatovic, Martin, 116s
Kane, Delancy Astor, 384
Kant, Immanuel, 53
Karolik, Martha (Codman), 442s
Karolik, Maxim, 441, 442s
Katy (ship), 190, 219s
Kay, Nathaniel, 109–110
Keith, Dr., 132
Kennedy, Jacqueline (Bouvier), 275, 443, 449s–450s; photograph of, 449
Kennedy, John F., 275, 434, 449s–450s, 452–453; photograph of, 449
Kensett, John F., 301
Kent, William, 159
A Key into the Language of America (Williams), 31–32, 48
King, Benjamin, 147s
King, Charles Bird, 276, 283–285; self-portrait, 283
King, Clarence, 337
King, David, 322, 338
King, Deborah Bird, 283
King, Edward, 317
King, Ernest J., 437
King, George, 319
King, Samuel, 276, 278, 283
King, Samuel Ward, 291
King, Theodore Wheaton, 322
King, William, 338
King, Zebulon, 283
King George's Wars, 131, 171–174
King Philip. *See* Metacomet (Wampanoag sachem)
King Philip's War (1675), 11, 67, 69–71, 75s, 197–198
Kings Arm Tavern, 446
Kingscote, 338, 442
King William's War, 87, 91, 94
Kneller, Godfrey, 116s

Know-Nothing Party, 319–320
Krupa, Gene, 455

L

lacrosse, 390
Ladies Auxiliary of the YMCA, 418
La Farge, John, 324, 325–326, 329–331, 333, 369
La Farge, Margaret Mason (Perry), 329–330
Lafayette, Marquis de, 209s, 213–216, 218, 224, 228, 231; portrait of, 214
Lake Erie, Battle of, 260, 262–265
Landholder's Constitution, 291, 292
Landon, Alfred M., 433
Land's End, 398–399
Langford, Mehitable, 133
Langley, Batty, 159
László Széchényi, Countess, 442
Laud, William, 9, 121
Law and Order Party, 292
Lawless, James, 424
USS *Lawrence*, 263–265
Lawrence, Peter, 92s
Lawrence, William Beach, 312, 362–363
Lawrence, William G., 389
Lawton, Polly, 230
Leathley (ship), 147s
Lechford, Thomas, 30
The Ledges, 402–403
Lee, Charles, 206
Lee, Robert E., 323
Lefuel, Hector, 363
Lehr, Harry, 408–409
Lenox, Massachusetts, 399
Lenox Library, New York, 364
Lenthal, Robert, 34s
HMS *Leopold*, 257
The Letter Book of Peleg Sanford, 64
Levi (Jewish immigrant), 63
Lewis, Ida, 337s
Lexington, Massachusetts, 190
Ley's Department Store, 450
HMS *Liberty*, 185, 187
Liberty (ship), 454
libraries, colonial, 114–115, 121, 135–136, 159–161
Lincoln, Abraham, 320–321, 322
Lincoln, Benjamin, 234
Lincoln Memorial, Washington, D. C., 370
Lindsey, Benjamin, 199
Lipton, Thomas, 451–452
Literary and Philosophical Society, 130, 132, 133, 135, 156s, 159, 178

Little, Nina, 280–281

Little, William, 382

Little Compton, Rhode Island, 175, 223

Livingston, Robert, 255s

Livingstone, David, 348–349

Locke, John, 53, 113

Lockyer, John, 121

London, England, 3, 32, 33, 38, 49

Longfellow, Henry Wadsworth, 75, 287, 310, 334

Lopez, Aaron, 106, 138, 147, 149, 151–154, 161, 165

Lopez, Moses, 151

Lords of Trade, 88, 110

Lorillard, Elaine, 455

Lorillard, Louis, 455

Lorillard, Pierre, 362–363

Lotus-Eating (Curtis), 301

Louisiana Purchase, 255s, 258

Louis XIV, King of France, 86s

Louis XVI, King of France, 209, 231

Low, Edward, 95

Lowell, James Russell, 287

Lowell, Robert, 380

Lowenthal, Larry, 377

Luce, Henry, 378s

Lusitania (ship), 416

Luther, Seth, 292

Lynn, Massachusetts, 48

Lysistrata (ship), 395

M

Macdonald, Charles Blair, 389

Mackenzie, Frederick, 197, 198, 202s, 205, 206, 208, 212, 219

Madison, Dolly, 167

Madison, James, 167, 235, 237s, 242, 257, 258, 259, 265, 276s

Mahan, Alfred Thayer, 381–382

HMS *Maidstone* (ship), 184

Malbone, an Oldport Romance (Higginson), 335

Malbone, Deborah, 184s

Malbone, Edward Greene, 276–278, 283, 286; self-portrait, 277

Malbone, Francis, 165

Malbone, Godfrey, 103, 106, 111, 132, 132s, 133, 135, 149, 155, 156, 172, 173, 178, 184s

Malbone, John, 133, 276

Malbone, Patience (Greene), 276

Malbone, Saunders, 165

Malkovich, Mark P. III, 457

Malthus, Thomas, 177s

Mann, Horace, 287

Mann, William, 404–405

Marble House, 347, 365, 367, 378s, 409, 410, 413, 427, 442, 454; picture of, 366

Marble House Tea House, 442

Marchant, Henry, 133

Mary Dyer on Her Way to Execution (Pyle), 61

Maryland, 33

Mason, Elizabeth Champlin, 260

Mason, George, 242

Mason, George Champlin, 280, 318, 335s, 339–341, 353, 361; portrait of, 339

Massachusetts Bay Colony, 3–4, 6–15, 17–20, 25–27, 29–35, 30, 31, 32, 34, 35, 37–38, 41, 43, 45, 46, 48, 50, 52, 59, 60–62, 67, 68, 82, 174–175, 402

Massachusetts Institute of Technology, 335

Mather, Cotton, 117

Mather, Increase, 117

Matthiessen, F. O., 329

Mawdsley, Captain, 73

Mawdsley House, 227, 230

Maxwell, Elsa, 409

May, Edith, 349

May, Fred, 349

Mayes, William, Jr., 90–92

Mayes, William, Sr., 71, 91

Mayflower (yacht), 395

McAllister, Sarah (Gibbons), 360

McAllister, Ward, 315, 355, 356, 357, 360, 405

McBean, Alletta, 442

McBean, Peter, 443

McGregor, Alexander, 275

McKim, Charles, 349–350, 361, 362, 365, 369–371; photograph of, 370

McKim, Mead & White, 361, 369, 371, 373, 381s

McLoughlin, William, 14, 291, 292

Mead, William, 369; photograph of, 370

Medus, Simon, 63

Melvill, David, 267

Melville, Robert, 180s

Mendon, Massachusetts, 136

Metacomet (Wampanoag sachem), 69–71; picture, 69

Methodists, 274, 287s

Metropolitan Museum of Art, New York, 139, 167, 170, 364, 441

Miantonomi (Narragansett sachem), 11, 18

Miantonomy Hill, 40

middle class, rise of, 295–296

Middleton, Henry, 299–300

Middletown, 99, 197, 217, 360, 392

Miller, Paul, 442

Millet, Jean-François, 328

Mills, C. Wright, 344

Milton, John, 32

Miranda, Francisco, 236

Missouri (ship), 438

Modern Society (Howe), 334

Moffatt, Thomas, 132, 164, 185

Molasses Act, 110, 182

money, paper. *See* currency

Monk, Thelonious, 455

Monroe, James, 168, 255s, 265, 284, 432

Montague, Admiral, 188

Montcalm, Louis Joseph de, 176

Montreal, 176

Moore, C. J., 137

Moore, Clement C., 334

Morgan, E. D., 388

Morgan, Edward III, 371

Morgan, J. P., 395, 412

Morgan Library, New York, 370

Morison, Samuel Eliot, 345, 425, 426

Morse, Samuel F. B., 279

Mosbacher, Emil ("Bus"), 452–453

motoring, 391–392

The Mount, 399

Mount Hope Bridge, 269s, 426, 459

Mrozek, Donald J., 385s

Mumford, Stephen, 75

Munday, Richard, 121, 130, 154–158

Murphy-Schlichting, Mary, 334, 397

Museum of Fine Arts, Boston, 279, 442s

Museum of Modern Art, New York, 443

Myles, Samuel, 120

N

Nahant, Massachusetts, 296

Nahma (ship), 395

Namouna (ship), 395

Nantucket, Massachusetts, 153, 254

Narragansett Bay, 3–4, 35, 38, 54, 68, 76. *See also* pirates and privateers

Narragansett Bay, described by Verrazzano, 22, 24

Narragansett Bay, map of, 199

Narragansett Indians, 6, 11–12, 18–19, 25–26, 32, 41s, 50, 68, 70, 197

Narragansett Pacers, 147

National Museum of American Illustration, 374

National Women's Party, 411

HMS *Nautilus*, 256

USS *Nautilus*, 260

Naval Academy, 321s, 367, 371, 380–381

The Naval Monument, 280

Naval Torpedo Station, 381–383, 418–420, 422, 428, 434, 436, 437, 438, 439

Naval Training Station, 381, 416, 418, 431, 437, 439

Naval War College, 340, 381, 417, 423s, 437, 439

Navigation Acts, 67, 85, 131, 182

Negro Emancipation Act, 180

Nesbit, Evelyn, 370

Netherlands, 43

New Amsterdam, 31, 36s, 42, 63

New Bedford, Massachusetts, 153, 254

Newbury, Walter, 64, 67, 68

New Deal, 426–427

New England, map of, 23

New England colonies, governance in, 9–10, 12–13, 81

New-England Courant, 117

A New-England Fire-Brand Quenched (Fox), 68s

New England Steamship Company. *See* Fall River Line

New Orleans, Battle of, 259

New Orleans, Louisiana, 255s

Newport: agriculture and husbandry, 8, 25, 26, 32, 41, 58–59, 68; British evacuation, 222–223; British occupation, 41, 197–198, 201, 202, 204–206, 208–209, 212, 219–224; building and architecture, 6, 24, 40, 58, 71–75, 96, 103, 136, 154–163, 273–275, 302–303, 311–317, 315, 338, 340, 347, 360–362, 365, 370–371, 373, 378–380, 415–416 (*see also specific site names*); 374; city directories, 317–318; climate, 25, 28, 114, 125, 419–420 (*see also* Great Gale of 1815; Hurricane of 1938); commerce and trade, 8, 28, 32, 40–41, 58, 64–66, 76, 94s, 96, 104–106, 123, 125, 150–151, 182, 184, 202, 223–224, 240, 252–253, 267 (*see also* pirates and privateers); Common Burying Ground, 106, 447; "cottages," 313, 347, 360–365, 367, 369–371, 373–374, 376–380, 377s, 413, 418, 430, 442–443 (*see also specific names*); crime, 395s; defense and fortifications, 172; ferry service, 269s, 271, 420, 460; founding of, 3–8, 22, 24; French occupation, 225, 227–228, 230; geography, 6; Gilded Age, 343–353, 411–413; government,

26, 27, 28, 311s, 314; harbor, 180s; Historic District, 442; historic preservation, 440–447; hotels and boarding houses, 300–305, 338; manufacturing, 288, 297, 437; map of, 127, 194, 200, 229; music festivals, 455–457; pictures and views of, 80, 102, 246, 251, 294, 297, 298, 312, 315, 316, 346, 379, 383, 394, 401, 406, 414, 420, 427, 430, 457, 458; population, 68, 96, 126, 128, 202, 267, 301, 318, 347, 436, 440; real estate business, 311–317, 323–324, 339; recognition by Crown, 26; religious tolerance in, 29–31, 59–62, 59–63, 76, 120, 121s, 126, 228, 230, 235, 249, 285, 288; reunions, 318s; road construction, 313–314, 316; ropewalk, 148–149; society, 99, 111s, 128–130, 153s, 168s, 305–310, 317, 324, 347, 349–350, 352–358, 360–361, 377s, 405, 407–411, 415; summer sojourners, 125–126, 151, 255, 269, 295, 296–303, 305–310, 337–338, 350, 354–355, 422; tercentenary celebrations, 434–437; topography, 6–7; tourism, 440–443, 447–448, 459–460; town records, 63, 223; urban renewal, 448–450

Newport: An Artist's Impression (Grosvenor), 371

Newport, East Shropshire, England, 6

Newport, Isle of Wight, England, 6

Newport Artillery Company, 322; picture of, 323

Newport Art Museum, 402, 403

Newport Casino, 348–352, 362, 369, 371, 379, 384–386, 390, 404–405, 407, 411, 422, 455; picture of, 351

Newport Compact, 22

Newport Constabulary, 418

Newport Country Club, 387–388, 393, 431, 449s; picture of clubhouse, 389

Newport Court of Trials, 43

Newport Daily News, 307–308

Newport Folk Festival, 273, 456–457

Newport Gazette, 204–205

Newport Golf Club, 389, 393

Newport Historical Society, 339, 444

Newport Horse Show, 390

Newport Hospital, 339, 356s

Newport Illustrated (Dix and Mason), 318

Newport-Jamestown Bridge Commission, 459

Newport Jazz Festival, 273, 455–456

Newport Junto, 185

Newport Mercury, 119, 299–300, 307–308, 339

Newport Music Festival, 457

Newport Racing Association, 390

Newport Reading Room, 317, 348, 386

Newport Redevelopment Agency, 448–449

Newport Restoration Foundation, 440, 444–448; 374

Newport Roller Skating Rink, 390

Newport (Senator Claiborne Pell) Bridge, 450, 459–460; picture of, 457

Newport Town Council, 71, 184, 314

Newton, Dudley, 361

Newton, Isaac, 113

Newtowne, Massachusetts, 14

New Travels in the United States (de Warville), 237

New York, New York, 101, 104, 126, 144, 195, 196, 222, 242, 267, 269–271, 296, 307s, 312, 330, 353, 354–355, 356, 357, 358, 360, 361, 364, 369

New York Herald, 348–349, 404

New York Mirror, 308

New York Times, 305, 404

New York Tribune Building, 364

New York Yacht Club, 348, 385, 393, 395, 438s, 450–454; picture of Newport Club-House, 394

USS *Niagara*, 263–265

Nicholas-Wanton-Hunter House, 164, 168–170, 227, 275, 441, 442; picture of, 169

Nichols, Jonathan, Jr., 168

Niessen, Greta, 438

Niles, Hezekiah, 83

Nina (ship), 424

Nixon, Richard, 440

North, Lord, 189, 196, 234s

Nottinghamshire, England, 8

Nourmahal (ship), 395, 452

La nuova Francia (Gastaldi), 23

O

Oakland Farm, 286, 416

Ocean Hall, 308

Ocean House, 302–305, 308, 310, 312, 314, 349; picture of, 304, 312

Ochre Court, 365, 378s, 448; picture of, 366

Ochre Point, 365, 371, 448

O'Doherty, Brian, 442s

Oelrichs, Blanche, 411

Oelrichs, Hermann, 361, 388

Oelrichs, Hermann, Mrs., 392

Oelrichs, Theresa ("Tessie") Alice Fair, 371, 371s, 373, 405, 408

O'Hara, Charles, 234

Old Colony House, 154

Old North Church, Boston, 141, 156

Oldport Association, 444, 447

Old Slater Mill, 251
Old Stone Mill, 73–75; picture of, 74
Olmsted, Frederick Law, 371
Operation Clapboard, 444–445, 447
origin of name, 6
Otis, Jonathan, 145
Ousamequin (Wampanoag sachem), 18
Outerbridge, Eugenius, 384
Outerbridge, Mary, 384, 386
Overing, Mr., 206
Oxford University, 46

P
Pachelbel, Charles, 116
Packeckoe, Moses, 63
Packer, Frank, 452
Palladio (Hoppus), 159
Panic of 1893, 345
Pardee, Bettie Bearden, 376
Pardee, Edmund W., 448
Parker, Peter, 197
Parliament, English, 3–4, 33, 38, 49, 52, 60,
    66, 67, 77, 82, 89, 100, 101, 110, 178–185, 189,
    272; Long Parliament, 32; Parliamentary
    Commission, 32
Parrish, Daniel, 317
Partridge, Alexander, 37–38, 42
Partridge, Richard, 111
Pate, William, 66
Patent for the Colony of Rhode Island and
    Providence Plantations (1644), 21, 32–35, 37, 38,
    41–42, 49, 61
Patience Island, Rhode Island, 12, 31
Patriarch Balls, 355, 357
Patterson, Charles, 442
Patterson, Jerry E., 357
Peabody, George, 354
Peabody & Stearns, 361, 363; 374
Pearl (ship), 92
Pedro II, Emperor of Brazil, 272s
Pelham, Elizabeth, 159
Pelham, Hermione, 149
Pell, Claiborne, 433–434
Pell, Herbert C., 433
Pell Grants, 434
Pell-Newport Bridge, 269s
Pencraig Cottage, 398
Penn, William, 89
Pennsylvania Railroad Station, New York, 370
People's Constitution, 291
People's Party, 290–291

Pepys, Nadine, 444
Pequot Indians, 25
Pequot War (1637), 25
Percy, Hugh, 202
Perkins Institute for the Blind, 333
Perrotti, M. Thomas, 448
Perry, Caroline Slidell, 353–354, 356
Perry, Christopher, 260
Perry, Margaret Mason, 329–330
Perry, Marsden, 402, 432
Perry, Matthew Calbraith, 313s–314s, 333, 353, 380;
    portrait of, 313s
Perry, Oliver Hazard, 260, 262–266, 314s, 325,
    353; portrait of, 261
Perry, Sarah Alexander, 260
Perry, Thomas Sergeant, 325, 326, 329
Perry (steamboat), 322
Peterson, Edward, 63
Philadelphia, 101, 126, 139, 141, 144, 167, 180, 195,
    204
Phillips Exeter Academy, 290
Pigot, Robert, 206, 209, 216, 218, 219
Pilgrims, 8–9
pirates and privateers, 66, 76, 85, 86, 88, 89–96,
    126, 147, 172–173, 256, 258–259, 260, 265
Pitt, William, 109s, 176, 183, 184
Plymouth Colony, 3, 7, 9, 11, 19, 31, 37–38, 38
Pocasset settlement. *See* Portsmouth
Poe, Edgar Allan, 334
Point Association, 445
Point Judith, Rhode Island, 55
polo, 386–387
Poor Robin's Almanack, 118
Pope, Alexander, 86s, 111
Pope, John Russell, 361
Portrait of a Clergyman (de Ville), 44, 47
Portsmouth, 3–5, 8, 19–22, 26–28, 29, 32–33, 34,
    36, 39, 46, 65, 97, 135, 202, 217, 289
Portsmouth Adventure (bark), 91
Potter, John, family portrait including, 129
Prescott, Richard, 150, 202, 206–207, 219, 222
Preservation Society of Newport County, 71, 170,
    313, 347, 367, 374, 440–443, 440s, 448
President (steamboat), 269
Prince, Frederick, 427
Prince of Wales (ship), 173
printing and publishing, 117
privateers. *See* pirates and privateers
Private Newport (Pardee), 376
Privy Council, 54, 85, 87, 94, 175
Prohibition, 420, 421–424

Proust, Marcel, 327
Providence, 3, 12, 17, 29, 31, 32–33, 34, 35, 36, 37,
    38, 41, 42, 49, 55, 60, 69, 70–71, 73, 82, 97, 103,
    108, 136, 153, 177–181, 197, 202, 206, 237, 243,
    250, 254–255, 266, 267, 269, 288, 289, 318, 370,
    381s
Providence Gazette, 178
Prudence Island, Rhode Island, 12, 31
Pulitzer, Joseph, 348
Pumpelly, Raphael, 337
Puritans, 3–4, 6, 8–9, 10, 11–12, 27, 32, 33, 35, 36s,
    38, 45, 46, 48, 49, 50, 51, 52, 59, 60s, 62, 113, 117

Q
Quaker Meeting House, 73; photograph, 74
Quakers and Quakerism, 31, 32s, 46, 59–62, 64,
    68, 68s, 70, 73, 75s, 85, 87, 92–93, 107, 109,
    119–120, 133, 136, 139, 202, 227, 254, 260
Quebec, 176
Queen Anne's War, 87, 94, 97–98
HMS *Queen Charlotte*, 264–265
Queen of Hungary (ship), 173

R
Radcliffe College, 336
railroads, 270–271, 323, 345, 358, 437s–438s
Rand, Larry, 319, 320
Randolph, Richard, 317
Ranger (ship), 95, 452
Record Book, 21–22, 26, 28, 41
Red Cross, 438
Redwood, Abraham, 100, 103, 130, 133, 147, 159,
    164, 165; 135–136; portrait of, 134
Redwood, Abraham, Sr., 133
Redwood, Jonas, 135
Redwood, Martha (Coggeshall), 135
Redwood, Mehetable, 230
Redwood, Mehitable (Langford), 133
Redwood Library and Athenæum, 130, 131, 133,
    135–136, 141, 159–161, 164, 165, 167, 168, 184s,
    190s, 202, 237, 266, 267, 276, 282, 284, 285, 286,
    302, 317, 318, 326, 335s, 338, 339, 380, 400, 448;
    picture of, 159, 334
Redwood Library Company. *See* Company of the
    Redwood Library
Reed, Mrs. Verner Z., 457
Reid, William, 187
religion and religious strife, 3–4, 8–9, 11–12, 30–
    31, 45–46, 48, 51–53, 55, 57, 58, 59–62, 67, 76–77,
    113, 115, 119–122, 177, 285–288
Reminiscences of Newport (Cornè), 280

René, Marc, 272

Restoration, 49

USS *Revenge*, 260

Revere, Paul, 144, 190

Revolutionary War, military engagements of, 196, 204, 205–208, 210, 212–219, 224–225, 233–234

Rhinelander, Mrs. LeBrun, 435

Rhode Island: boundary disputes, 54–55, 96–97, 174–175; colonial sovereignty, 50, 54–55, 68, 77, 82; governance, 288–289, 318–320, 381s (*see also* Landholder's Constitution; Patent for the Colony of Rhode Island and Providence Plantations (1644); People's Constitution; Rhode Island State Constitution; Royal Charter of 1663); immigration, 272–273, 289, 305, 319, 356s, 422–423; independence from Crown, 191–192; manufacturing, 247–248; politics, 239–243, 248, 250, 319–320, 381s, 432–434; textile industry, 250–252, 288

Rhode Island College. *See* Brown University

Rhode-Island Gazette, 118–119

Rhode Island General Assembly. *See* General Assembly of Rhode Island

Rhode Island State Constitution, 292

Rhode Island Suffrage Association, 290

Rhode Island Superior Court, 256

Rhode Island Supreme Court, 291, 292, 377

Richards, William Trost, 400–402

Richardson, Henry Hobson, 369

Richardson, Samuel, 109s

Richman, Irving B., 39–40, 41

The Rights of Colonies Examined (Hopkins), 178

Riis, Jacob, 344

Ritty, James, 345

Rivera, Jacob Rodriguez, 151–153, 165

Robert, Earl of Warwick, 32

Robinson, David, 285

Robinson, John, 185

Robinson, Willard B., 271

Robinson, William, 62

Robson, Lloyd, 6, 35, 322

Rochambeau, Jean-Baptiste Donatien de Vimeur, comte de, 73, 225, 227–228, 230–234, 234s, 249; portrait of, 226

Rochambeau, vicomte de, 227

Rochefoucauld-Liancourt, duc de la, 237

Rockefeller, John D., Jr., 432

Rocky Farm, 73, 388

Rodman, Samuel, 321

Rodney, George, 195, 228

Rogers, Fairman, 374, 376

Rogers, Robert, 271s

Rogers, William, 335

Rome, George, 185

Roos, Pieter, 29, 75, 288, 444

Roosevelt, Franklin D., 426, 434, 436, 452

Roosevelt, Theodore, 379

ropemaking, 148–149

HMS *Rose*, 189–190

Rosecliff, 376, 438, 442; 371, 373; picture of, 372

Roth, Leland, 373

Rough Point, 446, 447; 374; picture of, 375

Royal Charlotte (ship), 191

Royal Charter of 1663, 4, 45–46, 49, 52–53, 55, 57, 71, 77, 81–83, 88, 89s, 183, 288–289, 377, 461; picture of, 57

Royall, Anne, 300

Royal Yacht Squadron, 451

Ruggles, Nathiel, 319

rum, 104–105

Russell, Charles, 317

S

sailing. *See* yachting

Salem, Massachuetts, 10, 12

Salve Regina University, 365, 441, 448, 457

Samuel Tilton House, 370

Sanford, Peleg, 64–66, 67, 70, 75–76, 78, 85

San Francisco, California, 373

Saratoga Springs, New York, 296, 297, 306, 307

Sargent, John Singer, 334, 402

Savage, Edward, 284

Savannah, Georgia, 195, 221, 222

Sceptre (ship), 452

Schlesinger, Arthur, 9

Schumacher, Alan, 312, 313, 340, 385, 388–389

Scotti, R. A., 429

Scrooby Pilgrims, 8

Scully, Vincent, Jr., 338, 340, 350, 361–362, 374, 441

Sea Captains Carousing in Surinam (Greenwood), 172

Sea-Girt House, 303

Searing, James, 122

Sears, Richard, 385

Second Congregational Church, Newport, 190s, 198, 430

Seixas, Moses, 249

Serle, Ambrose, 208–209

servants, 404s

Seventh Day Baptist Meeting House, 154

Severens, Martha, 276–277

Shamrock (ship), 452

Shaw, George Bernard, 412

Shays's Rebellion, 240

Shelley, Percy Bysshe, 279

Shelter Island, Long Island, 62

Sheraton-Islander, 428

Sheridan, Richard, 177s

Sherman, William Watts, 384

shipbuilding, 32, 40, 59, 78, 94s, 104, 125, 145–147

Shirley, William, 174

Shorto, Russell, 30s

silversmithing, 143–145

Simister, Florence, 202

Sims, William S., 423s

Singer Sewing Machine, 345

Sisters of Mercy, 448

Skemp, Sheila, 153

Slater, Samuel, 250–251, 288

slaves and slave trade, 96, 104–108, 118, 119, 123, 128, 147, 148, 150, 180, 219, 253–254, 305

Slocum, John J., Jr., 443

Smibert, John, 113, 116s, 130, 136s, 276; portrait by, 112

Smith, Adam, 177s

Smith, Alfred, 311–317, 324, 360, 377, 393; portrait of, 311

Smith, Alva, 357–358, 364, 365, 367, 371, 405, 407, 408–411, 412–413, 416, 422; portrait of, 410

Smith, George B., 322

Smithsonian Institution, 285

Snell, George, 335s

Snydacker, Daniel, 426, 428

Society As I Have Found It (McAllister), 403

Society for the Promotion of Knowledge and Virtue, 115

Society for the Propogation of the Gospel in Foreign Parts (SPG), 121

Society of Friends. *See* Quakers and Quakerism

Solgard, Peter, 95

Sopwith, Thomas, 452

Southern Cross (ship), 453

southern planters and tourists, 255, 269, 295, 297–302, 299s, 305, 320

South Kingstown, 70, 97

Southwick, Solomon, 299

Sovereign (ship), 453

Spain, 63, 67

Spanish influenza, 421

Sparkman and Stephens, 453

Spencer, Joseph, 206–208, 213

Spencer-Churchill, Charles, 411

sporting clubs, 392–393

sports and recreation, 347, 355, 383–393, 396

sports culture, 385s

Spouting Rock Beach Association, 393

Sprague, William, 320

Spring Rice, Cecil, 352–353, 354, 355, 432

HMS *Squirrel*, 184

St. John (schooner), 184

St. Joseph's Roman Catholic Church, Newport, 441

St. Mary's Church, Newport, 275, 449s

St. Paul's Methodist Episcopal Church, Newport, 274

Stafford, Jean, 380

stagecoaches, 270

Stamp Act, 169, 182–183, 184, 189, 300

Stamp Act Congress, 184

Stanley, Henry, 348–349

Stanton, Joseph, Jr., 248

State House. *See* Colony House

Statue of Liberty, 364

steamboats and steamships, 269–271, 307s

Steele, Henry, 345

Steele, Richard, 86s, 111

Steffens, Lincoln, 432

Stelle, Isaac, 136s

Stephenson, Marmaduke, 62

Sterne, Laurence, 177s

Sterngass, Jon, 303, 313, 411, 412

Steuben, Baron von, 209s

Stevens, John, 146s, 447s

Stevens, Paran, 384–385

Stiles, Ezra, 75, 122, 154, 184s, 190–193, 190s, 197–198, 201, 223, 227, 230, 266, 288; map of Newport, 127

Stillman, James, 388

Stinson, Brian, 337s

Stone Villa, 349

Stonington, Connecticut, 270

Stonor, Nadine, 435

Stonor, Noreen, 435

Strange, Michael, 411

Strum, Harvey, 259

Stuart, Charlotte (Coates), 167

Stuart, Elizabeth (Anthony), 163

Stuart, Gilbert, 163–168, 170, 276, 281; *Portrait of a Gentleman Skating*, 167; portrait of Benjamin Waterhouse, 275; portrait of Christian Banister and son, 165; portrait of George Washington, 166; portrait of John Banister, 165; self-portrait, 164

Stuart, Gilbert, [Sr.], 163

Stuart, Jane, 168, 276, 281–282

Stubbs, George, 177s

Students of the Academy, Leiden, 46

Stuyvesant, Peter, 30s

Sudden Sea (Scotti), 429

suffrage. *See* voting rights

Sugar Act, 182

Sullivan, John, 213, 215, 216, 217, 218, 219, 221

Sully, Thomas, 283, 284

Sumner, Charles, 287

HMS *Swan*, 190

Swansea, Massachusetts, 153

Swedenborg, Emanuel, 325

Swift, Jonathan, 111

Swinburne House, 361

Swiss Village, 437s–438s

Sydney, Algernon, 53

Syrett, David, 204

T

Talleyrand, Charles Maurice de, 255s

Tartar (ship), 173

Taylor, H. A. C., 388

Tea Act, 189

tennis, 383–386, 387, 392

Ternay, Chevalier de, 225, 227

Tew, Henry, 90

Tew, Thomas, 90–92, 149

Thames River, Battle of, 265

Thaw, Harry, 370

The Age of Innocence (Wharton), 356

The Growth of the American Republic (Morison and Steele), 345

The Theory of the Leisure Class (Veblen), 344–345

This Was My Newport (Elliott), 352, 384, 387

Thoreau, Henry David, 285, 327

Thoroughbred racing, 354, 367

Ticonderoga, New York, 176

Tiffany, Louis, 331

Tiffany, Mrs. George, 369

Tilley, William, 149

Titanic (ship), 412

Tiverton, Rhode Island, 175, 196, 219, 223, 269

Tokyo, Japan, 314s

Top of the Hill Association, 445

Torpedo Station. *See* Naval Torpedo Station, Goat Island

Totten, Joseph, 272

Touro, Isaac, 161–162

Touro House, 301

Touro Synagogue, Newport, 156s, 161–162, 249, 442; interior view of, 161

Tousard, Louis de, 271, 274

Town and Country Club, 170, 335, 336, 337, 362, 435

Townsend, Christopher, 138

Townsend, Hannah, 140

Townsend, Job, Jr., 139

Townsend, Job, Sr., 137–140

Townsend, John, 137–141

Townsend, Nathan, 111

Townsend, Suzanna, 140

Townsend Coffee House, 300

Townshend Acts, 189

Townshild, Charles, 183

Town Topics: The Journal of the Society, 404–405

Trancendentalism, 285, 287

The Transformation of Rhode Island (Coleman), 254

Treatise Concerning the Principles of Human Knowledge (Berkeley), 111

Treaty of Ghent, 259

Treaty of Kanagawa, 314s

Treaty of Paris, 176, 177s, 181

Treaty of Paris of 1783, 234s, 236, 255s, 256

Treaty of Ryswick, 87

Treaty of Utrecht, 94s, 97–98, 105, 170

Trevett, E., 299s

Trevett, John, 240

Trial of Ann Hutchinson (Abbey), 15

Trinidad, 266

Trinity Church, Newport, 113–116, 121–122, 131, 141, 145, 153s, 154–156, 158, 164, 168s, 198, 227, 260, 317, 369, 423s, 447, 448; interior view of, 155

Truman, Harry, 433

Trumbauer, Horace, 361, 365, 373, 374

Turner, Ted, 453

Twain, Mark, 334

Tyler, John, 291

U

Underhill, John, 12

Union Club, 349

Union Congregational Church, Newport, 274, 356s

Unitarian Christianity (Channing), 287

United Colonies of New England, 31, 37, 60, 70

United Company of Spermaceti Chandlers, 152

United States Amateur Golf tournament, 388–389, 390

United States Bicentennial celebrations, 454

United States Coast Guard, 423–424

United States Department of Commerce, 307s

United States Geological Survey, 337

United States Golf Association, 389

United States Lawn Tennis Association, 384, 386

United States Military Academy, 271

United States Navy, 258–260, 265, 380–382, 447, 459. *See also* Naval Academy; Naval Torpedo Station; Naval Training Station; Naval War College

United States Revenue Cutter Service, 259

University of Virginia, 158

Updike, Daniel, 115

Upjohn, Richard, 338

U. S. Open Championships, 390

U-53 (submarine), 417–418

V

Valiant (ship), 395

Valley Forge, Pennsylvania, 209s

The Valley of Decision (Wharton), 399

Van Alen, James, 378s, 386, 390, 393

van Beuren, Archbold, 71, 442

van Beuren, Mrs. Michael M., 441

Vanderbilt, Alfred G., 416

Vanderbilt, Alva (Smith), 357–358, 364, 365, 367, 371, 405, 407, 408–411, 412–413, 416, 422; portrait of, 410

Vanderbilt, Consuelo, 410–411

Vanderbilt, Cornelius, 345, 358, 369, 393

Vanderbilt, Cornelius II, 358, 360, 362–363, 365, 367, 442; portrait of, 359

Vanderbilt, Frederick W., 370; 374

Vanderbilt, George, 364

Vanderbilt, Gertrude, 411

Vanderbilt, Harold S., 442, 452

Vanderbilt, Mrs. French, 418

Vanderbilt, William Henry, 358, 434, 436

Vanderbilt, William K., 347, 357–358, 358, 360, 365, 367, 395, 410, 416

Vanderbilt, William Kissam II, 371s

Vane, Henry, 13, 18, 27, 31, 32, 33, 35, 38, 39, 42, 50

van Horne, Mahlon, 356s

Van Rensselaer, Mrs. John King, 344, 360, 377

Varnum, James Mitchell, 198, 238–239

Vauban, Sébastien de, 272

Veblen, Thorstein, 344–345

Vernon, Samuel, 106, 133, 145, 149, 154, 185; tankard made by, 144

Vernon, William, 106, 133, 145, 149, 154, 191, 227, 380

Vernon Court, 374; picture of, 375

Vernon House, picture of, 232

Verrazzano, Giovanni da, 22, 24, 37s, 75

Verses (Wharton), 397

Vietnam War, 456

Vigilant (ship), 259

Villa, Alphonse, 376

Volstead Act. *See* Prohibition

voting rights, 154s, 289–291, 411, 422

W

Wadsworth House, Hartford, 228

Wady, James, 143

Wake, Thomas, 91

Wakehurst, 378s

Wallace, James, 189–192, 192

Walpole, Robert, 109s, 116, 171–172

Wampanoag Indians, 18, 25–26, 70, 197

wampum. *See* currency

Wanton, Edward, 92–93, 94

Wanton, Gideon, 133, 174

Wanton, John, 92–95, 100, 103, 106, 108–111, 123, 172, 173, 174, 177; portrait of, 93

Wanton, John, Jr., 138

Wanton, Joseph, Jr., 168–169, 187–188, 190, 201, 227; picture of, 170

Wanton, Joseph, Sr., 169, 172, 174

Wanton, Mrs. Joseph, 116s

Wanton, Ruth (Bryant), 93

Wanton, Sarah (Brenton), 169

Wanton, William, 92–94, 103, 108–109, 111, 123, 155, 174, 177

Wanton-Lyman-Hazard House, 71, 73, 444; photograph, 72

Warburton, Eileen, 388, 420, 448–449

Ward, Richard, 101, 105, 146, 173, 177, 333

Ward, Samuel, 138, 177–180, 219s, 313, 333

Ward, Samuel, Jr., 216, 333; portrait of, 218

Ward-Hopkins controversy, 177–180, 239, 248

Waring, George, 336, 369

Warner, Charles Dudley, 343

War of 1812, 255–260, 262–266, 271

War of Austrian Succession. *See* King George's Wars

War of Independence. *See* Revolutionary War, military engagements of

War of Spanish Succession, 87

Warren, Katherine, 170, 442–443, 447–448; portrait of, 443

Warren, Rhode Island, 175, 210, 254

Warren, Whitney, 388–389

Warville, Brissot de, 237

Warwick, 3, 21, 35, 37, 41s, 42, 51s, 69, 70–71, 97, 289

Washington, D. C., 368

Washington, George, 167, 175, 180, 190, 195–196, 196, 201, 202–204, 209s, 215, 217, 218–219, 221, 224–225, 228, 230–234, 238, 241, 242–243, 248–249, 256, 286, 432; portrait of, 166

Washington, Martha, 167

Washington (ship), 190, 219s

Washington (steamboat), 269

Waterhouse, Benjamin, 130, 136, 165, 237, 275s–276s; portrait of, 275

Water Works, 450

Weatherly (ship), 452

Weaver, John B., Jr., 304

Weaver, John G., 302–304, 311

Weaver, Joseph B., 302–304, 311

Webster, Daniel, 284, 319

Weeden, John, 240

Wein, George, 455–456

Welles, Gideon, 321s

Wellington Park, 391

West, Benjamin, 165, 276, 279, 284

Westchester Polo Club, 386–387

Westhorpe, Suffolk, England, 46

West Indies, 58, 63, 64–65, 87, 98, 103–106, 110, 125, 133, 135, 150–151, 153, 210, 222, 224, 256, 298

West Side Tennis Club, New York, 385

Wetmore, Edith, 441

Wetmore, George Peabody, 374

Wetmore, Maud, 441

Wetmore, William, 315, 317, 374

Wetmore, William S., 354

whaling, 151–153, 254

Wharton, Edith, 324, 378s, 390, 396–400, 407; portrait of, 397

Wharton, Edward, 393, 397–399

Wheatland, Marcus, portrait of, 356

Wheeler & Company, 312

Wheelwright, John, 15, 17

Whipple, Abraham, 188, 190–191, 219s

White, Stanford, 349, 361, 362, 364, 365, 369–370, 371; photograph of, 370

Whitefield, George, 121

Whitehall, 114, 115, 116, 208

Whitehone House, 447